NEW PERSPECTIVES ON
Microsoft® Office 2013

BRIEF

Ann Shaffer
Patrick Carey
Kathleen T. Finnegan
Katherine T. Pinard

Lisa Ruffolo
Joseph J. Adamski
June Jamrich Parsons
Dan Oja

S. Scott Zimmerman
Brigham Young University

Beverly B. Zimmerman
Brigham Young University

CENGAGE
Learning·

Australia • Brazil • Japan • Korea • Mexico • Singapore • Spain • United Kingdom • United States

CENGAGE
Learning·

New Perspectives on Microsoft Office 2013, Brief

Director of Development: Marah Bellegarde

Executive Editor: Donna Gridley

Associate Acquisitions Editor: Amanda Lyons

Product Development Manager: Leigh Hefferon

Senior Product Manager: Kathy Finnegan

Product Manager: Julia Leroux-Lindsey

Developmental Editors: Kim T. M. Crowley, Robin M. Romer, Mary Pat Shaffer, Sasha Vodnik

Editorial Assistant: Melissa Stehler

Brand Manager: Elinor Gregory

Market Development Managers: Kristie Clark, Gretchen Swann

Senior Content Project Managers: Jennifer Feltri-George, Jennifer Goguen McGrail

Composition: GEX Publishing Services

Art Director: GEX Publishing Services

Text Designer: Althea Chen

Cover Art: ©Michael Adendorff/Flickr Open/Getty Images

Copyeditors: Suzanne Huizenga, Michael Beckett

Proofreader: Lisa Weidenfeld

Indexer: Alexandra Nickerson

Some of the product names and company names used in this book have been used for identification purposes only and may be trademarks or registered trademarks of their respective manufacturers and sellers.

Microsoft and the Office logo are either registered trademarks or trademarks of Microsoft Corporation in the United States and/or other countries. Cengage Learning is an independent entity from the Microsoft Corporation, and not affiliated with Microsoft in any manner.

Disclaimer: Any fictional data related to persons or companies or URLs used throughout this book is intended for instructional purposes only. At the time this book was printed, any such data was fictional and not belonging to any real persons or companies.

Library of Congress Control Number: 2013946969

ISBN-13: 978-1-285-16765-7

ISBN-10: 1-285-16765-1

Cengage Learning
200 First Stamford Place, 4th Floor
Stamford, CT 06902
USA

Cengage Learning is a leading provider of customized learning solutions with office locations around the globe, including Singapore, the United Kingdom, Australia, Mexico, Brazil, and Japan. Locate your local office at: **www.cengage.com/global**

Cengage Learning products are represented in Canada by Nelson Education, Ltd.

For your course and learning solutions, visit **www.cengage.com**

Purchase any of our products at your local college store or at our preferred online store **www.cengagebrain.com**

ProSkills Icons © 2014 Cengage Learning.

Printed in the United States of America
1 2 3 4 5 6 7 19 18 17 16 15 14 13

Preface

The New Perspectives Series' critical-thinking, problem-solving approach is the ideal way to prepare students to transcend point-and-click skills and take advantage of all that Microsoft Office 2013 has to offer.

In developing the New Perspectives Series, our goal was to create books that give students the software concepts and practical skills they need to succeed beyond the classroom. We've updated our proven case-based pedagogy with more practical content to make learning skills more meaningful to students.

With the New Perspectives Series, students understand *why* they are learning *what* they are learning, and are fully prepared to apply their skills to real-life situations.

About This Book

This book provides essential coverage of Microsoft Office 2013, and includes the following:

- Detailed, hands-on instruction of Microsoft Word, Excel, Access, PowerPoint and Outlook
- Coverage of Windows 8 basics and file management
- Exploration of exciting new features in Microsoft Office 2013, including Read Mode and the enhanced DESIGN tab in Word, Flash Fill and the Quick Analysis tool in Excel, the updated Backstage view in Access, and theme variants and the improved Presenter view in PowerPoint
- Introduction to cloud computing

New for this edition!

- Each tutorial has been updated with new case scenarios throughout, which provide a rich and realistic context for students to apply the concepts and skills presented.
- A new Troubleshoot type of Case Problem, in which certain steps of the exercise require students to identify and correct errors—which are intentionally placed in the files students work with—promotes problem solving and critical thinking.
- The content has been developed so that students and instructors can work seamlessly on either the Windows 7 or Windows 8 operating system.

> *"This comprehensive and well-written text provides students with a thorough understanding of Microsoft Office, using real-world, relevant examples. This text works well in both a face-to-face and online environment."*
> —Diane Kosharek
> Madison Area Technical College

System Requirements

This book assumes a typical installation of Microsoft Office 2013 and Microsoft Windows 8. (You can also complete the material in this text using another version of Windows 8, or using Windows 7. You may see only minor differences in how some windows look.) The browser used for any steps that require a browser is Internet Explorer 10.

The New Perspectives Approach

Context

Each tutorial begins with a problem presented in a "real-world" case that is meaningful to students. The case sets the scene to help students understand what they will do in the tutorial.

Hands-on Approach

Each tutorial is divided into manageable sessions that combine reading and hands-on, step-by-step work. Colorful screenshots help guide students through the steps. **Trouble?** tips anticipate common mistakes or problems to help students stay on track and continue with the tutorial.

VISUAL OVERVIEW

Visual Overviews

Each session begins with a Visual Overview, a two-page spread that includes colorful, enlarged screenshots with numerous callouts and key term definitions, giving students a comprehensive preview of the topics covered in the session, as well as a handy study guide.

PROSKILLS

ProSkills Boxes and Exercises

ProSkills boxes provide guidance for how to use the software in real-world, professional situations, and related ProSkills exercises integrate the technology skills students learn with one or more of the following soft skills: decision making, problem solving, teamwork, verbal communication, and written communication.

KEY STEP

Key Steps

Important steps are highlighted in yellow with attached margin notes to help students pay close attention to completing the steps correctly and avoid time-consuming rework.

INSIGHT

InSight Boxes

InSight boxes offer expert advice and best practices to help students achieve a deeper understanding of the concepts behind the software features and skills.

TIP

Margin Tips

Margin Tips provide helpful hints and shortcuts for more efficient use of the software. The Tips appear in the margin at key points throughout each tutorial, giving students extra information when and where they need it.

REVIEW

APPLY

Assessment

Retention is a key component to learning. At the end of each session, a series of Quick Check questions helps students test their understanding of the material before moving on. Engaging end-of-tutorial Review Assignments and Case Problems have always been a hall-mark feature of the New Perspectives Series. Colorful bars and headings identify the type of exercise, making it easy to understand both the goal and level of challenge a particular assignment holds.

REFERENCE

TASK REFERENCE

GLOSSARY/INDEX

Reference

Within each tutorial, Reference boxes appear before a set of steps to provide a succinct summary and preview of how to perform a task. In addition, a complete Task Reference at the back of the book provides quick access to information on how to carry out common tasks. Finally, each book includes a combination Glossary/Index to promote easy reference of material.

Our Complete System of Instruction

BRIEF

INTRODUCTORY

COMPREHENSIVE

Coverage To Meet Your Needs

Whether you're looking for just a small amount of coverage or enough to fill a semester-long class, we can provide you with a textbook that meets your needs.

- Brief books typically cover the essential skills in just 2 to 4 tutorials.
- Introductory books build and expand on those skills and contain an average of 5 to 8 tutorials.
- Comprehensive books are great for a full-semester class, and contain 9 to 12+ tutorials.

So if the book you're holding does not provide the right amount of coverage for you, there's probably another offering available. Go to our Web site or contact your Cengage Learning sales representative to find out what else we offer.

COURSECASTS

CourseCasts – Learning on the Go. Always available…always relevant.

Want to keep up with the latest technology trends relevant to you? Visit http://coursecasts. course.com to find a library of weekly updated podcasts, CourseCasts, and download them to your mp3 player.

Ken Baldauf, host of CourseCasts, is a faculty member of the Florida State University Computer Science Department where he is responsible for teaching technology classes to thousands of FSU students each year. Ken is an expert in the latest technology trends; he gathers and sorts through the most pertinent news and information for CourseCasts so your students can spend their time enjoying technology, rather than trying to figure it out. Open or close your lecture with a discussion based on the latest CourseCast.

Visit us at http://coursecasts.course.com to learn on the go!

Instructor Resources

We offer more than just a book. We have all the tools you need to enhance your lectures, check students' work, and generate exams in a new, easier-to-use and completely revised package. This book's Instructor's Manual, ExamView testbank, PowerPoint presentations, data files, solution files, figure files, and a sample syllabus are all available on a single CD-ROM or for downloading at http://www.cengage.com.

SAM: Skills Assessment Manager

Get your students workplace-ready with SAM, the premier proficiency-based assessment and training solution for Microsoft Office! SAM's active, hands-on environment helps students master computer skills and concepts that are essential to academic and career success.

Skill-based assessments, interactive trainings, business-centric projects, and comprehensive remediation engage students in mastering the latest Microsoft Office programs on their own, allowing instructors to spend class time teaching. SAM's efficient course setup and robust grading features provide faculty with consistency across sections. Fully interactive MindTap Readers integrate market-leading Cengage Learning content with SAM, creating a comprehensive online student learning environment.

www.cengage.com/series/newperspectives

Acknowledgments

The entire New Perspectives team would like to extend its sincere thanks to the New Perspectives Office 2013 advisory board members and textbook reviewers listed below. We are extremely grateful to all of them for their contributions in the development of this text. Their valuable insights and excellent feedback helped us to shape this text, ensuring that it will meet the needs of instructors and students both in the classroom and beyond. Thank you all!

New Perspectives Office 2013 Advisory Board

Brian Ameling, Limestone College
Lynn Baldwin, Madison Area Technical College
Earl Belcher, Sinclair Community College
Lydia Bell, Rasmussen College
Melisa Bryant, Forsyth Technical Institute
Kathleen Bent, Cape Cod Community College
Jennifer Day, Sinclair Community College
Mackinzee Escamilla, South Plains College
Hazel Freeman, University of Alabama
Sherrie Geitgey, Northwest State Community College
Jean Graham, Rasmussen College
Judy Grotefendt, Kilgore College
Dana Hooper, University of Alabama
Ralph Hooper, University of Alabama
Rahndy Jadinak, Rasmussen College
Beata Jones, Texas Christian University
Jamie Kretsch, Monmouth University
Jackie Lamoureux, Central New Mexico Community College

Diane Larson, Indiana University Northwest
Judy Matteson, Oakland Community College
Karen Miller, Hohokus Hackensack School
Don Naff, Charter College
Barb Neuwerth, Southeast Community College
Kathy Niebur, Dakota County Technical College
Karen O'Connor, Cerro Coso Community College
Nathan Plitzuweit, Rasmussen College
Anastasia Rashtchian, Rasmussen College
Gail Schroeder, Northwest Wisconsin Technical College
Susan Taylor, Highline Community College
Valerie Thompson, West Kentucky Community and Technical College
Terri Tiedeman, Southeast Community College
Joseph Torok, Bryant & Stratton College

Textbook Reviewers

John Bojonny, Brown Mackie College
Cliff Brozo, Monroe College
Rollie Cox, Madison Area Technical College
Will Demeré, Michigan State University
Peggy Foreman, Texas State University
Deborah Franklin, Bryant & Stratton College
Maryann Gallant, Curry College
Debi Griggs, Bellevue College
Jennifer Gwizdala, Rasmussen College
Martha Huggins, Pitt Community College

Bill Hutchinson, Charter College
Diane Kosharek, Madison Area Technical College
Steve Luzier, Fortis Institute
Paul Smith, Brown Mackie College
Kerrie Specker, Rio Salado College
Bradley West, Sinclair Community College
Christine Yero, Madison Area Technical College

www.cengage.com/series/newperspectives

BRIEF CONTENTS

TABLE OF CONTENTS

WORD TUTORIALS

EXCEL TUTORIALS

Tutorial 1 Getting Started with Excel
Creating a Customer Order Report . . . .**EX 1**

ACCESS TUTORIALS

Tutorial 1 Creating a Database
Tracking Patient, Visit, and Billing Data . . . . **AC 1**

POWERPOINT

Tutorial 1 Creating a Presentation
Presenting Information About Community Supported Agriculture . . . . **PPT 1**

OBJECTIVES

- Start and turn off Windows 8
- Describe how to use Windows 8 with a touchscreen device
- Tour the Start screen and the desktop
- Start Windows 8 and desktop applications
- Switch between applications and close them
- Identify and use the controls in windows and dialog boxes
- Get help with Windows 8 tasks

Exploring the Basics of Windows 8

Investigating the Windows 8 Operating System

Case | *Behind the Scenes*

Behind the Scenes is a small but growing temporary employment agency in St. Louis, Missouri. The agency specializes in training and providing virtual assistants, high-quality support staff that work from home to perform office tasks and projects for clients. As the training manager at Behind the Scenes, Emma Garcia coordinates staff training sessions on a wide range of professional and computer skills.

Emma recently hired you as her assistant. She has asked you to lead the upcoming training sessions on the fundamentals of the Microsoft Windows 8 operating system. As you prepare for the sessions, she offers to help you identify the topics you should cover and the skills you should demonstrate while focusing on the new features in Windows 8.

In this tutorial, you will start Windows 8 and practice some fundamental computer skills. You will tour the Start screen, start applications, and then explore the desktop. You will also work with windows and their tools, use the Windows 8 Help system, and turn off Windows 8.

STARTING DATA FILES

There are no starting Data Files needed for this tutorial.

Visual Overview:

The four corners of the Start screen are **hot corners**; point to one to display objects for interacting with Windows.

The **Start screen** appears after you sign in to Windows; you use it to start applications.

Click the Desktop tile to display the Windows 8 desktop.

The **user icon** identifies the current user and provides access to your account settings.

The name you use to sign in to Windows appears next to the user icon.

Calendar is an example of a **Windows 8 app**, which uses the full screen and includes touch-friendly controls.

A **tile** represents an application or another resource, such as a Web page.

A **live tile** displays content that changes frequently.

An **app**, short for **application**, is software you use to perform specific tasks.

Scroll the Start screen to the right to display additional tiles.

Click the Zoom button to reduce the size of the tiles and display more tiles on the Start screen.

Windows 8 Start Screen & Desktop

The **Recycle Bin** holds deleted items until you remove them permanently.

The **desktop** is your work area for running many productivity applications and applications designed for previous versions of Windows.

This graphic is part of a **theme**, a set of coordinated desktop backgrounds, window colors, sounds, and screen savers.

Two applications are **pinned** to the taskbar, which means their buttons always appear on the left side of the taskbar.

The **taskbar** contains icons and buttons that give you quick access to common tools and running applications.

An **icon** is a small picture that represents a resource on your computer.

The **notification area** displays icons corresponding to services Windows provides, such as an Internet connection.

The **Date/time control** is an element that shows the current date and time and lets you set the clock.

Introducing Windows 8

The **operating system** is software that manages and coordinates activities on the computer and helps the computer perform essential tasks, such as displaying information on the screen and saving data on disks. Your computer uses the **Microsoft Windows 8** operating system—**Windows 8** for short. Windows is the name of the operating system, and 8 indicates the version you are using.

Computers can run two types of software—system software and applications. **System software** is the software that runs a computer, including the operating system. An application (abbreviated as "app") is the software you use most directly to perform tasks such as writing a screenplay or viewing a webpage. In general, a computer runs system software to perform computer tasks, and you run applications to carry out your work or personal tasks. On Windows 8, you can run applications created specifically for the Windows 8 operating system and for earlier versions of Windows, such as Windows 7. With both versions of Windows, you can use more than one application at a time and switch seamlessly from one application to another to perform your work effectively.

Windows 8 is designed to run on computers that use a touchscreen, such as tablets, those that use a keyboard and mouse, such as a desktop computer, and those that use a touchpad, such as a laptop. A **touchscreen** is a display that lets you touch areas of the screen to interact with software. See Figure 1.

Figure 1	Windows 8 on different types of computers

© 2014 Cengage Learning

Using Windows 8 with Pointing Devices

As shown in the Visual Overview, when you work with Windows 8, you interact with objects such as tiles and icons to start applications, provide information to Windows, and perform other computer tasks. If you are using a laptop or desktop computer, you most likely use a **pointing device** to interact with the objects on the screen. Pointing devices come in many shapes and sizes. The most common one is called a **mouse**, so this book uses that term. If you are using a different pointing device, such as a trackball or touchpad, substitute that device whenever you see the term "mouse."

You use a mouse to move the pointer over locations and objects on the screen, or to **point** to them. The **pointer** is an on-screen object, often shaped like an arrow, though it changes shape depending on its location on the screen and the tasks you are performing. As you move the mouse on a surface, such as a table top, the pointer moves in a corresponding direction.

You also use the mouse to interact with specific objects on the screen. For example, you can use the mouse to click an object. **Clicking** refers to pressing a mouse button and immediately releasing it. Clicking sends a signal to your computer that you want to perform an action with the object you click. In Windows 8, you perform most actions with the left mouse button. If a step instructs you to click an on-screen object, such as a Start screen tile, position the pointer on that object and click the left mouse button. Another common mouse action is **double-clicking**, which means to click the left mouse button twice in quick succession. You can also press and release the right button on a mouse, which is called **right-clicking**. (If your mouse has only one button, you right-click by pressing the right side of the button.) Finally, you can point to an object, press and hold down the mouse button, and then move the mouse, which is called **dragging** the object.

Using Windows 8 with Touchscreen Devices

If you are using a computer with a touchscreen, such as a tablet, you use your fingertips to interact with on-screen objects. The movements you make as you touch the screen with your fingertips are called **gestures**. The six basic gestures are tap, press, swipe, slide or drag, pinch, and rotate. For example, instead of clicking a tile on the Start screen, you tap the tile, which means you use your fingertip to touch the item briefly. Figure 2 illustrates the six gestures you use with touchscreen devices.

Figure 2   Gestures used with touchscreen devices

Touch Gesture	Description	Illustration
Tap	Touch an item with a fingertip	Tap to start an application or select an object
Press	Touch and hold an item	Press and hold to learn
Swipe	Drag a fingertip across the screen and then release	Swipe to display commands
Slide or drag	Drag a fingertip across the screen without releasing	Slide to scroll the screen or move an object
Pinch	Touch the screen with two fingers and then drag your fingertips toward each other to zoom out, or drag your fingertips away from each other to zoom in	Pinch and stretch to zoom
Rotate	Touch the screen with two fingers and then drag either clockwise or counterclockwise	Turn to rotate

© 2014 Cengage Learning

Many elements of Windows 8 are designed with touchscreen users in mind. For example, the Start screen includes large tiles instead of small icons because tiles are easier to tap. However, you are not required to use a touchscreen with Windows 8. In fact, this book assumes that you are using a computer with a keyboard and a mouse.

INSIGHT

The Windows 8 User Interface

The part of the operating system you use when you work with a computer is called the **user interface (UI)**. The UI includes everything that lets you interact with the computer, including the layout of the screen and the controls that the operating system provides so you can make selections and change settings. (**Controls** are graphical or textual objects you use to work with the operating system and applications.) On the Start screen, the Windows 8 UI uses a design that emphasizes large, clear graphical icons to identify screen objects. When you use a Windows 8 app, the focus is on the content, so the screen is not cluttered with tools and controls. The Windows 8 UI also uses animation and fluid motions to respond to your actions and selections, which make the system seem livelier than a collection of static objects. To take advantage of wide screens, multiple monitors, and touch-screen devices, the Windows 8 UI is more horizontally oriented than previous versions of Windows. For example, you scroll right and left to access content currently out of view.

Starting Windows 8

TIP

If you have a Microsoft account, you can use the username and password for that account to sign in to Windows 8. However, this tutorial assumes you are not signed in to a Microsoft account.

Windows 8 starts automatically when you turn on your computer. After completing some necessary startup tasks, Windows 8 might display a **lock screen**, which includes a picture, the date, and the time. You clear the lock screen to display the Welcome screen, which lists all the users for the computer. Before you start working with Windows 8, you might also need to click your **username** (a unique name that identifies you to Windows 8) and type a **password** (a confidential series of characters). After you provide this information, the Windows 8 Start screen appears, as shown in the Visual Overview.

PROSKILLS

Decision Making: Selecting a User Account Type

In order to use Windows 8, you must have a user account. A **user account** identifies you to the computer. You access your user account by selecting your username and typing your password, if required. You can create additional user accounts at any time. If you share a computer with other people, your user account allows you to keep your work and settings separate from the other users. When you create your user account, you must choose from one of the following types of accounts:

- Microsoft account—This is a user account that is associated with Microsoft's **SkyDrive**, a Microsoft server on the Internet on which you can store files and access some Microsoft programs. If you have a user account on more than one computer running Windows 8, you can access your applications, preferences, and other settings. In addition, you can use some Windows 8 applications only if you are signed in with a Microsoft account, including the Store app, which lets you add new applications to your computer, and the Music app, which you use to purchase songs and albums. You sign in to a Microsoft account using an email address. Any email address can be associated with a Microsoft account, and that email address then becomes the username for that account. You can also set up a Microsoft account when you create your user account in Windows 8.
- Local account—When you sign in with a local account, you are signed in to Windows 8 but you are not automatically connected to SkyDrive. This type of account accesses resources on your computer in the same way user accounts worked in earlier versions of Windows. You can, however, create a separate account on Microsoft SkyDrive to access SkyDrive features.

Make sure you understand the differences between these two types of user accounts so you can decide which one is the best type for you and your work habits.

To begin preparing for the Windows 8 training session you will deliver, Emma asks you to start Windows 8.

To start Windows 8:

▶ **1.** Turn on your computer. After a moment, Windows 8 starts and displays the Welcome screen.

Trouble? If you are asked to select an operating system, do not take action. Windows 8 should start automatically after a designated number of seconds. If it does not, ask your instructor or technical support person for help.

Trouble? If a lock screen appears before the Welcome screen does, press any key to clear the lock screen.

▶ **2.** If the Welcome screen is displayed for more than a few seconds, click your username, type your password, and then press the **Enter** key.

The Windows 8 Start screen appears, as shown in the Visual Overview. Your screen might look different.

Trouble? If your username does not appear on the Welcome screen, ask your instructor or technical support person for further assistance.

Trouble? If a blank screen or an animated design replaces the Start screen, your computer might be set to use a **screen saver**, a program that causes a monitor to go blank or to display an animated design after a specified amount of idle time. Press any key or move your mouse to restore the Start screen.

Trouble? If your computer is using a screen resolution other than 1366 x 768, the figures shown in this tutorial might not match exactly what you see in Windows 8 as you work through the steps. Take the screen resolution difference into account as you compare your screen to the figures.

Touring the Start Screen

The screen that appears after you sign in to Windows 8 is called the Start screen because you start working on your computer from this screen. The Start screen includes multicolored rectangles called tiles, which represent applications and other resources your computer can access. See Figure 3.

Figure 3   Tiles on the Start screen

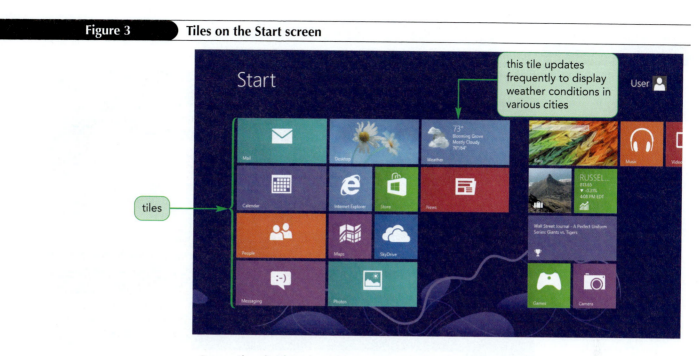

Some tiles display changing pictures or text that previews the contents of the tile. A tile that displays updated content is called a live tile. For example, the Weather tile is a live tile that displays current weather conditions in cities around the world. You click the Weather live tile to open the Weather app, a Windows 8 app that lets you check the current and forecasted weather in various locations.

The first time you start Windows 8, the computer uses **default settings**, which are preset by the operating system. The default Start screen you see after you first install Windows 8, for example, displays a number of tiles, including those for Internet Explorer (an application you use to access the Internet), Weather, and Photos. However, Microsoft designed Windows 8 so that you can easily change the appearance of the Start screen. You can, for example, move and add tiles and change the background color.

Emma suggests that during your class, you introduce Behind the Scenes employees to the Start screen by showing them how to scroll in case some tiles are out of view.

To scroll the Start screen:

TIP

Make sure you position the pointer on the very edge of the Start screen. You might also need to press and hold the mouse button as you scroll.

1. Use the mouse to point to the **right edge** of the Start screen. The screen scrolls to display additional tiles or those not shown on the main Start screen. See Figure 4.

   Trouble? If a bar of buttons appears on the right side of the screen, you pointed to the upper-right or lower-right corner. Point to the middle of the right edge of the screen to scroll.

   Trouble? If the screen does not scroll, your Start screen might not contain additional or half-shown tiles.

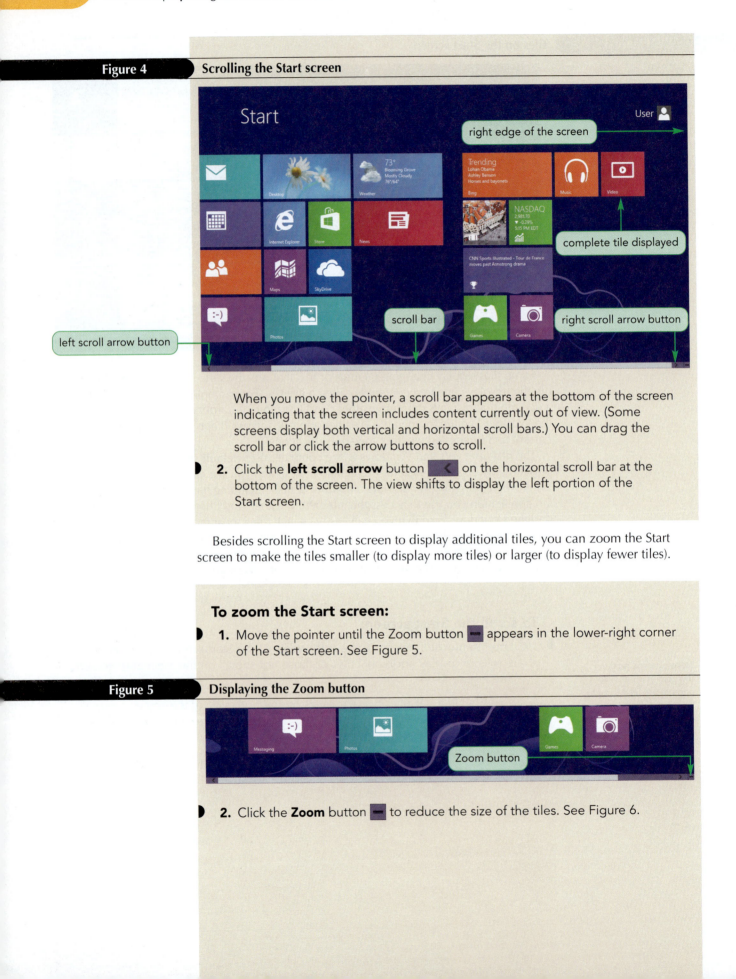

Figure 4 Scrolling the Start screen

When you move the pointer, a scroll bar appears at the bottom of the screen indicating that the screen includes content currently out of view. (Some screens display both vertical and horizontal scroll bars.) You can drag the scroll bar or click the arrow buttons to scroll.

2. Click the **left scroll arrow** button on the horizontal scroll bar at the bottom of the screen. The view shifts to display the left portion of the Start screen.

Besides scrolling the Start screen to display additional tiles, you can zoom the Start screen to make the tiles smaller (to display more tiles) or larger (to display fewer tiles).

To zoom the Start screen:

1. Move the pointer until the Zoom button appears in the lower-right corner of the Start screen. See Figure 5.

Figure 5 Displaying the Zoom button

2. Click the **Zoom** button to reduce the size of the tiles. See Figure 6.

Figure 6 | **Zooming the Start screen**

tiles are smaller to display more of them on the Start screen

3. Click a blank area on the Start screen to return the tiles to their original size.

When you moved the pointer to the Zoom button to click it, a bar appeared on the right edge of the Start screen. This is called the **Charms bar**, and it contains buttons, also called **charms**, for interacting with Windows 8. The Charms bar appears when you point to the upper-right or lower-right corner of the screen. These locations are two of the four hot corners Windows 8 provides for mouse users. When you point to the Charms bar, it appears with a black background, indicating it is the **active object**. You can interact with active objects by clicking them. For example, when you click some charms, such as the Settings charm, a menu opens. A **menu** is a list, or group, of commands, and a **menu command** is an item on the list that you can click to perform a task. The **Settings menu** lets you access options and information for your current task and your system. Emma suggests you use the Settings charm on the Charms bar to open the Settings menu.

To open the Settings menu:

1. Point to the upper-right corner of the screen to display the Charms bar.

2. Point to the **Charms bar** to display it with a black background, indicating it is active. See Figure 7. When you activate the Charms bar, a status box appears on the screen displaying the date and time. It might also display other status information, such as the strength of your network connection or battery level.

TIP

You can also press and hold the Windows key and then press the C key to display the Charms bar.

Figure 7 Active Charms bar

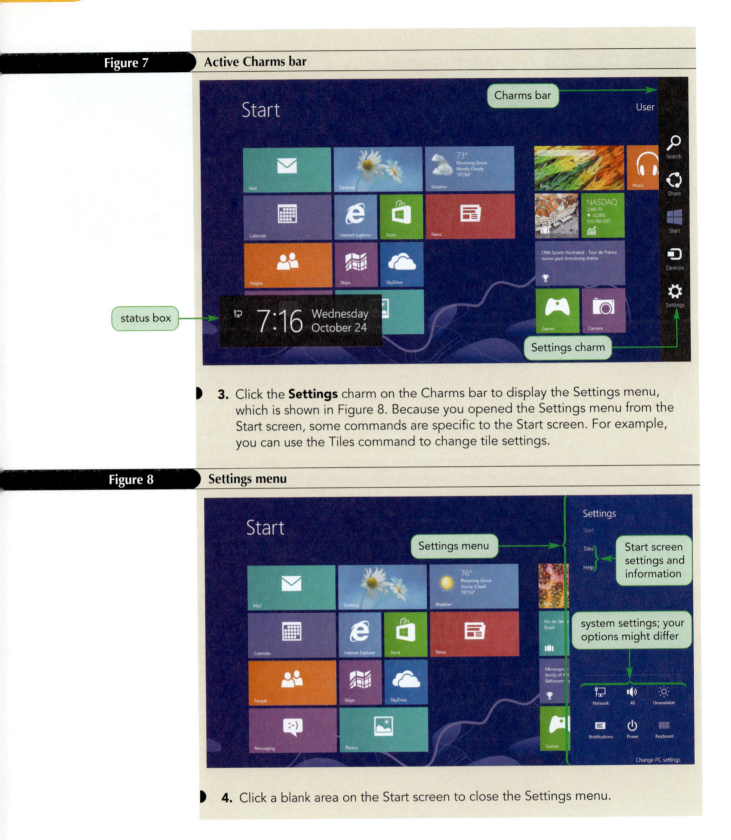

3. Click the **Settings** charm on the Charms bar to display the Settings menu, which is shown in Figure 8. Because you opened the Settings menu from the Start screen, some commands are specific to the Start screen. For example, you can use the Tiles command to change tile settings.

Figure 8 Settings menu

4. Click a blank area on the Start screen to close the Settings menu.

Starting Applications

Windows 8 runs two types of applications. Windows 8 applications, as the name suggests, are designed to use the Windows 8 interface and work with touchscreen devices. They are often called apps. When you start a Windows 8 application, it takes up the entire screen and provides an uncluttered workspace for performing tasks. You can also use Windows 8 to run **desktop applications**, programs that open and run on the desktop, which is shown in the Visual Overview. For example, WordPad is a desktop application you use to create basic word-processing documents.

REFERENCE

Starting an Application

- Click the application's tile on the Start screen.
or
- Right-click a blank area on the Start screen, click the All apps button on the Apps bar at the bottom of the screen, and then click the application on the Apps screen.
or
- On the Start screen, type the name of the application until the application appears in the search results on the Apps screen.
- Click the application in the search results.

The easiest way to start an application is to click its tile on the Start screen. Emma suggests you use this technique to start the Weather app.

To start the Weather app from the Start screen:

1. Click the **Weather** tile on the Start screen to start the Weather app.

Trouble? If a message appears asking if you want to allow Weather to use your location, click the Block button.

2. If an Enter Location box appears, type **St** to display a list of location names that start with "St," and then click **St Louis, Missouri, United States** in the list to display weather information for that location. See Figure 9. Your weather information will differ.

Trouble? If an Enter Location box does not appear after you click the Weather tile, your Weather app is set to use a specific location and shows the weather for that location. Continue to Step 3.

| Figure 9 | Weather app |

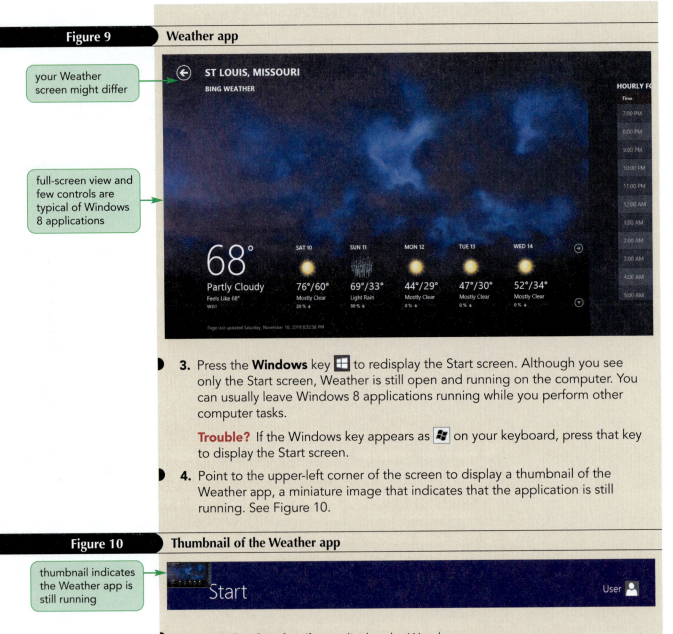

your Weather screen might differ

full-screen view and few controls are typical of Windows 8 applications

3. Press the **Windows** key ⊞ to redisplay the Start screen. Although you see only the Start screen, Weather is still open and running on the computer. You can usually leave Windows 8 applications running while you perform other computer tasks.

   Trouble? If the Windows key appears as 🪟 on your keyboard, press that key to display the Start screen.

4. Point to the upper-left corner of the screen to display a thumbnail of the Weather app, a miniature image that indicates that the application is still running. See Figure 10.

| Figure 10 | Thumbnail of the Weather app |

thumbnail indicates the Weather app is still running

Start   User 👤

5. Click the **thumbnail** to redisplay the Weather app.

Using the Apps Screen to Start an Application

If an application's tile does not appear on the Start screen, you can open the application using the **Apps screen**, which lists all the applications installed on your computer. One way to display the Apps screen is to right-click a blank area of the Start screen to display the **Apps bar**, which includes buttons related to your current task, and then click the All apps button.

Emma wants you to demonstrate how to use more than one technique to start applications, so you will use the Apps screen to start Reader, a Windows 8 application that does not appear on the Start screen by default. Reader lets you view and navigate **PDF documents**, which are files in the Portable Document Format that usually include text and graphics and are readable on most computer systems. First, you must return to the Start screen so you can display the Apps bar with the All apps button.

To start the Reader app from the Apps screen:

1. Press the **Windows** key ⊞ to display the Start screen.

2. Right-click a blank area on the Start screen to display the Apps bar at the bottom of the screen.

3. Click the **All apps** button on the right side of the Apps bar to display the Apps screen. See Figure 11. The Apps screen lists Windows 8 applications on the left and categories of desktop applications on the right.

Figure 11   Apps screen

categories of desktop applications; your list might differ

Apps screen

Windows 8 applications; your list might differ

Reader app

scroll to display additional applications

4. Click **Reader** to start the Reader app. A PDF document opens in Reader explaining how to edit PDF files using Microsoft Word.

   Trouble? You might have a different PDF document that opens in Reader, or no document will open at all and you will see the Recent screen for Reader. This is not a problem.

Windows 8 applications start and run as full-screen programs so you can focus on your task and the content on the screen. Occasionally, you need to refer to information in one application while you are working in another application. For example, you might want to keep the Weather app open so you can check the weather while you are reading a document in the Reader app. If you are using a high screen resolution (at least 1366 × 768), you can **snap** an app, which means you display a Windows 8 application on the left or right side of the screen and leave it open as you work in another Windows 8 application. You can snap only Windows 8 applications, not desktop applications.

If a Windows 8 application appears on the screen, you snap it by dragging it to the left or right. If the application is open and running but does not appear on the screen, you can display its thumbnail, and then right-click the thumbnail to open a **shortcut menu**, which lists actions you can take with the application. The thumbnail shortcut menu includes commands for snapping the application to the left or right side of the screen.

TIP

You can right-click other objects on the Start screen and the desktop to view a shortcut menu of commands associated with that object.

To snap the Weather app:

▶ 1. Point to the upper-left hot corner to display the Weather thumbnail.

▶ 2. Right-click the **Weather** thumbnail, and then click **Snap left** on the shortcut menu to snap the Weather app to the left side of the screen while the Reader app is open on the right. See Figure 12.

| Figure 12 | Weather app snapped on the left |

Weather app

drag this bar to the left edge of the screen to unsnap the Weather app

Reader app; your Reader app might show different content

TIP

You can also drag the bar between the applications to adjust the amount of screen space devoted to each one.

▶ 3. Drag the **bar** between the two applications to the left edge of the screen to unsnap the Weather app. Both Reader and Weather are still running, but the Weather app is no longer snapped to the screen.

Using the Search Menu to Start an Application

Besides using the Apps screen to start Windows 8 applications, you can also use it to start desktop applications. When you first install Windows 8, the Apps screen lists so many applications that you need to scroll to the right at least once to display all of them. As you add other applications to your computer, you might need to scroll a few more times to find the application you want to start. Instead of scrolling the Apps screen, you can use the **Search menu** as a time-saving shortcut for starting applications. You open the Search menu from the Charms bar. When you do, it appears on top of the Apps screen by default. See Figure 13.

Figure 13   **Apps screen and Search menu**

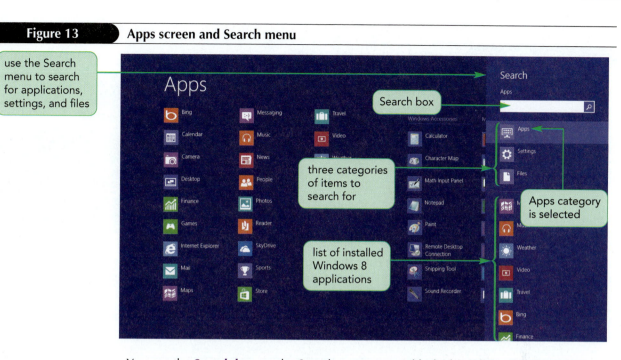

use the Search menu to search for applications, settings, and files

Search box

three categories of items to search for

list of installed Windows 8 applications

Apps category is selected

You use the **Search box** on the Search menu to quickly find anything stored on your computer including applications, documents, pictures, music, videos, and settings. Below the Search box, the Search menu lists three major categories of items you can search for—Apps, Settings, and Files. The Apps category is selected by default. Below the category list on the Search menu is a list of Windows 8 applications installed on your computer. To search for an application, click in the Search box and start typing the name of the application. As you type, the Apps screen displays the search results—applications containing words beginning with that text in their names. Another way to search for an application is to type some or all of the application name on the Start screen. (You don't need to click a particular part of the screen or open a box first.) When you start typing, the Search menu opens on the Apps screen and the text you typed appears in the Search box. The Apps screen displays the search results, which are the applications whose names start with the text in the Search box. You then click the application in the search results to start the application.

If you want to search for settings, you enter the text relating to the setting you are searching for, and then click Settings in the category list. Searching for files works the same way—in the Search box, type the text related to the file you are looking for, and then click Files in the category list.

Emma suggests you use the Search menu to locate and start the WordPad desktop application, which Behind the Scenes employees can use to write and open text documents.

To start WordPad:

1. Press the **Windows** key ⊞ to display the Start screen.

2. On the Start screen, type **wordp** to display the Search menu with "wordp" inserted in the Search box. The Apps screen lists the search results, which include the WordPad application. See Figure 14.

TIP

You can also display the Charms bar and then click the Search charm to open the Search menu.

Figure 14   WordPad in the search results

Apps   Results for "wordp"

WordPad is listed in the search results

search text entered

number of apps found

no settings or files associated with WordPad

Search

> **Trouble?** If settings or files appear in the search results, click Apps in the category list, and then repeat Step 2 if necessary, making sure the search text is displayed in the Search box.

> 3. Click **WordPad** in the search results. WordPad opens on the desktop, as shown in Figure 15.

Figure 15   WordPad open on the desktop

WordPad opens in a window; yours might be a different size or in a different location

WordPad taskbar button

When you open a desktop application such as WordPad, its **window**—a rectangular work area that contains tools for performing tasks in the application—is displayed on the desktop and a taskbar button for WordPad appears on the taskbar. You use **taskbar buttons** to identify and work with open desktop applications.

Manipulating Windows

After you open a window, you can manipulate it to display as much or as little information as you need. In most windows, three buttons appear on the right side of the title bar. See Figure 16. The first button is the Minimize button, which you can use to **minimize** a window, or hide it so that only its button is visible on the taskbar. Depending on the status of the window, the middle button either maximizes the window or restores it to a predefined size. **Maximizing** means to enlarge a window so that it fills the entire screen. The last button is the Close button, which closes the window.

Figure 16   **Window buttons**

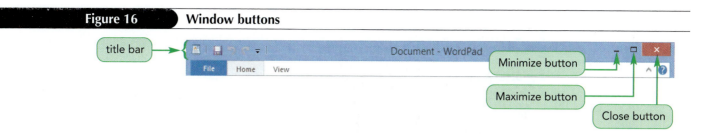

To make sure Behind the Scenes employees know how to manipulate windows, Emma suggests you show them how to use the WordPad taskbar button and the buttons on the WordPad title bar.

To manipulate the WordPad window:

1. Click the **Minimize** button ▬ on the WordPad title bar to minimize the WordPad window. The WordPad window shrinks so that only the WordPad button is visible on the taskbar. With the WordPad window hidden, you can view the entire desktop.

2. Click the **WordPad** button ▦ on the taskbar to redisplay the WordPad window.

3. Click the **Maximize** button ▢ on the WordPad title bar to maximize the WordPad window.

   Trouble? If the window is already maximized, it fills the entire screen and the Maximize button ▢ doesn't appear. Instead, you see the Restore Down button ▣. Skip Step 3.

4. Click the **Restore Down** button ▣ on the title bar to make the WordPad window smaller than the entire screen. After a window is restored, the Restore Down button ▣ changes to the Maximize button ▢.

> **TIP**
>
> You can also double-click a window's title bar to maximize the window. Double-click the title bar again to restore the window to its previous size.

You can also manipulate windows by moving and resizing them. To move a window, you drag the window by its title bar. You also drag to resize a window. When you point to an edge or a corner of a window, the pointer changes to a resize pointer, which is a double-headed arrow, similar to ⬂. You can use the resize pointer to drag an edge or a corner of the window and change the size of the window. If a window is maximized, you must click the Restore Down button before you can move or resize the window.

To move and resize the WordPad window:

1. Position the mouse pointer on the title bar of the WordPad window.

2. Press and hold the mouse button, and then move the pointer up or down a little to drag the window. The window moves as you move the pointer.

3. Drag the window to the middle of the desktop so it does not cover any part of the Recycle Bin icon that appears on the desktop, and then release the mouse button. The WordPad window remains in the new location.

   Trouble? If the WordPad window becomes maximized when you drag it, click the Restore Down button ▣ before performing Step 4.

4. Point to the lower-right corner of the WordPad window until the ⬉ pointer appears, and then drag down and to the right to enlarge the window.

5. Drag up and to the left until the window is about its original size.

In addition to the window manipulation buttons, the WordPad window contains other tools common in desktop applications.

Using Tools in Desktop Applications

In a desktop application, you use controls to manipulate the application window and perform your work in the application. Many desktop applications organize controls in two places—ribbons and dialog boxes.

Using the Ribbon

Many desktop applications use a **ribbon** to consolidate the application's features and commands. The ribbon is located at the top of a desktop application window, immediately below the title bar, and is organized into tabs. Each **tab** contains commands that perform a variety of related tasks. For example, the **Home tab** has commands for tasks you perform frequently, such as changing the appearance of a document. You use the commands on the **View tab** to change your view of the WordPad window. You use the commands on the **File tab** to work with WordPad documents, such as to save or print them.

To select a command and perform an action, you click a button or another type of control on the ribbon. Controls for related actions are organized on a tab in **groups**. For example, on the Home tab in the Font group, you click the Bold button to enter bold text in a WordPad document. If a button displays only an icon and not the button name, you can point to the button to display a **ScreenTip**, which is text that identifies the name or purpose of the button.

Figure 17 shows examples of the types of controls on the ribbon.

Figure 17   Examples of ribbon controls

If a button includes an arrow, you click the button to display a menu of related commands. To use a box, you click the box and type an entry, such as numbers or other text, or you click the arrow button to select an item from the list. A toggle button is like a switch; you click the button to turn on or apply a setting, and then click the button again to turn off the setting. When a toggle button is turned on, it is highlighted. To use a two-part button with an arrow, you first point to the button. If an arrow is displayed on a separate part of the button, click the arrow to display a menu of commands. Click the button itself to apply the current selection.

Most desktop applications, including WordPad, include a **Quick Access Toolbar**, which is a row of buttons on the title bar that let you perform common tasks such as saving your work and undoing an action. You can display the name of each button on the Quick Access Toolbar in a ScreenTip by pointing to the button, just as you do for buttons on the ribbon.

Emma mentions that the WordPad application displays the controls you are likely to see in most desktop application windows, including the ribbon, which might be unfamiliar to Behind the Scenes employees. She suggests that you identify the controls on the WordPad ribbon and in WordPad dialog boxes during your first training session.

To use buttons on the WordPad ribbon and the Quick Access Toolbar:

1. On the Home tab, in the Font group, click the **Bold** button **B**. Now any text you type will appear as bold text.

2. Type your full name in the WordPad window. See Figure 18.

| Figure 18 | Bold text in the WordPad window |

Undo button

Bold button is highlighted, indicating it is toggled on

Emma Garcia

3. On the Quick Access Toolbar, click the **Undo** button. WordPad reverses your last action by removing your name from the WordPad window.

Using Dialog Boxes

A **dialog box** is a special kind of window in which you enter or choose settings for performing a task. Dialog boxes can include tabs, option buttons, check boxes, and other controls to collect information about how you want to perform the task. Emma says a good way to learn how dialog box controls work is to open a typical WordPad dialog box, such as the Print dialog box, which you use to print a document.

To work with a typical Windows 8 dialog box:

1. On the ribbon, click the **File** tab, and then click **Print** on the menu to open the Print dialog box. See Figure 19.

Figure 19   Print dialog box

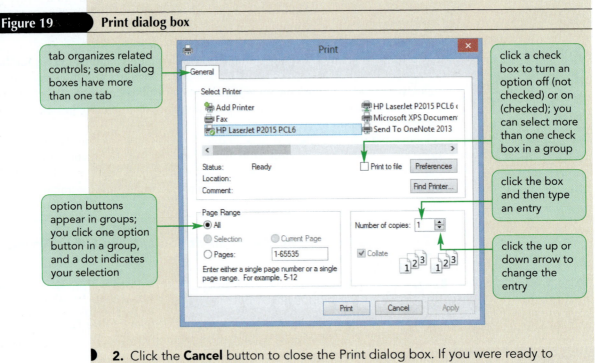

tab organizes related controls; some dialog boxes have more than one tab

click a check box to turn an option off (not checked) or on (checked); you can select more than one check box in a group

click the box and then type an entry

option buttons appear in groups; you click one option button in a group, and a dot indicates your selection

click the up or down arrow to change the entry

> **2.** Click the **Cancel** button to close the Print dialog box. If you were ready to print a document with the settings you specified, you would click the Print button instead of the Cancel button.

Working with Multiple Applications

One of the most useful features of Windows 8 is its ability to run multiple applications at the same time. This feature, known as **multitasking**, allows you to work on more than one task at a time and to switch quickly between open applications. When an application is open but not being used to complete tasks, it is said to be running in the **background**. Just as you saw when working with multiple Windows 8 apps on the Start screen, you can run multiple desktop applications and then switch from one to another so you can work efficiently. To demonstrate, Emma suggests that you open the Recycle Bin so that two applications are running on the desktop. (The Recycle Bin is part of an application that lets you explore the contents of your computer.)

To open the Recycle Bin on the desktop:

> **1.** Point to the **Recycle Bin** icon on the desktop, and then double-click the **Recycle Bin** icon by pressing the left mouse button twice quickly. The Recycle Bin window opens on top of the WordPad window, as shown in Figure 20.

Figure 20   **Recycle Bin and WordPad open on the desktop**

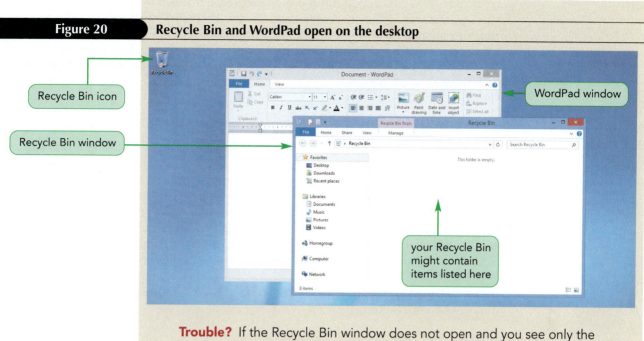

Recycle Bin icon

Recycle Bin window

WordPad window

your Recycle Bin
might contain
items listed here

Trouble? If the Recycle Bin window does not open and you see only the Recycle Bin name highlighted below the icon, you double-clicked too slowly. Double-click the icon again more quickly.

Trouble? If the Recycle Bin window opens as a maximized window, click the Restore Down button so the window does not fill the screen.

2. If necessary, drag the Recycle Bin window to a location on the desktop that allows you to see both it and the WordPad window open on the desktop.

Now that two application windows are open, Emma wants you to demonstrate how to switch from one to the other.

Switching Between Desktop Applications

When two or more applications are open and their windows are displayed on the desktop, only one can be the **active window**, which is the application window in which you are currently working. When a window is active, any keystroke or command you select applies only to that window. The active window appears on top of all other open windows, and its title bar and window borders are blue; the title bar and window border of all other open windows are gray. Right now, the Recycle Bin is the active window. To switch to the WordPad window, you can click its button on the taskbar or you can click in the window itself. If you minimize an active window, it is no longer active, and the window directly under it becomes the active window.

To switch between the Recycle Bin and WordPad:

1. Click the **WordPad** button on the taskbar. The WordPad window now appears on top of the Recycle Bin window, and the color of its title bar and borders changes to blue, indicating that WordPad is the active window.

2. Click any part of the Recycle Bin window to make it the active window.

3. Click the **Minimize** button on the Recycle Bin title bar to minimize the Recycle Bin window and make WordPad the active window.

In addition to the Recycle Bin and WordPad, recall that two Windows 8 apps are also running in the background—Weather and Reader. Although Weather and Reader are running right now, neither one is visible from the desktop. Only desktop applications have buttons on the taskbar, so you cannot use the taskbar to switch to a running Windows 8 app from the desktop. Next, you'll learn how to use a different technique to switch from a desktop application to a Windows 8 app running in the background.

Switching Between Windows 8 Applications

You use the **Switch List** to display thumbnails of the Windows 8 applications running in the background, and then select the one you want to work with. You can display the Switch List from the Start screen, while working with a Windows 8 app, or from the desktop by using the upper-left hot corner on the screen.

When you display the Switch List from the Start screen or a Windows 8 application, it displays one thumbnail for the desktop. Although the Switch List includes thumbnails for Windows 8 applications only, not desktop applications, Windows 8 treats the desktop as a Windows 8 application, so the Switch List includes a thumbnail for the desktop.

Emma encourages you to use the Switch List to switch between the running Windows 8 applications.

To switch between Windows 8 applications:

▶ **1.** Point to the upper-left hot corner of the desktop to display a thumbnail of the Reader app, and then move the pointer down along the left edge of the screen to display the Switch List. See Figure 21.

Figure 21   **Switch List displayed on the desktop**

thumbnail of the Reader app

thumbnail of the Weather app

Switch List

thumbnail of the Start screen appears at the bottom of the Switch List

▶ **2.** Click the **Weather** thumbnail to switch to the Weather app.

▶ **3.** Point to the upper-left hot corner of the screen to display a thumbnail, and then move the pointer down along the left edge of the screen to display the Switch List, which now includes a thumbnail for the desktop.

▶ **4.** Click the **Reader** thumbnail to switch to the Reader app.

TIP

You can also click the thumbnail that appears when you point to the upper-left hot corner to start the associated application without displaying the Switch List.

If you want to switch from the Start screen or a Windows 8 application to an inactive desktop application using the Switch List, you must click the Desktop thumbnail in the Switch List, and then activate the application's window on the desktop. A simpler way is to use a keyboard shortcut.

Using Keyboard Shortcuts

Windows 8 provides many keyboard shortcuts for streamlining your work. A **keyboard shortcut** is one or more keys you press on the keyboard to perform an action. The keyboard shortcut for switching to any type of running application is Alt+Tab. To use this keyboard shortcut, you press and hold the Alt key and then press the Tab key to display thumbnails of all running applications. Continue pressing the Alt key as you press the Tab key to select a thumbnail, and then release the Alt key to make that application active.

You can use the Alt+Tab keyboard shortcut to switch to any running application, such as from a Windows 8 application to an inactive desktop application. Right now, the Recycle Bin is inactive on the desktop. Emma wants you to show Behind the Scenes employees how to use the Alt+Tab keyboard shortcut to switch to the inactive Recycle Bin window.

To use the Alt+Tab keyboard shortcut:

1. Press and hold the **Alt** key, and then press the **Tab** key to display thumbnails of the running applications, including Windows 8 and desktop applications. See Figure 22.

| Figure 22 | Thumbnails of running applications |

2. While holding down the Alt key, press the **Tab** key as many times as necessary to select the Recycle Bin thumbnail, and then release the Alt key. You return to the desktop, where the Recycle Bin is no longer minimized but is now the active window.

Emma says you don't need to demonstrate any other skills with WordPad and the Recycle Bin. When you're finished working with an application, you can close it.

Closing Applications

When you finish working with applications, you can close them to keep the desktop and the Switch List free of clutter, and to allow your computer to run more efficiently. To close a desktop application, you close its window. To close a Windows 8 application, you can use a shortcut menu or drag the application off the screen. You can also use a keyboard shortcut to close either type of application.

Closing Desktop Applications

When you are finished working in a desktop application, you can close it. One way to close an application is to use the Close button on the window's title bar. Another way is to right-click the application window's taskbar button to display a shortcut menu that includes a command to close the window. The advantage of using the shortcut menu is that it lets you close active or inactive windows, even if they are minimized.

Emma suggests that you show Behind the Scenes employees two ways to close a desktop application. You'll start by using a shortcut menu to close the inactive WordPad window.

To close desktop applications:

► **1.** Right-click the **WordPad** button 🖼 on the taskbar. The shortcut menu for the WordPad taskbar button opens. See Figure 23.

| Figure 23 | Taskbar button shortcut menu |

► **2.** Click **Close window** on the shortcut menu.

► **3.** When a message appears asking if you want to save changes, click the **Don't Save** button. The WordPad window closes and its button no longer appears on the taskbar.

► **4.** Click the **Close** button ✕ in the title bar of the Recycle Bin window to close the application.

Now the WordPad and Recycle Bin windows are closed and only the desktop is displayed on the screen.

Closing Windows 8 Applications

TIP

You can also point to the top of a Windows 8 application until a hand pointer appears, drag the application down until it shrinks to a thumbnail, and then continue dragging to the bottom of the screen to close the application.

As you've seen, Windows 8 applications do not include a control such as a Close button that you can use to close the application. Instead, you close a Windows 8 application using its thumbnail when it appears on its own in the upper-left corner of the screen, or when it appears in the Switch List. You right-click the thumbnail and then click Close on the shortcut menu to close the application. You can also use the Alt+F4 keyboard shortcut to close any application. To do so, you press the Alt and F4 keys at the same time when the application is displayed on the screen.

To demonstrate how to close Windows 8 applications, Emma suggests that you use the shortcut menu and the keyboard shortcut to close the open Windows 8 applications.

To close Windows 8 applications:

▶ **1.** Point to the upper-left hot corner, and then click the **Reader** thumbnail to display the Reader app.

▶ **2.** Press the **Alt+F4** keys to close the Reader app and return to the Start screen.

▶ **3.** Point to the upper-left hot corner, and then move the mouse down to display the Switch List.

▶ **4.** Right-click the **Weather** thumbnail, and then click **Close** on the shortcut menu to close the Weather app.

▶ **5.** Click a blank area on the Start screen to close the Switch List.

Before you finish working with Windows 8, you should show Behind the Scenes employees how to get help when they need it.

Getting Help

Windows 8 **Help and Support** provides on-screen information about Windows 8 and its applications. Help and Support gives you access to Help files stored on your computer as well as Help information stored on the Microsoft website. If you are not connected to the web, you have access to only the Help files stored on your computer.

To start Windows 8 Help and Support:

▶ **1.** On the Start screen, type **help** to display the Apps screen and Search menu, with "help" inserted in the Search box.

▶ **2.** Click **Help and Support** in the search results to open the Windows Help and Support window on the desktop. By default, this window displays the Help home page when you start Help and Support.

▶ **3.** Click the **Maximize** button ⬜ to maximize the Windows Help and Support window. See Figure 24. The contents of the home page differ depending on whether you are connected to the Internet.

Trouble? If the Help and Support window does not display the home page, click the Help home link near the top of the window.

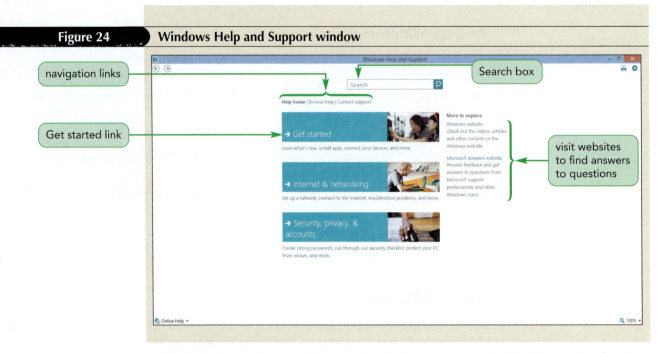

Figure 24   Windows Help and Support window

The Help home page provides tools for finding answers and other information about Windows 8. You can click links on the page to view information about popular topics, browse for a specific topic, or search to find an answer to a Windows 8 question.

Viewing the Get Started Topics

Windows Help and Support includes instructions on the basics of using Windows 8. You can learn more about these basic topics by using the Get started link on the Windows Help and Support home page.

To view Get started topics:

1. Click the **Get started** link. A list of topics related to using Windows 8 appears in the Windows Help and Support window.

2. Click the **Mouse and keyboard: What's new** topic. An article explaining how to use the mouse and keyboard appears.

3. Scroll down to the bottom of the page, and then click the **Get to know Windows** link. A page opens describing the new features in Windows 8.

4. Click the **Back** button ⊛ at the top of the window to return to the previous page you visited, which is the Mouse and keyboard page, and then click the **Back** button ⊛ to return to the Get started page.

Selecting a Topic from the Browse Help List

The Browse help list organizes the information in Windows Help and Support into topics and categories. You can click a link to display the titles of related categories, and then click a topic in a specific category to get help with a particular task or feature. For example, you can use the Browse help list to learn more about personalizing your computer.

To find a Help topic using the Browse help list:

1. Click the **Browse help** link. A list of Windows Help topics appears in the Windows Help and Support window.

2. Click the **Personalization** topic to display a list of topics divided by categories related to personalizing your computer.

3. In the Customize your PC category, click the **Adding apps, websites, and more to Start** topic. The Windows Help and Support window displays information about that topic.

4. Scroll down to review the information on this page, and then scroll up to return to the top of the page.

Searching the Help Pages

If you can't find the topic you need by clicking a link or browsing topics, or if you want to quickly find Help pages related to a particular topic, you can use the Search box. Suppose you want to know how to exit Windows 8, but you don't know if Windows refers to this as exiting, quitting, closing, or shutting down. Emma suggests you can search the Help pages to find just the right topic.

To search the Help pages for information on exiting Windows 8:

1. Click the **Help home** link to return to the home page.

2. Click the **Search** box, type **shut down**, and then press the **Enter** key. A list of Help pages containing the words "shut down" appears in the Windows Help and Support window. See Figure 25. (Your results might differ.)

Figure 25   Search Help results

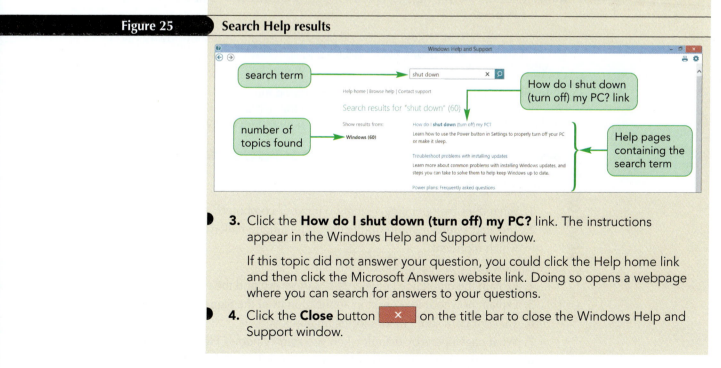

3. Click the **How do I shut down (turn off) my PC?** link. The instructions appear in the Windows Help and Support window.

   If this topic did not answer your question, you could click the Help home link and then click the Microsoft Answers website link. Doing so opens a webpage where you can search for answers to your questions.

4. Click the **Close** button ![X] on the title bar to close the Windows Help and Support window.

Now that you know how Windows 8 Help works, Emma reminds you to use it when you need to perform a new task or want a reminder about how to complete a procedure.

Turning Off Windows 8

When you're finished working in Windows 8, you should always turn it off properly. Doing so saves energy, preserves your data and settings, and makes sure your computer starts quickly the next time you use it.

You turn off Windows 8 using the Power button on the Settings menu. First, you use the Charms bar to display the Settings menu, and then you click the Power button to display a menu, which includes the Shut down option. Click Shut down to have Windows close all open programs, including Windows itself, and then completely turn off your computer.

The Power button menu might also include the Sleep option, which instructs Windows to save your work and then turn down the power to your monitor and computer, a condition called **sleep**. A light on the outside of your computer case blinks or changes color to indicate that the computer is sleeping. Because Windows saves your work, you do not need to close your programs or files before your computer goes to sleep. To wake a computer, you typically press the hardware power button on your computer case. Some computer manufacturers might set the computer to wake when you press a key or move the mouse. After you wake a computer, the screen looks exactly as it did when you put your computer to sleep.

To turn off Windows 8:

1. Point to the upper-right hot corner on the desktop to display the Charms bar, and then click the **Settings** charm to display the Settings menu.

2. Click the **Power** button, and then click **Shut down**. Windows 8 turns off the computer.

   Trouble? If the Power button displays the Update and shut down option instead of Shut down, click Update and shut down.

In this tutorial, you started Windows 8 and toured the Start screen and the desktop. You also worked with Windows 8 apps and desktop applications, and learned how to get help when you need it. Finally you learned how to turn off Windows 8.

Quick Check

REVIEW

1. What does the operating system do for your computer?
2. The Start screen includes multicolored rectangles called _____, which represent _____.
3. How can you display the Charms bar?
4. Explain the difference between the Start screen and the desktop.
5. Explain how to start a desktop application from the Start screen.
6. The keyboard shortcut for closing an application is _____.
7. What page opens by default when you start Windows Help and Support?
8. What option saves your work before turning off your computer?

PRACTICE

Review Assignments

There are no Data Files needed for the Review Assignments.

The day before your first Windows 8 training session for Behind the Scenes employees, Emma Garcia offers to observe your tour of the operating system and help you fine-tune your lesson. You'll start working on the Start screen, with no applications open. Complete the following steps, recording your answers to any questions according to your instructor's preferences:

1. Start Windows 8 and sign in, if necessary.
2. Use the mouse to scroll the Start screen. How many full tiles appear on the screen when you scroll?
3. Zoom the Start screen to reduce the size of the tiles. How many tiles appear on the screen now?
4. Display the desktop. List the major parts of the desktop, including any icons.
5. Start WordPad. Identify each object on the taskbar (not including the notification area). Minimize the WordPad window.
6. Open the Recycle Bin window and then maximize it. How do you know that the Recycle Bin window is active?
7. Redisplay the WordPad window. Which window is active now? How can you tell?
8. Start the Weather app, and then display the Switch List. Which thumbnails are displayed in the Switch List?
9. Display the Start screen, and then start the Reader app. How did you start the Reader app?
10. If possible, snap the Weather app to the left side of the screen, and then unsnap it. Explain how to snap a Windows 8 application to the left side of the screen and then unsnap it.
11. Use a keyboard shortcut to close the Reader app and then the Weather app. Which keyboard shortcut did you use?
12. Use a keyboard shortcut to switch back to the desktop. Which keyboard shortcut did you use?
13. Minimize the WordPad window. In the Recycle Bin window, click the Home tab. Which buttons are active (not gray)? Use any button on the Home tab to open a dialog box. What dialog box did you open? What do you think this dialog box is used for? Click the Cancel button to close the dialog box, and then close the Recycle Bin window.
14. Close the WordPad window from the taskbar. What command did you use?
15. Open Windows Help and Support. Use any link on the home page to learn something new about Windows 8. What did you learn? How did you find this topic?
16. Close Help and Support.
17. Turn off Windows 8 by using the Sleep option, shutting down, or signing out.

CHALLENGE

Case Problem 1

There are no Data Files needed for this Case Problem.

Up and Running   Up and Running is a computer support firm located in major electronics stores throughout the Midwest. Ken Mathias is the manager of a store in Red Wing, Minnesota. He hired you to work with customers in their homes or businesses. You are preparing for a visit to a customer who is new to Windows 8 and wants to learn about the applications installed on his computer. Complete the following steps:

1. Start Windows 8 and sign in, if necessary.
2. Examine the tiles on the Start screen and use one to start an application that plays music or videos. Which application did you start?
3. Search for an application installed on your computer related to photos. What application did you find?
4. Start the application you found in Step 3. Is it a Windows 8 application or a desktop application? How can you tell?

5. Search for an application installed on your computer that lets you perform calculations. What application did you find?

6. Start the application you found in Step 5. Is it a Windows 8 application or a desktop application? How can you tell?

✦ **Explore** 7. Use the Search menu to find settings related to music. (*Hint*: After you use the Search menu to search for "music," click the Settings category on the Search menu.) How many settings did you find?

8. Use the Apps screen to start the Paint application. Describe how you started this application.

✦ **Explore** 9. Point to the buttons in the Paint window until you find one that displays a "Paint Help (F1)" ScreenTip. Click this button, and then describe what happens.

10. Close all open Windows 8 applications only. Describe how you closed the applications.

11. Use Windows Help and Support to find and read about topics that describe two Windows features that make your PC more secure. Which two features did you read about?

12. Close all open windows.

RESEARCH

Case Problem 2

There are no Data Files needed for this Case Problem.

Home Care Therapy   After earning their certifications as physical and occupational therapists, Josh Cohen and Deborah Whiting decided to start a service called Home Care Therapy for people who need physical or occupational therapy in their homes. They have been using Windows 8 on laptops to schedule client appointments and track client progress, but recently purchased tablet computers to use when they are working with clients face to face. They hired you as a consultant to help them use and maintain their computers. Because Josh and Deborah learned to use Windows 8 on laptop computers, they anticipate that they might have trouble adapting to tablets. Josh asks you to research the skills and techniques they need to use Windows 8 on a tablet. Complete the following:

1. In Windows Help and Support, find information about how to perform the following tasks on a tablet computer:
   - Display the Charms bar.
   - Scroll the Start screen.
   - Zoom the Start screen.
   - Display the desktop.
   - Display app settings, such as Save and Edit.

2. Use the Windows website link to visit the Microsoft website to obtain more information about Windows 8 on a tablet computer. Watch a video that showcases Windows 8 touch features. Then, describe how to rearrange tiles on the Start screen.

3. Choose a topic that describes how to browse the web, and then watch the related video. Explain what's new and different in Internet Explorer for touchscreen devices.

4. Write one to two paragraphs for Josh and Deborah explaining the basics of using Windows 8 on a tablet with a touchscreen.

OBJECTIVES

- Explore the differences between Windows 7 and Windows 8
- Plan the organization of files and folders
- Use File Explorer to view and manage libraries, folders, and files
- Open and save files
- Create folders
- Copy and move files and folders
- Compress and extract files

Managing Your Files

Organizing Files and Folders with Windows 8

Case | *Savvy Traveler*

After spending a summer traveling in Italy, Matt Marino started Savvy Traveler, a travel company that organizes small tours in Europe. To market his company, Matt created flyers, brochures, webpages, and other materials that describe the tours he offers. Matt uses the Savvy Traveler office computer to locate and store photos, illustrations, and text documents he can include in his marketing materials. He recently hired you to help manage the office. To keep Matt connected to the office while traveling, he just purchased a new laptop computer running Windows 8. He is familiar with Windows 7, so he needs an overview explaining how Windows 8 is different. Matt asks you to train him on using Windows 8 to organize his files and folders. Although he has only a few files, he knows it's a good idea to set up a logical organization now so he can find his work later as he stores more files and folders on the computer.

In this tutorial, you'll explore the differences between Windows 7 and Windows 8, especially those related to file management tools. You'll also work with Matt to devise a plan for managing his files. You'll learn how Windows 8 organizes files and folders, and then create files and folders yourself and organize them on Matt's computer. You'll also use techniques to display the information you need in folder windows, and explore options for working with compressed files.

STARTING DATA FILES

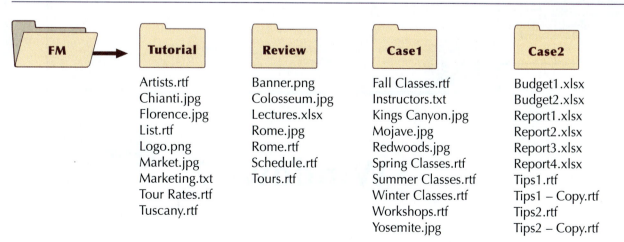

FM → Tutorial	Review	Case1	Case2
Artists.rtf	Banner.png	Fall Classes.rtf	Budget1.xlsx
Chianti.jpg	Colosseum.jpg	Instructors.txt	Budget2.xlsx
Florence.jpg	Lectures.xlsx	Kings Canyon.jpg	Report1.xlsx
List.rtf	Rome.jpg	Mojave.jpg	Report2.xlsx
Logo.png	Rome.rtf	Redwoods.jpg	Report3.xlsx
Market.jpg	Schedule.rtf	Spring Classes.rtf	Report4.xlsx
Marketing.txt	Tours.rtf	Summer Classes.rtf	Tips1.rtf
Tour Rates.rtf		Winter Classes.rtf	Tips1 – Copy.rtf
Tuscany.rtf		Workshops.rtf	Tips2.rtf
		Yosemite.jpg	Tips2 – Copy.rtf

Visual Overview:

You use the Change your view button to change the size of the icons in the window.

In Windows 7, you use **Windows Explorer** to navigate the contents of your computer.

Use the arrow buttons in the Address bar to navigate to other locations on your computer.

The **file path** is a notation that indicates a file's location on your computer.

Use the Search box to search for files in the current folder.

The Windows Explorer **toolbar** provides buttons for completing tasks.

Windows Explorer includes a **navigation pane**, which displays icons and links to resources and locations on your computer.

By default, Windows Explorer includes the **Details pane** at the bottom of the window, which displays the properties of the selected object.

Windows provides **libraries** so you can organize files by category—documents, music, pictures, and video.

A thumbnail image previews the file contents for certain types of files.

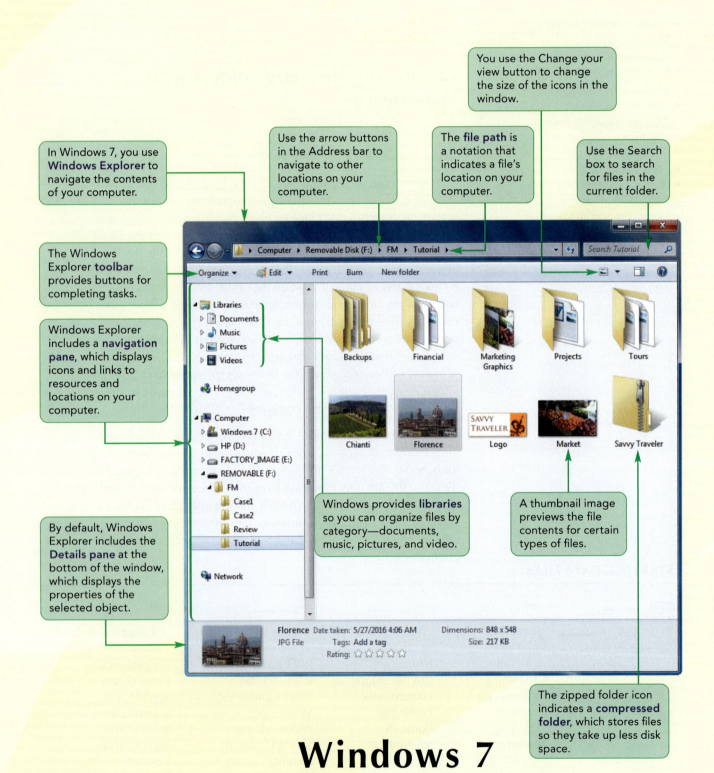

The zipped folder icon indicates a **compressed folder**, which stores files so they take up less disk space.

Windows 7

Comparing Windows 7 & Windows 8

The **View tab** on the ribbon contains options for specifying how the information displays in File Explorer.

Windows provides **libraries** so you can organize files by category—documents, music, pictures, and videos.

The **Quick Access toolbar** contains buttons for viewing properties and creating a folder.

Use the arrow buttons in the Address bar to navigate to other locations on your computer.

The **file path** in the Address bar shows a file's location on your computer.

In Windows 8, you use **File Explorer** to navigate the contents of your computer.

File Explorer includes a ribbon with tools organized on tabs for working with files and folders.

A thumbnail image previews the file contents for certain types of files.

A **filename** is the name you give to a file when you save it to identify the file's contents.

A **file icon** indicates the file type.

Clicking the Computer icon in the navigation pane shows the drives on your computer.

Data Files for this tutorial are stored on a removable disk on this computer.

You can use the Large icons view button on the status bar or in the Layout group on the View tab to switch to Large icons view.

File Explorer includes a **navigation pane**, which displays icons and links to resources and locations on your computer.

Windows 8

Exploring the Differences Between Windows 7 and Windows 8

Windows 8, the most recent version of the Microsoft operating system, is significantly different from Windows 7, the previous version. The major difference is that Windows 8 is designed for touchscreen computers such as tablets and laptops with touch-activated displays, though it runs on computers with more traditional pointing devices such as a mouse or a trackpad. This design change affects many of the fundamental Windows features you use to work on a computer. Figure 1 compares how to perform typical tasks in Windows 7 and Windows 8.

Figure 1	Comparing Windows 7 and Windows 8

Task	Windows 7 Method	Windows 8 Method
Start applications (sometimes called apps)	**Start menu** Open the Start menu by clicking the Start button.	**Start screen** The Start screen appears when you start Windows.
Access applications, documents, settings, and other resources	**Start menu** Use the Start menu, All Programs list, and Search box.	**Charms bar** The Charms bar appears when you point to the upper-right or lower-right corner of the screen, and displays buttons, called charms, for interacting with Windows 8 and accessing applications.
Select objects and commands	**Icons** Icons are small and detailed, designed for interaction with mechanical pointing devices.	**Icons and tiles** Icons and tiles are large and simplified, designed for interaction with your fingertips.
Open and work in applications	**Desktop** Applications all use a single desktop interface featuring windows and dialog boxes.	**Windows 8 and desktop** Applications use one of two interfaces: the Windows 8 interface (featuring tiles and a full-screen layout) or the desktop.
Display content out of view	**Vertical scrolling** Applications allow more vertical scrolling than horizontal scrolling.	**Horizontal scrolling** The Start screen and applications allow more horizontal scrolling than vertical scrolling to take advantage of wide-screen monitors.
Store files	**Physical storage devices** Windows primarily provides access to disks physically connected to the computer.	**Cloud storage locations** A Microsoft user account provides access to information stored online.
Enter text	**Physical keyboard** Type on the keyboard attached to the computer.	**On-screen keyboard** If your computer does not have a physical keyboard, type using the on-screen keyboard.

© 2014 Cengage Learning

Although Windows 7 introduced a few gestures for touchscreen users, Windows 8 expands the use of gestures and interactions. In Windows 8, you can use touch gestures to do nearly everything you can do with a pointing device. Figure 2 lists common Windows 8 interactions and their touch and mouse equivalents.

| Figure 2 | Windows 8 touch and mouse interactions |

Interaction	Touch Gesture	Mouse Action
Display a ScreenTip, text that identifies the name or purpose of the button	Touch and hold (or press) an object such as a button.	Point to an object such as a button.
Display an Apps bar, which displays options related to the current task and access to the Apps screen	Swipe from the top or bottom of the screen toward the center.	Right-click the bottom edge of the screen.
Display the Charms bar	Swipe from the right edge of the screen toward the center.	Point to the upper-right or lower-right corner of the screen.
Display thumbnails of open apps (the Switch List)	Swipe from the left edge of the screen toward the center.	Point to the upper-left corner of the screen, and then drag the pointer down.
Drag an object	Press and then drag.	Click, hold, and then drag.
Scroll the Start screen	Swipe from the right edge of the screen to the left.	Click the scroll arrows, or drag the scroll bar.
Select an object or perform an action such as starting an app	Tap the object.	Click the object.
Zoom	Pinch two fingers to zoom out or move the fingers apart to zoom in.	Click the Zoom button.

© 2014 Cengage Learning

Despite the substantial differences between how you interact with Windows 7 and Windows 8, the steps you follow to perform work in either operating system are the same. In a typical computer session, you start an application and open a **file**, often referred to as a document, which is a collection of data that has a name and is stored on a computer. You view, add, or change the file contents, and then save and close the file. You can complete all of these steps using Windows 7 or Windows 8. Because most of your work involves files, you need to understand how to save and organize files so you can easily find and open them when necessary.

Organizing Files and Folders

Knowing how to save, locate, and organize computer files makes you more productive when you are working with a computer. After you create a file, you can open it, edit its contents, print the file, and save it again—usually using the same application you used to create the file. You organize files by storing them in folders. A **folder** is a container for files. You need to organize files and folders so that you can find them easily and work efficiently.

A file cabinet is a common metaphor for computer file organization. As shown in Figure 3, a computer is like a file cabinet that has two or more drawers—each drawer is a storage device, or **disk**. Each disk contains folders that hold files. To make it easy to retrieve files, you arrange them logically into folders. For example, one folder might contain financial data, another might contain your creative work, and another could contain information you're gathering for an upcoming vacation.

| Figure 3 | Computer as a file cabinet |

disks contain folders

folders contain files

each drawer is a storage device, or disk

© 2014 Cengage Learning

A computer can store folders and files on different types of disks, ranging from removable media—such as **USB drives** (also called USB flash drives) and digital video discs (DVDs)—to **hard disks**, or fixed disks, which are permanently housed in a computer. Hard disks are the most popular type of computer storage because they provide an economical way to store many gigabytes of data. (A **gigabyte**, or **GB**, is about 1 billion bytes, with each byte roughly equivalent to a character of data.)

To have your computer access a removable disk, you must insert the disk into a **drive**, which is a device that can retrieve and sometimes record data on a disk. A computer's hard disk is already contained in a drive inside the computer, so you don't need to insert it each time you use the computer.

A computer distinguishes one drive from another by assigning each a drive letter. The hard disk is assigned to drive C. The remaining drives can have any other letters, but are usually assigned in the order that the drives were installed on the computer—so your USB drive might be drive D or drive F.

Understanding How to Organize Files and Folders

Windows stores thousands of files in many folders on the hard disk of your computer. These are system files that Windows needs to display the Start screen and desktop, use drives, and perform other operating system tasks. To keep the system stable and to find files quickly, Windows organizes the folders and files in a hierarchy, or **file system**. At the top of the hierarchy, Windows stores folders and important files that it needs when you turn on the computer. This location is called the **root directory** and is usually drive C (the hard disk). As Figure 4 shows, the root directory contains all the other folders and files on the computer. The figure also shows that folders can contain other folders. An effectively organized computer contains a few folders in the root directory, and those folders contain other folders, also called **subfolders**.

| Figure 4 | Organizing folders and files on a hard disk |

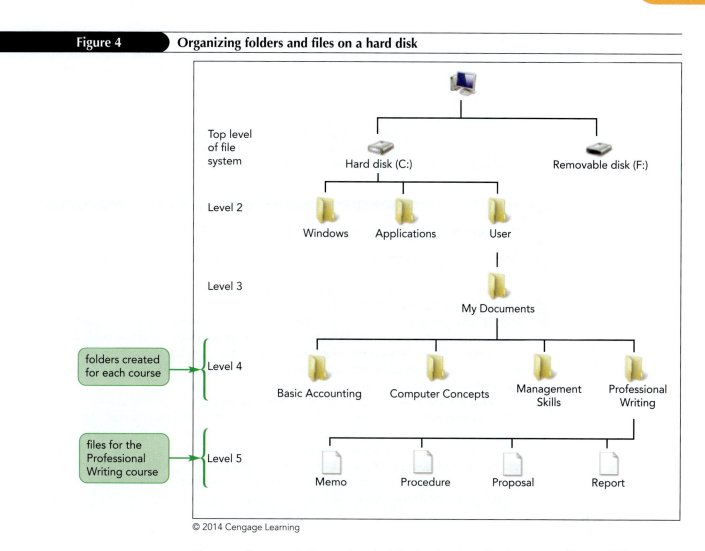

© 2014 Cengage Learning

The root directory is the top level of the hard disk and is for system files and folders only. You should not store your own work in the root directory because your files could interfere with Windows or an application. (If you are working in a computer lab, you might not be allowed to access the root directory.)

Do not delete or move any files or folders from the root directory of the hard disk; doing so could disrupt the system so that you can't start or run the computer. In fact, you should not reorganize or change any folder that contains installed software because Windows 8 expects to find the files for specific applications within certain folders. In Figure 4, folders containing software are stored at Level 2 of the file system. If you reorganize or change these folders, Windows 8 can't locate and start the applications stored in those folders. Likewise, you should not make changes to the folder (usually named Windows) that contains the Windows 8 operating system.

Level 2 of the file system also includes a folder for your user account, such as the User folder. This folder contains all of your system settings, preferences, and other user account information. It also contains subfolders, such as the My Documents folder, for your personal files. The folders in Level 3 of the file system are designed to contain subfolders for your personal files. You can create as many subfolders at Level 4 of the file system as you need to store other folders and files and keep them organized.

Figure 4 shows how you could organize your files on a hard disk if you were taking a full semester of business classes. To duplicate this organization, you would open the main folder for your documents, such as My Documents, create four folders—one each for the Basic Accounting, Computer Concepts, Management Skills, and Professional Writing courses—and then store the writing assignments you complete in the Professional Writing folder.

If you store your files on removable media, such as a USB drive, you can use a simpler organization because you do not have to account for system files. In general, the larger the storage medium, the more levels of folders you should use because large media can store more files and, therefore, need better organization. For example, if you were organizing your files on a 12 GB USB drive, you could create folders in the top level of the USB drive for each general category of documents you store—one each for Courses, Creative, Financials, and Vacation. The Courses folder could then include one folder for each course (Basic Accounting, Computer Concepts, Management Skills, and Professional Writing), and each of those folders could contain the appropriate files.

PROSKILLS

Decision Making: Determining Where to Store Files

When you create and save files on your computer's hard disk, you should store them in subfolders. The top level of the hard disk is off-limits for your files because they could interfere with system files. If you are working on your own computer, store your files within the My Documents folder in the Documents library, which is where many applications save your files by default. When you use a computer on the job, your employer might assign a main folder to you for storing your work. In either case, if you simply store all your files in one folder, you will soon have trouble finding the files you want. Instead, you should create subfolders within a main folder to separate files in a way that makes sense for you.

Even if you store most of your files on removable media, such as USB drives, you still need to organize those files into folders and subfolders. Before you start creating folders, whether on a hard disk or removable disk, you need to plan the organization you will use. Following your plan increases your efficiency because you don't have to pause and decide which folder to use when you save your files. A file organization plan also makes you more productive in your computer work—the next time you need a particular file, you'll know where to find it.

Exploring Files and Folders

As shown in the Visual Overview, you use File Explorer in Windows 8 to explore the files and folders on your computer. File Explorer displays the contents of your computer by using icons to represent drives, folders, and files. When you open File Explorer, it shows the contents of the Windows built-in libraries by default. Windows provides these libraries so you can organize files by category—documents, music, pictures, and video. A library can display these categories of files together, no matter where the files are actually stored. For example, you might keep some music files in a folder named Albums on your hard disk. You might also keep music files in a Songs folder on a USB drive. Although the Albums and Songs folders are physically stored in different locations, you can set up the Music library to display both folders in the same File Explorer window. You can then search and arrange the files as a single collection to quickly find the music you want to open and play. In this way, you use libraries to organize your files into categories so you can easily locate and work with files.

The File Explorer window is divided into two sections, called panes. The left pane is the navigation pane, which contains icons and links to locations on your computer. The right pane displays the contents of the location selected in the navigation pane. If the navigation pane showed all the contents on your computer at once, it could be a very long list. Instead, you open drives and folders only when you want to see what they contain. For example, to display the hierarchy of the folders and other locations on your computer, you select the Computer icon in the navigation pane, and then select the icon for a drive, such as Local Disk (C:) or Removable Disk (F:). You can then open and explore folders on that drive.

If a folder contains undisplayed subfolders, an expand icon appears to the left of the folder icon. (The same is true for drives.) To view the folders contained in an object, you click the expand icon. A collapse icon then appears next to the folder icon; click the collapse icon to hide the folder's subfolders. To view the files contained in a folder, you click the folder icon, and the files appear in the right pane. See Figure 5.

Figure 5   **Viewing files in File Explorer**

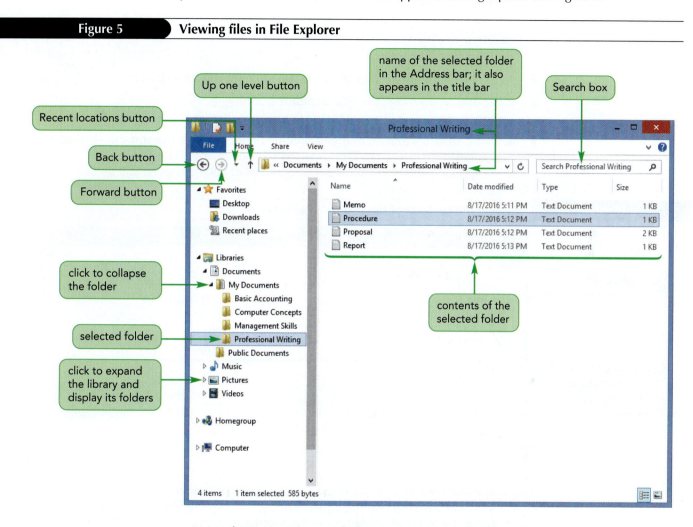

Using the navigation pane helps you explore your computer and orients you to your current location. As you move, copy, delete, and perform other tasks with the files and folders in the right pane of File Explorer, you can refer to the navigation pane to see how your changes affect the overall organization of the selected location.

In addition to using the navigation pane, you can explore your computer in File Explorer using the following navigation techniques:

- Opening drives and folders in the right pane—To view the contents of a drive or folder, double-click the drive or folder icon in the right pane of File Explorer.
- Using the Address bar—You can use the Address bar to navigate to a different folder. The Address bar displays the file path for your current folder. (Recall that a file path shows the location of a folder or file.) Click a folder name such as My Documents in the Address bar to navigate to that folder, or click an arrow button to navigate to a different location in the folder's hierarchy.
- Clicking the Back, Forward, Recent locations, and Up to buttons—Use the Back, Forward, and Recent locations buttons to navigate to other folders you have already opened. Use the Up to button to navigate up to the folder containing the current folder.
- Using the Search box—To find a file or folder stored in the current folder or its subfolders, type a word or phrase in the Search box. The search begins as soon as you

start typing. Windows finds files based on text in the filename, text within the file, and other properties of the file.

You'll practice using some of these navigation techniques later in the tutorial. Right now, you'll show Matt how to open File Explorer. Your computer should be turned on and displaying the Start screen.

To open File Explorer:

▶ **1.** On the Start screen, click the **Desktop** tile to display the desktop.

▶ **2.** On the taskbar, click the **File Explorer** button 📁. The File Explorer window opens, displaying the contents of the default libraries.

▶ **3.** In the Libraries section of the navigation pane, click the **expand** icon ▷ next to the Documents icon. The folders in the Documents library appear in the navigation pane; see Figure 6. The contents of your computer will differ.

Figure 6	Viewing the contents of the Documents library

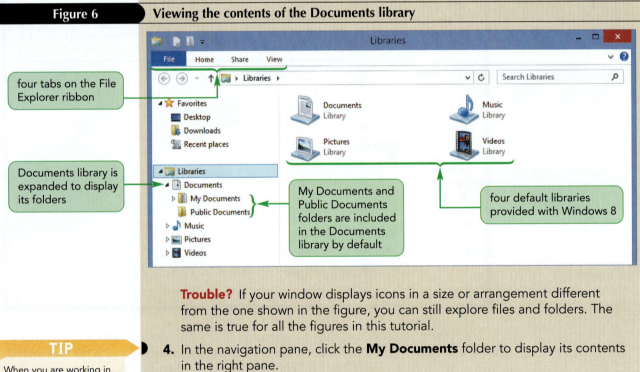

four tabs on the File Explorer ribbon

Documents library is expanded to display its folders

My Documents and Public Documents folders are included in the Documents library by default

four default libraries provided with Windows 8

Trouble? If your window displays icons in a size or arrangement different from the one shown in the figure, you can still explore files and folders. The same is true for all the figures in this tutorial.

▶ **4.** In the navigation pane, click the **My Documents** folder to display its contents in the right pane.

TIP

When you are working in the navigation pane, you only need to click a folder to open it; you do not need to double-click it.

As Figure 6 shows, the File Explorer window includes a ribbon, which is collapsed by default so it displays only tab names, such as File, Home, Share, and View. The Visual Overview shows the expanded ribbon, which displays the options for the selected tab. You'll work with the ribbon and learn how to expand it later in the tutorial.

Navigating to Your Data Files

To navigate to the files you want, it helps to know the file path because the file path tells you exactly where the file is stored in the hierarchy of drives and folders on your computer. For example, Matt has a file named "Logo," which contains an image of the company's logo. If Matt stored the Logo file in a folder named "Marketing" and saved that folder in a folder named "Savvy Traveler" on drive F (a USB drive) on his computer, the Address bar would show the following file path for the Logo file:

Computer ▸ Removable Disk (F:) ▸ Savvy Traveler ▸ Marketing ▸ Logo.png

This path has five parts, with each part separated by an arrow button:

- Computer—The main container for the file, such as "Computer" or "Network"
- Removable Disk (F:)—The drive name, including the drive letter followed by a colon, which indicates a drive rather than a folder
- Savvy Traveler—The top-level folder on drive F
- Marketing—A subfolder in the Savvy Traveler folder
- Logo.png—The name of the file

Although File Explorer uses arrow buttons to separate locations in a file path, printed documents use backslashes (\ ). For example, if you read an instruction to open the Logo file in the Savvy Traveler\Marketing folder on your USB drive, you know you must navigate to the USB drive attached to your computer, open the Savvy Traveler folder, and then open the Marketing folder to find the Logo file.

File Explorer displays the file path in the Address bar so you can keep track of your current location as you navigate between drives and folders. You can use File Explorer to navigate to the Data Files you need for this tutorial. Before you perform the following steps, you should know where you stored your Data Files, such as on a USB drive. The following steps assume that drive is Removable Disk (F:), a USB drive. If necessary, substitute the appropriate drive on your system when you perform the steps.

To navigate to your Data Files:

1. Make sure your computer can access your Data Files for this tutorial. For example, if you are using a USB drive, insert the drive into the USB port.

   Trouble? If you don't have the starting Data Files, you need to get them before you can proceed. Your instructor will either give you the Data Files or ask you to obtain them from a specified location (such as a network drive). If you have any questions about the Data Files, see your instructor or technical support person for assistance.

2. In the navigation pane of File Explorer, click the **expand** icon ▷ next to the Computer icon to display the drives on your computer, if necessary.

3. Click the **expand** icon ▷ next to the drive containing your Data Files, such as Removable Disk (F:). A list of the folders on that drive appears below the drive name.

4. If the list of folders does not include the FM folder, continue clicking the **expand** icon ▷ to navigate to the folder that contains the FM folder.

5. Click the **expand** icon ▷ next to the FM folder to expand the folder, and then click the **FM** folder so that its contents appear in the navigation pane and in the right pane of the folder window. The FM folder contains the Case1, Case2, Review, and Tutorial folders, as shown in Figure 7. The other folders on your computer might vary.

Figure 7   **Navigating to the FM folder**

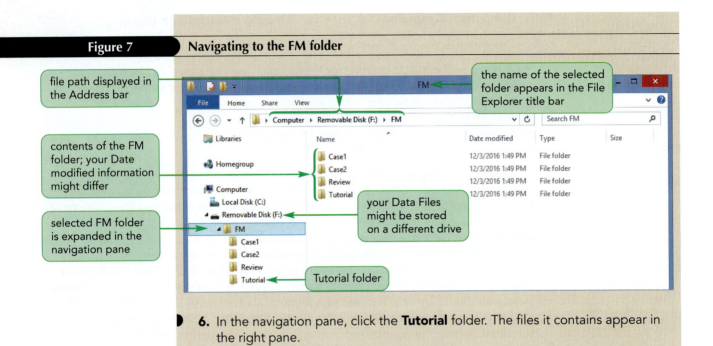

file path displayed in the Address bar

the name of the selected folder appears in the File Explorer title bar

contents of the FM folder; your Date modified information might differ

your Data Files might be stored on a different drive

selected FM folder is expanded in the navigation pane

Tutorial folder

6. In the navigation pane, click the **Tutorial** folder. The files it contains appear in the right pane.

You can change the appearance of the File Explorer window to suit your preferences. You'll do so next so you can see more details about folders and files.

Changing the View

TIP

The default view for any folder in the Pictures library is Large icons view, which provides a thumbnail image of the file contents.

File Explorer provides eight ways to view the contents of a folder: Extra large icons, Large icons, Medium icons, Small icons, List, Details, Tiles, and Content. For example, the files in the Tutorial folder are currently displayed in Details view, which is the default view for all folders except those stored in the Pictures library. Details view displays a small icon to identify each file's type and lists file details in columns, such as the date the file was last modified, the file type, and the size of the file. Although only Details view lists the file details, you can see these details in any other view by pointing to a file to display a ScreenTip.

To change the view of File Explorer to any of the eight views, you use the View tab on the ribbon. To switch to Details view or Large icons view, you can use the view buttons on the status bar.

REFERENCE

Changing the View in File Explorer

- Click a view button on the status bar.
  or
- Click the View tab on the ribbon.
- In the Layout group, click the view option; or click the More button, if necessary, and then click a view option.

You'll show Matt how to change the view of the Tutorial folder in the File Explorer window.

To change the view of the Tutorial folder in File Explorer:

1. On the ribbon, click the **View** tab.

2. In the Layout group, click **Medium icons**. The files appear in Medium icons view in File Explorer. See Figure 8.

| Figure 8 | Files in the Tutorial folder in Medium icons view |

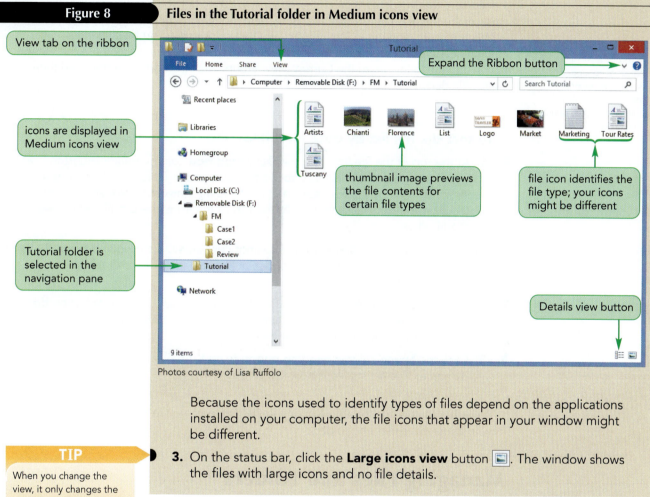

Photos courtesy of Lisa Ruffolo

Because the icons used to identify types of files depend on the applications installed on your computer, the file icons that appear in your window might be different.

TIP

When you change the view, it only changes the view for the currently selected folder.

3. On the status bar, click the **Large icons view** button ⊡. The window shows the files with large icons and no file details.

When you clicked the View tab in the previous steps, the ribbon expanded so you could select an option and then collapsed after you clicked the Medium icons option. You can keep the ribbon expanded in the File Explorer window so you can easily access all of its options. You'll show Matt how to expand the ribbon and then use the View tab to switch to Details view.

To expand the ribbon in File Explorer:

1. Click the **Expand the Ribbon** button ⌄ to expand the ribbon. The Expand the Ribbon button changes to the Minimize the Ribbon button, which you could click if you wanted to collapse the ribbon.

2. On the View tab, in the Layout group, click **Details**. The window shows the files with small icons and lists the file details.

No matter which view you use, you can sort the file list by the name of the files or another detail, such as size, type, or date. When you **sort** files, you list them in ascending order (A to Z, 0 to 9, or earliest to latest date) or descending order (Z to A, 9 to 0, or latest to earliest date) by a file detail. If you're viewing music files, you can sort by details such as contributing artists or album title; and if you're viewing picture files, you can sort by details such as date taken or size. Sorting can help you find a particular file in a long file listing. For example, suppose you want to work on a document that you know you edited on June 4, 2016, but you can't remember the name of the file. You can sort the file list by date modified to find the file you want.

When you are working in Details view in File Explorer, you sort by clicking a column heading that appears at the top of the file list. In other views, you use the View tab on the ribbon to sort. In the Current view group, click the Sort by button, and then click a file detail.

TIP

To sort by a file detail that does not appear as a column heading, right-click any column heading and then select a file detail.

To sort the file list by date modified:

1. At the top of the file list, click the **Date modified** column heading button. The down arrow that appears above the label of the Date modified button indicates that the files are sorted in descending (newest to oldest) order by the date the file was modified. At the top of the list is the List file, which was modified on June 18, 2016.

   Trouble? If your folder window does not contain a Date modified column, right-click any column heading, click Date modified on the shortcut menu, and then repeat Step 1.

2. Click the **Date modified** column heading button again. The up arrow on the Date modified button indicates that the sort order is reversed, with the files listed in ascending (oldest to newest) order.

3. Click the **Name** column heading button to sort the files in alphabetical order by name. The Artists file is now listed first.

Now that Matt is comfortable working in File Explorer, you're ready to show him how to manage his files and folders.

Managing Files and Folders

As discussed earlier, you manage your personal files and folders by storing them according to a logical organization so that they are easy to find later. You can organize files as you create, edit, and save them, or you can do so later by creating folders, if necessary, and then moving and copying files into the folders.

To create a file-organization plan for Matt's files, you can review Figure 8 and look for files that logically belong together. In the Tutorial folder, Chianti, Florence, Logo, and Market are all graphics files that Matt uses for marketing and sales. He created the Artists and Tuscany files to describe Italian tours. The Marketing and Tour Rates files relate to business finances. Matt thinks the List file contains a task list for completing a project, but he isn't sure of its contents. He does recall creating the file using WordPad.

If the List file does contain a project task list, you can organize the files by creating four folders—one for graphics, one for tours, another for the financial files, and a fourth folder for projects. When you create a folder, you give it a name, preferably one that describes its contents. A folder name can have up to 255 characters, and any character is allowed, except / \ : * ? " < > and |. Considering these conventions, you could create four folders to contain Matt's files, as follows:

- Marketing Graphics folder—Chianti, Florence, Logo, and Market files
- Tours folder—Artists and Tuscany files
- Financial folder—Marketing and Tour Rates files
- Projects folder—List file

Before you start creating folders according to this plan, you need to verify the contents of the List file. You can do so by opening the file.

Opening a File

TIP

To select the default application for opening a file, right-click the file in File Explorer, point to Open with, and then click Choose default application. Click an application in the list that opens, and then click OK.

You can open a file from a running application or from File Explorer. To open a file in a running application, you select the application's Open command to access the Open dialog box, which you use to navigate to the file you want, select the file, and then open it. In the Open dialog box, you use the same tools that are available in File Explorer to navigate to the file you want to open. If the application you want to use is not running, you can open a file by double-clicking it in the right pane of File Explorer. The file usually opens in the application that you used to create or edit it.

Occasionally, File Explorer will open the file in an application other than the one you want to use to work with the file. For example, double-clicking a digital picture file usually opens the picture in a picture viewer application. If you want to edit the picture, you must open the file in a graphics editing application. When you need to specify an application to open a file, you can right-click the file, point to Open with on the shortcut menu, and then click the name of the application that you want to use.

Matt says that he might want to edit the List file to add another task. You'll show him how to use File Explorer to open the file in WordPad, which he used to create the file, and then edit it.

To open and edit the List file:

▶ **1.** In the right pane of File Explorer, right-click the **List** file, and then point to **Open with** on the shortcut menu to display a list of applications that can open the file. See Figure 9.

Trouble? If a list does not appear when you point to Open with on the shortcut menu, click Open with to display a window asking how you want to open this file.

Figure 9	Shortcut menu for opening a file

List is the selected file

Open with command

applications on this computer that can open the List file

9 items   1 item selected 350 bytes

TIP

In File Explorer, you can also double-click a file to open it in the default application for that file type.

2. Click **WordPad** to open the List file in WordPad. The file contains a task list for the marketing project, which includes three items.

   Trouble? If you had to click Open with instead of pointing to it, in the window that asks how you want to open this file, click Keep using WordPad.

3. Press the **Ctrl+End** keys to move the insertion point to the end of the document, press the **Enter** key if necessary to start a new line, and then type **4. Review the Tours in Italy webpage.**

Now that you've added text to the List file, you need to save it to preserve the changes you made.

Saving a File

As you are creating or editing a file, you should save it frequently so you don't lose your work. When you save a file, you need to decide what name to use for the file and where to store it. Most applications provide a default location for saving a file, which makes it easy to find the file again later. However, you can select a different location depending on where you want to store the file.

Besides a storage location, every file must have a filename, which provides important information about the file, including its contents and purpose. A filename such as Italian Tours.docx has the following three parts:

- Main part of the filename—When you save a file, you need to provide only the main part of the filename, such as "Italian Tours."
- Dot—The dot (.) separates the main part of the filename from the extension.
- Extension—The **extension** includes the three or four characters that follow the dot in the filename and identify the file's type.

Similar to folder names, the main part of a filename can have up to 255 characters. This gives you plenty of room to name your file accurately enough so that you'll recognize the contents of the file just by looking at the filename. You can use spaces and certain punctuation symbols in your filenames. However, filenames cannot contain the symbols / \ : * ? " < > or | because these characters have special meanings in Windows 8.

Windows and other software add the dot and the extension to a filename, though File Explorer does not display them by default. Instead, File Explorer shows the file icon associated with the extension or a thumbnail for some types of files, such as graphics. For example, in a file named Italian Tours.docx, the docx extension identifies the file as one created in Microsoft Word, a word-processing application. File Explorer displays this file using a Microsoft Word icon and the main part of its filename. For a file named Italian Tours.png, the png extension identifies the file as one created in a graphics application such as Paint. In Details view or List view, File Explorer displays this file using a Paint icon and the main part of its filename. In other views, File Explorer does not use an icon, but displays the file contents in a thumbnail. File Explorer treats the Italian Tours.docx and Italian Tours.png files differently because their extensions distinguish them as different types of files, even though the main parts of their filenames are identical.

When you save a new file, you use the Save As dialog box to provide a filename and select a location for the file. You can create a folder for the new file at the same time you save the file. When you edit a file you saved previously, you can use the application's Save command to save your changes to the file, keeping the same name and location. If you want to save the edited file with a different name or in a different location, however, you need to use the Save As dialog box to specify the new name or location.

As with the Open dialog box, you specify the file location in the Save As dialog box using the same navigation techniques and tools that are available in File Explorer. You might need to click the Browse Folders button to expand the Save As dialog box so it displays these tools. In addition, the Save As dialog box always includes a File name box where you specify a filename.

INSIGHT

Saving Files on SkyDrive

Some Windows 8 applications, such as Microsoft Office, include SkyDrive as a location for saving and opening files. **SkyDrive** is a Microsoft service that provides up to 7 GB of online storage space for your files at no charge. You can purchase additional space if you need it. For example, if you create a document in Microsoft Word, your SkyDrive appears as a location for saving the document. (Your SkyDrive appears with your username, such as Matt's SkyDrive.) If you have a Microsoft account, you can select a folder on your SkyDrive to save the document online. (If you don't have a Microsoft account, you can sign up for one by visiting the SkyDrive website.) Because the file is stored online, it takes up no storage space on your computer and is available from any computer with an Internet connection. You access the document by opening it in Word or by visiting the SkyDrive website, and then signing in to your Microsoft account. To share the document with other people, you can send them a link to the document via email. They can use the link to access the document even if they do not have a Microsoft account.

One reason that Matt had trouble remembering the contents of the List file is that "List" is not a descriptive name. A better name for this file is Task List. You will save this document in the Tutorial subfolder of the FM folder provided with your Data Files. You will also use the Save As dialog box to specify a new name for the file as you save it.

To save the List file with a new name:

1. On the ribbon in the WordPad window, click the **File** tab to display commands for working with files.

2. Click **Save as** to open the Save As dialog box, as shown in Figure 10. The Tutorial folder is selected as the storage location for this file because you opened the file from this folder.

Figure 10 Saving a file using the Save As dialog box

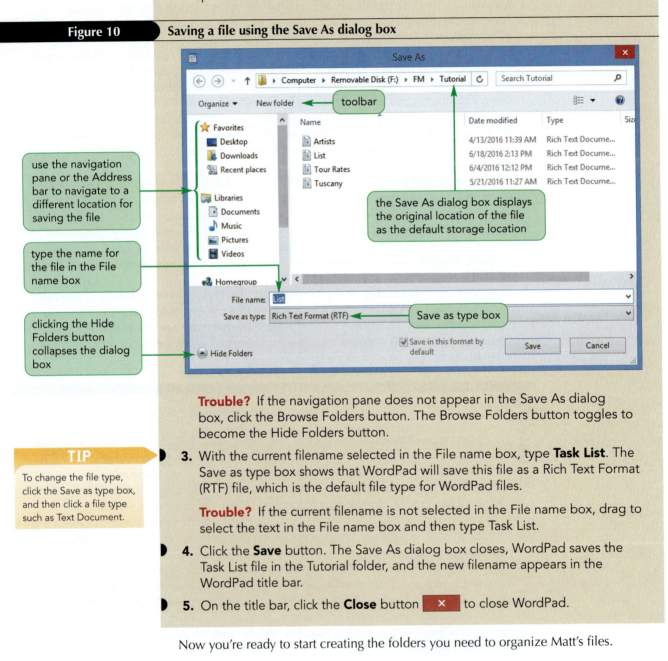

use the navigation pane or the Address bar to navigate to a different location for saving the file

type the name for the file in the File name box

clicking the Hide Folders button collapses the dialog box

the Save As dialog box displays the original location of the file as the default storage location

Save as type box

Trouble? If the navigation pane does not appear in the Save As dialog box, click the Browse Folders button. The Browse Folders button toggles to become the Hide Folders button.

3. With the current filename selected in the File name box, type **Task List**. The Save as type box shows that WordPad will save this file as a Rich Text Format (RTF) file, which is the default file type for WordPad files.

   Trouble? If the current filename is not selected in the File name box, drag to select the text in the File name box and then type Task List.

4. Click the **Save** button. The Save As dialog box closes, WordPad saves the Task List file in the Tutorial folder, and the new filename appears in the WordPad title bar.

5. On the title bar, click the **Close** button ✕ to close WordPad.

Now you're ready to start creating the folders you need to organize Matt's files.

Creating Folders

You originally proposed creating four new folders for Matt's files: Marketing Graphics, Tours, Financial, and Projects. Matt asks you to create these folders now. After that, you'll move his files to the appropriate folders. You create folders in File Explorer using one of three methods: using the New folder button in the New group on the Home tab; using the New folder button on the Quick Access Toolbar; or right-clicking to display a shortcut menu that includes the New command.

INSIGHT

Guidelines for Creating Folders

Consider the following guidelines as you create folders:
- Keep folder names short yet descriptive of the folder's contents. Long folder names can be more difficult to display in their entirety in folder windows, so use names that are short but clear. Choose names that will be meaningful later, such as project names or course numbers.
- Create subfolders to organize files. If a file list in File Explorer is so long that you must scroll the window, you should probably organize those files into subfolders.
- Develop standards for naming folders. Use a consistent naming scheme that is clear to you, such as one that uses a project name as the name of the main folder, and includes step numbers in each subfolder name (for example, 1-Outline, 2-First Draft, 3-Final Draft, and so on).

In the following steps, you will create the four folders for Matt in your Tutorial folder. Because it is easier to work with files using large file icons, you'll switch to Large icons view first.

To create the folders:

1. On the status bar in the File Explorer window, click the **Large icons view** button ▣ to switch to Large icons view.

2. Click the **Home** tab to display the Home tab on the ribbon.

3. In the New group, click the **New folder** button. A folder icon with the label "New folder" appears in the right pane of the File Explorer window. See Figure 11.

Figure 11	Creating a new folder in the Tutorial folder

Photos courtesy of Lisa Ruffolo

Trouble? If the "New folder" name is not selected, right-click the new folder, click Rename on the shortcut menu, and then continue with Step 4.

Windows uses "New folder" as a placeholder, and selects the text so that you can replace it immediately by typing a new name. You do not need to press the Backspace or Delete key to delete the text.

▸ 4. Type **Marketing Graphics** as the folder name, and then press the **Enter** key. The new folder is named Marketing Graphics and is the selected item in the right pane. To create a second folder, you can use a shortcut menu.

▸ 5. In the right pane, right-click a blank area, point to **New** on the shortcut menu, and then click **Folder**. A folder icon appears in the right pane with the "New folder" text selected.

▸ 6. Type **Tours** as the name of the new folder, and then press the **Enter** key. To create the third folder, you can use the Quick Access Toolbar.

▸ 7. On the Quick Access Toolbar, click the **New folder** button 📁, type **Financial**, and then press the **Enter** key to create and name the folder.

▸ 8. Create a new folder in the Tutorial folder named **Projects**.

After creating four folders, you're ready to organize Matt's files by moving them into the appropriate folders.

Moving and Copying Files and Folders

You can either move or copy a file from its current location to a new location. **Moving** a file removes it from its current location and places it in a new location that you specify. **Copying** a file places a duplicate version of the file in a new location that you specify, while leaving the original file intact in its current location. You can also move and copy folders. When you do, you move or copy all the files contained in the folder. (You'll practice copying folders in a Case Problem at the end of this tutorial.)

In File Explorer, you can move and copy files by using the Move to or Copy to buttons in the Organize group on the Home tab; using the Copy and Cut commands on a file's shortcut menu; or using keyboard shortcuts. When you copy or move files using these methods, you are using the **Clipboard**, a temporary storage area for files and information that you copy or move from one location to place in another.

You can also move files by dragging the files in the File Explorer window. You will now organize Matt's files by moving them to the appropriate folders you have created. You'll start by moving the Marketing file to the Financial folder by dragging the file.

To move the Marketing file by dragging it:

1. In File Explorer, point to the **Marketing** file in the right pane, and then press and hold the mouse button.

2. While still pressing the mouse button, drag the **Marketing** file to the **Financial** folder. See Figure 12.

| Figure 12 | Dragging a file to move it to a folder |

Marketing file is selected

Market

Marketing Graphics

Tours

Financial folder

Move to Financial ScreenTip

14 items   1 item selected 1.42 KB

TIP

If you drag a file or folder to a location on a different drive, the file is copied, not moved, to preserve the file in its original location.

3. When the Move to Financial ScreenTip appears, release the mouse button. The Marketing file is removed from the main Tutorial folder and stored in the Financial subfolder.

   Trouble? If you released the mouse button before the Move to Financial ScreenTip appeared, press the Ctrl+Z keys to undo the move, and then repeat Steps 1–3.

   Trouble? If you moved the Market file instead of the Marketing file, press the Ctrl+Z keys to undo the move, and then repeat Steps 1–3.

4. In the right pane, double-click the **Financial** folder to verify that it contains the Marketing file.

Trouble? If the Marketing file does not appear in the Financial folder, you probably moved it to a different folder. Press the Ctrl+Z keys to undo the move, and then repeat Steps 1–3.

▶ 5. Click the **Back** button ⊖ on the Address bar to return to the Tutorial folder.

You'll move the remaining files into the folders using the Clipboard.

To move files using the Clipboard:

▶ 1. Right-click the **Artists** file, and then click **Cut** on the shortcut menu. Although the file icon still appears selected in the right pane of File Explorer, Windows removes the Artists file from the Tutorial folder and stores it on the Clipboard.

▶ 2. In the right pane, right-click the **Tours** folder, and then click **Paste** on the shortcut menu. Windows pastes the Artists file from the Clipboard to the Tours folder. The Artists file icon no longer appears in the File Explorer window, which is currently displaying the contents of the Tutorial folder.

▶ 3. In the navigation pane, click the **expand** icon ▷ next to the Tutorial folder, if necessary, to display its contents, and then click the **Tours** folder to view its contents in the right pane. The Tours folder now contains the Artists file. See Figure 13.

| Figure 13 | Artists file in its new location |

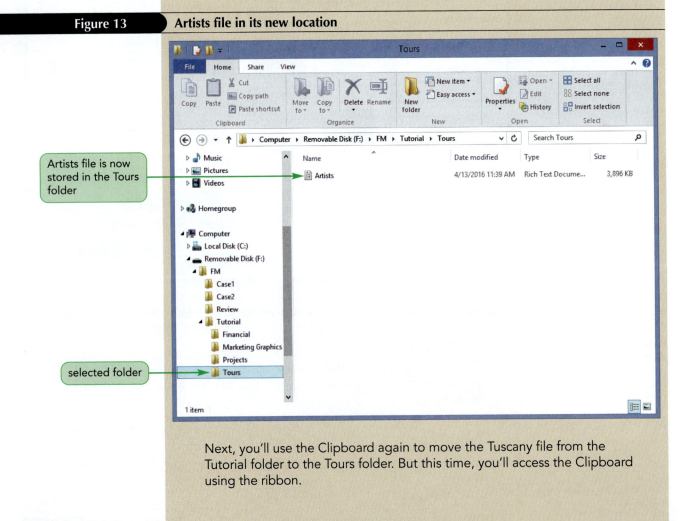

Next, you'll use the Clipboard again to move the Tuscany file from the Tutorial folder to the Tours folder. But this time, you'll access the Clipboard using the ribbon.

4. On the Address bar, point to the **Up to** button ⬆ to display its ScreenTip (Up to "Tutorial"), click the **Up to** button ⬆ to return to the Tutorial folder, and then click the **Tuscany** file to select it.

5. On the Home tab, in the Clipboard group, click the **Cut** button to remove the Tuscany file from the Tutorial folder and temporarily store it on the Clipboard.

6. In the Address bar, click the **arrow** button ▶ to the right of "Tutorial" to display a list of subfolders in the Tutorial folder, and then click **Tours** to display the contents of the Tours folder in File Explorer.

7. In the Clipboard group, click the **Paste** button to paste the Tuscany file in the Tours folder. The Tours folder now contains the Artists and Tuscany files.

Finally, you'll move the Task List file from the Tutorial folder to the Projects folder using the Move to button in the Organize group on the Home tab. This button and the Copy to button are ideal when you want to move or copy files without leaving the current folder. When you select a file and then click the Move to or Copy to button, a list of locations appears, including all of the Windows libraries and one or more folders you open frequently. You can click a location in the list to move the selected file to that library or folder. You can also select the Choose location option to open the Move Items or Copy Items dialog box, and then select a location for the file, which you'll do in the following steps.

To move the Task List file using the Move to button:

1. In the Address bar, click **Tutorial** to return to the Tutorial folder, and then click the **Task List** file to select it.

2. On the Home tab, in the Organize group, click the **Move to** button to display a list of locations to which you can move the selected file. The Projects folder is not included on this list because you haven't opened it yet.

3. Click **Choose location** to open the Move Items dialog box. See Figure 14.

| **Figure 14** | **Move Items dialog box** |

4. If necessary, scroll the list of locations, and then click the **expand** icon ▶ next to the drive containing your Data Files, such as Removable Disk (F:).

5. Navigate to the FM ▸ Tutorial folder, and then click the **Projects** folder to select it.

6. Click the **Move** button to close the dialog box and move the Task List file to the Projects folder.

7. Open the Projects folder to confirm that it contains the Task List file.

One way to save steps when moving or copying multiple files or folders is to select all the files and folders you want to move or copy, and then work with them as a group. You can use several techniques to select multiple files or folders at the same time, which are described in Figure 15.

Figure 15 Selecting multiple files or folders

Items to Select in the Right Pane of File Explorer	Method
Files or folders listed together	Click the first item, press and hold the Shift key, click the last item, and then release the Shift key. *or* Drag the pointer to create a selection box around all the items you want to include.
Files or folders not listed together	Press and hold the Ctrl key, click each item you want to select, and then release the Ctrl key.
All files and folders	On the Home tab, in the Select group, click the Select all button.
Items to Deselect in the Right Pane of File Explorer	**Method**
Single file or folder in a selected group	Press and hold the Ctrl key, click each item you want to remove from the selection, and then release the Ctrl key.
All selected files and folders	Click a blank area of the File Explorer window.

© 2014 Cengage Learning

Next, you'll copy the four graphics files from the Tutorial folder to the Marketing Graphics folder using the Clipboard. To do this efficiently, you will select multiple files at once.

To copy multiple files at once using the Clipboard:

1. Display the contents of the Tutorial folder in File Explorer.

2. Click the **Chianti** file, press and hold the **Shift** key, click the **Market** file, and then release the **Shift** key.

3. Press and hold the **Ctrl** key, click the **List** file to deselect it, and then release the **Ctrl** key. Four files—Chianti, Florence, Logo, and Market—are selected in the Tutorial folder window.

4. Right-click a selected file, and then click **Copy** on the shortcut menu. Windows copies the selected files to the Clipboard.

5. Right-click the **Marketing Graphics** folder, and then click **Paste** on the shortcut menu.

6. Open the **Marketing Graphics** folder to verify it contains the four files you copied, and then return to the Tutorial folder.

7. Right-click the **Tour Rates** file, and then click **Copy** on the shortcut menu.

8. In the right pane, double-click the **Financial** folder to open it, right-click a blank area of the right pane, and then click **Paste** on the shortcut menu.

INSIGHT

Duplicating Your Folder Organization

If you work on two computers, such as one computer at an office or school and another computer at home, you can duplicate the folders you use on both computers to simplify the process of transferring files from one computer to another. For example, if you have four folders in your My Documents folder on your work computer, create these same four folders on a USB drive and in the My Documents folder of your home computer. If you change a file on the hard disk of your home computer, you can copy the most recent version of the file to the corresponding folder on your USB drive so the file is available when you are at work. You also then have a **backup**, or duplicate copy, of important files. Having a backup of your files is invaluable if your computer has a fatal error.

All the files that originally appeared in the Tutorial folder are now stored in appropriate subfolders. You can streamline the organization of the Tutorial folder by deleting the duplicate files you no longer need.

Deleting Files and Folders

TIP

In most cases, a file deleted from a USB drive does not go into the Recycle Bin. Instead, it is deleted when Windows 8 removes its icon, and the file cannot be recovered.

You should periodically delete files and folders you no longer need so that your main folders and disks don't get cluttered. In File Explorer, you delete a file or folder by deleting its icon. When you delete a file from a hard disk, Windows 8 removes the file from the folder but stores the file contents in the Recycle Bin. The Recycle Bin is an area on your hard disk that holds deleted files until you remove them permanently. When you delete a folder from the hard disk, the folder and all of its files are stored in the Recycle Bin. If you change your mind and want to retrieve a deleted file or folder, you can double-click the Recycle Bin on the desktop, right-click the file or folder you want to retrieve, and then click Restore. However, after you empty the Recycle Bin, you can no longer recover the files it contained.

Because you copied the Chianti, Florence, Logo, Market, and Tour Rates files to the subfolders in the Tutorial folder, you can safely delete the original files. You can also delete the List file because you no longer need it. You can delete a file or folder using various methods, including using a shortcut menu or selecting one or more files and then pressing the Delete key.

To delete files in the Tutorial folder:

1. Display the Tutorial folder in the File Explorer window.

2. In the right pane, click **Chianti**, press and hold the **Shift** key, click **Tour Rates**, and then release the **Shift** key. All files in the Tutorial folder are now selected. None of the subfolders should be selected.

Make sure you have copied the selected files to the Marketing Graphics and Financial folders before completing this step.

3. Right-click the selected files, and then click **Delete** on the shortcut menu. A message box appears, asking if you're sure you want to permanently delete these files.

4. Click the **Yes** button to confirm that you want to delete the files.

Renaming Files

After creating and naming a file or folder, you might realize that a different name would be more meaningful or descriptive. You can easily rename a file or folder by using the Rename command on the file's shortcut menu.

Now that you've organized Matt's files into folders, he reviews your work and notes that the Artists file was originally created to store text specifically about Florentine painters and sculptors. You can rename that file to give it a more descriptive filename.

To rename the Artists file:

1. In the right pane of the File Explorer window, double-click the **Tours** folder to display its contents.

2. Right-click the **Artists** file, and then click **Rename** on the shortcut menu. The filename is highlighted and a box appears around it.

3. Type **Florentine Artists**, and then press the **Enter** key. The file now appears with the new name.

   Trouble? If you make a mistake while typing and you haven't pressed the Enter key yet, press the Backspace key until you delete the mistake and then complete Step 3. If you've already pressed the Enter key, repeat Steps 2 and 3 to rename the file again.

   Trouble? If your computer is set to display filename extensions, a message might appear asking if you are sure you want to change the filename extension. Click the No button, and then repeat Steps 2 and 3.

Working with Compressed Files

You compress a file or a folder of files so it occupies less space on the disk. It can be useful to compress files before transferring them from one location to another, such as from your hard disk to a removable disk or vice versa, or from one computer to another via email. You can then transfer the files more quickly. Also, if you or your email contacts can send and receive files only up to a certain size, compressing large files might make them small enough to send and receive. Compare two folders—a folder named Photos that contains files totaling about 8.6 MB, and a compressed folder containing the same files but requiring only 6.5 MB of disk space. In this case, the compressed files use about 25 percent less disk space than the uncompressed files.

You can compress one or more files in File Explorer using the Zip button, which is located in the Send group on the Share tab of the ribbon. Windows stores the compressed files in a special type of folder called an **archive**, or a compressed folder. File Explorer uses an icon of a folder with a zipper to represent a compressed folder. To compress additional files or folders, you drag them into the compressed folder. You can open a file directly from a compressed folder, although you cannot modify the file. To edit and save a compressed file, you must extract it first. When you **extract** a file, you create an uncompressed copy of the file in a folder you specify. The original file remains in the compressed folder.

Matt suggests that you compress the files and folders in the Tutorial folder so that you can more quickly transfer them to another location.

To compress the folders and files in the Tutorial folder:

TIP

Another way to compress files is to select the files, right-click the selection, point to Send to on the shortcut menu, and then click Compressed (zipped) folder.

1. In File Explorer, navigate to the Tutorial folder, and then select all the folders in the Tutorial folder.

2. Click the **Share** tab on the ribbon.

3. In the Send group, click the **Zip** button. After a few moments, a new compressed folder appears in the Tutorial window with the filename selected. By default, File Explorer uses the name of the first selected item as the name of the compressed folder. You'll replace the name with a more descriptive one.

4. Type **Savvy Traveler**, and then press the **Enter** key to rename the compressed folder. See Figure 16.

Figure 16 Compressing files and folders

5. Double-click the **Savvy Traveler** compressed folder to open it, open the **Tours** folder, and then note the size of the compressed Tuscany file, which is 1,815 KB.

6. Navigate back to the Tutorial folder.

You can move and copy the files and folders from an opened compressed folder to other locations, although you cannot rename the files. More often, you extract all of the files from the compressed folder to a new location that you specify, preserving the files in their original folders as appropriate.

To extract the compressed files:

1. Click the **Savvy Traveler** compressed folder to select it, and then click the **Compressed Folder Tools Extract** tab on the ribbon.

2. In the Extract all group, click the **Extract all** button. The Extract Compressed (Zipped) Folders Wizard starts and opens the Select a Destination and Extract Files dialog box.

3. Press the **End** key to deselect the path in the box and move the insertion point to the end of the path, press the **Backspace** key as many times as necessary to delete the Savvy Traveler text, and then type **Backups**. The final three parts of the path in the box should be \FM\Tutorial\Backups. See Figure 17.

Figure 17   **Extracting files from a compressed folder**

your path might differ, but should end with FM\Tutorial\Backups

check box should be selected

> Extract Compressed (Zipped) Folders
>
> Select a Destination and Extract Files
>
> Files will be extracted to this folder:
>
> F:\FM\Tutorial\Backups   Browse...
>
> ☑ Show extracted files when complete
>
> Extract   Cancel

4. Make sure the Show extracted files when complete check box is checked, and then click the **Extract** button. Windows extracts the files and then opens the Backups folder, showing the Financial, Marketing Graphics, Projects, and Tours folders.

5. Open each folder to make sure it contains the files you worked with in this tutorial. When you open the Tours folder, note the uncompressed size of the Tuscany file, which is about four times as large as its compressed version.

6. Close all open windows.

In this tutorial, you examined the purpose of organizing files and folders, and you planned and created an organization for a set of related files and folders. You also explored your computer using File Explorer and learned how to navigate to your Data Files using the navigation pane. You used File Explorer to manage files and folders by opening and saving files; creating folders; and selecting, moving, and copying files. You also renamed and deleted files according to your organization plan. Finally, you compressed and extracted files.

Quick Check

1. You organize files by storing them in _____.
2. What is the purpose of the Address bar in File Explorer?
3. A filename _____ identifies the file's type and indicates the application that created the file.
4. Explain how to use File Explorer to navigate to a file in the following location: E: ▸ Courses ▸ Computer Basics ▸ Operating Systems.txt.
5. One way to move files and folders is to use the _____, a temporary storage area for files and information that you copied or moved from one place and plan to use somewhere else.
6. What happens if you click the first file in a folder window, press the Shift key, click the last file, and then release the Shift key?
7. When you delete a file from a hard disk, Windows removes the file from the folder but stores the file contents in the _____.
8. Describe how to compress a file or folder.
9. What are the benefits of compressing files and folders?

PRACTICE

Review Assignments

Data Files needed for the Review Assignments: Banner.png, Colosseum.jpg, Lectures.xlsx, Rome.jpg, Rome.rtf, Schedule.rtf, Tours.rtf

Matt has saved a few files from his old computer to a removable disk. He gives you these files in a single, unorganized folder, and asks you to organize them logically into subfolders. To do this, you will need to devise a plan for managing the files, and then create the subfolders you need. Next, you will rename, copy, move, and delete files, and then perform other management tasks to make it easy for Matt to work with these files and folders. Complete the following steps:

1. Use File Explorer to navigate to and open the FM ▶ Review folder provided with your Data Files. Examine the seven files in this folder and consider the best way to organize the files.

2. Open the **Rome** text file in WordPad, and then add the following tip to the end of the document: **Dine on the Italian schedule, with the main meal in the middle of the day.**

3. Save the document as **Rome Dining Tips** in the Review folder. Close the WordPad window.

4. In the Review folder, create three folders: **Business**, **Destinations**, and **Supplements**.

5. To organize the files into the correct folders, complete the following steps:
   - Move the Banner and Schedule files from the Review folder to the Business folder.
   - Move the Colosseum and Rome JPEG image files and the Rome Dining Tips and Tours text files to the Destinations folder.
   - Copy the Lectures file to the Supplements folder.

6. Copy the Tours file in the Destinations folder to the Business folder.

7. Rename the Schedule file in the Business folder as **2016 Schedule**. Rename the Lectures file in the Supplements folder as **On-site Lectures**.

8. Delete the Lectures file and the Rome text file from the Review folder.

9. Create a compressed (zipped) folder in the Review folder named **Rome** that contains all the files and folders in the Review folder.

10. Extract the contents of the Rome compressed folder to a new folder named **Rome Backups** in the Review folder. (*Hint:* The file path will end with \FM\Review\Rome Backups.)

11. Close the File Explorer window.

Case Problem 1

APPLY

See the Starting Data Files section at the beginning of this tutorial for the list of Data Files needed for this Case Problem.

Bay Shore Arts Center   Casey Sullivan started the Bay Shore Arts Center in Monterey, California, to provide workshops and courses on art and photography. Attracting students from the San Francisco and San José areas, Casey's business has grown and she now holds classes five days a week. She recently started a course on fine art landscape photography, which has quickly become her most popular offering. Casey hired you to help her design new classes and manage other parts of her growing business, including maintaining electronic business files and communications. Your first task is to organize the files on her new Windows 8 computer. Complete the following steps:

1. Open File Explorer. In the FM ▶ Case1 folder provided with your Data Files, create three folders: **Classes**, **Landscapes**, and **Management**.
2. Move the Fall Classes, Spring Classes, Summer Classes, and Winter Classes files from the Case1 folder to the Classes folder.
3. Rename the four files in the Classes folder by deleting the word "Classes" from each filename.
4. Move the four JPEG image files from the Case1 folder to the Landscapes folder.
5. Copy the remaining two files to the Management folder.
6. Copy the Workshops file to the Classes folder.
7. Delete the Instructors and Workshops files from the Case1 folder.
8. Make a copy of the Landscapes folder in the Case1 folder. The name of the duplicate folder appears as Landscapes – Copy. Rename the Landscapes – Copy folder as **California Photos**.
9. Copy the Workshops file from the Classes folder to the California Photos folder. Rename this file **California Workshops**.
10. Compress the graphics files in the California Photos folder in a new compressed folder named **Photos**.
11. Move the compressed Photos folder to the Case1 folder.
12. Close File Explorer.

TROUBLESHOOT

Case Problem 2

See the Starting Data Files section at the beginning of this tutorial for the list of Data Files needed for this Case Problem.

Charlotte Area Business Incubator   Antoine Jackson is the director of the Charlotte Area Business Incubator, a service run by the University of North Carolina in Charlotte to consult with new and struggling small businesses. You work as an intern at the business incubator and spend part of your time organizing client files. Since Antoine started using Windows 8, he has been having trouble finding files on his computer. He sometimes creates duplicates of files and then doesn't know which copy is the most current. Complete the following steps:

1. Navigate to the FM ▶ Case2 folder provided with your Data Files, and then examine the files in this folder. Based on the filenames and file types, begin to create an organization plan for the files.

⚙ **Troubleshoot** 2. Open the Tips1 and the Tips1 – Copy files and consider the problem these files could cause. Close the files and then fix the problem, renaming one or more files as necessary to reflect the contents.

⚙ **Troubleshoot** 3. Open the Tips2 and the Tips2 – Copy files and compare their contents. Change the filenames to clarify the purpose and contents of the files.

4. Complete the organization plan for Antoine's files. In the FM ▶ Case2 folder, create the subfolders you need according to your plan.

5. Move the files in the Case2 folder to the subfolders you created. When you finish, the Case2 folder should contain at least two subfolders containing files.

6. Rename the spreadsheet files in each subfolder according to the following descriptions.
   - Budget1: **Website budget**
   - Budget2: **Marketing budget**
   - Report1: **Travel expense report**
   - Report2: **Project expense report**
   - Report3: **Balance sheet**
   - Report4: **Event budget**

⚙ **Troubleshoot** 7. Make sure all files have descriptive names that accurately reflect their contents.

⚙ **Troubleshoot** 8. Based on the work you did in Steps 6 and 7, move files as necessary to improve the file organization.

9. Close File Explorer.

WORD

Creating and Editing a Document

Writing a Business Letter and Formatting a Flyer

OBJECTIVES

Session 1.1
- Create and save a document
- Enter text and correct errors as you type
- Use AutoComplete and AutoCorrect
- Select text and move the insertion point
- Undo and redo actions
- Adjust paragraph spacing, line spacing, and margins
- Preview and print a document
- Create an envelope

Session 1.2
- Open an existing document
- Use the Spelling and Grammar task panes
- Change page orientation, font, font color, and font size
- Apply text effects and align text
- Copy formatting with the Format Painter
- Insert a paragraph border and shading
- Delete, insert, and edit a photo
- Use Word Help

Case | *Sandy Hill Portrait Studio*

Sandy Hill Portrait Studio in Baltimore, Maryland, specializes in wedding photography and family portraits. It also offers weekend and evening classes for new and experienced photographers. The sales manager, Tim Bartolutti, has asked you to create a cover letter to accompany a set of prints that he needs to send to a client, and an envelope for sending a class schedule to another client. He also wants your help creating a flyer announcing a class that focuses on photographing pets.

You will create the letter and flyer using **Microsoft Office Word 2013** (or simply **Word**), a word-processing program. You'll start by opening Word and saving a new document. Then you'll type the text of the cover letter and print it. In the process of entering the text, you'll learn several ways to correct typing errors and how to adjust paragraph and line spacing. When you create the envelope, you'll learn how to save it as part of a document for later use. As you work on the flyer, you will learn how to open an existing document, change the way text is laid out on the page, format text, and insert and resize a photo. Finally, you'll learn how to use Word's Help system.

STARTING DATA FILES

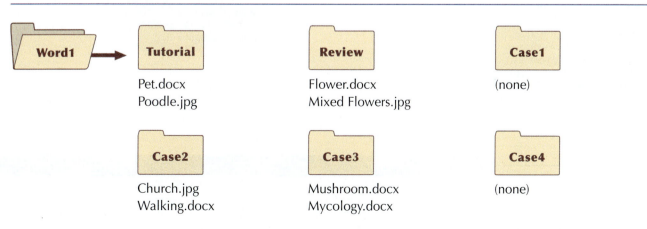

Word1 → **Tutorial**
Pet.docx
Poodle.jpg

Review
Flower.docx
Mixed Flowers.jpg

Case1
(none)

Case2
Church.jpg
Walking.docx

Case3
Mushroom.docx
Mycology.docx

Case4
(none)

Session 1.1 Visual Overview:

The **Quick Access Toolbar** is a collection of buttons that provides one-click access to commonly used commands, such as Save, Undo, and Repeat.

Each **tab** includes commands related to particular activities or tasks. The HOME tab includes options for formatting and editing text.

The **title bar** displays the name of the open file and the program.

The **ribbon** is the main set of buttons and other tools you can use to complete tasks. It is organized into tabs and groups.

The dark gray areas on the ruler represent the document's margins. **Margins** are the blank spaces around the edges of a document's content.

The **insertion point** shows where characters will appear when you start typing.

The **paragraph mark** indicates the end of a paragraph. It is only visible if nonprinting characters are turned on. **Nonprinting characters** appear on the screen but not on the printed page.

Buttons for related commands are organized on a tab in **groups**. The buttons in this group can be used to change the appearance of a paragraph.

The **status bar** provides information about the current document, such as the current page and number of words in the document; it also contains buttons and other controls for working with the document.

You can choose to display the rulers, which help you position elements in a document.

The Word Window

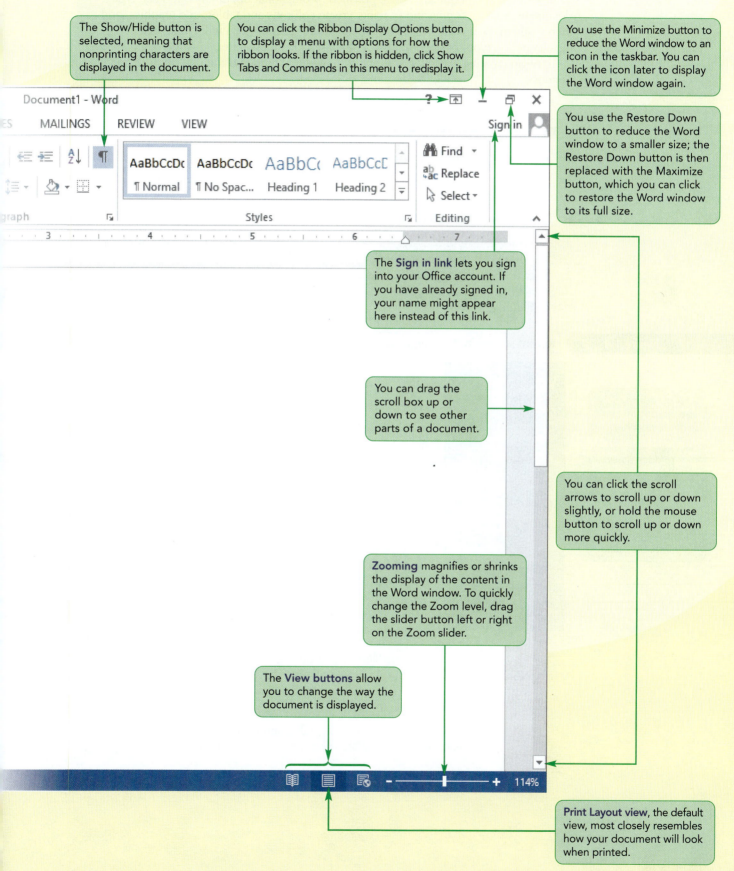

The Show/Hide button is selected, meaning that nonprinting characters are displayed in the document.

You can click the Ribbon Display Options button to display a menu with options for how the ribbon looks. If the ribbon is hidden, click Show Tabs and Commands in this menu to redisplay it.

You use the Minimize button to reduce the Word window to an icon in the taskbar. You can click the icon later to display the Word window again.

You use the Restore Down button to reduce the Word window to a smaller size; the Restore Down button is then replaced with the Maximize button, which you can click to restore the Word window to its full size.

The **Sign in link** lets you sign into your Office account. If you have already signed in, your name might appear here instead of this link.

You can drag the scroll box up or down to see other parts of a document.

You can click the scroll arrows to scroll up or down slightly, or hold the mouse button to scroll up or down more quickly.

Zooming magnifies or shrinks the display of the content in the Word window. To quickly change the Zoom level, drag the slider button left or right on the Zoom slider.

The **View buttons** allow you to change the way the document is displayed.

Print Layout view, the default view, most closely resembles how your document will look when printed.

Starting Word

With Word, you can quickly create polished, professional documents. You can type a document, adjust margins and spacing, create columns and tables, add graphics, and then easily make revisions and corrections. In this session, you will create one of the most common types of documents—a block style business letter.

To begin creating the letter, you first need to start Word and then set up the Word window.

To start Microsoft Word:

▶ **1.** Display the Windows Start screen, if necessary.

Using Windows 7? To complete Step 1, click the Start button on the taskbar.

▶ **2.** Click the **Word 2013** tile.

Word starts and displays the Recent screen in Backstage view, with template options for new documents on the right. A list of recently opened documents might appear on the left. **Backstage view** provides access to various screens with commands that allow you to manage files and Word options. See Figure 1-1.

Figure 1-1	Recent screen in Backstage view

a list of recently opened documents might appear here

click to open a new, blank document

your list of available templates may differ

Trouble? If you don't see Word 2013 on the Windows Start screen, type Word 2013 to display the Apps screen with the Word 2013 tile highlighted, and then click the tile. If you still can't find Word 2013, ask your instructor or technical support person for help.

Using Windows 7? To complete Step 2, point to All Programs on the Start menu, click Microsoft Office 2013, and then click Word 2013.

3. Click **Blank document**. The Word window opens, with the ribbon displayed.

> **Trouble?** If you don't see the ribbon, click the Ribbon Display Options button ⬆️, as shown in the Session 1.1 Visual Overview, and then click Show Tabs and Commands.

> Don't be concerned if your Word window doesn't match the Session 1.1 Visual Overview exactly. You'll have a chance to adjust its appearance shortly.

Working in Touch Mode

You can interact with the Word screen using a mouse, or, if you have a touch screen, you can work in Touch Mode, using a finger instead of the mouse pointer. In **Touch Mode**, extra space around the buttons on the ribbon allows your finger to tap the specific button you need. The figures in this text show the screen with Mouse Mode on, but it's helpful to learn how to switch back and forth between Touch Mode and Mouse Mode.

Note: The following steps assume that you are using a mouse. If you are instead using a touch device, please read these steps but don't complete them so that you remain working in Touch Mode.

To switch between Touch and Mouse Mode:

1. On the Quick Access Toolbar, click the **Customize Quick Access Toolbar** button ▾ to open the menu. The Touch/Mouse Mode command near the bottom of the menu does not have a checkmark next to it, indicating that it is currently not selected.

> **Trouble?** If the Touch/Mouse Mode command has a checkmark next to it, press the Esc key to close the menu, and then skip to Step 3.

2. On the menu, click **Touch/Mouse Mode**. The menu closes, and the Touch/Mouse Mode button 👆 appears on the Quick Access Toolbar.

3. On the Quick Access Toolbar, click the **Touch/Mouse Mode** button 👆. A menu opens with two options—Mouse and Touch. The icon next to Mouse is shaded blue to indicate it is selected.

> **Trouble?** If the icon next to Touch is shaded blue, press the Esc key to close the menu and skip to Step 5.

4. On the menu, click **Touch**. The menu closes, and the ribbon increases in height so that there is more space around each button on the ribbon. See Figure 1-2.

Figure 1-2   **Word window in Touch Mode**

expanded ribbon, with buttons farther apart than in Mouse Mode

Touch/Mouse Mode button

Customize Quick Access Toolbar button

insertion point

Trouble? If you are working with a touch screen and want to use Touch Mode, skip Steps 5 and 6.

▶ **5.** On the Quick Access Toolbar, click the **Touch/Mouse Mode** button 🔲, and then click **Mouse**. The ribbon changes back to its Mouse Mode appearance, as shown in the Session 1-1 Visual Overview.

▶ **6.** On the Quick Access Toolbar, click the **Customize Quick Access Toolbar** button ▾, and then click **Touch/Mouse Mode** to deselect it. The Touch/Mouse Mode button is removed from the Quick Access Toolbar.

Setting Up the Word Window

Before you start using Word, you should make sure you can locate and identify the different elements of the Word window, as shown in the Session 1.1 Visual Overview. In the following steps, you'll make sure your screen matches the Visual Overview.

To set up your Word window to match the figures in this book:

▶ **1.** If the Word window does not fill the entire screen, click the **Maximize** button 🔲 in the upper-right corner of the Word window.

The insertion point on your computer should be positioned about an inch from the top of the document, as shown in Figure 1-2, with the top margin visible.

Trouble? If the insertion point appears at the top of the document, with no white space above it, position the mouse pointer between the top of the document and the horizontal ruler, until it changes to ÷, double-click, and then scroll up to top of the document.

▶ **2.** On the ribbon, click the **VIEW** tab. The ribbon changes to display options for changing the appearance of the Word window.

▶ **3.** In the Show group, click the **Ruler** check box to insert a checkmark, if necessary. If the rulers were not displayed, they are displayed now.

Next, you'll change the Zoom level to a setting that ensures that your Word window will match the figures in this book. To increase or decrease the screen's magnification, you could drag the slider button on the Zoom slider in the lower-right corner of the Word window. But to choose a specific Zoom level, it's easier to use the Zoom dialog box.

TIP

Changing the Zoom level affects only the way the document is displayed on the screen; it does not affect the document itself.

▶ **4.** In the Zoom group, click the **Zoom** button to open the Zoom dialog box. Double-click the **Percent** box to select the current zoom percentage, type **120**, and then click the **OK** button to close the Zoom dialog box.

▶ **5.** On the status bar, click the **Print Layout** button 🔲 to select it, if necessary. As shown in the Session 1.1 Visual Overview, the Print Layout button is the middle of the three View buttons located on the right side of the status bar. The Print Layout button in the Views group on the View tab is also now selected.

Before typing a document, you should make sure nonprinting characters are displayed. Nonprinting characters provide a visual representation of details you might otherwise miss. For example, the (¶) character marks the end of a paragraph, and the (•) character marks the space between words.

To verify that nonprinting characters are displayed:

1. On the ribbon, click the **HOME** tab.

2. In the blank Word document, look for the paragraph mark (¶) in the first line of the document, just to the right of the blinking insertion point.

   Trouble? If you don't see the paragraph mark, click the Show/Hide ¶ button ¶ in the Paragraph group.

   In the Paragraph group, the Show/Hide ¶ button should be highlighted in blue, indicating that it is selected, and the paragraph mark (¶) should appear in the first line of the document, just to the right of the insertion point.

Saving a Document

Before you begin working on a document, you should save it with a new name. When you use the Save button on the Quick Access Toolbar to save a document for the first time, Word displays the Save As screen in Backstage view. In the Save As screen, you can select the location where you want to store your document. After that, when you click the Save button, Word saves your document to the same location you specified earlier, and with the same name.

To save the document:

1. On the Quick Access Toolbar, click the **Save** button 🖫. Word switches to the Save As screen in Backstage view, as shown in Figure 1-3.

Figure 1-3	Save As screen in Backstage view

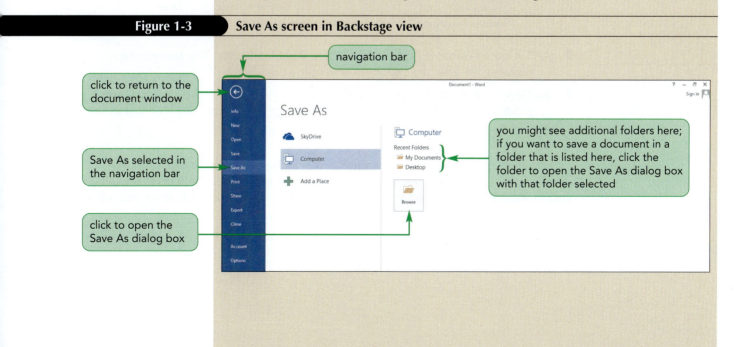

navigation bar

click to return to the document window

Save As selected in the navigation bar

click to open the Save As dialog box

you might see additional folders here; if you want to save a document in a folder that is listed here, click the folder to open the Save As dialog box with that folder selected

Because a document is now open, more commands are available in Backstage view than when you started Word. The **navigation bar** on the left contains commands for working with the open document and for changing settings that control how Word works.

2. Click **Computer**, if necessary, and then click the **Browse** button. The Save As dialog box opens.

   Trouble? If your instructor wants you to save your files to your SkyDrive account, click SkyDrive, log in to your account, if necessary, and then click the Browse button.

3. Navigate to the location specified by your instructor. The default filename, "Doc1," appears in the File name box. You will change that to something more descriptive. See Figure 1-4.

Figure 1-4	**Save As dialog box**

you might see something different here, depending on the location specified by your instructor

default filename

4. Click the File name box, and then type **Robbins Letter**. The text you type replaces the selected text in the File name box.

5. Click the **Save** button. The file is saved, the dialog box and Backstage view close, and the document window appears again, with the new filename in the title bar.

Now that you have saved the document, you can begin typing the letter. Tim has asked you to type a block style letter to accompany a set of family portraits that will be sent to Sonia Robbins, a regular client. Figure 1-5 shows the block style letter you will create in this tutorial.

Figure 1-5   Completed block style letter

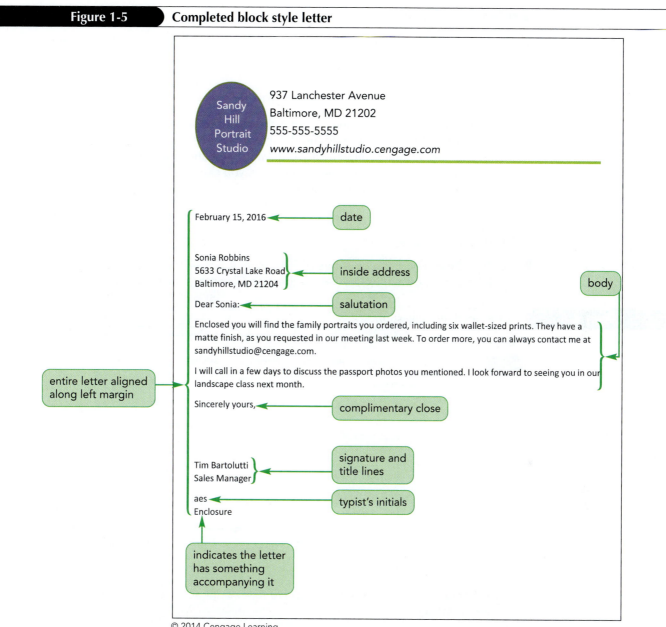

© 2014 Cengage Learning

PROSKILLS

Written Communication: Creating a Business Letter

Several styles are considered acceptable for business letters. The main differences among the styles have to do with how parts of the letter are indented from the left margin. In the block style, which you will use in this tutorial, each line of text starts at the left margin. In other words, nothing is indented. Another style is to indent the first line of each paragraph. The choice of style is largely a matter of personal preference, or it can be determined by the standards used in a particular business or organization. To further enhance your skills in writing business correspondence, you should consult an authoritative book on business writing that provides guidelines for creating a variety of business documents, such as *Business Communication: Process & Product,* by Mary Ellen Guffey.

Entering Text

The letters you type in a Word document appear at the current location of the blinking insertion point.

Inserting a Date with AutoComplete

The first item in a block style business letter is the date. Tim plans to send the letter to Sonia on February 15, so you need to insert that date into the document. To do so, you can take advantage of **AutoComplete**, a Word feature that automatically inserts dates and other regularly used items for you. In this case, you can type the first few characters of the month and let Word insert the rest.

To insert the date:

▶ 1. Type **Febr** (the first four letters of February). A ScreenTip appears above the letters, as shown in Figure 1-6, suggesting "February" as the complete word.

| Figure 1-6 | AutoComplete suggestion |

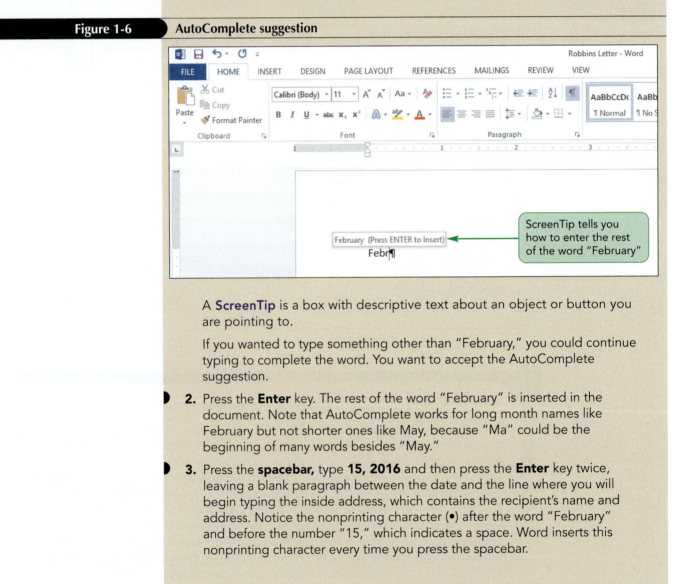

A **ScreenTip** is a box with descriptive text about an object or button you are pointing to.

If you wanted to type something other than "February," you could continue typing to complete the word. You want to accept the AutoComplete suggestion.

▶ 2. Press the **Enter** key. The rest of the word "February" is inserted in the document. Note that AutoComplete works for long month names like February but not shorter ones like May, because "Ma" could be the beginning of many words besides "May."

▶ 3. Press the **spacebar,** type **15, 2016** and then press the **Enter** key twice, leaving a blank paragraph between the date and the line where you will begin typing the inside address, which contains the recipient's name and address. Notice the nonprinting character (•) after the word "February" and before the number "15," which indicates a space. Word inserts this nonprinting character every time you press the spacebar.

Trouble? If February happens to be the current month, you will see a second AutoComplete suggestion displaying the current date after you press the spacebar. To ignore that AutoComplete suggestion, continue typing the rest of the date as instructed in Step 3.

Continuing to Type the Block Style Letter

In a block style business letter, the inside address appears below the date, with one blank paragraph in between. Some style guides recommend including even more space between the date and the inside address. But in the short letter you are typing, more space would make the document look out of balance.

To insert the inside address:

1. Type the following information, pressing the **Enter** key after each item:

   Sonia Robbins

   5633 Crystal Lake Road

   Baltimore, MD 21204

   Remember to press the Enter key after you type the zip code. Your screen should look like Figure 1-7. Don't be concerned if the lines of the inside address seem too far apart. You'll use the default spacing for now, and then adjust it after you finish typing the letter.

Figure 1-7	Letter with inside address

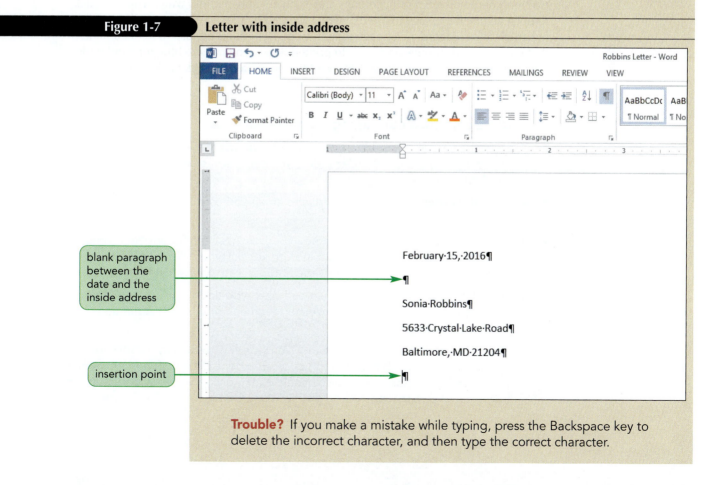

Trouble? If you make a mistake while typing, press the Backspace key to delete the incorrect character, and then type the correct character.

Now you can move on to the salutation and the body of the letter. As you type the body of the letter, notice that Word automatically moves the insertion point to a new line when the current line is full.

To type the salutation and the body of the letter:

1. Type **Dear Sonia:** and then press the **Enter** key to start a new paragraph for the body of the letter.

2. Type the following sentence, including the period: **Enclosed you will find the family portraits you ordered, including six wallet-sized prints.**

3. Press the **spacebar**. Note that you should only include one space between sentences.

4. Type the following sentence, including the period: **They have a matte finish, as you requested in our conversation last week.**

5. On the Quick Access Toolbar, click the **Save** button 🔲. Word saves the document as Robbins Letter to the same location you specified earlier.

The next sentence you need to type includes Tim's email address.

Typing a Hyperlink

When you type an email address and then press the spacebar or the Enter key, Word converts it to a hyperlink, with blue font and an underline. A **hyperlink** is text or a graphic you can click to jump to another file or to somewhere else in the same file. The two most common types of hyperlinks are: 1) an email hyperlink, which you can click to open an email message to the recipient specified by the hyperlink; and 2) a web hyperlink, which opens a webpage in a browser. Hyperlinks are useful in documents that you plan to distribute via email. In printed documents, where blue font and underlines can be distracting, you'll usually want to convert a hyperlink back to regular text.

To add a sentence containing an email address:

1. Press the **spacebar**, and then type the following sentence, including the period: **To order more, you can always contact me at sandyhillstudio@cengage.com.**

2. Press the **Enter** key. Word converts the email address to a hyperlink, with blue font and an underline.

3. Position the mouse pointer over the hyperlink. A ScreenTip appears, indicating that you could press and hold the Ctrl key and then click the link to follow it—that is, to open an email message addressed to Sandy Hill Portrait Studio.

4. With the mouse pointer positioned over the hyperlink, right-click—that is, press the right mouse button. A shortcut menu opens with commands related to working with hyperlinks.

You can right-click many items in the Word window to display a **shortcut menu** with commands related to the item you right-clicked. The **Mini toolbar** also appears when you right-click or select text, giving you easy access to the buttons and settings most often used when formatting text. See Figure 1-8.

Figure 1-8   **Shortcut menu**

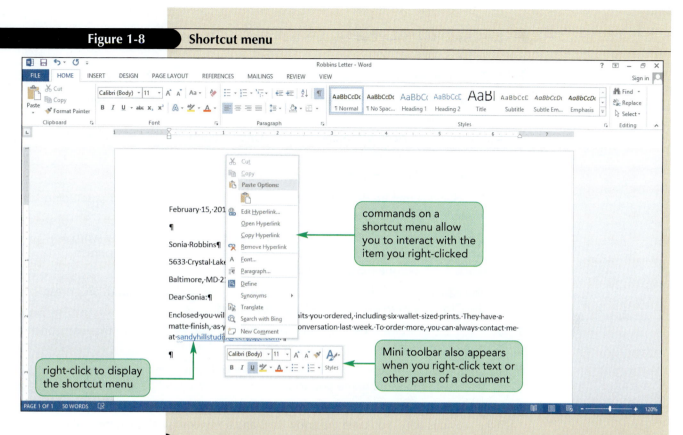

5. Click **Remove Hyperlink** in the shortcut menu. The shortcut menu and the Mini toolbar are no longer visible. The email address is now formatted in black, like the rest of the document text.

6. On the Quick Access Toolbar, click the **Save** button 💾.

Using the Undo and Redo Buttons

To undo (or reverse) the last thing you did in a document, click the Undo button on the Quick Access Toolbar. To restore your original change, click the Redo button, which reverses the action of the Undo button (or redoes the undo). To undo more than your last action, you can continue to click the Undo button, or you can click the Undo button arrow on the Quick Access Toolbar to open a list of your most recent actions. When you click an action in the list, Word undoes every action in the list up to and including the action you clicked.

Tim asks you to change the word "conversation" to "meeting" in the second-to-last sentence you typed. You'll make the change now. If Tim decides he doesn't like it after all, you can always undo it. To delete a character, space, or blank paragraph to the right of the insertion point, you use the Delete key; or to delete an entire word, you can use the Ctrl+Delete key combination. To delete a character, space, or blank paragraph to the left of the insertion point, you use the Backspace key; or to delete an entire word, you can use the Ctrl+Backspace key combination.

To change the word "conversation":

1. Press the ↑ key once and then press the → key as necessary to move the insertion point to the left of the "c" in the word "conversation."

▶ **2.** Press and hold the **Ctrl** key, and then press the **Delete** key to delete the word "conversation."

▶ **3.** Type **meeting** as a replacement, and then press the **spacebar**.

   After reviewing the sentence, Tim decides he prefers the original wording, so you'll undo the change.

▶ **4.** On the Quick Access Toolbar, click the **Undo** button ↶. The word "meeting" is removed from the sentence.

▶ **5.** Click the **Undo** button ↶ again to restore the word "conversation."

   Tim decides that he does want to use "meeting" after all. Instead of retyping it, you'll redo the undo.

▶ **6.** On the Quick Access Toolbar, click the **Redo** button ↷ twice. The word "meeting" replaces "conversation" in the document, so that the phrase reads "…in our meeting last week."

   You can also press the Ctrl+Z keys to execute the Undo command, and press the Ctrl+Y keys to execute the Redo command.

▶ **7.** Press and hold the **Ctrl** key, and then press the **End** key to move the insertion point to the blank paragraph at the end of the document.

▶ **8.** On the Quick Access Toolbar, click the **Save** button 🖫. Word saves your letter with the same name and to the same location you specified earlier.

In the previous steps, you used the arrow keys and a key combination to move the insertion point to specific locations in the document. For your reference, Figure 1-9 summarizes the most common keystrokes for moving the insertion point in a document.

Figure 1-9   **Keystrokes for moving the insertion point**

To Move the Insertion Point	Press
Left or right one character at a time	← or →
Up or down one line at a time	↑ or ↓
Left or right one word at a time	Ctrl+← or Ctrl+→
Up or down one paragraph at a time	Ctrl+↑ or Ctrl+↓
To the beginning or to the end of the current line	Home or End
To the beginning or to the end of the document	Ctrl+Home or Ctrl+End
To the previous screen or to the next screen	Page Up or Page Down
To the top or to the bottom of the document window	Alt+Ctrl+Page Up or Alt+Ctrl+Page Down

© 2014 Cengage Learning

Correcting Errors as You Type

As you have seen, you can use the Backspace or Delete keys to remove an error, and then you can type a correction. In many cases, however, Word's AutoCorrect feature will do the work for you. Among other things, **AutoCorrect** automatically corrects common typing errors, such as typing "adn" instead of "and." For example, you might have noticed AutoCorrect at work if you forgot to capitalize the first letter in a sentence as you typed the letter. After you type this kind of error, AutoCorrect automatically corrects it when you press the spacebar, the Tab key, or the Enter key.

Word draws your attention to other potential errors by marking them with wavy underlines. If you type a word that doesn't match the correct spelling in Word's dictionary, or if a word is not in the dictionary at all, a wavy red line appears beneath it. A wavy red underline also appears if you mistakenly type the same word twice in a row. Misused words (for example, "your" instead of "you're") are underlined with a wavy blue line. Likewise, punctuation errors, problems with possessives and plurals, and grammatical errors are marked with a wavy blue underline.

You'll see how this works as you continue typing the letter and make some intentional typing errors.

To learn more about correcting errors as you type:

▶ **1.** Type the following sentence, including the errors shown here: **i will call in a few few days to disuss teh pasport photos you mentioned.**

As you type, AutoCorrect changes the lowercase "i" at the beginning of the sentence to uppercase. It also changes "teh" to "the" and "pasport" to "passport." The spelling error "disuss" and the second "few" are marked with wavy red underlines. You will correct these errors after you finish typing the rest of the paragraph.

▶ **2.** Press the **spacebar**, and then type the following sentence, including the extra period and the other errors: **I look forward too seeing you in our landscape class next month..** The word "too" is underlined with a wavy blue line, indicating a misused word. The sentence also contains a punctuation error, but Word won't identify it until you start a new sentence or press the Enter key to begin a new paragraph.

▶ **3.** Press the **Enter** key to begin a new paragraph. As shown in Figure 1-10, the two periods at the end of the sentence are now underlined in blue.

Figure 1-10	Errors marked in the document

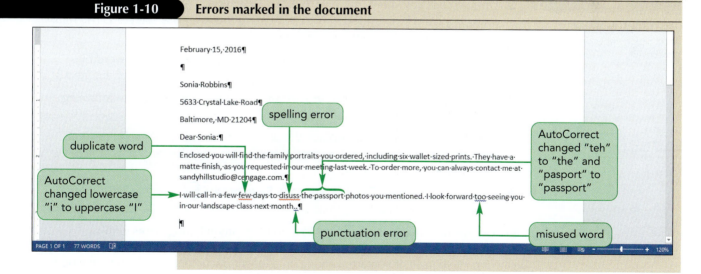

To correct an error marked with a wavy underline, you can right-click the error, and then click a replacement in the shortcut menu. If you don't see the correct word in the shortcut menu, click anywhere in the document to close the menu, and then type the correction yourself. You can also bypass the shortcut menu entirely, and simply delete the error and type a correction.

To correct the spelling and grammar errors:

▶ **1.** Right-click **disuss** to display the shortcut menu shown in Figure 1-11.

Figure 1-11 | **Shortcut menu with suggested spellings**

Trouble? If you see a shortcut menu other than the one shown in Figure 1-11, you didn't right-click exactly on the word "disuss." Press the Esc key to close the menu, and then repeat Step 1.

▶ **2.** On the shortcut menu, click **discuss**. The correct word is inserted into the sentence, and the shortcut menu closes. You could use a shortcut menu to remove the second instance of "few," but in the next step you'll try a different method—selecting the word and deleting it.

TIP

To deselect highlighted text, click anywhere in the document.

▶ **3.** Double-click anywhere in the underlined word **few**. The word and the space following it are highlighted in gray, indicating that they are selected. The Mini toolbar is also visible, but you can ignore it.

Trouble? If the entire paragraph is selected, you triple-clicked the word by mistake. Click anywhere in the document to deselect it, and then repeat Step 3.

▶ **4.** Press the **Delete** key. The second instance of "few" and the space following it are deleted from the sentence.

▶ **5.** Use the shortcut menu to replace the underlined word "too" with "to," and then click to the right of the second period after "month" and press the **Backspace** key to delete it.

▶ **6.** On the Quick Access Toolbar, click the **Save** button 💾.

You can see how quick and easy it is to correct common typing errors with AutoCorrect and the wavy red and blue underlines, especially in a short document that you are typing yourself. If you are working on a longer document or a document typed by someone else, you'll also want to have Word check the entire document for errors. You'll learn how to do this in Session 1.2.

Next, you'll finish typing the letter.

To finish typing the letter:

1. Press the **Ctrl+End** keys. The insertion point moves to the end of the document.

2. Type **Sincerely yours,** (including the comma).

3. Press the **Enter** key three times to leave space for the signature.

4. Type **Tim Bartolutti** and then press the **Enter** key. Because Tim's last name is not in Word's dictionary, a wavy red line appears below it. You can ignore this for now.

TIP

You only need to include your initials in a letter if you are typing it for someone else.

5. Type your first, middle, and last initials in lowercase, and then press the **Enter** key. AutoCorrect wrongly assumes your first initial is the first letter of a new sentence, and changes it to uppercase.

6. On the Quick Access Toolbar, click the **Undo** button. Word reverses the change, replacing the uppercase initial with a lowercase one.

7. Type **Enclosure**. At this point, your screen should look similar to Figure 1-12. Notice that as you continue to add lines to the letter, the top part of the letter scrolls off the screen. For example, in Figure 1-12, you can no longer see the date.

Figure 1-12 **Robbins Letter**

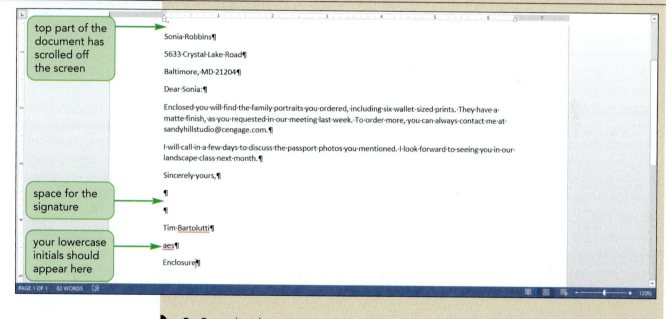

8. Save the document.

Now that you have finished typing the letter, you need to proofread it.

Proofreading a Document

After you finish typing a document, you need to proofread it carefully from start to finish. Part of proofreading a document in Word is removing all wavy underlines, either by correcting the text or by telling Word to ignore the underlined text because it isn't really an error. For example, Tim's last name is marked as an error, when in fact it is spelled correctly. You need to tell Word to ignore "Bartolutti" wherever it occurs in the letter. You need to do the same for your initials.

To proofread and correct the remaining marked errors in the letter:

▶ 1. Right-click **Bartolutti**. A shortcut menu opens.

▶ 2. On the shortcut menu, click **Ignore All** to indicate that Word should ignore the word "Bartolutti" each time it occurs in this document. (The Ignore All option can be particularly helpful in a longer document.) The wavy red underline disappears from below Tim's last name. If your initials do not form a word, a red wavy underline appears beneath them; otherwise, a blue wavy underline appears there.

▶ 3. If you see a wavy red underline below your initials, right-click your initials. On the shortcut menu, click **Ignore All** to remove the red wavy underline. If you didn't see a wavy blue underline below your initials before, you should see one now.

▶ 4. Right-click your initials again. On the shortcut menu, click **Ignore Once** to remove the blue underline.

▶ 5. Read the entire letter to proofread it for typing errors. Correct any errors using the techniques you have just learned.

▶ 6. Save the document.

The text of the letter is finished. Now you need to think about how it looks—that is, you need to think about the document's **formatting**. First, you need to adjust the spacing in the inside address.

Adjusting Paragraph and Line Spacing

When typing a letter, you might need to adjust two types of spacing—paragraph spacing and line spacing. **Paragraph spacing** is the space that appears directly above and below a paragraph. In Word, any text that ends with a paragraph mark symbol (¶) is a paragraph. So, a **paragraph** can be a group of words that is many lines long, a single word, or even a blank line, in which case you see a paragraph mark alone on a single line. Paragraph spacing is measured in points; a **point** is 1/72 of an inch. The default setting for paragraph spacing in Word is 0 points before each paragraph and 8 points after each paragraph. When laying out a complicated document, resist the temptation to simply press the Enter key to insert extra space between paragraphs. Changing the paragraph spacing gives you much more control over the final result.

Line spacing is the space between lines of text within a paragraph. Word offers a number of preset line spacing options. The 1.0 setting, which is often called **single-spacing**, allows the least amount of space between lines. All other line spacing options are measured as multiples of 1.0 spacing. For example, 2.0 spacing (sometimes called **double-spacing**) allows for twice the space of single-spacing. The default line spacing setting is 1.08, which allows a little more space between lines than 1.0 spacing.

Now consider the line and paragraph spacing in the Robbins letter. The three lines of the inside address are too far apart. That's because each line of the inside address is actually a separate paragraph. Word inserted the default 8 points of paragraph spacing after each of these separate paragraphs. See Figure 1-13.

| Figure 1-13 | Line and paragraph spacing in the letter to Sonia Robbins |

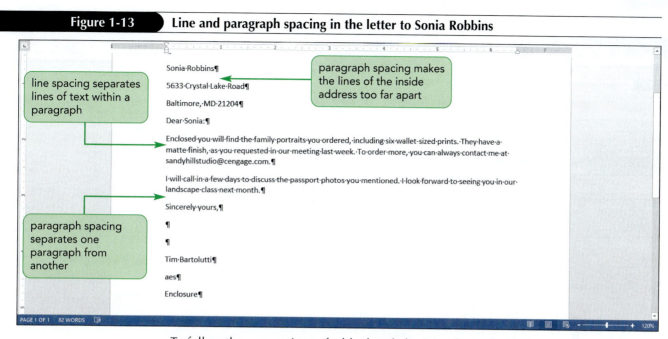

To follow the conventions of a block style business letter, the three paragraphs that make up the inside address should have the same spacing as the lines of text within a single paragraph—that is, they need to be closer together. You can accomplish this by removing the 8 points of paragraph spacing after the first two paragraphs in the inside address. To conform to the block style business letter format, you also need to close up the spacing between your initials and the word "Enclosure" at the end of the letter.

To adjust paragraph and line spacing in Word, you use the Line and Paragraph Spacing button in the Paragraph group on the HOME tab. Clicking this button displays a menu of preset line spacing options (1.0, 1.15, 2.0, and so on). The menu also includes two paragraph spacing options, which allow you to add 12 points before a paragraph or remove the default 8 points of space after a paragraph.

Next you'll adjust the paragraph spacing in the inside address and after your initials. In the process, you'll also learn some techniques for selecting text in a document.

To adjust the paragraph spacing in the inside address and after your initials:

1. Move the pointer to the white space just to the left of "Sonia Robbins" until it changes to a right-facing arrow ⤢.

2. Click the mouse button. The entire name, including the paragraph symbol after it, is selected.

3. Press and hold the mouse button, drag the pointer ⤢ down to select the next paragraph of the inside address as well, and then release the mouse button.

The name and street address are selected as well as the paragraph marks at the end of each paragraph. You did not select the paragraph containing the city, state, and zip code because you do not need to change its paragraph spacing. See Figure 1-14.

Figure 1-14 **Inside address selected**

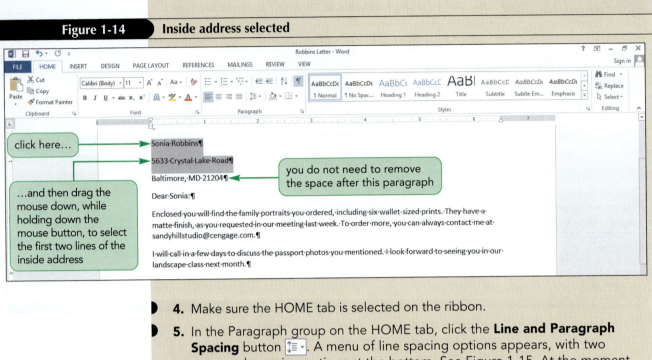

4. Make sure the HOME tab is selected on the ribbon.

5. In the Paragraph group on the HOME tab, click the **Line and Paragraph Spacing** button. A menu of line spacing options appears, with two paragraph spacing options at the bottom. See Figure 1-15. At the moment, you are only interested in the paragraph spacing options. Your goal is to remove the default 8 points of space after the first two paragraphs in the inside address.

Figure 1-15 **Line and paragraph spacing options**

6. Click **Remove Space After Paragraph**. The menu closes, and the paragraphs are now closer together.

7. Double-click your initials to select them and the paragraph symbol after them.

8. In the Paragraph group, click the **Line and Paragraph Spacing** button, click **Remove Space After Paragraph**, and then click anywhere in the document to deselect your initials.

Another way to compress lines of text is to press the Shift+Enter keys at the end of a line. This inserts a **manual line break**, also called a **soft return**, which moves the insertion point to a new line without starting a new paragraph. You will use this technique now as you add Tim's title below his name in the signature line.

To use a manual line break to move the insertion point to a new line without starting a new paragraph:

1. Click to the right of the "i" in "Bartolutti."

2. Press the **Shift+Enter** keys. Word inserts a small arrow symbol ↵, indicating a manual line break, and the insertion point moves to the line below Tim's name.

3. Type **Sales Manager**. Tim's title now appears directly below his name with no intervening paragraph spacing, just like the lines of the inside address.

4. Save the document.

INSIGHT

Understanding Spacing Between Paragraphs

When discussing the correct format for letters, many business style guides talk about single-spacing and double-spacing between paragraphs. In these style guides, to single-space between paragraphs means to press the Enter key once after each paragraph. Likewise, to double-space between paragraphs means to press the Enter key twice after each paragraph. With the default paragraph spacing in Word 2013, however, you only need to press the Enter key once after a paragraph. The space Word adds after a paragraph is not quite the equivalent of double-spacing, but it is enough to make it easy to see where one paragraph ends and another begins. Keep this in mind if you're accustomed to pressing the Enter key twice; otherwise, you could end up with more space than you want between paragraphs.

As you corrected line and paragraph spacing in the previous set of steps, you used the mouse to select text. Word provides multiple ways to select, or highlight, text as you work. Figure 1-16 summarizes these methods and explains when to use them most effectively.

Figure 1-16	Methods for selecting text

To Select	Mouse	Keyboard	Mouse and Keyboard
A word	Double-click the word	Move the insertion point to the beginning of the word, press and hold Ctrl+Shift, and then press →	
A line	Click in the white space to the left of the line	Move the insertion point to the beginning of the line, press and hold Shift, and then press ↓	
A sentence	Click at the beginning of the sentence, then drag the pointer until the sentence is selected		Press and hold Ctrl, then click any location within the sentence
Multiple lines	Click and drag in the white space to the left of the lines	Move the insertion point to the beginning of the first line, press and hold Shift, and then press ↓ until all the lines are selected	
A paragraph	Double-click in the white space to the left of the paragraph, or triple-click at any location within the paragraph	Move the insertion point to the beginning of the paragraph, press and hold Ctrl+Shift, and then press ↓	
Multiple paragraphs	Click in the white space to the left of the first paragraph you want to select, and then drag to select the remaining paragraphs	Move the insertion point to the beginning of the first paragraph, press and hold Ctrl+Shift, and then press ↓ until all the paragraphs are selected	
An entire document	Triple-click in the white space to the left of the document text	Press Ctrl+A	Press and hold Ctrl, and click in the white space to the left of the document text
A block of text	Click at the beginning of the block, then drag the pointer until the entire block is selected		Click at the beginning of the block, press and hold Shift, and then click at the end of the block
Nonadjacent blocks of text			Press and hold Ctrl, then drag the mouse pointer to select multiple blocks of nonadjacent text

© 2014 Cengage Learning

Adjusting the Margins

Another important aspect of document formatting is the amount of margin space between the document text and the edge of the page. You can check the document's margins by changing the Zoom level to display the entire page.

To change the Zoom level to display the entire page:

▶ **1.** On the ribbon, click the **VIEW** tab.

▶ **2.** In the Zoom group, click the **One Page** button. The entire document is now visible in the Word window. See Figure 1-17.

Figure 1-17   **Document zoomed to show entire page**

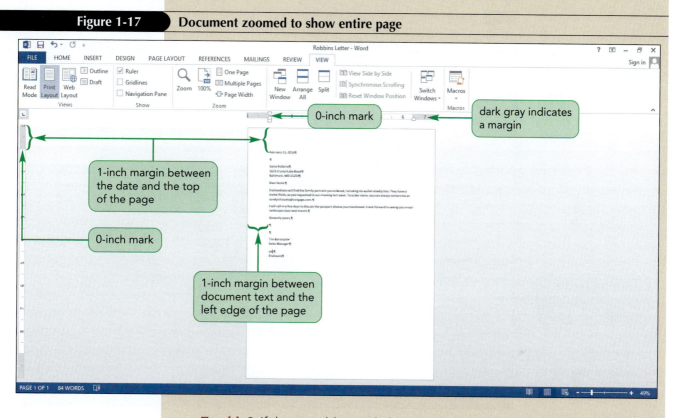

Trouble? If the wavy blue underline reappears under your initials, you can ignore it.

On the rulers, the margins appear dark gray. By default, Word documents include 1-inch margins on all sides of the document. By looking at the vertical ruler, you can see that the date in the letter, the first line in the document, is located 1 inch from the top of the page. Likewise, the horizontal ruler indicates the document text begins 1 inch from the left edge of the page.

Reading the measurements on the rulers can be tricky at first. On the horizontal ruler, the 0-inch mark is like the origin on a number line. You measure from the 0-inch mark to the left or to the right. On the vertical ruler, you measure up or down from the 0-inch mark.

Tim plans to print the letter on Sandy Hill Portrait Studio letterhead, which includes a graphic and the company's address. To allow more blank space for the letterhead, and to move the text down so it doesn't look so crowded at the top of the page, you need to increase the top margin. The settings for changing the page margins are located on the PAGE LAYOUT tab on the ribbon.

To change the page margins:

▶ **1.** On the ribbon, click the **PAGE LAYOUT** tab. The PAGE LAYOUT tab displays options for adjusting the layout of your document.

> **2.** In the Page Setup group, click the **Margins** button. The Margins gallery opens, as shown in Figure 1-18.

| Figure 1-18 | Margins gallery |

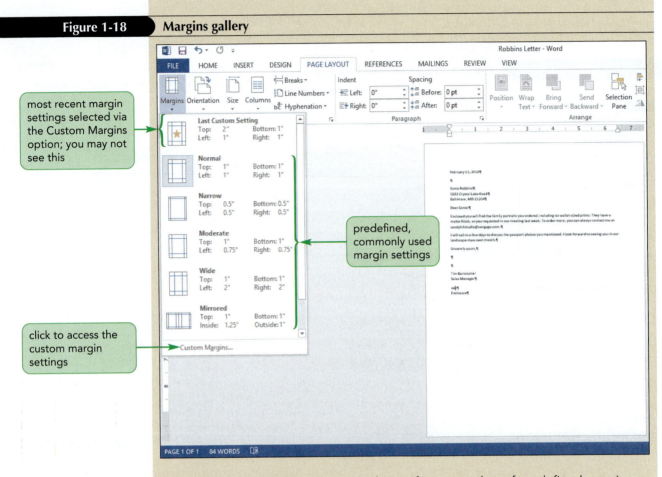

most recent margin settings selected via the Custom Margins option; you may not see this

predefined, commonly used margin settings

click to access the custom margin settings

In the Margins gallery, you can choose from a number of predefined margin options, or you can click the Custom Margins command to select your own settings. After you create custom margin settings, the most recent set appears as an option at the top of the menu. For the Robbins letter, you will create custom margins.

> **3.** Click **Custom Margins**. The Page Setup dialog box opens with the Margins tab displayed. The default margin settings are displayed in the boxes at the top of the Margins tab. The top margin of 1" is already selected, ready for you to type a new margin setting.

> **4.** In the Top box in the Margins section, type **2.5**. You do not need to type an inch mark ("). See Figure 1-19.

Figure 1-19   **Creating custom margins in the Page Setup dialog box**

enter a Top margin of 2.5

allows you to make this new margin setting the default for all new Word documents

> **5.** Click the **OK** button. The text of the letter is now lower on the page. The page looks less crowded, with room for the company's letterhead.

> **6.** Change the Zoom level back to **120%**, and then save the document.

For most documents, the Word default of 1-inch margins is fine. In some professional settings, however, you might need to use a particular custom margin setting for all your documents. In that case, define the custom margins using the Margins tab in the Page Setup dialog box, and then click the Set As Default button to make your settings the default for all new documents. Keep in mind that most printers can't print to the edge of the page; if you select custom margins that are too narrow for your printer's specifications, Word alerts you to change your margin settings.

Previewing and Printing a Document

To make sure the document is ready to print, and to avoid wasting paper and time, you should first review it in Backstage view to make sure it will look right when printed. Like the One Page zoom setting you used earlier, the Print option in Backstage view displays a full-page preview of the document, allowing you to see how it will fit on the printed page. However, you cannot actually edit this preview. It simply provides one last opportunity to look at the document before printing.

To preview the document:

> **1.** Proofread the document one last time and correct any remaining errors.

> **2.** Click the **FILE** tab to display Backstage view.

> **3.** In the navigation bar, click **Print**.

The Print screen displays a full-page version of your document, showing how the letter will fit on the printed page. The Print settings to the left of the preview allow you to control a variety of print options. For example, you can change the number of copies from the default setting of "1." The 1 Page Per Sheet button opens a menu where you can choose to print multiple pages on a single sheet of paper, or to scale the printed page to a particular paper size. You can also use the navigation controls at the bottom of the screen to display other pages in a document. See Figure 1-20.

Figure 1-20	Print settings in Backstage view

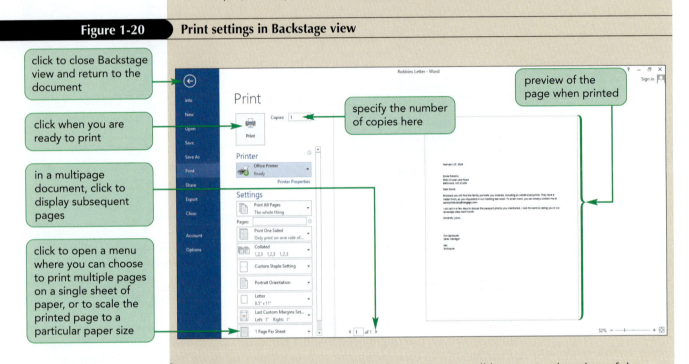

click to close Backstage view and return to the document

click when you are ready to print

in a multipage document, click to display subsequent pages

click to open a menu where you can choose to print multiple pages on a single sheet of paper, or to scale the printed page to a particular paper size

preview of the page when printed

specify the number of copies here

4. Review your document and make sure its overall layout matches that of the document in Figure 1-20. If you notice a problem with paragraph breaks or spacing, click the **Back** button ⬅ at the top of the navigation bar to return to the document, make any necessary changes, and then start again at Step 2.

At this point, you can print the document or you can leave Backstage view and return to the document in Print Layout view. In the following steps, you should only print the document if your instructor asks you to. If you will be printing the document, make sure your printer is turned on and contains paper.

To leave Backstage view or to print the document:

1. Click the **Back** button ⬅ at the top of the navigation bar to leave Backstage view and return to the document in Print Layout view, or click the **Print** button. Backstage view closes, and the letter prints if you clicked the Print button.

2. Click the **FILE** tab, and then click **Close** in the navigation bar to close the document without closing Word.

Next, Tim asks you to create an envelope he can use to send a class schedule to another client.

Creating an Envelope

Before you can create the envelope, you need to open a new, blank document. To create a new document, you can start with a blank document—as you did with the letter to Sonia Robbins—or you can start with one that already contains formatting and generic text commonly used in a variety of professional documents, such as a fax cover sheet or a memo. These preformatted files are called **templates**. You could use a template to create a formatted envelope, but first you'll learn how to create one on your own in a new, blank document. You'll have a chance to try out a template in the Case Problems at the end of this tutorial.

To create a new document for the envelope:

1. Click the **FILE** tab, and then click **New** in the navigation bar. The New screen is similar to the one you saw when you first started Word, with a blank document in the upper-left corner, along with a variety of templates. See Figure 1-21.

| Figure 1-21 | New options in Backstage view |

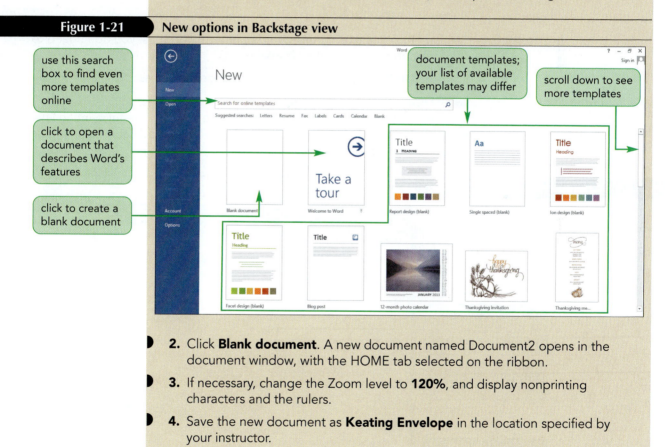

use this search box to find even more templates online

click to open a document that describes Word's features

click to create a blank document

document templates; your list of available templates may differ

scroll down to see more templates

2. Click **Blank document**. A new document named Document2 opens in the document window, with the HOME tab selected on the ribbon.

3. If necessary, change the Zoom level to **120%**, and display nonprinting characters and the rulers.

4. Save the new document as **Keating Envelope** in the location specified by your instructor.

To create the envelope:

1. On the ribbon, click the **MAILINGS** tab. The ribbon changes to display the various Mailings options.

2. In the Create group, click the **Envelopes** button. The Envelopes and Labels dialog box opens, with the Envelopes tab displayed. The insertion point appears in the Delivery address box, ready for you to type the recipient's address. Depending on how your computer is set up, and whether you are working on your own computer or a school computer, you might see an address in the Return address box.

3. In the Delivery address box, type the following address, pressing the Enter key to start each new line:

   Lakeisha Keating

   2245 Farley Lane

   Baltimore, MD 21206

   Because Tim will be using the studio's printed envelopes, you don't need to print a return address on this envelope.

4. Click the **Omit** check box to insert a checkmark, if necessary.

   At this point, if you had a printer stocked with envelopes, you could click the Print button to print the envelope. To save an envelope for printing later, you need to add it to the document. Your Envelopes and Labels dialog box should match the one in Figure 1-22.

Figure 1-22   Envelopes and Labels dialog box

5. Click the **Add to Document** button. The dialog box closes, and you return to the document window. The envelope is inserted at the top of your document, with 1.0 line spacing. The double line with the words "Section Break (Next Page)" is related to how the envelope is formatted, and will not be visible when you print the envelope. The envelope will print in the standard business envelope format.

6. Save the document. Tim will print the envelope later, so you can close the document now.

7. Click the **FILE** tab and then click **Close** in the navigation bar. The document closes, but Word remains open.

INSIGHT

Creating Documents with Templates

Microsoft offers predesigned templates for all kinds of documents, including calendars, reports, and thank you cards. You can use the scroll bar on the right of the New screen (shown earlier in Figure 1-21) to scroll down to see more templates, or you can use the Search for online templates box in the New screen to search among hundreds of other options available at Office.com. When you open a template, you actually open a new document containing the formatting and text stored in the template, leaving the original template untouched. A typical template includes placeholder text that you replace with your own information.

Templates allow you to create stylish, professional-looking documents quickly and easily. To use them effectively, however, you need to be knowledgeable about Word and its many options for manipulating text, graphics, and page layouts. Otherwise, the complicated formatting of some Word templates can be more frustrating than helpful. As you become a more experienced Word user, you'll learn how to create your own templates.

You're finished creating the cover letter and the envelope. In the next session, you will modify a flyer that announces an upcoming class by formatting the text and adding a photo.

REVIEW

Session 1.1 Quick Check

1. In a block style letter, does each line of text start at the left or right margin?
2. What do you call the recipient's address, which appears below the date in a block style letter?
3. Explain how to use a hyperlink in a Word document to open a new email message.
4. Explain how to display nonprinting characters.
5. Define the term "paragraph spacing."
6. How does Word indicate a potential spelling error?

Session 1.2 Visual Overview:

Alignment buttons control the text's **alignment**—that is, the way it lines up between the left and right margins. Here, the Center button is selected because the text containing the insertion point is center-aligned.

You can click the Clear All Formatting button to restore selected text to the default font, font size, and color.

Clicking the Format Painter button displays the Format Painter pointer, which you can use to copy formatting from the selected text to other text in the document.

The Font group on the HOME tab includes the Font box and the Font size box for setting the text's font and the font size, respectively. A **font** is a set of characters that uses the same typeface.

This document has a landscape orientation, meaning it is wider than it is tall.

You can insert a photo or another type of picture in a document by using the **Pictures button** located on the INSERT tab of the ribbon. After you insert a photo or another picture, you can format it with a style that adds a border or a shadow, or changes its shape.

You click the Shading button arrow to apply a colored background to a selected paragraph.

Pet Flyer - Word

FILE | HOME | INSERT | DESIGN | PAGE LAYOUT | REFERENCES | MAILINGS | REVI

Arial | 22

Paste

Clipboard

Font

Paragraph

Do·you·want·the·perfect·portrait·of·your·furry·frend

Learn·how·the·pet·pros·do·it·at·Sandy·Hill·Portra

Beginning·Pet·Photography¶

Tuesdays,·March·1·-·April·4·from·7·to·8·p.m.¶

Contact·Tim·Bartolutti·at·sandyhillstudio@cengage.com·to·re

PAGE 1 OF 1 | 1 OF 44 WORDS

The boldface and blue font color applied to this text are examples of formatting that you would use sparingly to draw attention to a specific part of a document.

Formatting a Document

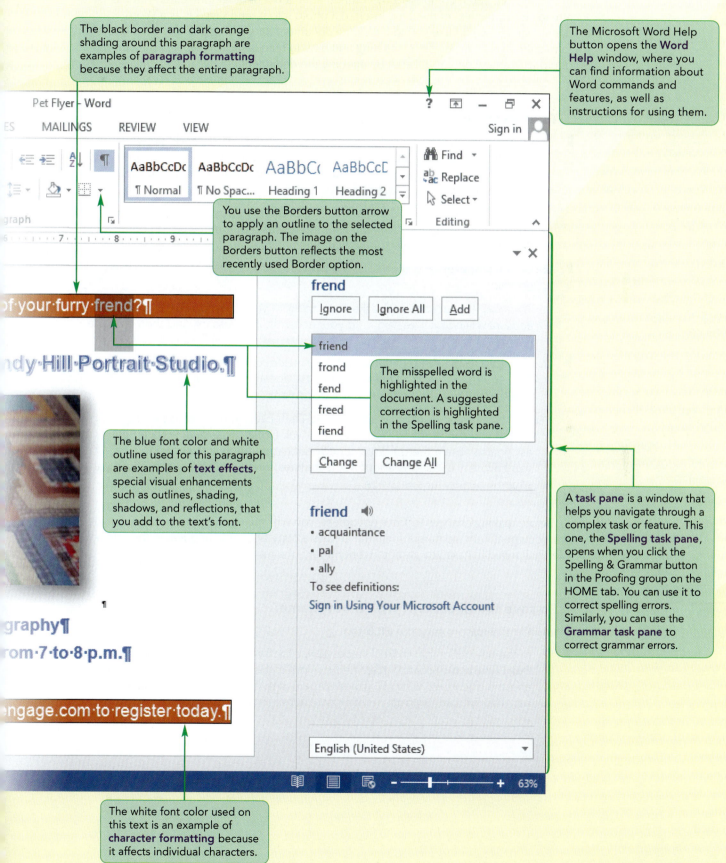

The black border and dark orange shading around this paragraph are examples of **paragraph formatting** because they affect the entire paragraph.

The Microsoft Word Help button opens the **Word Help** window, where you can find information about Word commands and features, as well as instructions for using them.

You use the Borders button arrow to apply an outline to the selected paragraph. The image on the Borders button reflects the most recently used Border option.

The misspelled word is highlighted in the document. A suggested correction is highlighted in the Spelling task pane.

The blue font color and white outline used for this paragraph are examples of **text effects**, special visual enhancements such as outlines, shading, shadows, and reflections, that you add to the text's font.

A **task pane** is a window that helps you navigate through a complex task or feature. This one, the **Spelling task pane**, opens when you click the Spelling & Grammar button in the Proofing group on the HOME tab. You can use it to correct spelling errors. Similarly, you can use the **Grammar task pane** to correct grammar errors.

The white font color used on this text is an example of **character formatting** because it affects individual characters.

Opening an Existing Document

In this session, you'll complete a flyer announcing a pet photography class. Tim has already typed the text of the flyer, inserted a photo into it, and saved it as a Word document. He would like you to check the document for spelling and grammar errors, format the flyer to make it eye-catching and easy to read, and then replace the current photo with a new one. You'll start by opening the document.

To open the flyer document:

▶ 1. On the ribbon, click the **FILE** tab to open Backstage view, and then verify that **Open** is selected in the navigation bar. On the left side of the Open screen is a list of places you can go to locate other documents, and on the right is a list of recently opened documents.

   Trouble? If you closed Word at the end of the previous session, start Word now, click Open Other Documents at the bottom of the navigation bar in Backstage view, and then begin with Step 2.

▶ 2. Click **Computer**, and then click the **Browse** button. The Open dialog box opens.

   Trouble? If your instructor asked you to store your files to your SkyDrive account, click SkyDrive, log in to your account, if necessary, and then click the Browse button.

▶ 3. Navigate to the Word1 ▸ Tutorial folder included with your Data Files, click **Pet**, and then click the **Open** button. The document opens with the insertion point blinking in the first line of the document.

   Trouble? If you don't have the starting Data Files, you need to get them before you can proceed. Your instructor will either give you the Data Files or ask you to obtain them from a specified location (such as a network drive). If you have any questions about the Data Files, see your instructor or technical support person for assistance.

Before making changes to Tim's document, you will save it with a new name. Saving the document with a different filename creates a copy of the file and leaves the original file unchanged in case you want to work through the tutorial again.

To save the document with a new name:

▶ 1. On the ribbon, click the **FILE** tab.

▶ 2. In the navigation bar in Backstage view, click **Save As**. Save the document as **Pet Flyer** in the location specified by your instructor. Backstage view closes, and the document window appears again with the new filename in the title bar. The original Pet document closes, remaining unchanged.

Decision Making: Creating Effective Documents

Before you create a new document or revise an existing document, take a moment to think about your audience. Ask yourself these questions:

- Who is your audience?
- What do they know?
- What do they need to know?
- How can the document you are creating change your audience's behavior or opinions?

Every decision you make about your document should be based on your answers to these questions. To take a simple example, if you are creating a flyer to announce an upcoming seminar on college financial aid, your audience would be students and their parents. They probably all know what the term "financial aid" means, so you don't need to explain that in your flyer. Instead, you can focus on telling them what they need to know—the date, time, and location of the seminar. The behavior you want to affect, in this case, is whether or not your audience will show up for the seminar. By making the flyer professional looking and easy to read, you increase the chance that they will.

You might find it more challenging to answer these questions about your audience when creating more complicated documents, such as corporate reports. But the focus remains the same—connecting with the audience. As you are deciding what information to include in your document, remember that the goal of a professional document is to convey the information as effectively as possible to your target audience.

Before revising a document for someone else, it's a good idea to familiarize yourself with its overall structure.

To review the document:

1. Verify that the document is displayed in Print Layout view and that nonprinting characters are displayed. For now, you can ignore the wavy underlines that appear in the document.

2. Change the Zoom level to **120%**, if necessary.

   At this point, the document is very simple. By the time you are finished, it will look like the document shown in the Session 1.2 Visual Overview, with the spelling and grammar errors corrected. Figure 1-23 summarizes the tasks you will perform.

| Figure 1-23 | Formatting changes requested by Tim |

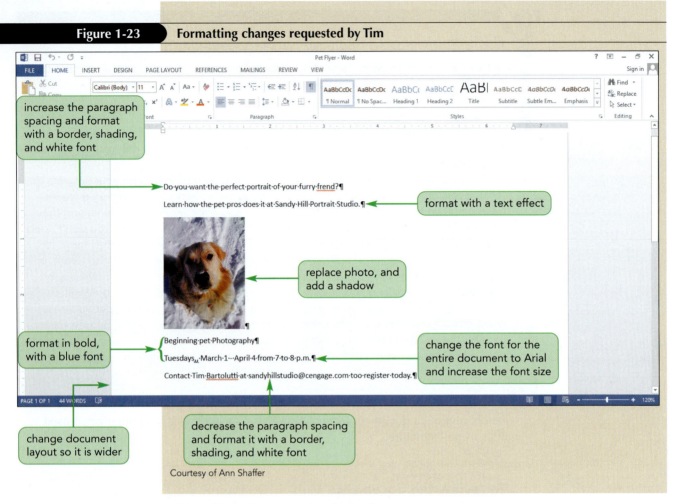

increase the paragraph spacing and format with a border, shading, and white font

format with a text effect

replace photo, and add a shadow

format in bold, with a blue font

change the font for the entire document to Arial and increase the font size

change document layout so it is wider

decrease the paragraph spacing and format it with a border, shading, and white font

Courtesy of Ann Shaffer

You will start by correcting the spelling and grammar errors.

Using the Spelling and Grammar Task Panes

As you learned in Tutorial 1, Word marks possible spelling and grammatical errors with wavy underlines as you type so you can quickly go back and correct those errors. A more thorough way of checking the spelling in a document is to use the Spelling and Grammar task panes to check a document word by word for a variety of errors. You can customize the spelling and grammar settings to add or ignore certain types of errors.

Tim asks you to use the Spelling and Grammar task panes to check the flyer for mistakes. Before you do, you'll configure the grammar settings to look for subject/verb agreement, in addition to other types of errors.

To customize the grammar settings:

1. On the ribbon, click the **FILE** tab, and then click **Options** in the navigation bar. The Word Options dialog box opens. You can use this dialog box to change a variety of settings related to how Word looks and works.

2. In the left pane, click **Proofing**, and then, in the "When correcting spelling and grammar in Word" section, click the **Settings** button. The Grammar Settings dialog box opens.

3. If necessary, scroll down in the Grammar Settings dialog box to display all the check boxes under "Grammar," and then click the **Subject-verb agreement** check box to insert a checkmark. See Figure 1-24.

Figure 1-24   Grammar Settings dialog box

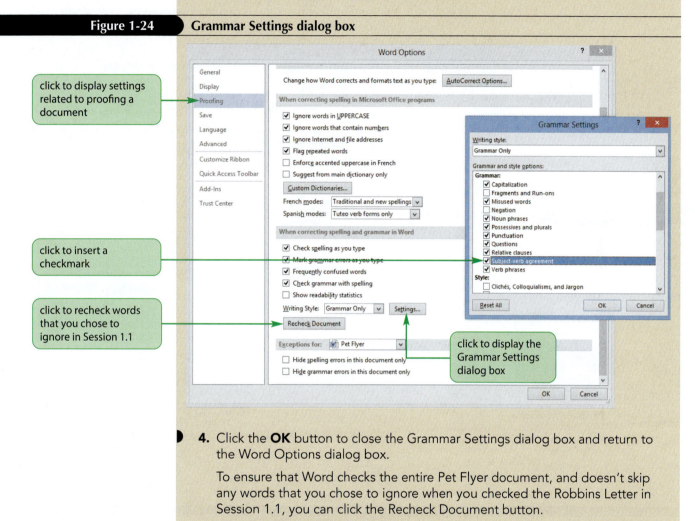

click to display settings related to proofing a document

click to insert a checkmark

click to recheck words that you chose to ignore in Session 1.1

click to display the Grammar Settings dialog box

4. Click the **OK** button to close the Grammar Settings dialog box and return to the Word Options dialog box.

To ensure that Word checks the entire Pet Flyer document, and doesn't skip any words that you chose to ignore when you checked the Robbins Letter in Session 1.1, you can click the Recheck Document button.

5. Click the **Recheck Document** button, and then click **Yes** in the warning dialog box.

6. In the Word Options dialog box, click the **OK** button to close the dialog box.

You return to the Pet Flyer document, where three errors are now marked with wavy blue underlines. The two new errors are related to subject-verb agreement. You should also see two words marked with wavy red underlines, including Tim's last name in the final paragraph.

Now you are ready to check the document's spelling and grammar. All errors marked with red underlines are considered spelling errors, while all errors marked with blue underlines are considered grammatical errors.

To check the Pet Flyer document for spelling and grammatical errors:

1. Press the **Ctrl+Home** keys, if necessary, to move the insertion point to the beginning of the document, to the left of the "D" in "Do." By placing the insertion point at the beginning of the document, you ensure that Word will check the entire document from start to finish without having to go back and check an earlier part.

2. On the ribbon, click the **REVIEW** tab. The ribbon changes to display reviewing options.

3. In the Proofing group, click the **Spelling & Grammar** button.

   The Spelling task pane opens on the right side of the Word window, with the word "frend" listed as a possible spelling error. The same word is highlighted in gray in the document. In the task pane's list of possible corrections, the correctly spelled word "friend" is highlighted in light blue. See Figure 1-25.

Figure 1-25	Spelling task pane

Courtesy of Ann Shaffer

4. In the task pane, click the **Change** button. The misspelled word "frend" is replaced with "friend."

   Next, Word highlights the entire second sentence, indicating another possible error. The Spelling task pane changes to the Grammar task pane, and the information at the bottom of the task pane explains that the error is related to subject-verb agreement.

5. Verify that "pros do" is selected in the Grammar task pane, and then click the **Change** button. The second to last paragraph of text is now highlighted in the document. The explanation at the bottom of the task pane indicates that the error is related to punctuation.

6. Verify that the comma is selected in the Grammar task pane, and then click the **Change** button.

   Tim's last name is now highlighted in the document, and the Grammar task pane changes to the Spelling task pane. Although the Spelling task pane doesn't recognize "Bartolutti" as a word, it is spelled correctly, so you can ignore it.

7. Click the **Ignore** button in the Spelling task pane.

   The last paragraph in the document is highlighted, and the Grammar task pane indicates a possible subject-verb agreement problem related to the word "register." However, the real problem is the word "too," just before "register." It should be replaced with "to." You can fix this problem by typing directly in the document.

8. In the document, click to the right of the word "too," delete the second letter "o," and then click the **Resume** button in the task pane. The task pane closes and a dialog box opens indicating that the spelling and grammar check is complete.

9. Click the **OK** button to close the dialog box.

   Finally, you'll restore the grammar settings to their original configuration.

10. Click the **FILE** tab, and then click **Options**.

11. In the Word Options dialog box, click **Proofing**, and then click the **Settings** button.

12. Scroll down, and then click the **Subject-verb agreement** check box to remove the checkmark.

13. Click the **OK** button to close the Grammar Settings dialog box, and then click the **OK** button to close the Word Options dialog box.

PROSKILLS

Written Communication: Proofreading Your Document

Although the Spelling and Grammar task panes are useful tools, they won't always catch every error in a document, and they sometimes flag "errors" that are actually correct. This means there is no substitute for careful proofreading. Always take the time to read through your document to check for errors the Spelling and Grammar task panes might have missed. Keep in mind that the Spelling and Grammar task panes cannot pinpoint inaccurate phrases or poorly chosen words. You'll have to find those yourself. To produce a professional document, you must read it carefully several times. It's a good idea to ask one or two other people to read your documents as well; they might catch something you missed.

You still need to proofread the Pet Flyer document. You'll do that next.

To proofread the Pet Flyer document:

1. Review the document text for any remaining errors. In the third paragraph of text, change the lowercase "p" in "pet" to an uppercase "P."

2. In the last line of text, replace "Tim Bartolutti" with your first and last name, and then save the document. Including your name in the document will make it easier for you to find your copy later if you print it on a shared printer.

Now you're ready to begin formatting the document. You will start by turning the page so it is wider than it is tall. In other words, you will change the document's **orientation**.

Changing Page Orientation

Portrait orientation, with the page taller than it is wide, is the default page orientation for Word documents because it is the orientation most commonly used for letters, reports, and other formal documents. However, Tim wants you to format the pet flyer in **landscape orientation**—that is, with the page turned so it is wider than it is tall to better accommodate the photo. You can accomplish this task by using the Orientation button located on the PAGE LAYOUT tab on the ribbon. After you change the page orientation, you will select narrower margins so you can maximize the amount of color on the page.

To change the page orientation:

1. Change the document zoom setting to **One Page** so that you can see the entire document.

2. On the ribbon, click the **PAGE LAYOUT** tab. The ribbon changes to display options for formatting the overall layout of text and images in the document.

3. In the Page Setup group, click the **Orientation** button, and then click **Landscape** on the menu. The document changes to landscape orientation.

4. In the Page Setup group, click the **Margins** button, and then click the **Narrow** option on the menu. The margins shrink from 1 inch to .5 inch on all four sides. See Figure 1-26.

| Figure 1-26 | Document in landscape orientation with narrow margins |

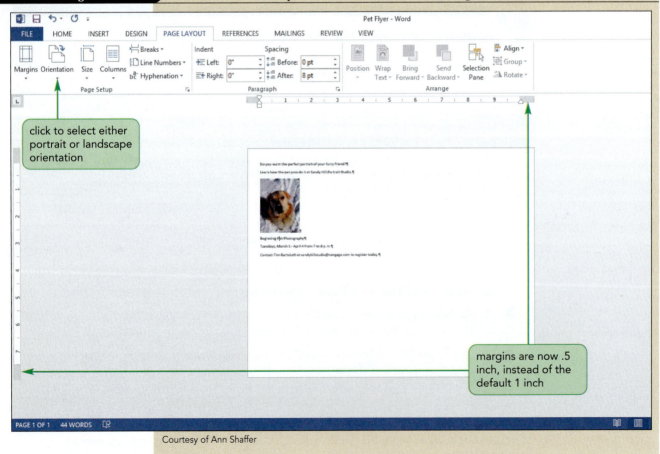

click to select either portrait or landscape orientation

margins are now .5 inch, instead of the default 1 inch

Courtesy of Ann Shaffer

Changing the Font and Font Size

Tim typed the document in the default font size, 11 point, and the default font, Calibri, but he would like to switch to the Arial font instead. Also, he wants to increase the size of all five paragraphs of the document text. To apply these changes, you start by selecting the text you want to format. Then you select the options you want in the Font group on the HOME tab.

To change the font and font size:

   1. On the ribbon, click the HOME tab.

   2. Change the document Zoom level to **120%**.

   3. To verify that the insertion point is located at the beginning of the document, press the **Ctrl+HOME** keys.

   4. Press and hold the **Shift** key, and then click to the right of the second paragraph marker, at the end of the second paragraph of text. The first two paragraphs of text are selected, as shown in Figure 1-27.

Figure 1-27	Selected text, with default font displayed in Font box

Courtesy of Ann Shaffer

The Font box in the Font group displays the name of the font applied to the selected text, which in this case is Calibri. The word "Body" next to the font name indicates that the Calibri font is intended for formatting body text. **Body text** is ordinary text, as opposed to titles or headings.

   5. In the Font group on the HOME tab, click the **Font** arrow. A list of available fonts appears, with Calibri Light and Calibri at the top of the list. Calibri is highlighted in blue, indicating that this font is currently applied to the selected text. The word "Headings" next to the font name "Calibri Light" indicates that Calibri Light is intended for formatting headings.

Below Calibri Light and Calibri, you might see a list of fonts that have been used recently on your computer, followed by a complete alphabetical list of all available fonts. (You won't see the list of recently used fonts if you just installed Word.) You need to scroll the list to see all the available fonts. Each name in the list is formatted with the relevant font. For example, the name "Arial" appears in the Arial font. See Figure 1-28.

Figure 1-28 Font list

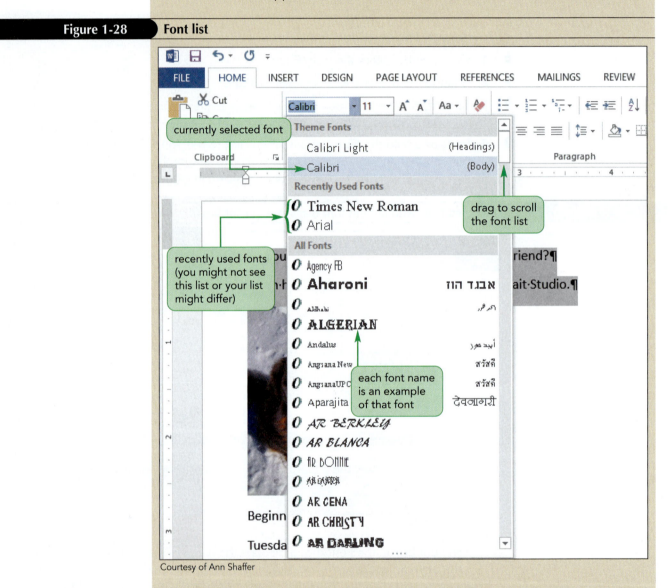

Courtesy of Ann Shaffer

▸ **6.** Without clicking, move the pointer over a dramatic-looking font in the font list, such as Algerian or Arial Black, and then move the pointer over another font.

The selected text in the document changes to show a Live Preview of the font the pointer is resting on. **Live Preview** shows the results that would occur in your document if you clicked the option you are pointing to.

▸ **7.** When you are finished reviewing the Font list, click **Arial**. The Font menu closes, and the selected text is formatted in Arial.

Next, you will make the text more eye-catching by increasing the font size. The Font Size box currently displays the number "11," indicating that the selected text is formatted in 11-point font.

8. Verify that the two paragraphs are still selected, and then click the **Font Size** arrow in the Font group to display a menu of font sizes. As with the Font menu, you can move the pointer over options in the Font Size menu to see a Live Preview of that option.

9. On the Font Size menu, click **22**. The selected text increases significantly in size and the Font Size menu closes.

10. Select the three paragraphs of text below the photo, format them in the Arial font, and then increase the paragraphs' font size to 22 points.

11. Click a blank area of the document to deselect the text, and then save the document.

Tim examines the flyer and decides he would like to apply more character formatting, which affects the appearance of individual characters, in the middle three paragraphs. After that, you can turn your attention to paragraph formatting, which affects the appearance of the entire paragraph.

Applying Text Effects, Font Colors, and Font Styles

To really make text stand out, you can use text effects. You access these options by clicking the Text Effects button in the Font group on the HOME tab. Keep in mind that text effects can be very dramatic. For formal, professional documents, you probably only need to use **bold** or *italic* to make a word or paragraph stand out.

Tim suggests applying text effects to the second paragraph.

To apply text effects to the second paragraph:

1. Scroll up, if necessary, to display the beginning of the document, and then click in the selection bar to the left of the second paragraph. The entire second paragraph is selected.

2. In the Font group on the HOME tab, click the **Text Effects and Typography** button ⓐ ▾ .

   A gallery of text effects appears. Options that allow you to fine-tune a particular text effect, perhaps by changing the color or adding an even more pronounced shadow, are listed below the gallery. A **gallery** is a menu or grid that shows a visual representation of the options available when you click a button.

3. In the middle of the bottom row of the gallery, place the pointer over the blue letter "A." This displays a ScreenTip with the text effect's full name, which is "Fill - Blue, Accent 1, Outline - Background 1, Hard Shadow - Accent 1." A Live Preview of the effect appears in the document. See Figure 1-29.

Figure 1-29	Live Preview of a text effect

Courtesy of Ann Shaffer

▶ **4.** In the bottom row of the gallery, click the blue letter "A." The text effect is applied to the selected paragraph and the Text Effects gallery closes. The second paragraph is formatted in blue, as shown in the Session 1.2 Visual Overview. The Bold button in the Font group is now highlighted because bold formatting is part of this text effect.

Next, to make the text stand out a bit more, you'll increase the font size. This time, instead of using the Font Size button, you'll use a different method.

▶ **5.** In the Font group, click the **Increase Font Size** button A˄. The font size increases from 22 points to 24 points.

▶ **6.** Click the **Increase Font Size** button A˄ again. The font size increases to 26 points. If you need to decrease the font size of selected text, you can use the Decrease Font Size button.

Tim asks you to emphasize the third and fourth paragraphs by adding bold and a blue font color.

To apply a font color and bold:

▶ **1.** Select the third and fourth paragraphs of text, which contain the class name as well as the dates and times.

▶ **2.** In the Font group on the Home tab, click the **Font Color button arrow** A▾. A gallery of font colors appears. Black is the default font color and appears at the top of the Font Color gallery, with the word "Automatic" next to it.

The options in the Theme Colors section of the menu are complementary colors that work well when used together in a document. The options in the Standard Colors section are more limited. For more advanced color options, you could use the More Colors or Gradient options. Tim prefers a simple blue.

Trouble? If the class name turned red, you clicked the Font Color button A instead of the arrow next to it. On the Quick Access Toolbar, click the Undo button ↩, and then repeat Step 2.

3. In the Theme Colors section, place the mouse pointer over the square that's second from the right in the top row. A ScreenTip with the color's name, "Blue, Accent 5," appears. A Live Preview of the color appears in the document, where the text you selected in Step 1 now appears formatted in blue. See Figure 1-30.

Figure 1-30	Font Color gallery showing a Live Preview

black is the default font color

point to this color

Blue, Accent 5

Do·you·want·the·p[...]·ait·of·your·furry·friend?¶

Learn·how·the[...]s·do·it·at·Sandy·Hill·Portrait·Studio.¶

Live Preview of Blue, Accent 5 color in the document

Beginning·Pet·Photography¶

Tuesdays,·March·1·-·April·4·from·7·to·8·p.m.¶

Courtesy of Ann Shaffer

4. Click the **Blue, Accent 5** square. The Font color gallery closes, and the selected text is formatted in blue. On the Font Color button, the bar below the letter "A" is now blue, indicating that if you select text and click the Font Color button, the text will automatically change to blue.

5. In the Font group, click the **Bold** button [B]. The selected text is now formatted in bold, with thicker, darker lettering.

TIP

You can use other buttons in the Font group on the HOME tab to apply other character attributes, such as underline, italic, or superscript.

Next, you will complete some paragraph formatting, starting with paragraph alignment.

Aligning Text

Alignment refers to how text and graphics line up between the page margins. By default, Word aligns text along the left margin, with the text along the right margin **ragged**, or uneven. This is called **left alignment**. With **right alignment**, the text is aligned along the right margin and is ragged along the left margin. With **center alignment**, text is centered between the left and right margins and is ragged along both the left and right margins. With **justified alignment**, full lines of text are spaced between both the left and the right margins, and no text is ragged. Text in newspaper columns is often justified. See Figure 1-31.

Figure 1-31	Varieties of text alignment

left alignment

The term "alignment"
refers to the way a
paragraph lines up
between the margins. The
term "alignment" refers to
the way a paragraph lines
up between the margins.

right alignment

The term "alignment"
refers to the way a
paragraph lines up
between the margins.
The term "alignment"
refers to the way a
paragraph lines up
between the margins.

center alignment

The term
"alignment"
refers to the
way a
paragraph lines
up between
the margins.

justified alignment

The   term   "alignment"
refers   to   the   way   a
paragraph   lines   up
between   the   margins.
The   term   "alignment"
refers   to   the   way   a
paragraph   lines   up
between   the   margins.

© 2014 Cengage Learning

The Paragraph group on the HOME tab includes a button for each of the four major types of alignment described in Figure 1-31: the Align Left button, the Center button, the Align Right button, and the Justify button. To align a single paragraph, click anywhere in that paragraph, and then click the appropriate alignment button. To align multiple paragraphs, select the paragraphs first, and then click an alignment button.

You need to center all the text in the flyer now. You can center the photo at the same time.

To center-align the text:

Use the Ctrl+A keys to select the entire document, instead of dragging the mouse pointer. It's easy to miss part of the document when you drag the mouse pointer.

1. Press the **Ctrl+A** keys to select the entire document, and make sure the HOME tab is still selected.

2. In the Paragraph group, click the **Center** button , and then click a blank area of the document to deselect the selected paragraphs. The text and photo are now centered on the page, similar to the centered text shown earlier in the Session 1.2 Visual Overview.

3. Save the document.

Adding a Paragraph Border and Shading

A **paragraph border** is an outline that appears around one or more paragraphs in a document. You can choose to apply only a partial border—for example, a bottom border that appears as an underline under the last line of text in the paragraph—or an entire box around a paragraph. You can select different colors and line weights for the border as well, making it more prominent or less prominent as needed. You apply paragraph borders using the Borders button in the Paragraph group on the HOME tab. **Shading** is background color that you can apply to one or more paragraphs and can be used in conjunction with a border for a more defined effect. You apply shading using the Shading button in the Paragraph group on the HOME tab.

Now you will apply a border and shading to the first paragraph, as shown earlier in the Session 1.2 Visual Overview. Then you will use the Format Painter to copy this formatting to the last paragraph in the document.

To add shading and a paragraph border:

1. Select the first paragraph. Be sure to select the paragraph mark at the end of the paragraph.

2. On the HOME tab, in the Paragraph group, click the **Borders button arrow**. A gallery of border options appears, as shown in Figure 1-32. To apply a complete outline around the selected text, you use the Outside Borders option.

| Figure 1-32 | Border gallery |

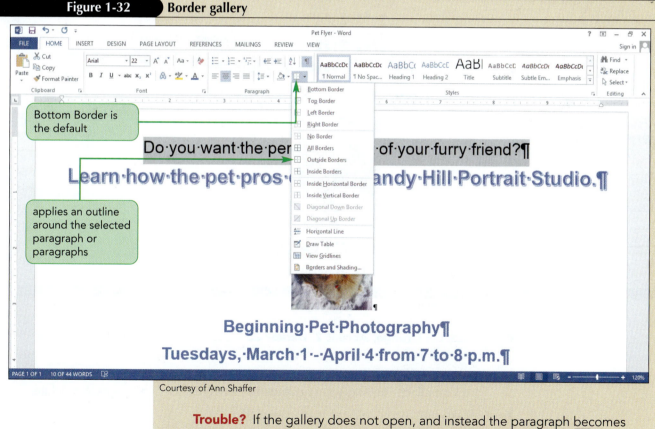

Courtesy of Ann Shaffer

Trouble? If the gallery does not open, and instead the paragraph becomes underlined with a single underline, you clicked the Borders button instead of the arrow next to it. On the Quick Access Toolbar, click the Undo button , and then repeat Step 2.

3. In the Border gallery, click **Outside Borders**. The menu closes and a black border appears around the selected paragraph, spanning the width of the page. In the Paragraph group, the Borders button changes to show the Outside Borders option.

    Trouble? If the border around the first paragraph doesn't extend all the way to the left and right margins, and instead only encloses the text, you didn't select the paragraph mark as directed in Step 1. Click the Undo button repeatedly to remove the border, and begin again with Step 1.

4. In the Paragraph group, click the **Shading button arrow**. A gallery of shading options opens, divided into Theme Colors and Standard Colors. You will use a shade of orange in the sixth column from the left.

5. In the second row from the bottom in the Theme Colors section, move the pointer over the square in the sixth column from the left to display a ScreenTip that reads "Orange, Accent 2, Darker 25%." A Live Preview of the color appears in the document. See Figure 1-33.

Figure 1-33   **Shading gallery with a Live Preview displayed**

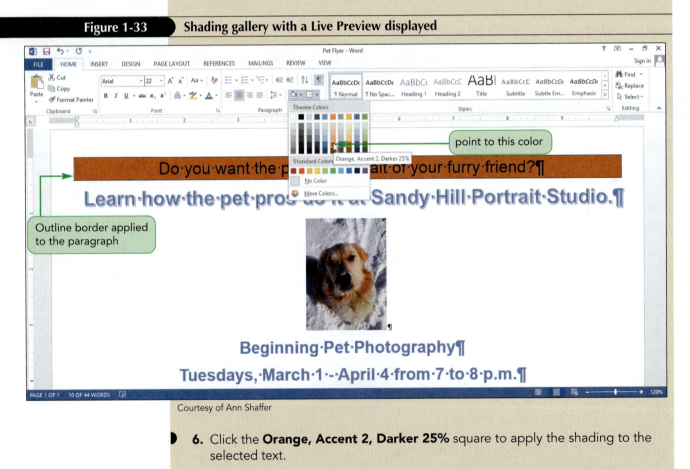

Courtesy of Ann Shaffer

6. Click the **Orange, Accent 2, Darker 25%** square to apply the shading to the selected text.

    On a dark background like the one you just applied, a white font creates a striking effect. Tim asks you to change the font color for this paragraph to white.

7. Make sure the HOME tab is still selected.

8. In the Font group, click the **Font Color button arrow** to open the Font Color gallery, and then click the **white** square in the top row of the Theme Colors. The Font Color gallery closes and the paragraph is now formatted with white font.

9. Click a blank area of the document to deselect the text, review the change, and then save the document. See Figure 1-34.

| Figure 1-34 | Paragraph formatted with dark orange shading, a black border, and white font |

To add balance to the flyer, Tim suggests formatting the last paragraph in the document with the same shading, border, and font color as the first paragraph. You'll do that next.

Copying Formatting with the Format Painter

You could select the last paragraph and then apply the border, shading, and font color one step at a time. But it's easier to copy all the formatting from the first paragraph to the last paragraph using the Format Painter button in the Clipboard group on the HOME tab.

Using the Format Painter

- Select the text whose formatting you want to copy.
- On the HOME tab, in the Clipboard group, click the Format Painter button; or to copy formatting to multiple sections of nonadjacent text, double-click the Format Painter button.
- The mouse pointer changes to the Format Painter pointer, the I-beam pointer with a paintbrush.
- Click the words you want to format, or drag to select and format entire paragraphs.
- When you are finished formatting the text, click the Format Painter button again to turn off the Format Painter.

You'll use the Format Painter now.

To use the Format Painter:

1. Change the document Zoom level to **One Page** so you can easily see both the first and last paragraphs.

2. Select the first paragraph, which is formatted with the dark orange shading, the border, and the white font color.

3. On the ribbon, click the HOME tab.

4. In the Clipboard group, click the **Format Painter** button to activate, or turn on, the Format Painter.

5. Move the pointer over the document. The pointer changes to the Format Painter pointer 🖌 when you move the mouse pointer near an item that can be formatted. See Figure 1-35.

Figure 1-35   **Format Painter**

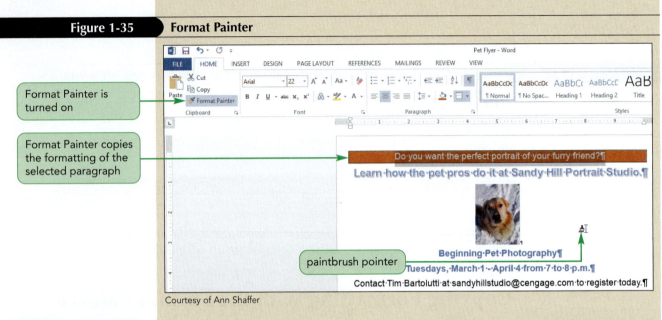

Format Painter is turned on

Format Painter copies the formatting of the selected paragraph

paintbrush pointer

Courtesy of Ann Shaffer

6. Click and drag the Format Painter pointer ▲Ị to select the last paragraph in the document. The paragraph is now formatted with dark orange shading, a black border, and white font. The mouse pointer returns to its original I-beam shape Ị.

Trouble? If the text in the newly formatted paragraph wrapped to a second line, replace your full name with your first name, or, if necessary, use only your initials so the paragraph is only one line long.

7. Click anywhere in the document to deselect the text, review the change, and then save the document.

You're almost finished working on the document's paragraph formatting. Your last step is to increase the paragraph spacing below the first paragraph and above the last paragraph. This will give the shaded text even more weight on the page. To complete this task, you will use the settings on the PAGE LAYOUT tab, which offer more options than the Line and Paragraph Spacing button on the HOME tab.

To increase the paragraph spacing below the first paragraph and above the last paragraph:

1. Click anywhere in the first paragraph, and then click the **PAGE LAYOUT** tab. On this tab, the Paragraph group contains settings that control paragraph spacing. Currently, the paragraph spacing for the first paragraph is set to the default 0 points before the paragraph and 8 points after.

2. In the Paragraph group, click the **After** box to select the current setting, type **42**, and then press the **Enter** key. The added space causes the second paragraph to move down 42 points.

3. Click anywhere in the last paragraph.

4. On the PAGE LAYOUT tab, in the Paragraph group, click the **Before** box to select the current setting, type **42**, and then press the **Enter** key. The added space causes the last paragraph to move down 42 points.

Formatting Professional Documents

In more formal documents, use color and special effects sparingly. The goal of letters, reports, and many other types of documents is to convey important information, not to dazzle the reader with fancy fonts and colors. Such elements only serve to distract the reader from your main point. In formal documents, it's a good idea to limit the number of colors to two and to stick with left alignment for text. In a document like the flyer you're currently working on, you have a little more leeway because the goal of the document is to attract attention. However, you still want it to look professional.

Finally, Tim wants you to replace the photo of the golden retriever with one that will look better in the document's new landscape orientation. You'll replace the photo, and then you'll resize it so the flyer fills the entire page.

Working with Pictures

A **picture** is a photo or another type of image that you insert into a document. To work with a picture, you first need to select it. Once a picture is selected, a contextual tab— the PICTURE TOOLS FORMAT tab—appears on the ribbon, with options for editing the picture and adding effects such as a border, a shadow, a reflection, or a new shape. A **contextual tab** appears on the ribbon only when an object is selected. It contains commands related to the selected object so you can manipulate, edit, and format the selected object. You can also use the mouse to resize or move a selected picture. To insert a new picture, you use the Pictures button in the Illustrations group on the INSERT tab.

To delete the current photo and insert a new one:

1. Click the photo to select it.

   The squares, called **handles**, around the edge of the photo indicate the photo is selected. The Layout Options button, to the right of the photo, gives you access to options that control how the document text flows around the photo. You don't need to worry about these options now. Finally, note that the PICTURE TOOLS FORMAT tab appeared on the ribbon when you selected the photo. See Figure 1-36.

Figure 1-36   **Selected photo**

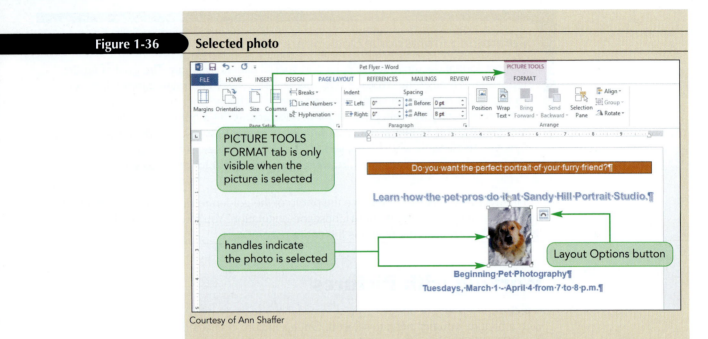

Courtesy of Ann Shaffer

▶ **2.** Press the **Delete** key. The photo is deleted from the document. The insertion point blinks next to the paragraph symbol. You will insert the new photo in that paragraph.

▶ **3.** On the ribbon, click the **INSERT** tab. The ribbon changes to display the Insert options.

▶ **4.** In the Illustrations group, click the **Pictures** button. The Insert Picture dialog box opens.

▶ **5.** Navigate to the Word1 ▶ Tutorial folder included with your Data Files, and then click **Poodle** to select the file. The name of the selected file appears in the File name box.

▶ **6.** Click the **Insert** button to close the Insert Picture dialog box and insert the photo. An image of a black poodle appears in the document, below the text. The photo is selected, as indicated by the handles that appear on its border.

Now you need to enlarge the photo to fit the available space on the page. You could do so by clicking one of the picture's corner handles, holding down the mouse button, and then dragging the handle to resize the picture. But using the Shape Height and Shape Width boxes on the PICTURE TOOLS FORMAT tab gives you more precise results.

To resize the photo:

▶ **1.** Make sure the PICTURE TOOLS FORMAT tab is still selected on the ribbon.

▶ **2.** In the Size group on the far right edge of the ribbon, locate the Shape Height box, which tells you that the height of the selected picture is currently 2.46". The Shape Width box tells you that the width of the picture is 3.69". As you'll see in the next step, when you change one of these measurements, the other changes accordingly, keeping the overall shape of the picture the same. See Figure 1-37.

Figure 1-37 | **Shape Height and Shape Width boxes**

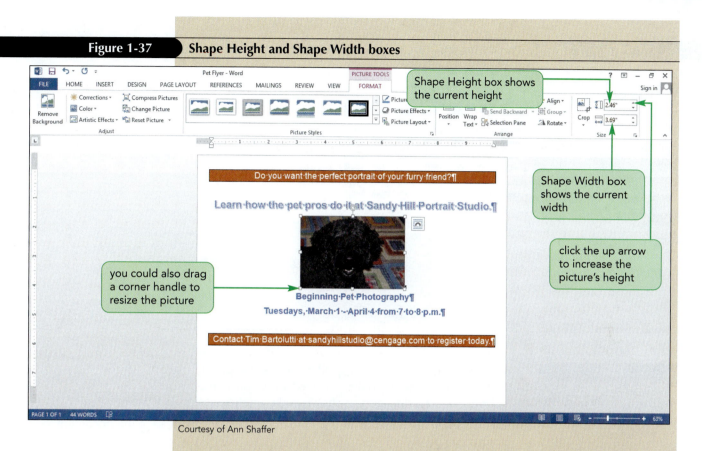

Courtesy of Ann Shaffer

> **3.** Click the **up arrow** in the Shape Height box in the Size group. The photo increases in size slightly. The measurement in the Shape Height box increases to 2.5" and the measurement in the Shape Width box increases to 3.75".

> **4.** Click the **up arrow** in the Shape Height box repeatedly until the picture is 3.3" tall and 4.95" wide.

Finally, to make the photo more noticeable, you can add a **picture style**, which is a collection of formatting options, such as a frame, a rounded shape, and a shadow. You can apply a picture style to a selected picture by clicking the style you want in the Picture Styles gallery on the PICTURE TOOLS FORMAT tab. In the following steps, you'll start by displaying the gallery.

To add a style to the photo:

> **1.** Make sure the PICTURE TOOLS FORMAT tab is still selected on the ribbon.

> **2.** In the Picture Styles group, click the **More** button to the right of the Picture Styles gallery to open the gallery and display more picture styles. Some of the picture styles simply add a border, while others change the picture's shape. Other styles combine these options with effects such as a shadow or a reflection.

> **3.** Place the mouse pointer over various styles to observe the Live Previews in the document, and then place the mouse pointer over the Drop Shadow Rectangle style, which is the middle style in the top row. See Figure 1-38.

Figure 1-38   Previewing a picture style

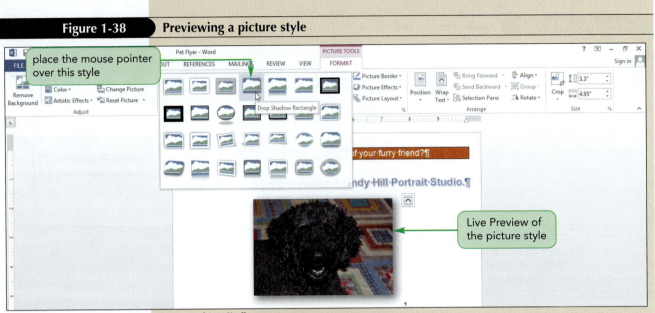

Courtesy of Ann Shaffer

TIP

To return a picture to its original appearance, click the Reset Picture button in the Adjust group on the PICTURE TOOLS FORMAT tab.

4. In the gallery, click the **Drop Shadow Rectangle** style to apply it to the photo and close the gallery. The photo is formatted with a shadow on the bottom and right sides, as shown earlier in the Session 1.2 Visual Overview.

5. Click anywhere outside the photo to deselect it, and then, save the document.

6. Click the **FILE** tab, and then click **Close** in the navigation bar to close the document without closing Word.

INSIGHT

Working with Inline Pictures

By default, when you insert a picture in a document, it is treated as an inline object, which means its position changes in the document as you add or delete text. Also, because it is an inline object, you can align the picture just as you would align text, using the alignment buttons in the Paragraph group on the HOME tab. Essentially, you can treat an inline picture as just another paragraph.

When you become a more advanced Word user, you'll learn how to wrap text around a picture so that the text flows around the picture—with the picture maintaining its position on the page no matter how much text you add to or delete from the document. The alignment buttons don't work on pictures that have text wrapped around them. Instead, you can drag the picture to the desired position on the page.

The flyer is complete and ready for Tim to print later. Because Tim is considering creating a promotional brochure that would include numerous photographs, he asks you to look up information about other ways to format a picture. You can do that using Word's Help system.

Getting Help

To get the most out of Help, your computer must be connected to the Internet so it can access the reference information stored at Office.com.

To look up information in Help:

TIP

You can also open the Word Help window by pressing the F1 key.

1. Verify that your computer is connected to the Internet, and then, on the title bar, click the **Microsoft Word Help** button ⍰. The Word Help window opens, with its Home page displayed. You might see the topics shown in Figure 1-39, or you might see other topics. You can click the various options in the Word Help window to browse among topics, or you can use the Search online help box to look up information on a particular topic.

Figure 1-39   Word Help window

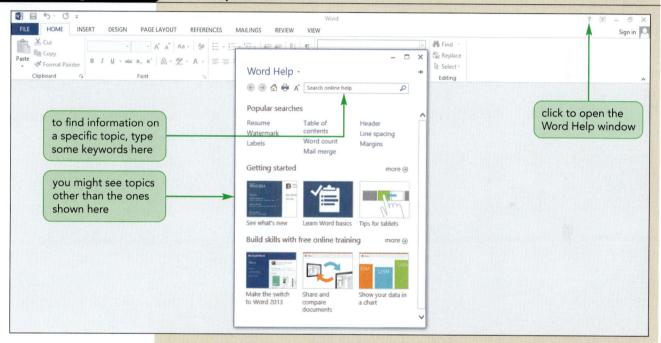

to find information on a specific topic, type some keywords here

you might see topics other than the ones shown here

click to open the Word Help window

2. Click in the **Search online help** box, type **format picture**, and then press the **Enter** key. The Word Help window displays a list of articles related to inserting pictures in a document.

3. Click the first topic listed, and then read the article to see if it contains any information about formatting pictures that might be useful to Tim. Note that to print information about a topic, you can click the Print button near the top of the Word Help window.

4. When are you finished reading the article, click the **Back** button ⬅ near the top of the Word Help window to return to the previous list of topics.

5. Click the **Home** button ⌂ to return to the Home page.

6. Click the **Close** button ✖ in the upper-right corner to close the Word Help window.

Word Help is a great way to learn more about Word's many features. Articles on basic skills provide step-by-step guides for completing tasks, while more elaborate, online tutorials walk you through more complicated tasks. Be sure to take some time on your own to explore Word Help so you can find the information you want when you need it.

REVIEW

Session 1.2 Quick Check

1. Explain how to open the Spelling and Grammar task panes.
2. What is the default page orientation for Word documents?
3. What is the default font size?
4. Explain how to use the Format Painter button.
5. What button do you use to insert a photo in a document?
6. Explain how to open the Help window.

ASSESS

SAM Projects

Put your skills into practice with SAM Projects! SAM Projects for this tutorial can be found online. If you have a SAM account, go to www.cengage.com/sam2013 to download the most recent Project Instructions and Start Files.

PRACTICE

Review Assignments

Data Files needed for the Review Assignments: Flower.docx, Mixed Flowers.jpg

Tim asks you to write a cover letter to accompany a wedding photography contract. After that, he wants you to create an envelope for the letter, and to format a flyer announcing a class about photographing flowers. Change the Zoom level as necessary while you are working. Complete the following steps:

1. Open a new, blank document and then save the document as **Sommer Letter** in the location specified by your instructor.
2. Type the date **February 16, 2016** using AutoComplete for "February."
3. Press the Enter key twice, and then type the following inside address, using the default paragraph spacing and pressing the Enter key once after each line:
   Kiley Sommer
   2355 Greenwillow Drive
   Baltimore, MD 21204
4. Type **Dear Ms. Sommer:** as the salutation, press the Enter key, and then type the following as the body of the letter:
   Enclosed you will find the contract summarizing our plans for your wedding. Please return your signed copy to me by next Monday, along with the down payment specified in the contract.
   As you'll see, the second page of the contract lists the specific shots we've already agreed on. For more ideas about possible group shots, please see our website at www.sandyhillstudio. cengage.com. Of course, the photographer will be taking candid shots throughout the day.
5. Press the Enter key, type **Sincerely yours,** as the complimentary closing, press the Enter key three times, type **Tim Bartolutti** as the signature line, insert a manual line break, and type **Sales Manager** as his title.
6. Press the Enter key, type your initials, insert a manual line break, and then use the Undo button to make your initials all lowercase, if necessary.
7. Type **Enclosure** and save the document.
8. Scroll to the beginning of the document and proofread your work. Remove any wavy underlines by using a shortcut menu or by typing a correction yourself. Remove the hyperlink formatting from the web address.
9. Remove the paragraph spacing from the first two lines of the inside address.
10. Change the top margin to 2.75 inches. Leave the other margins at their default settings.
11. Save your changes to the letter, preview it, print it if your instructor asks you to, and then close it.
12. Create a new, blank document, and then create an envelope. Use Kiley Sommer's address (from Step 3) as the delivery address. Use your school's name and address for the return address. Add the envelope to the document. If you are asked if you want to save the return address as the new return address, click No.

13. Save the document as **Sommer Envelope** in the location specified by your instructor, and then close the document.

14. Open the file **Flower**, located in the Word1 ▶ Review folder included with your Data Files, and then check your screen to make sure your settings match those in the tutorial.

15. Save the document as **Flower Flyer** in the location specified by your instructor.

16. Configure the grammar settings to check for subject-verb agreement errors, and then use the Spelling and Grammar task panes to correct any errors marked with wavy underlines. When you are finished, return the grammar settings to their original configuration.

17. Proofread the document and correct any other errors. Be sure to change "gardens" to "garden's" in the first paragraph.

18. Change the page orientation to Landscape and the margins to Narrow.

19. Format the document text in 22-point Times New Roman font.

20. Center the text and the photo.

21. Format the first paragraph with an outside border, and then add green shading, using the Green, Accent 6, Darker 25% color in the Theme Colors section of the Shading gallery. Format the paragraph text in white.

22. Format the last paragraph in the document using the same formatting you applied to the first paragraph.

23. Increase the paragraph spacing after the first paragraph to 42 points. Increase the paragraph spacing before the last paragraph in the document to 42 points.

24. Format the second paragraph with the Fill - Orange, Accent 2, Outline - Accent 2 text effect. Increase the paragraph's font size to 26 points.

25. Format the third and fourth paragraphs (containing the class name, date, and time) in green, using the Green, Accent 6, Darker 50% font color, and then add bold and italic.

26. Delete the photo and replace it with the **Mixed Flowers.jpg** photo, located in the Word1 ▶ Review folder included with your Data Files.

27. Resize the new photo so that it is 3.8" tall, and then add the Soft Edge Rectangle style in the Pictures Styles gallery.

28. Save your changes to the flyer, preview it, and then close it.

29. Start Word Help and look up the topic "work with pictures." Read the article, return to the Help home page, and then close Help.

Case Problem 1

There are no Data Files needed for this Case Problem.

Prairie Public Health Consultants   You are a program administrator at Prairie Public Health Consultants. Over the past few months, you have collected handwritten surveys from high school students about their exercise habits. Now you need to send the surveys to the researcher in charge of compiling the data. Create a cover letter to accompany the surveys by completing the following steps. Because your office is currently out of letterhead, you'll start the letter by typing a return address. As you type the letter, remember to include the appropriate number of blank paragraphs between the various parts of the letter. Complete the following steps:

1. Open a new, blank document, and then save the document as **Prairie Letter** in the location specified by your instructor. If necessary, change the Zoom level to 120%.

APPLY

2. Type the following return address, using the default paragraph spacing, and replacing [Your Name] with your first and last names:

   [Your Name]

   Prairie Public Health Consultants

   6833 Erickson Lane

   Des Moines, IA 50301

3. Type **November 7, 2016** as the date, leaving a blank paragraph between the last line of the return address and the date.

4. Type the following inside address, using the default paragraph spacing and leaving the appropriate number of blank paragraphs after the date:

   Dr. Anna Witinski

   4643 University Circle

   Ames, IA 50010

5. Type **Dear Dr. Witinski:** as the salutation.

6. To begin the body of the letter, type the following paragraph:

   Enclosed please find the surveys I have collected so far. I hope to have another 200 for you in a week, but I thought you would like to get started on these now. After you've had a chance to review the surveys, please call or email me with your answers to these questions:

7. Add the following questions as separate paragraphs, using the default paragraph spacing:

   Do you need help tabulating the survey responses?

   Should we consider expanding the survey to additional schools?

   Should we rephrase any of the survey questions?

8. Insert a new paragraph before the second question, and then add the following as the new second question in the list:

   Have you hired a student to help you with your analysis?

9. Insert a new paragraph after the last question, and then type the complimentary closing **Sincerely,** (including the comma).

10. Leave the appropriate amount of space for your signature, type your full name, insert a manual line break, and then type **Program Administrator**.

11. Type **Enclosure** in the appropriate place.

12. Use the Spelling and Grammar task panes to correct any errors. Instruct the Spelling task pane to ignore the recipient's name.

13. Italicize the four paragraphs containing the questions.

14. Remove the paragraph spacing from the first three lines of the return address. Do the same for the first two paragraphs of the inside address.

15. Center the four paragraphs containing the return address, format them in 16-point font, and then add the Fill - Black, Text 1, Shadow text effect.

16. Save the document, preview it, and then close it.

17. Create a new, blank document, and create an envelope. Use Dr. Witinski's address (from Step 4) as the delivery address. Use the return address shown in Step 2. Add the envelope to the document. If you are asked if you want to save the return address as the new return address, click No.

18. Save the document as **Witinski Envelope** in the location specified by your instructor, and then close the document.

Case Problem 2

Data Files needed for this Case Problem: Church.jpg, Walking.docx

CREATE

Walking Tours of Old San Juan   You work as the guest services coordinator at Hotel Azul, a luxury resort hotel in San Juan, Puerto Rico. You need to create a flyer promoting a daily walking tour of Old San Juan, the historic Colonial section of Puerto Rico's capital city. Complete the following steps:

1. Open the file **Walking** located in the Word1 ▸ Case2 folder included with your Data Files, and then save the document as **Walking Tour Flyer** in the location specified by your instructor.
2. In the document, replace "Student Name" with your first and last names.
3. Use the Spelling and Grammar task panes to correct any errors, including problems with subject-verb agreement. Instruct the Spelling task pane to ignore the Spanish church names, as well as your name if Word marks it with a wavy underline.
4. Change the page margins to Narrow.
5. Complete the flyer as shown in Figure 1-40. Use the file **Church.jpg** located in the Word1 ▸ Case2 folder included with your Data Files. Use the default line spacing and paragraph spacing unless otherwise specified in Figure 1-40.

Figure 1-40   **Formatted Walking Tour flyer**

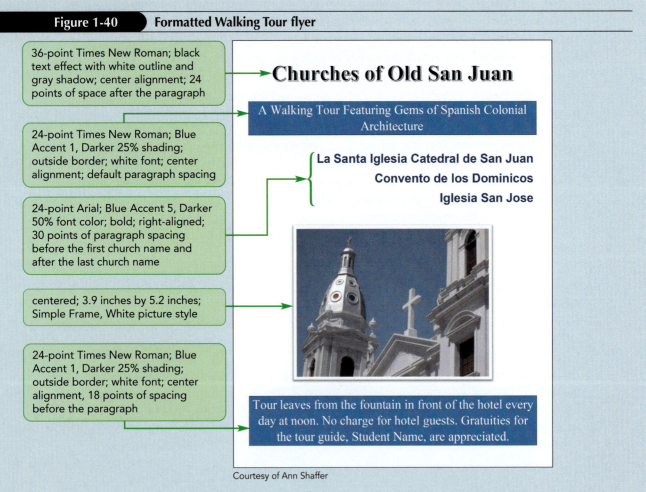

Courtesy of Ann Shaffer

6. Save the document, preview it, and then close it.

TROUBLESHOOT

Case Problem 3

Data Files needed for this Case Problem: Mushroom.docx, Mycology.docx

Green Valley Arborists   You work as the office manager for Green Valley Arborists, a tree care service in Billings, Montana. One of the company's arborists noticed a bright orange fungus growing on a tree stump in a client's backyard. She has started writing a letter to a mycologist at the local community college to ask if he can identify the fungus. The letter is almost finished, but the arborist needs help correcting errors and formatting the text to match the block style. The photo itself is stored in a separate document. The arborist mistakenly applied a picture style to the photo that is inappropriate for professional correspondence. She asks you to remove the picture style and then format the page. Complete the following steps:

1. Open the file **Mycology** located in the Word1 ▶ Case3 folder included with your Data Files, and then save the document as **Mycology Letter** in the location specified by your instructor.

2. Use the Spelling and Grammar task panes to correct any errors, including subject-verb errors. When you are finished, return the Grammar settings to their original configuration.

⚙ **Troubleshoot** 3. Make any necessary changes to ensure that the letter matches the formatting of a block style business letter, including the appropriate paragraph spacing. Keep in mind that the letter will include an enclosure. Include your initials where appropriate.

⚙ **Troubleshoot** 4. The letterhead for Green Valley Arborists requires a top margin of 2.5 inches. Determine if the layout of the letter will work with the letterhead, make any necessary changes, and then save the letter.

5. Save the document and preview it.

6. With the letter still open, create an envelope. Use the delivery address taken from the letter, but edit the delivery address. Click the Omit check box to deselect it (if necessary), and then, for the return address, type your school's name and address. Add the envelope to the document. If you are asked if you want to save the return address as the new default return address, answer No.

7. Save the document, preview it, and then close it.

8. Open the file **Mushroom** located in the Word1 ▶ Case3 folder included with your Data Files, and then save the document as **Mushroom Photo** in the location specified by your instructor.

⚙ **Troubleshoot** 9. Reset the picture to its original appearance, before the arborist mistakenly added the style with the reflection.

⚙ **Troubleshoot** 10. Modify the page layout and adjust the size of the photo so the photo fills as much of the page as possible without overlapping the page margins.

11. Save the document, preview it, and then close it.

CHALLENGE

Case Problem 4

There are no Data Files needed for this Case Problem.

Hapsburg Interior Design As a design assistant at Hapsburg Interior Design, you are responsible for distributing manufacturer samples throughout the office so the firm's designers can stay up to date on newly available paint colors, wallpaper patterns, and fabrics. Along with each sample, you need to include an explanatory memo. Complete the following steps:

⊕ **Explore** 1. Open a new document—but instead of selecting the Blank document option, search for a memo template online. In the list of search results, click the Memo (Simple design) template, and then click the Create button. A memo template opens in the Word window. Above the memo template is the Document Properties panel, where you could enter information about the document that might be useful later. You don't need the panel for this project, so you can ignore it, as well as any entries in the text boxes in the panel.

2. Save the document as **Samples Memo** in the location specified by your instructor. If you see a dialog box indicating that the document will be upgraded to the newest file format, click the OK button. Note that of the hundreds of templates available online, only a small portion have been created in the most recent version of Word, so you will often see this dialog box when working with templates.

⊕ **Explore** 3. In the document, click the text "[Company name]." The placeholder text appears in a box with gray highlighting. The box containing the highlighted text (with the small rectangle attached) is called a document control. You can enter text in a document control just as you enter text in a dialog box. Type **Hapsburg Interior Design**, and then press the Tab key. The "[Recipient names]" placeholder text now appears in a document control next to the word "To." (*Hint*: As you work on the memo in the following steps, keep in mind that if you accidentally double-click the word "memo" at the top of the document, you will access the header portion of the document, which is normally closed to editing. In that case, press the Esc key to return to the main document.)

4. Type **All Designers** and then press the Tab key twice. A document control is now visible to the right of the word "From." Depending on how your computer is set up, you might see your name or another name here, or the document control might be empty. Delete the name, if necessary, and then type your first and last names.

⊕ **Explore** 5. Continue using the Tab key to edit the remaining document controls as indicated below. If you press the Tab key too many times and accidentally skip a document control, you can click the document control to select it.
   - In the CC: document control, delete the placeholder text.
   - In the Date document control, click the down arrow, and then click the current date in the calendar.
   - In the Re: document control, type **Rowley Fabrics**.
   - In the Comments document control, type **Here are the latest offerings from Rowley Fabrics. After you have reviewed the collection, please write your initials at the bottom of this memo and pass the collection on to another designer. If you are the last of the group to review the samples, please return them to my desk. Thank you.**

6. Use the Spelling and Grammar task panes to correct any underlined errors, and then proofread the document to look for any additional errors.

7. Save the document, preview it, and then close it.

WORD

Navigating and Formatting a Document

Editing an Academic Document According to MLA Style

OBJECTIVES

Session 2.1
- Read, reply to, delete, and add comments
- Create bulleted and numbered lists
- Move text using drag and drop
- Cut and paste text
- Copy and paste text
- Navigate through a document using the Navigation pane
- Find and replace text
- Format text with styles
- Apply a theme to a document

Session 2.2
- Review the MLA style for research papers
- Indent paragraphs
- Insert and modify page numbers
- Create citations
- Create and update a bibliography
- Modify a source

Case | *Rivas-Garcia College*

Kaya Cho, a student at Rivas-Garcia College, works part-time in the college's Media Studies department. She has written a handout describing the requirements for a Media Studies major, and asks you to help her finish it. The text of the handout needs some reorganization and other editing. It also needs formatting so the finished document looks professional and is easy to read.

Kaya is also taking a Media Studies class this semester, and is writing a research paper on the history of newspapers. To complete the paper, she needs to follow a set of very specific formatting and style guidelines for academic documents.

Kaya has asked you to help her edit these two very different documents. In Session 2.1, you will review and respond to some comments in the handout, and then revise and format that document. In Session 2.2, you will review the MLA style for research papers, and then format Kaya's research paper to match the MLA specifications.

STARTING DATA FILES

Word2 → Tutorial
Media.docx
Newspaper.docx

Review
Broadcast.docx
Situation.docx

Case1
Yoga.docx

Case2
Hamlet.docx

Case3
Capital.docx
Sarah.docx

Case4
Movie.docx

Session 2.1 Visual Overview:

Use the Bullets button to create a bulleted list from selected paragraphs.

Use the Numbering button to create a numbered list from selected paragraphs.

Click the **Search for more things button** to access advanced search tools, or to select something to search for besides text.

The **Navigation pane** allows you to search for text in the document, with the results highlighted in yellow in the document.

You can type the text you want to search for here.

This text is formatted with the Heading 1 style for the Office theme.

The **bullet** before each of these paragraphs identifies the four paragraphs as items in a list.

This document has two pages.

Navigation

communication

2 results

HEADINGS   PAGES   **RESULTS**

that explores everything having to do with **communication**, journalism and entertainment, including

and entertainment, including mass **communication**, electronic journalism, online

Media Studies - Word

FILE   HOME   INSERT   DESIGN   PAGE LAYOUT   REFERENCES   MAILINGS   REV

Calibri (Body)   11   A˄ A˅   Aa

B   I   U   abc   x₂   x²   A   A

Paste

Clipboard   Font   Paragraph

Majoring i

Media·Studies·is·an·exciting·academic·field·th journalism·and·entertainment,·including·mass and·television.·In·your·Media·Studies·classes, take·classes·in·many·different·departments.·F literature·and·popular·culture,·or·a·history·cla might·bring·you·to·the·Psychology,·Economics

Prerequisites¶

Before·you·can·officially·declare·yourself·a·Me courses,·drawn·from·four·different·academic·

- → Media·Studies·101:·General·Media·St
- → History·200:·North·American·History·
- → Political·Science·101:·Introduction·to·
- → Sociology·101:·Introduction·to·the·So

It·is·possible·to·substitute·another·introducto need·to·submit·a·formal·request·to·your·Med enough·time·to·complete·your·upper-level·co your·sophomore·year.¶

Core·Courses¶

PAGE 1 OF 2   527 WORDS

Working with Lists and Styles

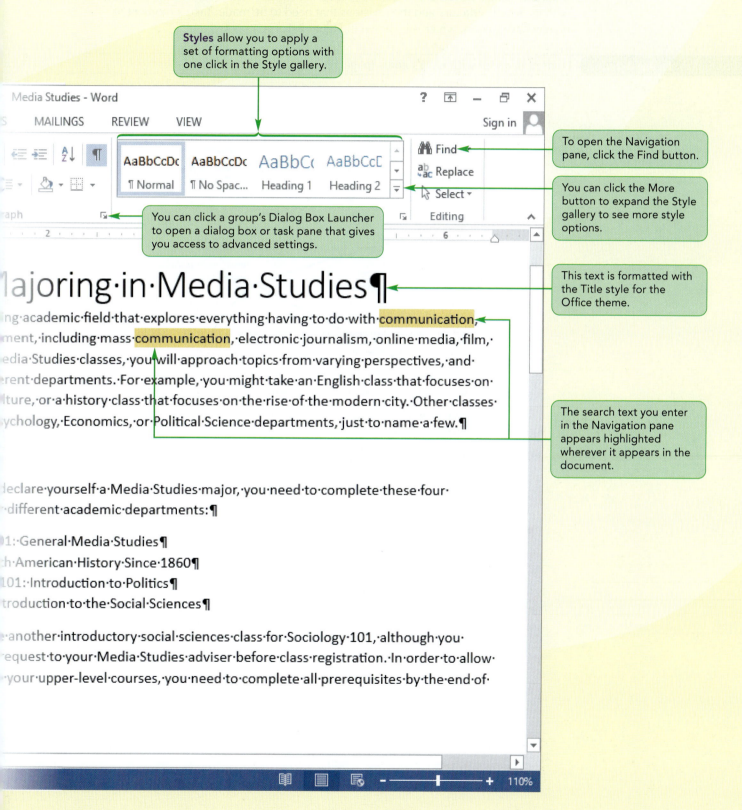

Styles allow you to apply a set of formatting options with one click in the Style gallery.

You can click a group's Dialog Box Launcher to open a dialog box or task pane that gives you access to advanced settings.

To open the Navigation pane, click the Find button.

You can click the More button to expand the Style gallery to see more style options.

This text is formatted with the Title style for the Office theme.

The search text you enter in the Navigation pane appears highlighted wherever it appears in the document.

Reviewing the Document

Before revising a document for someone else, it's a good idea to familiarize yourself with its overall structure and the revisions that need to be made. Take a moment to review Kaya's notes, which are shown in Figure 2-1.

Figure 2-1   **Draft of handout with Kaya's notes (page 1)**

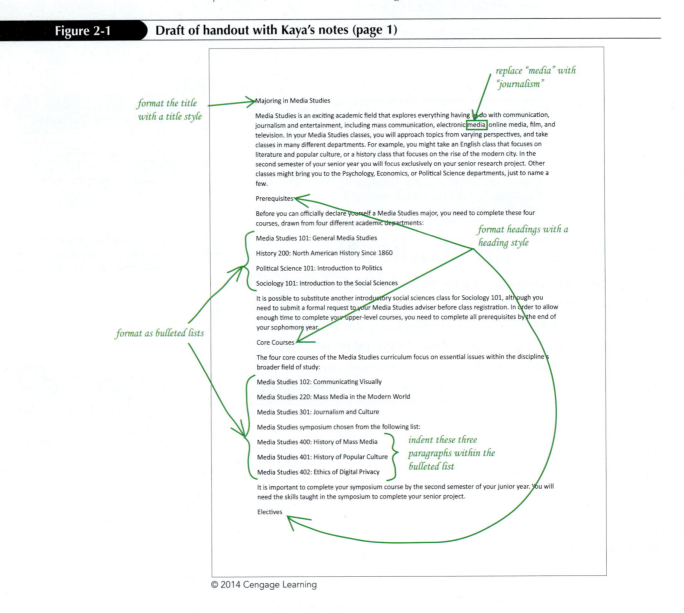

© 2014 Cengage Learning

Figure 2-1   Draft of handout with Kaya's notes (page 2)

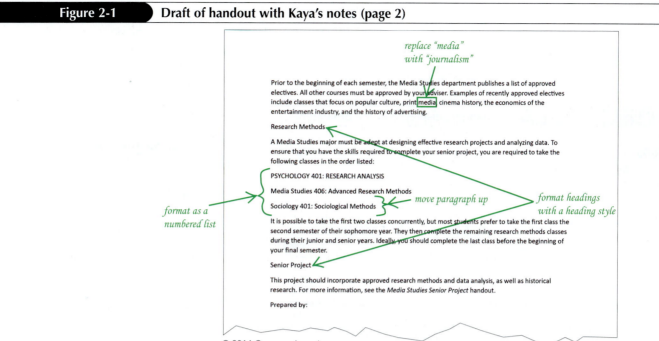

© 2014 Cengage Learning

Kaya also included additional guidance in some comments she added to the document file. A **comment** is like an electronic sticky note attached to a word, phrase, or paragraph in a document. Comments appear in the margin, along with the name of the person who added them. Within a single document, you can add new comments, reply to existing comments, and delete comments.

You will open the document now, save it with a new name, and then review Kaya's comments in Word.

To open and rename the document:

1. Open the document named **Media** located in the Word2 ▶ Tutorial folder included with your Data Files.

2. Save the document as **Media Studies** in the location specified by your instructor.

3. Verify that the document is displayed in Print Layout view, that the zoom is set to **120%**, and that the rulers and nonprinting characters are displayed.

4. On the ribbon, click the **REVIEW** tab to display the tools used for working with comments. Comments can be displayed in several different ways, so your first step is to make sure the comments in the Media Studies document are displayed to match the figures in this book—using Simple Markup view.

5. In the Tracking group, click the **Display for Review** arrow, and then click **Simple Markup** to select it, if necessary. At this point, you might see comment icons to the right of the document text, or you might see the full text of each comment.

6. In the Comments group, click the **Show Comments** button several times to practice displaying and hiding the comments, and then, when you are finished, make sure the Show Comments button is selected so the full text of each comment is displayed.

7. At the bottom of the Word window, drag the horizontal scroll bar all the way to the right so you can read the full text of each comment. See Figure 2-2. Note that the comments on your screen might be a different color than the ones shown in the figure.

Figure 2-2 Comments displayed in the document

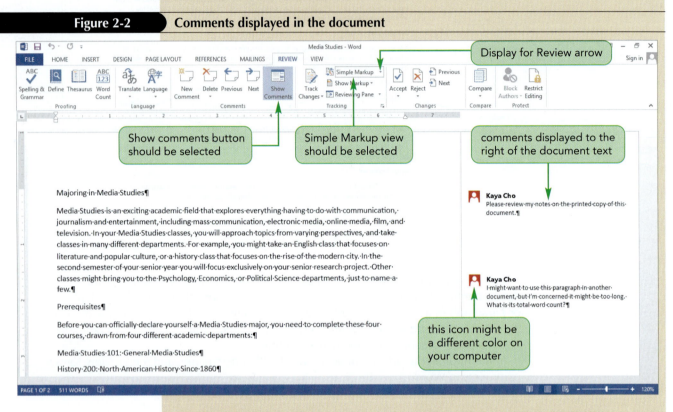

Note that when working on a small monitor, it can be helpful to switch the document Zoom level to Page Width, in which case Word automatically reduces the width of the document to accommodate the comments on the right.

8. Read the document, including the comments. The handout includes the title "Majoring in Media Studies" at the top, as well as headings (such as "Prerequisites" and "Core Courses") that divide the document into parts. Right now the headings are hard to spot because they don't look different from the surrounding text. Kaya used the default font size, 11-point, and the default font, Calibri (Body), for all the text in the document. Note, too, that the document includes some short paragraphs that would work better as bulleted or numbered lists.

9. Scroll down until you can see the first line on page 2, which begins "Prior to the beginning of each semester…." and then click anywhere in that sentence. The message "PAGE 2 OF 2" in the status bar, in the lower-left corner of the Word window, tells you that the insertion point is currently located on page 2 of the two-page document. The shaded space between the first and second pages of the document indicates a page break. To hide the top and bottom margins in a document, as well as the space between pages, you can double-click the shaded space between any two pages.

10. Position the mouse pointer over the shaded space between page 1 and page 2 until the pointer changes to ⊞, and then double-click. The shaded space disappears. Instead, the two pages are now separated by a gray, horizontal line.

Trouble? If the HEADER & FOOTER TOOLS DESIGN tab appears on the ribbon, you double-clicked the top or bottom of one of the pages, instead of in the space between them. Click the Close Header and Footer button on the DESIGN tab, and then repeat Step 10.

▶ **11.** Use the ✛ pointer to double-click the gray horizontal line between pages 1 and 2. The shaded space between the two pages is redisplayed.

Working with Comments

Now that you are familiar with the Media Studies document, you can review and respond to Kaya's comments. The Comment group on the REVIEW tab includes helpful tools for working with comments.

Working with Comments

- On the ribbon, click the REVIEW tab.
- To display comments in an easy-to-read view, in the Tracking group, click the Display for Review button, and then click Simple Markup.
- To see the text of each comment in Simple Markup view, click the Show Comments button in the Comments group.
- To move the insertion point to the next or previous comment in the document, click the Next button or the Previous button in the Comments group.
- To delete a comment, click anywhere in the comment, and then click the Delete button in the Comments group.
- To delete all the comments in a document, click the Delete button arrow in the Comments group, and then click Delete All Comments in Document.
- To add a new comment, select the document text you want to comment on, click the New Comment button in the Comments group, and then type the comment text.
- To reply to a comment, click the Reply button to the right of the comment, and then type your reply.
- To indicate that a comment or an individual reply to a comment is no longer a concern, right-click the comment or reply, and then click Mark Comment Done in the shortcut menu. To mark a comment and all of the replies attached to it as done, right-click the original comment and then click Mark Comment Done.

To review and respond to the comments in the document:

▶ **1.** Press the **Ctrl+Home** keys to move the insertion point to the beginning of the document.

▶ **2.** On the REVIEW tab, in the Comments group, click the **Next** button. The first comment now has an outline, indicating that it is selected. See Figure 2-3.

In the document, the word "Majoring" is highlighted. A line connects the comment to the word "Majoring," indicating that the comment is attached to that word. Because Kaya created the comment, her name appears at the beginning of the comment, followed by the date on which she created it. The insertion point blinks at the beginning of the comment, and is ready for you to edit the comment if you want.

Figure 2-3 Comment attached to document text

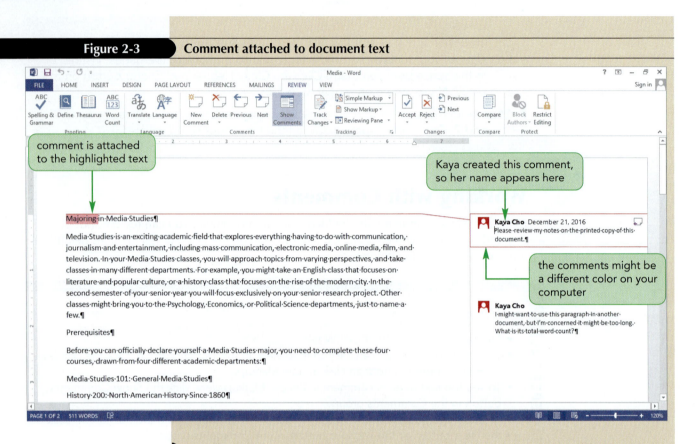

3. Read the comment, and then in the Comments group, click the **Next** button to select the next comment. According to this comment, Kaya wants to know the total word count of the paragraph the comment is attached to. You can get this information by selecting the entire paragraph and locating the word count in the status bar.

4. Triple-click anywhere in the second paragraph of the document (which begins "Media studies is an exciting academic field…") to select the paragraph. In the status bar, the message "110 of 511" tells you that 110 of the document's 511 words are currently selected. So the answer to Kaya's question is 110.

5. Point to the second comment to select it again, click the **Reply** button ⬚, and then type **110**. Your reply appears below Kaya's original comment.

Trouble? If you do not see the Reply button in the comment box, drag the horizontal scroll bar at the bottom of the Word window to the right until you can see it.

The name that appears in your reply comment is taken from the User name box in the General tab of the Word Options dialog box. If your name is the username for your computer, your name appears attached to the comment. If you are working on a shared computer at school, or on a computer owned by someone else, another name will appear in the comment.

You can quickly open the General tab of the Word Options dialog box by clicking the Dialog Box Launcher in the Tracking group on the REVIEW tab, and then clicking Change User Name. From there, you can change the username and the initials associated with your copy of Word. However, there is no need to change these settings for this tutorial, and you should never change them on a shared computer at school unless specifically instructed to do so by your instructor.

6. In the Comments group, click the **Next** button to move the insertion point to the next comment, which asks you to insert your name after "Prepared by:" at the end of the document.

7. Click after the colon in "Prepared by:", press the **spacebar**, and then type your first and last name. To indicate that you have complied with Kaya's request by adding your name, you could right-click the comment, and then click Mark Comment Done. However, in this case, you'll simply delete the comment. Kaya also asks you to delete the first comment in the document.

8. Click anywhere in the final comment, and then in the Comments group, click the **Delete** button.

9. In the Comments group, click the **Previous** button three times to select the comment at the beginning of the document, and then click the **Delete** button to delete the comment.

As you reviewed the document, you might have noticed that, on page 2, one of the class names in the Research Methods section appears in all uppercase letters. This is probably just a typing mistake. You can correct it, and then add a comment that points out the change to Kaya.

To correct the mistake and add a comment:

1. Scroll down to page 2, and then select the fourth paragraph on the page, which contains the text "PSYCHOLOGY 401: RESEARCH ANALYSIS."

2. On the ribbon, click the **HOME** tab.

3. In the Font group, click the **Change Case** button Aa ▾, and then click **Capitalize Each Word**. The text changes to read "Psychology 401: Research Analysis."

4. Verify that the paragraph is still selected, and then click the **REVIEW** tab on the ribbon.

5. In the Comments group, click the **New Comment** button. A new comment appears, with the insertion point ready for you to begin typing.

6. In the new comment, type **I assumed you didn't want this all uppercase, so I changed it.** and then save the document.

   You can now hide the text of the comments because you are finished working with them.

7. In the Comments group, click the **Show Comments** button. You now see a comment icon in the document margin rather than on the right side of the Word screen. A comment icon alerts you to the presence of a comment without taking up all the space required to display the comment text. You can click a comment icon to read a particular comment without displaying the text of all the comments.

8. Click the comment icon 💬. The comment icon is highlighted, and the full comment is displayed, as shown in Figure 2-4.

| Figure 2-4 | Document with the comment icon |

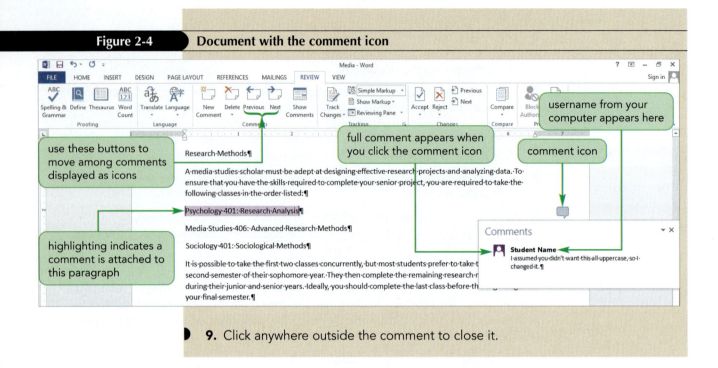

use these buttons to move among comments displayed as icons

full comment appears when you click the comment icon

username from your computer appears here

comment icon

highlighting indicates a comment is attached to this paragraph

9. Click anywhere outside the comment to close it.

Creating Bulleted and Numbered Lists

A **bulleted list** is a group of related paragraphs with a black circle or other character to the left of each paragraph. For a group of related paragraphs that have a particular order (such as steps in a procedure), you can use consecutive numbers instead of bullets to create a **numbered list**. If you insert a new paragraph, delete a paragraph, or reorder the paragraphs in a numbered list, Word adjusts the numbers to make sure they remain consecutive.

PROSKILLS

Written Communication: Organizing Information in Lists

Bulleted and numbered lists are both great ways to draw the reader's attention to information. But it's important to know how to use them. Use numbers when your list contains items that are arranged by priority in a specific order. For example, in a document reviewing the procedure for performing CPR, it makes sense to use numbers for the sequential steps. Use bullets when the items in the list are of equal importance, or when they can be accomplished in any order. For example, in a resume, you could use bullets for a list of professional certifications.

To add bullets to a series of paragraphs, you use the Bullets button in the Paragraph group on the HOME tab. To create a numbered list, you use the Numbering button in the Paragraph group instead. Both the Bullets button and the Numbering button have arrows you can click to open a gallery of bullet or numbering styles.

Kaya asks you to format the list of prerequisites on page 1 as a bulleted list. She also asks you to format the list of core courses on page 1 as a separate bulleted list. Finally, you need to format the list of research methods classes on page 2 as a numbered list.

To apply bullets to paragraphs:

▶ **1.** Scroll up until you see the paragraphs containing the list of prerequisites, which begins with "Media Studies 101: General Media Studies," and then select this paragraph and the three that follow it.

▶ **2.** On the ribbon, click the **HOME** tab.

▶ **3.** In the Paragraph group, click the **Bullets** button ▤. Black circles appear as bullets before each item in the list. Also, the bulleted list is indented and the paragraph spacing between the items is reduced.

After reviewing the default, round bullet in the document, Kaya decides she would prefer square bullets.

▶ **4.** In the Paragraph group, click the **Bullets button arrow** ▤▾. A gallery of bullet styles opens. See Figure 2-5.

Figure 2-5	Bullets gallery

The Recently Used Bullets section appears at the top of the gallery of bullet styles; it displays the bullet styles that have been used since you started Word, which, in this case, is just the round black bullet style that was applied by default when you clicked the Bullets button. The **Bullet Library**, which offers a variety of bullet styles, is shown below the Recently Used Bullets. To create your own bullets from a picture file or from a set of predesigned symbols including diamonds, hearts, or Greek letters, click Define New Bullet, and then click the Symbol button or the Picture button in the Define New Bullet dialog box.

▶ **5.** Move the mouse pointer over the bullet styles in the Bullet Library to see a Live Preview of the bullet styles in the document. Kaya prefers the black square style.

▶ **6.** In the Bullet Library, click the **black square**. The round bullets are replaced with square bullets.

Next, you need to format the list of core courses on page 1 with square bullets. When you first start Word, the Bullets button applies the default, round bullets you saw earlier. But after you select a new bullet style, the Bullets button applies the last bullet style you used. So, to add square bullets to the decorating styles list, you just have to select the list and click the Bullets button.

To add bullets to the list of core courses:

1. Scroll down in the document and select the paragraphs listing the core courses, starting with "Media Studies 102: Communicating Visually" and ending with "Media Studies 402: Ethics of Digital Privacy."

2. In the Paragraph group, click the **Bullets** button ⊞. The list is now formatted with square black bullets.

The list is finished except for one issue. A Media Studies major only needs to take one of the last three classes in the list, but that's not clear because of the way the list is currently formatted. To clarify this information, you can use the Increase Indent button in the Paragraph group to indent the last three bullets. When you do this, Word inserts a different style bullet to make the indented paragraphs visually subordinate to the bulleted paragraphs above.

To indent the last three bullets:

1. In the list of core courses, select the last three paragraphs.

TIP

To remove the indent from selected text, click the Decrease Indent button in the Paragraph group.

2. In the Paragraph group, click the **Increase Indent** button ⊞. The three paragraphs move to the right, and the black square bullets are replaced with open circle bullets.

Next, you will format the list of research methods classes on page 2. Kaya wants you to format this information as a numbered list because the classes must be taken in a specific order.

To apply numbers to the list of research methods classes:

1. Scroll down to page 2 until you see the "Psychology 401: Research Analysis" paragraph. You added a comment to this paragraph earlier, but that will have no effect on the process of creating the numbered list.

2. Select the three paragraphs containing the list of research methods classes, starting with "Psychology 401: Research Analysis" and ending with "Sociology 401: Sociological Methods."

3. In the Paragraph group, click the **Numbering** button ⊞. Consecutive numbers appear in front of each item in the list. See Figure 2-6.

| Figure 2-6 | Numbered list |

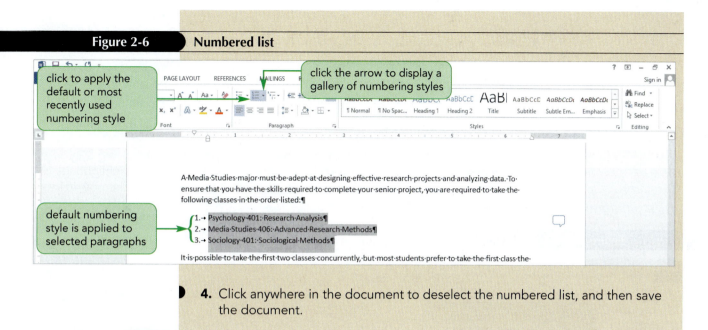

click to apply the default or most recently used numbering style

click the arrow to display a gallery of numbering styles

default numbering style is applied to selected paragraphs

A·Media·Studies·major·must·be·adept·at·designing·effective·research·projects·and·analyzing·data.·To·ensure·that·you·have·the·skills·required·to·complete·your·senior·project,·you·are·required·to·take·the·following·classes·in·the·order·listed:¶

1.→ Psychology·401:·Research·Analysis¶
2.→ Media·Studies·406:·Advanced·Research·Methods¶
3.→ Sociology·401:·Sociological·Methods¶

It·is·possible·to·take·the·first·two·classes·concurrently,·but·most·students·prefer·to·take·the·first·class·the·

> **4.** Click anywhere in the document to deselect the numbered list, and then save the document.

As with the Bullets button arrow, you can click the Numbering button arrow and then select from a library of numbering styles. You can also indent paragraphs in a numbered list to create an outline, in which case the indented paragraphs will be preceded by lowercase letters instead of numbers. To apply a different list style to the outline (for example, with Roman numerals and uppercase letters), select the list, click the Multilevel List button in the Paragraph group, and then click a multilevel list style.

Moving Text in a Document

One of the most useful features of a word-processing program is the ability to move text easily. For example, Kaya wants to reorder the information in the numbered list. You could do this by deleting a paragraph and then retyping it at a new location. However, it's easier to select and then move the text. Word provides several ways to move text—drag and drop, cut and paste, and copy and paste.

Dragging and Dropping Text

To move text with **drag and drop**, you select the text you want to move, press and hold the mouse button while you drag the selected text to a new location, and then release the mouse button.

In the numbered list you just created, Kaya wants you to move the paragraph that reads "Sociology 401 Sociological Methods" up so it is the first item in the list.

To move text using drag and drop:

> **1.** Select the third paragraph in the numbered list, "Sociology 401: Sociological Methods," being sure to include the paragraph marker at the end. The number 3 remains unselected because it's not actually part of the paragraph text.

> **2.** Position the pointer over the selected text. The pointer changes to a left-facing arrow ⟍.

3. Press and hold the mouse button until the drag-and-drop pointer ⬚ appears. A dark black insertion point appears within the selected text.

4. Without releasing the mouse button, drag the pointer to the beginning of the list until the insertion point is positioned to the left of the "P" in "Psychology 401: Research Analysis." Use the insertion point, rather than the mouse pointer, to guide the text to its new location. See Figure 2-7.

Trouble? If the numbers in the numbered list appear highlighted in gray, you moved the mouse pointer too close to the numbers. Ignore the highlighting and position the insertion point just to the left of the "P" in "Psychology 401: Research Analysis."

Figure 2-7 | Moving text with the drag-and-drop pointer

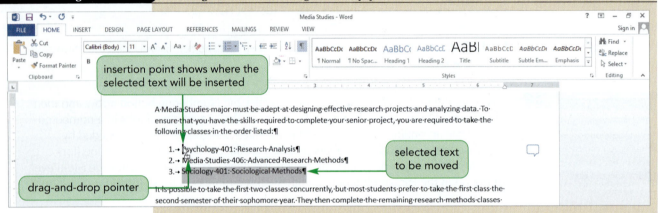

5. Release the mouse button, and then click a blank area of the document to deselect the text. The text "Sociology 401: Sociological Methods" is now the first item in the list, and the remaining paragraphs have been renumbered as paragraphs 2 and 3. See Figure 2-8.

Figure 2-8 | Text in new location

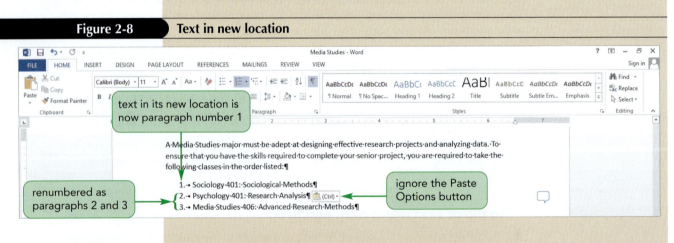

The Paste Options button appears near the newly inserted text, providing access to more advanced options related to pasting text. You don't need to use the Paste Options button right now; it will disappear when you start performing another task.

Trouble? If the selected text moves to the wrong location, click the Undo button ↩ on the Quick Access Toolbar, and then repeat Steps 2 through 5.

▶ **6.** Save the document.

Dragging and dropping works well when you are moving text a short distance. When you are moving text from one page to another, it's easier to cut, copy, and paste text using the Clipboard.

Cutting or Copying and Pasting Text Using the Clipboard

The **Office Clipboard** is a temporary storage area on your computer that holds objects such as text or graphics until you need them. To **cut** means to remove text or another item from a document and place it on the Clipboard. Once you've cut something, you can paste it somewhere else. To **copy** means to copy a selected item to the Clipboard, leaving the item in its original location. To **paste** means to insert a copy of whatever is on the Clipboard into the document, at the insertion point. When you paste an item from the Clipboard into a document, the item remains on the Clipboard so you can paste it again somewhere else if you want. The buttons for cutting, copying, and pasting are located in the Clipboard group on the HOME tab.

By default, Word pastes text in a new location in a document with the same formatting it had in its old location. To select other ways to paste text, you can use the Paste Options button, which appears next to newly pasted text, or the Paste button arrow in the Clipboard group. Both buttons display a menu of paste options. Two particularly useful paste options are Merge Formatting, which combines the formatting of the copied text with the formatting of the text in the new location, and Keep Text Only, which inserts the text using the formatting of the surrounding text in the new location.

When you need to keep track of multiple pieces of cut or copied text, it's helpful to open the **Clipboard task pane**, which displays the contents of the Clipboard. You open the Clipboard task pane by clicking the Dialog Box Launcher in the Clipboard group on the HOME tab. When the Clipboard task pane is displayed, the Clipboard can store up to 24 text items. When the Clipboard task pane is *not* displayed, the Clipboard can hold only the most recently copied item.

Kaya would like to move the second-to-last sentence under the heading "Majoring in Media Studies" on page 1. You'll use cut and paste to move this sentence to a new location.

To move text using cut and paste:

▶ **1.** Make sure the HOME tab is selected on the ribbon.

▶ **2.** Scroll up until you can see the second paragraph in the document, just below the heading "Majoring in Media Studies."

▶ **3.** Press and hold the **Ctrl** key, and then click anywhere in the sentence near the end of the second paragraph, which begins "In the second semester of your senior year...." The entire sentence and the space following it are selected.

TIP

You can also press the Ctrl+X keys to cut selected text. Press the Ctrl+V keys to paste the most recently copied item.

4. In the Clipboard group, click the **Cut** button. The selected text is removed from the document and copied to the Clipboard.

5. Scroll down to page 2, and then click at the beginning of the second-to-last paragraph in the document, just to the left of the "T" in "This project should...."

6. In the Clipboard group, click the **Paste** button. The sentence and the space following it are displayed in the new location. The Paste Options button appears near the newly inserted sentence.

   Trouble? If a menu opens below the Paste button, you clicked the Paste button arrow instead of the Paste button. Press the Esc key to close the menu, and then repeat Step 6, taking care not to click the arrow below the Paste button.

7. Save the document.

Kaya explains that she'll be using some text from the Media Studies document as the basis for another department handout. She asks you to copy that information and paste it into a new document. You can do this using the Clipboard task pane.

To copy text to paste into a new document:

1. In the Clipboard group, click the **Dialog Box Launcher**. The Clipboard task pane opens on the left side of the document window, as shown in Figure 2-9.

Figure 2-9   **Clipboard task pane**

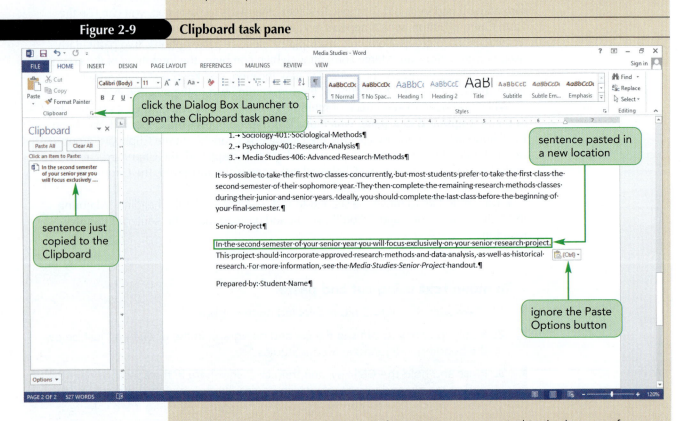

Notice the Clipboard contains the sentence you copied in the last set of steps, although you can only see the first part of the sentence. You'll copy the last two sentences in the current paragraph for use in Kaya's other document.

2. Select the text **This project should incorporate approved research methods and data analysis, as well as historical research. For more information, see the *Media Studies Senior Project* handout.** Do not select the paragraph mark.

3. In the Clipboard group, click the **Copy** button. The first few words of the text appear at the top of the Clipboard task pane, but in fact the entire two sentences are now stored on the Clipboard.

TIP

You can also copy selected text by pressing the Ctrl+C keys.

4. Click anywhere in the document to deselect the text, scroll up, if necessary, and then locate the first sentence on page 2.

5. Press and hold the **Ctrl** key, and then click anywhere in the first sentence on page 2, which begins "A Media Studies major must be adept…." The sentence and the space following it are selected.

6. In the Clipboard group, click the **Copy** button. The first part of the sentence appears at the top of the Clipboard task pane, as shown in Figure 2-10.

Figure 2-10	Items in the Clipboard task pane

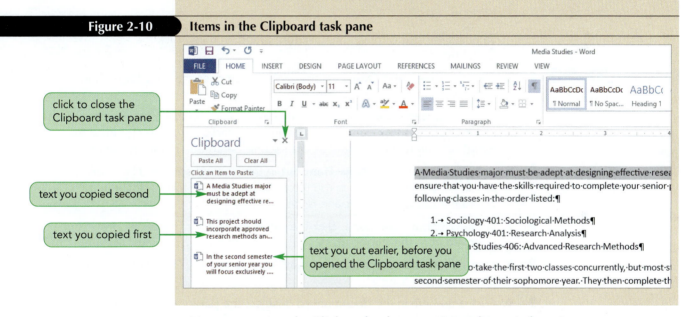

Now you can use the Clipboard task pane to insert the copied text into a new document.

To insert the copied text into a new document:

1. Open a new, blank document. If necessary, open the Clipboard task pane.

2. In the Clipboard task pane, click the second item in the list of copied items, which begins "This project should incorporate…." The text is inserted in the document and the "*Media Studies Senior Project*" title retains its italic formatting.

   Kaya doesn't want to keep the italic formatting in the newly pasted text. You can remove this formatting by using the Paste Options button, which is visible just below the pasted text.

3. Click the **Paste Options** button in the document. The Paste Options menu opens, as shown in Figure 2-11.

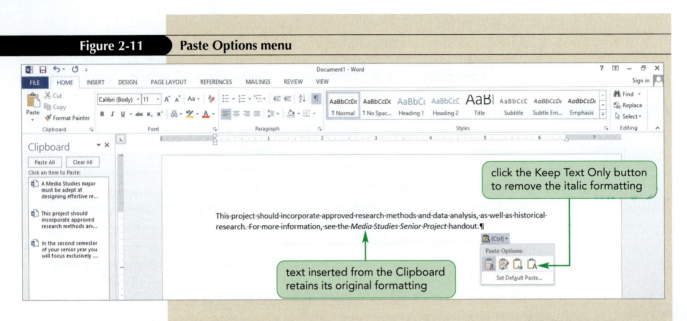

Figure 2-11 **Paste Options menu**

> click the Keep Text Only button to remove the italic formatting

This·project·should·incorporate·approved·research·methods·and·data·analysis,·as·well·as·historical·research.·For·more·information,·see·the·*Media·Studies·Senior·Project*·handout.¶

> text inserted from the Clipboard retains its original formatting

To paste the text without the italic formatting, you can click the Keep Text Only button.

4. Click the **Keep Text Only** button. Word removes the italic formatting from "Media Studies Senior Project."

5. Press the **Enter** key to start a new paragraph, and then click the first item in the Clipboard task pane, which begins "A Media Studies major must be adept...." The text is inserted as the second paragraph in the document.

6. Save the document as **New Handout** in the location specified by your instructor, and then close it. You return to the Media Studies document, where the Clipboard task pane is still open.

7. In the Clipboard task pane, click the **Clear All** button. The copied items are removed from the Clipboard.

8. In the Clipboard task pane, click the **Close** button. The Clipboard task pane closes.

9. Click anywhere in the document to deselect the paragraph, and then save the document.

TIP

To select a paste option before pasting an item, click the Paste button arrow in the Clipboard group, and then click the paste option you want.

Using the Navigation Pane

The Navigation pane simplifies the process of moving through a document page by page. You can also use the Navigation pane to locate a particular word or phrase. You start by typing the text you're searching for—the **search text**—in the Search box at the top of the Navigation pane. As shown in the Session 2.1 Visual Overview, Word highlights every instance of the search text in the document. At the same time, a list of the **search results** appears in the Navigation pane. You can click a search result to go immediately to that location in the document.

To become familiar with the Navigation pane, you'll use it to navigate through the Media Studies document page by page. You'll start by moving the insertion point to the beginning of the document.

To navigate through the document page by page:

1. Press the **Ctrl+Home** keys to move the insertion point to the beginning of the document, making sure the HOME tab is still selected on the ribbon.

2. In the Editing group, click the **Find** button. The Navigation pane opens on the left side of the Word window.

   In the Search document box at the top, you can type the text you want to find. The three links below the Search document box—HEADINGS, PAGES, and RESULTS—allow you to navigate through the document in different ways. As you become a more experienced Word user, you'll learn how to use the HEADINGS link; for now, you'll ignore it. To move quickly among the pages of a document, you can use the PAGES link.

3. In the Navigation pane, click the **PAGES** link. The Navigation pane displays thumbnail icons of the document's two pages, as shown in Figure 2-12. You can click a page in the Navigation pane to display that page in the document window.

Figure 2-12   Document pages displayed in the Navigation pane

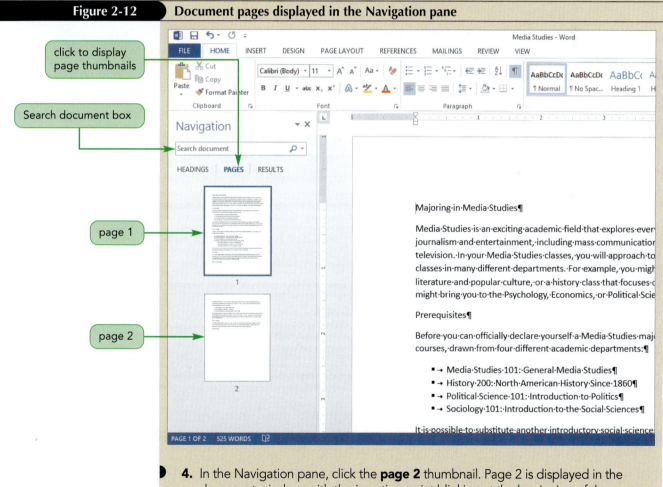

4. In the Navigation pane, click the **page 2** thumbnail. Page 2 is displayed in the document window, with the insertion point blinking at the beginning of the page.

5. In the Navigation pane, click the **page 1** thumbnail to move the insertion point back to the beginning of the document.

Kaya thinks she might have mistakenly used the word "media" when she actually meant to use "journalism" in certain parts of the document. She asks you to use the Navigation pane to find all instances of "media."

To search for the word "media" in the document:

1. In the Navigation pane, click the **RESULTS** link, click the **Search document** box, and then type **media**. You do not have to press the Enter key.

   Every instance of the word "media" is highlighted in yellow in the document. The yellow highlight is only temporary; it will disappear as soon as you begin to perform any other task in the document. A full list of the 24 search results is displayed in the Navigation pane. Some of the search results contain the word "Media" (with an uppercase "M") while others contain the word "media" (with a lowercase "m"). To narrow the search results, you need to tell Word to match the case of the search text.

2. In the Navigation pane, click the **Search for more things** button ▼. This displays a two-part menu. In the bottom part, you can select other items to search for, such as graphics or tables. The top part provides more advanced search tools. See Figure 2-13.

Figure 2-13   Navigation pane with Search for more things menu

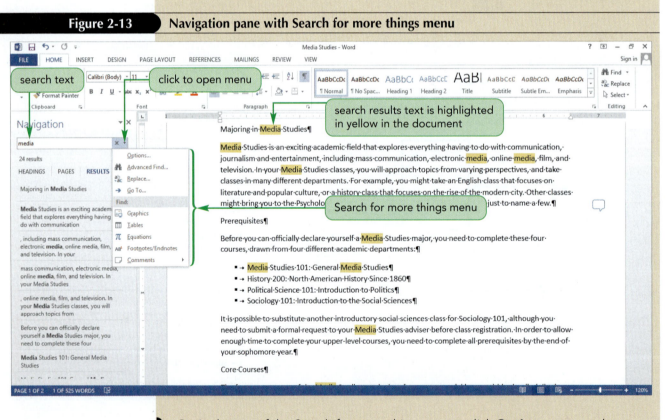

3. At the top of the Search for more things menu, click **Options** to open the Find Options dialog box.

The check boxes in this dialog box allow you to fine-tune your search. For example, to ensure that Word finds the search text only when it appears as a separate word, and not when it appears as part of another word, you could select the Find whole words only check box. Right now, you are only concerned with making sure the search results have the same case as the search text.

4. Click the **Match case** check box to select it, and then click the **OK** button to close the Find Options dialog box. Now you can search the document again.

5. Press the **Ctrl+Home** keys to move the insertion point to the beginning of the document, click the **Search document** box in the Navigation pane, and then type **media**. This time, there are only three search results in the Navigation pane, and they all start with a lowercase "m."

   To move among the search results, you can use the up and down arrows in the Navigation pane.

6. In the Navigation pane, click the **down arrow** button [▼]. Word selects the first instance of "media" in the Navigation pane, as indicated by a blue outline. Also, in the document, the first instance has a gray selection highlight over the yellow highlight. See Figure 2-14.

Figure 2-14	**Navigation pane with the first search result selected**

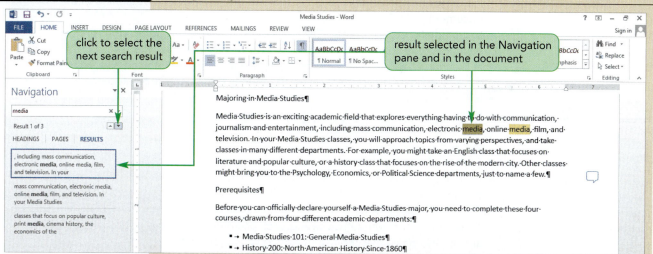

Trouble? If the second instance of "media" is selected in the Navigation pane, then you pressed the Enter key after typing "media" in Step 5. Click the up arrow button [▲] to select the first instance.

7. In the Navigation pane, click the **down arrow** button [▼]. Word selects the second instance of "media" in the document and in the Navigation pane.

8. Click the **down arrow** button [▼] again to select the third search result, in the paragraph after "Electives," and then click the **up arrow** button [▲] to select the second search result again.

   You can also select a search result in the document by clicking a search result in the Navigation pane.

9. In the Navigation pane, click the third search result, which begins "classes that focus on popular culture...." The third search result is selected in the document and in the Navigation pane.

After reviewing the search results, Kaya decides she would like to replace two of the three instances of "media" with the word "journalism." You can do that by using the Find and Replace dialog box.

Finding and Replacing Text

To open the Find and Replace dialog box from the Navigation pane, click the Find more things button, and then click Replace. This opens the **Find and Replace dialog box**, with the Replace tab displayed by default. The Replace tab provides options for finding a specific word or phrase in the document and replacing it with another word or phrase. To use the Replace tab, type the search text in the Find what box, and then type the text you want to substitute in the Replace with box. You can also click the More button on the Replace tab to display the Search Options section, which includes the same options you saw earlier in the Find Options dialog box, including the Find whole words only check box and the Match case check box.

After you have typed the search text and selected any search options, you can click the Find Next button to select the first occurrence of the search text; you can then decide whether or not to substitute the search text with the replacement text.

REFERENCE

Finding and Replacing Text

- Press the Ctrl+Home keys to move the insertion point to the beginning of the document.
- In the Editing group on the HOME tab, click the Replace button; or, in the Navigation pane, click the Search for more things button, and then click Replace.
- In the Find and Replace dialog box, click the More button, if necessary, to expand the dialog box and display the Search Options section of the Replace tab.
- In the Find what box, type the search text.
- In the Replace with box, type the replacement text.
- Select the appropriate check boxes in the Search Options section of the dialog box to narrow your search.
- Click the Find Next button.
- Click the Replace button to substitute the found text with the replacement text and find the next occurrence.
- Click the Replace All button to substitute all occurrences of the found text with the replacement text without reviewing each occurrence. Use this option only if you are absolutely certain that the results will be what you expect.

You'll use the Find and Replace dialog box now to replace two instances of "media" with "journalism."

To replace two instances of "media" with "journalism":

1. Press the **Ctrl+Home** keys to move the insertion point to the beginning of the document.

2. In the Navigation pane, click the **Search for more things** button ▼ to open the menu, and then click **Replace**. The Find and Replace dialog box opens with the Replace tab on top.

   The search text you entered earlier in the Navigation pane, "media," appears in the Find what box. If you hadn't already conducted a search, you would need to type your search text now. Because you selected the Match case check box earlier in the Find Options dialog box, "Match Case" appears below the Find what box.

3. In the lower-left corner of the dialog box, click the **More** button to display the search options. Because you selected the Match case check box earlier in the Find Options dialog box, it is selected here.

   Trouble? If you see the Less button instead of the More button, the search options are already displayed.

4. Click the **Replace with** box, and then type **journalism**.

5. Click the **Find Next** button. Word highlights the first instance of "media" in the document. See Figure 2-15.

Figure 2-15   **Find and Replace dialog box**

6. Click the **Replace** button. Word replaces "media" with "journalism," so the text reads "electronic journalism." Then, Word selects the next instance of "media," which happens to be in the same sentence. Kaya does not want to replace this instance, so you can find the next one.

7. Click the **Find Next** button. Word selects the last instance of "media," located in the sentence just before the "Research Methods" heading.

8. Click the **Replace** button. Word makes the substitution, so the text reads "print journalism," and then displays a message box telling you that Word has finished searching the document.

9. Click the **OK** button to close the message box, and then in the Find and Replace dialog box, click the **Close** button.

You are finished with the Navigation pane, so you can close it. But first you need to restore the search options to their original settings. It's a good practice to restore the original search settings so that future searches are not affected by any settings that might not apply.

To restore the search options to their original settings:

1. In the Navigation pane, open the Find Options dialog box, deselect the Match case check box, and then click the **OK** button to close the Find Options dialog box.

2. Click the **Close** button ✖ in the upper-right corner of the Navigation pane.

3. Save the document.

INSIGHT

Searching for Formatting

You can search for formatting just as you can search for text. For example, you might want to check a document to look for text formatted in bold and the Arial font. To search for formatting from within the Navigation pane, click the Search for more things button to display the menu, and then click Advanced Find. The Find and Replace dialog box opens with the Find tab displayed. Click the More button, if necessary, to display the Search Options section of the Find tab. Click the Format button at the bottom of the Search Options section, click the category of formatting you want to look for (such as Font or Paragraph), and then select the formatting you want to find.

You can look for formatting that occurs only on specific text, or you can look for formatting that occurs anywhere in a document. If you're looking for text formatted in a certain way (such as all instances of "Media Studies" that are bold), enter the text in the Find what box and then specify the formatting you're looking for. To find formatting on any text in a document, leave the Find what box empty, and then specify the formatting. Use the Find Next button to move through the document, from one instance of the specified formatting to another.

You can follow the same basic steps on the Replace tab to replace one type of formatting with another. First, click the Find what box and select the desired formatting. Then click the Replace with box and select the desired formatting. If you want, type search text and replacement text in the appropriate boxes. Then proceed as with any Find and Replace operation.

Now that the text in the Media Studies document is final, you will turn your attention to styles and themes, which affect the look of the entire document.

Working with Styles

A style is a set of formatting options that you can apply by clicking an icon in the Style gallery on the HOME tab. Each style is designed for a particular use. For example, the Title style is intended for formatting the title at the beginning of a document.

All the text you type into a document has a style applied to it. By default, text is formatted in the Normal style, which applies 11-point Calibri font, left alignment, 1.08 line spacing, and a small amount of extra space between paragraphs. In other words, the Normal style applies the default formatting you learned about when you first began typing a Word document.

Note that some styles apply **paragraph-level formatting**—that is, they are set up to format an entire paragraph, including the paragraph and line spacing. The Normal, Heading, and Title styles all apply paragraph-level formatting. Other styles apply **character-level formatting**—that is, they are set up to format only individual characters or words (for example, emphasizing a phrase by adding italic formatting and changing the font color).

One row of the Style gallery is always visible on the HOME tab. To display the entire Style gallery, click the More button in the Styles group. After you begin applying styles in a document, the visible row of the Style gallery changes to show the most recently used styles.

You are ready to use the Style gallery to format the document title.

To display the entire Style gallery and then format the document title with a style:

1. Press the **Ctrl+Home** keys to move the insertion point to the beginning of the document, if necessary.

2. Make sure the HOME tab is still selected and locate the More button in the Styles group, as shown earlier in the Session 2.1 Visual Overview.

3. In the Styles group, click the **More** button. The Style gallery opens, displaying a total of 16 styles arranged in two rows, as shown in Figure 2-16. If your screen is set at a lower resolution than the screenshots in this book, the Style gallery on your screen might contain more than two rows.

| Figure 2-16 | Displaying the Style gallery |

You don't actually need any of the styles in the bottom row now, so you can close the Style gallery.

4. Press the **Esc** key to close the Style gallery.

5. Click anywhere in the first paragraph, "Majoring in Media Studies," and then point to (but don't click) the **Title** style, which is the fifth style from the left in the top row of the gallery. The ScreenTip "Title" is displayed, and a Live Preview of the style appears in the paragraph containing the insertion point, as shown in Figure 2-17. The Title style changes the font to 28-point Calibri Light.

Figure 2-17   **Title style in the Style gallery**

6. Click the **Title** style. The style is applied to the paragraph. To finish the title, you need to center it.

7. In the Paragraph group, click the **Center** button. The title is centered in the document.

Next, you will format the document headings using the heading styles, which have different levels. The highest level, Heading 1, is used for the major headings in a document, and it applies the most noticeable formatting with a larger font than the other heading styles. (In heading styles, the highest, or most important, level has the lowest number.) The Heading 2 style is used for headings that are subordinate to the highest level headings; it applies slightly less dramatic formatting than the Heading 1 style.

The Media Studies handout only has one level of headings, so you will only apply the Heading 1 style.

To format text with the Heading 1 style:

1. Click anywhere in the "Prerequisites" paragraph.

2. On the HOME tab, in the Style gallery, click the **Heading 1** style. The paragraph is now formatted in blue, 16-point Calibri Light. The Heading 1 style also inserts some paragraph space above the heading.

3. Scroll down, click anywhere in the "Core Courses" paragraph, and then click the **Heading 1** style in the Style gallery.

4. Repeat Step 3 to apply the Heading 1 style to the "Electives" paragraph, the "Research Methods" paragraph and the "Senior Project" paragraph. When you are finished, scroll up to the beginning of the document to review the new formatting. See Figure 2-18.

TIP

On most computers, you can press the F4 key to repeat your most recent action.

Figure 2-18   **Document with Title and Heading 1 styles**

Understanding the Benefits of Heading Styles

INSIGHT

By default, the Style gallery offers 16 styles, each designed for a specific purpose. As you gain more experience with Word, you will learn how to use a wider array of styles. You'll also learn how to create your own styles. Styles allow you to change a document's formatting in an instant. But the benefits of heading styles go far beyond attractive formatting. Heading styles allow you to reorganize a document or generate a table of contents with a click of the mouse. Also, the heading styles are set up to keep a heading and the body text that follows it together, so a heading is never separated from its body text by a page break. Each Word document includes nine levels of heading styles, although only the Heading 1 and Heading 2 styles are available by default in the Style gallery. Whenever you use the lowest heading style in the Style gallery, the next-lowest level is added to the Style gallery. For example, after you use the Heading 2 style, the Heading 3 style appears in the Styles group in the Style gallery.

After you format a document with a variety of styles, you can alter the look of the document by changing the document's theme.

Working with Themes

A **theme** is a coordinated collection of fonts, colors, and other visual effects designed to give a document a cohesive, polished look. A variety of themes are installed with Word, with more available online at Office.com. When you open a new blank document in Word, the Office theme is applied by default. To change a document's theme, you click the Themes button, which is located in the Document Formatting group on the DESIGN tab, and then click the theme you want. Pointing to the Themes button displays a ScreenTip that tells you what theme is currently applied to the document.

When applying color to a document, you usually have the option of selecting a color from a palette of colors designed to match the current theme, or from a palette of standard colors. For instance, recall that the colors in the Font Color gallery are divided into Theme Colors and Standard Colors. When you select a Standard Color, such as Dark Red, that color remains the same no matter which theme you apply to the document. But when you click one of the Theme Colors, you are essentially telling Word to use the color located in that particular spot on the Theme Colors palette. Then, if you change the document's theme later, Word substitutes a color from the same location on the Theme Colors palette. This ensures that all the colors in a document are drawn from a group of colors coordinated to look good together. So as a rule, if you are going to use multiple colors in a document (perhaps for paragraph shading and font color), it's a good idea to stick with the Theme Colors.

A similar substitution takes place with fonts when you change the theme. However, to understand how this works, you need to understand the difference between headings and body text. Kaya's document includes the headings "Prerequisites," "Core Courses," "Electives," "Research Methods," and "Senior Project"—all of which you have formatted with the Heading1 style. The title of the document, "Majoring in Media Studies," is now formatted with the Title style, which is also a type of heading style. Everything else in the Media Studies document is body text.

To ensure that your documents have a harmonious look, each theme assigns a font for headings and a font for body text. Typically, in a given theme, the same font is used for both headings and body text, but not always. In the Office theme, for instance, they are slightly different; the heading font is Calibri Light, and the body font is Calibri. These two fonts appear at the top of the Font list as "Calibri Light (Headings)" and "Calibri (Body)" when you click the Font box arrow in the Font group on the HOME tab. When you begin typing text in a new document with the Office theme, the text is formatted as body text with the Calibri font by default.

When applying a font to selected text, you can choose one of the two theme fonts at the top of the Font list, or you can choose one of the other fonts in the Font list. If you choose one of the other fonts and then change the document theme, that font remains the same. But if you use one of the theme fonts and then change the document theme, Word substitutes the appropriate font from the new theme. When you paste text into a document that has a different theme, Word applies the theme fonts and colors of the new document. To retain the original formatting, use the Keep Source Formatting option in the Paste Options menu.

Figure 2-19 compares elements of the default Office theme with the Integral theme. The Integral theme was chosen for this example because, like the Office theme, its heading and body fonts are different.

Figure 2-19 | Comparing the Office theme to the Integral theme

© 2014 Cengage Learning

Each document theme is designed to convey a specific look and feel. The Office theme is designed to be appropriate for standard business documents. Other themes are designed to give documents a flashier look. Because Kaya has not yet selected a new theme, the Office theme is currently applied to the Media Studies document. However, she thinks the Facet theme might be more appropriate for the Media Studies document. She asks you to apply it now.

To change the document's theme:

1. If necessary, press the **Ctrl+Home** keys to move the insertion point to the beginning of the document. With the title and first heading visible, you will more easily see what happens when you change the document's theme.

2. On the ribbon, click the **DESIGN** tab.

3. In the Document Formatting group, point to the **Themes** button. A ScreenTip appears containing the text "Current: Office Theme" as well as general information about themes.

4. In the Document Formatting group, click the **Themes** button. The Themes gallery opens. See Figure 2-20.

Figure 2-20 Themes gallery displayed

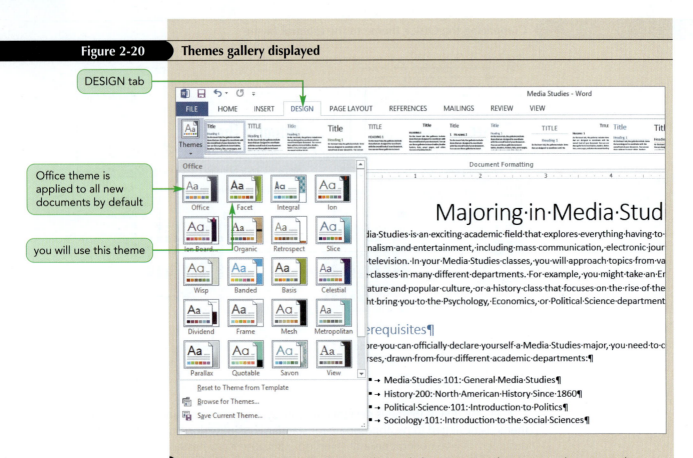

DESIGN tab

Office theme is applied to all new documents by default

you will use this theme

5. Move the mouse pointer (without clicking it) over the various themes in the gallery to see a Live Preview of each theme in the document. The heading and body fonts as well as the heading colors change to reflect the fonts associated with the various themes.

6. In the Themes gallery, click the **Facet** theme. The text in the Media Studies document changes to the body and heading fonts of the Facet theme, with the headings formatted in green. To see exactly what the Facet theme fonts are, you can point to the Fonts button in the Document Formatting group.

7. In the Document Formatting group, point to the **Fonts** button. A ScreenTip appears, listing the currently selected theme (Facet), the heading font (Trebuchet MS), and the body font (Trebuchet MS). See Figure 2-21.

Figure 2-21   **Fonts for the Facet theme**

Trouble? If a menu appears, you clicked the Fonts button instead of pointing to it. Press the Esc key, and then repeat Step 7.

8. Save your changes and then close the document.

Kaya's Media Studies document is ready to be handed in to her supervisor. The use of styles, bulleted and numbered lists, and a new theme gives the document a professional look appropriate for use in a department handout.

Session 2.1 Quick Check

REVIEW

1. Explain how to display comments to the right of the document text in Simple Markup view.
2. What term refers to the process of using the mouse to drag text to a new location?
3. How can you ensure that the Navigation pane will find "ZIP code" instead of "zip code"?
4. What is a style?
5. What style is applied to all text in a new document by default?
6. Explain the relationship between a document's theme and styles.

Session 2.2 Visual Overview:

Use an easy-to-read font, such as the default Calibri, set to 12 point.

An MLA-style research paper does not require a separate title page; instead, type your name, your instructor's name, the course number, and the date in the upper-left corner of the first page.

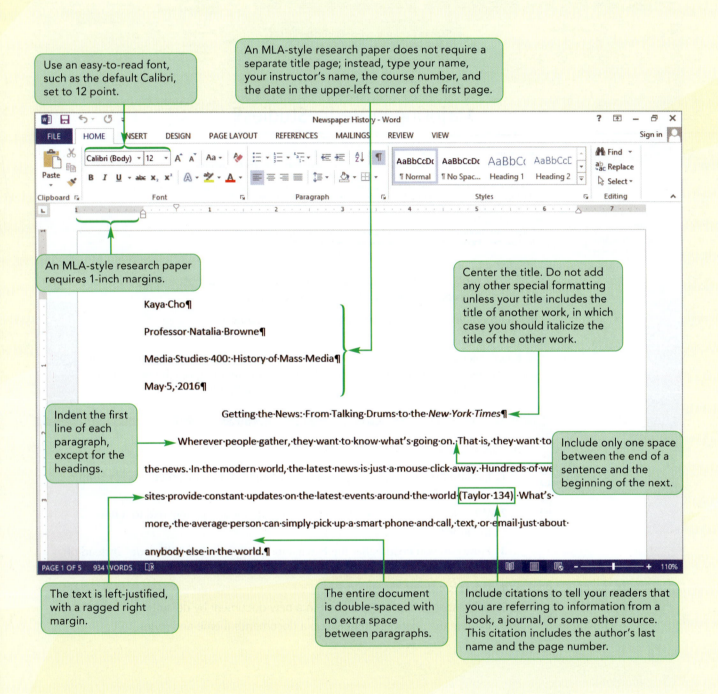

An MLA-style research paper requires 1-inch margins.

Center the title. Do not add any other special formatting unless your title includes the title of another work, in which case you should italicize the title of the other work.

Kaya·Cho¶

Professor·Natalia·Browne¶

Media·Studies·400:·History·of·Mass·Media¶

May·5,·2016¶

Getting·the·News:·From·Talking·Drums·to·the·*New·York·Times*¶

Indent the first line of each paragraph, except for the headings.

Wherever·people·gather,·they·want·to·know·what's·going·on.·That·is,·they·want·to

the·news.·In·the·modern·world,·the·latest·news·is·just·a·mouse·click·away.·Hundreds·of·we

sites·provide·constant·updates·on·the·latest·events·around·the·world.·(Taylor·134)··What's·

more,·the·average·person·can·simply·pick·up·a·smart·phone·and·call,·text,·or·email·just·about·

anybody·else·in·the·world.¶

Include only one space between the end of a sentence and the beginning of the next.

PAGE 1 OF 5   934 WORDS

The text is left-justified, with a ragged right margin.

The entire document is double-spaced with no extra space between paragraphs.

Include citations to tell your readers that you are referring to information from a book, a journal, or some other source. This citation includes the author's last name and the page number.

MLA Formatting Guidelines

The REFERENCES tab includes options that help you create a research paper.

In the Style box, specify the style of research paper you are creating. For college research papers, the MLA style is commonly used.

After you create all the citations, click the Bibliography button to create a list of all the sources mentioned in your citations. This list is known as a **bibliography** or, in the MLA style, a **works cited list**.

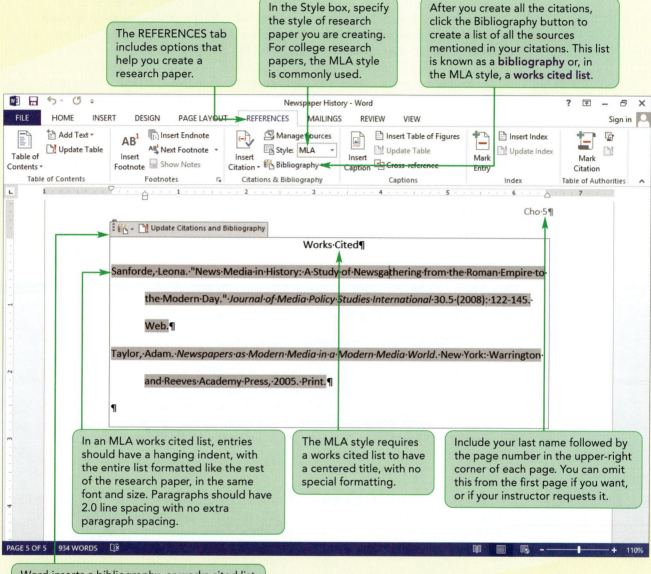

In an MLA works cited list, entries should have a hanging indent, with the entire list formatted like the rest of the research paper, in the same font and size. Paragraphs should have 2.0 line spacing with no extra paragraph spacing.

The MLA style requires a works cited list to have a centered title, with no special formatting.

Include your last name followed by the page number in the upper-right corner of each page. You can omit this from the first page if you want, or if your instructor requests it.

Word inserts a bibliography, or works cited list, contained in a special feature, known as a **content control**, used to display information that is inserted automatically and that may need to be updated later. You can use the buttons in the content control tab to make changes to material inside the content control.

Reviewing the MLA Style

A **style guide** is a set of rules that describe the preferred format and style for a certain type of writing. People in different fields use different style guides, with each style guide designed to suit the needs of a specific discipline. For example, journalists commonly use the *Associated Press Stylebook*, which focuses on the concise writing style common in magazines and newspapers. In the world of academics, style guides emphasize the proper way to create **citations**, which are formal references to the work of others. Researchers in the social and behavioral sciences use the **American Psychological Association (APA) style**, which is designed to help readers scan an article quickly for key points and emphasizes the date of publication in citations. Other scientific and technical fields have their own specialized style guides.

In the humanities, the **Modern Language Association (MLA) style** is widely used. This is the style Kaya has used for her research paper. She followed the guidelines specified in the *MLA Handbook for Writers of Research Papers*, published by the Modern Language Association of America. These guidelines focus on specifications for formatting a research document and citing the sources used in research conducted for a paper. The major formatting features of an MLA-style research paper are illustrated in the Session 2.2 Visual Overview. Compared to style guides for technical fields, the MLA style is very flexible, making it easy to include citations without disrupting the natural flow of the writing. MLA-style citations of other writers' works take the form of a brief parenthetical entry, with a complete reference to each item included in the alphabetized bibliography, also known as the works cited list, at the end of the research paper.

INSIGHT

Formatting an MLA-Style Research Paper

The MLA guidelines were developed, in part, to simplify the process of transforming a manuscript into a journal article or a chapter of a book. The style calls for minimal formatting; the simpler the formatting in a manuscript, the easier it is to turn the text into a published document. The MLA guidelines were also designed to ensure consistency in documents, so that all research papers look alike. Therefore, you should apply no special formatting to the text in an MLA-style research paper. Headings should be formatted like the other text in the document, with no bold or heading styles.

Kaya has started writing a research paper on the history of newspapers for her Media Studies class. You'll open the draft of Kaya's research paper and determine what needs to be done to make it meet the MLA style guidelines for a research paper.

To open the document and review it for MLA style:

1. Open the document named **Newspaper** located in the Word2 ▸ Tutorial folder included with your Data Files, and then save the document as **Newspaper History** in the location specified by your instructor.

2. Verify that the document is displayed in Print Layout view, and that the rulers and nonprinting characters are displayed. Make sure the Zoom level is set to **120%**.

3. Review the document to familiarize yourself with its structure. First, notice the parts of the document that already match the MLA style. Kaya included a block of information in the upper-left corner of the first page, giving her name, her instructor's name, the course name, and the date. The title at the top of the first page also meets the MLA guidelines in that it is centered and does not have any special formatting except for "*New York Times*," which is italicized because it is the name of a newspaper. The headings ("Early News Media," "Merchant Newsletters," "Modern American Newspapers," and "Looking to the Future") have no special formatting; but unlike the title, they are left-aligned. Finally, the body text is left-aligned with a ragged right margin, and the entire document is formatted in the same font, Calibri, which is easy to read.

What needs to be changed in order to make Kaya's paper consistent with the MLA style? Currently, the entire document is formatted using the default settings, which are the Normal style for the Office theme. To transform the document into an MLA-style research paper, you need to complete the checklist shown in Figure 2-22.

Figure 2-22	Checklist for formatting a default Word document to match the MLA style

✓ Double-space the entire document.

✓ Remove paragraph spacing from the entire document.

✓ Increase the font size for the entire document to 12 points.

✓ Indent the first line of each body paragraph .5 inch from the left margin.

✓ Add the page number (preceded by your last name) in the upper-right corner of each page. If you prefer, you can omit this from the first page.

© 2014 Cengage Learning

You'll take care of the first three items in the checklist now.

To begin applying MLA formatting to the document:

1. Press the **Ctrl+A** keys to select the entire document.

2. Make sure the HOME tab is selected on the ribbon.

3. In the Paragraph group, click the **Line and Paragraph Spacing** button, and then click **2.0**.

4. Click the **Line and Spacing** button again, and then click **Remove Space After Paragraph**. The entire document is now double-spaced, with no paragraph spacing, and the entire document is still selected.

5. In the Font group, click the **Font Size** arrow, and then click **12**. The entire document is formatted in 12-point font.

6. Click anywhere in the document to deselect the text.

7. In the first paragraph of the document, replace Kaya's name with your first and last name, and then save the document.

Now you need to indent the first line of each body paragraph.

Indenting a Paragraph

Word offers a number of options for indenting a paragraph. You can move an entire paragraph to the right, or you can create specialized indents, such as a **hanging indent**, where all lines except the first line of the paragraph are indented from the left margin. As you saw in the Session 2.2 Visual Overview, all the body paragraphs (that is, all the paragraphs except the information in the upper-left corner of the first page, the title, and the headings) have a first-line indent in MLA research papers. Figure 2-23 shows some examples of other common paragraph indents.

Figure 2-23	Common paragraph indents

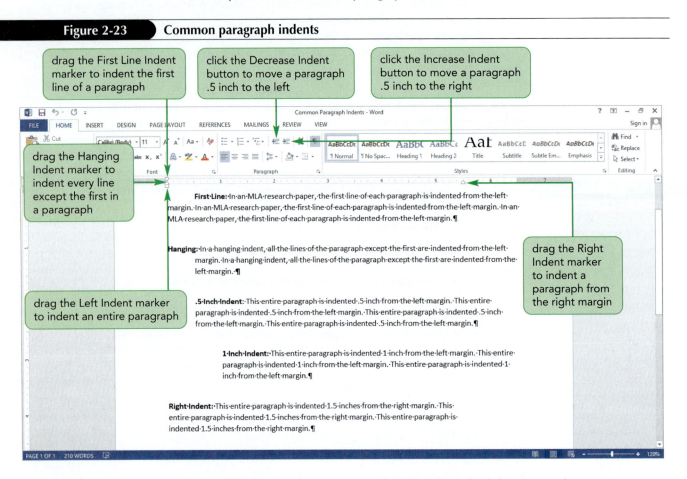

To quickly indent an entire paragraph .5 inch from the left, position the insertion point in the paragraph you want to indent and then click the Increase Indent button in the Paragraph group on the HOME tab. You can continue to indent the paragraph in increments of .5 inch by repeatedly clicking the Increase Indent button. To move an indented paragraph back to the left .5 inch, click the Decrease Indent button.

To create first line, hanging, or right indents, you can use the indent markers on the ruler. First, click in the paragraph you want to indent, or select multiple paragraphs. Then drag the appropriate indent marker to the left or right on the horizontal ruler. The indent markers are small and can be hard to see. As shown in Figure 2-23, the **First Line Indent marker** looks like the top half of an hourglass; the **Hanging Indent marker** looks like the bottom half. The rectangle below the Hanging Indent marker is the **Left Indent marker**. The **Right Indent Marker** looks just like the Hanging Indent marker except that it is located on the far-right side of the horizontal ruler.

Note that when you indent an entire paragraph using the Increase Indent button, the three indent markers, shown stacked on top of one another in Figure 2-23, move as a unit along with the paragraphs you are indenting.

In Kaya's paper, you will indent the first lines of the body paragraphs .5 inch from the left margin, as specified by the MLA style.

To indent the first line of each paragraph:

1. On the first page of the document, just below the title, click anywhere in the first main paragraph, which begins "Wherever people gather…."

2. On the horizontal ruler, position the mouse pointer over the First Line Indent marker ▽. When you see the ScreenTip that reads "First Line Indent," you know the mouse is positioned correctly.

3. Press and hold the mouse button as you drag the **First Line Indent** marker ▽ to the right, to the .5-inch mark on the horizontal ruler. As you drag, a vertical guide line appears over the document, and the first line of the paragraph moves right. See Figure 2-24.

Figure 2-24   Dragging the First Line Indent marker

First Line Indent marker

.5-inch mark

as you drag the indent marker, a guide line appears and the first line of the paragraph moves right

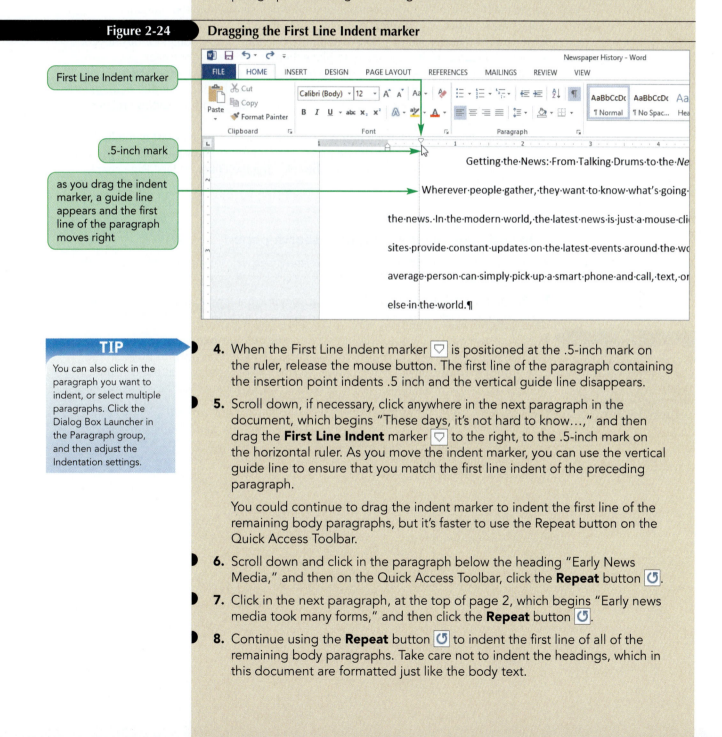

4. When the First Line Indent marker ▽ is positioned at the .5-inch mark on the ruler, release the mouse button. The first line of the paragraph containing the insertion point indents .5 inch and the vertical guide line disappears.

5. Scroll down, if necessary, click anywhere in the next paragraph in the document, which begins "These days, it's not hard to know…," and then drag the **First Line Indent** marker ▽ to the right, to the .5-inch mark on the horizontal ruler. As you move the indent marker, you can use the vertical guide line to ensure that you match the first line indent of the preceding paragraph.

   You could continue to drag the indent marker to indent the first line of the remaining body paragraphs, but it's faster to use the Repeat button on the Quick Access Toolbar.

6. Scroll down and click in the paragraph below the heading "Early News Media," and then on the Quick Access Toolbar, click the **Repeat** button ↻.

7. Click in the next paragraph, at the top of page 2, which begins "Early news media took many forms," and then click the **Repeat** button ↻.

8. Continue using the **Repeat** button ↻ to indent the first line of all of the remaining body paragraphs. Take care not to indent the headings, which in this document are formatted just like the body text.

9. Scroll to the top of the document, verify that you have correctly indented the first line of each body paragraph, and then save the document.

Next, you need to insert page numbers.

Inserting and Modifying Page Numbers

When you insert page numbers in a document, you don't have to type a page number on each page. Instead, you insert a **page number field**, which is an instruction that tells Word to insert a page number on each page, no matter how many pages you eventually add to the document. Word inserts page number fields above the top margin, in the blank area known as the **header**, or below the bottom margin, in the area known as the **footer**. You can also insert page numbers in the side margins, although for business or academic documents, it's customary to place them in the header or footer.

After you insert a page number field, Word switches to Header and Footer view. In this view, you can add your name or other text next to the page number field, or use the HEADER & FOOTER TOOLS DESIGN tab to change various settings related to headers and footers.

The MLA style requires a page number preceded by the student's last name in the upper-right corner of each page. If you prefer (or if your instructor requests it), you can omit the page number from the first page by selecting the Different First Page check box on the DESIGN tab.

To add page numbers to the research paper:

1. Press the **Ctrl+Home** keys to move the insertion point to the beginning of the document.

2. On the ribbon, click the **INSERT** tab. The ribbon changes to display the Insert options, including options for inserting page numbers.

3. In the Header & Footer group, click the **Page Number** button to open the Page Number menu. Here you can choose where you want to position the page numbers in your document—at the top of the page, at the bottom of the page, in the side margins, or at the current location of the insertion point.

4. Point to **Top of Page**. A gallery of page number styles opens. You can scroll the list to review the many styles of page numbers. Because the MLA style calls for a simple page number in the upper-right corner, you will use the Plain Number 3 style. See Figure 2-25.

TIP

To remove page numbers from a document, click the Remove Page Numbers command on the Page Number menu.

Figure 2-25   **Gallery of page number styles**

5. In the gallery, click the **Plain Number 3** style. The Word window switches to Header and Footer view, with the page number for the first page in the upper-right corner. The page number has a gray background, indicating that it is actually a page number field and not simply a number that you typed.

The HEADER & FOOTER TOOLS DESIGN tab is displayed on the ribbon, giving you access to a variety of formatting options. The insertion point blinks to the left of the page number field, ready for you to add text to the header if you wish. Note that in Header and Footer view, you can only type in the header or footer areas. The text in the main document area is a lighter shade of gray, indicating that it cannot be edited in this view.

6. Type your last name, and then press the **spacebar**. If you see a wavy red line below your last name, right-click your name, and then click **Ignore** on the Shortcut menu. See Figure 2-26.

Figure 2-26 **Last name inserted next to the page number field**

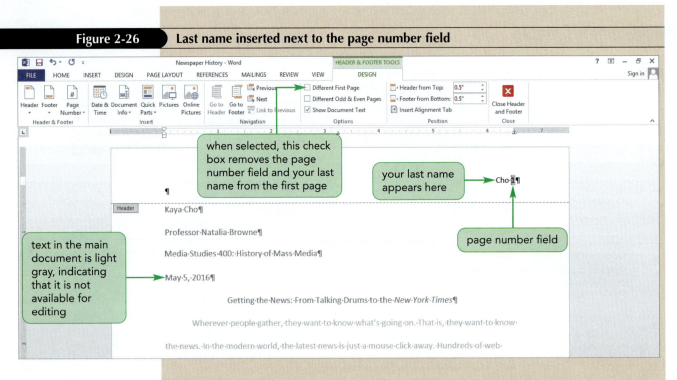

when selected, this check box removes the page number field and your last name from the first page

your last name appears here

Cho·1¶

text in the main document is light gray, indicating that it is not available for editing

May·5,·2016¶

Kaya·Cho¶

Professor·Natalia·Browne¶

Media·Studies·400:·History·of·Mass·Media¶

page number field

Getting·the·News:·From·Talking·Drums·to·the·*New·York·Times*¶

Wherever·people·gather,·they·want·to·know·what's·going·on.·That·is,·they·want·to·know·

the·news.·In·the·modern·world,·the·latest·news·is·just·a·mouse·click·away.·Hundreds·of·web·

7. Scroll down and observe the page number (with your last name) at the top of pages 2, 3, and 4. As you can see, whatever you insert in the header on one page appears on every page of the document by default.

8. Press the **Ctrl+Home** keys to return to the header on the first page.

9. On the HEADER & FOOTER TOOLS DESIGN tab, in the Options group, click the **Different First Page** check box to insert a check. The page number field and your last name are removed from the first page header. The insertion point blinks at the header's left margin in case you want to insert something else for the first page header. In this case, you don't.

10. In the Close group, click the **Close Header and Footer** button. You return to Print Layout view, and the HEADER & FOOTER TOOLS DESIGN tab is no longer displayed on the ribbon.

11. Scroll down to review your last name and the page number in the headers for pages 2, 3, and 4. In Print Layout view, the text in the header is light gray, indicating that it is not currently available for editing.

TIP

After you insert page numbers, you can reopen Header and Footer view by double-clicking a page number in Print Layout view.

You have finished all the tasks related to formatting the MLA-style research paper. Now Kaya wants your help with creating the essential parts of any research paper—the citations and the bibliography.

Creating Citations and a Bibliography

A bibliography (or, as it is called in the MLA style, the works cited list) is an alphabetical list of all the books, magazine articles, websites, movies, and other works referred to in a research paper. The items listed in a bibliography are known as **sources**. The entry for each source includes information such as the author, the title of the work, the publication date, and the publisher.

Within the research paper itself, you include a parenthetical reference, or citation, every time you quote or refer to a source. Every source included in your citations then has a corresponding entry in the works cited list. A citation should include enough information to identify the quote or referenced material so the reader can easily locate the source in the accompanying works cited list. The exact form for a citation varies depending on the style guide you are using and the type of material you are referencing.

Some style guides are very rigid about the form and location of citations, but the MLA style offers quite a bit of flexibility. Typically, though, you insert an MLA citation at the end of a sentence in which you quote or refer to material from a source. For books or journals, the citation itself usually includes the author's last name and a page number. However, if the sentence containing the citation already includes the author's name, you only need to include the page number in the citation. Figure 2-27 provides some sample MLA citations for books and journals. For detailed guidelines, you can consult the *MLA Handbook for Writers of Research Papers, Seventh Edition,* which includes many examples.

Figure 2-27 **MLA guidelines for citing a book or journal**

Citation Rule	Example
If the sentence includes the author's name, the citation should only include the page number.	Peterson compares the opening scene of the movie to a scene from Shakespeare (188).
If the sentence does not include the author's name, the citation should include the author's name and the page number.	The opening scene of the movie has been compared to a scene from Shakespeare (Peterson 188).

© 2014 Cengage Learning

Word greatly simplifies the process of creating citations and a bibliography. You specify the style you want to use, and then Word takes care of setting up the citation and the works cited list appropriately. Every time you create a citation for a new source, Word prompts you to enter the information needed to create the corresponding entry in the works cited list. If you don't have all of your source information available, Word also allows you to insert a temporary, placeholder citation, which you can replace later with a complete citation. When you are finished creating your citations, Word generates the bibliography automatically. Note that placeholder citations are not included in the bibliography.

PROSKILLS

Written Communication: Acknowledging Your Sources

A research paper is a means for you to explore the available information about a subject and then present this information, along with your own understanding of the subject, in an organized and interesting way. Acknowledging all the sources of the information presented in your research paper is essential. If you fail to do this, you might be subject to charges of plagiarism, or trying to pass off someone else's thoughts as your own. Plagiarism is an extremely serious accusation for which you could suffer academic consequences ranging from failing an assignment to being expelled from school.

To ensure that you don't forget to cite a source, you should be careful about creating citations in your document as you type. It's very easy to forget to go back and cite all your sources correctly after you've finished typing a research paper. Failing to cite a source could lead to accusations of plagiarism and all the consequences that entails. If you don't have the complete information about a source, you should at least insert a placeholder citation. But take care to go back later and substitute complete citations for any placeholders.

Creating Citations

Before you create citations, you need to select the style you want to use, which in the case of Kaya's paper is the MLA style. Then, to insert a citation, you click the Insert Citation button in the Citations & Bibliography group on the REFERENCES tab. If you are citing a source for the first time, Word prompts you to enter all the information required for the source's entry in the bibliography or works cited list. If you are citing an existing source, you simply select the source from the Insert Citation menu.

By default, an MLA citation includes only the author's name in parentheses. However, you can use the Edit Citation dialog box to add a page number. You can also use the Edit Citation dialog box to remove, or suppress, the author's name, so only the page number appears in the citation. However, in an MLA citation, Word will replace the suppressed author name with the title of the source, so you need to suppress the title as well, by selecting the Title check box in the Edit Citation dialog box.

Creating Citations

- On the ribbon, click the REFERENCES tab. In the Citations & Bibliography group, click the Style button arrow, and then select the style you want.
- Click in the document where you want to insert the citation. Typically, a citation goes at the end of a sentence, before the ending punctuation.
- To add a citation for a new source, click the Insert Citation button in the Citations & Bibliography group, click Add New Source, enter information in the Create Source dialog box, and then click the OK button.
- To add a citation for an existing source, click the Insert Citation button, and then click the source.
- To add a placeholder citation, click the Insert Citation button, click Add New Placeholder, and then, in the content control, type placeholder text, such as the author's last name, that will serve as a reminder about which source you need to cite. Note that a placeholder citation cannot contain any spaces.
- To add a page number to a citation, click the citation in the document, click the Citation Options button, click Edit Citation, type the page number, and then click the OK button.
- To display only the page number in a citation, click the citation in the document, click the Citation Options button, and then click Edit Citation. In the Edit Citation dialog box, select the Author and Title check boxes to suppress this information, and then click the OK button.

So far, Kaya has referenced information from two different sources in her research paper. You'll select a style and then begin adding the appropriate citations.

To select a style for the citation and bibliography:

1. On the ribbon, click the **REFERENCES** tab. The ribbon changes to display references options.

2. In the Citations & Bibliography group, click the **Style button arrow**, and then click **MLA Seventh Edition** if it is not already selected.

3. Press the **Ctrl+F** keys to open the Navigation pane.

4. Use the Navigation pane to find the phrase "As at least one historian has observed," which appears on page 1, and then click in the document at the end of that sentence (between the end of the word "medium" and the closing period).

5. Close the Navigation pane, and then click the **REFERENCES** tab on the ribbon, if necessary. You need to add a citation that informs the reader that historian Adam Taylor made the observation described in the sentence. See Figure 2-28.

Figure 2-28 **MLA style selected and insertion point positioned for new citation**

selected citation and bibliography style

As at least one historian has observed, the ability to distribute news to a geographically diverse group of people depends on the availability of a reliable medium. But what is a medium exactly? Leona Sanford defines "medium" as a way or a means of accomplishing something extension, then, a news medium is a way or means of delivering news to other people. ¶

citation will appear at the insertion point

6. In the Citations & Bibliography group, click the **Insert Citation** button to open the menu. At this point, you could click Add New Placeholder on the menu to insert a temporary, placeholder citation. However, because you have all the necessary source information, you can go ahead and create a complete citation.

7. On the menu, click **Add New Source**. The Create Source dialog box opens, ready for you to add the information required to create a bibliography entry for Adam Taylor's book.

8. If necessary, click the **Type of Source** arrow, scroll up or down in the list, and then click **Book**.

TIP

When entering information in a dialog box, you can press the Tab key to move the insertion point from one box to another.

9. In the Author box, type **Adam Taylor**.

10. Click in the **Title** box, and then type **Newspapers as Modern Media in a Modern Media World**.

11. Click in the **Year** box, and then type **2005**. This is the year the book was published. Next, you need to enter the name and location of the publisher.

12. Click the **City** box, type **New York**, click the **Publisher** box, and then type **Warrington and Reeves Academy Press**.

Finally, you need to indicate the medium used to publish the book. In this case, Kaya used a printed copy, so the medium is "Print." For books or journals published online, the correct medium would be "Web."

13. Click the **Medium** box, and then type **Print**. See Figure 2-29.

Figure 2-29 **Create Source dialog box with information for the first source**

▶ **14.** Click the **OK** button. Word inserts the parenthetical "(Taylor)" at the end of the sentence in the document.

Although the citation looks like ordinary text, it is actually contained inside a content control, a special feature used to display information that is inserted automatically and that may need to be updated later. You can only see the content control itself when it is selected. When it is unselected, you simply see the citation. In the next set of steps, you will select the content control, and then edit the citation to add a page number.

To edit the citation:

TIP

To delete a citation, click the citation to display the content control, click the tab on the left side of the content control, and then press the Delete key.

▶ **1.** In the document, click the citation **(Taylor)**. The citation appears in a content control, which is a box with a tab on the left and an arrow button on the right. The arrow button is called the Citation Options button.

▶ **2.** Click the **Citation Options** button ⬚. A menu of options related to editing a citation opens, as shown in Figure 2-30. To edit the information about the source, you click Edit Source. To change the information that is displayed in the citation itself, you use the Edit Citation option.

Figure 2-30   **Citation Options menu**

▶ **3.** On the Citation Options menu, click **Edit Citation**. The Edit Citation dialog box opens, as shown in Figure 2-31.

Figure 2-31   **Edit Citation dialog box**

To add a page number for the citation, you type the page number in the Pages box. If you want to display only the page number in the citation (which would be necessary if you already mentioned the author's name in the same sentence in the text), then you would also select the Author and Title check boxes in this dialog box to suppress this information.

▶ **4.** Type **45** to insert the page number in the Pages box, click the **OK** button to close the dialog box, and then click anywhere in the document outside the citation content control. The revised citation now reads "(Taylor 45)."

Next, you will add two more citations, both for the same journal article.

To insert two more citations:

▶ **1.** Click at the end of the second-to-last sentence of the current paragraph (which begins "Leona Sanford defines…"), between the word "something" and the period. This sentence mentions historian Leona Sanford; you need to add a citation to one of her journal articles.

▶ **2.** In the Citations & Bibliography group, click the **Insert Citation** button to open the Insert Citation menu. Notice that Adam Taylor's book is now listed as a source on this menu. You could click Taylor's book on the menu to add a citation to it, but right now you need to add a new source.

▶ **3.** Click **Add New Source** to open the Create Source dialog box, click the **Type of Source** arrow, and then click **Journal Article**.

The Create Source dialog box displays the boxes, or fields, appropriate for a journal article. The information required to cite a journal article differs from the information you entered earlier for the citation for the Taylor book. For journal articles, you are prompted to enter the page numbers for the entire article. If you want to display a particular page number in the citation, you can add it later.

By default, Word displays boxes, or fields, for the information most commonly included in a bibliography. In this case, you also want to include the volume and issue numbers for Leona Sanford's article, so you need to display more fields.

▶ **4.** In the Create Source dialog box, click the **Show All Bibliography Fields** check box to select this option. The Create Source dialog box expands to allow you to enter more detailed information. Red asterisks highlight the fields that are recommended, but these recommended fields don't necessarily apply to every source.

▶ **5.** Enter the following information, scrolling down to display the necessary boxes:

Author: **Leona Sanford**

Title: **News Media in History: A Study of Newsgathering from the Roman Empire to the Modern Day**

Journal Name: **Journal of Media Policy Studies International**

Year: **2008**

Pages: **122–145**

Volume: **30**

Issue: **5**

Medium: **Web**

When you are finished, your Create Source dialog box should look like the one shown in Figure 2-32.

Figure 2-32   **Create Source dialog box with information for the journal article**

Callouts in figure:
- scroll up or down to display more boxes
- new citation will appear here
- select this check box to display more fields

6. Click the **OK** button. The Create Source dialog box closes, and the citation "(Sanford)" is inserted in the text. Because the sentence containing the citation already includes the author's name, you will edit the citation to include the page number and suppress the author's name.

7. Click the **(Sanford)** citation to display the content control, click the **Citation Options** button , and then click **Edit Citation** to open the Edit Citation dialog box.

8. In the Pages box, type **142**, and then click the **Author** and **Title** check boxes to select them. You need to suppress both the author's name and the title because otherwise Word will replace the suppressed author name with the title. When using the MLA style, you don't ever have to suppress the year because the year is never included as part of an MLA citation. When working in other styles, however, you might need to suppress the year.

9. Click the **OK** button to close the Edit Citation dialog box, and then click anywhere outside the content control to deselect it. The end of the sentence now reads "…accomplishing something (142)."

10. Use the Navigation pane to find the sentence that begins "Throughout history…" on the second page. Click at the end of the sentence, to the left of the period after "news," and then close the Navigation pane.

11. On the REFERENCES tab, in the Citations & Bibliography group, click the **Insert Citation** button, and then click the **Sanford, Leona** source at the top of the menu. You want the citation to refer to the entire article instead of just one page, so you will not edit the citation to add a specific page number.

12. Save the document.

You have entered the source information for two sources.

Generating a Bibliography

Once you have created a citation for a source in a document, you can generate a bibliography. When you do, Word scans all the citations in the document, collecting the source information for each citation, and then it creates a list of information for each unique source. The format of the entries in the bibliography will reflect the style you specified when you created your first citation, which in this case is the MLA style. The bibliography itself is a **field**, similar to the page number field you inserted earlier in this session. In other words, it is really an instruction that tells Word to display the source information for all the citations in the document. Because it is a field and not actual text, you can update the bibliography later to reflect any new citations you might add.

You can choose to insert a bibliography as a field directly in the document, or you can insert a bibliography enclosed within a content control that also includes the heading "Bibliography" or "Works Cited." Inserting a bibliography enclosed in a content control is best because the content control includes a useful button that you can use to update your bibliography if you make changes to the sources.

In the MLA style, the bibliography (or works cited list) starts on a new page. So your first step is to insert a manual page break. A **manual page break** is one you insert at a specific location; it doesn't matter if the previous page is full or not. To insert a manual page break, use the Page Break button in the Pages group on the INSERT tab.

To insert a manual page break:

1. Press the **Ctrl+End** keys to move the insertion point to the end of the document.

2. On the ribbon, click the **INSERT** tab.

3. In the Pages group, click the **Page Break** button. Word inserts a new, blank page at the end of the document, with the insertion point blinking at the top. Note that you could also use the Ctrl+Enter keyboard shortcut to insert a manual page break.

4. Scroll up to see the dotted line with the words "Page Break" at the bottom of the text on page 4. See Figure 2-33.

TIP

Use the Blank Page button to insert a new, blank page in the middle of a document.

Figure 2-33 Manual page break inserted into the document

this·type·of·arrangement·will·allow·newspapers·to·thrive,·or·if·the·current·trend·of·newspaper·

closures·will·continue.¶

page break → Page Break ¶

Now you can insert the bibliography on the new page 5.

To insert the bibliography:

1. Scroll down so you can see the insertion point at the top of page 5.

2. On the ribbon, click the **REFERENCES** tab.

3. In the Citations & Bibliography group, click the **Bibliography** button. The Bibliography menu opens, displaying three styles with preformatted headings—"Bibliography," "References," and "Works Cited." The Insert Bibliography command at the bottom inserts a bibliography without a preformatted heading. See Figure 2-34.

Figure 2-34	Bibliography menu

inserts a bibliography field in a content control with a heading; use for an MLA research paper

inserts a bibliography field without a content control or heading

4. Click **Works Cited**. Word inserts the bibliography, with two entries, below the "Works Cited" heading.

   The bibliography text is formatted in Calibri, the default font for the Office theme. The "Works Cited" heading is formatted with the Heading 1 style. To see the content control that contains the bibliography, you need to select it.

5. Click anywhere in the bibliography. Inside the content control, the bibliography is highlighted in gray, indicating that it is a field and not regular text. The content control containing the bibliography is also now visible in the form of a rectangular border and a tab with two buttons. See Figure 2-35.

Figure 2-35 | **Bibliography displayed in a content control**

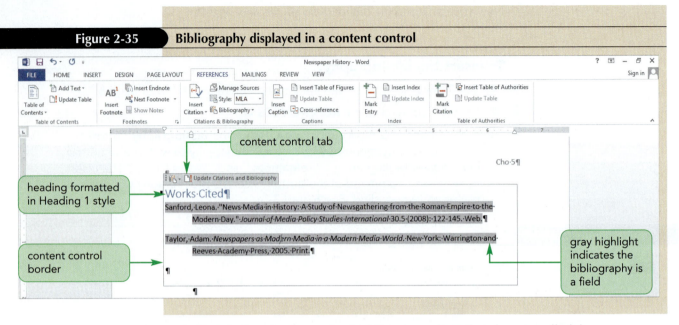

As Kaya looks over the works cited list, she realizes that she misspelled the last name of one of the authors. You'll correct the error now, and then update the bibliography.

INSIGHT

Managing Sources

When you create a source, Word adds it to a Master List of sources, which is available to any document created using the same user account on that computer. Word also adds each new source to the Current List of sources for that document. Both the Master List and the Current List are accessible via the Source Manager dialog box, which you open by clicking the Manage Sources button in the Citations & Bibliography group on the REFERENCES tab. Using this dialog box, you can copy sources from the Master List into the Current List, and vice versa. As you begin to focus on a particular academic field and turn repeatedly to important works in your chosen field, you'll find this ability to reuse sources very helpful.

Modifying an Existing Source

To modify information about a source, you click a citation to that source in the document, click the Citation Options button on the content control, and then click Edit Source. After you are finished editing the source, Word prompts you to update the master list and the source information in the current document. In almost all cases, you should click Yes to ensure that the source information is correct in all the places it is stored on your computer.

To edit a source in the research paper:

▶ **1.** Click in the blank paragraph below the bibliography content control to deselect the bibliography.

▶ **2.** Scroll up to display the last paragraph on page 2, and then click the **(Sanford)** citation you entered earlier in the first line of the paragraph. The content control appears around the citation.

  3. Click the **Citation Options** button ⬚, and then click **Edit Source**. The Edit Source dialog box opens. Note that Word displays the author's last name first in the Author box, just as it would appear in a bibliography.

  4. Click the **Author** box, and then add an "e" to the last name "Sanford" to change it to "Sanforde."

  5. Click the **OK** button. A message dialog box opens, asking if you want to update the master source list and the current document.

  6. Click the **Yes** button, and then click anywhere on the second page to deselect the citation content control. The revised author name in the citation now reads "Sanforde."

  7. Scroll up to the last paragraph on page 1, locate "Sanford" in the last paragraph on the page, and then change "Sanford" to "Sanforde."

  8. Save the document.

You've edited the document text and the citation to include the correct spelling of "Sanforde," but now you need to update the bibliography to correct the spelling.

Updating and Finalizing a Bibliography

The bibliography does not automatically change to reflect edits you make to existing citations or to show new citations. To incorporate the latest information stored in the citations, you need to update the bibliography. To update a bibliography in a content control, click the bibliography, and then, in the content control tab, click Update Citations and Bibliography. To update a bibliography field that is not contained in a content control, right-click the bibliography, and then click Update Field on the shortcut menu.

To update the bibliography:

  1. Scroll down to page 5 and click anywhere in the works cited list to display the content control.

  2. In the content control tab, click **Update Citations and Bibliography**. The works cited list is updated, with "Sanford" changed to "Sanforde" in the first entry.

Kaya still has a fair amount of work to do on her research paper. After she finishes writing it and adding all the citations, she will update the bibliography again to include all her cited sources. At that point, you might think the bibliography would be finished. However, a few steps remain to ensure that the works cited list matches the MLA style. To finalize Kaya's works cited list to match the MLA style, you need to make the changes shown in Figure 2-36.

| Figure 2-36 | Steps for finalizing a bibliography to match MLA guidelines for a Works Cited list |

1. Format the "Works Cited" heading to match the formatting of the rest of the text in the document.

2. Center the "Works Cited" heading.

3. Double-space the entire works cited list, including the heading, and remove extra space after the paragraphs.

4. Change the font size for the entire works cited list to 12 points.

To format the bibliography as an MLA style works cited list:

1. Click in the **Works Cited** heading, and then click the **HOME** tab on the ribbon.

2. In the Styles group, click the **Normal** style. The "Works Cited" heading is now formatted in Calibri body font like the rest of the document. The MLA style for a works cited list requires this heading to be centered.

3. In the Paragraph group, click the **Center** button.

4. Select the entire works cited list, including the heading. Change the font size to **12** points, change the line spacing to **2.0**, and then remove the paragraph spacing after each paragraph.

5. Click below the content control to deselect the works cited list, and then review your work. See Figure 2-37.

Figure 2-37 MLA-style Works Cited list

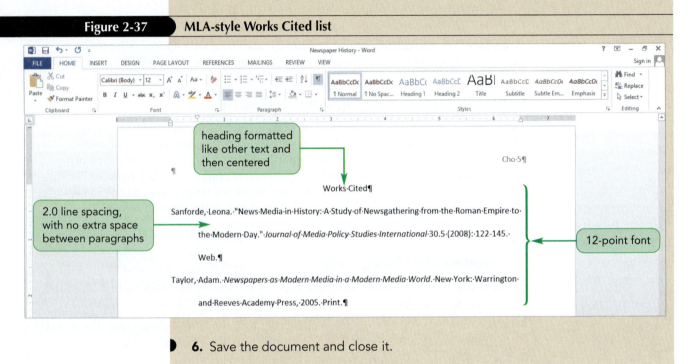

6. Save the document and close it.

Kaya's research paper now meets the MLA style guidelines.

Session 2.2 Quick Check

REVIEW

1. List the five tasks you need to perform to make a default Word document match the MLA style.

2. How do you indent a paragraph one inch from the left margin using an option on the ribbon?

3. Explain how to remove a page number from the first page of a document.

4. What is a bibliography called according to the MLA style?

5. Explain how to create a citation for a new source.

6. Explain how to edit a citation to display only the page number.

SAM Projects

Put your skills into practice with SAM Projects! SAM Projects for this tutorial can be found online. If you have a SAM account, go to www.cengage.com/sam2013 to download the most recent Project Instructions and Start Files.

Review Assignments

Data Files needed for the Review Assignments: Broadcast.docx, Situation.docx

Because the Media Studies document turned out so well, Kaya has been asked to help a student assistant in the Journalism department create a handout describing the classes required for a major in Broadcast Journalism. Kaya asks you to help her revise and format the document. She also asks you to create a document listing the prerequisites and core courses. Finally, as part of her Media Studies class, Kaya is working on a research paper on the history of situation comedy. She asks you to help her format the paper according to the MLA style, and to create some citations and a bibliography. She has inserted the uppercase word "CITATION" wherever she needs to insert a citation. Complete the following steps:

1. Open the file **Broadcast** located in the Word2 ▶ Review folder included with your Data Files, and then save the document as **Broadcast Journalism** in the location specified by your instructor.

2. Read the first comment, which provides an overview of the changes you will be making to the document in the following steps. Perform the task described in the second comment, and then delete both comments.

3. On page 2, in the second paragraph, revise the name of the first public speaking class so that only the first letter of each word is capitalized. Attach a comment to this paragraph that explains the change.

4. On page 2, move the "Senior Project" heading up to position it before the paragraph that begins "This project should incorporate…."

5. Replace the first instance of "journalism" with "media," being sure to match the case.

6. On page 1, format the list of four prerequisite classes as a bulleted list with square bullets. Do the same for the list of core courses, and then indent the three symposium names so they are formatted with an open circle bullet.

7. At the top of page 2, format the list of three public speaking classes as a numbered list, using the "1), 2), 3)" numbering style.

8. In the numbered list, move paragraph 3 ("Broadcast Journalism 220: Video Reporting") up to make it paragraph 2.

9. Format the title "Majoring in Broadcast Journalism" using the Title style. Format the following headings with the Heading 1 style: "Prerequisites," "Core Courses," "Electives," "Public Speaking," and "Senior Project."

10. Change the document theme to the Integral theme.

11. Display the Clipboard task pane. Copy the bulleted list of prerequisites to the Clipboard, and then copy the heading "Prerequisites" to the Clipboard. To ensure that you copy the heading formatting, be sure to select the paragraph mark after "Prerequisites" before you click the Copy button.

12. Open a new, blank document, and then save the document as **Prerequisite List** in the location specified by your instructor.

13. At the beginning of the document, paste the heading "Prerequisites," and then, from the Paste Options menu, apply the Keep Source Formatting option. Below the heading, paste the list of prerequisites, which begins with the text "Journalism 101…."

14. At the end of the document, insert a new paragraph, and then type **Prepared by:** followed by your first and last names.

15. Save the Prerequisite List document and close it.

16. In the Broadcast Journalism document, clear the contents of the Clipboard task pane, close the Clipboard task pane, save the document, and then close it.

17. Open the file **Situation** located in the Word2 ▶ Review folder included with your Data Files.

18. Save the document as **Situation Comedy** in the location specified by your instructor.

19. In the first paragraph, replace Kaya's name with your own.

20. Adjust the font size, line spacing, paragraph spacing, and paragraph indents to match the MLA style.

21. Insert your last name and a page number on every page except the first.

22. If necessary, select MLA Seventh Edition as the citations and bibliography style.

23. Use the Navigation pane to highlight all instances of the uppercase word "CITATION." Keep the Navigation pane open so you can continue to use it to find the locations where you need to insert citations in Steps 24–28.

24. Delete the first instance of "CITATION" and the space before it, and then create a new source with the following information:
    Type of Source: **Book**
    Author: **Cecile Webster**
    Title: **The Comedy of Situations: A History in Words and Pictures**
    Year: **2008**
    City: **Boston**
    Publisher: **Boston Valley Press**
    Medium: **Print**

25. Edit the citation to add **203** as the page number. Display only the page number in the citation.

26. Delete the second instance of "CITATION" and the space before it, and then create a new source with the following information:
    Type of Source: **Journal Article**
    Author: **Oliver Bernault**
    Title: **How Slapstick Conquered the World**
    Journal Name: **Pacific Film Quarterly: Criticism and Comment**
    Year: **2011**
    Pages: **68–91**
    Volume: **11**
    Issue: **2**
    Medium: **Web**

27. Edit the citation to add "80" as the page number.

28. Delete the third instance of "CITATION" and the space before it, and then insert a citation for the book by Cecile Webster.

29. At the end of the document, start a new page and insert a bibliography in a content control with the heading "Works Cited."

30. In the second source you created, add an "e" to change the last name "Bernault" to "Bernaulte," and then update the bibliography.

31. Finalize the bibliography to create an MLA-style Works Cited list.

32. Save the **Situation Comedy** document and close it.

33. Close any other open documents.

Case Problem 1

APPLY

Data File needed for this Case Problem: Yoga.docx

Green Willow Yoga Studio and Spa   Karl Boccio, the manager of Green Willow Yoga Studio and Spa, created a flyer to inform clients of the studio's move to a new location. The flyer also lists classes for the summer session and explains the registration process. It's your job to format the flyer to make it look professional and easy to read. Karl included comments in the document explaining what he wants you to do. Complete the following steps:

1. Open the file **Yoga** located in the Word2 ▶ Case1 folder included with your Data Files, and then save the file as **Yoga Flyer** in the location specified by your instructor.

2. Format the document as directed in the comments. After you complete a task, delete the relevant comment. Respond "Yes" to the comment asking if twenty is the correct number of years. When you are finished with the formatting, the comment with the question and the comment with your reply should be the only remaining comments.

3. Move the third bulleted item (which begins "Yoga for Relaxation...") up to make it the first bulleted item in the list.

4. Change the theme to the Ion theme, and then attach a comment to the title listing the heading and body fonts applied by the Ion theme.

5. Save the document and then close it.

Case Problem 2

APPLY

Data File needed for this Case Problem: Hamlet.docx

South Valley Community College   Jaleel Reynolds is a student at South Valley Community College. He's working on a research paper about Shakespeare's tragic masterpiece, *Hamlet*. The research paper is only partly finished, with notes in brackets indicating the material Jaleel still plans to write. He also inserted the uppercase word "CITATION" wherever he needs to insert a citation. Jaleel asks you to help him format this early draft to match the MLA style. He also asks you to help him create some citations and a first attempt at a bibliography. He will update the bibliography later, after he finishes writing the research paper. Complete the following steps:

1. Open the file **Hamlet** located in the Word2 ▶ Case2 folder included with your Data Files, and then save the document as **Hamlet Paper** in the location specified by your instructor.

2. In the first paragraph, replace "Jaleel Reynolds" with your name, and then adjust the font size, line spacing, paragraph spacing, and paragraph indents to match the MLA style.

3. Insert your last name and a page number in the upper-right corner of every page except the first page in the document.

4. If necessary, select MLA Seventh Edition as the citations and bibliography style.

5. Use the Navigation pane to find three instances of the uppercase word "CITATION."

6. Delete the first instance of "CITATION" and the space before it, and then create a new source with the following information:
   Type of Source: **Book**
   Author: **Andre Kahn**
   Title: **Tragic Drama in a Tragic Age**
   Year: **2000**
   City: **Chicago**
   Publisher: **Houghton University Press**
   Medium: **Print**

7. Edit the citation to add **127** as the page number.

8. Delete the second instance of "CITATION" and the space before it, and then create a new source with the following information:

    Type of Source: **Sound Recording**

    Performer: **Avery Pohlman**

    Title: **Live From New York's Golden Arch Theater**

    Production Company: **Prescott**

    Year: **1995**

    Medium: **CD**

    City: **New York**

9. Edit the citation to suppress the Author and the Year, so that it displays only the title.

10. Delete the third instance of "CITATION" and the space before it, and then insert a second reference to the book by Andre Kahn.

11. Edit the citation to add **35** as the page number.

12. At the end of the document, start a new page, and then insert a bibliography with the preformatted heading "Works Cited."

13. Edit the first source you created, changing the last name from "Kahn" to **Klann.**

14. Update the bibliography so it shows the revised name "Klann."

15. Finalize the bibliography so that it matches the MLA style.

16. Save the Hamlet Paper document and close it.

Case Problem 3

CREATE

Data Files needed for this Case Problem: Capital.docx, Sarah.docx

Sports Training   Sarah Vang has more than a decade of experience as an athletic trainer in several different settings. After moving to a new city, she is looking for a job as a trainer in a hospital. She has asked you to edit and format her resume. As part of the application process, she will have to upload her resume to the hospitals' employee recruitment websites. Because these sites typically request a simple page design, Sarah plans to rely primarily on heading styles and bullets to organize her information. When the resume is complete, she wants you to remove any color applied by the heading styles. She also needs help formatting a document she created for a public health organization for which she volunteers. Complete the following steps:

1. Open the file **Sarah** located in the Word2 ▸ Case3 folder included with your Data Files, and then save the file as **Sarah Resume** in the location specified by your instructor.

2. Read the comment included in the document, and then perform the task it specifies.

3. Respond to the comment with the response **I think that's a good choice for the theme.**, and then mark Sarah's comment as done.

4. Replace all occurrences of "Mesacrest" with **Mesa Crest**.

5. Format the resume as shown in Figure 2-38. To ensure that the resume fits on one page, pay special attention to the paragraph spacing settings specified in Figure 2-38.

Figure 2-38 Formatting for Sarah Vang's resume

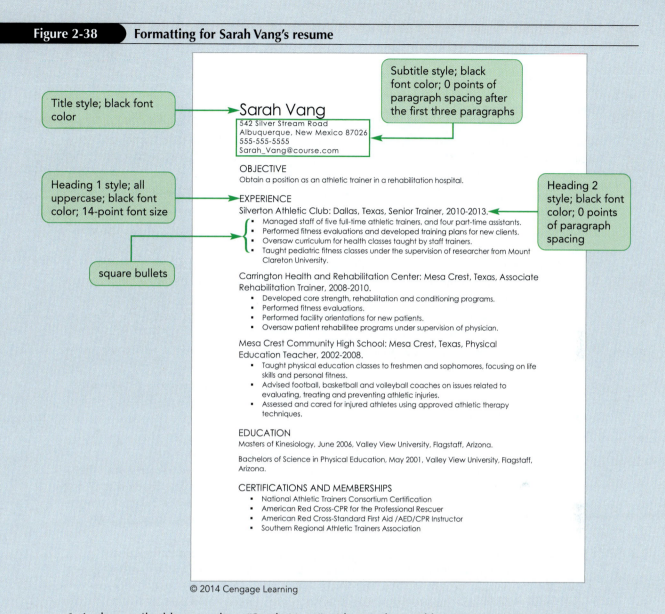

© 2014 Cengage Learning

6. In the email address, replace "Sarah_Vang" with your first and last names, separated by an underscore, and then save the document and close it.

7. Open the file **Capital** located in the Word2 ▸ Case4 folder included with your Data Files, and then save the file as **Capital Campaign** in the location specified by your instructor. Search for the text "Your Name", and then replace it with your first and last names.

8. Select the three paragraphs below your name, and then decrease the indent for the selected paragraphs so that they align at the left margin. Create a .5-inch hanging indent for the selected paragraphs instead.

9. Change the document theme to Ion, and then add a comment to the first word in the document that reads "I changed the theme to Ion."

10. Use the Advanced Find dialog box to search for bold formatting. Remove the bold formatting from the fourth bold element in the document, and then add a comment to that element that reads "I assumed bold here was a mistake, so I removed it."

11. Save and close the document.

CHALLENGE

Case Problem 4

Data File needed for this Case Problem: Movie.docx

Winona College Tristan Giroux is a student at Winona College. She's working on a research paper about disaster movies for Film Studies 105, taught by Professor Douglas Fischer. The research paper is only partly finished, but before she does more work on it, she asks you to help format this early draft to match the MLA style. She also asks you to help her create some citations, add a placeholder citation, and manage her sources. Complete the following steps:

1. Open the file **Movie** located in the Word2 ▸ Case4 folder included with your Data Files, and then save the document as **Movie Paper** in the location specified by your instructor.

2. Revise the paper to match the MLA style, seventh edition. Instead of Tristan's name, use your own. Also, use the current date.

3. Locate the sentences in which the authors Dana Someya and Peter Williams are mentioned. At the end of the appropriate sentence, add a citation for page 135 in the following book and one for page 152 in the following journal article:

   Someya, Dana. *Society and Disaster in the Silent Era: A Modern Analysis.* New York: Movie House Academy Press, 1997. Print.

   Williams, Peter. "Romance in the Shadow of Disaster." *New England Journal of Cinema Studies* (2012): 133–155. Web.

4. At the end of the second-to-last sentence in the document, insert a placeholder citation that reads "Candela." At the end of the last sentence in the document, insert a placeholder citation that reads "Goldman."

✪ Explore 5. Use Word Help to look up the topic "Create a bibliography," and then, within that article, read the sections titled "Find a source" and "Edit a citation placeholder."

✪ Explore 6. Open the Source Manager, and search for the name "Someya." From within the Current List in the Source Manager, edit the Dana Someya citation to delete "Society and" from the title, so that the title begins "Disaster in the Silent Era…." Click Yes when asked if you want to update the source in both lists. When you are finished, delete "Someya" from the Search box to redisplay all the sources in both lists.

✪ Explore 7. From within the Source Manager, copy a source not included in the current document from the Master List to the Current List. Examine the sources in the Current List and note the checkmarks next to the two sources for which you have already created citations, and the question marks next to the placeholder sources. Sources in the Current list that are not actually cited in the text have no symbol next to them in the Current List. For example, if you copied a source from the Master List into your Current List, that source has no symbol next to it in the Current List.

8. Close the Source Manager, create a bibliography in the MLA style, and note which works appear in it.

✪ Explore 9. Open the Source Manager, and then edit the Goldman placeholder source to include the following information about a journal article:

   Goldman, Simon. "Attack of the Killer Disaster Movie." *Cinema International Journal* (2009): 72–89. Web.

10. Update the bibliography.

✪ Explore 11. Open Internet Explorer and use the Web to research the difference between a works cited list and a works consulted list. If necessary, open the Source Manager, and then delete any uncited sources from the Current List to ensure that your document contains a true works cited list, as specified by the MLA style, and not a works consulted list. (Tristan will create a full citation for the "Candela" placeholder later.)

12. Update the bibliography, finalize it so it matches the MLA style, save the document and close it.

Written Communication

Writing Clear and Effective Business Documents

Whether it's a simple email message sent to a group, a memo to provide information on an upcoming event, or a press release introducing a new product to the market, the quality of your written communication tells the world how prepared, informed, and detail-oriented you are. When searching for a job, the ability to write clearly and effectively is essential. After all, your first contact with a company is often a cover letter and resume. For a prospective employer, these documents provide the first indicators of the kind of employee you might be. To make the best possible impression, follow these important rules in all types of business communication.

Rule One: Identify Your Audience

Who will read your document? What do they already know about your subject? For starters, you can assume your audience is made up of busy people who will only take the time to read what is important and relevant to them. They don't want to be entertained. They just want to read the information as quickly as possible. In the case of a resume and cover letter, your audience is typically one or more professional people who don't know you. Therefore, the goal of your resume and cover letter should be to introduce yourself quickly and efficiently.

Rule Two: Do Your Research

Provide all the information the reader will need to make a decision or take action. Be absolutely certain that the facts you present are correct. Don't assume that something is true just because a friend told you it was, or because you read it online. Verify all your facts using reputable sources. Remember, your goal as a writer is to make the reader trust you. Nothing alienates a reader faster than errors or misleading statements. When applying for a job, make sure you are knowledgeable about the company so that you can mention relevant and accurate details in your cover letter.

Rule Three: State Your Purpose

At the beginning of the document, explain why you are writing. The reader shouldn't have to wonder. Are you writing to inform, or do you want action to be taken? Do you hope to change a belief or simply state your position? In a cover letter accompanying your resume, state clearly that you are writing to apply for a job, and then explain exactly what job you are applying for. That might sound obvious, but many job applicants forget about directness in their efforts to come across as clever or interesting. This only hurts their chances because prospective employers typically have many cover letters to read, with no time to spare for sorting through irrelevant information.

Rule Four: Write Succinctly

Use as few words as possible. Don't indulge in long, complicated words and sentences because you think they make you sound smart. The most intelligent writing is usually short and to the point. Keep in mind that hiring a new employee is a very time-consuming process. In small companies, people in charge of hiring often have to do it while performing their regular duties. Thus, the more succinct your resume and cover letter, the greater the chances that a potential employer will actually read both documents.

Rule Five: Use the Right Tone

Be professional and courteous. In the case of writing to a prospective employer, don't make the mistake of being overly friendly because it might indicate to the reader that you are not taking the job application process seriously.

Rule Six: Revise, Revise, Revise

After you finish a document, set it aside for a while, and then proofread it when it's no longer fresh in your mind. Even a small grammar or punctuation error can cause a potential employer to set aside your resume in favor of a more polished one with no errors. Remember, the best writers in the world seek out readers who can provide constructive suggestions, so consider having a friend or colleague read it and provide feedback. If someone points out an unclear passage, make every attempt to improve it.

Following these basic rules will help to ensure that you develop strong, professional written communication skills.

PROSKILLS

Create a Resume and Cover Letter

You've seen how Microsoft Word 2013 allows you to create polished, professional-looking documents in a variety of business settings. The word-processing skills you've learned will be useful to you in many areas of your life. In the following exercise, you'll use the skills you learned in Word Tutorials 1 and 2 to create a resume and a cover letter to send to prospective employers.

Note: Please be sure *not* to include any personal information of a sensitive nature in the documents you create to be submitted to your instructor for this exercise. Later on, you can update the documents with such information for your own personal use.

1. Pick a career field that interests you, and then go online and look up information about four companies or organizations in that field for which you would like to work.

2. Create a document that summarizes your research. Your document should include four bulleted lists with information about how to apply for a job at the four different companies or organizations you researched. Does each company require you to email your resume and cover letter as PDFs, to submit them as Word documents via a website, to paste them into a form on a website, or to mail printed copies? The process of applying for a job can vary widely from one company to another—and from one industry to another—so make sure you clearly explain the process for each company and include any relevant website addresses. Include general information that would be useful for you in a job interview. For example, you might include a "Most Important Product" bullet and a "Facts About Company Founder" bullet. Use styles and a theme of your choice to make your document attractive.

3. Create a resume that you could use to apply for jobs at the four companies you researched. To ensure that your resume is suitable for your chosen field, search the web for sample resumes in your field. Find a resume design that you like, and then adapt the design for your resume. Your goal should be to create the most elegant, professional-looking resume you can, using styles, a theme of your choice, and other formatting options.

4. After creating your resume, proofread it for any errors, and then revise it for proper tone and clear and succinct content. If possible, ask a classmate or a family member to read it and provide constructive feedback.

5. Create a copy of your resume, and then revise this new version to use the simplest possible formatting. This time, your goal should be to create a resume that you could easily paste into a form on a website.

6. Create a cover letter to accompany your resume. Make sure that your letter clearly states your purpose, and that the letter is formatted correctly and written succinctly. When reviewing your cover letter and revising it, make sure your writing is professional and uses an appropriate tone.

7. Spell check all your documents and carefully proofread them a final time.

8. Review all your documents carefully in Print Preview, make any necessary changes, and then save the documents.

EXCEL

OBJECTIVES

Session 1.1
- Open and close a workbook
- Navigate through a workbook and worksheet
- Select cells and ranges
- Plan and create a workbook
- Insert, rename, and move worksheets
- Enter text, dates, and numbers
- Undo and redo actions
- Resize columns and rows

Session 1.2
- Enter formulas and the SUM and COUNT functions
- Copy and paste formulas
- Move or copy cells and ranges
- Insert and delete rows, columns, and ranges
- Create patterned text with Flash Fill
- Add cell borders and change font size
- Change worksheet views
- Prepare a workbook for printing
- Save a workbook with a new filename

Getting Started with Excel

Creating a Customer Order Report

Case | **Sparrow & Pond**

Sally Hughes is part owner of Sparrow & Pond, a small bookstore in Hudson, New Hampshire. Among her many tasks is to purchase new books from publishers. She also purchases rare and first edition books from online auctions as well as local library, estate, and garage sales.

Sally needs to quickly track sales data, compile customer profiles, and generate financial reports. She can perform all of these tasks with **Microsoft Excel 2013** (or **Excel**), an application used to enter, analyze, and present quantitative data. Sally asks you to use Excel to record a recent book order from a regular Sparrow & Pond customer.

STARTING DATA FILES

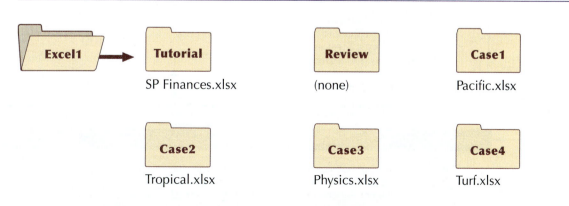

Excel1 → Tutorial
SP Finances.xlsx

Review
(none)

Case1
Pacific.xlsx

Case2
Tropical.xlsx

Case3
Physics.xlsx

Case4
Turf.xlsx

Session 1.1 Visual Overview:

The ribbon is organized into tabs. Each **tab** has commands related to particular activities or tasks.

The **formula bar** displays the value or formula entered in the active cell.

Excel stores spreadsheets in files called **workbooks**. The name of the current workbook appears in the title bar.

The **ribbon** contains buttons that you click to execute commands to work with Excel. You can pin the ribbon to leave it fully displayed, as shown here.

The **Name box** displays the cell reference of the active cell. In this case, the active cell is cell B104.

A group of cells in a rectangular block is called a **cell range** (or **range**). If the blocks are not connected, as shown here, it is a **nonadjacent range**.

The currently selected cell is the **active cell**.

The **row headings** are numbers along the left side of the workbook window that identify the different rows of the worksheet.

A workbook is made up of **sheets**. Each sheet is identified by a sheet name, which appears in a **sheet tab**.

The **status bar** provides information about the workbook.

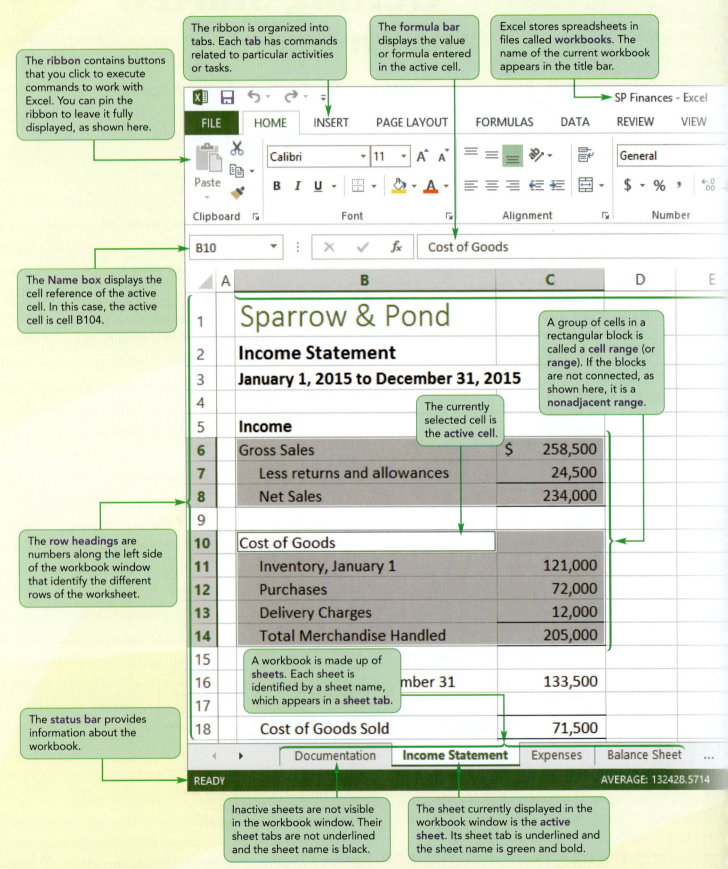

Inactive sheets are not visible in the workbook window. Their sheet tabs are not underlined and the sheet name is black.

The sheet currently displayed in the workbook window is the **active sheet**. Its sheet tab is underlined and the sheet name is green and bold.

The Excel Window

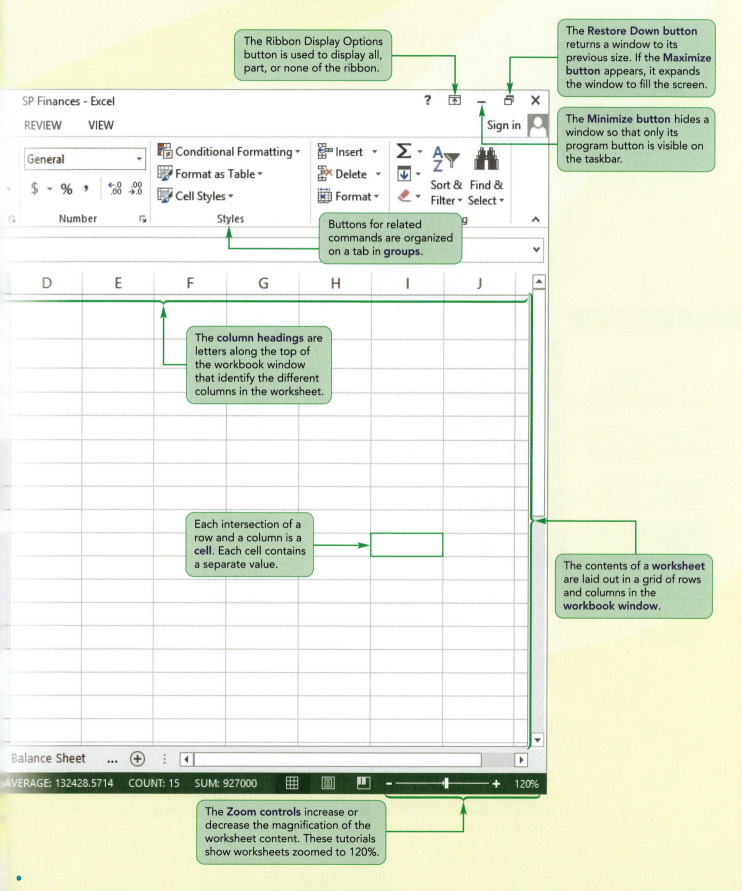

The Ribbon Display Options button is used to display all, part, or none of the ribbon.

The **Restore Down button** returns a window to its previous size. If the **Maximize button** appears, it expands the window to fill the screen.

The **Minimize button** hides a window so that only its program button is visible on the taskbar.

Buttons for related commands are organized on a tab in **groups**.

The **column headings** are letters along the top of the workbook window that identify the different columns in the worksheet.

Each intersection of a row and a column is a **cell**. Each cell contains a separate value.

The contents of a **worksheet** are laid out in a grid of rows and columns in the **workbook window**.

The **Zoom controls** increase or decrease the magnification of the worksheet content. These tutorials show worksheets zoomed to 120%.

Introducing Excel and Spreadsheets

A **spreadsheet** is a grouping of text and numbers in a rectangular grid or table. Spreadsheets are often used in business for budgeting, inventory management, and financial reporting because they unite text, numbers, and charts within one document. They can also be employed for personal use for planning a personal budget, tracking expenses, or creating a list of personal items. The advantage of an electronic spreadsheet is that the content can be easily edited and updated to reflect changing financial conditions.

To start Excel:

  1. Display the Windows Start screen, if necessary.

     Using Windows 7? To complete Step 1, click the Start button on the taskbar.

  2. Click the **Excel 2013** tile. Excel starts and displays the Recent screen in Backstage view. **Backstage view** provides access to various screens with commands that allow you to manage files and Excel options. On the left is a list of recently opened workbooks. On the right are options for creating new workbooks. See Figure 1-1.

Figure 1-1	Recent screen in Backstage view

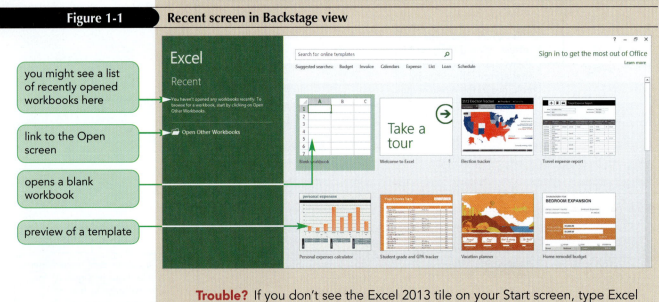

you might see a list of recently opened workbooks here

link to the Open screen

opens a blank workbook

preview of a template

Trouble? If you don't see the Excel 2013 tile on your Start screen, type Excel to display the Apps screen with the Excel 2013 tile highlighted, and then click the tile.

Using Windows 7? To complete Step 2, point to All Programs on the Start menu, click Microsoft Office 2013, and then click Excel 2013.

Opening an Existing Workbook

Excel documents are called workbooks. From the Recent screen in Backstage view, you can open a blank workbook, open an existing workbook, or create a new workbook based on a template. A **template** is a preformatted workbook with many design features and some content already filled in. Templates can speed up the process of creating a workbook because much of the work in designing the appearance of the workbook and entering its data and formulas is already done for you.

Sally created an Excel workbook that contains several worksheets describing the current financial status of Sparrow & Pond. You will open that workbook now.

To open Sally's workbook:

1. In the navigation bar on the Recent screen, click the **Open Other Workbooks** link. The Open screen is displayed and provides access to different locations where you might store files. The Recent Workbooks list shows the workbooks that were most recently opened on your computer.

2. Click **Computer**. The list of recently opened workbooks is replaced with a list of recently accessed folders on your computer and a Browse button.

   Trouble? If you are storing your files on your SkyDrive, click SkyDrive, and then log in if necessary.

3. Click the **Browse** button. The Open dialog box appears.

4. Navigate to the **Excel1 ▸ Tutorial** folder included with your Data Files.

   Trouble? If you don't have the starting Data Files, you need to get them before you can proceed. Your instructor will either give you the Data Files or ask you to obtain them from a specified location (such as a network drive). If you have any questions about the Data Files, see your instructor or technical support person for assistance.

5. Click **SP Finances** in the file list to select it.

6. Click the **Open** button. The SP Finances workbook opens in Excel.

   Trouble? If you don't see the full ribbon as shown in the Session 1.1 Visual Overview, the ribbon may be partially or fully hidden. To pin the ribbon so that the tabs and groups are fully displayed and remain visible, click the Ribbon Display Options button 🔼, and then click Show Tabs and Commands.

7. If the Excel window doesn't fill the screen, click the **Maximize** button ☐ in the upper-right corner of the title bar. See Figure 1-2.

| Figure 1-2 | SP Finances workbook |

Using Keyboard Shortcuts to Work Faster

Keyboard shortcuts can help you work faster and more efficiently because you can keep your hands on the keyboard. A **keyboard shortcut** is a key or combination of keys that you press to access a feature or perform a command. Excel provides keyboard shortcuts for many commonly used commands. For example, Ctrl+S is the keyboard shortcut for the Save command, which means you hold down the Ctrl key while you press the S key to save the workbook. (Note that the plus sign is not pressed; it is used to indicate that an additional key is pressed.) When available, a keyboard shortcut is listed next to the command's name in a ScreenTip. A **ScreenTip** is a box with descriptive text about a command that appears when you point to a button on the ribbon. Figure 1-3 lists some of the keyboard shortcuts commonly used in Excel. The tutorials in this text show the corresponding keyboard shortcuts for accomplishing an action when available.

Figure 1-3 Excel keyboard shortcuts

Press	To	Press	To
Alt	Display the Key Tips for the commands and tools on the ribbon	Ctrl+V	Paste content that was cut or copied
Ctrl+A	Select all objects in a range	Ctrl+W	Close the current workbook
Ctrl+C	Copy the selected object(s)	Ctrl+X	Cut the selected object(s)
Ctrl+G	Go to a location in the workbook	Ctrl+Y	Repeat the last command
Ctrl+N	Open a new blank workbook	Ctrl+Z	Undo the last command
Ctrl+O	Open a saved workbook file	F1	Display the Excel Help window
Ctrl+P	Print the current workbook	F5	Go to a location in the workbook
Ctrl+S	Save the current workbook	F12	Save the current workbook with a new name or to a new location

© 2014 Cengage Learning

You can also use the keyboard to quickly select commands on the ribbon. First, you press the Alt key to display the **Key Tips**, which are labels that appear over each tab and command on the ribbon. Then, you press the key or keys indicated to access the corresponding tab, command, or button while your hands remain on the keyboard.

Getting Help

If you are unsure about the function of an Excel command or you want information about how to accomplish a particular task, you can use the Help system. To access Excel Help, you either press the F1 key or click the Microsoft Excel Help button in the title bar of the Excel window or dialog boxes. From the Excel Help window, you can search for a specific topic or click a topic in a category.

Using Excel 2013 in Touch Mode

In Office 2013, you can work with a mouse or, if you have a touchscreen, you can work in Touch Mode. In **Touch Mode**, the ribbon increases in height, the buttons are bigger, and more space appears around each button so you can more easily use your finger or a stylus to tap the button you need. As you work with Excel on a touchscreen, you tap objects instead of clicking them. Note that the figures in these tutorials show the screen with Mouse Mode on, but it's helpful to learn how to switch back and forth between Touch Mode and Mouse Mode. You'll switch to Touch Mode and then back to Mouse Mode now.

Note: The following steps assume that you are using a mouse. If you are instead using a touch device, please read these steps but don't complete them, so that you remain working in Touch Mode.

To switch between Touch Mode and Mouse Mode:

1. On the Quick Access Toolbar, click the **Customize Quick Access Toolbar** button ⏷. A menu opens listing buttons you can add to the Quick Access Toolbar as well as other options for customizing the toolbar.

   Trouble? If the Touch/Mouse Mode command on the menu has a checkmark next to it, press the Esc key to close the menu, and then skip Step 2.

2. Click **Touch/Mouse Mode**. The Quick Access Toolbar now contains the Touch/Mouse Mode button 👆, which you can use to switch between Mouse Mode, the default display, and Touch Mode.

3. On the Quick Access Toolbar, click the **Touch/Mouse Mode** button 👆. A menu opens listing Mouse and Touch, and the icon next to Mouse is shaded to indicate it is selected.

   Trouble? If the icon next to Touch is shaded, press the Esc key to close the menu and skip Step 4.

4. Click **Touch**. The display switches to Touch Mode with more space between the commands and buttons on the ribbon. See Figure 1-4.

Figure 1-4	Ribbon displayed in Touch Mode

Touch/Mouse Mode button

buttons are larger with more space around them

Now you'll return to Mouse Mode.

Trouble? If you are working with a touchscreen and want to use Touch Mode, skip Steps 5 and 6.

5. On the Quick Access Toolbar, click the **Touch/Mouse Mode** button 👆, and then click **Mouse**. The ribbon returns to the Mouse Mode display shown in Figure 1-2.

6. On the Quick Access Toolbar, click the **Customize Quick Access Toolbar** button ⏷, and then click **Touch/Mouse Mode** to deselect it. The Touch/Mouse Mode button is removed from the Quick Access Toolbar.

Exploring a Workbook

Workbooks are organized into separate pages called sheets. Excel supports two types of sheets: worksheets and chart sheets. A worksheet contains a grid of rows and columns into which you can enter text, numbers, dates, and formulas, and display charts. A **chart sheet** contains a chart that provides a visual representation of worksheet data. The contents of a workbook are shown in the workbook window.

Changing the Active Sheet

The sheets in a workbook are identified in the sheet tabs at the bottom of the workbook window. The SP Finances workbook includes five sheets labeled Documentation, Income Statement, Expenses, Balance Sheet, and Cash Flow. The sheet currently displayed in the workbook window is the active sheet, which in this case is the Documentation sheet. To make a different sheet active and visible, you click its sheet tab. You can tell which sheet is active because its name appears in bold green.

If a workbook includes so many sheets that not all of the sheet tabs can be displayed at the same time in the workbook window, you can use the sheet tab scrolling buttons to scroll through the list of tabs. Scrolling the sheet tabs does not change the active sheet; it only changes which sheet tabs are visible.

You will view the different sheets in the SP Finances workbook.

To change the active sheet:

1. Click the **Income Statement** sheet tab. The Income Statement worksheet becomes the active sheet, and its name is in bold green type. See Figure 1-5.

Figure 1-5   Income Statement worksheet

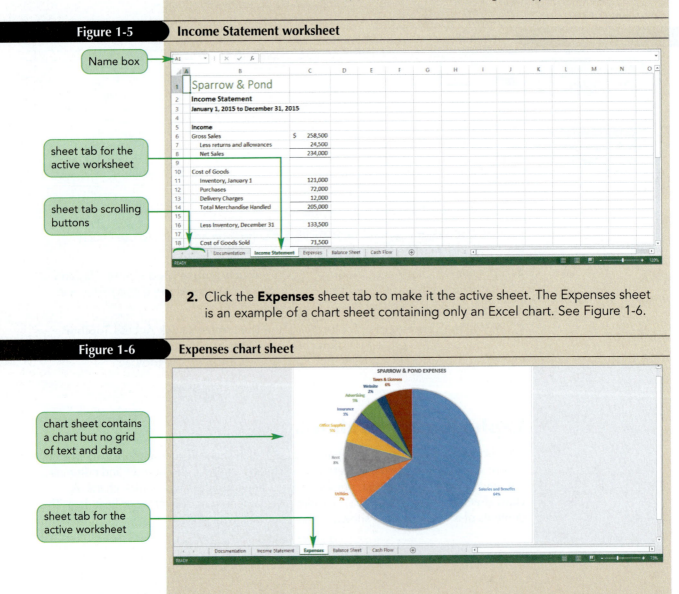

2. Click the **Expenses** sheet tab to make it the active sheet. The Expenses sheet is an example of a chart sheet containing only an Excel chart. See Figure 1-6.

Figure 1-6   Expenses chart sheet

TIP

You can move to the previous or next sheet in the workbook by pressing the Ctrl+PgUp or Ctrl+PgDn keys.

3. Click the **Balance Sheet** sheet tab to make it the active sheet. Note that this sheet contains a chart embedded into the grid of data values. A worksheet can contain data values, charts, pictures, and other design elements.

4. Click the **Cash Flow** sheet tab. The worksheet with information about the company's cash flow is now active.

5. Click the **Income Statement** sheet tab to make the Income Statement worksheet the active sheet.

Navigating Within a Worksheet

The worksheet is organized into individual cells. Each cell is identified by a **cell reference**, which is based on the cell's column and row location. For example, in Figure 1-5, the company name, Sparrow & Pond, is in cell B1, which is the intersection of column B and row 1. The column letter always appears before the row number in any cell reference. The cell that is currently selected in the worksheet is referred to as the active cell. The active cell is highlighted with a thick green border, its cell reference appears in the Name box, and the corresponding column and row headings are highlighted. The active cell in Figure 1-5 is cell A1.

Row numbers range from 1 to 1,048,576, and column labels are letters in alphabetical order. The first 26 column headings range from A to Z. After Z, the next column headings are labeled AA, AB, AC, and so forth. Excel allows a maximum of 16,384 columns in a worksheet (the last column has the heading XFD). This means that you can create large worksheets whose content extends well beyond what is visible in the workbook window.

To move different parts of the worksheet into view, you can use the horizontal and vertical scroll bars located at the bottom and right edges of the workbook window, respectively. A scroll bar has arrow buttons that you can click to shift the worksheet one column or row in the specified direction, and a scroll box that you can drag to shift the worksheet in the direction you drag.

You will scroll the active worksheet so you can review the rest of the Sparrow & Pond income statement.

To scroll through the Income Statement worksheet:

1. On the vertical scroll bar, click the down arrow button ▼ to scroll down the Income Statement worksheet until you see cell C36, which displays the company's net income value of $4,600.

2. On the horizontal scroll bar, click the right arrow button ▶ three times. The worksheet scrolls three columns to the right, moving columns A through C out of view.

3. On the horizontal scroll bar, drag the scroll box to the left until you see column A.

4. On the vertical scroll bar, drag the scroll box up until you see the top of the worksheet and cell A1.

Scrolling the worksheet does not change the location of the active cell. Although the active cell might shift out of view, you can always see the location of the active cell in the Name box. To make a different cell active, you can either click a new cell or use the keyboard to move between cells, as described in Figure 1-7.

Figure 1-7 **Excel navigation keys**

Press	To move the active cell
↑ ↓ ← →	Up, down, left, or right one cell
Home	To column A of the current row
Ctrl+Home	To cell A1
Ctrl+End	To the last cell in the worksheet that contains data
Enter	Down one row or to the start of the next row of data
Shift+Enter	Up one row
Tab	One column to the right
Shift+Tab	One column to the left
PgUp, PgDn	Up or down one screen
Ctrl+PgUp, Ctrl+PgDn	To the previous or next sheet in the workbook

© 2014 Cengage Learning

You will use both your mouse and your keyboard to change the location of the active cell in the Income Statement worksheet.

To change the active cell:

1. Move your pointer over cell **B5**, and then click the mouse button. The active cell moves from cell A1 to cell B5. A green border appears around cell B5, the column heading for column B and the row heading for row 5 are both highlighted, and the cell reference in the Name box changes from A1 to B5.

2. Press the → key. The active cell moves one cell to the right to cell C5.

3. Press the **PgDn** key. The active cell moves down one full screen.

4. Press the **PgUp** key. The active cell moves up one full screen, returning to cell C5.

5. Press the **Ctrl+Home** keys. The active cell returns to the first cell in the worksheet, cell A1.

The mouse and keyboard provide quick ways to navigate the active worksheet. For larger worksheets that span several screens, you can move directly to a specific cell using the Go To command or by typing a cell reference in the Name box. You will try both of these methods.

To use the Go To dialog box and the Name box:

1. On the HOME tab, in the Editing group, click the **Find & Select** button, and then click **Go To** on the menu that opens (or press the **F5** key). The Go To dialog box opens.

2. Type **C36** in the Reference box. See Figure 1-8.

Figure 1-8   **Go To dialog box**

cell reference of the cell you want to make active

3. Click the **OK** button. Cell C36 becomes the active cell, displaying $4,600, which is Sparrow & Pond's net income for the year. Because cell C36 is the active cell, its cell reference appears in the Name box.

4. Click in the Name box, type **A1**, and then press the **Enter** key. Cell A1 is again the active cell.

Selecting a Cell Range

Many tasks in Excel require you to work with a group of cells. You can use your mouse or keyboard to select those cells. A group of cells in a rectangular block is called a cell range (or simply a range). Each range is identified with a **range reference** that includes the cell reference of the upper-left cell of the rectangular block and the cell reference of the lower-right cell separated by a colon. For example, the range reference A1:G5 refers to all of the cells in the rectangular block from cell A1 through cell G5.

As with individual cells, you can select cell ranges using your mouse, the keyboard, or commands. You will select a range in the Income Statement worksheet.

To select a cell range:

1. Click cell **B5** to select it, and without releasing the mouse button, drag down to cell **C8**.

2. Release the mouse button. The range B5:C8 is selected. See Figure 1-9. The selected cells are highlighted and surrounded by a green border. The first cell you selected in the range, cell B5, is the active cell in the worksheet. The active cell in a selected range is white. The Quick Analysis button appears, providing options for working with the range; you will use this button in another tutorial.

TIP

You can also select a range by clicking the upper-left cell of the range, holding down the Shift key as you click the lower-right cell in the range, and then releasing the Shift key.

Figure 1-9 **Range B5:C8 selected**

3. Click cell **A1** to deselect the range.

A nonadjacent range is a collection of separate ranges. The range reference for a nonadjacent range includes the range reference to each range separated by a semicolon. For example, the range reference A1:G5;A10:G15 includes two ranges—the first range is the rectangular block of cells from cell A1 to cell G5, and the second range is the rectangular block of cells from cell A10 to cell G15.

You will select a nonadjacent range in the Income Statement worksheet.

To select a nonadjacent range in the Income Statement worksheet:

1. Click cell **B5**, hold down the **Shift** key as you click cell **C8**, and then release the **Shift** key to select the range B5:C8.

2. Hold down the **Ctrl** key as you select the range **B10:C14**, and then release the **Ctrl** key. The two separate blocks of cells in the nonadjacent range B5:C8;B10:C14 are selected. See Figure 1-10.

| Figure 1-10 | Nonadjacent range B5:C8;B10:C14 selected |

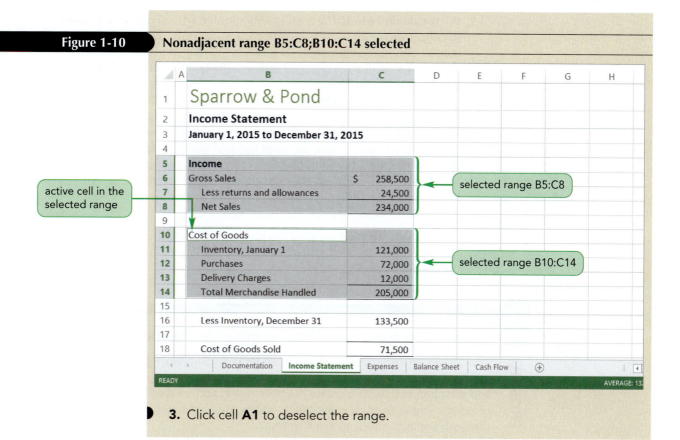

3. Click cell **A1** to deselect the range.

Closing a Workbook

When you close a workbook, a dialog box might open, asking whether you want to save the workbook. If you have made changes that you want to keep, you should save the workbook. You have finished reviewing the SP Finances workbook, so you will close it. You will not save the workbook because you want the original version to remain unchanged.

To close the SP Finances workbook:

1. On the ribbon, click the **FILE** tab to display Backstage view, and then click **Close** in the navigation bar (or press the **Ctrl+W** keys).

2. If a dialog box opens asking whether you want to save your changes to the workbook, click the **Don't Save** button. The workbook closes without saving any changes. Excel remains opens, ready for you to create or open another workbook.

Planning a Workbook

Before you begin creating a new workbook, you should develop a plan. You can do this by using a **planning analysis sheet**, which includes the following questions that help you think about the workbook's purpose and how to achieve your desired results:

1. What problems do I want to solve? The answer identifies the goal or purpose of the workbook. For example, Sally needs an easy way to record customer orders and analyze details from these orders.

2. **What data do I need?** The answer identifies the type of data that you need to collect and enter into the workbook. For example, Sally needs customer contact information, an order ID number, the date the order shipped, the shipping method, a list of books ordered, the quantity of each book ordered, and the price of each book.

3. **What calculations do I need to enter?** The answer identifies the formulas you need to apply to the data you have collected and entered. For example, Sally needs to calculate the charge for each book ordered, the number of books ordered, the shipping cost, the sales tax, and the total cost of the order.

4. **What form should my solution take?** The answer describes the appearance of the workbook content and how it should be presented to others. For example, Sally wants the information stored in a single worksheet that is easy to read and prints clearly.

Based on Sally's plan, you will create a workbook containing the details of a recent customer order. Sally will use this workbook as a model for future workbooks detailing other customer orders.

PROSKILLS

Written Communication: Creating Effective Workbooks

Workbooks convey information in written form. As with any type of writing, the final product creates an impression and provides an indicator of your interest, knowledge, and attention to detail. To create the best impression, all workbooks—especially those you intend to share with others such as coworkers and clients—should be well planned, well organized, and well written.

A well-designed workbook should clearly identify its overall goal and present information in an organized format. The data it includes—both the entered values and the calculated values—should be accurate. The process of developing an effective workbook includes the following steps:

- Determine the workbook's purpose, content, and organization before you start.
- Create a list of the sheets used in the workbook, noting each sheet's purpose.
- Insert a documentation sheet that describes the workbook's purpose and organization. Include the name of the workbook author, the date the workbook was created, and any additional information that will help others to track the workbook to its source.
- Enter all of the data in the workbook. Add labels to indicate what the values represent and, if possible, where they originated so others can view the source of your data.
- Enter formulas for calculated items rather than entering the calculated values into the workbook. For more complicated calculations, provide documentation explaining them.
- Test the workbook with a variety of values; edit the data and formulas to correct errors.
- Save the workbook and create a backup copy when the project is completed. Print the workbook's contents if you need to provide a hard-copy version to others or for your files.
- Maintain a history of your workbook as it goes through different versions, so that you and others can quickly see how the workbook has changed during revisions.

By including clearly written documentation, explanatory text, a logical organization, and accurate data and formulas, you will create effective workbooks that others can use easily.

Creating a New Workbook

You create new workbooks from the New screen in Backstage view. Similar to the Recent screen that opened when you started Excel, the New screen include templates for a variety of workbook types. You can see a preview of what the different workbooks will look like. You will create a new workbook from the Blank workbook template, in which you can add all of the content and design Sally wants for the Sparrow & Pond customer order worksheet.

To start a new, blank workbook:

TIP

You can also create a new, blank workbook by pressing the Ctrl+N keys.

1. On the ribbon, click the **FILE** tab to display Backstage view.

2. Click **New** in the navigation bar to display the New screen, which includes access to templates for a variety of workbooks.

3. Click the **Blank workbook** tile. A blank workbook opens. See Figure 1-11.

Figure 1-11	Blank workbook

Save button on the Quick Access Toolbar

workbook is named Book1 until you save it with a new name

Restore Down button appears when the window is maximized

active sheet is named Sheet1

inserts a new sheet

zoom controls

In these tutorials, the workbook window is zoomed to 120% for better readability. If you want to zoom your workbook window to match the figures, complete Step 4. If you prefer to work in the default zoom of 100% or at another zoom level, read but do not complete Step 4; you might see more or less of the worksheet on your screen, but this will not affect your work in the tutorials.

4. If you want your workbook window zoomed to 120% to match the figures, click the **Zoom In** button ➕ on the status bar twice to increase the zoom level to 120%. The 120% magnification increases the size of each cell, but reduces the number of worksheet cells visible in the workbook window.

The name of the active workbook, Book1, appears in the title bar. If you open multiple blank workbooks, they are named Book1, Book2, Book3, and so forth until you save them with a more descriptive name.

Renaming and Inserting Worksheets

Blank workbooks open with a single blank sheet named Sheet1. You can give sheets more descriptive and meaningful names. This is a good practice so that you and others can easily tell what a sheet contains. Sheet names cannot exceed 31 characters, but they can contain blank spaces and include upper- and lowercase letters.

Because Sheet1 is not a very descriptive name, Sally wants you to rename the worksheet as Customer Order.

To rename the Sheet1 worksheet:

▶ 1. Double-click the **Sheet1** tab. The Sheet1 label in the tab is selected.

▶ 2. Type **Customer Order** as the new name, and then press the **Enter** key. The width of the sheet tab expands to fit the longer sheet name.

Many workbooks include multiple sheets so that data can be organized in logical groups. A common business practice is to include a worksheet named Documentation that contains a description of the workbook, the name of the person who prepared the workbook, and the date it was created.

You will create two new worksheets. You will rename one worksheet as Documentation and you will rename the other worksheet as Customer Contact to record the customer's contact information.

To insert and name the Documentation and Customer Contact worksheets:

▶ 1. To the right of the Customer Order sheet tab, click the **New sheet** button ⊕. A new sheet named Sheet2 is inserted to the right of the Customer Order sheet.

▶ 2. Double-click the **Sheet2** sheet tab, type **Documentation** as the new name, and then press the **Enter** key. The second worksheet is renamed.

▶ 3. To the right of the Documentation sheet, click the **New sheet** button ⊕, and then rename the inserted worksheet as **Customer Contact**.

Moving Worksheets

A good practice is to place the most important sheets at the beginning of the workbook (the leftmost sheet tabs) and less important sheets at the end (the rightmost sheet tabs). To change the placement of sheets in a workbook, you drag them by their sheet tabs to the new location.

Sally wants you to move the Documentation worksheet to the front of the workbook, so that it appears before the Customer Order sheet.

To move the Documentation worksheet:

▶ 1. Point to the **Documentation** sheet tab.

TIP

To copy a sheet, hold down the Ctrl key as you drag and drop its sheet tab.

▶ 2. Press and hold the mouse button. The pointer changes to ⬚, and a small arrow appears in the upper-left corner of the tab.

▶ 3. Drag to the left until the small arrow appears in the upper-left corner of the Customer Order sheet tab, and then release the mouse button. The Documentation worksheet is now the first sheet in the workbook.

Deleting Worksheets

In some workbooks, you will want to delete an existing sheet. The easiest way to delete a sheet is by using a **shortcut menu**, which is a list of commands related to a selection that opens when you click the right mouse button. Sally asks you to include the customer's contact information on the Customer Order worksheet so all of the information is on one sheet.

To delete the Customer Contact worksheet from the workbook:

▶ **1.** Right-click the **Customer Contact** sheet tab. A shortcut menu opens.

▶ **2.** Click **Delete**. The Customer Contact worksheet is removed from the workbook.

Saving a Workbook

As you modify a workbook, you should save it regularly—every 10 minutes or so is a good practice. The first time you save a workbook, the Save As dialog box opens so you can name the file and choose where to save it. You can save the workbook on your computer or network, or to your account on SkyDrive.

To save your workbook for the first time:

▶ **1.** On the Quick Access Toolbar, click the **Save** button 🖫 (or press the **Ctrl+S** keys). The Save As screen in Backstage view opens.

▶ **2.** Click **Computer** in the Places list, and then click the **Browse** button. The Save As dialog box opens.

   Trouble? If your instructor wants you to save your files to your SkyDrive account, click SkyDrive, and then log in to your account, if necessary.

▶ **3.** Navigate to the location specified by your instructor.

▶ **4.** In the File name box, select **Book1** (the suggested name) if it is not already selected, and then type **SP Customer Order**.

▶ **5.** Verify that **Excel Workbook** appears in the Save as type box.

▶ **6.** Click the **Save** button. The workbook is saved, the dialog box closes, and the workbook window reappears with the new filename in the title bar.

As you modify the workbook, you will need to resave the file. Because you already saved the workbook with a filename, the next time you save, the Save command saves the changes you made to the workbook without opening the Save As dialog box.

Entering Text, Dates, and Numbers

Workbook content is entered into worksheet cells. Those cells can contain text, numbers, or dates and times. **Text data** is any combination of letters, numbers, and symbols. Text data is often referred to as a **text string** because it contains a series, or string, of text characters. **Numeric data** is any number that can be used in a mathematical calculation. **Date** and **time data** are commonly recognized formats for date and time values. For example, Excel interprets the cell entry April 15, 2016 as a date and not as text. New data is placed into the active cell of the current worksheet. As you enter data, the entry appears in both the active cell and the formula bar. By default, text is left-aligned in cells, and numbers, dates, and times are right-aligned.

Entering Text

Text is often used in worksheets to label other data and to identify areas of a sheet. Sally wants you to enter some of the information from the planning analysis sheet into the Documentation sheet.

To enter the text for the Documentation sheet:

1. Press the **Ctrl+Home** keys to make sure cell A1 is the active cell on the Documentation sheet.

2. Type **Sparrow and Pond** in cell A1. As you type, the text appears in cell A1 and in the formula bar.

3. Press the **Enter** key twice. The text is entered into cell A1 and the active cell moves down two rows to cell A3.

4. Type **Author** in cell A3, and then press the **Tab** key. The text is entered and the active cell moves one column to the right to cell B3.

5. Type your name in cell B3, and then press the **Enter** key. The text is entered and the active cell moves one cell down and to the left to cell A4.

6. Type **Date** in cell A4, and then press the **Tab** key. The text is entered and the active cell moves one column to the right to cell B4, where you would enter the date you created the worksheet. For now, you will leave the cell for the date blank.

7. Click cell **A5** to make it the active cell, type **Purpose** in the cell, and then press the **Tab** key. The active cell moves one column to the right to cell B5.

8. Type **To record customer book orders**. in cell B5, and then press the **Enter** key. Figure 1-12 shows the text entered in the Documentation sheet.

Figure 1-12 **Documentation sheet**

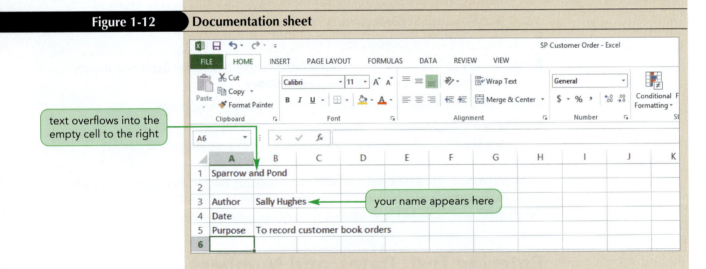

text overflows into the empty cell to the right

your name appears here

The text you entered in cell A1 is so long that it appears to overflow into cell B1. The same is true for the text you entered in cells B3 and B5. Any text you enter in a cell that doesn't fit within that cell will cover the adjacent cells to the right as long as they are empty. If the adjacent cells contain data, only the text that fits into the cell is displayed. The rest of the text entry is hidden from view. The text itself is not affected. The complete text is still entered in the cell; it is just not displayed. (You will learn how to display all text in a cell in the next session.)

Undoing and Redoing an Action

As you enter data in a workbook, you might need to undo a previous action. Excel maintains a list of the actions you performed in the workbook during the current session, so you can undo most of your actions. You can use the Undo button on the Quick Access Toolbar or press the Ctrl+Z keys to reverse your most recent actions one at a time. If you want to undo more than one action, you can click the Undo button arrow and then select the earliest action you want to undo—all of the actions after the earliest action you selected are also undone.

You will undo the most recent change you made to the Documentation sheet—the text you entered into cell B5. Then you will enter more descriptive and accurate description of the worksheet's purpose.

To undo the text entry in cell B5:

1. On the Quick Access Toolbar, click the **Undo** button ↺ (or press the **Ctrl+Z** keys). The last action is reversed, removing the text you entered in cell B5.

2. In cell B5, type **To record book orders from a Sparrow & Pond customer.** and then press the **Enter** key.

If you want to restore actions you have undone, you can redo them. To redo one action at a time, you can click the Redo button ↻ on the Quick Access Toolbar or press the Ctrl+Y keys. To redo multiple actions at once, you can click the Redo button arrow and then click the earliest action you want to redo. After you undo or redo an action, Excel continues the action list starting from any new changes you make to the workbook.

Editing Cell Content

As you work, you might find mistakes you need to correct or entries that you want to change. If you want to replace all of the content in a cell, you simply select the cell and then type the new entry to overwrite the previous entry. However, if you need to replace only part of a cell's content, you can work in **Edit mode**. To switch to Edit mode, you double-click the cell. A blinking insertion point indicates where the new content you type will be inserted. In the cell or formula bar, the pointer changes to an I-beam, which you can use to select text in the cell. Anything you type replaces the selected content.

You need to edit the text in cell A1 to Sparrow & Pond. You will switch to Edit mode to correct the text.

To edit the text in cell A1:

1. Double-click cell **A1** to select the cell and switch to Edit mode. A blinking insertion point appears within the text of cell A1. The status bar displays EDIT instead of READY to indicate that the cell is in Edit mode.

2. Press the arrow keys to move the insertion point directly to the right of the word "and" in the company name.

3. Press the **Backspace** key three times to delete the word "and."

4. Type **&** to enter the new text, and then press the **Enter** key. The cell text changes to Sparrow & Pond. See Figure 1-13.

Figure 1-13 Revised Documentation sheet

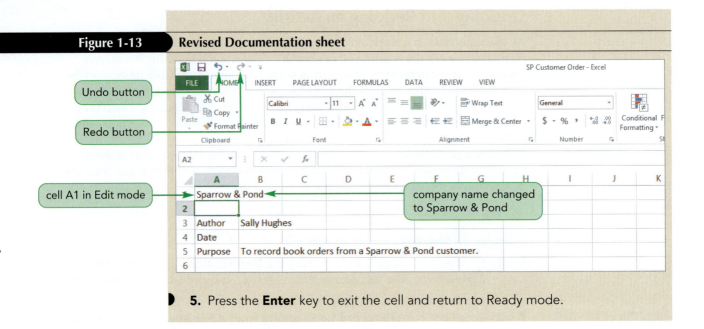

5. Press the **Enter** key to exit the cell and return to Ready mode.

Understanding AutoComplete

As you type text in the active cell, Excel tries to anticipate the remaining characters by displaying text that begins with the same letters as a previous entry in the same column. This feature, known as **AutoComplete**, helps make entering repetitive text easier. To accept the suggested text, press the Tab or Enter key. To override the suggested text, continue to type the text you want to enter in the cell. AutoComplete does not work with dates or numbers, or when a blank cell is between the previous entry and the text you are typing.

Next, you will enter the contact information for Tobias Gregson, a customer who recently placed an order with Sparrow & Pond. You will enter the contact information on the Customer Order worksheet.

To enter Tobias Gregson's contact information:

1. Click the **Customer Order** sheet tab to make it the active sheet.

2. In cell A1, type **Customer Order** as the worksheet title, and then press the **Enter** key twice. The worksheet title is entered in cell A1, and the active cell is cell A3.

3. Type **Ship To** in cell A3, and then press the **Enter** key. The label is entered in the cell, and the active cell is now cell A4.

4. In the range A4:A10, enter the following labels, pressing the **Enter** key after each entry and ignoring any AutoComplete suggestions: **First Name, Last Name, Address, City, State, Postal Code**, and **Phone**.

5. Click cell **B4** to make that cell the active cell.

6. In the range B4:B10, enter the following contact information, pressing the **Enter** key after each entry and ignoring any AutoComplete suggestions: **Tobias, Gregson, 412 Apple Grove St., Nashua, NH, 03061,** and **(603) 555-4128.** See Figure 1-14.

Figure 1-14   **Text entered in the Customer Order worksheet**

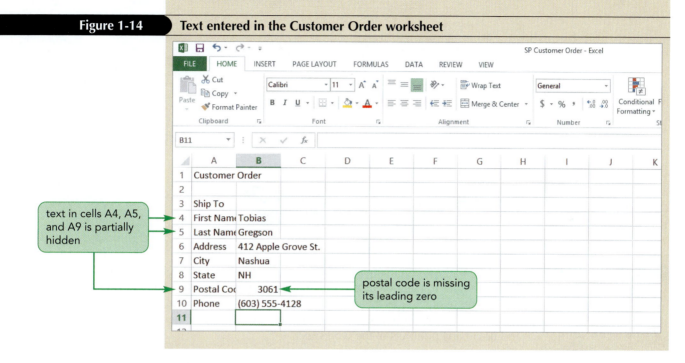

text in cells A4, A5, and A9 is partially hidden

postal code is missing its leading zero

Displaying Numbers as Text

When you type numbers in the active cell, Excel treats the entry as a number and ignores any leading zero. For example, in cell B9, the first digit of the postal code 03061 is missing; Excel displays 3061 because the numbers 3061 and 03061 have the same value. To specify that a number entry should be considered text and all digits should be displayed, you include an apostrophe (') before the numbers.

You will make this change in cell B9 so that Excel treats the postal code as text and displays all of the digits you type.

To enter the postal code as text:

1. Click cell **B9** to select it. Notice that the postal code is right-aligned in the cell, unlike the other text entries, which are left-aligned—another indication that the entry is being treated as a number.

2. Type **'03061** in cell B9, and then press the **Enter** key. The text 03061 appears in cell B9 and is left-aligned in the cell, matching all of the other text entries. See Figure 1-15.

Figure 1-15 Number displayed as text

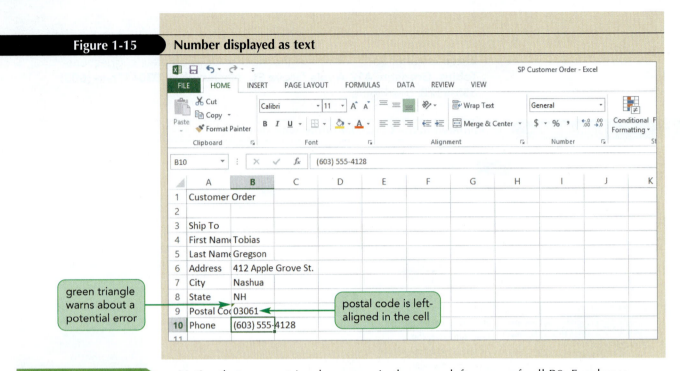

green triangle warns about a potential error

postal code is left-aligned in the cell

TIP

To remove a green triangle, click the cell, click the yellow caution icon that appears to the left of the cell, and then click Ignore Error.

Notice that a green triangle appears in the upper-left corner of cell B9. Excel uses green triangles to flag potential errors in cells. In this case, it is simply a warning that you entered a number as a text string. Because this is intentional, you do not have to edit the cell to fix the "error." Green triangles appear only in the workbook window and not in any printouts of the worksheet.

Entering Dates

You can enter dates in any of the standard date formats. For example, all of the following entries are recognized by Excel as the same date:

- 4/6/2016
- 4/6/16
- 4-6-2016
- April 6, 2016
- 6-Apr-16

Even though you enter a date as text, Excel stores the date as a number equal to the number of days between the specified date and January 0, 1900. Times are also entered as text and stored as fractions of a 24-hour day. For example, the date and time April 4, 2016 @ 6:00 PM is stored by Excel as 42,464.75. Dates and times are stored as numbers so that Excel can easily perform date and time calculations, such as determining the elapsed time between one date and another.

Based on the default date format your computer uses, Excel might alter the format of a date after you type it. For example, if you enter the date 4/6/16 into the active cell, Excel might display the date with the four-digit year value, 4/6/2016; if you enter the text April 6, 2016, Excel might convert the date format to 6-Apr-16. Changing the date or time format does not affect the underlying date or time value.

INSIGHT

International Date Formats

As business transactions become more international in scope, you may need to adopt international standards for expressing dates, times, and currency values in your workbooks. For example, a worksheet cell might contain 06/05/16. This format could represent any of the following dates: the 5th of June, 2016; the 6th of May, 2016; and the 16th of May, 2006.

The date depends on which country the workbook has been designed for. You can avoid this problem by entering the full date, as in June 5, 2016. However, this might not work with documents written in foreign languages, such as Japanese, that use different character symbols.

To solve this problem, many international businesses adopt ISO (International Organization for Standardization) dates in the format *yyyy-mm-dd*, where *yyyy* is the four-digit year value, *mm* is the two-digit month value, and *dd* is the two-digit day value. So, a date such as June 5, 2016 is entered as 2016/06/05. If you choose to use this international date format, make sure that people using your workbook understand this format so they do not misinterpret the dates. You can include information about the date format in the Documentation sheet.

For the SP Customer Order workbook, you will enter dates in the format *mm/dd/yyyy*, where *mm* is the 2-digit month number, *dd* is the 2-digit day number, and *yyyy* is the 4-digit year number.

To enter the current date into the Documentation sheet:

1. Click the **Documentation** sheet tab to make the Documentation sheet the active worksheet.

2. Click cell **B4** to make it active, type the current date in the *mm/dd/yyyy* format, and then press the **Enter** key. The date is entered in the cell.

   Trouble? Depending on your system configuration, Excel might change the date to the date format *dd-mmm-yy*. This difference will not affect your work.

3. Make the **Customer Order** worksheet the active sheet.

The next part of the Customer Order worksheet will list the books the customer purchased from Sparrow & Pond. As shown in Figure 1-16, the list includes identifying information about each book, its price, and the quantity ordered.

Figure 1-16   Book order from Tobias Gregson

ISBN	CATEGORY	BINDING	TITLE	AUTHOR(S)	PRICE	QTY
0-374-25385-4	Used	Hardcover	Samurai William: The Englishman Who Opened Japan	Milton, Giles	$5.95	2
4-889-96213-1	New	Softcover	Floral Origami Globes	Fuse, Tomoko	$24.95	3
0-500-27062-7	New	Hardcover	Tao Magic: The Secret Language of Diagrams and Calligraphy	Legeza, Laszlo	$8.95	1
0-785-82169-4	Used	Hardcover	The Holy Grail	Morgan, Giles	$3.75	1
0-854-56516-7	New	Softcover	Murder on the Links	Christie, Agatha	$7.50	2

You will enter the first five columns of the book order into the worksheet.

To enter the first part of the book order:

▶ 1. In the Customer Order worksheet, click cell **A12** to make it the active cell, type **ISBN** as the column label, and then press the **Tab** key to move to cell B12.

▶ 2. In the range B12:E12, type the following labels, pressing the **Tab** key to move to the next cell: **CATEGORY**, **BINDING**, **TITLE**, and **AUTHOR(S)**.

▶ 3. Press the **Enter** key to go to the next row of the worksheet, making cell A13 the active cell.

▶ 4. In the range A13:E17, enter the ISBN, category, binding, title, and author text for the five books listed in Figure 1-16, pressing the **Tab** key to move from one cell to the next, and pressing the **Enter** key to move to a new row. See Figure 1-17. The text in some cells will be partially hidden; you will fix that problem shortly.

Figure 1-17	Tobias Gregson's partial book order

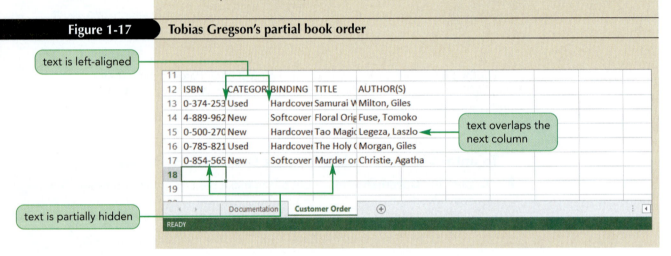

text is left-aligned

text overlaps the next column

text is partially hidden

Entering Numbers

In Excel, numbers can be integers such as 378, decimals such as 1.95, or negatives such as −5.2. In the case of currency and percentages, you can include the currency symbol and percent sign when you enter the value. Excel treats a currency value such as $87.25 as the number 87.25, and a percentage such as 95% as the decimal 0.95. Much like dates, currency and percentages are formatted in a convenient way for you to read, but only the number is stored within the cell. This makes it easier to perform calculations with currency and percentage values.

You will complete the information for Tobias Gregson's order by entering the price for each title and the quantity of each title he ordered.

To enter the price and quantity of books ordered:

▶ 1. In the range F12:G12, enter **PRICE** and **QTY** as the labels.

▶ 2. In cell F13, enter **$5.95** as the price of the first book. The book price is stored as a number but displayed with the $ symbol.

▶ 3. In cell G13, enter **2** as the quantity of books ordered.

▶ 4. In the range F14:G17, enter the remaining prices and quantities shown in Figure 1-16. See Figure 1-18.

Figure 1-18 **Price and quantity data**

	ISBN	CATEGOR	BINDING	TITLE	AUTHOR(S	PRICE	QTY	
11								
12	ISBN	CATEGOR	BINDING	TITLE	AUTHOR(S	PRICE	QTY	
13	0-374-253	Used	Hardcover	Samurai W	Milton, Gil	$5.95	2	numbers are right-aligned
14	4-889-962	New	Softcover	Floral Orig	Fuse, Tom	$24.95	3	
15	0-500-270	New	Hardcover	Tao Magic	Legeza, La	$8.95	1	
16	0-785-821	Used	Hardcover	The Holy (	Morgan, G	$3.75	1	
17	0-854-565	New	Softcover	Murder or	Christie, A	$7.50	2	
18								
19								

price stored as a number formatted as currency

Documentation   **Customer Order**   ⊕

READY

5. On the Quick Access Toolbar, click the **Save** button 🖫 (or press the **Ctrl+S** keys) to save the workbook.

Resizing Columns and Rows

Much of the information in the Customer Order worksheet is difficult to read because of the hidden text. You can make the cell content easier to read by changing the size of the columns and rows in the worksheet.

Changing Column Widths

Column widths are expressed as the number of characters the column can contain. The default column width is 8.43 standard-sized characters. In general, this means that you can type eight characters in a cell; any additional text is hidden or overlaps the adjacent cell. Column widths are also expressed in terms of pixels. A **pixel** is a single point on a computer monitor or printout. A column width of 8.43 characters is equivalent to 64 pixels.

INSIGHT

Setting Column Widths

On a computer monitor, pixel size is based on screen resolution. As a result, cell contents that look fine on one screen might appear very different when viewed on a screen with a different resolution. If you work on multiple computers or share your workbooks with others, you should set column widths based on the maximum number of characters you want displayed in the cells rather than pixel size. This ensures that everyone sees the cell contents the way you intended.

You will increase the width of column A so that the contact information labels in cells A4 and A5 and the ISBN numbers in the range A13:A17 are completely displayed.

To increase the width of column A:

1. Move the pointer over the right border of the column A heading until the pointer changes to ↔.

2. Click and drag to the right until the width of the column heading reaches **15** characters, but do not release the mouse button. The ScreenTip that appears as you resize the column shows the new column width in characters and in pixels.

3. Release the mouse button. The width of column A expands to 15 characters, and all of the text within that column is visible within the cells. See Figure 1-19.

| Figure 1-19 | Width of column A increased |

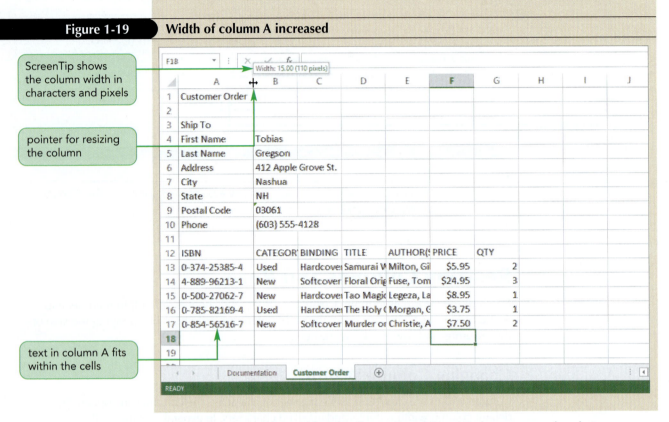

ScreenTip shows the column width in characters and pixels

pointer for resizing the column

text in column A fits within the cells

You will increase the widths of columns B and C to 18 characters so that their complete entries are visible. Rather than resizing each column separately, you can select both columns and adjust their widths at the same time.

To increase the widths of columns B and C:

1. Click the **column B** heading. The entire column is selected.

2. Hold down the **Ctrl** key, click the **column C** heading, and then release the **Ctrl** key. Both columns B and C are selected.

3. Move the pointer to the right border of the column C heading until the pointer changes to ↔.

4. Drag to the right until the column width changes to **18** characters, and then release the mouse button. Both column widths increase to 18 characters and display all of the entered text.

The book titles in column D are partially hidden. You will increase the width of this column to 30 characters. Rather than using your mouse, you can set the column width using the Format command on the HOME tab. The Format command gives you precise control over setting column widths and row heights.

To set the width of column D with the Format command:

1. Click the **column D** heading. The entire column is selected.

2. On the HOME tab, in the Cells group, click the **Format** button, and then click **Column Width**. The Column Width dialog box opens.

3. Type **30** in the Column width box to specify the new column width.

4. Click the **OK** button. The width of column D changes to 30 characters.

5. Change the width of column E to **15** characters.

6. Click cell **A1**. The revised column widths are shown in Figure 1-20.

Figure 1-20   Resized columns

Even with the width of column D increased, some of the book titles still don't fit within the allotted space. Instead of manually changing the column width to display all of the text, you can autofit the column. **AutoFit** changes the column width or row height to display the longest or tallest entry within the column or row. You autofit a column or a row by double-clicking the right border of the column heading or the bottom border of the row heading.

TIP

If the row or column is blank, autofitting restores its default height or width.

To autofit the contents of column D:

1. Move the pointer over the right border of column D until the pointer changes to ✛.

2. Double-click the right border of the column D heading. The width of column D increases to about 54 characters so that the longest book title is completely visible.

Wrapping Text Within a Cell

Sometimes, resizing a column width to display all of the text entered in the cells makes the worksheet more difficult to read. This is the case with column D in the Customer Order worksheet. Another way to display long text entries is to wrap text to a new line when it extends beyond the column width. When text wraps within a cell, the row height increases so that all of the text within the cell is displayed.

You will resize column D, and then wrap the text entries in the column.

To wrap text in column D:

1. Resize the width of column D to **30** characters.

2. Select the range **D13:D17**. These cells include the titles that extend beyond the new cell width.

3. On the HOME tab, in the Alignment group, click the **Wrap Text** button. The Wrap Text button is toggled on, and text in the selected cells that exceeds the column width wraps to a new line.

4. Click cell **A12** to make it the active cell. See Figure 1-21.

| Figure 1-21 | Text wrapped within cells |

If you want to create a new line within a cell, press the Alt+Enter keys to move the insertion point to the next line within the cell. Whatever you type next will appear on the new line in the cell.

Changing Row Heights

The height of a row is measured in points or pixels. A **point** is approximately 1/72 of an inch. The default row height is 15 points or 20 pixels. Row heights are set in the same way as column widths. You can drag the bottom border of the row heading to a new row height, specify a row height using the Format command, or autofit the row's height to match its content.

Sanjit wants you add more space above the labels in the book list by resizing row 12.

To increase the height of row 12:

1. Move the pointer over the bottom border of the row 12 heading until the pointer changes to ✛.

2. Drag the bottom border down until the height of the row is equal to **30** points (or **40** pixels), and then release the mouse button. The height of row 12 is set to 30 points.

3. Press the **Ctrl+S** keys to save the workbook.

TIP

You can also set the row height by clicking the Format button in the Cells group on the HOME tab and then using the Row Height command.

You have entered most of the data for Tobias Gregson's order at Sparrow & Pond. In the next session, you will calculate the total charge for the order and print the worksheet.

Session 1.1 Quick Check

REVIEW

1. What are the two types of sheets used in a workbook?
2. What is the cell reference for the cell located in the fourth column and third row of a worksheet?
3. What is the range reference for the block of cells B10 through C15?
4. What is the reference for the nonadjacent block of cells B10 through C15 and cells B20 through D25?
5. What keyboard shortcut changes the active cell to cell A1?
6. What is text data?
7. Cell A4 contains *May 3, 2016*; why doesn't Excel consider this entry a text string?
8. How do you resize a column or row?

Session 1.2 Visual Overview:

The **font size** refers to how big the text is.

You use the PAGE LAYOUT tab to change how the worksheet will appear on the printed page.

In Excel, every formula begins with an equal sign (=).

When the active cell contains a formula, the formula appears in the formula bar but the result of the formula appears in the cell.

The gridlines that surround cells appear on the worksheet as a guide; they do not print.

A **border** is a line you can add along an edge of a cell. Borders are used to improve the readability of data.

SP Customer Order - Excel

FILE | HOME | INSERT | PAGE LAYOUT | FORMULAS | DATA | REVIEW | VIEW

Calibri | 11 | A A
B I U
Paste
Clipboard | Font | Alignment | Number
Currency
$ % , .00 .00

I23   fx   =G23*H23

	A	B	C	D	E
9	Ship To				
10	First Name	Tobias			
11	Last Name	Gregson			
12	Address	412 Apple Grove St.			
13	City	Nashua			
14	State	NH			
15	Postal Code	03061			
16	Phone	(603) 555-4128			
17					
18	BOOK ID	ISBN	CATEGORY	BINDING	TITLE
19	25385-Used	0-374-25385-4	Used	Hardcover	Samurai William: The Who Opened Japan
20	96213-New	4-889-96213-1	New	Softcover	Floral Origami Globes
21	01089-Used	0-151-01089-7	Used	Hardcover	Pops: A Life of Louis A
22	27062-New	0-500-27062-7	New	Hardcover	Tao Magic: The Secret Diagrams and Calligra
23	56516-New	0-854-56516-7	New	Softcover	Murder on the Links
24					
25					
26					
27					
28					

◄ ►   Documentation   **Customer Order**   ⊕

READY

6. With the insertion point still blinking in cell B6, select the range **G19:G23**. The range reference is entered as the argument for the COUNT function.

7. Type **)** to complete the function, and then press the **Enter** key. Cell B6 displays the value 5, indicating that five items were ordered by Tobias Gregson. Cell A7 is the active cell.

8. Type **Total Charge** as the label in cell A7, and then press the **Tab** key to make cell B7 the active cell.

9. Type **=** to start the formula, and then click cell **H28** to enter its cell reference in the formula in cell B7. The formula =H28 tells Excel to display the contents of cell H28 in the current cell.

10. Press the **Enter** key to complete the formula. See Figure 1-29.

Figure 1-29	Customer order summary

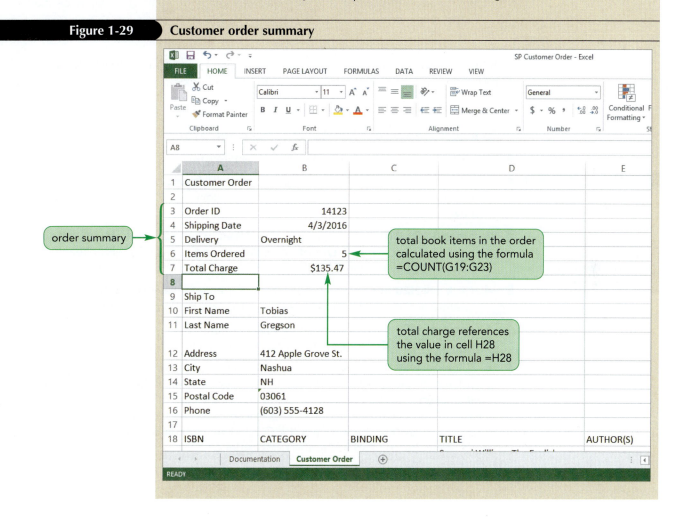

Inserting a Column or Row

You can insert a new column or row anywhere within a worksheet. When you insert a new column, the existing columns are shifted to the right and the new column has the same width as the column directly to its left. When you insert a new row, the existing rows are shifted down and the new row has the same height as the row above it. Because inserting a new row or column moves the location of the other cells in the worksheet, any cell references in a formula or function are updated to reflect the new layout.

Inserting or Deleting a Column or Row

To insert a column or row:
- Select the column(s) or row(s) where you want to insert the new column(s) or row(s). Excel will insert the same number of columns or rows as you select to the *left* of the selected columns or *above* the selected rows.
- On the HOME tab, in the Cells group, click the Insert button (or right-click a column or row heading or selected column and row headings, and then click Insert on the shortcut menu; or press the Ctrl+Shift+= keys).

To delete a column or row:
- Select the column(s) or row(s) you want to delete.
- On the HOME tab, in the Cells group, click the Delete button (or right-click a column or row heading or selected column and row headings, and then click Delete on the shortcut menu; or press the Ctrl+− keys).

Tobias Gregson's order is missing an item. You need to insert a row directly below *Floral Origami Globes* in which to enter the additional book.

To insert a new row for the missing book order:

1. Click the **row 21** heading to select the entire row.

2. On the HOME tab, in the Cells group, click the **Insert** button (or press the **Ctrl+Shift+=** keys). A new row is inserted below row 20 and becomes the new row 21.

3. Enter **0-151-01089-7** in cell A21, enter **Used** in cell B21, enter **Hardcover** in cell C21, enter **Pops: A Life of Louis Armstrong** in cell D21, enter **Teachout, Terry** in cell E21, enter **$11.95** in cell F21, and then enter **2** in cell G21.

4. Click cell **H20** to select the cell with the formula for calculating the book charge, and then press the **Ctrl+C** keys to copy the formula in that cell.

5. Click cell **H21** to select the cell where you want to insert the formula, and then press the **Ctrl+V** keys to paste the formula into the cell.

6. Click cell **H26**. The formula in this cell is now =SUM(H19:H24); the range reference was updated to reflect the inserted row. Also, the tax amount increased to $6.92 based on the new subtotal value of $138.35, and the total charge increased to $160.57 because of the added book order. See Figure 1-30. Also, the result of the COUNT function in cell B6 increased to 6 to reflect the item added to the book order.

> **TIP**
>
> You can insert multiple columns or rows by selecting that number of column or row headings, and then clicking the Insert button or pressing the Ctrl+Shift+= keys.

Figure 1-30   New row inserted

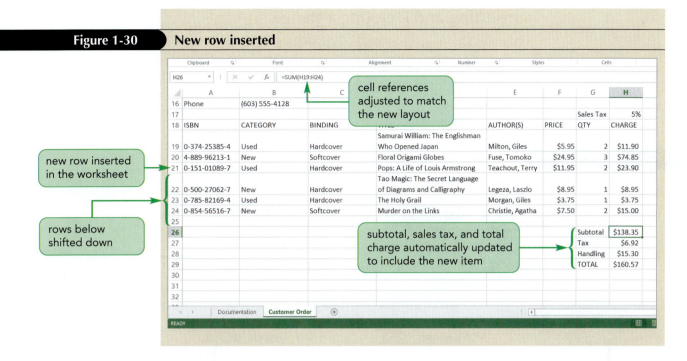

new row inserted
in the worksheet

rows below
shifted down

cell references
adjusted to match
the new layout

subtotal, sales tax, and total
charge automatically updated
to include the new item

Deleting a Row or Column

You can delete rows or columns from a worksheet. **Deleting** removes the data from the row or column as well as the row or column itself. The rows below the deleted row shift up to fill the vacated space. Likewise, the columns to the right of the deleted column shift left to fill the vacated space. Also, all cell references in the worksheet are adjusted to reflect the change. You click the Delete button in the Cells group on the HOME tab to delete selected rows or columns.

Deleting a column or row is not the same as clearing a column or row. **Clearing** removes the data from the selected row or column but leaves the blank row or column in the worksheet. You press the Delete key to clear the contents of the selected row or column, which leaves the worksheet structure unchanged.

Tobias Gregson did not order *The Holy Grail* by Giles Morgan, so that book needs to be removed from the order. You will delete the row containing that book.

To delete the *The Holy Grail* row from the book order:

▸ **1.** Click the **row 23** heading to select the entire row.

▸ **2.** On the HOME tab, in the Cells group, click the **Delete** button (or press the **Ctrl+−** keys). Row 23 is deleted, and the rows below it shift up to fill the space.

All of the cell references in the worksheet are again updated automatically to reflect the impact of deleting row 23. The subtotal value in cell H25 now returns a value of $134.60 based on the sum of the cells in the range H19:H23. The sales tax amount in cell H26 decreases to $6.73. The total cost of the order decreases to $156.63. Also, the result of the COUNT function in cell B6 decreases to 5 to reflect the item deleted from the book order. As you can see, one of the great advantages of using Excel is that it modifies the formulas to reflect the additions and deletions you make to the worksheet.

Inserting and Deleting a Range

You can also insert or delete ranges within a worksheet. When you use the Insert button to insert a range of cells, the existing cells shift down when the selected range is wider than it is long, and they shift right when the selected range is longer than it is wide, as shown in Figure 1-31. When you use the Insert Cells command, you specify whether the existing cells shift right or down, or whether to insert an entire row or column into the new range.

Figure 1-31	Cells being inserted in a worksheet

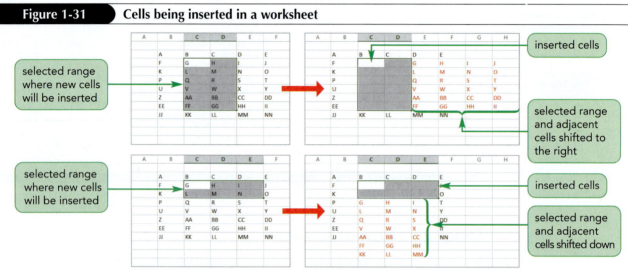

selected range where new cells will be inserted

inserted cells

selected range and adjacent cells shifted to the right

selected range where new cells will be inserted

inserted cells

selected range and adjacent cells shifted down

© 2014 Cengage Learning

The process works in reverse when you delete a range. As with deleting a row or column, the cells adjacent to the deleted range either move up or left to fill in the space vacated by the deleted cells. The Delete Cells command lets you specify whether you want to shift the adjacent cells left or up, or whether you want to delete the entire column or row.

When you insert or delete a range, cells that shift to a new location adopt the width of the columns they move into. As a result, you might need to resize columns and rows in the worksheet.

REFERENCE

Inserting or Deleting a Range

- Select a range that matches the range you want to insert or delete.
- On the HOME tab, in the Cells group, click the Insert button or the Delete button.

or

- Select the range that matches the range you want to insert or delete.
- On the HOME tab, in the Cells group, click the Insert button arrow and then click Insert Cells, or click the Delete button arrow and then click Delete Cells (or right-click the selected range, and then click Insert or Delete on the shortcut menu).
- Click the option button for the direction to shift the cells, columns, or rows.
- Click the OK button.

Sally wants you to insert cells in the book list that will contain the Sparrow & Pond book ID for each book. You will insert these new cells into the range A17:A28, shifting the adjacent cells to the right.

To insert a range in the book list:

1. Select the range **A17:A28**. You want to insert cells in this range.

2. On the HOME tab, in the Cells group, click the **Insert button arrow**. A menu of insert options appears.

3. Click **Insert Cells**. The Insert dialog box opens.

4. Verify that the **Shift cells right** option button is selected.

5. Click the **OK** button. New cells are inserted into the selected range, and the adjacent cells move to the right. The cell contents do not fit well in the columns and rows they shifted into, so you will resize the columns and rows.

6. Resize columns C and D to **12** characters, resize column E to **30** characters, and then resize column F to **15** characters. The text is easier to read in the resized columns.

7. Select the row **19** through row **23** headings.

8. In the Cells group, click the **Format** button, and then click **AutoFit Row Height**. The selected rows autofit to their contents.

9. Click cell **A18**, type **BOOK ID** as the label, and then press the **Enter** key. See Figure 1-32.

TIP

You can also autofit by double-clicking the bottom border of row 23.

Figure 1-32 **Range added to the worksheet**

Why did you insert cells in the range A17:A28 even though the book ID values will be entered only in the range A18:A23? You did this to retain the layout of the page design. Selecting the additional rows ensures that the sales tax and summary values still line up with the QTY and CHARGE columns. Whenever you insert a new range, be sure to consider its impact on the layout of the entire worksheet.

Hiding and Unhiding Rows, Columns, and Worksheets

Workbooks can become long and complicated, filled with formulas and data that are important for performing calculations but are of little interest to readers. In those situations, you can simplify these workbooks for readers by **hiding** rows, columns, and even worksheets. Although the contents of hidden cells cannot be seen, the data in those cells is still available for use in formulas and functions throughout the workbook.

Hiding a row or column essentially decreases that row height or column width to 0 pixels. To a hide a row or column, select the row or column heading, click the Format button in the Cells group on the HOME tab, point to Hide & Unhide on the menu that appears, and then click Hide Rows or Hide Columns. The border of the row or column heading is doubled to mark the location of hidden rows or columns.

A worksheet often is hidden when the entire worksheet contains data that is not of interest to the reader and is better summarized elsewhere in the document. To hide a worksheet, make that worksheet active, click the Format button in the Cells group on the HOME tab, point to Hide & Unhide, and then click Hide Sheet.

Unhiding redisplays the hidden content in the workbook. To unhide a row or column, click in a cell below the hidden row or to the right of the hidden column, click the Format button, point to Hide & Unhide, and then click Unhide Rows or Unhide Columns. To unhide a worksheet, click the Format button, point to Hide & Unhide, and then click Unhide Sheet. The Unhide dialog box opens. Click the sheet you want to unhide, and then click the OK button. The hidden content is redisplayed in the workbook.

Although hiding data can make a worksheet and workbook easier to read, be sure never to hide information that is important to the reader.

Sally wants you to add one more piece of data to the worksheet—a book ID that is used by Sparrow & Pond to identify each book in stock. You will use Flash Fill to create the book IDs.

Using Flash Fill

Flash Fill enters text based on patterns it finds in the data. As shown in Figure 1-33, Flash Fill generates customer names from the first and last names stored in the adjacent columns in the worksheet. To enter the rest of the names, you press the Enter key; to continue typing the names yourself, you press the Esc key.

Figure 1-33   **Entering text with Flash Fill**

	A	B	C	D	E
1	First	M.I.	Last	Full Name	
2	Tobias	A.	Gregson	Tobias Gregson	
3	Maria	R.	Sanchez	Maria Sanchez	
4	Andrew	T.	Lewis	Andrew Lewis	
5	Brett	K.	Carls	Brett Carls	
6	Carmen	A.	Hzu	Carmen Hzu	
7	Karen	M.	Schultz	Karen Schultz	
8	Howard	P.	Gary	Howard Gary	
9	Natalia	N.	Shapiro	Natalia Shapiro	
10	Paul	O.	Douglas	Paul Douglas	
11					

you enter the full name twice to begin the pattern

Flash Fill generates the remaining full names based on the pattern in the first two cells

Flash Fill works best when the pattern is clearly recognized from the values in the data. Be sure to enter the data pattern in the column or row right next to the related data. The data used to generate the pattern must be in a rectangular grid and cannot have blank columns or rows. Also, Flash Fill enters text, not formulas. If you edit or replace an entry originally used by Flash Fill, the content generated by Flash Fill will not be updated.

The Sparrow & Pond book ID combines five digits of the book's ISBN and its category (used or new). For example, *Floral Origami Globes* has the ISBN 4-889-96213-1 and is new, so its book ID is 96213-New. The book IDs follow a consistent and logical pattern. Rather than typing every book ID, you will use Flash Fill to enter the book IDs into the worksheet.

To enter the book IDs using Flash Fill:

1. Make sure that cell **A19** is the active cell.

2. Type **25385-Used** as the ID for the first book in the list, and then press the **Enter** key.

3. Type **9** in cell A20. As soon as you start typing, Flash Fill generates the remaining entries in the column based on the pattern you entered. See Figure 1-34.

Figure 1-34 **Book IDs generated by Flash Fill**

book ID is based on the ISBN and Category values

book ID values suggested by Flash Fill

4. Press the **Enter** key to accept the suggested entries.

Formatting a Worksheet

Formatting changes a workbook's appearance to make the content of a worksheet easier to read. Two common formatting changes are adding borders to cells and changing the font size of text.

Adding Cell Borders

Sometimes you want to include lines along the edges of cells to enhance the readability of rows and columns of data. You can do this by adding borders to the left, top, right, or bottom edge of a cell or range. You can also specify the thickness of and the number of lines in the border. This is especially helpful when a worksheet is printed because the gridlines that surround the cells are not printed by default; they appear on the worksheet only as a guide.

Sally wants add borders around the cells that contain content in the Customer Order worksheet to make the content easier to read.

To add borders around the worksheet cells:

1. Select the range **A3:B7**. You will add borders around all of the cells in the selected range.

2. On the HOME tab, in the Font group, click the **Borders button arrow** ⊞ ▾, and then click **All Borders**. Borders are added around each cell in the range. The Borders button changes to reflect the last selected border option, which in this case is All Borders. The name of the selected border option appears in the button's ScreenTip.

3. Select the nonadjacent range **A9:B16;H17:I17**. You will add borders around each cell in the selected range.

4. In the Font group, click the **All Borders** button ⊞ to add borders to all of the cells in the selected range.

5. Click cell **A17** to deselect the cells. See Figure 1-35.

Figure 1-35   Borders added to selected cells

6. Select the nonadjacent range **A18:I23;H25:I28**, and then click the **All Borders** button ⊞ to add borders to all of the cells in the selected range.

Changing the Font Size

Changing the size of text in a sheet provides a way to identify different parts of a worksheet, such as distinguishing a title or section heading from data. The size of the text is referred to as the font size and is measured in points. The default font size for worksheets is 11 points, but it can be made larger or smaller as needed. You can resize text in selected cells using the Font Size button in the Font group on the HOME tab. You can also use the Increase Font Size and Decrease Font Size buttons to resize cell content to the next higher or lower standard font size.

Sally wants you to increase the size of the worksheet title to 26 points to make it stand out more.

To change the font size of the worksheet title:

▶ **1.** Click cell **A1** to select it. The worksheet title is in this cell.

▶ **2.** On the HOME tab, in the Font group, click the **Font Size button arrow** to display a list of font sizes, and then click **28**. The worksheet title changes to 28 points. See Figure 1-36.

| Figure 1-36 | Font size of cell content increased |

Font Size button arrow

title is now 28 points

▶ **3.** Press the **Ctrl+S** keys to save the workbook.

Printing a Workbook

Now that you have finished the workbook, Sally wants you to print a copy of the book order. Before you print a workbook, you should preview it to ensure that it will print correctly.

Changing Worksheet Views

You can view a worksheet in three ways. Normal view, which you have been using throughout this tutorial, shows the contents of the worksheet. Page Layout view shows how the worksheet will appear when printed. Page Break Preview displays the location of the different page breaks within the worksheet. This is useful when a worksheet will span several printed pages and you need to control what content appears on each page.

Sally wants you to see how the Customer Order worksheet will appear on printed pages. You will do this by switching between views.

To switch the Customer Order worksheet to different views:

1. Click the **Page Layout** button 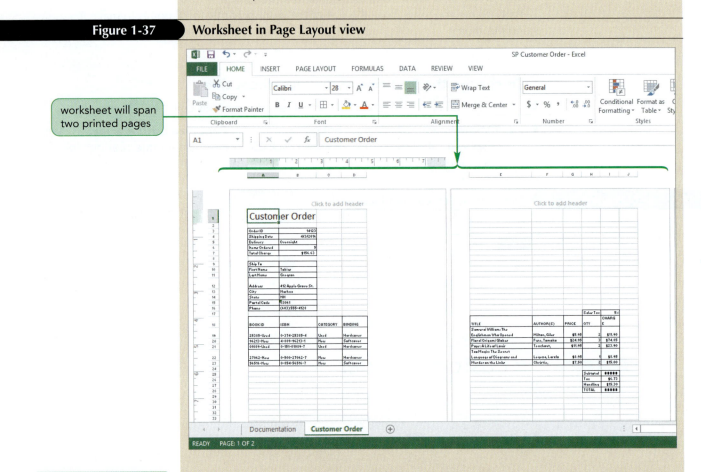 on the status bar. The page layout of the worksheet appears in the workbook window.

2. Drag the **Zoom slider** to reduce the zoom level to 50%. The reduced magnification makes it clear that the worksheet will spread over two pages when printed. See Figure 1-37.

Figure 1-37	Worksheet in Page Layout view

worksheet will span two printed pages

3. Click the **Page Break Preview** button on the status bar. The view switches to Page Break Preview, which shows only those parts of the current worksheet that will print. A dotted blue border separates one page from another.

4. Zoom the worksheet to **70%** so that you can more easily read the contents of the worksheet. See Figure 1-38.

TIP

You can relocate a page break by dragging the dotted blue border in the Page Break Preview window.

Figure 1-38   **Worksheet in Page Break Preview**

page 1 of the printout   page 2 of the printout

5. Click the **Normal** button ⊞ on the status bar. The worksheet returns to Normal view. A dotted black line indicates where the page break will occur.

Changing the Page Orientation

Page orientation specifies in which direction content is printed on the page. In **portrait orientation**, the page is taller than it is wide. In **landscape orientation**, the page is wider than it is tall. By default, Excel displays pages in portrait orientation. Changing the page orientation affects only the active sheet.

As you saw in Page Layout view and Page Break Preview, the Customer Order worksheet will print on two pages—columns A through D will print on the first page, and columns E through I will print on the second page, although the columns that print on each page may differ slightly depending on the printer. Sally wants the entire worksheet to print on a single page, so you'll change the page orientation from portrait to landscape.

To change the page orientation of the Customer Order worksheet:

1. On the ribbon, click the **PAGE LAYOUT** tab. The tab includes options for changing how the worksheet is arranged.

2. In the Page Setup group, click the **Orientation** button, and then click **Landscape**. The worksheet switches to landscape orientation.

3. Click the **Page Layout** button 🔲 on the status bar to switch to Page Layout view. The worksheet will still print on two pages.

Setting the Scaling Options

You change the size of the worksheet on the printed page by **scaling** it. You can scale the width or the height of the printout so that all of the columns or all of the rows fit on a single page. You can also scale the printout to fit the entire worksheet (both columns and rows) on a single page. If the worksheet is too large to fit on one page, you can scale the print to fit on the number of pages you select. You can also scale the worksheet to a percentage of its size. For example, scaling a worksheet to 50% reduces the size of the sheet by half when it is sent to the printer. When scaling a printout, make sure that the worksheet is still readable after shrinking. Scaling affects only the active worksheet, so you can scale each worksheet to best fit its contents.

Sally asks you to scale the printout so that all of the Customer Order worksheet fits on one page in landscape orientation.

To scale the printout of the Customer Order worksheet:

1. On the PAGE LAYOUT tab, in the Scale to Fit group, click the **Width arrow**, and then click **1 page** on the menu that appears. All of the columns in the worksheet now fit on one page.

2. In the Scale to Fit group, click the **Height arrow**, and then click **1 page**. All of the rows in the worksheet now fit on one page. See Figure 1-39.

Figure 1-39 | **Printout scaled to fit on one page**

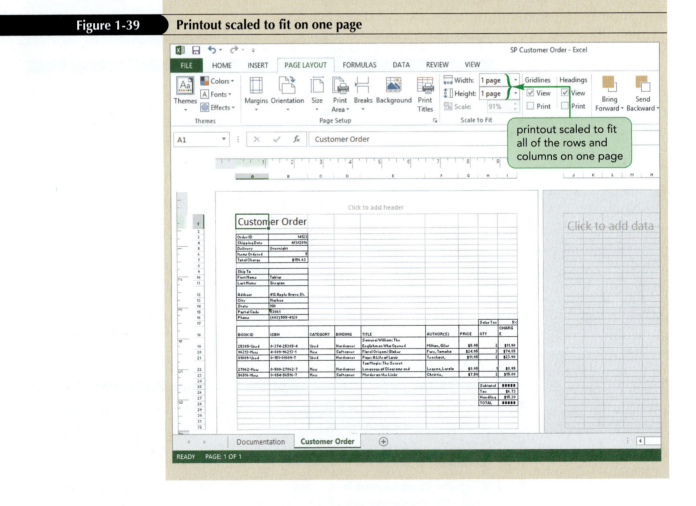

printout scaled to fit all of the rows and columns on one page

Setting the Print Options

TIP

To print the gridlines or the column and row headings, click the corresponding Print check box in the Sheet Options group on the PAGE LAYOUT tab.

You can print the contents of a workbook by using the Print screen in Backstage view. The Print screen provides options for choosing where to print, what to print, and how to print. For example, you can specify the number of copies to print, which printer to use, and what to print. You can choose to print only the selected cells, only the active sheets, or all of the worksheets in the workbook that contain data. The printout will include only the data in the worksheet. The other elements in the worksheet, such as the row and column headings and the gridlines around the worksheet cells, will not print by default. The preview shows you exactly how the printed pages will look with the current settings. You should always preview before printing to ensure that the printout looks exactly as you intended and avoid unnecessary reprinting.

Sally asks you to preview and print the Sparrow & Pond workbook now.

Note: Check with your instructor first to make sure you should complete the steps for printing the workbook.

To preview and print the workbook:

 1. On the ribbon, click the **FILE** tab to display Backstage view.

 2. Click **Print** in the navigation bar. The Print screen appears with the print options and a preview of the Customer Order worksheet printout. See Figure 1-40.

Figure 1-40 | **Print screen in Backstage view**

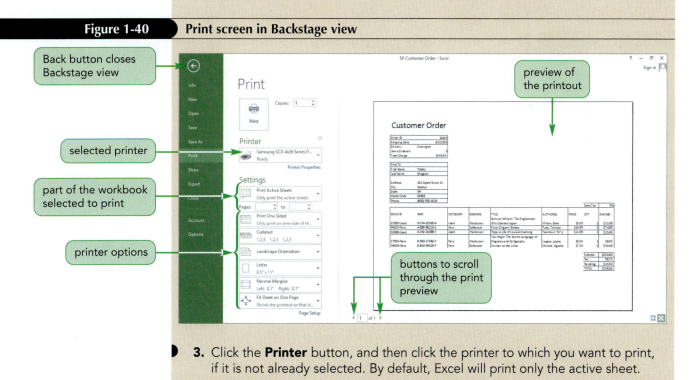

 3. Click the **Printer** button, and then click the printer to which you want to print, if it is not already selected. By default, Excel will print only the active sheet.

 4. In the Settings options, click the top button, and then click **Print Entire Workbook** to print all of the sheets in the workbook—in this case, both the Documentation and the Customer Order worksheets. The preview shows the first sheet in the workbook—the Documentation worksheet. Note that this sheet is still in the default portrait orientation.

 5. Below the preview, click the **Next Page** button ▶ to view the Customer Order worksheet. As you can see, the Customer Order worksheet will print on a single page in landscape orientation.

▶ **6.** If you are instructed to print, click the **Print** button to send the contents of the workbook to the specified printer. If you are not instructed to print, click the **Back** button ⬅ in the navigation bar to exit Backstage view.

Viewing Worksheet Formulas

Most of the time, you will be interested in only the final results of a worksheet, not the formulas used to calculate those results. However, in some cases, you might want to view the formulas used to develop the workbook. This is particularly useful when you encounter unexpected results and you want to examine the underlying formulas, or you want to discuss your formulas with a colleague. You can display the formulas instead of the resulting values in cells.

If you print the worksheet while the formulas are displayed, the printout shows the formulas instead of the values. To make the printout easier to read, you should print the worksheet gridlines as well as the row and column headings so that cell references in the formulas are easy to find in the printed version of the worksheet.

You will look at the Customer Order worksheet with the formulas displayed.

To display the formulas in cells in the Customer Order worksheet:

▶ **1.** Make sure the Customer Order worksheet is in Page Layout view.

TIP

You can also display formulas in a worksheet by clicking the Show Formulas button in the Formula Auditing group on the FORMULAS tab.

▶ **2.** Press the **Ctrl+`** keys (the grave accent symbol ` is usually located above the Tab key). The worksheet changes to display all of the formulas instead of the resulting values. Notice that the columns widen to display all of the formula text in the cells.

▶ **3.** Look at the entry in cell B4. The underlying numeric value of the shipping date (42463) is displayed instead of the formatted date value (4/3/2016). See Figure 1-41.

Figure 1-41 | **Worksheet with formulas displayed**

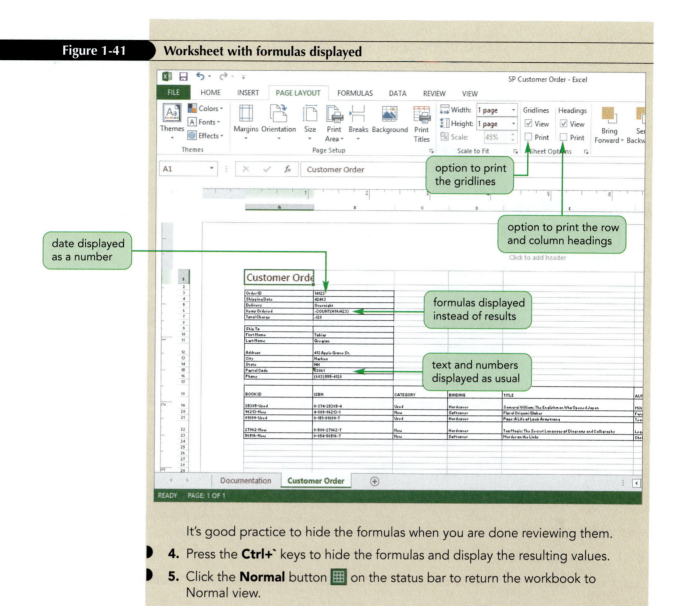

It's good practice to hide the formulas when you are done reviewing them.

4. Press the **Ctrl+`** keys to hide the formulas and display the resulting values.

5. Click the **Normal** button on the status bar to return the workbook to Normal view.

Saving a Workbook with a New Filename

Whenever you click the Save button on the Quick Access Toolbar or press the Ctrl+S keys, the workbook file is updated to reflect the latest content. If you want to save a copy of the workbook with a new filename or to a different location, you need to use the Save As command. When you save a workbook with a new filename or to a different location, the previous version of the workbook remains stored as well.

You have completed the SP Customer Order workbook. Sally wants to use the workbook as a model for other customer order reports. You will save the workbook with a new filename to avoid overwriting the Tobias Gregson book order. Then you'll clear the information related to Tobias Gregson, leaving the formulas intact. This new, revised workbook will then be ready for a new customer order.

To save the workbook with a new filename:

1. Press the **Ctrl+S** keys to save the workbook. This ensures that the final copy of the SP Customer Order workbook contains the latest content.

2. On the ribbon, click the **FILE** tab to display Backstage view, and then click **Save As** on the navigation bar. The Save As screen is displayed.

3. Click **Computer**, and then click the **Browse** button. The Save As dialog box opens so you can save the workbook with a new filename or to a new location.

4. Navigate to the location specified by your instructor.

TIP

Save the workbook with the new name *before* making your changes to avoid inadvertently saving your edits to the wrong file.

5. In the File name box, type **SP Customer Order Form** as the new filename.

6. Click the **Save** button. The workbook is saved with the new filename and is open in Excel.

7. Select the range **B3:B5**, right-click the selected range to open the shortcut menu, and then click **Clear Contents** to clear the contents of the order ID, shipping date, and delivery type cells.

8. Select the nonadjacent range **B10:B16;A19:H23**, and then press the **Delete** key to clear the contact information for Tobias Gregson and the list of books he ordered from those cells.

9. Select cell **I27**, and then clear the handling fee.

10. Click cell **A3** to make that cell the active cell. The next time someone opens this workbook, cell A3 will still be the active cell.

11. Press the **Ctrl+S** keys to save the workbook.

12. Click the **Close** button ☒ on the title bar (or press the **Ctrl+W** keys). The workbook closes, and the Excel program closes.

Sally is pleased with the workbook you created. With the calculations already in place in the new workbook, she will be able to quickly enter new customer orders and see the calculated book charges without having to recreate the worksheet.

REVIEW

Session 1.2 Quick Check

1. What formula would you enter to add the values in cells B4, B5, and B6? What function would you enter to achieve the same result?

2. What formula would you enter to count the number of numeric values in the range B2:B100?

3. What formula would you enter to find the maximum value of the cells in the range B2:B100?

4. If you insert cells into the range C1:D10 shifting the cells to the right, what is the new location of the data that was previously in cell E5?

5. Cell E11 contains the formula =SUM(E1:E10). How does this formula change if a new row is inserted above row 5?

6. Describe four ways of viewing the content of a workbook in Excel.

7. How are page breaks indicated in Page Break Preview?

8. How do you display the formulas used in a worksheet instead of the formula results?

ASSESS

SAM Projects

Put your skills into practice with SAM Projects! SAM Projects for this tutorial can be found online. If you have a SAM account, go to www.cengage.com/sam2013 to download the most recent Project Instructions and Start Files.

PRACTICE

Review Assignments

There are no Data Files needed for the Review Assignments.

Sally wants you to create a workbook to record the recent book purchases made by Sparrow & Pond. The workbook should list the recent acquisitions from private sellers, libraries, and other vendors; include a description of each book; and calculate the total number of books acquired and the total amount spent by Sparrow & Pond. Complete the following:

1. Create a new, blank workbook, and then save the workbook as **Book List** in the location specified by your instructor.
2. Rename the Sheet1 worksheet as **Documentation**, and then enter the data shown in Figure 1-42 in the specified cells.

Figure 1-42   Documentation sheet data

Cell	Data
A1	Sparrow & Pond
A3	Author
A4	Date
A5	Purpose
B3	*your name*
B4	*current date*
B5	To record book acquisitions by Sparrow & Pond

© 2014 Cengage Learning

3. Set the font size of the title text in cell A1 to 26 points.
4. Add a new worksheet after the Documentation sheet, and then rename the sheet as **Books**.
5. In cell A1, enter the text **Book Acquisitions**. Set the font size of this text to 26 points.
6. In cell A2, enter the text **DATE** as the label. In cell B2, enter the date **4/3/2016**.
7. In the range A4:G9, enter the data shown in Figure 1-43.

Figure 1-43	Book list

ISBN	STATUS	BINDING	TITLE	AUTHOR	CONDITION	PRICE
0-670-02103-2	New	Softcover	Rocket Men: The Epic Story of the First Men on the Moon	Nelson, Craig	Excellent	$12.95
0-195-09076-4	Used	Hardcover	Buildings of Colorado	Noel, Thomas J.	Good	$22.50
0-375-70365-9	New	Softcover	American Visions: The Epic History of Art in America	Hughes, Robert	Excellent	$22.50
1-564-77848-7	New	Softcover	Simple Comforts: 12 Cozy Lap Quilts	Diehl, Kim	Very Good	$9.25
1-851-70006-4	Used	Hardcover	Beautiful Stories About Children	Dickens, Charles	Good	$33.50

© 2014 Cengage Learning

8. Insert cells into the range A4:A9, shifting the other cells to the right.

9. Enter the label **BOOK ID** in cell A4, type **02103-New** in cell A5, and then type **09076-Used** in cell A6.

10. Use Flash Fill to fill in the remaining book IDs.

11. Set the width of columns A through D to 15 characters each. Set the width of column E to 30 characters. Set the width of column F to 20 characters. Set the width of column G to 15 characters.

12. Set the book titles in the range E4:E9 to wrap to a new line.

13. Autofit the heights of rows 4 through 9.

14. Move the book list in the range A4:H9 to the range A8:H13.

15. In cell G15, enter the text **TOTAL**. In cell H15, enter a function to add the prices in the range H9:H13.

16. In cell A4, enter the text **TOTAL BOOKS**. In cell B4, enter a function to count the number of numeric values in the range H9:H13.

17. In cell A5, enter the text **TOTAL PRICE**. In cell B5, display the value from cell H15.

18. In cell A6, enter the text **AVERAGE PRICE**. In cell B6, enter a formula to calculate the total price paid for the books (listed in cell B5) divided by the number of books purchased (listed in cell B4).

19. Add borders around each cell in the nonadjacent range A4:B6;A8:H13;G15:H15.

20. For the Books worksheet, change the page orientation to landscape and scale the worksheet to print on a single page for both the width and the height. If you are instructed to print, print the entire workbook.

21. Display the formulas in the Books worksheet, and set the gridlines and row/column headings to print. If you are instructed to print, print the entire worksheet.

22. Save and close the workbook.

Case Problem 1

Data File needed for this Case Problem: Pacific.xlsx

American Wheel Tours   Kevin Bennett is a tours manager at American Wheel Tours, a bicycle touring company located in Philadelphia, Pennsylvania, that specializes in one- and two-week supported tours in destinations across the United States. Kevin wants you to create a workbook that details the itinerary of the company's Pacific Coast tour. The workbook will list the tour itinerary shown in Figure 1-44 and calculate the total number of riding days, total mileage, and average mileage per ride.

Figure 1-44   **Pacific Tour itinerary**

DATE	START	FINISH	CAMPSITE	MILES	DESCRIPTION
10-Oct-16	Eugene	Eugene	Richardson Park		Orientation day. Meet at Richardson Park, located at the Fern Ridge Reservoir.
11-Oct-16	Eugene	Florence	Honeyman State Park	66	Cycle over Low Pass to Honeyman State Park.
12-Oct-16	Florence	Charleston	Sunset Bay State Park	56	Cycle through Oregon Dunes National Recreation Area to Sunset Bay State Park.
13-Oct-16	Charleston	Port Orford	Humbug Mountain State Park	60	Cycle around Bullards Beach State Park and camp at Humbug Mountain State Park.
14-Oct-16	Port Orford	Brookings	Harris Beach State Park	52	Cycle past the mouth of the Rogue River to Harris Beach State Park.
15-Oct-16	Brookings	Crescent City	Jedediah State Park	48	Pass into California and camp at Jedediah State Park.
16-Oct-16	Crescent City	Eureka	Eureka Fairgrounds	72	A long day through Del Norte Coast Redwoods State Park to Eureka.

© 2014 Cengage Learning

Complete the following:

1. Open the **Pacific** workbook located in the Excel1 ▸ Case1 folder included with your Data Files, and then save the workbook as **Pacific Coast** in the location specified by your instructor.
2. In the Documentation worksheet, enter your name in cell B3 and the date in cell B4.
3. Add a new sheet to the end of the workbook and rename it as **Itinerary**.
4. In cell A1, enter the text **Pacific Coast Tour** and set the font size to 28 points.
5. In the range A3:A8, enter the following labels: **Start Date**, **End Date**, **Total Days**, **Riding Days**, **Total Miles**, and **Miles per Day**.
6. Enter the date **October 10, 2016** in cell B3, and then enter the date **October 16, 2016** in cell B4.
7. In the range D3:D8, enter the labels **Type**, **Surface**, **Difficulty**, **Tour Leader**, **Cost**, and **Deposit**.
8. In the range E3:E8, enter **Van Supported**, **Paved**, **Intermediate**, **Kevin Bennett**, **$1,250**, and **$350**.
9. In the range A11:F18, enter the data shown in Figure 1-44, including the column labels. Leave the mileage value for October 10th blank.
10. In cell B5, enter a formula to calculate the total number of days in the tour by subtracting the starting date (cell B3) from the ending date (cell B4) and adding 1.

11. In cell B6, enter a function to count the total number of riding days based on the numbers in the range E12:E18.

12. In cell B7, enter a function to add the total number of miles in the range E12:E18.

13. In cell B8, enter a formula to calculate the average miles per day by dividing the total miles by the number of riding days.

14. Insert cells in the range A11:A18, shifting the cells to the right. In cell A11, enter **DAY**. In the range A12:A18, enter the numbers 1 through 7 to number each day of the tour.

15. Set the column widths so that column A is 12 characters, columns B through E are 14 characters each, column F is 6 characters, and column G is 50 characters.

16. Wrap text in the range A11:G18 as needed so that any hidden entries are displayed on multiple lines within the cell.

17. Autofit the height of rows 11 through 18.

18. Add borders around the ranges A3:B8, D3:E8, and A11:G18.

19. Format the Itinerary worksheet so that it prints on a single page in landscape orientation. If you are instructed to print, print the entire workbook.

20. Display the formulas in the Itinerary worksheet, and set the gridlines and column/row headings to print. If you are instructed to print, print the worksheet.

21. Return the Itinerary worksheet to Normal view, hide the formulas, set the gridlines and column/row headings so that they won't print, and then save the workbook.

22. Save the workbook as **Pacific Coast Revised** in the location specified by your instructor.

23. Determine what the total mileage and average mileage per day of the tour would be if Kevin adds a 10-mile warm-up ride on October 10th but decreases the length of the October 15th ride to 41 miles. Save the workbook.

Case Problem 2

APPLY

Data File needed for this Case Problem: Tropical.xlsx

Tropical Foods   Tropical Foods is a health food grocery store located in Keizer, Oregon. Monica Li is working on the store's annual financial report. One part of the financial report will be the company's balance sheet for the previous two years. Monica already entered the labels for the balance sheet. You will enter the numeric data and formulas to perform the financial calculations. Complete the following:

1. Open the **Tropical** workbook located in the Excel1 ▶ Case2 folder included with your Data Files, and then save the workbook as **Tropical Foods Balance Sheet** in the location specified by your instructor.

2. In cells B3 and B4 of the Documentation sheet, enter your name and the date. In cell A1, increase the font size of the title to 28 points.

3. Go to the Balance Sheet worksheet. Increase the font size of the title in cell A1 to 28 points, and then increase the font size of the subtitle in cell A2 to 20 points.

4. In the corresponding cells of columns C and D, enter the numbers shown in Figure 1-45 for the company's assets and liabilities.

Figure 1-45   **Tropical Foods assets and liabilities**

		2015	2014
Assets	Cash	$645,785	$627,858
	Accounts Receivable	431,982	405,811
	Inventories	417,615	395,648
	Prepaid Expenses	2,152	4,151
	Other Assets	31,252	26,298
	Fixed Assets @ Cost	1,800,000	1,750,000
	Accumulated Depreciation	82,164	$77,939
Liabilities	Accounts Payable	$241,191	$193,644
	Accrued Expenses	31,115	32,151
	Current Portion of Debt	120,000	100,000
	Income Taxes Payable	144,135	126,524
	Long-Term Debt	815,000	850,000
	Capital Stock	1,560,000	1,525,000
	Retain Earnings	335,181	304,508

© 2014 Cengage Learning

5. Set the width of column A to 12 characters, column B to 28 characters, columns C and D to 14 characters each, column E to 2 characters, and column F to 10 characters.

6. In cells C8 and D8, enter formulas to calculate the current assets value for 2014 and 2015, which is equal to the sum of the cash, accounts receivable, inventories, and prepaid expenses values.

7. In cells C14 and D14, enter formulas to calculate the net fixed assets value for 2014 and 2015, which is equal to the difference between the fixed assets value and the accumulated depreciation value.

8. In cells C16 and D16, enter formulas to calculate the total assets value for 2014 and 2015, which is equal to the sum of the current assets, other assets, and net fixed assets value.

9. In cells C23 and D23, enter formulas to calculate the sum of the accounts payable, accrued expenses, current portion of debt, and income taxes payable values for 2014 and 2015.

10. In cells C29 and D29, enter formulas to calculate the shareholders' equity value for 2014 and 2015, which is equal to the sum of the capital stock and retained earnings.

11. In cells C31 and D31, enter formulas to calculate the total liabilities & equity value for 2014 and 2015, which is equal to the sum of the current liabilities, long-term debt, and shareholders' equity.

12. In a balance sheet, the total assets should equal the total liabilities & equity. Compare the values in cells C16 and C31, and then compare the values in cells D16 and D31 to confirm that this is the case for the Tropical Foods balance sheet in 2014 and 2015. If the account doesn't balance, check your worksheet for errors in either values or formulas.

13. In cell F4, enter a formula to calculate the percentage change in cash from 2014 to 2015, which is equal to (C4–D4)/D4.

14. Copy the formula in cell F4 and paste it in the nonadjacent range F5:F8;F10;F12:F14;F16; F19:F23;F25;F27:F29;F31 to show the percentage change in all values of the balance sheet.

15. Add borders around the cells in columns B, C, D, and F of the balance sheet, excluding the cells in rows 9, 11, 15, 17, 18, 24, 26, and 30.

16. Set the page layout of the Balance Sheet worksheet to portrait orientation and scaled to print on a single page. If you are instructed to print, print the entire workbook.

17. Display the formulas in the Balance Sheet worksheet, and then set the gridlines and row/column headings to print. If you are instructed to print, print the worksheet.

18. Display the Balance Sheet worksheet in Normal view, hide the formulas, set the gridlines and column/row headings so that they won't print, and then save the workbook.

Case Problem 3

CHALLENGE

Data File needed for this Case Problem: Physics.xlsx

Gladstone Country Day School   Beatrix Melendez teaches Introduction to Physics at Gladstone Country Day School in Gladstone, Missouri. She wants to record students' quiz scores, and then calculate each student's total and average scores. She also wants to calculate the class average, high score, and low score for each quiz in her records. Beatrix has entered scores from 10 quizzes for 20 students in a worksheet. You will summarize these grades by student and by quiz using the functions listed in Figure 1-46.

Figure 1-46   Excel summary functions

Function	Description
=AVERAGE (*range*)	Calculates the average of the values from the specified *range*
=MEDIAN (*range*)	Calculates the median or midpoint of the values from the specified *range*
=MIN (*range*)	Calculates the minimum of the values from the specified *range*
=MAX (*range*)	Calculates the maximum of the values from the specified *range*

© 2014 Cengage Learning

Complete the following:

1. Open the **Physics** workbook located in the Excel1 ▶ Case3 folder included with your Data Files, and then save the workbook as **Physics Grading Sheet** in the location specified by your instructor.

2. In the Documentation sheet, enter your name in cell B3 and the date in cell B4. Increase the font size of the title in cell A1 to 28 points.

3. Go to the Grades worksheet. Increase the font size of cell A1 to 28 points, and then increase the font size of cell A2 to 22 points.

✦ Explore 4. In cell M5, enter a formula to calculate the median or midpoint of the quiz scores for Debra Alt. In cell N5, enter a formula to calculate the average of Debra Alt's quiz scores.

5. Copy the formulas in the range M5:N5 to the range M6:N24 to summarize the scores for the remaining students.

✦ Explore 6. In cell B26, enter a formula to calculate the minimum class score from the first quiz. In cell B27, enter a formula to calculate the median class score.

✦ Explore 7. In cell B28, use the MAX function to calculate the high score from the first quiz.

8. In cell B30, enter a formula to calculate the average score from the first quiz.

9. Copy the formulas in the range B26:B30 to the range C26:K30 to calculate the summary statistics for the rest of the quizzes.

10. Insert 10 new rows above row 4, shifting the student grade table and summary from the range A4:N30 to the range A14:N40. You will enter a summary of all of the students from all of the quizzes at the top of the worksheet.

11. In cell A4, enter the text **Class Size**. In cell B4, enter a formula to calculate the count of scores from the range N15:N34.

12. In the range A6:A9, enter the labels **Overall Scores**, **Lowest Average**, **Median Average**, and **Highest Average**. In cell A11, enter **Class Average**.

13. Using the average scores in the range N15:N34, enter formulas to calculate the overall lowest average score in cell B7, the median of the class averages in cell B8, the overall highest average in cell B9, and the average overall class score in cell B11.

14. Add cell borders around the ranges A4:B4, A7:B9, A11:B11, A14:K34, M14:N34, A36:K38, and A40:K40.

15. Set the page layout of the Grades worksheet to landscape orientation and scaled to print on a single page. If you are instructed to print, print the entire workbook.

16. Display the formulas in the Grades worksheet. Set the gridlines and the row/column headings to print. If you are instructed to print, print the worksheet.

17. Display the Grades worksheet in Normal view, hide the formulas, set the gridlines and column/row headings so that they won't print, and then save the workbook.

18. Determine the effect of raising each student's score on the first quiz by 10 points to curve the results. Report what impact this has on the overall class average from all 10 quizzes.

19. Save the workbook as **Physics Grading Sheet Revised**. If you are instructed to print, print the Grades worksheet.

TROUBLESHOOT

Case Problem 4

Data File needed for this Case Problem: Turf.xlsx

Turf Toughs   Tim Gables is the owner and operator of Turf Toughs, a lawn and tree removal service located in Chicopee, Massachusetts. He created a workbook to record and analyze the service calls made by his company. So far, the workbook calculates the cost of each service call, the total charges for all of the calls, and the total number of billable hours. Unfortunately, the workbook contains several errors. You will fix these errors and then complete the workbook. Complete the following:

1. Open the **Turf** workbook located in the Excel1 ▸ Case4 folder included with your Data Files, and then save the workbook as **Turf Toughs Service Calls** in the location specified by your instructor.

2. In the Documentation sheet, enter your name in cell B3 and the date in cell B4.

3. Go to the Service Log worksheet. The log lists the contact information and the service calls for each customer.

   Tim wants you to insert a column of IDs for each customer. The customer ID is in the form *last-phone*, where *last* is the customer's last name and *phone* is the last four digits of the customer's phone number.

4. Insert cells in the range A4:A34, shifting the other cells to the right. Type **Cust ID** in cell A4, and then enter **Morris-4380** as the customer ID for Michael Morris. Use Flash Fill to fill in the remaining customer IDs in the column.

5. Add borders around the cells in the range A4:A32.

⚙ **Troubleshoot** 6. There is a problem with the all of the customer zip codes. Each zip code should begin with zero. Make the necessary changes to fix this problem.

7. Resize the columns of the worksheet so that all of the column labels in the service calls list are displayed entirely.

⚙ **Troubleshoot** 8. The formula in cell L5 is not correctly calculating the number of hours for each service call. Fix the formula so that it multiplies the difference between the starting and ending time by 24.

9. Copy the formula you created for cell L5 to the range L6:L32, replacing the previous calculated values.

10. Calculate the service charge for each service call so that it equals the base fee added to the hourly rate times the number of hours worked.

⚙ **Troubleshoot** 11. Cell N34 contains a formula to calculate the total service charges for all customer visits. Is it calculating the value correctly? If not, edit the formula to fix any errors you find.

12. Above row 4, insert six new rows, shifting the range A4:N34 down to the range A10:N40.

13. In the range A4:A8, enter the labels **From**, **To**, **Total Service Calls**, **Billable Hours**, and **Total Charges**.

14. In cell B4, calculate the starting date of the service calls by entering a formula that finds the minimum value of the dates in the Date column.

15. In cell B5, calculate the ending date of the service calls by entering a formula that finds the maximum value of the dates in the Date column.

16. In cell B6, enter a formula that counts the total number of service calls using the values in the Date column.

17. In cell B7, enter a formula that calculates the sum of hours from the Hours column.

18. In cell B8, enter a formula that references the value of cell N40.

19. Add borders around each cell in the range A4:B8.

20. Set the page layout of the Service Log worksheet so that it prints on a single page in landscape orientation. If you are instructed to print, print the entire workbook.

21. Display the formulas in the Service Log worksheet, scale the worksheet to fit on a single page, and then set the gridlines and row/column headings to print. If you are instructed to print, print the Service Log worksheet.

22. Return the Service Log worksheet to Normal view, hide the formulas, set the gridlines and column/row headings so that they won't print, and then save the workbook.

EXCEL

OBJECTIVES

Session 2.1
- Change fonts, font style, and font color
- Add fill colors and a background image
- Create formulas to calculate sales data
- Apply Currency and Accounting formats and the Percent style
- Format dates and times
- Align, indent, and rotate cell contents
- Merge a group of cells

Session 2.2
- Use the AVERAGE function
- Apply cell styles
- Copy and paste formats with the Format Painter
- Find and replace text and formatting
- Change workbook themes
- Highlight cells with conditional formats
- Format a worksheet for printing
- Set the print area, insert page breaks, add print titles, create headers and footers, and set margins

Formatting Workbook Text and Data

Designing a Sales Report

Case | *Big Red Wraps*

Sanjit Chandra is a sales manager for Big Red Wraps, a growing restaurant chain that specializes in preparing made-to-order sandwich wraps, seasonal soups, and fresh salads. The first Big Red Wraps opened in Madison, Wisconsin, and has since expanded to 20 restaurants across six states. Four of these restaurants were opened this year. Each spring, the company has a sales conference where the restaurant managers meet to discuss sales concerns and review marketing plans for the upcoming year. Sanjit created a workbook that summarizes the sales data for the previous year and is part of a sales report that will be given to all conference attendees. He wants you to calculate some summary statistics and format the workbook.

STARTING DATA FILES

Excel2 → Tutorial
Background.jpg
Sales.xlsx

Review
Background2.png
Menu.xlsx

Case1
Salon.xlsx

Case2
Waist.xlsx

Access3 →
Wind.xlsx

Case4
Office.xlsx

Session 2.1 Visual Overview:

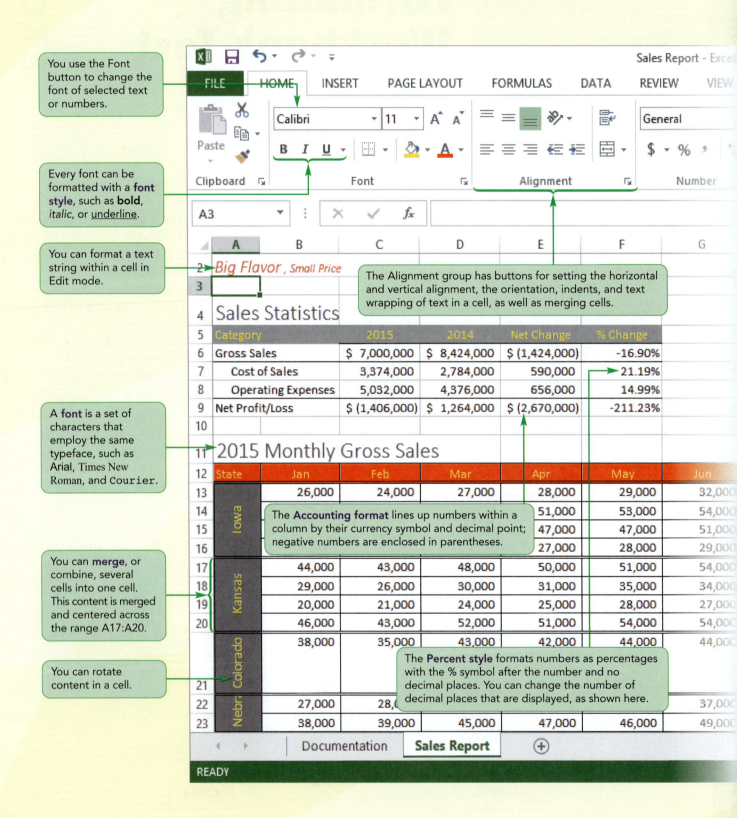

You use the Font button to change the font of selected text or numbers.

Every font can be formatted with a **font style**, such as **bold**, *italic*, or <u>underline</u>.

You can format a text string within a cell in Edit mode.

A **font** is a set of characters that employ the same typeface, such as Arial, Times New Roman, and Courier.

You can **merge**, or combine, several cells into one cell. This content is merged and centered across the range A17:A20.

You can rotate content in a cell.

The Alignment group has buttons for setting the horizontal and vertical alignment, the orientation, indents, and text wrapping of text in a cell, as well as merging cells.

The **Accounting format** lines up numbers within a column by their currency symbol and decimal point; negative numbers are enclosed in parentheses.

The **Percent style** formats numbers as percentages with the % symbol after the number and no decimal places. You can change the number of decimal places that are displayed, as shown here.

Big Flavor , Small Price

Sales Statistics

Category	2015	2014	Net Change	% Change
Gross Sales	$ 7,000,000	$ 8,424,000	$ (1,424,000)	-16.90%
Cost of Sales	3,374,000	2,784,000	590,000	21.19%
Operating Expenses	5,032,000	4,376,000	656,000	14.99%
Net Profit/Loss	$ (1,406,000)	$ 1,264,000	$ (2,670,000)	-211.23%

2015 Monthly Gross Sales

State	Jan	Feb	Mar	Apr	May	Jun
Iowa	26,000	24,000	27,000	28,000	29,000	32,000
				51,000	53,000	54,000
				47,000	47,000	51,000
				27,000	28,000	29,000
Kansas	44,000	43,000	48,000	50,000	51,000	54,000
	29,000	26,000	30,000	31,000	35,000	34,000
	20,000	21,000	24,000	25,000	28,000	27,000
	46,000	43,000	52,000	51,000	54,000	54,000
Colorado	38,000	35,000	43,000	42,000	44,000	44,000
Nebr	27,000	28,0				37,000
	38,000	39,000	45,000	47,000	46,000	49,000

Documentation   **Sales Report**   +

READY

Worksheet with Formatting

The Number group has buttons for formatting numbers in the Accounting format, Percent style, and Comma style, as well as changing the number of decimal places displayed.

A **fill color** is a background color that can be added to cells to help differentiate parts of a worksheet or highlight data.

You can increase or decrease the number of decimal places that are displayed in a value. These values show no decimal places.

The **Comma style** adds a thousands separator to numbers, adds two decimal places, and lines up values within a column by their decimal points. You can change the number of decimal places that are displayed, as shown here.

Jun	Jul	Aug	Sep	Oct	Nov
32,000	33,000	34,000	30,000	32,000	30,000
54,000	54,000	58,000	54,000	55,000	51,000
51,000	52,000	54,000	50,000	49,000	46,000
29,000	32,000	30,000	30,000	28,000	27,000
54,000	54,000	55,000	54,000	52,000	51,000
34,000	37,000	37,000	34,000	34,000	34,000
27,000	27,000	29,000	24,000	26,000	24,000
54,000	58,000	58,000	55,000	54,000	50,000
44,000	47,000	48,000	47,000	48,000	44,000
37,000	37,000	38,000	35,000	33,000	35,000
49,000	51,000	49,000	47,000	49,000	47,000

Formatting Cell Text

You can add formatting to a workbook by choosing its fonts, styles, colors, and decorative features. Formatting changes only the appearance of data—it does not affect the data itself. In Excel, formatting options are organized into themes. A **theme** is a collection of formatting for text, colors, and graphical effects that are applied throughout a workbook to create a specific look and feel. Each theme has a name. Although the Office theme is the default theme, you can apply other themes or create your own. You can also add formatting to a workbook using fonts and colors that are not part of the current theme.

As you format a workbook, galleries and Live Preview show how a workbook would be affected by a formatting selection. A **gallery** is a menu or grid that shows a visual representation of the options available for the selected button. As you point to options in a gallery, **Live Preview** shows the results of clicking each option. By pointing to different options, you can quickly see different results before selecting the format you want.

PROSKILLS

Written Communication: Formatting Workbooks for Readability and Appeal

Designing a workbook requires the same care as designing any written document or report. A well-formatted workbook is easy to read and establishes a sense of professionalism with readers. Do the following to improve the appearance of your workbooks:

- **Clearly identify each worksheet's purpose.** Include column or row titles and a descriptive sheet name.
- **Include only one or two topics on each worksheet.** Don't crowd individual worksheets with too much information. Place extra topics on separate sheets. Readers should be able to interpret each worksheet with a minimal amount of horizontal and vertical scrolling.
- **Place worksheets with the most important information first in the workbook.** Position worksheets summarizing your findings near the front of the workbook. Position worksheets with detailed and involved analysis near the end as an appendix.
- **Use consistent formatting throughout the workbook.** If negative values appear in red on one worksheet, format them in the same way on all sheets. Also, be consistent in the use of thousands separators, decimal places, and percentages.
- **Pay attention to the format of the printed workbook.** Make sure your printouts are legible with informative headers and footers. Check that the content of the printout is scaled correctly to the page size, and that page breaks divide the information into logical sections.

Excel provides many formatting tools. However, too much formatting can be intrusive, overwhelm data, and make the document difficult to read. Remember that the goal of formatting is not simply to make a "pretty workbook," but also to accentuate important trends and relationships in the data. A well-formatted workbook should seamlessly convey your data to the reader. If the reader is thinking about how your workbook looks, it means he or she is not thinking about your data.

Sanjit has already entered the data and some formulas in a workbook, which is only a rough draft of what he wants to submit to the company. The Documentation sheet describes the workbook's purpose and content. The Sales Report sheet displays a summary of the previous year's sales including a table of monthly gross sales broken down by the 20 franchise stores. In its current form, the data is difficult to read and interpret. Sanjit wants you to format the contents of the workbook to improve its readability and visual appeal.

To open the workbook:

▶ **1.** Open the **Sales** workbook located in the Excel2 ▶ Tutorial folder included with your Data Files, and then save the workbook as **Sales Report** in the location specified by your instructor.

▶ **2.** In the Documentation sheet, enter your name in cell B4 and the date in cell B5.

Applying Fonts and Font Styles

Excel organizes fonts into theme and non-theme fonts. A **theme font** is associated with a particular theme and used for headings and body text in the workbook. These fonts change automatically when you change the theme applied to the workbook. Text formatted with a **non-theme font** retains its appearance no matter what theme is used with the workbook.

Fonts appear in different character styles. **Serif fonts**, such as Times New Roman, have extra strokes at the end of each character that aid in reading passages of text. **Sans serif fonts**, such as Arial, do not include these extra strokes. Other fonts are purely decorative, such as a font used for specialized logos. Every font can be further formatted with a font style such as *italic*, **bold**, or ***bold italic***; with underline; and with special effects such as ~~strikethrough~~ and color. You can also increase or decrease the font size.

REFERENCE

Formatting Cell Content

- To change the font, select the cell or range. On the HOME tab, in the Font group, click the Font arrow, and then click a font.
- To change the font size, select the cell or range. On the HOME tab, in the Font group, click the Font Size arrow, and then click a font size.
- To change a font style, select the cell or range. On the HOME tab, in the Font group, click the Bold, Italic, or Underline button.
- To change a font color, select the cell or range. On the HOME tab, in the Font group, click the Font Color button arrow, and then click a color.
- To format a text selection, double-click the cell to enter Edit mode, and then select the text to format. Change the font, size, style, or color, and then press the Enter key.

Sanjit wants the company name at the top of each worksheet to appear in large, bold letters using the default heading font from the Office theme. He wants the slogan "Big Flavor, Small Price" displayed below the company name to appear in the heading font, but in smaller, italicized letters.

To format the company name and slogan in the Documentation sheet:

▶ **1.** In the Documentation sheet, select cell **A1** to make it the active cell. The cell with the company name is selected.

▶ **2.** On the HOME tab, in the Font group, click the **Font button arrow** to display a gallery of fonts available on your computer. Each name is displayed in its corresponding font. When you point to a font in the gallery, Live Preview shows how the text in the selected cell will look with that font. The first two fonts are the theme fonts for headings and body text—Calibri Light and Calibri.

3. Point to **Algerian** (or another font) in the All Fonts list. Live Preview shows the effect of the Algerian font on the text in cell A1. See Figure 2-1.

Figure 2-1   **Font gallery**

fonts in the Office theme

Live Preview of the Algerian font

all available fonts

pointer on the Algerian font

Big Red Wraps sales conference

4. Point to three other fonts in the Font gallery to see the Live Preview showing how cell A1 could look with those fonts.

5. Click **Calibri Light** in the Theme Fonts list. The company name in cell A1 changes to the Calibri Light font, the default headings font in the current theme.

6. In the Font group, click the **Font Size button arrow** to display a list of font sizes, and then click **26**. The company name changes to 26 points.

7. In the Font group, click the **Bold** button **B** (or press the **Ctrl+B** keys). The company name is set in bold.

8. Select cell **A2** to make it active. The cell with the slogan text is selected.

9. In the Font group, click the **Font Size button arrow**, and then click **10**. The slogan text changes to 10 points.

10. In the Font group, click the **Italic** button **I** (or press the **Ctrl+I** keys). The slogan in cell A2 is italicized.

11. Select the range **A4:A6**, and then press the **Ctrl+B** keys to change the font to bold.

12. Select cell **A7** to deselect the range. The column labels are set in bold. See Figure 2-2.

Figure 2-2   **Formatted cell text**

Applying a Font Color

Color can transform a plain workbook filled with numbers and text into a powerful presentation that captures the user's attention and adds visual emphasis to the points you want to make. By default, Excel displays text in a black font color.

Like fonts, colors are organized into theme and non-theme colors. **Theme colors** are the 12 colors that belong to the workbook's theme. Four colors are designated for text and backgrounds, six colors are used for accents and highlights, and two colors are used for hyperlinks (followed and not followed links). These 12 colors are designed to work well together and to remain readable in all combinations. Each theme color has five variations, or accents, in which a different tint or shading is applied to the theme color.

Ten **standard colors**—dark red, red, orange, yellow, light green, green, light blue, blue, dark blue, and purple—are always available regardless of the workbook's theme. You can open an extended palette of 134 standard colors. You can also create a custom color by specifying a mixture of red, blue, and green color values, making available 16.7 million custom colors—more colors than the human eye can distinguish. Some dialog boxes have an automatic color option that uses your Windows default text and background colors, usually black text on a white background.

Creating Custom Colors

Custom colors let you add subtle and striking colors to a formatted workbook. To create custom colors, you use the **RGB Color model** in which each color is expressed with varying intensities of red, green, and blue. RGB color values are often represented as a set of numbers in the format

(*red*, *green*, *blue*)

where *red* is an intensity value assigned to red light, *green* is an intensity value assigned to green light, and *blue* is an intensity value assigned to blue light. The intensities are measured on a scale of 0 to 255—0 indicates no intensity (or the absence of the color) and 255 indicates the highest intensity. So, the RGB color value (255, 255, 0) represents a mixture of high-intensity red (255) and high-intensity green (255) with the absence of blue (0), which creates the color yellow.

To create colors in Excel using the RGB model, click the More Colors option located in a color menu or dialog box to open the Colors dialog box. In the Colors dialog box, click the Custom tab, and then enter the red, green, and blue intensity values. A preview box shows the resulting RGB color.

Sanjit wants the labels in the Documentation sheet to stand out, so you will change the Big Red Wraps company name and slogan to red.

To change the company name and slogan font color:

1. Select the range **A1:A2**. The company name and slogan are selected.

2. On the HOME tab, in the Font group, click the **Font Color button arrow** to display the gallery of theme and standard colors. (The two colors for hyperlinked text are not shown.)

3. Point to the **Red** color (the second color) in the Standard Colors section. The color name appears in a ScreenTip and you see a Live Preview of the text with the red font color. See Figure 2-3.

Figure 2-3 **Font color gallery**

4. Click the **Red** color. The company name and slogan change to red.

Formatting Text Selections

In Edit mode, you can select and format selections of text within a cell. When the Big Red Wraps slogan is used in marketing materials, "Big Flavor" is set slightly larger than "Small Price." Sanjit wants you to recreate this effect in the workbook by increasing the font size of "Big Flavor" while leaving the rest of the text unchanged. You will use Edit mode to apply a different format to part of the cell text.

To format part of the company slogan:

1. Double-click cell **A2** to select the cell and enter Edit mode (or click cell **A2** and press the **F2** key). The status bar shows EDIT to indicate that you are working with the cell in Edit mode. The pointer changes to the I-beam pointer.

2. Drag the pointer over the phrase **Big Flavor** to select it. The Mini toolbar appears above the selected text with buttons to change the font, size, style, and color of the selected text in the cell. See Figure 2-4.

Figure 2-4   Mini toolbar in Edit mode

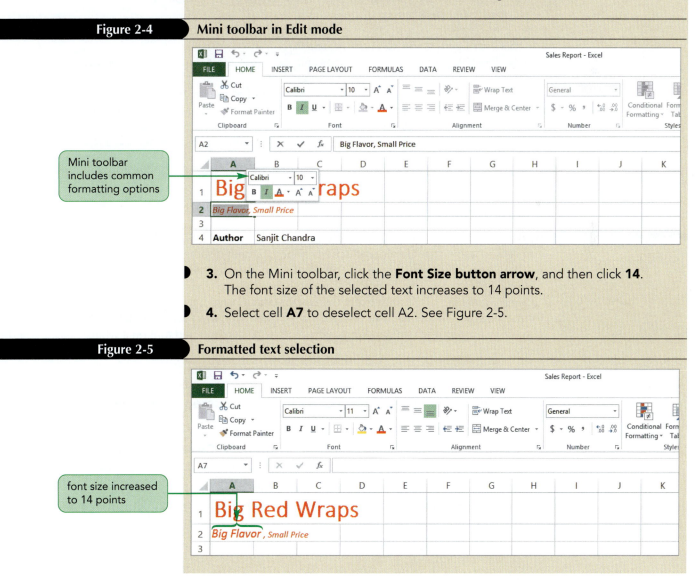

3. On the Mini toolbar, click the **Font Size button arrow**, and then click **14**. The font size of the selected text increases to 14 points.

4. Select cell **A7** to deselect cell A2. See Figure 2-5.

Figure 2-5   Formatted text selection

Working with Fill Colors and Backgrounds

Another way to distinguish sections of a worksheet is by formatting the cell background. You can fill the cell background with color or an image. Sanjit wants you to add fill colors and background images to the Documentation worksheet.

INSIGHT

Using Color to Enhance a Workbook

When used wisely, color can enhance any workbook. However, when used improperly, color can distract the user, making the workbook more difficult to read. As you format a workbook, keep in mind the following tips:

- Use colors from the same theme to maintain a consistent look and feel across the worksheets. If the built-in themes do not fit your needs, you can create a custom theme.
- Use colors to differentiate types of cell content and to direct users where to enter data. For example, format a worksheet so that formula results appear in cells without a fill color and users enter data in cells with a light gray fill color.
- Avoid color combinations that are difficult to read.
- Print the workbook on both color and black-and-white printers to ensure that the printed copy is readable in both versions.
- Understand your printer's limitations and features. Colors that look good on your monitor might not look as good when printed.
- Be sensitive to your audience. About 8 percent of all men and 0.5 percent of all women have some type of color blindness and might not be able to see the text when certain color combinations are used. Red-green color blindness is the most common, so avoid using red text on a green background or green text on a red background.

Changing a Fill Color

TIP

You can also change a sheet tab's color. Right-click a sheet tab, point to Tab Color on the shortcut menu, and then click a color.

By default, worksheet cells do not include any background color. But background colors, also known as fill colors, can be helpful for distinguishing different parts of a worksheet or adding visual interest. You add fill colors to selected cells in the worksheet from the Fill Color gallery, which has the same options as the Font Color gallery.

Sanjit wants the labels and text in the Documentation sheet to stand out. You will format the labels in a white font on a red background, and then you'll format the author's name, current date, and purpose of the worksheet in a red font on a white background.

To change the fill and font colors in the Documentation worksheet:

1. Select the range **A4:A6**.

2. On the HOME tab, in the Font group, click the **Fill Color button arrow** 🖌️ ▾, and then click the **Red** color (the second color) in the Standard Colors section.

3. In the Font group, click the **Font Color button arrow** 🅰 ▾, and then click the **White, Background 1** color in the Theme Colors section. The labels are formatted in white text on a red background.

4. Select the range **B4:B6**, and then format the cells with a red font and a white background.

5. Increase the width of column B to **30** characters, and then wrap the text in the selected range.

6. Select the range **A4:B6**, and then add all borders around each of the selected cells.

7. Click cell **A7** to deselect the range. See Figure 2-6.

Figure 2-6   **Font and fill colors in the Documentation sheet**

Adding a Background Image

A background image can provide a textured appearance, like that of granite, wood, or fibered paper, to a worksheet. The image is repeated until it fills the entire sheet. The background image does not affect any cell's format or content. Fill colors added to cells appear on top of the image, covering that portion of the image. Background images are visible only on the screen; they do not print.

Sanjit has provided an image that he wants you to use as the background of the Documentation sheet.

To add a background image to the Documentation sheet:

1. On the ribbon, click the **PAGE LAYOUT** tab to display the page layout options.

2. In the Page Setup group, click the **Background** button. The Insert Pictures dialog box opens with options to select a picture from a file, select Office.com Clip Art, or perform a Bing Image Search.

3. Click the **Browse** button next to the From a file label. The Sheet Background dialog box opens.

4. Navigate to the **Excel2 ▶ Tutorial** folder included with your Data Files, click the **Background** JPEG image file, and then click the **Insert** button. The image is added to the background of the Documentation sheet, and the Background button changes to the Delete Background button, which you can use to remove the background image. See Figure 2-7.

Figure 2-7   **Background image in the Documentation sheet**

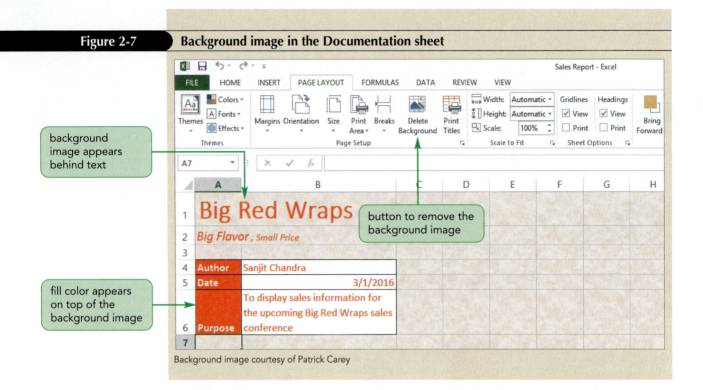

background image appears behind text

button to remove the background image

fill color appears on top of the background image

Background image courtesy of Patrick Carey

Using Functions and Formulas to Calculate Sales Data

In the Sales Report worksheet, you will format the gross sales from each of the store's 20 restaurants and the summary statistics for those stores. The Sales Report worksheet is divided into two areas. The table at the bottom of the worksheet displays gross sales for the past year for each month by restaurant. The section at the top of the worksheet summarizes the sales data for the past two years. Sanjit collected the following sales data:

- **Gross Sales**—the total amount of sales at all of the restaurants
- **Cost of Sales**—the cost of producing the store's menu items
- **Operating Expenses**—the cost of running the stores including the employment and insurance costs
- **Net Profit/Loss**—the difference between the income from the gross sales and the total cost of sales and operating expenses
- **Units Sold**—the total number of menu items sold by the company during the year
- **Customers Served**—the total number of customers served by the company during the year

Sanjit wants you to calculate these sales statistics for the entire company and per store so he can track how well the stores are performing. First, you will calculate the total gross sales for Big Red Wraps and the company's overall net profit and loss.

To calculate the company's sales and profit/loss:

▶ 1. Click the **Sales Report** sheet tab to make the Sales Report worksheet active.

2. Click cell **C6**, type the formula **=SUM(C27:N46)** to calculate the total gross sales from all stores in the previous year, and then press the **Enter** key. Cell C6 displays 9514000, which means that Big Red Wraps' total gross sales for the previous year were more than $9.5 million.

TIP

To enter content in a cell, you select the cell, type the specified content, and then press the Enter key.

3. In cell **C9**, enter the formula **=C6–(C7+C8)** to calculate the current year's net profit/loss, which is equal to the difference between the gross sales and the sum of the cost of sales and operating expenses. Cell C9 displays 1108000, which means that the company's net profit for 2015 was more than $1.1 million.

4. Copy the formula in cell **C9**, and then paste it into cell **D9** to calculate the net profit/loss for 2014. Cell D9 displays 1264000, which means that the company's net profit for that year was more than $1.26 million.

Next, Sanjit asks you to summarize the sales statistics for each store. Sanjit wants the same per-store statistics calculated for the 2015 and 2014 sales data. Per-store sales statistics are calculated by dividing the overall statistics by the number of stores. In this case, you will divide the overall statistics by the value in cell C23, which contains the total number of stores in the Big Red Wraps chain. After you enter the 2015 formulas, you can copy and paste them to calculate the 2014 results.

To calculate the per-store statistics:

1. In cell **C16**, enter the formula **=C6/C23** to calculate the gross sales per store in 2015. The formula returns 475700, which means that the annual gross sales amount for a Big Red Wraps store in 2015 was more than $475,000.

2. In cell **C17**, enter the formula **=C7/C23** to calculate the cost of sales per store in 2015. The formula returns the value 168700, which means that the cost of sales for a Big Red Wraps store in 2015 was typically $168,700.

3. In cell **C18**, enter the formula **=C8/C23** to calculate the operating expenses per store in 2015. The formula returns the value 251600, which means that operating expenses of a typical store in 2015 were $251,600.

4. In cell **C19**, enter the formula **=C9/C23** to calculate the net profit/loss per store in 2015. The formula returns the value 55400, indicating that the net profit/loss of a typical store in 2015 was $55,400.

5. In cell **C21**, enter the formula **=C11/C23** to calculate the units sold per store in 2015. The formula returns the value 67200, indicating that a typical store sold 67,200 units during 2015.

6. In cell **C22**, enter the formula **=C12/C23** to calculate the customers served per store in 2015. The formula returns the value 7770, indicating that a typical store served 7,770 customers during that year.

7. Copy the formulas in the range **C16:C22** and paste them into the range **D16:D22**. The cell references in the formulas change to calculate the sales data for the year 2014.

8. Select cell **B24** to deselect the range. See Figure 2-8.

Figure 2-8 **Sales statistics for the entire company and per store**

overall store sales statistics

per-store sales statistics are calculated by dividing the overall statistics by the number of stores

number of stores in 2014 and 2015

	A	B	C	D	E	F	G	H	I
5		Category	2015	2014	Net Change	% Change			
6		Gross Sales	9514000	8424000					
7		Cost of Sales	3374000	2784000					
8		Operating Expenses	5032000	4376000					
9		Net Profit/Loss	1108000	1264000					
10									
11		Units Sold	1344000	1104000					
12		Customers Served	155400	129600					
13									
14		Sales Statistics per Store							
15		Category	2015	2014	Net Change	% Change			
16		Gross Sales	475700	526500					
17		Cost of Sales	168700	174000					
18		Operating Expenses	251600	273500					
19		Net Profit/Loss	55400	79000					
20									
21		Units Sold	67200	69000					
22		Customers Served	7770	8100					
23		Stores	20	16					

Documentation Sales Report ⊕

READY

Sanjit also wants to explore how the company's sales and expenses have changed from 2014 to 2015. To do this, you will calculate the net change in sales from 2014 to 2015 as well as the percent change. The percent change is calculated using the following formula:

$$percent\ change = \frac{2015\ value - 2014\ value}{2014\ value}$$

You will calculate the net and percent changes for all of the sales statistics.

To calculate the net and percent changes for 2015 and 2014:

1. In cell **E6**, enter the formula **=C6–D6** to calculate the difference between the 2015 and 2014 gross sales. The formula returns 1090000, indicating that gross sales increased by $1.09 million between 2014 and 2015.

2. In cell **F6**, enter the formula **=(C6–D6)/D6** to calculate the percent change in gross sales from 2014 to 2015. The formula returns 0.129392213, indicating a nearly 13% increase in gross sales from 2014 to 2015.

Be sure to include the parentheses as shown to calculate the percent change correctly.

Next, you'll copy and paste the formulas in cells E6 and F6 to the rest of the sales data to calculate the net change and percent change from 2014 to 2015.

3. Select the range **E6:F6**, and then copy the selected range. The two formulas are copied to the Clipboard.

4. Select the nonadjacent range **E7:F9;E11:F12;E16:F19;E21:F23**, and then paste the formulas from the Clipboard into the selected range. The net and percent changes are calculated for the remaining sales data.

5. Click cell **B24** to deselect the range, and then scroll the worksheet up to display row 5. See Figure 2-9.

Figure 2-9	Net and percent changes calculated

column E displays the change in sales values from 2014 to 2015

	A	B		C	D	E	F	G	H	I	J	K
5		Category		2015	2014	Net Change	% Change					
6		Gross Sales		9514000	8424000	1090000	0.129392213					
7		Cost of Sales		3374000	2784000	590000	0.211925287					
8		Operating Expenses		5032000	4376000	656000	0.149908592					
9		Net Profit/Loss		1108000	1264000	-156000	-0.12341772					
10												
11		Units Sold		1344000	1104000	240000	0.217391304					
12		Customers Served		155400	129600	25800	0.199074074					
13												
14		Sales Statistics per Store										
15		Category		2015	2014	Net Change	% Change					
16		Gross Sales		475700	526500	-50800	-0.09648623					
17		Cost of Sales		168700	174000	-5300	-0.03045977					
18		Operating Expenses		251600	273500	-21900	-0.08007313					
19		Net Profit/Loss		55400	79000	-23600	-0.29873418					
20												
21		Units Sold		67200	69000	-1800	-0.02608696					
22		Customers Served		7770	8100	-330	-0.04074074					
23		Stores		20	16	4	0.25					

column F displays the percent change in sales values from 2014 to 2015

percentages are displayed as decimals

Documentation   Sales Report

READY   120%

The bottom part of the worksheet contains the sales for each restaurant from 2015. You will use the SUM function to calculate the total gross sales for each restaurant during the entire year, the total monthly sales of all 20 restaurants, and the total gross sales of all restaurants and months.

To calculate different subtotals of the gross sales:

1. Select cell **O26**, type **TOTAL** as the label, and then press the **Enter** key. Cell O27 is now the active cell.

2. On the HOME tab, in the Editing group, click the **AutoSum** button, and then press the **Enter** key to accept the suggested range reference and enter the formula =SUM(C27:N27) in cell O27. The cell displays 355000, indicating gross sales in 2015 for the 411 Elm Drive restaurant were $355,000.

3. Copy the formula in cell **O27**, and then paste that formula into the range **O28:O46** to calculate the total sales for each of the remaining 19 restaurants in the Big Red Wraps chain.

4. Select cell **B47**, type **TOTAL** as the label, and then press the **Tab** key. Cell C47 is now the active cell.

5. Select the range **C47:O47** so that you can calculate the total monthly sales for all of the stores.

6. On the HOME tab, in the Editing group, click the **AutoSum** button, and then press the **Enter** key to calculate the total sales for each month as well as the total sales for all months. For example, cell C47 displays 680000, indicating that monthly sales for January 2015 for all stores were $680,000.

7. Select cell **O48** to deselect the range. See Figure 2-10.

Figure 2-10   **Gross sales summarized by store and month**

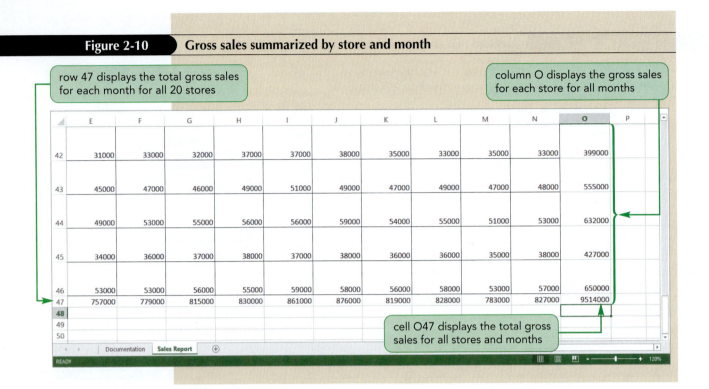

row 47 displays the total gross sales for each month for all 20 stores

column O displays the gross sales for each store for all months

cell O47 displays the total gross sales for all stores and months

	E	F	G	H	I	J	K	L	M	N	O	P
42	31000	33000	32000	37000	37000	38000	35000	33000	35000	33000	399000	
43	45000	47000	46000	49000	51000	49000	47000	49000	47000	48000	555000	
44	49000	53000	55000	56000	56000	59000	54000	55000	51000	53000	632000	
45	34000	36000	37000	38000	37000	38000	36000	36000	35000	38000	427000	
46	53000	53000	56000	55000	59000	58000	56000	58000	53000	57000	650000	
47	757000	779000	815000	830000	861000	876000	819000	828000	783000	827000	9514000	
48												
49												
50												

Documentation   Sales Report   +

READY   120%

Formatting Numbers

The goal in formatting any workbook is to make the content easier to interpret. For numbers, this can mean adding a comma to separate thousands, setting the number of decimal places, and using percentage and currency symbols to make numbers easier to read and understand. Sanjit asks you to format the numbers in the Sales Report worksheet to improve their readability.

Applying Number Formats

You can use a number format to display values in a way that makes them easier to read and understand. Changing the number format of the displayed value does not affect the stored value. Numbers are originally formatted in the **General format**, which, for the most part, displays numbers exactly as they are typed. If the number is calculated from a formula or function, the cell displays as many digits after the decimal point as will fit in the cell with the last digit rounded. Calculated values too large to fit into the cell are displayed in scientific notation.

The General format is fine for small numbers, but some values require additional formatting to make the numbers easier to interpret. For example, you might want to:

- Change the number of digits displayed to the right of the decimal point
- Add commas to separate thousands in large numbers
- Apply currency symbols to numbers to identify the monetary unit being used
- Display percentages using the % symbol

Excel supports two monetary formats: currency and accounting. Both formats add a thousands separator to the currency values and display two digits to the right of the decimal point. However, the **Currency format** places a currency symbol directly to the left of the first digit of the currency value and displays negative numbers with a negative sign. The **Accounting format** fixes a currency symbol at the left edge of the column, and displays negative numbers within parentheses and zero values with a dash. It also slightly indents the values from the right edge of the cell to allow room for parentheses around negative values. Figure 2-11 compares the two formats.

Figure 2-11	Currency and Accounting number formats

Currency Format	Accounting Format
$95,000.00	$ 95,000.00
-$3,300.00	$ (3,300.00)
$0.00	$ -
$1,108.00	$ 1,108.00

negative values displayed with a negative sign

$ symbols placed to the left of the leading digit

negative values displayed in parentheses

zeros displayed with a dash

$ symbols fixed on the left edge of the cell

values slightly indented from the right cell edge

PROSKILLS

Written Communication: Formatting Monetary Values

Spreadsheets commonly include monetary values. To make these values simpler to read and comprehend, keep in mind the following guidelines when formatting the currency data in a worksheet:

- **Format for your audience.** For general financial reports, round values to the nearest hundred, thousand, or million. Investors are generally more interested in the big picture than in exact values. However, for accounting reports, accuracy is important and often legally required. So, for those reports, be sure to display the exact monetary value.
- **Use thousands separators.** Large strings of numbers can be challenging to read. For monetary values, use a thousands separator to make the amounts easier to comprehend.
- **Apply the Accounting format to columns of monetary values.** The Accounting format makes columns of numbers easier to read than the Currency format. Use the Currency format for individual cells that are not part of long columns of numbers.
- **Use only two currency symbols in a column of monetary values.** Standard accounting format displays one currency symbol with the first monetary value in the column, and optionally displays a second currency symbol with the last value in that column. Use the Accounting format to fix the currency symbols, lining them up within the column.

Following these standard accounting principles will make your financial data easier to read both on the screen and in printouts.

Sanjit wants you to format the gross sales amounts in the Accounting format so that they are easier to read.

To format the gross sales in the Accounting format:

▶ 1. Select the range **C6:E6** with the gross sales.

▶ 2. On the HOME tab, in the Number group, click the **Accounting Number Format** button $. The numbers are formatted in the Accounting format. You cannot see the format because the cells display ##########.

The cells display ########## because the formatted number doesn't fit into the column. One reason for this is that monetary values, by default, show both dollars and cents in the cell. However, you can increase or decrease the number of decimal places displayed in a cell. The displayed value might then be rounded. For example, the stored value 11.7 will appear in the cell as 12 if no decimal places are displayed to the right of the decimal point. Changing the number of decimal places displayed in a cell does not change the value stored in the cell.

Because Sanjit and the other conference attendees are interested only in whole dollar amounts, he wants you to hide the cents values of the gross sales by decreasing the number of decimal places to zero.

To decrease the number of decimal places displayed in the gross sales:

▶ 1. Make sure the range **C6:E6** is selected.

▶ 2. On the HOME tab, in the Number group, click the **Decrease Decimal** button twice. The cents are hidden for gross sales.

▶ 3. Select cell **C4** to deselect the range. See Figure 2-12.

Figure 2-12 ▶ **Formatted gross sales values**

The Comma style is identical to the Accounting format except that it does not fix a currency symbol to the left of the number. The advantage of using the Comma style and the Accounting format together is that the numbers will be aligned in the column.

Sanjit asks you to apply the Comma style to the remaining sales statistics.

To apply the Comma style to the sales statistics:

▶ 1. Select the nonadjacent range **C7:E9;C11:E12** containing the sales figures for all stores in 2014 and 2015.

▶ 2. On the HOME tab, in the Number group, click the **Comma Style** button ⸲. In some instances, the number is now too large to be displayed in the cell.

▶ 3. In the Number group, click the **Decrease Decimal** button ⸲⁰⁰ twice to remove two decimal places. Digits to the right of the decimal point are hidden for all of the selected cells.

▶ 4. Select cell **C13** to deselect the range. See Figure 2-13.

Figure 2-13   **Formatted sales values**

numbers with the Accounting format and no decimal places

numbers with the Comma style and no decimal places

4	Sales Statistics				
5	Category	2015	2014	Net Change	% Change
6	Gross Sales	$ 9,514,000	$ 8,424,000	$ 1,090,000	0.129392213
7	Cost of Sales	3,374,000	2,784,000	590,000	0.211925287
8	Operating Expenses	5,032,000	4,376,000	656,000	0.149908592
9	Net Profit/Loss	1,108,000	1,264,000	(156,000)	-0.12341772
10					
11	Units Sold	1,344,000	1,104,000	240,000	0.217391304
12	Customers Served	155,400	129,600	25,800	0.199074074
13					
14	Sales Statistics per Store				
15	Category	2015	2014	Net Change	% Change
16	Gross Sales	475700	526500	-50800	-0.09648623
17	Cost of Sales	168700	174000	-5300	-0.03045977
18	Operating Expenses	251600	273500	-21900	-0.08007313
19	Net Profit/Loss	55400	79000	-23600	-0.29873418

numbers aligned within each column

Documentation   **Sales Report**   ⊕

READY

The Percent style formats numbers as percentages. When you format values as percentages, the % symbol appears after the number and no digits appear to the right of the decimal point. You can always change how many decimal places are displayed in the cell if that is important to show with your data.

Sanjit wants you to format the percent change from the 2014 to 2015 sales statistics with a percent symbol to make the percent values easier to read.

To format percentages:

▶ 1. Select the nonadjacent range **F6:F9;F11:F12** containing the percent change values.

▶ 2. On the HOME tab, in the Number group, click the **Percent Style** button % (or press the **Ctrl+Shift+%** keys). The values are displayed as percentages.

▶ 3. In the Number group, click the **Increase Decimal** button ⁰⁰ twice. The displayed number includes two decimal places.

▶ 4. Select cell **F13** to deselect the range. See Figure 2-14.

Figure 2-14   **Formatted percent changes**

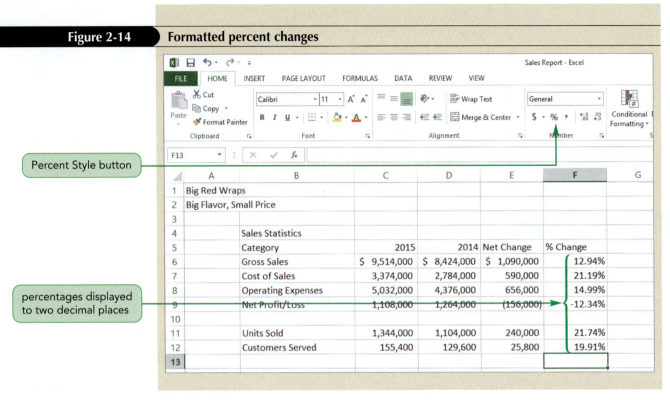

With the data reformatted, the worksheet clearly shows that Big Red Wraps' gross sales increased from 2014 to 2015 by almost 13 percent. However, both the cost of sales and the operating expenses increased by about 21.2 percent and 15 percent, respectively, probably due to the cost of building four new stores. As a result, the company's net profit decreased by $156,000 or about 12.3 percent.

Formatting Dates and Times

TIP

To view the underlying date and time value, apply the General format to the cell or display the formulas instead of the formula results.

Because Excel stores dates and times as numbers and not as text, you can apply different formats without affecting the date and time value. The abbreviated format, *mm/dd/yyyy*, entered in the Documentation sheet is referred to as the **Short Date format**. You can also apply a **Long Date format** that displays the day of the week and the full month name in addition to the day of the month and the year. Other built-in formats include formats for displaying time values in 12- or 24-hour time format.

You will change the date in the Documentation sheet to the Long Date format.

To format the date in the Long Date format:

1. Go to the **Documentation** sheet, and then select cell **B5**.

2. On the ribbon, make sure the HOME tab is displayed.

3. In the Number group, click the **Number Format button arrow** to display a list of number formats, and then click **Long Date**. The date is displayed with the weekday name, month name, day, and year. Notice that the date in the formula bar did not change because you changed only the display format, not the date value.

Formatting Worksheet Cells

You can format the appearance of individual cells by modifying the alignment of text within the cell, indenting cell text, or adding borders of different styles and colors.

Aligning Cell Content

By default, text is aligned with the left and bottom borders of a cell, and numbers are aligned with the right and bottom borders. You might want to change the alignment to make the text and numbers more readable or visually appealing. In general, you should center column titles, left-align other text, and right-align numbers to keep their decimal places lined up within a column. Figure 2-15 describes the buttons you use to set these alignment options, which are located in the Alignment group on the HOME tab.

Figure 2-15   **Alignment buttons**

Button	Name	Description
	Top Align	Aligns the cell content with the cell's top edge
	Middle Align	Vertically centers the cell content within the cell
	Bottom Align	Aligns the cell content with the cell's bottom edge
	Align Left	Aligns the cell content with the cell's left edge
	Center	Horizontally centers the cell content within the cell
	Align Right	Aligns the cell content with the cell's right edge
	Decrease Indent	Decreases the size of the indentation used in the cell
	Increase Indent	Increases the size of the indentation used in the cell
	Orientation	Rotates the cell content to any angle within the cell
	Wrap Text	Forces the cell text to wrap within the cell borders
	Merge & Center	Merges the selected cells into a single cell

© 2014 Cengage Learning

The date in the Documentation sheet is right-aligned in the cell because Excel treats dates and times as numbers. Sanjit wants you to left-align the date and center the column titles in the Sales Report worksheet.

To left-align the date and center the column titles:

1. In the Documentation sheet, make sure cell **B5** is still selected.

2. On the HOME tab, in the Alignment group, click the **Align Left** button. The date shifts to the left edge of the cell.

3. Make the **Sales Report** worksheet the active worksheet.

4. Select the range **C5:F5**. The column titles are selected.

5. In the Alignment group, click the **Center** button. The column titles are centered in the cells.

Indenting Cell Content

Sometimes you want a cell's content moved a few spaces from the cell's left edge. This is particularly useful to create subsections in a worksheet or to set off some entries from others. You can increase the indent to shift the contents of a cell away from the left edge of the cell, or you can decrease the indent to shift a cell's contents closer to the left edge of the cell.

Sanjit wants the Cost of Sales and Operating Expenses labels in the sales statistics table offset from the other labels because they represent expenses to the company. You will increase the indent for the expense categories.

To indent the expense categories:

1. Select the range **B7:B8** containing the expense categories.

2. On the HOME tab, in the Alignment group, click the **Increase Indent** button ⬛ twice to indent each label two spaces in its cell.

Adding Cell Borders

Common accounting practices provide guidelines on when to add borders to cells. In general, a single black border appears above a subtotal, a single bottom border is added below a calculated number, and a double black bottom border appears below the total.

Sanjit wants you to follow these common accounting practices in the Sales Report worksheet. You will add borders below the column titles and below the gross sales values. You will add a top border to the net profit/loss values. Finally, you will add a top and bottom border to the Units Sold and Customers Served rows.

To add borders to the sales statistics data:

1. Select the range **B5:F5** containing the table headings.

2. On the HOME tab, in the Font group, click the **All Borders button arrow** ⬛ ▾, and then click **Bottom Border**. A border is added below the column titles.

3. Select the range **B6:F6** containing the gross sales amounts.

4. In the Font group, click the **Bottom Border** button ⬛ to add a border below the selected gross sales amounts.

5. Select the range **B9:F9**, click the **Bottom Border button arrow** ⬛ ▾, and then click **Top Border** to add a border above the net profit/loss amounts.

   The Units Sold and Customers Served rows do not contain monetary values as the other rows do. You will distinguish these rows by adding a top and bottom border.

6. Select the range **B11:F12**, click the **Top Border button arrow** ⬛ ▾, and then click **Top and Bottom** to add a border above the number of units sold and below the number of customers served.

7. Select cell **B3** to deselect the range. See Figure 2-16.

Figure 2-16   **Worksheet with formatted cells**

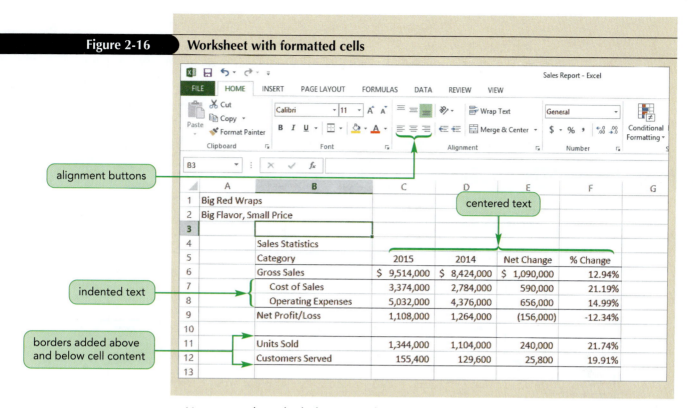

You can apply multiple formats to the same cell to create the look that best fits the data. For example, one cell might be formatted with a number format, alignments, borders, indents, fonts, font sizes, and so on. The monthly sales data needs to be formatted with number styles, alignment, indents, and borders. You'll add these formats now.

To format the monthly sales table:

▶ 1. Click the **Name** box to select the cell reference, type **C27:O47**, and then press the **Enter** key to quickly select the range C27:O47 containing the monthly gross sales for each restaurant.

▶ 2. On the HOME tab, in the Number group, click the **Comma Style** button ⟨,⟩ to add a thousands separator to the values.

▶ 3. In the Number group, click the **Decrease Decimal** button ⟨.00→.0⟩ twice to hide the cents from the sales results.

▶ 4. In the Alignment group, click the **Top Align** button ⟨≡⟩ to align the sales numbers with the top of each cell.

▶ 5. Select the range **C26:O26** containing the labels for the month abbreviations and the TOTAL column.

▶ 6. In the Alignment group, click the **Center** button ⟨≡⟩ to center the column labels.

▶ 7. Select the range **B27:B46** containing the store addresses.

▶ 8. Reduce the font size of the store addresses to **9** points.

▶ 9. In the Alignment group, click the **Increase Indent** button ⟨≡≡⟩ to indent the store addresses.

▶ 10. In the Alignment group, click the **Top Align** button ⟨≡⟩ to align the addresses at the top of each cell.

▶ 11. Select the range **B47:O47** containing the monthly totals.

▶ **12.** In the Font group, click the **Top and Bottom Borders button arrow** ▦ ▾, and then click **All Borders** to add borders around each monthly totals cell.

▶ **13.** Select the range **O26:O46**, which contains the annual totals for each restaurant, and then click the **All Borders** button ▦ to add borders around each restaurant total.

▶ **14.** Select cell **A24** to deselect the range. See Figure 2-17.

Figure 2-17   **Formatted monthly gross sales figures**

gross sales values aligned with the top of the cell

month abbreviations are centered

address text is 9 points

thousands separators displayed

Merging Cells

You can merge, or combine, several cells into one cell. A merged cell contains two or more cells with a single cell reference. When you merge cells, only the content from the upper-left cell in the range is retained. The cell reference for the merged cell is the upper-left cell reference. So, if you merge cells A1 and A2, the merged cell reference is cell A1. After you merge cells, you can align the content within the merged cell. The Merge & Center button in the Alignment group on the HOME tab includes the following options:

- **Merge & Center**—merges the range into one cell and horizontally centers the content
- **Merge Across**—merges each row in the selected range across the columns in the range
- **Merge Cells**—merges the range into a single cell, but does not horizontally center the cell content
- **Unmerge Cells**—reverses a merge, returning the merged cell to a range of individual cells

The first column of the monthly sales data lists the states in which Big Red Wraps has stores. You will merge the cells for each state name.

To merge the state name cells:

▶ **1.** Select the range **A27:A33** containing the cells for the Wisconsin stores. You will merge these seven cells into a single cell.

2. On the HOME tab, in the Alignment group, click the **Merge & Center** button. The range A27:A33 merges into one cell with the cell reference A27, and the text is centered and bottom-aligned within the cell.

3. Select the range **A34:A36**, and then click the **Merge & Center** button in the Alignment group to merge and center the Minnesota cells.

4. Select the range **A37:A40**, and then click the **Merge & Center** button to merge and center the Iowa cells.

5. Select cell **A41**, and then center it horizontally to align the Colorado text with the text in the other state cells.

6. Merge and center the range **A42:A43** containing the Nebraska cells.

7. Merge and center the range **A44:A46** containing the Kansas cells. See Figure 2-18. The merged cells make it easier to distinguish restaurants in each state.

Figure 2-18   Merged cells

	A	B	C	D	E	F	G
40	Iowa	414 Main St. Des Moines, IA 50311 (515) 555 - 3134	46,000	43,000	52,000	51,000	54
41	Colorado	112 Reservoir Ln. Greeley, CO 80631 (970) 555 - 2138	38,000	35,000	43,000	42,000	44
42		5155 Pocane Dr. Grand Island, NE 68801 (402) 555 - 7734	27,000	28,000	31,000	33,000	32
43	Nebraska	42 East River Rd. Omaha, NE 68111 (402) 555 - 9148	38,000	39,000	45,000	47,000	46
44		975 Business Dr. Manhattan, KS 66502 (785) 555 - 0444	46,000	45,000	49,000	53,000	55
45		47 Valley View Ln. Topeka, KS 66604 (785) 555 - 6106	31,000	31,000	34,000	36,000	37
46	Kansas	87210 Causeway Dr. Salina, KS 67401 (785) 555 - 8103	47,000	45,000	53,000	53,000	56
47		TOTAL	680,000	659,000	757,000	779,000	815
48							

merged cell A42 contains the range A42:A43

merged cell A44 contains the range A44:A46

Documentation   **Sales Report**

READY

Rotating Cell Contents

Text and numbers are displayed horizontally within cells. However, you can rotate cell text to any angle to save space or to provide visual interest to a worksheet. The state names at the bottom of the merged cells would look better and take up less room if they were rotated vertically within their cells. Sanjit asks you to rotate the state names.

To rotate the state names:

1. Select the merged cell **A27**.

2. On the HOME tab, in the Alignment group, click the **Orientation** button to display a list of rotation options, and then click **Rotate Text Up**. The state name rotates 90 degrees counterclockwise.

▶ **3.** In the Alignment group, click the **Middle Align** button ☰ to vertically center the rotated text in the merged cell.

▶ **4.** Select the merged cell range **A34:A44**, and then repeat Steps 2 and 3 to rotate and vertically center the rest of the state names in their cells.

▶ **5.** Select cell **A41** to deselect the range, and then increase the height of row 41 (the Colorado row) to **75** points (**100** pixels) so that the entire state name appears in the cell.

▶ **6.** Reduce the width of column A to **7** characters because the rotated state names take up less space.

▶ **7.** Select cell **A47**. See Figure 2-19.

Figure 2-19   ▶   **Rotated cell content**

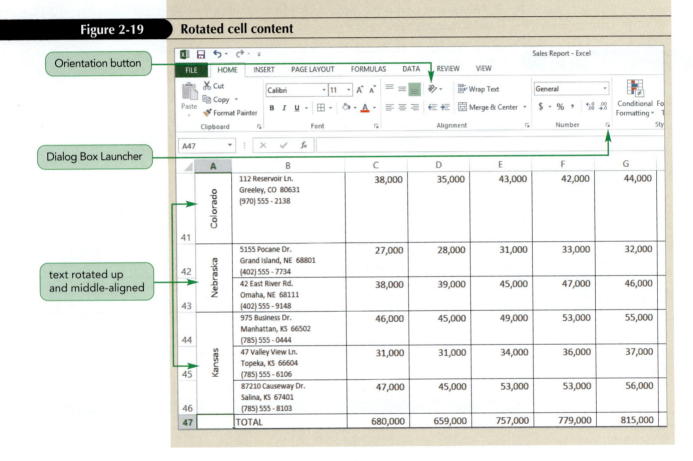

Exploring the Format Cells Dialog Box

The buttons on the HOME tab provide quick access to the most commonly used formatting choices. For more options, you can use the Format Cells dialog box. You can apply the formats in this dialog box to the selected worksheet cells. The Format Cells dialog box has six tabs, each focusing on a different set of formatting options, as described below:

- **Number**—provides options for formatting the appearance of numbers, including dates and numbers treated as text such as telephone or Social Security numbers
- **Alignment**—provides options for how data is aligned within a cell
- **Font**—provides options for selecting font types, sizes, styles, and other formatting attributes such as underlining and font colors

- **Border**—provides options for adding and removing cell borders as well as selecting a line style and color
- **Fill**—provides options for creating and applying background colors and patterns to cells
- **Protection**—provides options for locking or hiding cells to prevent other users from modifying their contents

Although you have applied many of these formats from the HOME tab, the Format Cells dialog box presents them in a different way and provides more choices. You will use the Font and Fill tabs to format the column titles with a white font on a red background.

To use the Format Cells dialog box to format the column labels:

1. Select the range **A26:O26** containing the column labels for the table.

TIP

You can also open the Format Cells dialog box by right-clicking the selected range, and then clicking Format Cells on the shortcut menu.

2. On the HOME tab, in the Number group, click the **Dialog Box Launcher** located to the right of the group name (refer to Figure 2-19). The Format Cells dialog box opens with the Number tab displayed.

3. Click the **Font** tab to display the font formatting options.

4. Click the **Color** box to display the color palette, and then click the **White, Background 1** theme color. The font is set to white. See Figure 2-20.

Figure 2-20   Font tab in the Format Cells dialog box

5. Click the **Fill** tab to display background options.

6. In the Background Color palette, click the **red** standard color (the second color in the last row). The background is set to red, as you can see in the Sample box.

7. Click the **OK** button. The dialog box closes, and the font and fill options you selected are applied to the column titles.

You will also use the Format Cells dialog box to change the appearance of the row titles. You'll format them to be displayed in a larger white font on a gray background.

To format the row labels:

▶ 1. Select the range **A27:A46** containing the rotated state names.

▶ 2. Right-click the selected range, and then click **Format Cells** on the shortcut menu. The Format Cells dialog box opens with the last tab used displayed—in this case, the Fill tab.

▶ 3. In the Background Color palette, click the **gray** theme color (the first color in the seventh column). Its preview is shown in the Sample box.

▶ 4. Click the **Font** tab to display the font formatting options.

▶ 5. Click the **Color** box, and then click the **White, Background 1** theme color to set the font color to white.

▶ 6. Scroll down the **Size** box, and then click **16** to set the font size to 16 points.

▶ 7. Click the **OK** button. The dialog box closes, and the font and fill formats are applied to the state names.

The Border tab in the Format Cells dialog box provides options for changing the border style and color as well as placing the border anywhere around a cell or cells in a selected range. Sanjit wants you to format the borders in the monthly sales data so that the sales result from each state is surrounded by a double border.

To add a double border to the state results:

▶ 1. Select the range **A27:O33** containing the monthly sales totals for the Wisconsin restaurants.

▶ 2. Open the Format Cells dialog box, and then click the **Border** tab to display the border options.

▶ 3. In the Style box, click the **double line** in the lower-right corner of the box.

▶ 4. In the Presets section, click the **Outline** option. The double border appears around the outside of the selected cells in the Border preview. See Figure 2-21.

Figure 2-21   Border tab in the Format Cells dialog box

5. Click the **OK** button. The selected border is applied to the Wisconsin monthly sales.

6. Repeat Steps 2 through 5 to apply double borders to the ranges **A34:O36**, **A37:O40**, **A41:O41**, **A42:O43**, and **A44:O46**.

7. Select cell **A48** to deselect the range. See Figure 2-22.

Figure 2-22   **Worksheet with font, fill, and border formatting**

state names in a 16-point white font on a gray background

double borders around state sales rows

8. Save the Sales Report worksheet.

You have completed much of the formatting that Sanjit wants in the Sales Report worksheet for the Big Red Wraps sales conference. In the next session, you will explore other formatting options.

Session 2.1 Quick Check

REVIEW

1. What is the difference between a serif font and a sans serif font?

2. What is the difference between a theme color and a standard color?

3. A cell containing a number displays ######. Why does this occur and what can you do to fix it?

4. What is the General format?

5. Describe the differences between Currency format and Accounting format.

6. The range A1:C5 is merged into a single cell. What is its cell reference?

7. How do you format text so that it is set vertically within the cell?

8. Where can you access all the formatting options for worksheet cells?

Session 2.2 Visual Overview:

The PAGE LAYOUT tab has options for setting how the worksheet will print.

The **Format Painter** copies and pastes formatting from one cell or range to another without duplicating any data.

Print titles are rows and columns that are included on every page of the printout. In this case, the text in rows 1 and 2 will print on every page.

A **manual page break** is one you set to indicate where a new page of the printout should start and is identified by a solid blue line.

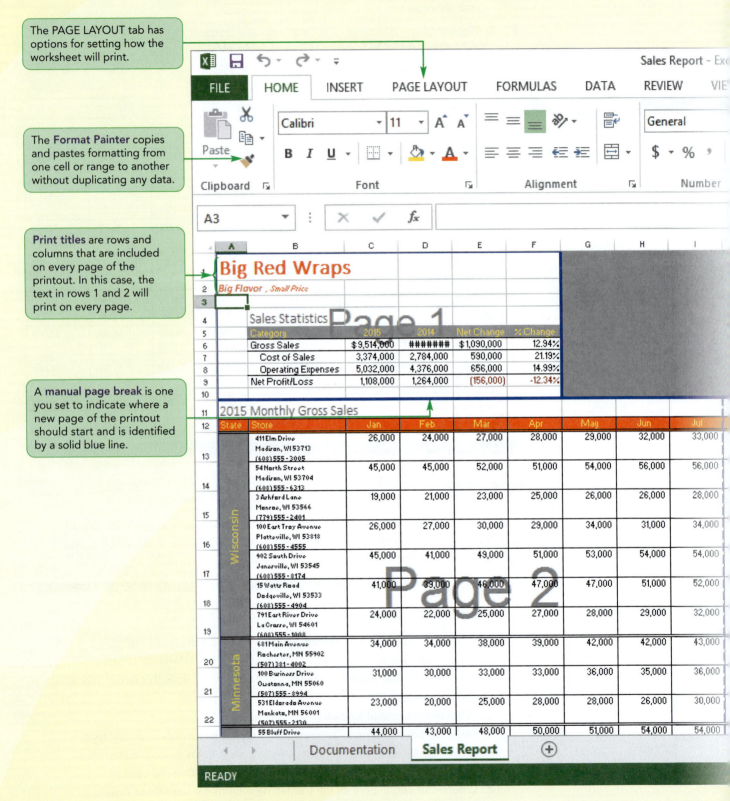

Worksheet Formatted for Printing

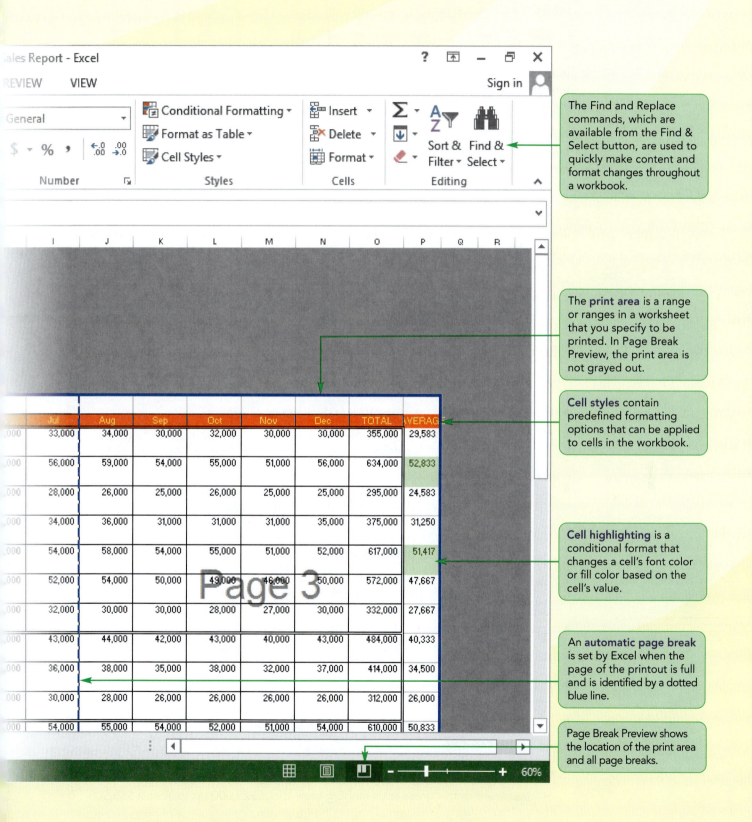

The Find and Replace commands, which are available from the Find & Select button, are used to quickly make content and format changes throughout a workbook.

The **print area** is a range or ranges in a worksheet that you specify to be printed. In Page Break Preview, the print area is not grayed out.

Cell styles contain predefined formatting options that can be applied to cells in the workbook.

Cell highlighting is a conditional format that changes a cell's font color or fill color based on the cell's value.

An **automatic page break** is set by Excel when the page of the printout is full and is identified by a dotted blue line.

Page Break Preview shows the location of the print area and all page breaks.

Using the Average Function

The **AVERAGE function** calculates the average value from a collection of numbers. The syntax of the Average function is

```
AVERAGE (number1, number2, number3, …)
```

where *number1, number2, number3,* and so forth are either numbers or cell references to the cells or a range where the numbers are stored. For example, the following formula uses the AVERAGE function to calculate the average of 1, 2, 5, and 8, returning the value 4:

```
=AVERAGE(1, 2, 5, 8)
```

However, functions usually reference values entered in a worksheet. So, if the range A1:A4 contains the values 1, 2, 5, and 8, the following formula also returns the value 4:

```
=AVERAGE(A1:A4)
```

The advantage of using cell references is that the values used in the function are visible and can be easily edited.

Sanjit wants to show the average monthly sales for each of the 20 Big Red Wraps stores in addition to the total sales for each store. You will use the AVERAGE function to calculate these values.

To calculate the average monthly sales for each store:

▶ **1.** If you took a break after the previous session, make sure the Sales Report workbook is open and the Sales Report worksheet is active.

▶ **2.** In cell **P26**, enter the text **AVERAGE** as the label.

▶ **3.** Select cell **P27**. You will enter the AVERAGE function in this cell to calculate the average monthly sales for the store on 411 Elm Drive in Madison, Wisconsin.

▶ **4.** On the HOME tab, in the Editing group, click the **AutoSum button arrow**, and then click **AVERAGE**. The formula =AVERAGE(C27:O27) appears in the cell. The range reference that was included in the function is incorrect. It includes cell O27, which contains the total gross sales for all months. You need to correct the range reference.

▶ **5.** Select **O27** in the function's argument, and then click cell **N27** to replace the cell reference. The range reference now correctly includes only the gross sales for each month.

▶ **6.** Press the **Enter** key to complete the formula. The formula results show 29,583, which is the monthly gross sales from the store on 411 Elm Drive in Madison, Wisconsin.

▶ **7.** Select cell **P27**, and then change the alignment to **Top Align** so that the calculated value is aligned with the top of the cell.

▶ **8.** Copy the formula in cell **P27**, and then paste the copied formula into the range **P28:P47**.

▶ **9.** Select cell **P48** to deselect the range. As shown in Figure 2-23, the average monthly sales from all of the stores are $792,833. Individual stores have average monthly gross sales ranging from about $25,000 up to almost $55,000.

Figure 2-23 | **AVERAGE function results**

average gross sales for each store per month

average gross sales for all stores per month

With the last formulas added to the worksheet, Sanjit wants you to continue formatting the workbook.

Applying Cell Styles

A workbook often contains several cells that store the same type of data. For example, each worksheet might have a cell displaying the sheet title, or a range of financial data might have several cells containing totals and averages. It is good design practice to apply the same format to worksheet cells that contain the same type of data.

One way to ensure that similar data is displayed consistently is with styles. A **style** is a collection of formatting options that include a specified font, font size, font styles, font color, fill color, and borders. The Cell Styles gallery includes a variety of built-in styles that you can use to format titles and headings, different types of data such as totals or calculations, and cells that you want to emphasize. For example, you can use the Heading 1 style to display sheet titles in a bold, blue-gray, 15-point Calibri font with no fill color and a blue bottom border. You can then apply the Heading 1 style to all titles in the workbook. If you later revise the style, the appearance of any cell formatted with that style is updated automatically. This saves you the time and effort of reformatting each cell individually.

You already used built-in styles when you formatted data in the Sales Report worksheet with the Accounting, Comma, and Percent styles. You can also create your own cell styles by clicking New Cell Style at the bottom of the Cell Styles gallery.

Sanjit wants you to add more color and visual interest to the Sales Report worksheet. You'll use some of the styles in the Cell Styles gallery to do this.

To apply cell styles to the Sales Report worksheet:

1. Select cell **B4** containing the text "Sales Statistics."

2. On the HOME tab, in the Styles group, click the **Cell Styles** button. The Cell Styles gallery opens.

3. Point to the **Heading 1** style in the Titles and Headings section. Live Preview shows cell B4 in a 15-point, bold font with a solid blue bottom border. See Figure 2-24.

Figure 2-24   Cell Styles gallery

4. Move the pointer over different styles in the Cell Styles gallery to see cell B4 with a Live Preview of each style.

5. Click the **Title** style. The Title style is applied to cell B4.

6. Select the range **B5:F5** containing the column labels for the Sales Statistics data.

7. In the Styles group, click the **Cell Styles** button, and then click the **Accent3** style in the Themed Cell Styles section of the Cell Styles gallery.

8. Select cell **A25** containing the text "2015 Monthly Gross Sales," and then apply the **Title** cell style to the cell.

9. Select cell **A3**. See Figure 2-25.

Figure 2-25 | **Cell styles applied to the worksheet**

Accent3 style applied to the range B5:F5

Title style applied to cell B4

Copying and Pasting Formats

Large workbooks often use the same formatting on similar data throughout the workbook, sometimes in widely scattered cells. Rather than repeating the same steps to format these cells, you can copy the format of one cell or range and paste it to another.

Copying Formats with the Format Painter

The Format Painter provides a fast and efficient way of copying and pasting formats, ensuring that a workbook has a consistent look and feel. The Format Painter does not copy formatting applied to selected text within a cell, and it does not copy data.

Sanjit wants the Sales Report worksheet to use the same formats you applied to the Big Red Wraps company name and slogan in the Documentation sheet. You will use the Format Painter to copy and paste the formats.

To use the Format Painter to copy and paste a format:

1. Go to the **Documentation** worksheet, and then select the range **A1:A2**.

2. On the HOME tab, in the Clipboard group, click the **Format Painter** button. The formats from the selected cells are copied to the Clipboard, and a flashing border appears around the selected range and the pointer changes to ⊕🖌.

3. Return to the **Sales Report** worksheet, and then click cell **A1**. The formatting from the Documentation worksheet is removed from the Clipboard and applied to the range A1:A2. Notice that the larger font size you applied to the text "Big Flavor" was not included in the pasted formats.

4. Double-click cell **A2** to enter Edit mode, select **Big Flavor**, and then increase the font size to **14** points. The format for the slogan now matches the slogan on the Documentation sheet.

5. Select cell **A3** to exit Edit mode. See Figure 2-26.

Figure 2-26 Formats pasted in the Sales Report worksheet

Format Painter button

format copied from Documentation sheet

You can use the Format Painter to copy all of the formats within a selected range and then apply those formats to another range that has the same size and shape by clicking the upper-left cell of the range. Sanjit wants you to copy all of the formats you applied to the Sales Statistics data to the sales statistics per store.

To copy and paste multiple formats:

1. Select the range **B4:F12** in the Sales Report worksheet.

2. On the HOME tab, in the Clipboard group, click the **Format Painter** button.

3. Click cell **B14**. All of the number formats, cell borders, fonts, and fill colors are pasted into the range B14:F22.

4. Select the range **C23:E23**.

5. On the HOME tab, in the Number group, click the **Comma Style** button ❜, and then click the **Decrease Decimal** button twice to remove the decimal places to the right of the decimal point. The numbers are vertically aligned in their columns.

6. Select cell **F23**.

7. In the Number group, click the **Percent Style** button % to change the number to a percentage, and then click the **Increase Decimal** button twice to display two decimal places in the percentage.

8. Click cell **B24**. See Figure 2-27.

Figure 2-27   Formats pasted from a range

	A	B	C	D	E	F	G	H
6		Gross Sales	$ 9,514,000	$ 8,424,000	$ 1,090,000	12.94%		
7		Cost of Sales	3,374,000	2,784,000	590,000	21.19%		
8		Operating Expenses	5,032,000	4,376,000	656,000	14.99%		
9		Net Profit/Loss	1,108,000	1,264,000	(156,000)	-12.34%		
10								
11		Units Sold	1,344,000	1,104,000	240,000	21.74%		
12		Customers Served	155,400	129,600	25,800	19.91%		
13								
14		Sales Statistics per Store						
15		Category	2015	2014	Net Change	% Change		
16		Gross Sales	$ 475,700	$ 526,500	$ (50,800)	-9.65%		
17		Cost of Sales	168,700	174,000	(5,300)	-3.05%		
18		Operating Expenses	251,600	273,500	(21,900)	-8.01%		
19		Net Profit/Loss	55,400	79,000	(23,600)	-29.87%		
20								
21		Units Sold	67,200	69,000	(1,800)	-2.61%		
22		Customers Served	7,770	8,100	(330)	-4.07%		
23		Stores	20	16	4	25.00%		
24								

copied formats

pasted formats

Documentation   **Sales Report**   ⊕

READY

Copying Formats with the Paste Options Button

Another way to copy and paste formats is with the Paste Options button (Ctrl) ▾ , which provides options for pasting only values, only formats, or some combination of values and formats. Each time you paste, the Paste Options button appears in the lower-right corner of the pasted cell or range. You click the Paste Options button to open a list of pasting options, shown in Figure 2-28, such as pasting only the values or only the formatting. You can also click the Transpose button to paste the column data into a row, or to paste the row data into a column.

Figure 2-28   Paste Options button

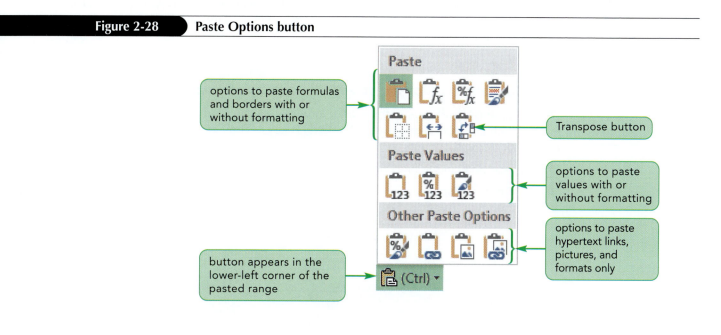

options to paste formulas and borders with or without formatting

Transpose button

options to paste values with or without formatting

options to paste hypertext links, pictures, and formats only

button appears in the lower-left corner of the pasted range

Copying Formats with Paste Special

The Paste Special command provides another way to control what you paste from the Clipboard. To use Paste Special, select and copy a range, select the range where you want to paste the Clipboard contents, click the Paste button arrow in the Clipboard group on the HOME tab, and then click Paste Special to open the dialog box shown in Figure 2-29.

specifies what to paste

applies the specified arithmetic operation to the copied value

avoids pasting into empty cells

pastes column data into a row or row data into a column

From the Paste Special dialog box, you can control exactly how to paste the copied range.

Finding and Replacing Text and Formats

The Find and Replace commands let you make content and design changes to a worksheet or the entire workbook quickly. The Find command searches through the current worksheet or workbook for the content or formatting you want to locate, and the Replace command then substitutes it with the new content or formatting you specify.

Sanjit wants you to replace all the street title abbreviations (such as Ave.) in the Sales Report with their full names (such as Avenue). You will use Find and Replace to make these changes.

To find and replace the street title abbreviations:

1. On the HOME tab, in the Editing group, click the **Find & Select** button, and then click **Replace** (or press the **Ctrl+H** keys). The Find and Replace dialog box opens.

2. Type **Ave.** in the Find what box.

3. Press the **Tab** key to move the insertion point to the Replace with box, and then type **Avenue**. See Figure 2-30.

Figure 2-30   Find and Replace dialog box

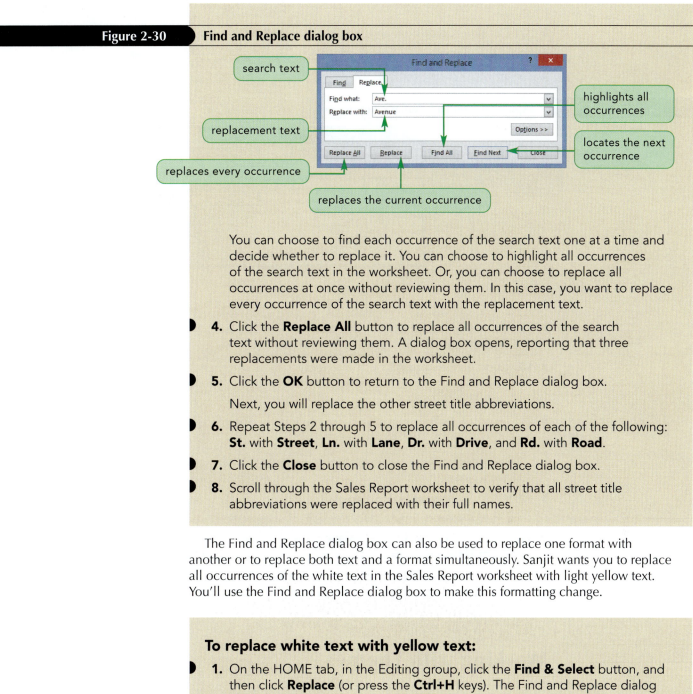

You can choose to find each occurrence of the search text one at a time and decide whether to replace it. You can choose to highlight all occurrences of the search text in the worksheet. Or, you can choose to replace all occurrences at once without reviewing them. In this case, you want to replace every occurrence of the search text with the replacement text.

4. Click the **Replace All** button to replace all occurrences of the search text without reviewing them. A dialog box opens, reporting that three replacements were made in the worksheet.

5. Click the **OK** button to return to the Find and Replace dialog box.

Next, you will replace the other street title abbreviations.

6. Repeat Steps 2 through 5 to replace all occurrences of each of the following: **St.** with **Street**, **Ln.** with **Lane**, **Dr.** with **Drive**, and **Rd.** with **Road**.

7. Click the **Close** button to close the Find and Replace dialog box.

8. Scroll through the Sales Report worksheet to verify that all street title abbreviations were replaced with their full names.

The Find and Replace dialog box can also be used to replace one format with another or to replace both text and a format simultaneously. Sanjit wants you to replace all occurrences of the white text in the Sales Report worksheet with light yellow text. You'll use the Find and Replace dialog box to make this formatting change.

To replace white text with yellow text:

1. On the HOME tab, in the Editing group, click the **Find & Select** button, and then click **Replace** (or press the **Ctrl+H** keys). The Find and Replace dialog box opens.

2. Click the **Options** button to expand the dialog box.

3. Click the **Format** button in the Find what row to open the Find Format dialog box, which is similar to the Format Cells dialog box you used earlier to format a range.

4. Click the **Font** tab to make it active, click the **Color** box, and then click the **White, Background 1** theme color.

5. Click the **OK** button to close the dialog box and return to the Find and Replace dialog box.

6. Click the **Format** button in the Replace with row to open the Replace Format dialog box.

7. Click the **Color** box, and then click the **Yellow** standard color.

8. Click the **OK** button to close the dialog box and return to the Find and Replace dialog box. See Figure 2-31.

Figure 2-31   **Expanded Find and Replace dialog box**

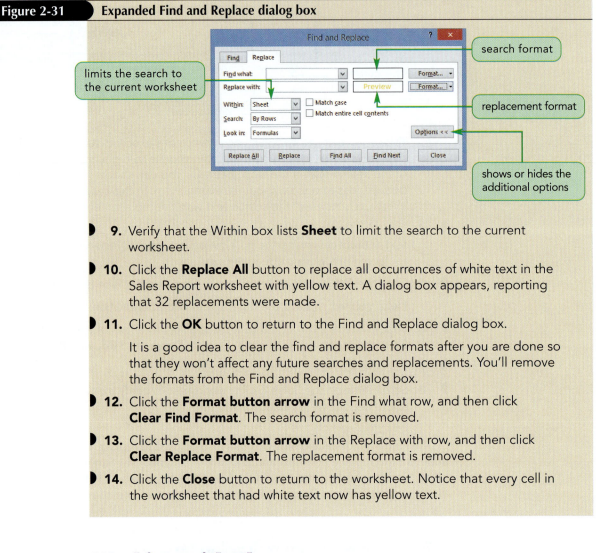

9. Verify that the Within box lists **Sheet** to limit the search to the current worksheet.

10. Click the **Replace All** button to replace all occurrences of white text in the Sales Report worksheet with yellow text. A dialog box appears, reporting that 32 replacements were made.

11. Click the **OK** button to return to the Find and Replace dialog box.

It is a good idea to clear the find and replace formats after you are done so that they won't affect any future searches and replacements. You'll remove the formats from the Find and Replace dialog box.

12. Click the **Format button arrow** in the Find what row, and then click **Clear Find Format**. The search format is removed.

13. Click the **Format button arrow** in the Replace with row, and then click **Clear Replace Format**. The replacement format is removed.

14. Click the **Close** button to return to the worksheet. Notice that every cell in the worksheet that had white text now has yellow text.

Working with Themes

Recall that a theme is a coordinated selection of fonts, colors, and graphical effects that are applied throughout a workbook to create a specific look and feel. When you switch to a different theme, the theme-related fonts, colors, and effects change throughout the workbook to reflect the new theme. The appearance of non-theme fonts, colors, and effects remains unchanged no matter which theme is applied to the workbook.

Most of the formatting you have applied to the Sales Report workbook is based on the Office theme. Sanjit wants you to change the theme to see how it affects the workbook's appearance.

To change the workbook's theme:

1. Click the **PAGE LAYOUT** tab on the ribbon.

2. In the Themes group, click the **Themes** button. The Themes gallery opens. Office—the current theme—is the default.

3. Point to the **Organic** theme in the Themes gallery. Live Preview shows how the appearance of the Sales Report worksheet will change if you select the Organic theme. See Figure 2-32.

Figure 2-32   **Live Preview of the Organic theme**

4. Point to several other themes in the Themes gallery to see how the worksheet appearance would change.

5. Click the **Wisp** theme to apply that theme to the workbook.

Changing the theme made a significant difference in the worksheet's appearance. The most obvious changes to the worksheet are the fill colors and the fonts. Only formatting options directly tied to a theme change when you select a different theme. Any formatting options you selected that were not theme-based remain unaffected by the change. For example, the yellow standard color you just applied to the different column labels is still yellow, even with the Wisp theme applied, because yellow is not a theme color. For the same reason, the red fill color used in the column labels of the monthly sales table remains unchanged under the new theme.

Sanjit informs you that Big Red Wraps requires all documents to be formatted with the Office theme. You will reapply the Office theme to the workbook.

To reapply the Office theme to the workbook:

▶ **1.** On the PAGE LAYOUT tab, in the Themes group, click the **Themes** button, and then click the **Office** theme from the gallery of themes.

The workbook now complies with the company's standard formatting.

Sharing Styles and Themes

Using a consistent look and feel for all the files you create in Microsoft Office is a simple way to project a professional image. This consistency is especially important when a team is collaborating on a set of documents. When all team members work from a common set of style and design themes, readers will not be distracted by inconsistent or clashing formatting.

To quickly copy the styles from one workbook to another, open the workbook with the styles you want to copy, and then open the workbook in which you want to copy those styles. On the HOME tab, in the Styles group, click the Cell Styles button, and then click Merge Styles. The Merge Styles dialog box opens, listing the currently open workbooks. Select the workbook with the styles you want to copy, and then click the OK button to copy those styles into the current workbook. If you modify any styles, you must copy the styles to the other workbook; Excel does not update styles between workbooks.

Because other Office files, including those created with Word or PowerPoint, use the same file format for themes, you can create one theme to use with all of your Office files. To save a theme, click the Themes button in the Themes group on the PAGE LAYOUT tab, and then click Save Current Theme. The Save Current Theme dialog box opens. Select a save location (in a default Theme folder on your computer or another folder), type a descriptive name in the File name box, and then click the Save button. If you saved the theme file in a default Theme folder, the theme appears in the Themes gallery, and any changes made to the theme are reflected in any Office file that uses that theme.

Highlighting Cells with Conditional Formats

Conditional formats are often used to help analyze data. A **conditional format** applies formatting to a cell when its value meets a specified condition. For example, a conditional format can be used to format negative numbers in red and positive numbers in black. Conditional formats are dynamic, which means that the formatting can change when the cell's value changes. Each conditional format has a set of rules that define how the formatting should be applied and under what conditions the format will be changed.

Highlighting Cells with a Conditional Format

- Select the range in which you want to highlight cells.
- On the HOME tab, in the Styles group, click the Conditional Formatting button, point to Highlight Cells Rules or Top/Bottom Rules, and then click the appropriate rule.
- Select the appropriate options in the dialog box.
- Click the OK button.

Excel has four conditional formats—data bars, highlighting, color scales, and icon sets. In this tutorial, you will apply cell highlighting, which changes the cell's font color or fill color based on the cell's value, as described in Figure 2-33. You can enter a value or a cell reference if you want to compare other cells with the value in a certain cell.

Figure 2-33	Highlight Cells rules

Rule	Highlights Cell Values
Greater Than	Greater than a specified number
Less Than	Less than a specified number
Between	Between two specified numbers
Equal To	Equal to a specified number
Text that Contains	That contain specified text
A Date Occurring	That contain a specified date
Duplicate Values	That contain duplicate or unique values

© 2014 Cengage Learning

Highlighting Cells Based on Their Values

Sanjit wants to highlight important trends and sales values in the Sales Report worksheet. He wants you to use a conditional format to display sales statistics that showed a negative net or percent change in a red font so that they stand out. You will do this by creating a rule to format the cells in ranges E6:F12 and E16:F22 with numbers that are less than 0.

To highlight negative numbers in red:

1. Select the nonadjacent range **E6:F12;E16:F22** in the Sales Report worksheet.

2. On the ribbon, click the **HOME** tab.

3. In the Styles group, click the **Conditional Formatting** button, and then point to **Highlight Cells Rules** to display a menu of the available rules.

4. Click **Less Than**. The Less Than dialog box opens so you can select the value and formatting to highlight negative values.

5. Type **0** (a zero) in the Format cells that are LESS THAN box, click the **with** arrow, and then click **Red Text**. Live Preview shows that the rule formats any cells in the selected range that have a negative value in a red font. See Figure 2-34.

Figure 2-34 **Live Preview of the Less Than conditional format**

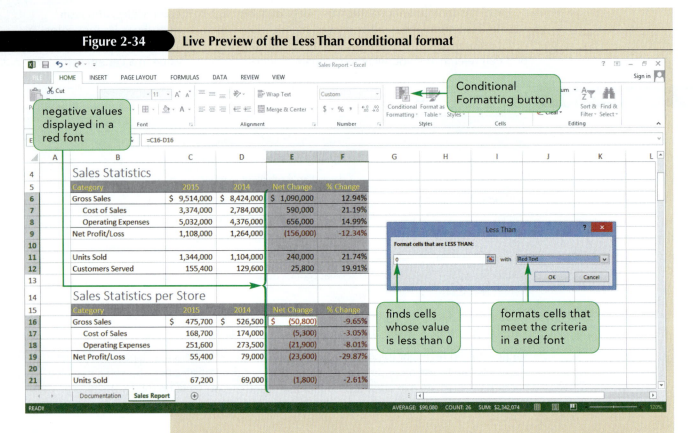

6. Click the **OK** button to apply the highlighting rule. You will verify that this format is conditional.

7. In cell D8, enter **4,576,000** to change the Operating Expenses value. The now positive values in cells E9 and F9 are formatted in a black font.

8. Press the **Ctrl+Z** keys to return the value in cell D8 to 4,376,000. The values in cells E9 and F9 are again negative and in a red font.

The highlighted values show at a glance that Big Red Wraps' gross sales, units sold, and customers served increased from 2014 to 2015, while the company's net profit declined during the same period. The average gross sales per store also declined in 2015. Big Red Wraps opened four new stores in 2015, and Sanjit will argue that the cost of this expansion and low sales from the new stores caused this apparent decline.

Highlighting Cells with a Top/Bottom Rule

Another way of applying conditional formats is with the Quick Analysis tool. The **Quick Analysis tool**, which appears whenever you select a range of cells, provides access to the most common tools for data analysis and formatting. The FORMATTING category includes buttons for the Greater Than and Top 10% conditional formatting rules. You can highlight cells based on their values in comparison to other cells. For example, you can highlight cells with the 10 highest or lowest values in a selected range, or you can highlight the cells with above-average values in a range.

Sanjit wants you to highlight the five stores in the Big Red Wraps chain that had the highest gross sales in the last fiscal year. You will use a Top/Bottom rule to do this.

To use a Top/Bottom Rule to highlight the stores with the highest gross sales:

1. Select the range **P27:P46** containing the average monthly gross sales for each of the 20 Big Red Wraps stores. The Quick Analysis button appears in the lower-right corner of the selected range.

2. Click the **Quick Analysis** button ▣, and then point to **Top 10%**. Live Preview colors the cells in the top 10 percent with red font and a red fill. See Figure 2-35.

Figure 2-35   Quick Analysis tool

Sanjit wants to see the top five items rather than the cells with values in the top 10 percent, so you won't apply this conditional formatting.

3. Press the **Esc** key to close the Quick Analysis tool. The range P27:P46 remains selected.

4. On the HOME tab, in the Styles group, click the **Conditional Formatting** button, and then point to **Top/Bottom Rules** to display a menu of available rules.

5. Click **Top 10 Items** to open the Top 10 Items dialog box.

6. Click the down arrow on the spin box five times to change the value from 10 to 5. This specifies that the top five values in the selected range will be formatted.

7. Click the **with** arrow, and then click **Green Fill with Dark Green Text** to specify the formatting to apply to the five cells with the top values. Live Preview highlights the top five stores in terms of gross sales. See Figure 2-36.

Figure 2-36 **Live Preview of the top five selling stores**

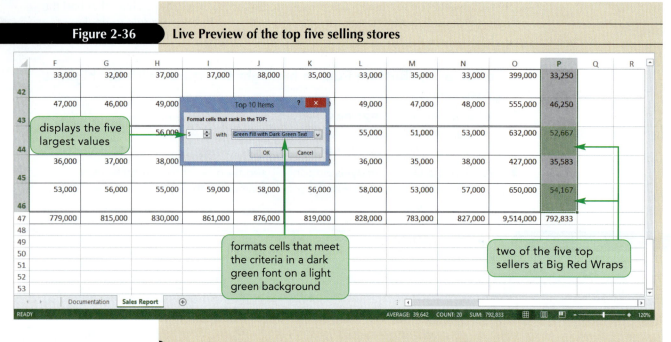

> **8.** Click the **OK** button to accept the conditional formatting.

The Top/Bottom rule highlights the average monthly gross sales for the five top-selling stores: the North Street store in Madison, Wisconsin; the South Drive store in Janesville, Wisconsin; the Main Street store in Des Moines, Iowa; the Business Drive store in Manhattan, Kansas; and the Causeway Drive store in Salina, Kansas.

Clearing a Conditional Format

You can remove a conditional format at any time without affecting the underlying data by selecting the range containing the conditional format, clicking the Conditional Formatting button, and then clicking the Clear Rules button. A menu opens, providing options to clear the conditional formatting rules from the selected cells or the entire worksheet. You can also click the Quick Analysis button that appears in the lower-right corner of the selected range, and then click the Clear Format button in the FORMATTING category.

Creating a Conditional Formatting Legend

When you use conditional formatting to highlight cells in a worksheet, the purpose of the formatting is not always immediately apparent. To ensure that everyone knows why certain cells are highlighted, you should include a **legend**, which is a key that identifies each color and its meaning.

You will add a legend to the Sales Report worksheet to document the Top 5 highlighting rule you just created.

To create a conditional formatting legend:

> **1.** Select cell **P49**, type **light green**, and then press the **Enter** key. You will use a highlight rule to fill this cell with a dark green font on a light green fill.

> **2.** Select cell **P49** to make it the active cell.

> **3.** On the HOME tab, in the Styles group, click the **Conditional Formatting** button, point to **Highlight Cells Rules**, and then click **Text that Contains**. The Text That Contains dialog box opens.

4. Verify that **light green** appears in the Format cells that contain the text box. The box shows the text entered in the selected cell.

5. Click the **with** arrow, and then click **Green Fill with Dark Green Text** to format cell P49 with the same format used for the top five gross sales.

6. Click the **OK** button. Cell P49 remains selected.

7. In the Alignment group, click the **Center** button ☰ to center the text in the cell.

8. In cell **O49**, enter **Top 5 Stores** to identify the format's purpose, and then select cell **O49**.

9. In the Styles group, click the **Cell Styles** button, and then click the **Explanatory Text** style (the third style in the first row of the Data and Model section). The cell style is applied to the selected cell.

10. Click cell **O51**. The legend is complete, as shown in Figure 2-37.

| Figure 2-37 | Conditional formatting legend |

The conditional formatting makes the top-selling stores stand out.

Written Communication: Using Conditional Formatting Effectively

Conditional formatting is an excellent way to highlight important trends and data values to clients and colleagues. However, be sure to use it judiciously. Overusing conditional formatting might obscure the very data you want to emphasize. Keep in mind the following tips as you make decisions about what to highlight and how it should be highlighted:

- **Document the conditional formats you use.** If a bold, green font means that a sales number is in the top 10 percent of all sales, include that information in a legend in the worksheet.
- **Don't clutter data with too much highlighting.** Limit highlighting rules to one or two per data set. Highlights are designed to draw attention to points of interest. If you use too many, you will end up highlighting everything—and, therefore, nothing.
- **Use color sparingly in worksheets with highlights.** It is difficult to tell a highlight color from a regular fill color, especially when fill colors are used in every cell.
- **Consider alternatives to conditional formats.** If you want to highlight the top 10 sales regions, it might be more effective to simply sort the data with the best-selling regions at the top of the list.

Remember that the goal of highlighting is to provide a strong visual clue to important data or results. Careful use of conditional formatting helps readers to focus on the important points you want to make rather than distracting them with secondary issues and facts.

Formatting a Worksheet for Printing

You should format any worksheets you plan to print so that they are easy to read and understand. You can do this using the print settings, which enable you to set the page orientation, the print area, page breaks, print titles, and headers and footers. Print settings can be applied to an entire workbook or to individual sheets. Because other people will likely see your printed worksheets, you should format the printed output as carefully as you format the electronic version. Sanjit wants you to format the Sales Report worksheet so he can distribute the printed version at the upcoming sales conference.

Using Page Break Preview

Page Break Preview shows only those parts of the active sheet that will print and how the content will be split across pages. A dotted blue border indicates a page break, which separates one page from another. As you format the worksheet for printing, you can use this view to control what content appears on each page.

Sanjit wants to know how the Sales Report worksheet would print in portrait orientation and how many pages would be required. You will look at the worksheet in Page Break Preview to find these answers.

To view the Sales Report worksheet in Page Break Preview:

1. Click the **Page Break Preview** button 🖳 on the status bar. The worksheet switches to Page Break Preview.

2. Change the zoom level of the worksheet to **30%** so you can view the entire contents of this large worksheet. See Figure 2-38.

| Figure 2-38 | Sales Report worksheet in Page Break Preview |

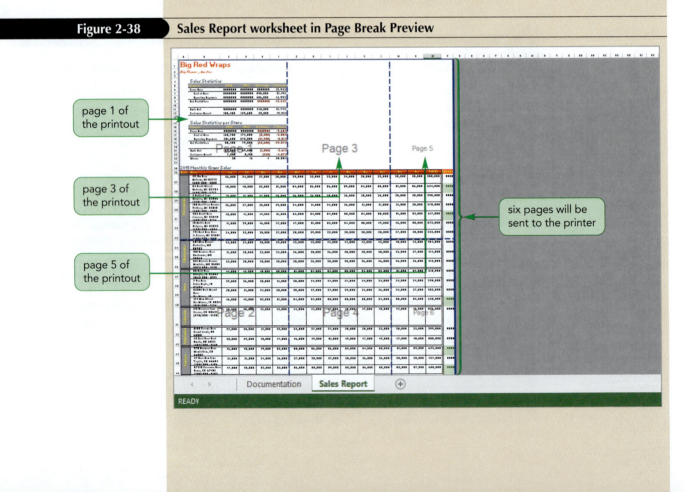

page 1 of the printout

page 3 of the printout

page 5 of the printout

six pages will be sent to the printer

Trouble? If you see a different page layout or the worksheet is split onto a different number of pages, don't worry. Each printer is different, so the layout and pages might differ from what is shown in Figure 2-38.

Page Break Preview shows that a printout of the Sales Report worksheet requires six pages in portrait orientation, and that pages 3 and 5 would be mostly blank. Note that each printer is different, so your Page Break Preview might show a different number of pages. With this layout, each page would be difficult to interpret because the data is separated from the descriptive labels. Sanjit wants you to fix the layout so that the contents are easier to read and understand.

Defining the Print Area

By default, all cells in a worksheet containing text, formulas, or values are printed. If you want to print only part of a worksheet, you can set a print area, which is the region of the worksheet that is sent to the printer. Each worksheet has its own print area. Although you can set the print area in any view, Page Break Preview shades the areas of the worksheet that are not included in the print area, making it simple to confirm what will print.

Sanjit doesn't want the empty cells in the range G1:O24 to print, so you will set the print area to eliminate those cells.

To set the print area of the Sales Report worksheet:

1. Change the zoom level of the worksheet to **80%** to make it easier to select cells and ranges.

2. Select the nonadjacent range **A1:F24;A25:P49** containing the cells with content.

3. On the ribbon, click the **PAGE LAYOUT** tab.

4. In the Page Setup group, click the **Print Area** button, and then click **Set Print Area**. The print area changes to cover only the nonadjacent range A1:F24;A25:P49. The rest of the worksheet content is shaded to indicate that it will not be part of the printout.

5. Select cell **A1** to deselect the range.

6. Change the zoom level to **50%** so you can view more of the worksheet. See Figure 2-39.

Figure 2-39 **Print area set for the Sales Report worksheet**

range A1:F24 prints on its own page

print area covers the nonadjacent range A1:F24;A25:P49

solid line indicates a manual page break

dotted lines indicate automatic page breaks

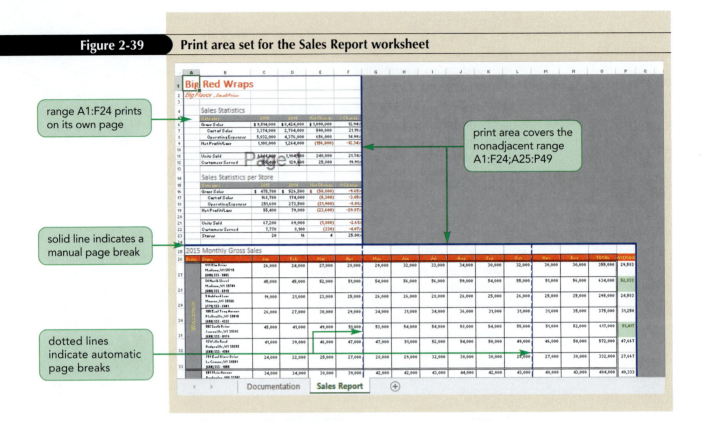

Inserting Page Breaks

Often, the contents of a worksheet will not fit onto a single printed page. When this happens, Excel prints as much of the content that fits on a single page without resizing, and then inserts automatic page breaks to continue printing the remaining worksheet content on successive pages. The resulting printouts might split worksheet content in awkward places, such as within a table of data.

To split the printout into logical segments, you can insert manual page breaks. Page Break Preview identifies manual page breaks with a solid blue line and automatic page breaks with a dotted blue line. When you specify a print area for a nonadjacent range, as you did for the Sales Report worksheet, you also insert manual page breaks around the adjacent ranges. So a manual page break already appears in the print area you defined (see Figure 2-39). You can remove a page break in Page Break Preview by dragging it out of the print area.

TIP

When you remove a page break, Excel will automatically rescale the printout to fit into the allotted pages.

REFERENCE

Inserting and Removing Page Breaks

To insert a page break:
- Click the first cell below the row where you want to insert a page break, click a column heading, or click a row heading.
- On the PAGE LAYOUT tab, in the Page Setup group, click the Breaks button, and then click Insert Page Break.

To remove a page break:
- Select any cell below or to the right of the page break you want to remove.
- On the PAGE LAYOUT tab, in the Page Setup group, click the Breaks button, and then click Remove Page Break.

or
- In Page Break Preview, drag the page break line out of the print area.

The Sales Report worksheet has automatic page breaks along columns F and L. You will remove these automatic page breaks from the Sales Report worksheet.

To remove the automatic page breaks and insert manual page breaks:

1. Point to the dotted blue page break directly to the right of column L until the pointer changes to ✛.

2. Drag the page break to the right and out of the print area. The page break is removed from the worksheet.

3. Point to the page break located in cell F31 until the pointer changes to ✛, and then drag the page break to the right and out of the print area.

   On the PAGE LAYOUT tab, in the Scale to Fit section, notice that the Scale box shows 43%. After removing the two page breaks from the Sales Report printout, Excel scaled the printout from 100% of its actual size to 43% to fit the printout onto two pages.

4. Click the **column I** heading to select the entire column. You will add a manual page break between columns H and I to split the monthly gross sales data onto two pages so the printout will be larger and easier to read.

5. On the PAGE LAYOUT tab, in the Page Setup group, click the **Breaks** button, and then click **Insert Page Break**. A manual page break is added between columns H and I, forcing the monthly gross sales onto a new page after the June data.

6. Select cell **A1** to deselect the column. The printout of the Sales Report worksheet is now limited to three pages. However, the gross sales data in the range A25:O49 is split across pages. See Figure 2-40.

| Figure 2-40 | Manual page break added to the print area |

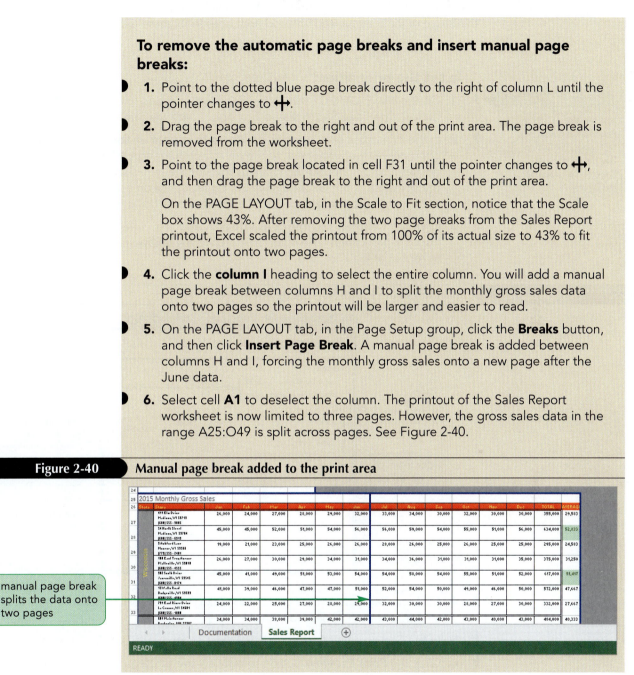

manual page break splits the data onto two pages

Adding Print Titles

It is a good practice to include descriptive information such as the company name, logo, and worksheet title on each page of a printout in case a page becomes separated from the other pages. You can repeat information, such as the company name, by specifying which rows or columns in the worksheet act as print titles. If a worksheet contains a large table, you can print the table's column headings and row headings on every page of the printout by designating those columns and rows as print titles.

In the Sales Report worksheet, the company name and slogan currently appear on the first page of the printout, but do not appear on subsequent pages. Also, the descriptive row labels for the monthly sales table in column A do not appear on the third page of the printout. You will add print titles to fix these issues.

To set the print titles:

TIP

You can also open the Page Setup dialog box by clicking the Dialog Box Launcher in the Page Setup group on the PAGE LAYOUT tab.

1. On the PAGE LAYOUT tab, in the Page Setup group, click the **Print Titles** button. The Page Setup dialog box opens with the Sheet tab displayed.

2. In the Print titles section, click the **Rows to repeat at top** box, move the pointer over the worksheet, and then select the range **A1:A2**. A flashing border appears around the first two rows of the worksheet to indicate that the contents of the first two rows will be repeated on each page of the printout. The row reference $1:$2 appears in the Rows to repeat at top box.

3. Click the **Columns to repeat at left** box, and then select columns A and B from the worksheet. The column reference $A:$B appears in the Columns to repeat at left box. See Figure 2-41.

Figure 2-41   **Sheet tab in the Page Setup dialog box**

4. Click the **Page** tab in the Page Setup dialog box. You will rescale the worksheet so that it doesn't appear too small in the printout.

5. In the Scaling section, change the Adjust to amount to **65%** of normal size.

6. Click the **Print Preview** button to preview the three pages of printed material on the Print screen in Backstage view.

7. Verify that each of the three pages has the Big Red Wraps title and slogan at the top of the page, and that the state and store names appear in the leftmost columns of pages 2 and 3. See Figure 2-42.

Figure 2-42   **Print titles on page 3 of the Sales Report worksheet**

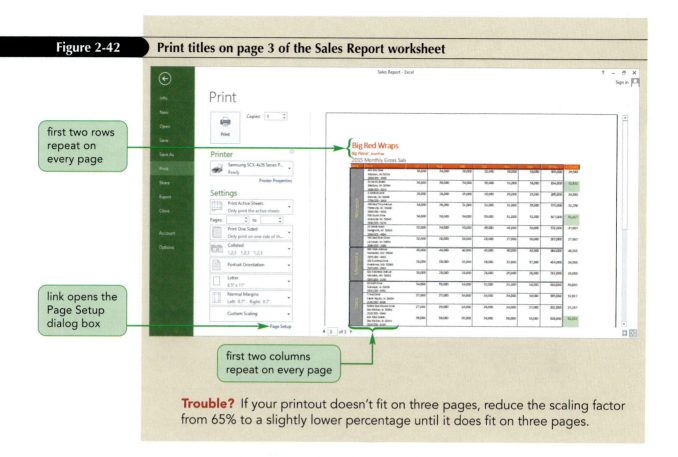

first two rows repeat on every page

link opens the Page Setup dialog box

first two columns repeat on every page

Trouble? If your printout doesn't fit on three pages, reduce the scaling factor from 65% to a slightly lower percentage until it does fit on three pages.

Creating Headers and Footers

You can also use headers and footers to repeat information on each printed page. A **header** appears at the top of each printed page; a **footer** appears at the bottom of each printed page. Headers and footers contain helpful and descriptive text that is usually not found within the worksheet, such as the workbook's author, the current date, or the workbook's filename. If the printout spans multiple pages, you can display the page number and the total number of pages in the printout to help ensure you and others have all the pages.

Each header and footer has three sections—a left section, a center section, and a right section. Within each section, you type the text you want to appear, or you insert elements such as the worksheet name or the current date and time. These header and footer elements are dynamic; if you rename the worksheet, for example, the name is automatically updated in the header or footer. Also, you can create one set of headers and footers for even and odd pages, and you can create another set for the first page in the printout.

Sanjit wants the printout to display the workbook's filename in the header's left section, and the current date in the header's right section. He wants the center footer to display the page number and the total number of pages in the printout, and the right footer to display your name as the workbook's author.

To create the header and footer:

1. Click the **Page Setup** link near the bottom of the Print screen to open the Page Setup dialog box.

2. Click the **Header/Footer** tab to display the header and footer options.

3. Click the **Different first page** check box to select it. This lets you create one set of headers and footers for the first page, and one set for the rest of the pages. See Figure 2-43.

Figure 2-43 | **Header/Footer tab in the Page Setup dialog box**

when selected, displays a different header and footer for even- and odd-numbered pages

displays a different header or footer for the first page

4. Click the **Custom Header** button to open the Header dialog box. The dialog box contains two tabs—Header and First Page Header—because you selected the Different first page option.

TIP

You can create or edit headers and footers in Page Layout view by clicking in the header/footer section and using the tools on the DESIGN tab.

5. On the Header tab, type **Filename:** in the Left section box, press the **spacebar**, and then click the **Insert File Name** button 🗐. The code &[File], which displays the filename of the current workbook, is added to the left section of the header.

6. Press the **Tab** key twice to move to the right section of the header, and then click the **Insert Current Date** button 🗐. The code &[Date] is added to the right section of the header. See Figure 2-44.

Figure 2-44 | **Header dialog box**

inserts the current date

inserts the workbook's filename

code to print the workbook's filename

code to print the current date

7. Click the **OK** button to return to the Header/Footer tab in the Page Setup dialog box. You did not define a header for the first page of the printout, so no header information will be added to that page.

Now you will format the page footer for all pages of the printout.

▶ **8.** Click the **Custom Footer** button to open the Footer dialog box, which is similar to the Header dialog box.

▶ **9.** Click the **Center section** box, type **Page**, press the **spacebar**, and then click the **Insert Page Number** button 🄳. The code &[Page], which inserts the current page number, appears after the label "Page."

▶ **10.** Press the **spacebar**, type **of**, press the **spacebar**, and then click the **Insert Number of Pages** button 🄳. The code &[Pages], which inserts the total number of pages in the printout, is added to the Center section box. See Figure 2-45.

Figure 2-45   **Footer dialog box**

click to set footer options for the first page

inserts the total number of pages

inserts the page number

prints the current page number out of the total page count

▶ **11.** Click the **First Page Footer** tab so you can create the footer for the first page of the printout.

▶ **12.** Click the **Right section** box, type **Prepared by:**, press the **spacebar**, and then type your name.

▶ **13.** Click the **OK** button to return to the Page Setup dialog box.

Setting the Page Margins

A **margin** is the space between the page content and the edges of the page. By default, Excel sets the page margins to 0.7 inch on the left and right sides, and 0.75 inch on the top and bottom; and it allows for 0.3-inch margins around the header and footer. You can reduce or increase these margins as needed by selecting predefined margin sizes or setting your own.

Sanjit's reports need a wider margin along the left side of the page to accommodate the binding. He asks you to increase the left margin for the printout from 0.7 inch to 1 inch.

To set the left margin:

TIP

To select preset margins, click the Margins button in the Page Setup group on the PAGE LAYOUT tab.

▶ **1.** Click the **Margins** tab in the Page Setup dialog box to display options for changing the page margins.

▶ **2.** Double-click the **Left** box to select the setting, and then type **1** to increase the size of the left margin. See Figure 2-46.

Figure 2-46   Margins tab in the Page Setup dialog box

sets the size of individual page margins

centers the workbook contents horizontally or vertically on the printout

▶ **3.** Click the **OK** button to close the dialog box and return to the worksheet.

Sanjit is happy with the appearance of the worksheet and the layout of the printout. You'll save the workbook, and then print the Documentation and Sales Report sheets.

To save and print the workbook:

▶ **1.** Return the Sales Report worksheet to **Normal** view, and then save the workbook.

▶ **2.** Display the Print screen in Backstage view, and then change the first Settings box to **Print Entire Workbook**. Both the Sales Report worksheet and the Documentation sheet appear in the preview. As you can see, the printout will include a header with the filename and date on every page except the first page, and a footer with your name on the first page and the page number along with the total number of pages on subsequent pages.

▶ **3.** If you are instructed to print, print the entire workbook, and then close it.

REVIEW

Session 2.2 Quick Check

1. Describe two methods of applying the same format to different ranges.
2. Red is a standard color. What happens to red text when you change the workbook's theme?
3. What is a conditional format?
4. How would you highlight the top five values in the range A1:C20?
5. How do you insert a manual page break in a worksheet?
6. What is a print area?
7. What are print titles?
8. Describe how to add the workbook filename to the center section of the footer on every page of the printout.

ASSESS

SAM Projects

Put your skills into practice with SAM Projects! SAM Projects for this tutorial can be found online. If you have a SAM account, go to www.cengage.com/sam2013 to download the most recent Project Instructions and Start Files.

PRACTICE

Review Assignments

Data Files needed for the Review Assignments: Menu.xlsx, Background2.png

Sanjit has a worksheet that details the sales of individual items from the Big Red Wraps menu. He asks you to format the sales figures and design a layout for the printed sheet as you did for the Sales Report workbook. Complete the following:

1. Open the **Menu** workbook located in the Excel2 ▸ Review folder included with your Data Files, and then save the workbook as **Menu Sales** in the location specified by your instructor.

2. In the Documentation sheet, enter your name in cell B4 and the date in cell B5.

3. Make the following formatting changes to the Documentation sheet:

   a. Set the background image to the **Background2.png** file located in the Excel2 ▸ Review folder.

   b. Format the text in cell A1 in red 26-point bold Calibri Light.

   c. Format the text in cell A2 to red 10-point italic Calibri Light. Change the text string "Big Flavor" to 14 points.

   d. Apply the Accent2 cell style to the range A4:A6.

   e. Change the font color of range B4:B6 to red and change its fill color to white.

   f. Format the date in the Long Date format and left-align the cell contents.

4. Use the Format Painter to copy the formatting in the range A1:A2 in the Documentation sheet and paste it to the same range in the Menu Sales worksheet. (*Hint*: You must increase the size of the text "Big Flavor" manually.)

5. Apply the Title cell style to the titles in cells B4, B12, and A20.

6. Make the following changes to the Units Sold table in the range B5:F10:

   a. In cell C6, calculate the total number of wraps sold by the company (found in the range C22:N31). In cell C7, calculate the total number of soups. In cell C8, calculate the total number of sides. In cell C9, calculate the total number of salads.

   b. In cell C10, calculate the sum of the range C6:C9. Copy the formula to cell D10.

   c. In the range E6:E10, calculate the difference between the 2015 and 2014 values. In the range F6:F10, calculate the percent change from 2014 to 2015.

   d. Apply the Accent2 cell style to the headings in the range B5:F5. Center the headings in the range C5:F5.

   e. Apply the Comma style to the values in the range C6:E10. Do not display any numbers to the right of the decimal point.

   f. Apply the Percent style to the values in the range F6:F10 and show two decimal places.

   g. Add a top border to the values in the range B10:F10.

7. Make the following changes to the range B13:F18:

   a. In cells C18 and D18, calculate the totals of the 2014 and 2015 sales. In the range E14:F18, calculate the change in sales and the percent change.

   b. Copy the format from the range B5:F10 and paste it into the range B13:F18.

   c. Change the format for the values in the ranges C14:E14 and C18:E18 to Accounting format with no decimal places.

8. Make the following changes to the Units Sold per Month table in the range A21:O46:
   a. In the range O22:O45, calculate the total units sold for each menu item. In the range C46:O46, calculate the total items sold per month and overall.
   b. Format the headings in the range A21:O21 with the Accent2 cell style. Center the headings in the range C21:O21.
   c. Format the units sold values in the range C22:O46 with the Comma style and no decimal places.
   d. Change the fill color of the subtotals in the range O22:O45 and C46:N46 to White, Background 1, Darker 15% (the first color in the third row of the theme colors).
   e. Merge each of the menu categories in the range A22:A45 into single cells. Rotate the text of the cells up. Increase the font size to 18 points and middle-align the cell contents.
   f. Format cell A22 with the "Wraps" label in a white font on a Gray-25%, Background 2, Darker 50% fill. Format cell A32 with the "Soups" label in a white font on Blue, Accent 1, Darker 25% fill. Format of cell A37 with the "Sides" label in a white font on a Gold, Accent 4, Darker 25% fill. Format cell A42 with the "Salads" label in a white font on a Green, Accent 6, Darker 25% fill.
   g. Add a thick box border around each category of menu item in the ranges A22:O31, A32:O36, A37:O41, and A42:O45.
9. Create a conditional format for the subtotals in the range O22:O45 highlighting the top five selling items with a yellow fill and dark yellow text.
10. Create a legend for the conditional format. Enter the text **Top 5 Sellers** in cell O48. Add a thick box border around the cell, and then use a conditional format that displays this text in dark yellow text on a yellow fill.
11. Set the following print formats for the Menu Sales worksheet:
   a. Set the print area to the nonadjacent range A1:F19;A20:O48.
   b. Remove any automatic page breaks in the large Units Sold table. Insert a manual page break to separate the June and July sales figures. The printout of the Menu Sales worksheet should fit on three pages.
   c. Scale the printout to 70 percent of normal size.
   d. Define the print titles to repeat the first three rows at the top of the sheet, and the first two columns at the left of the sheet.
   e. Increase the left margin of the printout from 0.7 inch to 1 inch.
   f. Create headers and footers for the printout with a different header for the first page.
   g. For the first page header, print **Prepared by** *your name* in the right section. For every other page, print **Filename:** *file* in the left section and *date* in the right section, where *file* is the name of the workbook file and *date* is the current date. (*Hint:* Use the buttons in the Header dialog box to insert the filename and date.)
   h. For every footer, print **Page** *page* **of** *pages* in the center section, where *page* is the page number and *pages* is the total number of pages in the printout.
12. If you are instructed to print, print the entire workbook in portrait orientation. Verify that the company name and slogan appear on every page of the Menu Sales worksheet printout, and that the menu category and menu item name appear on both pages with the Units Sold table.
13. Save and close the workbook.

Case Problem 1

Data File needed for this Case Problem: Salon.xlsx

APPLY

Special Highlights Hair Salon   Sarah Jones is developing a business plan for a new hair salon, Special Highlights Hair Salon, located in Hatton, North Dakota. As part of the business plan, she needs a projected income statement for the company. You will help her develop and format the income statement. Complete the following:

1. Open the **Salon** workbook located in the Excel2 ▸ Case1 folder included with your Data Files, and then save the workbook as **Salon Income Statement** in the location specified by your instructor.

2. In the Documentation sheet, enter your name in cell B3 and the date in cell B4.

3. Apply the following formatting to the Documentation sheet:
   a. Format cell A1 using the Title cell style.
   b. Format the range A3:A5 using the Accent6 cell style.
   c. In cell B4, format the date value using the long date format, and left-align the cell contents.
   d. In cell B5, format the text string "Special Highlights Hair Salon" in italic.

4. In the Income Statement worksheet, format cell A1 using the Title cell style.

5. Calculate the following items in the Income Statement worksheet:
   a. In cell C7, calculate the Gross Profit, which is equal to the Gross Sales minus the Cost of Sales.
   b. In cell C21, calculate the Total Operating Expenses, which is equal to the sum of the operating expenses.
   c. In cell C22, calculate the Total Operating Profit/Loss, which is equal to the Gross Profit minus the Total Operating Expenses.
   d. In cell C23, calculate the projected Income Taxes, which is equal to 35 percent of the Total Operating Profit/Loss.
   e. In cell C24, calculate the Net Profit/Loss, which is equal to the Total Operating Profit/Loss minus the projected Income Taxes.

6. Set the following formats to the Income Statement worksheet:
   a. Format cells A3 and A26 using the Heading 2 cell style.
   b. Format cells A4 and A9 and the range A27:A38 in bold.
   c. Format cells B5, C7, B10, C21, and C24 using the Accounting format with no decimal places.
   d. Format cells B6, B11:B19, C22, and C23 using the Comma style with no decimal places.
   e. Indent the text in the ranges A5:A6 and A10:A19 two spaces. Indent the text in cell A7 and the range A21:A24 four spaces.
   f. Add a bottom border to cells B6, C7, C21, C22, and C23. Add a double bottom border to cell C24.

7. Merge cells A26:E26 and then left-align the merged cell's contents.

8. Merge the contents of the range B27:E27. Left-align the merged cell's contents and wrap the text within the cell. Increase the height of row 27 to display the entire contents of the cell.

9. Top-align and left-align the range A27:B38.

10. Copy the format from the range A27:B27 to the range A28:B38. Merge columns B through E in each row, left-align the text, and resize the row heights to display the complete contents of the cells.

11. Italicize the text string "National Salon News" in cells B27 and B28.

12. Set the following printing formats to the Income Statement worksheet:

   a. Insert a manual page break directly above row 26 so that the Income Statement prints on two pages.

   b. Set rows 1 and 2 as a print title to print on both pages.

   c. Change the page margins to 1 inch on every side.

   d. On the first page of the printout, print **Prepared by** *your name* in the left section of the header, where *your name* is your name. Print the **current date** in the right section of the header. Do not display header text on any other page.

   e. For every page, add a footer that prints the workbook *filename* in the left section, **Page** *page* in the center section, and the *worksheet name* in the right section.

13. If you are instructed to print, print the entire contents of the workbook in portrait orientation.

14. Save and close the workbook.

Case Problem 2

Data File needed for this Case Problem: Waist.xlsx

Waist Trainers   Alexandra Roulez is a dietician at Waist Trainers, a company in Fort Smith, Arkansas, that specializes in personal improvement, particularly in areas of health and fitness. Alexandra wants to create a meal-planning workbook for her clients who want to lose weight and improve their health. One goal of meal planning is to decrease the percentage of fat in the diet. Alexandra thinks it would be helpful to highlight foods that have a high percentage of fat as well as list their total fat calories. She already created a workbook that contains a few sample food items and lists the number of calories and grams of fat in each item. She wants you to format this workbook. Complete the following:

1. Open the **Waist** workbook located in the Excel2 ▶ Case2 folder included with your Data Files, and then save the workbook as **Waist Trainers Nutrition Table** in the location specified by your instructor.

2. In the Documentation sheet, enter your name in cell B3 and the date in cell B4.

3. Set the following formatting to the Documentation sheet:

   a. In cell A1, apply the Title cell style, increase the font size to 24 points, and then change the font color to a medium orange.

   b. Apply the Accent2 cell style to the range A3:A5.

   c. Wrap the text within the range B3:B5, and then left- and top-align the text in the cells.

   d. Change the format of the date in cell B4 to the long date format.

   e. Add borders around all of the cells in the range A3:B5.

4. Copy the cell format for cell A1 in the Documentation sheet to cell A1 in the Meal Planner worksheet.

5. In cell F4, enter the text **Calories from Fat**. In cell G4, enter the text **Fat Percentage**.

6. In the range F5:F54, calculate the calories from fat for each food item, which is equal to the Grams of Fat multiplied by 9. In the range G5:G54, calculate the fat percentage of each food item, which is equal to the Calories from Fat divided by the Calories.

7. Format cell A3 using the Heading 4 cell style.

8. Format the range A4:G4 using the Accent2 cell style.

9. Format the range D5:F54 with the Comma style and display one decimal place.

10. Format the range G5:G54 with the Percent style and display two decimal places.

11. Merge the cells in the range A5:A8, rotate the text up, and then center-align the cell content both horizontally and vertically. Change the fill color to medium gold, increase the font size to 14 points, and then change the font color to white.

12. Place a thick box border around the beef food items in the range A5:G8.

13. Repeat Steps 11 and 12 for the other six food categories.

14. For good health, the FDA recommends that the fat percentage in a person's diet should not exceed 30 percent of the total calories per day. Create a Conditional Formatting rule for the fat percentages to highlight those food items that exceed the FDA recommendation in dark red text on a light red fill.

15. In cell G2, enter the text **High Fat Food**. Center the text in the cell. Change the format of the cell to dark red text on a light red fill. Add a thick black border around the cell.

16. Set the following print formats for the Meal Planner worksheet:
    a. Change the page orientation to landscape.
    b. Scale the printout so that the width of the worksheet fits on a single page.
    c. If necessary, create manual page breaks directly above row 25 and above row 44. The worksheet should print on three separate pages.
    d. Repeat the first four rows of the worksheet on every printed page.
    e. For every page, add a footer that prints **Prepared by** *your name* in the left section, **Page** *page* in the center section, and the ***worksheet name*** in the right section.

17. If you are instructed to print, print the entire contents of the workbook.

18. Save and close the workbook.

Case Problem 3

Data File needed for this Case Problem: Wind.xlsx

Winds of Change   Odette Ferris is a researcher at Winds of Change, a privately run wind farm providing supplemental power for communities near Topeka, Kansas. One of Odette's jobs is to record wind speeds from different sectors of the wind farm. She has entered the wind speed data into a workbook as a table with wind speed measures laid out in a grid. Because the numbers are difficult to read and interpret, she wants you to color code the wind speed values using conditional formatting. Complete the following:

1. Open the **Wind** workbook located in the Excel2 ▸ Case3 folder included with your Data Files, and then save the workbook as **Wind Speed Grid** in the location specified by your instructor.

2. In the Documentation sheet, enter your name in cell B3 and the date in cell B4.

3. In the Wind Speed Grid worksheet, merge the range A1:V1, and then apply the Heading 1 cell style to the merged cell and set the font size to 20 points.

4. Format the range B3:V3 as white text on a black background. Copy this formatting to the grid coordinates in the range A4:A64.

✛ **Explore** 5. Create a conditional format that highlights cells in the range B4:V64 whose value equals 18 with fill color equal to (99, 37, 35). (*Hint*: In the Equal To dialog box, select Custom Format in the with box to open the Format Cells dialog box. On the Fill tab, in the Background Color section, click the More Colors button, and then click the Custom tab to enter the RGB color value.)

✛ **Explore** 6. Repeat Step 5 to continue creating conditional formats that set highlight colors for the wind speed values in the range B4:V64 using the wind speeds and color values shown in Figure 2-47.

Figure 2-47 **Wind speed color values**

Wind Speed	RGB Color Value
16 m/s	(150, 54, 52)
14 m/s	(218, 150, 148)
12 m/s	(230, 184, 183)
10 m/s	(242, 220, 219)
8 m/s	(242, 242, 242)
6 m/s	(255, 255, 255)
4 m/s	(197, 217, 241)
2 m/s	(141, 180, 226)
0 m/s	(83, 141, 213)

© 2014 Cengage Learning

7. Reduce the font size of the values in the range B4:V64 to 1 point.

Explore 8. Enclose each cell in the range B4:V64 in a light gray border. (*Hint*: Use the Border tab in the Format Cells dialog box.)

9. Use the Format Painter to copy the formats from the range B4:V64 and apply them to the range X3:X12. Increase the font size of the cells in that range to 11 points.

10. Merge the range Y3:Y12, center the contents of the merged cell horizontally and vertically, and then rotate the text down. Format the text in a bold 18-point font.

11. Set the following print formats to the Wind Speed Grid worksheet:

   a Change the page orientation to landscape.

   b. Set the print area to the range A1:Y64.

   c. Scale the worksheet so that the width and the height of the sheet fit on a single page.

   d. Add a header to the printed page with your name in the left section of the header and the worksheet name in the right section of the header.

12. Save and close the workbook.

Case Problem 4

Data File needed for this Case Problem: Office.xlsx

Office Cart Robert Trenton is a shipping manager at Office Cart, an online office supply store located in Muncie, Indiana. He wants to use an Excel workbook to track shipping orders. Robert asks you to create and format a worksheet that he can use to enter information for packing slips. Complete the following:

1. Open the **Office** workbook located in the Excel2 ▶ Case4 folder included with your Data Files, and then save the workbook as **Office Cart Packing Slip** in the location specified by your instructor.

2. In the Documentation sheet, enter your name in cell B3 and the date in cell B4.

3. Set the following formats in the Documentation sheet:

   a. Merge cells A1 and B1, and then left-align the contents of the merged cell. Change the font to 28-point white Calibri Light on a dark green background.

   b. Change the font of the range A3:A5 to 14-point white Calibri Light on a dark green background.

   c. Change the format of the date value in cell B4 to the Long Date style, and then left-align the date in the cell.

   d. Italicize the text "Office Cart" in cell B5.

   e. Add a border around each cell in the range A3:B5.

4. Insert a new worksheet at the end of the workbook and name it **Packing Slip**.

5. In the Packing Slip worksheet, select all of the cells in the worksheet. (*Hint*: Click the Select All button at the intersection of the row and column headings, or press the Ctrl+A keys.) Change the font to 10-point dark green Calibri.

6. Add a thick box border around the range A1:D40.

7. For the range A1:D3, change the format to a white Calibri Light font on a dark green background.

8. Set the width of column A to 15 characters. Set the width of column B to 20 characters. Set the width of column C to 30 characters. Set the width of column D to 20 characters.

9. Merge the range A1:B3. Merge the range C1:D3, and then right- and top-align the merged cell. Set the row height of row 1 to 36 points and the heights of rows 2 and 3 to 15 points.

10. In cell A1, enter the following three lines of text, pressing the Alt+Enter keys to start a new line within the cell:
Office Cart
14 Trenke Lane
Muncie, IN 47303
Format the first line in a 26-point bold font.

11. In cell C1, enter **Packing Slip**, and then format the text in a 26-point bold font using the Headings font of the current theme.

12. In the range A5:A7, enter the following three lines of text in a bold font, and then right-align the text and indent the text one character:
Order Date
Order Number
Purchase Order

13. Format cell B5 in the Long Date format and left-align the cell contents. Insert border lines around each of the cells in the range B5:B7.

14. In the range C5:C7, enter the following three lines of text, and then use the Format Painter to copy the formats from the range A5:B7 to the range C5:D7:
Date
Sales Rep
Account Num

15. In cell B9, enter **Ship To**. In cell D9, enter **Bill To**. Format the text in both cells in bold.

16. In cell A10, enter **Address**, format the text in bold, right-align the text, and then indent it one character.

17. Merge the cells in the range B10:B15, left- and top-align the cell contents, insert a border around the merged cell, and then wrap the text within this cell.

18. In cell C10, enter **Address**. Copy the format from the range A10:B15 to the range C10:D15.

19. Enter the following data in the indicated cells in the worksheet:
cell A17: **Item**
cell B17: **Product No.**
cell C17: **Description**
cell D17: **Order Quantity**

20. Format the range A17:D17 in bold white Calibri on a dark green background.

21. Format the range A18:D18 with a bottom border and a light green background. Format the range A19:D19 with a bottom border and a white background. Copy the format in the range A18:D19 to the range A20:D27.

22. Apply a Top and Double Bottom Border to the range A28:D28. Merge the contents of the range A28:C28. Enter **Total** in cell A28, bold the text, and right-align the cell contents.

23. In cell D28, enter a formula to calculate the sum of the values in the range D18:D27. Bold the text.

24. In cell A30, enter **Comments** and then bold the text.

25. Merge the range A31:D39, left- and top-align the cell contents, and then add a thick box border around the merged cell.

26. In cell D40, enter **Thank you for your business!** in italic 16-point Calibri, and then right-align the cell contents.

27. Make sure the worksheet is set to portrait orientation, and then add a footer that displays your name in the left section, the filename in the center section, and the current date in the right section. Scale the printout so that it fits onto a single page.

28. Enter the packing slip data shown in Figure 2-48. Save and close the workbook.

Figure 2-48   Office Cart packing slip form

Office Cart

14 Trenke Lane
Muncie, IN 47303

Packing Slip

Order Date	Thursday, June 09, 2016	Date	Thursday, June 09, 2016
Order Number	OC414-0608	Sales Rep	Helen Richards
Purchase Order	OC912-1418-3	Account Num	97

Ship To
Address
c/o Kevin Davidson
Unger and Associates
550 Commerce Drive
Jefferson City, MO 65101

Bill To
Address
Unger and Associates
550 Commerce Drive
Jefferson City, MO

Item	Product No.	Description	Order Quantity
1	MC10R	Multiuse Copy Paper 10 ream	5
2	SGP10	Select Gel Pens	15
3	QCLPT4C	QS Laser Print Toner Kit	2
4	OCBE200	OC Business Envelopes (200 ct)	3
5	OCSL200	OC Shipping Labels (200 ct)	5
6			
7			
8			
9			
10			
		Total	30

Comments
Please contact shipping manager Robert Trenton (ext. 311) regarding discount shipping rates.

Thank you for your business!

OBJECTIVES

Session 3.1
- Make a workbook user-friendly
- Translate an equation into an Excel formula
- Understand function syntax
- Enter formulas and functions with the Quick Analysis tool
- Enter functions with the Insert Function dialog box
- Interpret error values
- Change cell references between relative and absolute

Session 3.2
- Use the AutoFill tool to enter formulas and data and complete a series
- Display the current date with the TODAY function
- Find the next weekday with the WORKDAY function
- Use the COUNT and COUNTA functions to tally cells
- Use an IF function to return a value based on a condition
- Perform an exact match lookup with the VLOOKUP function
- Perform what-if analysis using trial and error and Goal Seek

Calculating Data with Formulas and Functions

Creating a Fitness Tracker

Case | *Fit Fathers Inc.*

Ken Dorsett is a certified fitness professional and founder of Fit Fathers Inc., which is a fitness program he developed to help fathers stay fit and active. From its beginnings in Blue Springs, Missouri, where Ken led daily workouts with three other dads, his program has grown to an enrollment of 318 fathers in five different cities in the northwest corner of the state.

Ken wants to help his members evaluate their fitness goals and track their workouts. He has been working on an Excel workbook that can assess each participant's fitness level and track his workout progress. Ken has developed the basic structure of the workbook, but still needs to enter the formulas to calculate the different statistics and data that are important for his clients. He asks you to enter the appropriate formulas to complete the workbook. To do this, you will use a variety of formulas and functions.

STARTING DATA FILES

Excel3 → Tutorial
Fitness.xlsx

Review
Mothers.xlsx

Case1
Hernandez.xlsx

Case2
Econ.xlsx

Case3
Homes.xlsx

Case4
Quality.xlsx

Session 3.1 Visual Overview:

Functions are organized by category in the Function Library group. Select a function to open the Function Arguments dialog box.

The Insert Function button opens the Insert Function dialog box from which you can select a function.

The SUM function adds the values in the range.

The AVERAGE function calculates the average value of the range.

The MEDIAN function determines the middle value in the range.

The MAX function displays the maximum value in the range.

The MIN function displays the minimum value in the range.

Fitness Tracker - Excel

FILE   HOME   INSERT   PAGE LAYOUT   FORMULAS   DATA   REVIEW   VIEW

Insert Function

Σ AutoSum
Recently Used
Financial

Logical
Text
Date & Time

Lookup & Reference
Math & Trig
More Functions

Name Manager

Define Name
Use in Formu
Create from

Function Library

Defined Names

J17   =MEDIAN(K23:K45)

	F	G	H	I	J	K
14		Exercise Statistics	Jogging	Calisthenics	Strength	
15		SUM	278	245	347	
16		AVERAGE	16.4	14.4	20.4	
17		MEDIAN	15.0	15.0	20.0	
18		MAX	22	20	30	
19		MIN	10	8	12	

Jogging (min.)

=SUM(I23:I45)
=AVERAGE(I23:I45)
=MEDIAN(I23:I45)
=MAX(I23:I45)
=MIN(I23:I45)

	Jogging	Calisthenics	Streng
21		10	10
		10	8
		12	18
26			
27	x	12	15
28	6	x	15	10
29	7		
30	8	x	15	15
31	9	x	15	13
32	10	x	20	15

Documentation   Fitness Report   Explanation of Formulas

READY

Functions and Cell References

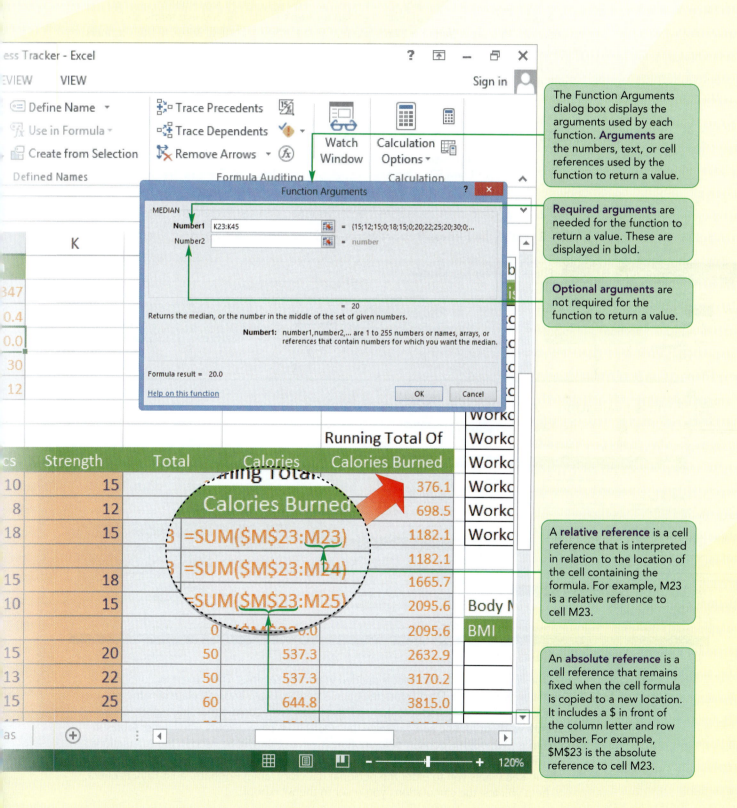

The Function Arguments dialog box displays the arguments used by each function. **Arguments** are the numbers, text, or cell references used by the function to return a value.

Required arguments are needed for the function to return a value. These are displayed in bold.

Optional arguments are not required for the function to return a value.

A **relative reference** is a cell reference that is interpreted in relation to the location of the cell containing the formula. For example, M23 is a relative reference to cell M23.

An **absolute reference** is a cell reference that remains fixed when the cell formula is copied to a new location. It includes a $ in front of the column letter and row number. For example, $M$23 is the absolute reference to cell M23.

Making Workbooks User-Friendly

Every workbook should be accessible to its intended users. When a workbook is user-friendly, anyone who needs to enter data in the workbook or interpret its results can understand the workbook's contents, including any jargon or unusual terms, what is being calculated, and how the equations make those calculations.

Many of the fitness calculations needed for Ken's workbook involve terms and equations that are unfamiliar to people not in the fitness industry. Because both trainers and clients will access this workbook, these terms and equations need to be explained. Ken has already included information about the fitness equations in the workbook. You will open the workbook, and examine its layout and structure.

To open and review the Fitness workbook:

1. Open the **Fitness** workbook located in the Excel3 ► Tutorial folder included with your Data Files, and then save the workbook as **Fitness Tracker** in the location specified by your instructor.

2. In the Documentation sheet, enter your name in cell B3 and the date in cell B4.

3. Go to the **Fitness Report** worksheet. See Figure 3-1.

Figure 3-1 | **Fitness Tracker workbook**

The Fitness Report worksheet is divided into three sections. The Fitness Evaluation in columns B through D will store the client's personal data and calculate his fitness status. The Workout Report in columns F through M will contain monthly reports on the client's workout routine and calculate the results from his workouts. The Fitness Tables in columns O through P contain different fitness values that will be used in the calculations.

The Fitness Evaluation contains a section for personal information on a Fit Fathers client. Ken wants you to enter the personal data for Daniel Pridham, a Fit Fathers client, to help you test the calculations you enter in the workbook.

To enter Daniel's personal data:

▸ **1.** In cell **C8**, enter **Daniel Pridham** as the client's name.

▸ **2.** In cell **C9**, enter **Sedentary** to describe Daniel's activity level.

▸ **3.** In the range **C10:C14**, enter **45** for his age, **193** for his weight in pounds, **70** for his height in inches, **37** for his waist size in inches, and **15.5** for his neck size in inches.

Documenting Formulas

Documenting the contents of a workbook helps to avoid errors and confusion. This type of information can make a workbook easier for other people to understand. For workbooks that include many calculations, as the Fitness Tracker workbook does, it is helpful to explain the formulas and terms used in the calculations. Such documentation also can serve as a check that the equations are accurate. Another way to document formulas and terms is to include notes of explanation within the worksheet where the equations are used.

Ken has included explanations of different fitness terms and equations in the Explanation of Formulas worksheet, and explanatory notes in cells B26 and F46 of the Fitness Report worksheet. Before proceeding, he wants you to review the documentation in these worksheets.

To review the documentation in the Fitness Tracker workbook:

▸ **1.** Click the **Explanation of Formulas** sheet tab to make it the active sheet.

▸ **2.** Read the sheet contents, reviewing the descriptions of common fitness terms and formulas. As you continue developing the Fitness Tracker workbook, you'll learn about these terms and formulas in more detail.

▸ **3.** Click the **Fitness Report** sheet tab to return to the Fitness Report worksheet.

▸ **4.** Read the explanatory notes in cells B26 and F46.

Using Constants in Formulas

The first fitness equation Ken wants you to enter is BMI, or body mass index, which estimates the amount of human body fat. The BMI equation is based on the individual's body weight divided by the square of his or her height. The specific formula is

$$BMI = \frac{703w}{h^2}$$

where w is the body weight in pounds and h is the height in inches. BMI values from 18.5 to 24.9 are considered normal; anything higher is considered overweight.

One common skill you need when creating a workbook is to translate an equation like the BMI equation into an Excel formula. Some equations use constants. A **constant** is a value in a formula that doesn't change. In the BMI equation, 703 is a constant because that value never changes when calculating the body mass index.

Deciding Where to Place a Constant

Should a constant be entered directly into the formula or placed in a separate worksheet cell and referenced in the formula? The answer depends on the constant being used, the purpose of the workbook, and the intended audience. Placing constants in separate cells that you reference in the formulas can help users better understand the worksheet because no values are hidden within the formulas. Also, when a constant is entered in a cell, you can add explanatory text next to each constant to document how it is being used in the formula. On the other hand, you don't want a user to inadvertently change the value of a constant and throw off all the formula results. You will need to evaluate how important it is for other people to immediately see the constant, and whether the constant requires any explanation for other people to understand the formula. For example, Ken wants you to include the 703 constant in the BMI formula rather than in a separate cell because he doesn't feel that clients need to see this constant to understand BMI.

To convert the BMI equation into a formula, you need to replace w and h in the equation with Daniel's actual weight and height. Because Daniel's weight is stored in cell C11 and his height is stored in cell C12, you replace the w in the formula with the C11 cell reference, and replace the h in the formula with the C12 cell reference. The resulting Excel formula is:

```
=703*C11/C12^2
```

Note that the exponent operator ^ is used to square the height value in the denominator of the fraction. Recall that exponentiation raises a value to a power; in this case, the value in cell C12 is raised to the second power, or squared. Following the order of operations, Excel will first square the height value, then multiply the weight value by 703, and finally divide that product by the squared height. You will enter the BMI formula in the Fitness Report worksheet now.

To enter the BMI formula in the Fitness Report worksheet:

1. In cell **C19**, enter the formula **=703*C11/C12^2**. The formula multiplies the weight in cell C11 by the constant 703, and then divides the resulting value by the square of the height in cell C12. The calculated BMI value that is displayed in cell C19 is 27.68959184.

   Trouble? If your BMI formula results differ from 27.68959184, you probably entered the formula incorrectly. Edit your formula as needed so that the numbers and cell references match those shown in the formula in Step 1.

2. Select cell **C19**, and then reduce the number of displayed decimals to one. Cell C19 displays 27.7 as the formula results.

The next fitness equation, which calculates the individual's resting basal metabolic rate (BMR), includes four constants. The resting BMR estimates the number of calories a person expends daily (not counting any actual activity). For men, the BMR is calculated with the equation

$$BMR = 6.23w + 12.7h - 6.76a + 66$$

where *w* is the weight in pounds, *h* is the height in inches, and *a* is the age in years. BMR is calculated by multiplying the weight, height, and age by different constants, and then adding the results to another constant. Heavier and taller people require more daily calories to sustain them. As people age, their metabolism slows, resulting in a lower BMR. Daniel's weight, height, and age are stored in cells C11, C12, and C10, respectively, so the BMR equation translates to the following Excel formula:

```
=6.23*C11+12.7*C12-6.76*C10+66
```

You will enter this formula in the Fitness Report worksheet to calculate Daniel's BMR.

To enter the BMR formula in the Fitness Report worksheet:

▶ **1.** In cell **C21**, enter the formula **=6.23*C11+12.7*C12–6.76*C10+66**. Cell C21 displays 1853.19, indicating that Daniel burns about 1853 calories per day before performing any activity.

   Trouble? If your BMR formula results differ from 1853.19, you might have entered the formula incorrectly. Edit the formula as needed so that the numbers and cell references match those shown in the formula in Step 1.

▶ **2.** Select cell **C21**, and then reduce the number of decimals displayed in the cell to zero. The number of calories per day displayed in cell C21 is 1853.

The 1853 calories per day amount assumes no physical activity. However, even the most sedentary person moves a little bit during the day, which increases the BMR value. The table in the range O7:P12 in the Fitness Report worksheet lists the constant multipliers for different activity levels. For example, the BMR of a sedentary man like Daniel is multiplied by 1.2 (shown in cell P8) to account for daily movements. If Daniel were to increase his activities to a moderate level, the multiplier would increase to 1.55 (as shown in cell P10).

You will enter the formula to calculate Daniel's active BMR based on his sedentary lifestyle. Ken wants you to use the constant value stored in the table rather entering it into the formula because he anticipates that Daniel will increase his activity level under the direction of Fit Fathers, and it is easier to update the amount in a cell rather than editing a formula.

To calculate Daniel's active BMR:

▶ **1.** In cell **C22**, enter the formula **=C21*P8** to multiply Daniel's resting BMR by the sedentary activity level. Based on this calculation, Daniel's active BMR is 2223.828 calories per day.

▶ **2.** Select cell **C22**, and then decrease the number of decimal places displayed in the cell to zero. The displayed value changes to 2224. See Figure 3-2.

Figure 3-2 BMI and BMR calculated values

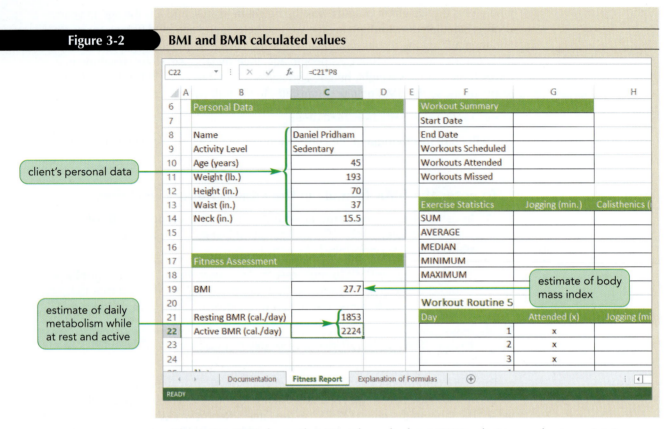

The active BMR shows that Daniel needs about 2224 calories per day to maintain his current weight.

Identifying Notes, Input Values, and Calculated Values

When worksheets involve notes and many calculations, it is useful to distinguish input values that are used in formulas from calculated values that are returned by formulas. Formatting that clearly differentiates input values from calculated values helps others more easily understand the worksheet. Such formatting also helps prevent anyone from entering a value in a cell that contains a formula.

You can use cell styles to identify cells as containing explanatory text, input values, and calculated values. When you use cell styles or other formatting to identify a cell's purpose, you should include a legend in the worksheet describing the purpose of the formatting.

Ken wants to be sure that whenever he and his staff members update a client's workbook, they can easily see where to enter numbers. You will apply cell styles to distinguish between notes, input cells, and formula cells.

To apply cell styles to differentiate cells with notes, input values, and calculated values:

1. Select the merged cell **B26**.

2. On the HOME tab, in the Styles group, click the **Cell Styles** button to open the Cell Styles gallery.

3. Click the **Explanatory Text** cell style located in the Data and Model group. Cell B26 is formatted with the Explanatory Text cell style.

4. Format cell **F46** with the **Explanatory Text** cell style.

5. Format the range **C8:C14** with the **Input** cell style. These cells contain the personal information about Daniel that you entered earlier.

6. Format the nonadjacent range **C19;C21:C22** containing the calculated BMI and BMR values with the **Calculation** cell style.

7. Format the range **G22:J44** with the **Input** cell style. These cells store information about Daniel's workout routine, which Ken enters after each workout.

   Next, you'll create a legend to identify which cells are input cells and which cells are calculated cells.

8. In cell **C2**, enter **Input Values** as the label, format the cell with the **Explanatory Text** cell style, and then right-align the text in the cell.

9. In cell **C4**, enter **Calculated Values** as the label, and then use the Format Painter to copy the formatting in cell C2 and paste it to cell C4.

10. Format cell **D2** with the **Input** cell style, and then format cell **D4** with the **Calculation** cell style.

11. Select cell **C19**. See Figure 3-3.

Figure 3-3	Input and calculated values formatted with cell styles

The built-in cell styles are a quick way of marking different types of values in your worksheet. If the formats do not match what you want for your workbook, you can create your own cell styles. However you design your worksheet, your purpose is to make the values easy to interpret.

PROSKILLS

Written Communication: Displaying Significant Digits

Excel stores numbers with up to 15 digits and displays as many digits as will fit into the cell. So even the result of a simple formula such as =10/3 will display 3.33333333333333 if the cell is wide enough.

A number with 15 digits is difficult to read, and calculations rarely need that level of accuracy. Many scientific disciplines, such as chemistry or physics, have rules for specifying exactly how many digits should be displayed with any calculation. These digits are called **significant digits** because they indicate the accuracy of the measured and calculated values. For example, an input value of 19.32 has four significant digits.

The rules are based on several factors and vary from one discipline to another. Generally, a calculated value should display no more digits than are found in any of the input values. For example, because the input value 19.32 has four significant digits, any calculated value based on that input should have no more than four significant digits. Showing more digits would be misleading because it implies a level of accuracy beyond that which was actually measured.

Because Excel displays calculated values with as many digits as can fit into a cell, you need to know the standards for your profession and change the display of your calculated values accordingly.

Using Excel Functions

Functions provide a quick way to calculate summary data such as the total, average, and median values in a collection of values. Ken recorded the amount of time Daniel spent at each workout doing brisk jogging, calisthenics, and strength exercise. Ken wants you to analyze the results from Daniel's workout routine. You will use Excel functions to summarize these results.

Excel supports an extensive library of functions, organized into the 12 categories shown in Figure 3-4. You can use Excel functions to perform statistical analysis, work with financial data, retrieve information from databases, and generate text strings, among many other tasks.

Figure 3-4   **Excel function categories**

Category	Description
Cube	Retrieve data from multidimensional databases involving online analytical processing (OLAP)
Database	Retrieve and analyze data stored in databases
Date & Time	Analyze or create date and time values and time intervals
Engineering	Analyze engineering problems
Financial	Analyze information for business and finance
Information	Return information about the format, location, or contents of worksheet cells
Logical	Return logical (true-false) values
Lookup & Reference	Look up and return data matching a set of specified conditions from a range
Math & Trig	Perform math and trigonometry calculations
Statistical	Provide statistical analyses of data sets
Text	Return text values or evaluate text
Web	Provide information on web-based connections

© 2014 Cengage Learning

The Excel Help system provides information on all of the Excel functions.

Exploring Function Syntax

Before you use functions, you should understand the function syntax. Recall that the syntax of an Excel function follows the general pattern

FUNCTION(argument1,argument2,...)

where *FUNCTION* is the name of the function, and *argument1*, *argument2*, and so forth are arguments used by the function. An argument can be any type of value including text, numbers, cell references, or even other formulas or functions. Not all functions require arguments.

TIP

Optional arguments are always placed last in the argument list.

Some arguments are optional. You can include an optional argument in the function or omit it from the function. Some optional arguments have default values associated with them, so that if you omit the optional argument, Excel will use the default value. These tutorials show optional arguments within square brackets along with the argument's default value (if any), as

FUNCTION(argument1[, argument2=value2,...])

where *argument1* is a required argument, *argument2* is optional, and *value2* is the default value for *argument2*. As you work with specific functions, you will learn which arguments are required and which are optional as well as any default values associated with optional arguments.

Figure 3-5 describes some of the more common Math, Trig, and Statistical functions and provides the syntax of those functions.

Figure 3-5	Common Math, Trig, and Statistical functions

Function	Category	Description
AVERAGE(number1[, number2, number3, ...])	Statistical	Calculates the average of a collection of numbers, where *number1*, *number2*, and so forth are numbers or cell references; only *number1* is required
COUNT(value1[, value2, value3, ...])	Statistical	Counts how many cells in a range contain numbers, where *value1*, *value2*, and so forth are text, numbers, or cell references; only *value1* is required
COUNTA(value1[, value2, value3, ...])	Statistical	Counts how many cells are not empty in ranges *value1*, *value2*, and so forth, or how many numbers are listed within *value1*, *value2*, etc.
INT(number)	Math & Trig	Displays the integer portion of *number*
MAX(number1[, number2, number3, ...])	Statistical	Calculates the maximum value of a collection of numbers, where *number1*, *number2*, and so forth are either numbers or cell references
MEDIAN(number1[, number2, number3, ...])	Statistical	Calculates the median, or middle, value of a collection of numbers, where *number1*, *number2*, and so forth are either numbers or cell references
MIN(number1[, number2, number3, ...])	Statistical	Calculates the minimum value of a collection of numbers, where *number1*, *number2*, and so forth are either numbers or cell references
RAND()	Math & Trig	Returns a random number between 0 and 1
ROUND(number, num_digits)	Math & Trig	Rounds *number* to the number of digits specified by *num_digits*
SUM(number1[, number2, number3, ...])	Math & Trig	Adds a collection of numbers, where *number1*, *number2*, and so forth are either numbers or cell references

© 2014 Cengage Learning

For example, the ROUND function rounds a number to a specified number of decimal places and has the syntax

`ROUND(number, num_digits)`

where `number` is the number to be rounded and `num_digits` is the number of decimal places to which you want to round the `number` argument. The following function rounds 2.718282 to two decimal places, resulting in 2.72:

`ROUND(2.718282, 2)`

However, you usually reference data values stored in worksheet cells rather than entering the numbers directly in the function. For example, the following function rounds the number in cell A10 to three decimal places:

`ROUND(A10, 3)`

Both arguments in the ROUND function are required. An example of a function that uses optional arguments is the AVERAGE function, which can calculate averages from several ranges or entered values. For example, the function

`AVERAGE(A1:A10)`

averages the values in the range A1:A10, while the function

`AVERAGE(A1:A10, C5:C10, E10)`

includes two optional arguments and averages the values from the cells in range A1:A10, range C5:C10, and cell E10.

Functions can be included as part of larger formulas. The following formula calculates the average of the values in the range A1:A100, and then squares that result using the ^ operator:

`=AVERAGE(A1:A100)^2`

Functions can also be placed inside another function, or **nested**. If a formula contains several functions, Excel starts with the innermost function and then moves outward. For example, the following formula first calculates the average of the values in the range A1:A100 using the AVERAGE function, and then rounds that value to two decimal places:

`=ROUND(AVERAGE(A1:A100),2)`

One challenge of nesting functions is to make sure that you include all of the parentheses. You can check this by counting the number of opening parentheses and making sure that number matches the number of closing parentheses. Excel also displays each level of nested parentheses in different colors to make it easier for you to match the opening and closing parentheses in the formula. If the number of parentheses doesn't match, Excel will not accept the formula and will provide a suggestion for how to rewrite the formula so the number of opening and closing parentheses does match.

There are several ways to enter a function. You have already entered a function by typing directly in a cell and using the AutoSum button. Another way to enter a function is with the Quick Analysis tool.

Entering Functions with the Quick Analysis Tool

The Quick Analysis tool, which you have already used to apply conditional formats that highlight specific data values, can also be used to generate columns and rows of summary statistics that can be used for analyzing data.

Columns F through M in the Fitness Report worksheet will contain the workout report. The range H22:J44 records the number of minutes Daniel spent at each workout jogging, doing calisthenics, and doing strength training. Ken needs to know the total minutes Daniel spent at each exercise to evaluate Daniel's workout effort during the past month. The most efficient way to calculate these totals is with the SUM function. You will use the Quick Analysis tool to enter the SUM function to calculate the total minutes spent at each exercise.

To calculate the total minutes spent on each exercise:

1. Select the range **H22:J44** containing the minutes spent on each exercise during each workout. The Quick Analysis button 🖼 appears in the lower-right corner of the selected range.

2. Click the **Quick Analysis** button 🖼 (or press the **Ctrl+Q** keys) to display the Quick Analysis tool.

3. Click the **TOTALS** category to display Quick Analysis tools for calculating totals.

4. Point to the **Sum** button. Live Preview shows the results of Sum. See Figure 3-6.

Figure 3-6	Quick Analysis tool to calculate totals

5. Click **Sum** to enter the SUM function for each cell in the selected range. The results show that Daniel spent 278 minutes jogging, 245 minutes doing calisthenics, and 347 minutes doing strength exercises during the previous month's workouts.

   The Quick Analysis tool automatically inserts the formulas containing the SUM function at the bottom of the table. Ken wants you to move this information near the top of the worksheet where it can be viewed first.

6. Select the range **H45:J45**, and then cut the selected range.

7. Select cell **G14**, and then paste the formulas with the SUM functions. The totals now appear in the range G14:I14.

The Quick Analysis tool can also be used to quickly calculate averages. An average provides an estimate of the most typical value from a data sample. Ken wants to know the average number of minutes that Daniel spent on each exercise during his sessions.

To calculate the average minutes spent per exercise:

▶ 1. Select the range **H22:J44**, and then click the **Quick Analysis** button 📊 that appears in the lower-right corner of the selected range (or press the **Ctrl+Q** keys).

▶ 2. Click the **TOTALS** category, and then click **Average** to enter the AVERAGE function in the range H45:J45 and calculate the average minutes per exercise type.

▶ 3. Cut the formulas from the range **H45:J45**, and then paste them into the range **G15:I15**.

   Excel displays the averages to eight decimal places, which implies a far greater accuracy in measuring the exercise time than could be recorded.

▶ 4. In the range **G15:I15**, decrease the number of decimal places displayed to one. On average, Daniel spent about 16.4 minutes per session jogging, 14.4 minutes on calisthenics, and 20.4 minutes on strength exercises. See Figure 3-7.

Figure 3-7 | Sums and averages of exercise times

The Quick Analysis tool can be used to summarize values across rows as well as down columns. Ken wants to calculate how long Daniel worked out each day. You will use the Quick Analysis tool to calculate the total exercise minutes per workout.

To calculate the total workout times per session:

▶ 1. In cell **K21**, enter **Total Minutes** as the heading.

▶ 2. Select the range **H22:J44**, and then open the Quick Analysis tool.

▶ 3. Click the **TOTALS** category, and then click the right scroll button to scroll to the right through the list of calculations.

▶ 4. Click the **Sum** button for the column of summary statistics. SUM functions are entered in the range K22:K44, calculating the sum of the workout minutes per session.

   The Quick Analysis tool applies its own style to the formulas it generates. Instead of the bold text, you want the formulas to be formatted with the Calculation style.

▶ 5. Format the range **K22:K44** with the **Calculation** cell style.

6. In cell **J13**, enter **Total Minutes** as the heading.

7. Copy the formulas in the range **I14:I15**, and then paste them into the range **J14:J15** to calculate the sum and average of the total exercise minutes from all of the workouts. As shown in Figure 3-8, Daniel worked out for 870 minutes during the month with an average of 37.8 minutes per workout.

Figure 3-8	Total exercise time per workout

Entering Functions with the Insert Function Dialog Box

Functions are organized in the Function Library group on the FORMULAS tab. In the Function Library, you can select a function from a function category. You can also open the Insert Function dialog box to search for a particular function based on a description you enter. When you select a function, the Function Arguments dialog box opens, listing all of the arguments associated with that function. Required arguments are in bold type; optional arguments are in normal type.

Ken wants his report to include the median exercise times for the three exercise categories. The **median** provides the middle value from a data sample. You can use the MEDIAN function to determine the middle value in a range of numbers. The Quick Analysis tool doesn't include median, so you will use the Insert Function and Function Arguments dialog boxes to help you correctly insert the MEDIAN function.

To calculate the median exercise time:

1. Select cell **G16**. This is the cell in which you will enter the MEDIAN function.

2. Click the **Insert Function** button f_x to the left of the formula bar to open the Insert Function dialog box. From the Insert Function dialog box, you can describe the function you want to search for.

3. In the Search for a function box, type **middle value**, and then click the **Go** button. Functions for finding a middle value appear in the Select a function box. The second entry in the list, MEDIAN, is the one you want to use. See Figure 3-9.

Figure 3-9 **Insert Function dialog box**

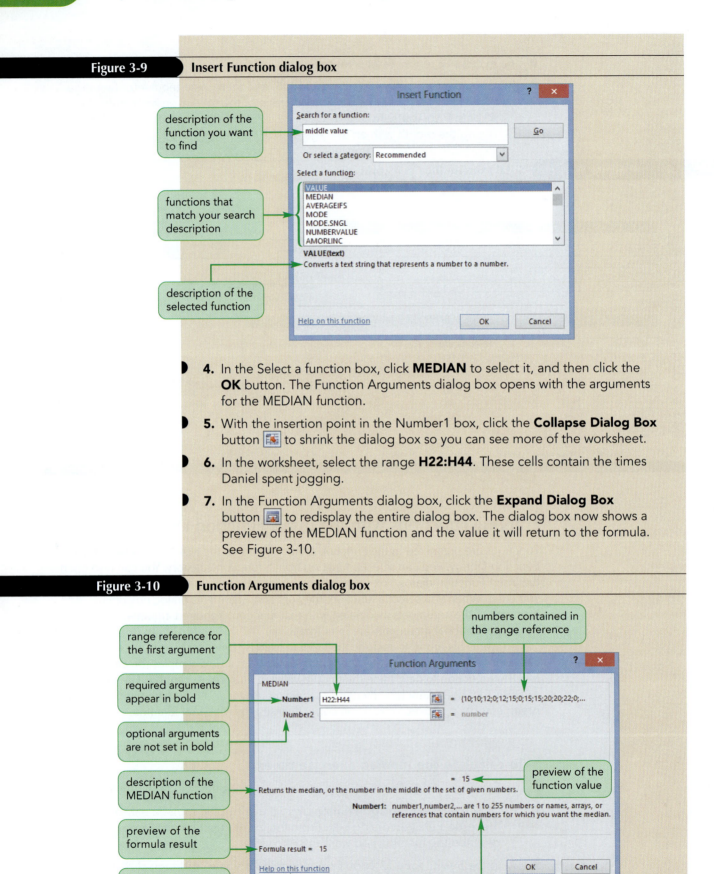

description of the function you want to find

functions that match your search description

description of the selected function

4. In the Select a function box, click **MEDIAN** to select it, and then click the **OK** button. The Function Arguments dialog box opens with the arguments for the MEDIAN function.

5. With the insertion point in the Number1 box, click the **Collapse Dialog Box** button to shrink the dialog box so you can see more of the worksheet.

6. In the worksheet, select the range **H22:H44**. These cells contain the times Daniel spent jogging.

7. In the Function Arguments dialog box, click the **Expand Dialog Box** button to redisplay the entire dialog box. The dialog box now shows a preview of the MEDIAN function and the value it will return to the formula. See Figure 3-10.

Figure 3-10 **Function Arguments dialog box**

range reference for the first argument

required arguments appear in bold

optional arguments are not set in bold

description of the MEDIAN function

preview of the formula result

click to view help about the function

numbers contained in the range reference

preview of the function value

description of the selected argument

8. Click the **OK** button. The formula =MEDIAN(H22:H44) is entered in cell G16, which displays 15 (the median exercise time for jogging).

9. Copy cell **G16**, and then paste the copied formula into the range **H16:J16** to calculate the median exercise times for calisthenics, strength training, and all exercises. See Figure 3-11.

Figure 3-11   Median exercise times

Daniel spent a median time of 15 minutes on calisthenics and 20 minutes on strength training. The median total exercise time was 50 minutes, which is quite a bit higher than the average total exercise time of 37.8 minutes. Why this difference? One reason is that averages are greatly influenced by extremely low or high values. Because Daniel missed several workouts, his exercise time for those days was 0, bringing down the overall average. A median, or middle value, is not as affected by these extreme values, which is why some statisticians advocate medians over averages for analyzing data with widely spaced values.

Ken also wants to know the minimum and maximum minutes Daniel spent exercising during the month. You can access functions by scrolling through the Function Library. You will use this method to enter the functions to calculate the minimum and maximum exercise times.

To calculate the minimum and maximum minutes of exercise:

1. Select cell **G17**, which is where you will calculate the minimum exercise time.

2. On the ribbon, click the **FORMULAS** tab to display the function categories in the Function Library.

3. Click the **More Functions** button to display the rest of the function categories. Calculations involving maximums and minimums are included with the Statistical functions.

4. Click **Statistical** to display the statistical functions, and then scroll down and point to **MIN**. A ScreenTip appears, displaying the MIN function syntax and a description of the function. See Figure 3-12.

Figure 3-12   **MIN function in the Function Library**

functions organized into categories

syntax of the selected function

list of statistical functions

5. Click **MIN** to open the Function Arguments dialog box.

6. With the insertion point in the Number1 box, select the range **H22:H44** in the worksheet. These cells store the amount of time Daniel spent jogging.

7. Click the **OK** button. The dialog box closes, and the formula =MIN(H22:H44) is entered in cell G17, which displays 10, the minimum minutes that Daniel spent jogging during the month.

8. Select cell **G18**, click the **More Functions** button in the Function Library group, click **Statistical**, and then scroll down and click **MAX**. The Function Arguments dialog box opens.

9. With the insertion point in the Number1 box, select the range **H22:H44** in the worksheet, and then click the **OK** button. The formula =MAX(H22:H44) is entered in cell G18, which displays 22, the maximum minutes that Daniel spent jogging.

10. Copy the range **G17:G18**, and then paste the formulas in the range **H17:J18** to calculate the minimum and maximum times for the other exercises and overall.

11. Format the range **G14:J18** with the **Calculation** cell style, and then select cell **F19**. See Figure 3-13.

Figure 3-13   **Summary statistics of the exercise times**

	E	F	G	H	I	J	K
13		Exercise Statistics	Jogging (min.)	Calisthenics (min.)	Strength (min.)	Total Minutes	
14		SUM	278	245	347	870	
15		AVERAGE	16.4	14.4	20.4	37.8	
16		MEDIAN	15	15	20	50	
17		MINIMUM	10	8	12	0	
18		MAXIMUM	22	20	30	60	
19							

sum, average, median, minimum, and maximum values of each exercise time

Referencing Function Results in a Formula

The amount of calories burned during exercise is a function of intensity and time. The more intense the exercise or the longer it lasts, the more calories burned. Ken uses the fitness equation

$$\text{Calories} = \frac{METS \times w \times t}{125.7143}$$

to calculate how many calories will be used during exercise, where *METS* is a metabolic factor that measures the intensity of the exercise, *w* is the individual's weight in pounds, *t* is the exercise time in minutes, and 125.7143 is a constant that converts the quantity into calories. Ken listed the METS values for the different workout routines he created in the range O15:P25 of the Fitness Report worksheet. For example, the METS for Workout Routine 5 is 7.0 and the METS for Workout Routine 10 is 16.0. Using the METS information and the weight and exercise times, you can calculate the total calories burned during each workout.

The fitness equation that calculates calories burned during the first workout translates into the formula

```
=P20*C11*K22/125.7143
```

where `P20` references the cell with the METS for Workout Routine 5, `C11` references the cell that stores Daniel's weight, and `K22` references the cell that calculates the total exercise time of the first workout.

You will enter this formula in cell L22, and then copy it to the remaining cells in the column to calculate the calories burned during each workout.

To calculate the calories burned during Daniel's first workout:

1. In cell **L21**, enter **Calories Burned** as the label.

2. In cell **L22**, enter the formula **=P20*C11*K22/125.7143** to calculate the calories Daniel burned at his first workout. Cell P20 stores the METS value, cell C11 contains Daniel's weight, and cell K22 is the total exercise time for Workout Routine 5 on the first day of the month. Cell L22 displays 376.1306391, which is the number of calories burned at the first workout.

Trouble? If your value differs from 376.1306391, edit your formula as needed so it exactly matches the formula shown in Step 2.

3. Select cell **L22**, and then decrease the number of decimal places shown to one. The displayed value is 376.1.

4. Copy the formula in cell **L22**, and then paste the formula to the range **L23:L44** to calculate the calories burned for the rest of the workouts. See Figure 3-14.

Figure 3-14 | **Formulas incorrectly calculating the calories burned per workout**

The first few values seem somewhat reasonable, but then several workouts show no calories burned. These are followed by cells displaying #VALUE! rather than a number. Obviously something went wrong when you copied and pasted the formula.

Interpreting Error Values

The #VALUE! that appears in some of the cells in the Fitness Report worksheet is an error value. An **error value** indicates that some part of a formula is preventing Excel from returning a calculated value. An error value begins with a pound sign (#) followed by an error name that indicates the type of error. Figure 3-15 describes common error values that you might see instead of the results from formulas and functions. For example, the error value #VALUE! indicates that the wrong type of value is used in a function or formula. You will need to examine the formulas in the cells with error values to determine exactly what went wrong.

Figure 3-15	Excel error values

Error Value	Description
#DIV/0!	The formula or function contains a number divided by 0.
#NAME?	Excel doesn't recognize text in the formula or function, such as when the function name is misspelled.
#N/A	A value is not available to a function or formula, which can occur when a workbook is initially set up prior to entering actual data values.
#NULL!	A formula or function requires two cell ranges to intersect, but they don't.
#NUM!	Invalid numbers are used in a formula or function, such as text entered in a function that requires a number.
#REF!	A cell reference used in a formula or function is no longer valid, which can occur when the cell used by the function was deleted from the worksheet.
#VALUE!	The wrong type of argument is used in a function or formula. This can occur when you reference a text value for an argument that should be strictly numeric.

© 2014 Cengage Learning

The error value messages are not particularly descriptive or helpful. To help you locate the error, an error indicator appears in the upper-left corner of the cell with the error value. When you point to the error indicator, a ScreenTip appears with more information about the source of the error.

INSIGHT

Deciding When to Correct an Error Value

An error value does not mean that you must correct the cell's formula or function. Some error values appear simply because you have not yet entered any data into the workbook. For example, if you use the AVERAGE function to find the average value of an empty column, the #DIV/0! error value appears because the formula cannot calculate the average of a collection of empty cells. However, as soon as you begin entering data, the #DIV/0! message will disappear.

Ken wants you to figure out why the #VALUE error value appears in some of the cells where you copied the calories burned formula. To figure this out, you will examine the formula in cell L31, which is the first cell that displays the error value instead of the expected number results.

To view the formula in cell L31 that results in an error value:

1. Double-click cell **L31**, which displays the #VALUE! error value. In Edit mode, the cell references used in the formula are color coded to match the corresponding cells, making it easier to see which cells are used in the formula.

2. Observe that cell L31 contains the formula =P29*C20*K31/125.7143.

> **3.** Look at the first cell reference in the formula. The first cell reference is to cell P29 containing the text "Fitness Level" instead of cell P20 containing the METS value for Workout Routine 5. The formula is attempting to multiply the text in cell P29, but multiplication can be done only with numbers. This is the problem causing the #VALUE! error value.

> **4.** Look at the second cell reference in the formula. The second cell reference is to cell C20, an empty cell, rather than to cell C11 containing Daniel's weight.

> **5.** Look at the third cell reference in the formula. The third cell reference is to cell K31, which contains the total exercise times for the tenth workout—the correct cell reference.

Exploring Cell References

Most workbooks include data entered in cells that are then referenced in formulas to perform calculations on that data. The formulas can be simple, such as the formulas you entered to add the total minutes of each workout, or they can be more complex, such as the formulas you entered to calculate the calories burned during each workout. Each of these formulas includes one or more cell references.

Understanding Relative References

When a formula includes a cell reference, Excel interprets that cell reference as being located relative to the position of the current cell. For example, Excel interprets the following formula entered in cell A1 to mean "add the value of the cell one column to the right of this cell to the value of the cell one column to the right and one row below this cell":

    =B1+B2

This relative interpretation is retained when the formula is copied to a new location. So, if the formula in cell A1 is copied to cell A3 (two rows down in the worksheet), the relative references in the formula also shift two rows down, resulting in the following formula:

    =B3+B4

Figure 3-16 shows another example of how relative references change when a formula is copied to new cell locations. In this figure, the formula =A4 entered in cell D7 displays 10, which is the number entered in cell A4. When pasted to a new location, each of the pasted formulas contains a reference to a cell that is three rows up and three rows to the left of the current cell's location.

Figure 3-16   **Formulas using relative references**

formula references a cell
three rows up and three
columns to the left of
the active cell

when copied to new
cells, each formula still
references a cell three
rows up and three
columns to the left

values returned by
each formula

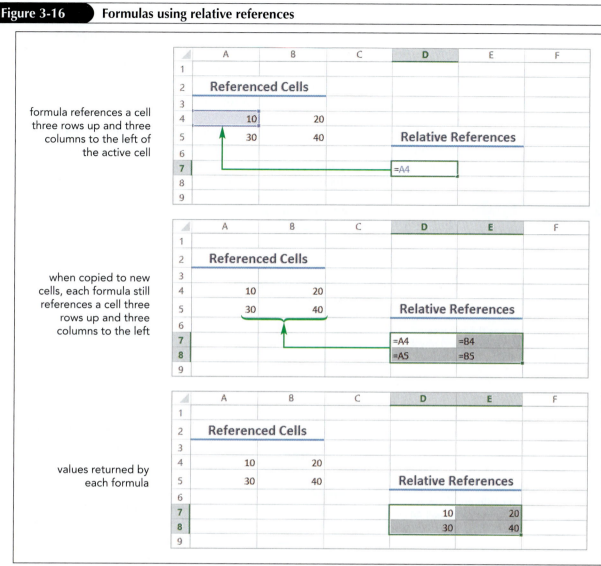

This explains what happened with the relative references you used to calculate calories burned for each workout. When you entered the following formula in cell L22, cell C11 correctly references the client's weight and the other cells correctly reference the METS for Workout Routine 5 and the total exercise time:

    =P20*C11*K22/125.7143

When you copied the formula down to cell L31, all of the cell references contained in that formula also shifted down nine rows, resulting in the following formula, which accurately references the total exercise time for the corresponding workout but no longer references Daniel's weight or the METS for Workout Routine 5—both of which are necessary for the calculation:

    =P29*C20*K31/125.7143

What you need is a cell reference that remains fixed when the formula is copied to a new location.

Understanding Absolute References

A fixed reference—one that always references the same cell no matter where it is moved—is called an absolute reference. In Excel, absolute references include a $ (dollar sign) before each column and row designation. For example, B8 is a relative reference to cell B8, and $B$8 is an absolute reference to that cell. When you copy a formula that contains an absolute reference to a new location, that cell reference does not change.

Figure 3-17 shows an example of how copying a formula with an absolute reference results in the same cell reference being pasted in different cells regardless of their position compared to the location of the original copied cell. In this example, the formula =$A$4 will always reference cell A4 no matter where the formula is copied to, because the cell is referenced with the absolute reference $A$4.

Figure 3-17   Formulas using absolute references

formula absolutely references the cell located in column A and row 4

when copied to new cells, the reference remains fixed on cell A4

values returned by each formula

© 2014 Cengage Learning

Understanding Mixed References

A formula can also include cell references that are mixed. A **mixed reference** contains both relative and absolute references. For example, a mixed reference for cell A2 can be either $A2 or A$2. In the mixed reference $A2, the reference to column A is absolute and the reference to row 2 is relative. In the mixed reference A$2, the column reference is relative and the row reference is absolute. A mixed reference "locks" one part of the cell reference while the other part can change. When you copy and paste a cell with a mixed reference to a new location, the absolute portion of the cell reference remains fixed and the relative portion shifts along with the new location of the pasted cell.

Figure 3-18 shows an example of using mixed references to complete a multiplication table. The first cell in the table, cell B3, contains the formula =$A3*B$2, which multiplies the first column entry (A3) by the first row entry (B2), returning 1. When this formula is copied to another cell, the absolute portions of the cell references remain unchanged and the relative portions of the references change. For example, if the formula is copied to cell E6, the first mixed cell reference changes to $A6 because the column reference is absolute and the row reference is relative, and the second cell reference changes to E$2 because the row reference is absolute and the column reference is relative. The result is that cell E6 contains the formula =$A6*E$2 and returns 16. Other cells in the multiplication table are similarly modified so that each entry returns the multiplication of the intersection of the row and column headings.

Figure 3-18   **Formulas using mixed references**

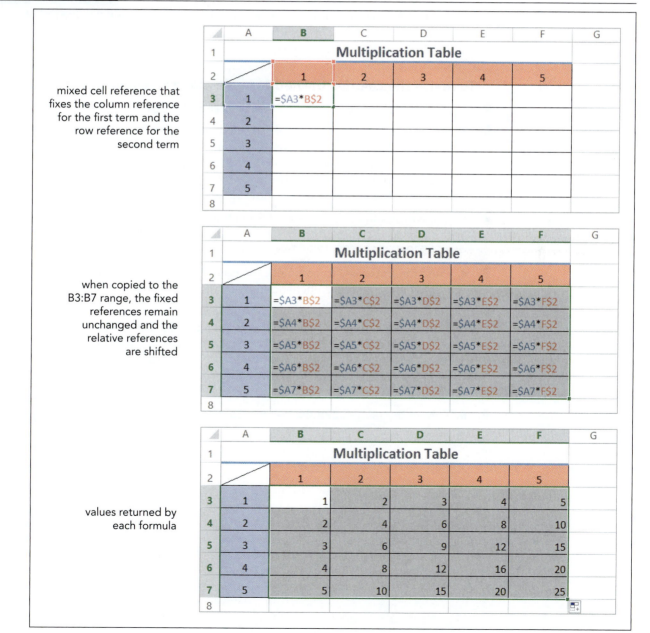

mixed cell reference that fixes the column reference for the first term and the row reference for the second term

when copied to the B3:B7 range, the fixed references remain unchanged and the relative references are shifted

values returned by each formula

Changing Cell References in a Formula

You can quickly switch a cell reference from relative to absolute or mixed. Rather than retyping the formula, you can select the cell reference in Edit mode and then press the F4 key. As you press the F4 key, Excel cycles through the different reference types— starting with the relative reference, followed by the absolute reference, then to a mixed reference with the row absolute, and finally to a mixed reference with the column absolute.

Ken wants you to fix the problem with the cell references in the calories burned formulas. You need to revise the formula to use absolute references to Daniel's weight and the METS value that will not change when the formula is copied to new locations. You will leave the relative reference to the total exercise time so that the copied formulas will retrieve the exercise times from the corresponding workouts. The revised formula in cell L22 uses an absolute reference to the METS values in $P$20 and an absolute reference to Daniel's weight in $C$11, as follows:

```
=$P$20*$C$11*K22/125.7143
```

You will edit the calories burned formula in cell L22, and then paste it to the rest of the workouts.

To revise the calories burned formulas to use absolute references:

1. Double-click cell **L22** to select it and enter Edit mode.

2. Click immediately to the left of cell reference **P20** in the formula to move the insertion point before the letter P, type **$** to change the column reference to absolute, press the → key to move the insertion point between the letter P and 20, and then type **$** to change the row reference to absolute. The complete absolute reference is now $P$20.

3. Double-click the cell reference **C11** in the formula to select it, and then press the **F4** key to change it to the absolute reference $C$11. The formula is now =$P$20*$C$11*K22/125.7143.

> Select only the cell reference you want to change before you press the F4 key.

4. Press the **Enter** key to complete the edit. The 376.1 calories burned displayed in the cell is unchanged because the relative references were accurate in this first formula.

5. Copy cell **L22** and paste it into the range **L23:L44**. The worksheet shows 322.4 calories burned for the second workout and 483.6 calories burned for the third workout. The next row in the list shows 0 calories burned because Daniel did not work out that day. As you can see, the remaining formulas now correctly calculate the calories burned at each workout.

6. Format the range **L22:L44** with the **Calculation** cell style. See Figure 3-19.

Figure 3-19 | **Formulas with absolute and relative references**

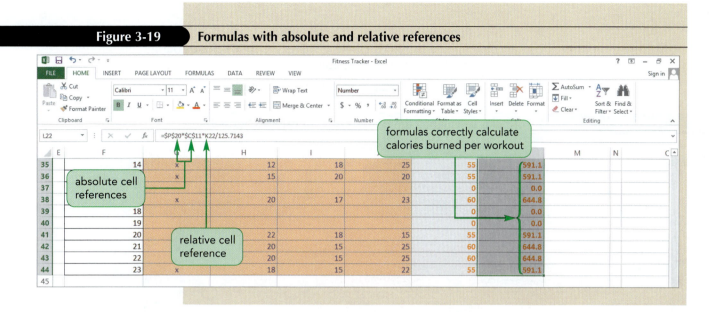

Planning Which Cell Reference to Use in a Formula

You can include the correct type of cell reference in a formula as you create the formula. This requires a little more thought up front, as you consider how each cell in a formula needs to be referenced before you create the formula. Ken wants you to create a running total of the calories burned during each workout. You can use the SUM function with a combination of absolute and relative cell references to add the values in a range. The formula to calculate the total in the first cell is:

=SUM($L$22:L22)

In this formula, the starting cell of the range is fixed at cell L22, but the ending cell of the range is relative. When you copy this formula down the column, the starting cell remains absolutely referenced to cell L22, but the ending cell changes to include the current row. For example, when the formula is pasted three rows down, the formula changes to add the numbers in cells L22, L23, L24, and L25, as follows:

=SUM($L$22:L25)

Continuing in this way, the last cell will contain the sum of all of the calories burned totals using the following formula:

=SUM($L$22:L44)

Instead of entering the formulas yourself, you can use the Quick Analysis tool to calculate the total calories burned up through the end of each workout session.

To calculate the running total of calories burned:

1. In cell **M21**, enter **Calories Subtotal** as the label.

2. Select the range **L22:L44** containing the calories burned during each workout, and then click the **Quick Analysis** button (or press the **Ctrl+Q** keys).

3. Click the **TOTALS** category, and then scroll right to the end of the TOTALS tools.

4. Click **Running Total** (the last entry in the list, which is the Running Total of a column). The range M22:M44 displays the total calories burned up through the end of each workout session.

5. Format the range **M22:M44** with the **Calculation** cell style. See Figure 3-20.

Figure 3-20   **Formulas calculating the running total of calories burned**

Daniel burned 698.5 calories during the first two workouts and more than 1180 calories after the first three workouts. The formula used to calculate the running totals for the column includes both absolute and relative references. You will review the formulas in column M to see the formulas calculating the running totals.

To view the formulas for the running totals:

1. Select cell **M22**, and then review the formula, which is =SUM($L$22:L22). Notice the absolute and relative references to cell L22.

2. Select cell **M23**, and then review the formula, which is =SUM($L$22:L23). Notice that the absolute reference to cell L22 remains unchanged, but the relative reference is now cell L23, expanding the range being added with the SUM function.

3. Select each cell in column M and review its formula, noticing that the absolute reference $L$22 always appears as the top cell of the range but the relative reference for the last cell of the range changes.

4. Save the workbook.

You can see that the running total is calculated with the SUM function using a combination of absolute and relative cell references. The top of the range used in the SUM function is locked at cell L22, but the bottom of the range is relative, expanding in size as the formula was copied down column M. Entered this way, with absolute and relative cell references, the SUM function calculates partial sums, providing the total calories burned up through the end of each workout session.

INSIGHT

Understanding When to Use Relative, Absolute, and Mixed References

Part of effective workbook design is knowing when to use relative, absolute, and mixed references. Use relative references when you want to apply the same formula with input cells that share a common layout or pattern. Relative references are commonly used when copying a formula that calculates summary statistics across columns or rows of data values. Use absolute references when you want your copied formulas to always refer to the same cell. This usually occurs when a cell contains a constant value, such as a tax rate, that will be referenced in formulas throughout the worksheet. Mixed references are seldom used other than when creating tables of calculated values such as a multiplication table in which the values of the formula or function can be found at the intersection of the rows and columns of the table.

So far, you have entered the fitness formulas and summary statistics in the Fitness Tracker workbook. In the next session, you will explore date and time functions, and then look up values to use in formulas and functions.

REVIEW

Session 3.1 Quick Check

1. What is an optional argument? What does Excel do if you do not include an optional argument?
2. Write the function to return the middle value from the values in the range X1:X10.
3. Write the function to round the value in cell A5 to the fourth decimal place.
4. The range of a set of values is defined as the maximum value minus the minimum value. Write the formula to calculate the range of values in the range Y1:Y10.
5. If cell A11 contains the formula =SUME(A1:A10), what error value will appear in the cell?
6. You need to reference cell Q57 in a formula. What is its relative reference? What is its absolute reference? What are the two mixed references?
7. If cell R10 contains the formula =R1+R2, which is then copied to cell S20, what formula is entered in cell S20?
8. If cell V10 contains the formula = AVERAGE($U1:$U5), which is then copied to cell W20, what formula is entered in cell W20?

Session 3.2 Visual Overview:

A **lookup table** stores the data you want to retrieve in categories. This is a vertical lookup table that organizes the categories in the first column of the table.

Compare values are the categories located in the first column of the lookup table and are used for matching to a lookup value specified by the user.

Return values are the data values you want to retrieve from the lookup table and are located in the second and subsequent columns.

A **lookup value** is the category you want to find in a lookup table.

The **VLOOKUP function** returns values from a vertical lookup table by specifying the lookup value to match to a compare value, the location of the lookup table, and the column in the table that contains the return values.

Basal Metabolic Rate Activity Factors

Activity Level	BMR Factor
Sedentary	1.200
Light	1.375
Moderate	1.550
High	1.725
Extreme	1.900

Fitness Tracker – Excel

REVIEW VIEW

Number

$ - % ,

Number

C2... ...LSE)*C21

	B	C	D	E	F	G
6	Personal Data				Workout Summary	
7					Start Date	8/1/2016
8	Name	Daniel Pridham			Ending Date	8/31/2016
9	Activity Level	Light			Workouts Scheduled	23
10	Age (years)	45			Workouts Attended	17
11	Weight (lb.)	173			Workouts Missed	6
12	Height (in.)	70				
13	Waist (in.)	37			Exercise Statistics	Jogging (min.)
14	Neck (in.)	15.5			SUM	278
15					AVERAGE	16.4
16					MEDIAN	15.0
17	Fitness Assessment				MAXIMUM	22.0
18					MINIMUM	10.0
19	BMI	24.8				
20					Workout Routine 5	
21	Resting BMR (cal./day)	1729			Day	Attended (x)
22	Active BMR (cal./d...	2377			8/1/2016	x
23					8/2/2016	x
24					8/3/2016	x
25	Notes...				8/4/2016	
26					8/5/2016	x
	...y)	=6.23*C11+12.7*C12-6.76*C10+			8/8/2016	x
	...)	=VLOOKUP(C9,O8:P12,2,FALSE)			8/9/2016	
					8/10/2016	x
					8/11/2016	x
31					8/12/2016	x

...tness Report   Explanation of Formulas   ⊕

READY

Logical and Lookup Functions

The **COUNT function** tallies how many cells in the specified range contain numbers or dates.

The **COUNTA function** tallies how many cells in the specified range are not blank (contain numbers, dates, or text).

A **logical function** is a function that works with statements that are either true or false. This logical function tests whether the value of cell G22 equals x.

The **IF function** is a logical function that tests a condition and then returns one value if the condition is true and another value if the condition is false.

The **WORKDAY function** displays the date of a weekday that is a specified number of weekdays past a starting date.

AutoFilling Formulas and Data

AutoFill provides a quick way to enter content and formatting in cells based on existing entries in adjacent cells. Ken wants you to include summary statistics for calories burned across all of the scheduled workouts. To add these statistics, you'll use the AutoFill tool.

REFERENCE

Copying Formulas and Formats with AutoFill

- Select the cell or range that contains the formula or formulas you want to copy.
- Drag the fill handle in the direction you want to copy the formula(s), and then release the mouse button.
- To copy only the formats or only the formulas, click the Auto Fill Options button and select the appropriate option.

or

- Select the cell or range that contains the formula or formulas you want to copy.
- On the HOME tab, in the Editing group, click the Fill button.
- Select a fill direction and fill type.

or

- On the HOME tab, in the Editing group, click Series.
- Enter the desired fill series options, and then click the OK button.

Using the Fill Handle

After you select a range, a **fill handle** appears in the lower-right corner of the selection. When you drag the fill handle over an adjacent cell or range, AutoFill copies the content and formats from the original cell or range into the adjacent cell or range. This process is often more efficient than the two-step process of copying and pasting.

Ken wants you to calculate the same summary statistics for the calories burned during the workouts as you did for the total minutes of each workout. Because the total minutes formulas use relative references, you can use the fill handle to copy these for the calories burned statistics.

To copy the calories burned summary statistics and formatting with the fill handle:

1. In cell **K13**, enter **Calories Burned** as the label.

2. Select the range **J14:J18**, which contains the cells with formulas for calculating the sum, average, median, minimum, and maximum total minutes. A fill handle appears in the lower-right corner of the selected range, directly above and to the left of the Quick Analysis button.

TIP

You can also fill a series to the right by selecting both the cells to copy and the cells to be filled in, and then pressing the Ctrl+R keys.

3. Point to the **fill handle**. The pointer changes to **+**.

4. Click and drag the fill handle over the range **K14:K18**. A solid outline appears around the selected range as you move the pointer.

5. Release the mouse button. The selected range is filled in with the formulas and formatting from the range J14:J18, and the Auto Fill Options button appears in the lower-right corner of the selected cells. See Figure 3-21.

| Figure 3-21 | Formulas and formatting copied with AutoFill |

6. Format the range **K14:K18** to display one decimal place.

Based on the summary statistics, Ken can see that Daniel burned 9349.5 calories during the month, burned an average of 406.5 calories per session, burned a median of 537.3 calories per session, and burned a minimum of 0.0 calories and a maximum of 644.8 calories per session during the month.

Using the Auto Fill Options Button

By default, AutoFill copies both the content and the formatting of the original range to the selected range. However, sometimes you might want to copy only the content or only the formatting. The Auto Fill Options button that appears after you release the mouse button lets you specify what is copied. As shown in Figure 3-22, clicking this button provides a menu of AutoFill options. The Copy Cells option, which is the default, copies both the content and the formatting. The Fill Formatting Only option copies the formatting into the selected cells but not any content. The Fill Without Formatting option copies the content but not the formatting.

| Figure 3-22 | Auto Fill Options button |

Because you want to copy the content and the formatting of the summary statistics, you don't need to use the Auto Fill Options button.

Filling a Series

AutoFill can also be used to create a series of numbers, dates, or text based on a pattern. To create a series of numbers, you enter the initial values in the series in a selected range and then use AutoFill to complete the series.

REFERENCE

Creating a Series with AutoFill

- Enter the first few values of the series into a range.
- Select the range, and then drag the fill handle of the selected range over the cells you want to fill.

or

- Enter the first few values of the series into a range.
- Select the entire range into which you want to extend the series.
- On the HOME tab, in the Editing group, click the Fill button, and then click Down, Right, Up, Left, Series, or Justify to set the direction in which you want to extend the series.

Figure 3-23 shows how AutoFill can be used to insert the numbers from 1 to 10 in a selected range. You enter the first few numbers in the range A2:A4 to establish the pattern you want AutoFill to use—consecutive positive numbers in this example. Then, you select the range and drag its fill handle over the cells where you want the pattern continued—in this case, the range A5:A11—and Excel fills in the rest of the series.

Figure 3-23 AutoFill extends a numeric sequence

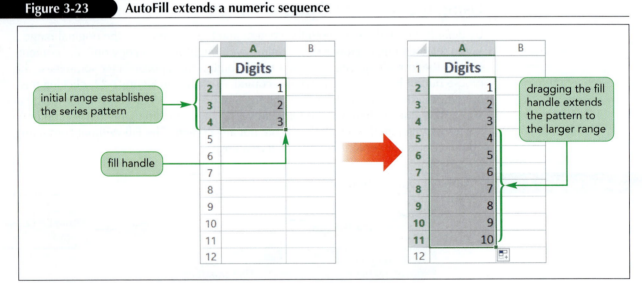

© 2014 Cengage Learning

AutoFill can extend a wide variety of series, including dates and times and patterned text. Figure 3-24 shows some examples of series that AutoFill can generate. In each case, you must provide enough information for AutoFill to identify the pattern. AutoFill can recognize some patterns from only a single entry—such as Jan or January, to create a series of month abbreviations or names, or Mon or Monday, to create a series of the days of the week. A text pattern that includes text and a number such as Region 1, Region 2, and so on can also be automatically extended using AutoFill. You can start the series at any point, such as Weds, June, or Region 10, and AutoFill will complete the next days, months, or text.

| **Figure 3-24** | **AutoFill extends numbers, dates and times, and patterned text** |

Type	Initial Pattern	Extended Series
Numbers	1, 2, 3	4, 5, 6, ..
	2, 4, 6	8, 10, 12, ...
Dates and Times	Jan	Feb, Mar, Apr, ...
	January	February, March, April, ...
	15-Jan, 15-Feb	15-Mar, 15-Apr, 15-May, ...
	12/30/2016	12/31/2016, 1/1/2017, 1/2/2017, ...
	12/31/2016, 1/31/2017	2/29/2017, 3/31/2017, 4/30/2017, ...
	Mon	Tue, Wed, Thu, ...
	Monday	Tuesday, Wednesday, Thursday, ...
	11:00AM	12:00PM, 1:00PM, 2:00PM, ...
Patterned Text	1st period	2nd period, 3rd period, 4th period, ...
	Region 1	Region 2, Region 3, Region 4, ...
	Quarter 3	Quarter 4, Quarter 1, Quarter 2, ...
	Qtr3	Qtr4, Qtr1, Qtr2, ...

© 2014 Cengage Learning

Ken wants you to fill in the dates of the workouts, replacing the numbers in the range F22:F44. You will use AutoFill to insert the calendar dates starting with 8/1/2016.

To use AutoFill to enter the calendar dates:

1. In cell **F22**, enter **8/1/2016**. This is the first date you want to use for the series.

2. Select cell **F22** to select the cell with the first date in the series.

3. Drag the fill handle over the range **F23:F44**.

4. Release the mouse button. AutoFill enters the calendar dates ending with 8/23/2016 in cell F44.

TIP

You can also fill a series down by selecting both the cells to copy and the cells to be filled in, and then pressing the Ctrl+D keys.

For more complex AutoFill patterns, you can use the Series dialog box to specify a linear or growth series for numbers; a date series for dates that increase by day, weekday, month, or year; or an AutoFill series for patterned text. With numbers, you can also specify the step value (how much each number increases over the previous entry) and a stop value (the endpoint for the entire series).

Ken notices that the workout dates are wrong in the Fitness Report worksheet. Fit Fathers meets only Monday through Friday. He asks you to change the fill pattern to include only weekdays. You will use the Series dialog box to set the fill pattern for the rest of the weekdays in the month.

To fill the dates of weekdays in August:

1. Make sure the range **F22:F44** is selected. Cell F22 contains the first value for the series that will be entered in the range F23:F44.

2. On the HOME tab, in the Editing group, click the **Fill** button, and then click **Series**. The Series dialog box opens.

3. In the Type section, make sure that the **Date** option button is selected.

4. In the Date unit section, click the **Weekday** option button so that the series includes only dates for Mondays through Fridays. See Figure 3-25.

| Figure 3-25 | Series dialog box |

fills the series columns

specifies date as the type of series

specifies weekdays as the date unit

5. Click the **OK** button. The dates of weekdays in August are filled into the selected range ending with 8/31/2016. See Figure 3-26.

| Figure 3-26 | Weekday values filled in |

only weekdays are entered in the selected range

⊿	E	F	G	H	I	J	
20		Workout Routine 5					
21		Day	Attended (x)	Jogging (min.)	Calisthenics (min.)	Strength (min.)	Tota
22		8/1/2016	x	10	10	15	
23		8/2/2016	x	10	8	12	
24		8/3/2016	x	12	18	15	
25		8/4/2016					
26		8/5/2016	x	12	15	18	
27		8/8/2016	x	15	10	15	
28		8/9/2016					
29		8/10/2016	x	15	15	20	
30		8/11/2016	x	15	13	22	
31		8/12/2016	x	20	15	25	
32		8/15/2016	x	20	15	20	
33		8/16/2016	x	22	8	30	
34		8/17/2016					
35		8/18/2016	x	12	18	25	
36		8/19/2016	x	15	20	20	
37		8/22/2016					
38		8/23/2016	x	20	17	23	

| ‹ › | Documentation | **Fitness Report** | Explanation of Formulas | ⊕ | |

READY   AVERAGE: 8

Working with Date Functions

Excel has several functions that work with dates and times. **Date functions** insert or calculate dates and times. They are particularly useful in business workbooks that involve production schedules and calendar applications. Figure 3-27 describes some of the commonly used Date functions.

Figure 3-27   Date functions

Function	Description
DATE(*year, month, day*)	Creates a date value for the date represented by the *year*, *month*, and *day* arguments
DAY(*date*)	Extracts the day of the month from *date*
MONTH(*date*)	Extracts the month number from *date* where 1=January, 2=February, and so forth
YEAR(*date*)	Extracts the year number from *date*
NETWORKDAYS(*start, end*[, *holidays*])	Calculates the number of whole working days between *start* and *end*; to exclude holidays, add the optional *holidays* argument containing a list of holiday dates to skip
WEEKDAY(*date*[, *return_type*])	Calculates the weekday from *date*, where 1=Sunday, 2=Monday, and so forth; to choose a different numbering scheme, set *return_type* to 1 (1=Sunday, 2=Monday, ...), 2 (1=Monday, 2=Tuesday, ...), or 3 (0=Monday, 1=Tuesday, ...)
WORKDAY(*start, days*[, *holidays*])	Returns the workday after *days* workdays have passed since the *start* date; to exclude holidays, add the optional *holidays* argument containing a list of holiday dates to skip
NOW( )	Returns the current date and time
TODAY( )	Returns the current date

© 2014 Cengage Learning

Displaying the Current Date with the TODAY function

Many workbooks include the current date. You can use the **TODAY function** to display the current date in a worksheet. The TODAY function has the following syntax:

=TODAY( )

Note that although the TODAY function doesn't have any arguments, you still must include the parentheses for the function to work. The date displayed by the TODAY function is updated automatically whenever you reopen the workbook or enter a new calculation.

Ken wants the Fitness Report worksheet to show the current date each time it is used or printed. You will use the TODAY function to display the current date in cell G2.

To display the current date with the TODAY function:

1. Select cell **G2**.
2. On the FORMULAS tab, in the Function Library group, click the **Date & Time** button to display the date and time functions.
3. Click **TODAY**. The Function Arguments dialog box opens and indicates that the TODAY function requires no arguments.
4. Click the **OK** button. The formula =TODAY() is entered in cell G2.
5. Verify that the current date is displayed in the cell.
6. Format the cell using the **Calculation** style.

Finding the Next Weekday with the WORKDAY function

Instead of using AutoFill to enter a series of dates in a range, you can use the WORKDAY function to fill in the remaining weekdays based on the start date you specify. The WORKDAY function displays the date of the weekday a specific number of weekdays past a starting date. The syntax of the WORKDAY function is

```
=WORKDAY(start, days[, holiday])
```

where *start* is a start date, *days* is the number of weekdays after *start*, and *holiday* is an optional list of dates to skip. If you do not include anything for the optional *holiday* argument, the WORKDAY function does not skip any days. For example, if cell A1 contains the date 11/4/2016, a Friday, the following formula displays the date 11/9/2016, a Wednesday that is three working days after 11/4/2016:

```
=WORKDAY(A1, 3)
```

Ken wants to automate the process of inserting the exercise dates. You will use the WORKDAY function to do this.

To insert the exercise dates using the WORKDAY function:

1. In cell **G7**, enter **8/1/2016** to specify the date the workouts will begin, and then format the cell using the **Input** cell style.

2. In cell **G8**, enter the formula **=F44** to display the date of the last scheduled workout, which is 8/31/2016 in this instance, and then format the cell using the **Calculation** cell style.

3. In cell **F22**, enter the formula **=G7** to replace the date with a reference to the start date you specified in cell G7. The cell still displays 8/1/2016.

4. Select cell **F23**, if necessary, and then click the **Insert Function** button f_x next to the formula bar. The Insert Function dialog box opens.

5. Type **working days** in the Search for a function box, and then click the **Go** button to find all of the functions related to working days.

6. In the Select a function box, click **WORKDAY** to select the function, and then click the **OK** button. The WORKDAY Function Arguments dialog box opens.

7. In the Start_date box, type the cell reference **F22** to specify that cell F22 contains the start date you want to use.

8. In the Days box, type **1** to specify the number of workdays after the date in cell F22 that you want the formula results to show. See Figure 3-28.

Figure 3-28   Function Arguments dialog box for the WORKDAY function

cell reference for the cell with the start date

number of workdays after the start date

preview of the formula result

TIP

To select a working day prior to the start date, enter a negative number rather than a positive number.

9. Click the **OK** button. Cell F23 contains the formula =WORKDAY(F22, 1) and displays the date 8/2/2016, which is the next workday after 8/1/2016.

   You want to use the same formula to calculate the rest of the workout dates. You can use AutoFill to quickly repeat the formula.

10. Select cell **F23**, and then drag the fill handle down over the range **F23:F44** to copy the formula and enter the rest of the workdays in the month.

   Because the copied formulas use relative references, each cell displays a date that is one workday after the date in the previous cell. The dates should not be different from the dates you entered previously using AutoFill.

11. Format the range **F22:F44** with the **Calculation** cell style to show that these dates are calculated by a formula rather than entered manually.

   You will test that the formulas in the range F22:F44 are working correctly by entering a different start date.

12. In cell **G7**, enter **9/1/2016** as the new start date.

13. Review the dates in the range F22:F44, verifying that the workout dates start with 9/2/2016 in cell F23, continue with 9/5/2016 in cell F24, and end with 10/3/2016 in cell F44.

   Trouble? If the workout dates do not end with 10/3/2016, compare the formula in cell F23 to the formula shown in Step 9, make any edits needed, and then repeat Step 10.

14. In cell **G7**, enter **8/1/2016** to return to the original start date.

INSIGHT

Selecting the Days in the Work Week

Different countries, regions, and even businesses might have different rules for what constitutes a workday. If you need to create a schedule that doesn't follow the standard U.S. business days (Monday through Friday), you can use the WORKDAY.INTL function to specify the days to use as the work week. The syntax of the WORKDAY.INTL function is:

```
=WORKDAY.INTL(start, days[, weekend=1, holidays])
```

The only difference between the syntax of the WORKDAY.INTL function and the syntax of the WORKDAY function is the optional *weekend* argument, which specifies the days of the week considered to be weekend or nonworking days. If you omit the *weekend* argument, weekends are considered to occur only on Saturday and Sunday. If you include the *weekend* argument, you enter one of the following numbers to specify the two days or the one day to consider as the weekend:

Weekend	Two-Day Weekend	Weekend	One-Day Weekend
1	Saturday, Sunday	11	Sunday
2	Sunday, Monday	12	Monday
3	Monday, Tuesday	13	Tuesday
…		…	
7	Friday, Saturday	17	Saturday

For example, a business that is open every day except Sunday would use a *weekend* value of 11 to indicate that only Sunday is considered a nonworking day, and a business that is closed on Monday and Tuesday would use a *weekend* value of 3 to specify a work week of Wednesday through Sunday. For other working week schedules, you can enter text to specify which days are workdays. See Excel Help for more information.

Counting Cells

Excel has two functions for counting cells—the COUNT function and the COUNTA function. The COUNT function tallies how many cells in a range contain numbers or dates (because they are stored as numeric values). The COUNT function does not count blank cells or cells that contain text. Its syntax is

```
COUNT(value1[, value2, value3, ...])
```

where *value1* is the first item or cell reference containing the numbers you want to count. The remaining *value* arguments are used primarily when you want to count numbers and dates in nonadjacent ranges. For example, the following function counts how many cells in the range A1:A10, the range C1:C5, and cell E5 contain numbers or dates:

```
COUNT(A1:A10, C1:C5, E5)
```

If you want to know how many cells contain entries—whether those entries are numbers, dates, or text—you use the COUNTA function, which tallies the nonblank cells in a range. The following is the syntax of the COUNTA function, which has the same arguments as the COUNT function:

```
COUNTA(value1[, value2, value3, ...])
```

Ken wants the Workout Summary to show the total number of scheduled workouts for the month, the number of attended workouts, and the number of missed workouts. You will use the COUNT function to count the total number of workout dates in the Workout Routine 5 table. Then, you will use the COUNTA function to count the number of workouts actually attended. Each attended workout is marked by an "x" in column G of the Workout Routine 5 table; missing workouts are left blank. Finally, you will enter a formula to calculate the missed workouts.

To count the scheduled, attended, and missed workouts:

1. In cell **G9**, enter the formula **=COUNT(F22:F44)**. Cell G9 displays 23, indicating that Ken scheduled 23 workouts for the month.

2. In cell **G10**, enter the formula **=COUNTA(G22:G44)**. Cell G10 displays 17, indicating that Daniel attended 17 of the 23 scheduled workouts.

3. In cell **G11**, enter the formula **=G9–G10** to calculate the difference between the number of scheduled workouts and the number of attended workouts. Cell G11 displays 6, which is the number of missed workouts.

4. Format the range **G9:G11** with the **Calculation** cell style.

5. Select cell **G10**. See Figure 3-29.

Figure 3-29   Completed Workout Summary

COUNTA function counts the number of nonblank cells in the specified range

number of scheduled workouts

workouts marked with an "x" in the Attended column

difference between the scheduled and attended workouts

It is important to understand the difference between the COUNT and COUNTA functions. For example, if you had used the COUNT function in cell G10 to tally the number of attended workouts, the result would have been 0 because the range G22:G44 contains no entries with numbers.

Like the COUNT function, many of Excel's statistical functions ignore cells that are blank or contain text. This can create unexpected results with calculated values if you are not careful. Figure 3-30 shows how some of the common summary statistics change when blank cells are used in place of zeroes.

Figure 3-30   Calculations involving blank cells and zeroes

cells with zeroes

cells left blank

Excel returns a different value depending on whether zeroes or blank cells are used

Some of the fitness statistics for total exercise minutes and calories burned include the six workouts that Daniel missed. For example, the minimum exercise minutes and calories burned are both listed as 0 because the calculated values show up as 0 in the worksheet when the workout session was missed. Ken wants the summary statistics based on only the workouts actually attended. One way to exclude missed workouts is to delete the zeroes, leaving blank cells. However, Ken wants the worksheet to be user-friendly and not require anyone to double-check and edit entries for missed workouts. Instead of editing the worksheet, you can use a logical function to automatically replace zeroes with blanks for missed workouts.

Working with Logical Functions

A logical function returns a different value depending on whether the given condition is true or false, such as whether or not a scheduled workout was attended. In Excel, the condition is expressed as a formula. Consider a condition that includes the expression A5=3. If cell A5 is equal to 3, this expression and condition are true; if cell A5 is not equal to 3, this expression and condition are false. The IF function is one of the many logical functions you can use in Excel.

Using the IF Function

The IF function is a logical function that returns one value if a condition is true, and returns a different value if that condition is false. The syntax of the IF function is

    IF(logical_test, value_if_true, value_if_false)

where *logical_test* is a condition that is either true or false, *value_if_true* is the value returned by the function if the condition is true, and *value_if_false* is the value returned if the condition is false. The value can be a number, text, a date, or a cell reference. For example, the following formula tests whether the value in cell A1 is equal to the value in cell B1:

    =IF(A1=B1, 100, 50)

If the value in cell A1 equals the value in cell B1, the formula result is 100; otherwise, the formula result is 50.

In many cases, however, you will not use values directly in the IF function. The following formula uses cell references, returning the value of cell C1 if A1 equals B1; otherwise, it returns the value of cell C2:

    =IF(A1=B1, C1, C2)

The = symbol in these formulas is a comparison operator. A **comparison operator** is a symbol that indicates the relationship between two values. Figure 3-31 describes the comparison operators that can be used within a logical function.

Figure 3-31 Comparison operators

Operator	Expression	Description
=	A1 = B1	Tests whether the value in cell A1 is equal to the value in cell B1
>	A1 > B1	Tests whether the value in cell A1 is greater than the value in cell B1
<	A1 < B1	Tests whether the value in cell A1 is less than the value in cell B1
>=	A1 >= B1	Tests whether the value in cell A1 is greater than or equal to the value in cell B1
<=	A1 <= B1	Tests whether the value in cell A1 is less than or equal to the value in cell B1
<>	A1 <> B1	Tests whether the value in cell A1 is not equal to the value in cell B1

The IF function also works with text. For example, the following formula tests whether the value of cell A1 is equal to "yes":

```
=IF(A1="yes", "done", "restart")
```

If true (the value of cell A1 is equal to "yes"), the formula returns the text "done"; otherwise, it returns the text "restart". Notice that the text in the function is enclosed in quotation marks.

In addition, you can nest other functions inside an IF statement. The following formula first tests whether cell A5 is equal to the maximum of values within the range A1:A100:

```
=IF(A5=MAX(A1:A100), "Maximum", "")
```

If it is, the formula returns the text "Maximum"; otherwise, it returns no text.

In the Fitness Report worksheet, you need to rewrite the formulas that calculate the total minutes and total calories from each workout as IF functions that test whether Daniel actually attended the workout. Because every attended workout is marked with an "x" in column G, you can test whether the cell entry in column G is an "x". For example, the following formula in cell K22 is currently being used to calculate the total minutes from the first workout:

```
=SUM(H22:J22)
```

This formula can be revised to the following IF function, which first determines if cell G22 contains an "x" (indicating that the workout was attended), and then uses the SUM function to calculate the total minutes if there is an "x":

```
=IF(G22="x", SUM(H22:J22), "")
```

Otherwise, the formula displays nothing, leaving the cell blank.

You will use relative references in the revised formula so that you can copy it for the other workouts and total columns. You will create the formula with the IF function for the total minutes column now.

To use an IF function to calculate total minutes for attended workouts:

1. Select cell **K22**, and then press the **Delete** key to clear the original formula from the cell.

2. Click the **Insert Function** button f_x next to the formula bar to open the Insert Function dialog box.

3. Type **if function** in the Search for a function box, and then press the **Enter** key. Functions that match your description appear in the Select a function box.

4. Click **IF** in the Select a function box, and then click the **OK** button to open the Function Arguments dialog box.

5. In the Logical_test box, type **G22="x"** as the expression that tests whether cell G22 is equal to x.

6. Press the **Tab** key to move the insertion point to the Value_if_true box, and then type **SUM(H22:J22)**. If cell G22 does contain an x (the logical test is true), the sum of the values in the range H22:J22 will be displayed in cell K22.

7. Press the **Tab** key to move the insertion point to the Value_if_false box, and then type **""** (opening and closing quotation marks). If cell G22 does not contain an x (the logical test is false), the cell will be left blank. See Figure 3-32.

Figure 3-32   **Function Arguments dialog box for the IF function**

8. Click the **OK** button. The formula =IF(G22="x", SUM(H22:J22), "") is entered into cell K22. The cell displays 35, which is the number of minutes Daniel spent exercising at that workout session.

   You will copy the formula with the IF function to calculate the total minutes for the rest of the workouts.

9. Select cell **K22**, and then drag the fill handle down over the range **K22:K44** to copy the IF formula to the remaining cells in the column. The total number of minutes for each workout is recalculated so that the missed workouts in cells K25, K28, K34, K37, K39, and K40 are now left blank.

10. Select cell **K22**. The #VALUE! error value appears in columns L and M for each of the missed workouts because the current formulas cannot calculate calories burned when no total minutes are provided. See Figure 3-33.

Figure 3-33   **IF function excludes the total minutes for missed workouts**

Next, you will update the calories burned formulas so that they don't display the #VALUE! error value when a workout is missed. This requires another IF statement similar to the one you used to calculate total minutes. As with the total minutes calculation, any missed workout will display a blank cell for the calories burned in place of a 0. Rather than reentering the complete formula for calories burned, you can edit the existing formula, inserting the IF function.

To change the calories burned formulas to IF functions:

1. Double-click cell **L22** to enter Edit mode.

2. Press the **Home** key to move the insertion point to the beginning of the formula, and then press the → key to move the insertion point one space to the right, directly after = (the equal sign). You will begin the IF function after the equal sign.

3. Type **IF(G22="x",** to insert the function name and the expression for the logical test.

4. Press the **Ctrl+End** keys to move the insertion point to the end of the formula.

Make sure your formula matches the one shown here.

5. Type **, "")** to enter the value if false and complete the IF function. The complete formula is now =IF(G22="x", $P$20*$C$11*K22/125.7143, "").

6. Press the **Enter** key to exit Edit mode and make cell L23 active. Cell L22 still displays 376.1 because Ken did not miss the first workout.

   You will use AutoFill to copy the IF function to the rest of the cells in the Calories Burned column.

7. Select cell **L22**, and then drag the fill handle down over the range **L22:L44**. As shown in Figure 3-34, the missed workouts now display blank cells instead of zeroes, and the attended workouts show the same calculated values as earlier.

| Figure 3-34 | IF function excludes the calories burned for missed workouts |

By excluding the missed workouts, Daniel's average exercise time increased from 37.8 minutes to 51.2 minutes, and the average calories burned increased to 550 calories. These averages more closely match the median values because zeroes were removed from the calculations. The minimum values for Total Minutes and Calories Burned now also reflect only attended workouts, changing from 0 (when they were based on a missed workout) to 30 minutes and 322.4 calories, respectively. These measures reflect the true results of the workouts Daniel attended.

Using a Lookup Function

Lookup functions find values in tables of data and insert them in another location in the worksheet such as cells or in formulas. For example, consider the active BMR calculated in cell C22, which adjusts the calculation of Daniel's metabolic rate to account for his activity level. The more active Daniel is, the more calories he can consume without gaining weight. The multiplying factors for each activity level (Sedentary, Light, Moderate, High, or Extreme) are stored in a table in the range O8:P12; you used the value in cell P8 to adjust Daniel's BMR value for his sedentary lifestyle. Instead of including a direct reference to one of the multiplying factors in the table, you can use a function to have Excel choose the multiplying factor that corresponds to the specified activity level.

The table that stores the data you want to retrieve is called a lookup table. A lookup table organizes numbers or text into categories. This particular lookup table organizes the BMR factors by activity levels, as shown in Figure 3-35. Every activity level category in the first column of the lookup table has a corresponding BMR factor in the second column of the table. This table is a vertical lookup table because the categories are arranged vertically. The entries in the first column of a vertical lookup table are referred to as the compare values because they are compared to the category you want to find (called the lookup value). When a match is found, the corresponding value in one of the subsequent columns is returned. For example, to find the return value for the Moderate lookup value, you look down the first column of the lookup table until you find the Moderate entry. Then, you move to the second column to locate the corresponding return value, which is 1.550, in this case.

| Figure 3-35 | Finding an exact match from a vertical lookup table |

© 2014 Cengage Learning

Lookup tables can be constructed for exact match or approximate match lookups. An **exact match lookup** is when the lookup value must match one of the compare values in the first column of the lookup table. The table in Figure 3-35 is an exact match lookup because the activity level must match one of the compare values in the table or a value is not returned. An **approximate match lookup** occurs when the lookup value falls within a range of numbers in the first column of the lookup table. You will work with exact match lookups in this tutorial.

Finding an Exact Match with the VLOOKUP Function

To retrieve the return value from a vertical lookup table, you use the VLOOKUP function. The syntax of the VLOOKUP function is

```
VLOOKUP(lookup_value, table_array, col_index_num[, range_lookup=TRUE])
```

where *lookup_value* is the compare value to find in the first column of the lookup table, *table_array* is the range reference to the lookup table, and *col_index_num* is the number of the column in the lookup table that contains the return value. Keep in mind that *col_index_num* refers to the number of the column within the lookup table, not the worksheet column. For example, *col_index_num* 2 refers to the second column of the table, *col_index_num* 3 refers to the third column of the table, and so forth. Finally, *range_lookup* is an optional argument that specifies whether the compare values are an exact match or a range of values (for an approximate match). For an exact match, you set the *range_lookup* value to FALSE. For approximate match lookups, you set the *range_lookup* value to TRUE or you can omit it because its default value is TRUE.

For example, the following formula performs an exact match lookup to find the BMR factor for an Extreme activity level based on the values from the lookup table in the range O8:P12 (shown earlier in Figure 3-35):

```
=VLOOKUP("Extreme", O8:P12, 2, FALSE)
```

> **TIP**
>
> If the VLOOKUP function cannot find the lookup value, the #N/A error value is displayed in the cell.

The *col_index_num* is 2 because the BMR factors are in the second column of the table. The *range_lookup* is FALSE because this is an exact match. The function looks through the compare values in the first column of the table to locate the "Extreme" entry. When the exact entry is found, the function returns the corresponding value in the second column of the table, which in this case is 1.900.

Daniel's activity level in cell C9 is entered as Sedentary, which has a BMR factor of 1.2. The following active BMR formula you entered earlier calculated that Daniel can consume about 2224 calories per day and maintain his current weight:

```
=P8*C21
```

In this formula, P8 references the Sedentary BMR value in cell P8 and C21 references Daniel's base or resting metabolic rate. To have Excel look up the BMR value, you need to replace the P8 cell reference with a VLOOKUP function, as follows:

```
=VLOOKUP(C9, O8:P12, 2, FALSE)*C21
```

In this formula, C9 contains Daniel's activity level (Sedentary), O8:P12 references the lookup table, 2 specifies the table column to find the BMR factors, and FALSE indicates that this is an exact match lookup. You will enter this formula into the worksheet now.

To use the VLOOKUP function to calculate Daniel's active BMR:

1. Select cell **C22**, and then press the **Delete** key to clear the formula currently in the cell.

2. On the ribbon, click the **FORMULAS** tab. Because VLOOKUP has several arguments to manage, you will enter the function using the Function Arguments dialog box.

3. In the Function Library group, click **Lookup & Reference** to display a list of functions, and then click **VLOOKUP**. The Function Arguments dialog box opens.

4. With the insertion point in the Lookup_value box, click cell **C9** in the worksheet to enter that cell reference as the location containing the value to look up in the first column of the lookup table.

5. Press the **Tab** key to move the insertion point into the Table_array box, and then select the range **O8:P12**, which contains the vertical lookup table in the worksheet.

6. Press the **Tab** key to move the insertion point to the Col_index_num box, and then type **2** to return a value from the second column of the lookup table.

7. Press the **Tab** key to move the insertion point to the Range_lookup box, and then type **FALSE** to specify an exact match lookup. The dialog box shows the resulting value of the function with these arguments, which in this case is 1.2. See Figure 3-36.

Figure 3-36   **Function Arguments dialog box for the VLOOKUP function**

8. Click the **OK** button to close the dialog box.

9. Double-click cell **C22** to enter Edit mode, press the **Ctrl+End** keys to move the insertion point to the end of the formula, type ***C21** to complete the formula, and then press the **Enter** key. The completed formula in cell C22 is =VLOOKUP(C9,O8:P12,2,FALSE)*C21, resulting in an active BMR of 2224 calories per day for a Sedentary activity level.

You will change the activity level to ensure that the formula works correctly.

10. In cell **C9**, enter **Moderate** to change the activity level from Sedentary. The active BMR value changes to 2872 because the VLOOKUP function returns a 1.55 BMR factor from the lookup table.

Ken decides that Light is a more accurate description of Daniel's activity level.

TIP

Exact matches are not case sensitive, so the lookup values Light, light, and LIGHT are considered to be the same.

11. In cell **C9**, enter **Light** as the activity level. At that activity level, the active BMR changes to 2548. With a Light activity level, Daniel can consume about 2548 calories per day and maintain his current weight.

12. Select cell **C22** to view the formula. See Figure 3-37.

Figure 3-37   VLOOKUP function calculates the active BMR

VLOOKUP function looks up the BMR factor from the table in the range O8:P12

updated activity level

formula results show the daily calories for light activity

Performing What-If Analysis

A **what-if analysis** lets you explore the impact that changing input values has on the calculated values in the workbook. For example, Ken could perform a what-if analysis to determine how many pounds Daniel needs to lose to reach a more healthy weight. Current fitness standards suggest that a body mass index between 18.5 and 24.9 is considered to be within the "normal" classification. Daniel's body mass index is 27.7, which is rated as overweight. So Ken wants to know how many pounds Daniel needs to lose to reduce his body mass index to 24.9.

Using Trial and Error

One way to perform a what-if analysis is by changing one or more of the input values to see how they affect the calculated results. This **trial-and-error method** requires some guesswork as you estimate which values to change and by how much. In this case, Ken wants you to find out the weight at which Daniel would reach a BMI of 24.9. You'll start by checking the resulting body mass index if Daniel were to lose 10 pounds, reducing his weight to 183 pounds.

To perform a what-if analysis by trial and error:

1. In cell **C11**, change the weight from 193 pounds to **183** pounds. Daniel's body mass index decreases from 27.7 to 26.3, as shown in cell C19. At this weight, he is still considered overweight.

> **2.** In cell **C11**, enter **163** pounds. At this weight, Daniel's BMI shown in cell C19 is 23.4. So losing 30 pounds is more than enough to classify Daniel's body weight as normal.
>
> Ken wants to know if Daniel can lose fewer than 30 pounds to reach that classification.

> **3.** In cell **C11**, enter **168** pounds. At this weight, Daniel's BMI value is 24.1, which is still within the normal classification, but not exactly equal to 24.9.

If you want to find the exact weight that will result in a body mass index of 24.9, you would have to continue trying different weight values as you close in on the correct weight. This is why the method is called "trial and error." For some calculations, trial and error can be a very time-consuming way to locate the exact input value. A more direct approach to this problem is to use Goal Seek.

Using Goal Seek

Goal Seek automates the trial-and-error process by allowing you to specify a value for a calculated item, which Excel uses to determine the input value needed to reach that goal. In this case, because Ken wants to know how Daniel can reach a body mass index of exactly 24.9 (the upper level of the normal classification), the question that Goal Seek answers is: "What weight value is required to reach that goal?" Goal Seek starts by setting the calculated value and works backward to determine the correct input value.

REFERENCE

Performing What-If Analysis and Goal Seek

To perform a what-if analysis by trial and error:
- Change the value of a worksheet cell (the input cell).
- Observe its impact on one or more calculated cells (the result cells).
- Repeat until the desired results are achieved.

To perform a what-if analysis using Goal Seek:
- On the DATA tab, in the Data Tools group, click the What-If Analysis button, and then click Goal Seek.
- Select the result cell in the Set cell box, and then specify its value (goal) in the To value box.
- In the By changing cell box, specify the input cell.
- Click the OK button. The value of the input cell changes to set the value of the result cell.

You will use Goal Seek to find the weight that will result in Daniel's BMI reaching exactly 24.9.

To use Goal Seek to find a weight resulting in a 24.9 BMI:

> **1.** On the ribbon, click the **DATA** tab.

> **2.** In the Data Tools group, click the **What-If Analysis** button, and then click **Goal Seek**. The Goal Seek dialog box opens.

> **3.** Make sure the value in the Set cell box is selected, and then click cell **C19** in the Fitness Report worksheet. The absolute cell reference $C$19 appears in the Set cell box. The set cell is the calculated value you want Goal Seek to change to meet your goal.

4. Press the **Tab** key to move the insertion point to the To value box, and then type **24.9**. This indicates that you want Goal Seek to set this value to 24.9 (the highest body mass index in the normal classification).

5. Press the **Tab** key to move the insertion point to the By changing cell box. There are often various input values you can change to meet a goal. In this case, you want to change the weight value in cell C11.

6. Click cell **C11**. The absolute reference $C$11 appears in the By changing cell box. See Figure 3-38.

Figure 3-38   **Goal Seek dialog box**

Goal Seek	
Set cell:	$C$19 ← cell whose value should be set
To value:	24.9 ← value to set cell to
By changing cell:	$C$11

input cell whose value should be changed to meet the set goal

7. Click the **OK** button. The Goal Seek dialog box closes, and the Goal Seek Status dialog box opens, indicating that Goal Seek found a solution.

8. Click the **OK** button. A weight value of about 173 pounds is displayed in cell C11. Daniel would need to lose roughly 20 pounds, reducing his weight to 173 pounds to reach a weight within the normal classification for BMI. See Figure 3-39.

Figure 3-39   **Target weight determined by Goal Seek**

	A	B	C	D	E	F	G	H
6		Personal Data				Workout Summary		
7						Start Date	8/1/2016	
8		Name	Daniel Pridham			End Date	8/31/2016	
9		Activity Level	Light			Workouts Scheduled	23	
10		Age (years)	45			Workouts Attended	17	
11		Weight (lb.)	173.5561878			Workouts Missed	6	
12		Height (in.)	70					
13		Waist (in.)	37			Exercise Statistics	Jogging (min.)	Calistheni
14		Neck (in.)	15.5			SUM	278	
15						AVERAGE	16.4	
16						MEDIAN	15	
17		Fitness Assessment				MINIMUM	10	
18						MAXIMUM	22	
19		BMI	24.9					
20						Workout Routine 5		
21		Resting BMR (cal./day)	1732			Day	Attended (x)	Jogging
22		Active BMR (cal./day)	2382			8/1/2016	x	
23						8/2/2016	x	
24						8/3/2016	x	

solution weight → (cell C11)

desired BMI → (cell C19)

Documentation | **Fitness Report** | Explanation of Formulas | ⊕

READY

9. Save and close the workbook.

Ken appreciates all of the work you have done in developing the Fitness Tracker workbook. He will use this workbook as a model for all of his other clients at Fit Fathers.

Session 3.2 Quick Check

1. The first three values in a selected series are 3, 6, and 9. What are the next three values that will be inserted by AutoFill?
2. Write a formula to display the current date.
3. Write a formula to find the date four workdays after the date value stored in cell B10. There are no holidays.
4. Explain the difference between the COUNT function and the COUNTA function.
5. If cell Q3 is greater than cell Q4, you want to display the text "OK"; otherwise, display the text "RETRY". Write the formula that accomplishes this.
6. Jan is entering hundreds of temperature values into an Excel worksheet for a climate research project, and she wants to save time on data entry by leaving freezing point values as blanks rather than typing zeroes. Will this cause complications if she later tries to calculate an average temperature from her data values? Explain why or why not.
7. Provide the formula to perform an exact match lookup with the lookup value from cell G5 using a lookup table located in the range A1:F50. Return the value from the third column of the table.
8. What is the difference between a what-if analysis by trial and error and by Goal Seek?

ASSESS

SAM Projects

Put your skills into practice with SAM Projects! SAM Projects for this tutorial can be found online. If you have a SAM account, go to www.cengage.com/sam2013 to download the most recent Project Instructions and Start Files.

PRACTICE

Review Assignments

Data File needed for the Review Assignments: Mothers.xlsx

Ken and his wife, Sally, are expanding the business, changing its name to Fit Fathers and Mothers Inc., and adding fitness classes for mothers with a special emphasis on pregnant women. The fitness equations for women are different from those for men. Ken and Sally want you to create a workbook similar to the one you created for fathers, but focused on the fitness needs of women. Sally also wants you to calculate the total fat burned in the course of completing the workout schedule. She has already designed much of the workbook's contents, but she needs you to add the formulas and functions. Complete the following:

1. Open the **Mothers** workbook located in the Excel3 ► Review folder included with your Data Files, and then save the workbook as **Mothers Fitness** in the location specified by your instructor.

2. In the Documentation sheet, enter your name and the date.

3. Go to the Fitness Analysis worksheet. In the range C8:C15, enter the personal data for **Dorothy Young**. Her activity level is **Moderate**, she is **38** years old, **152** pounds, **64** inches tall, with a **33**-inch waist, **35**-inch hips, and a **14**-inch neck.

4. In cell C20, enter a formula to calculate Dorothy's body mass index based on the equation
   $BMI = 703w/h^2$

   where w is the weight in pounds and h is the height in inches. Display the formula results with one decimal place.

5. In cell C22, enter a formula to calculate the resting metabolism rate for women based on the equation
   $BMR = 4.338w + 4.698h - 4.68a + 655$

   where w is the weight in pounds, h is the height in inches, and a is the age in years. Display the formula results with no decimal places.

6. In cell C23, enter a formula using the VLOOKUP function to calculate the active BMR based on the equation
   Active BMR = *Activity Factor* $\times$ *BMR*

   where *Activity Factor* is an exact match lookup for the value in the range O8:Q12 that corresponds to the activity level entered in cell C9, and *BMR* is the value in cell C22. Display the formula results with no decimal places.

7. In cell K22, enter a formula using an IF function to calculate the total minutes for the first workout that displays a blank cell if Dorothy did not attend a workout that day.

8. Use AuotFill to copy the formula you entered in cell K22 to the range K23:K44 to calculate the total minutes for each workout.

9. In cell L22, enter a formula to calculate the calories burned at the first workout based on the equation
   $$\text{Calories} = \frac{METS \times w \times t}{125.7143}$$

   where *METS* is the metabolic factor for the exercise, w is the client's weight, and t is the exercise time. Use the METS value located in cell P19, the weight value located in cell C11, and the time value located in the corresponding cell in column K. Be sure to use an absolute reference for both weight and METS.

10. Edit the formula you entered in cell L22 to be included as part of an IF function that returns a blank cell if Dorothy did not attend the workout that day. Display the formula results with one decimal place.

11. Use AutoFill to copy the formula you entered in cell L22 to the range L23:L44 to calculate the calories burned at each workout.

12. In the range M22:M44, use the Quick Analysis tool to calculate a column running total of the calories burned in the range L22:L44. Display the formula results with two decimal places.

13. Complete the exercise statistics in the range G14:K18 by entering formulas calculating the sum, average, median, maximum, and minimum values of the exercise times, and calories burned values from the workout log. Display the averages and the calories burned statistics with one decimal place.

14. In cell G2, use a function to display the current date whenever the workbook is opened.

15. In cell F22, enter a formula to reference the start date entered in cell G7.

16. In the range F23:F44, use a function to increase the value of the date in the previous row by 1 workday. Format the formula results with the Short Date format.

17. In cell G8, enter a formula to display the ending date entered in cell F44.

18. In cell G9, enter a formula to count the number of days included in the range F22:F44.

19. In cell G10, enter a formula to count the number of attended workouts as indicated in the range G22:G44.

20. In cell G11, enter a formula to calculate the difference between the number of scheduled workouts and the number of attended workouts. Save the workbook.

21. Use Goal Seek to determine the weight Dorothy must attain to reach a body mass index of 22.

22. Save the revised workbook as **Mothers Fitness Goal**, and then close the workbook.

Case Problem 1

Data File needed for this Case Problem: Hernandez.xlsx

Hernandez Family   Juan and Olivia Hernandez are a recently married couple in Fort Wayne, Indiana. Juan is currently in graduate school and Olivia is the manager at a local bakery. They want to use Excel to help manage their family budget, but they need help setting up the formulas and functions to project their monthly expenses and help them meet their financial goals. Complete the following:

1. Open the **Hernandez** workbook located in the Excel3 ▸ Case1 folder included with your Data Files, and then save the workbook as **Hernandez Budget** in the location specified by your instructor.

2. In the Documentation sheet, enter your name and the date.

3. Go to the Budget worksheet. In cell B7, calculate the couple's total monthly income.

4. In row 23, use AutoFill to replace the numbers 1 through 12 with the month abbreviations **Jan** through **Dec**.

5. In rows 24 and 25, enter the couple's monthly income by referencing the monthly income estimates in cells B5 and B6. Use an absolute cell reference.

6. In row 26, calculate the couple's monthly income.

7. In row 37, enter formulas to calculate the total estimated expenses for each month.

8. In row 38, calculate each month's net cash flow, which is equal to the total income minus the total expenses.

9. In row 39, calculate the running total of the net cash flow so that Olivia and Juan can see how their net cash flow changes as the year progresses.

10. In the range B10:B19, calculate the average monthly expenses by category based on the values previously entered in rows 27 through 36.

11. In cell B20, calculate the total average monthly expenses.

12. The couple currently has $7,350 in their savings account. Each month the couple will either take money out of their savings account or deposit money. In row 41, calculate the end-of-month balance in their savings account by adding the value in cell E5 to the running total values of the net cash flow in row 39. Use an absolute cell reference for cell E5.

13. In cell E6, enter a formula to display the value of the savings balance at the end of December.

14. Juan and Olivia would like to have $15,000 in their savings account by the end of the year. Olivia is planning to ask for a raise at her job. Use Goal Seek to determine the value of cell B6 that will achieve a final savings balance of $15,000.

15. Save and close the workbook.

Case Problem 2

CHALLENGE

Data File needed for this Case Problem: Econ.xlsx

Introduction to Economics 102   Alice Keyes teaches Introduction to Economics 102 at Mountain View Business School in Huntington, West Virginia. She wants to use Excel to track the grades from her class. Alice has already entered the homework, quiz, and final exam scores for all of her students in a workbook, and she has asked you to set up the formulas and functions for her.

You will calculate each student's final average based on his or her homework score, quiz scores, and final exam. Homework counts for 20 percent of the student's final grade. The first two quizzes count for 10 percent each. The second two quizzes count for 15 percent each. The final exam counts for 30 percent of the final grade.

You will also calculate each student's rank in the class. The rank will display which student placed first in terms of his or her overall score, which student placed second, and so forth. Ranks are calculated using the function

```
RANK(number, ref, [order=0])
```

where *number* is the value to be ranked, *ref* is a reference to the cell range containing the values against which the ranking is done, and *order* is an optional argument that specifies whether to rank in descending order or ascending order. The default *order* value is 0 to rank the values in descending order.

Finally, you will create formulas that will look up information on a particular student based on that student's ID so Alice doesn't have to scroll through the complete class roster to find a particular student. Complete the following:

1. Open the **Econ** workbook located in the Excel3 ▸ Case2 folder included with your Data Files, and then save the workbook as **Econ Grades** in the location specified by your instructor.

2. In the Documentation sheet, enter your name and the date.

3. Go to the Grade Book worksheet. In cell B5, count the number of student IDs in the range A22:A57.

⊕ **Explore** 4. Cells C15 through H15 contain the weights assigned to each assignment, quiz, or exam. In cell J22, calculate the weighted average of the first student's scores by entering a formula that multiplies each score by its corresponding weight and adds the resulting products.

5. Edit the formula in cell J22, changing the references to the weights in cells C15 through H15 from relative references to absolute references.

6. Use AutoFill to copy the formula from cell J22 into the range J23:J57.

⊕ **Explore** 7. In cell K22, use the RANK function to calculate how the first student compares to the other students in the class. Use the weighted average from cell J22 for the *number* argument and the range of weighted averages in the cell range $J$22:$J$57 for the *ref* argument. You do not need to specify a value for the *order* argument.

8. Use AutoFill to copy the formula you entered in cell K22 into the range K23:K57.

9. In the range C16:H18, calculate the class average, minimum, and maximum for each of the six grading components (homework, quizzes, and final exam).

10. In cell B8, enter the student ID **14858**.

⊕ **Explore** 11. Using the VLOOKUP function with an exact match and the student data table in the range A22:K57, retrieve the first name, last name, weighted average, and class rank for student 14858 in the range B9:B12. Use an absolute reference to the lookup table. Note that the first name is found in the third column of the student data table, the last name is found in the second column, the weighted average is found in the tenth column, and the class rank is found in the eleventh column.

12. Brenda Dunford missed the final exam and will be taking a make-up exam. She wants to know what score she would need on the final exam to achieve an overall weighted average of 90. Use Goal Seek to calculate what final exam score Brenda needs to result in a weighted average of 90.

13. Save and close the workbook.

Case Problem 3

CHALLENGE

Data File needed for this Case Problem: Homes.xlsx

Homes of Dreams   Larry Helt is a carpenter and a woodcrafter in Coventry, Rhode Island, who loves to design and build custom dollhouses. He started his business, Homes of Dreams, a few years ago and it has expanded into a very profitable sideline to his ongoing carpentry work. Larry wants to create a shipping form that will calculate the cost for the purchased items, including taxes, shipping, and handling. Larry already designed the worksheet, which includes a table of shipping rates, shipping surcharges, and items sold by Homes of Dreams. He asks you to complete the worksheet. Complete the following:

1. Open the **Homes** workbook located in the Excel3 ▶ Case3 folder included with your Data Files, and then save the workbook as **Homes of Dreams** in the location specified by your instructor.

2. In the Documentation sheet, enter your name and the date.

3. Go to the Order Form worksheet.

4. In cell B21, enter the Item ID **DH007**.

5. In cell C21, enter the VLOOKUP function with an exact match to return the name of the item referenced in cell B21. Reference the lookup table in the range M4:O50 using an absolute cell reference. Return the value from the second column of the table.

6. In cell E21, enter the VLOOKUP function with an exact match to return the price of the item referenced in cell B21. Use an absolute reference to the lookup table in the range M4:O50. Return the value from the third column of the table.

7. In cell F21, enter **1** as the quantity of the item ordered.

8. In cell G21, calculate the price of the item multiplied by the quantity ordered.

⊕ **Explore** 9. Revise your formulas in cells C21, E21, and G21, nesting them within an IF formula. For each cell, test whether the value of cell B21 is not equal to "" (a blank). If it is not, return the value of the VLOOKUP function in cells C21 and E21 and the calculated value in cell G21. Otherwise, those cells should return a blank ("") value.

10. Use AutoFill to copy the formulas in cells C21, E21, and G21 through row 30 in the order items table.

11. In row 22, enter **BD002** as the Item ID and **3** as the quantity of items ordered. Verify that the formulas you created automatically enter the name, price, and charge for the item.

12. In rows 23 through 25, enter **1** order for item **BH003**, **1** order for item **DR002**, and **1** order for item **KR009**.

13. In cell G32, calculate the sum of the item charges from all possible orders.

14. In cell G33, calculate the sales tax on the order, which is equal to the subtotal multiplied by the tax rate (entered in cell J9).

15. In cell C15, enter a function to insert the current date whenever the workbook is opened.

16. In cell C16, enter **3 Day** as the type of delivery for this order.

17. In cell C17, calculate the number of working days it will take to ship the order by inserting a VLOOKUP function using an exact match lookup. Use the delivery type in cell C16 as the lookup value, and use the shipping data in the range I4:K7 as the lookup table. Return the value from the third column of the table.

Explore 18. In cell C18, estimate the date of delivery. Use cell C15 as the start date and cell C17 as the number of working days after the start date.

Explore 19. The shipping and handling fee is based on the delivery method (Standard, 3 Day, 2 Day, or Overnight). In cell G34, calculate the shipping and handling fee for the order using an exact match lookup with the data in the range I4:J7. Use the delivery method specified in cell C16 to find the corresponding shipping and handling fee in the Delivery table.

20. In cell G36, calculate the sum of the merchandise subtotal, sales tax, and shipping and handling fee.

21. Save the workbook, and then delete the item IDs and quantities from the order table.

22. Save the workbook as **Homes of Dreams 2**, calculate the cost of ordering 1 of item BD001 using overnight delivery, and then save the workbook.

23. Save the workbook as **Homes of Dreams 3**, and then delete the item IDs and quantities from the order table. Calculate the cost of ordering 1 of item KR001, 2 of item BH004, and 1 of item DR001 using standard delivery. Save and close the workbook.

TROUBLESHOOT

Case Problem 4

Data File needed for this Case Problem: Quality.xlsx

Karleton Manufacturing   Carmen Garza is a quality control manager at Karleton Manufacturing, a manufacturing plant located in Trotwood, Ohio. One project that Carmen oversees is the manufacture of tin cans for a major food company. The can widths must be consistent. To compensate for the fact that metal working tools tend to wear down during the day, the pressure behind the tools is increased as the blades become worn. Quality control technicians monitor the process to check that it remains "in control" creating cans whose widths are neither too narrow nor too wide. Carmen has recorded the widths of four cans from 39 batches in an Excel workbook that she wants to use to determine whether the process is "in control." One standard for determining whether a process is "in control" is whether the average value from a process batch falls within the lower and upper control limits. The workbook itself is in need of quality control as some of the formulas are not calculating correctly. You will fix these and then enter the remainder of the formulas needed in the worksheet. Complete the following:

1. Open the **Quality** workbook located in the Excel3 ▸ Case4 folder included with your Data Files, and then save the workbook as **Quality Control Analysis** in the location specified by your instructor.

2. In the Documentation sheet, enter your name and the date.

3. In the Quality Control worksheet, use AutoFill with the value in cell A7 and fill the series of batch numbers from B-1 to B-39 into the range A7:A45.

Troubleshoot 4. In the Quality Control worksheet, cells M3 and M4 display the #NAME? error value instead of the averages. Make the necessary changes to correct the formulas.

Troubleshoot 5. The formulas in the range H7:H45 are supposed to calculate the range of values (maximum minus minimum) within each batch. However, the formula results display 6.2 for every batch. Make the necessary changes in the formulas to fix the problem.

Troubleshoot 6. The formulas in the range I7:I45 are supposed to calculate the average width of the four cans tested in each batch. Unfortunately, the formulas' results don't equal the average widths. Make the necessary changes in the formulas to fix the problem.

7. In cell J7, calculate the lower control limit for the first batch based on the equation

$LCL=XBAR-A2\times RBAR$

where LCL is the lower and upper control limits, $XBAR$ is the average value from all batches, $RBAR$ is the average range from all batches, and $A2$ is a correction factor that depends on the sample size of the batch. In this case, use the $XBAR$ value from cell M3 and the $RBAR$ value from cell M4. Determine the $A2$ value using an exact match lookup with the sample size in cell G7 as the reference value, and the second column from the table in the range O7:P30 as the return value.

8. AutoFill the lower control limit formula from cell J7 into the rest of the LCL column in the Control Limits table. Check to make sure your formulas were properly copied and that they still reference the correct cells.

9. In cell K7, calculate the upper control limit for the first batch based on the equation

   $UCL=XBAR+A2×RBAR$

   where UCL is the upper control limit. Copy your formula into the rest of the UCL column in the Control Limits table.

10. In cell L7, indicate whether the B-1 batch process is "in control low" by testing whether the batch's average is less than its LCL value. If it is, display "NO"; otherwise, display a blank cell.

11. In cell M7, indicate whether the B-1 batch process is "in control high" by testing whether the batch's average is greater than its UCL value. If it is, display "NO"; otherwise, display a blank cell.

12. Fill the in control low and in control high formulas for the rest of the batches.

13. Add conditional formatting to the range L7:M45 so that cells displaying "NO" are formatted in dark red text on a light red background.

⚙ **Troubleshoot** 14. The computer program that recorded the width values entered a missing width value as a 0 instead of leaving the cells blank. This affects the calculations about sample size and which batches are in control. Fix this in the data set and any formulas so that the worksheet accurately indicates which batches are not in control on the low side or not in control on the high side.

15. Save and close the workbook.

Decision Making

Creating a Budget Worksheet to Make Financial Decisions

Decision making is the process of choosing between alternative courses of action, usually in response to a problem that needs to be solved. Having an understanding of decision-making processes will lead to better decisions and greater confidence in carrying out those decisions. This is especially important when making financial decisions.

Gather Relevant Information

Begin by collecting data and information related to the decision you need to make. This information can include data expressed as currency or numbers, as well as data that cannot be measured numerically. For example, when creating a budget, numerical data includes your income and expenses, current savings, future savings and purchases, and so on. Other data might include the amount of savings you need in order to feel comfortable before making a large purchase, such as buying a car or paying tuition.

Evaluate the Gathered Information and Develop Alternatives

Evaluate the data you collected and determine possible alternatives. Excel workbooks are well suited to evaluating numerical data. You can also use workbooks to evaluate potential outcomes based on other data by assigning numerical weights to them. For example, you can enter your monthly income and fixed expenses into a worksheet along with variable expenses to determine your cash flow. You can then consider this information along with your current savings to determine how much money to contribute to savings or earmark for a purchase. Based on these results, you can develop alternatives for how to distribute your available money among variable expenses (such as entertainment), savings, and a large purchase.

Select the Best Alternative

Carefully evaluate the alternatives you developed based on your analysis. Before making a decision, be sure to take into account all factors. Consider such questions as:

- Does this alternative make sense for the long term? For example, does this budget allow you to achieve all your financial goals?
- Can you realistically carry out this alternative? For example, does this budget provide enough for necessities such as food and housing as well as for luxuries such as entertainment?
- Will this alternative be acceptable even if its outcome is not perfect or some unconsidered factors emerge? For example, will this budget cover unforeseen expenses such as car repairs or an unexpected trip?
- How comfortable are you with this decision? For example, does this budget relieve or add stress about managing your finances?

After analyzing all the factors, one alternative should begin to emerge as the best alternative. If it doesn't, you might need to develop additional alternatives.

Prepare an Action Plan

After making a decision, you need to plan how to implement that decision. Consider what steps you need to take to achieve the final outcome. For example, do you need to open a bank account or change services to reduce expenses (such as switching to a less expensive cell phone plan)? Determine a reasonable time table. When do you want to start? How long will each task take? What tasks must be completed before others start? Can tasks be performed at the same time? Develop milestones to track the success of your plan. For example, one milestone might be to increase your savings by 10 percent in three months. Finally, identify what resources you need to be successful. For example, do you need to talk to a financial advisor at your bank?

Take Action and Monitor the Results

After you develop the action plan, the actual plan begins. For example, you can open bank accounts, change telephone services, and so forth as outlined in your action plan. Be sure to check off completed tasks and assess how well those actions produce the desired outcome. For example, is the budget achieving the financial goals you set? If so, then continue to follow the established plan. If not, you may need to modify the action plan or reevaluate your decision.

PROSKILLS

Develop a Budget Worksheet

Excel is valuable to a wide audience of users: from accountants of Fortune 500 companies to homeowners managing their budgets. An Excel workbook can be a complex document, recording data from thousands of financial transactions, or it can track a few monthly household expenses. Anyone who has to balance a budget, track expenses, or project future income can use the financial tools in Excel to help them make good financial decisions about their financing and future expenditures.

In this exercise, you will use Excel to create a sample budget workbook that will contain information of your choice, using the Excel skills and features presented in Tutorials 1 through 3. Use the following steps as a guide to completing your workbook.

Note: Please be sure *not* to include any personal information of a sensitive nature in any workbooks you create to be submitted to your instructor for this exercise. Later, you can update the workbooks with such information for your personal use.

1. Gather the data related to your monthly cash inflows and outflows. For example, how much do you take home in your paychecks each month? What other sources of income do you have? What expenses do you have—rent, utilities, gas, insurance, groceries, entertainment, car payments, and so on?

2. Create a new workbook for the sample financial data. Use the first worksheet as a documentation sheet that includes your name, the date on which you start creating the workbook, and a brief description of the workbook's purpose.

3. Plan the structure of the second worksheet, which will contain the budget. Include a section to enter values that remain consistent from month to month, such as monthly income and expenses. As you develop the budget worksheet, reference these cells in formulas that require those values. Later, you can update any of these values and see the changes immediately reflected throughout the budget.

4. In the budget worksheet, enter realistic monthly earnings for each month of the year. Use formulas to calculate the total earnings each month, the average monthly earnings, and the total earnings for the entire year.

5. In the budget worksheet, enter realistic personal expenses for each month. Divide the expenses into at least three categories, providing subtotals for each category and a grand total of all the monthly expenses. Calculate the average monthly expenses and total expenses for the year.

6. Calculate the monthly net cash flow (the value of total income minus total expenses).

7. Use the cash flow values to track the savings throughout the year. Use a realistic amount for savings at the beginning of the year. Use the monthly net cash flow values to add or subtract from this value. Project the end-of-year balance in the savings account under your proposed budget.

8. Format the worksheet's contents using appropriate text and number formats. Add colors and borders to make the content easier to read and interpret. Use cell styles and themes to provide your worksheet with a uniform appearance.

9. Use conditional formatting to automatically highlight negative net cash flow months.

10. Insert new rows at the top of the worksheet and enter titles that describe the worksheet's contents.

11. Examine your assumptions. How likely are certain events to occur? Perform several what-if analyses on your budget, providing the impact of (a) reducing income with expenses remaining constant; (b) increasing expenses with income remaining constant; (c) reducing income and expenses; and (d) increasing income and expenses. Discuss the different scenarios you explored. How much cushion does your projected income give you if expenses increase? What are some things you can do in your budget to accommodate this scenario?

12. After settling on a budget, develop an action plan for putting your budget into place. What are some potential pitfalls that will prohibit you from following through on your proposed budget? How can you increase the likelihood that you will follow the budget? Be specific, and write down a list of goals and benchmarks that you'll use to monitor your progress in following your financial plan.

13. With the worksheet set up and your budget in place, you can take action and monitor your results. You will want to update your worksheet each month as income or expense items change to be sure you remain on track to meet your goals. You will also want to confirm that you made a good decision. If not, evaluate your budget and determine what new action you need to take to get yourself back on track.

14. Format the worksheets for your printer. Include headers and footers that display the workbook filename, the workbook's author, and the date on which the report is printed. If the report extends across several pages, repeat appropriate print titles on all of the pages, and include page numbers and the total number of pages on every printed page.

15. Save and close the workbook.

OBJECTIVES

Session 1.1
- Learn basic database concepts and terms
- Start and exit Access
- Explore the Microsoft Access window and Backstage view
- Create a blank database
- Create and save a table in Datasheet view
- Enter field names and records in a table datasheet
- Open a table using the Navigation Pane

Session 1.2
- Open an Access database
- Copy and paste records from another Access database
- Navigate a table datasheet
- Create and navigate a simple query
- Create and navigate a simple form
- Create, preview, navigate, and print a simple report
- Use Help in Access
- Learn how to compact, back up, and restore a database

Creating a Database

Tracking Patient, Visit, and Billing Data

ACCESS

Case | *Chatham Community Health Services*

Chatham Community Health Services, a nonprofit health clinic located in Hartford, Connecticut, provides a range of medical services to patients of all ages. The clinic specializes in the areas of pulmonology, cardiac care, and chronic disease management. Cindi Rodriguez, the office manager for Chatham Community Health Services, oversees a small staff and is responsible for maintaining the medical records of the clinic's patients.

In order to best manage the clinic, Cindi and her staff rely on electronic medical records for patient information, billing, inventory control, purchasing, and accounts payable. Several months ago, the clinic upgraded to **Microsoft Access 2013** (or simply **Access**), a computer program used to enter, maintain, and retrieve related data in a format known as a database. Cindi and her staff want to use Access to store information about patients, billing, vendors, and products. She asks for your help in creating the necessary Access database.

STARTING DATA FILES

Access1 → Tutorial
Cindi.accdb

Review
Company.accdb

Case1
Program.accdb

Case2
Consulting.accdb

Case3
Animal.accdb

Case4
Tour.accdb

Session 1.1 Visual Overview:

The **Quick Access Toolbar** provides one-click access to commonly used commands, such as Save.

The **Shutter Bar Open/Close Button** allows you to close and open the Navigation Pane; you might want to close the pane so that you have more room on the screen to view the object's contents.

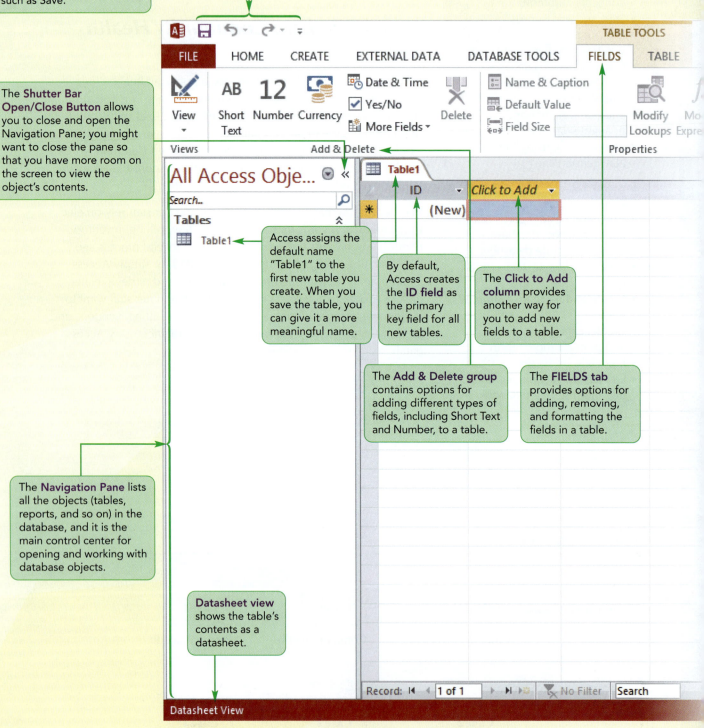

Access assigns the default name "Table1" to the first new table you create. When you save the table, you can give it a more meaningful name.

By default, Access creates the **ID field** as the primary key field for all new tables.

The **Click to Add column** provides another way for you to add new fields to a table.

The **Add & Delete group** contains options for adding different types of fields, including Short Text and Number, to a table.

The **FIELDS tab** provides options for adding, removing, and formatting the fields in a table.

The **Navigation Pane** lists all the objects (tables, reports, and so on) in the database, and it is the main control center for opening and working with database objects.

Datasheet view shows the table's contents as a datasheet.

The Access Window

The **Access window** is the program window that appears when you create a new database or open an existing database.

You use the window buttons to minimize, maximize, and close the Access window.

The **Sign in link** lets you sign into your Office account. If you have already signed in, your name might appear here instead of this link.

The **ribbon** provides the main Access commands organized by task into tabs and groups.

The **title bar** displays the name of the open file and the program.

A **datasheet** displays the table's contents in rows and columns, similar to a table that you create in a Word document or an Excel spreadsheet. Each row will be a separate record in the table, and each column will contain the field values for one field in the table.

The **status bar** provides information about the program or open file, as well as buttons for working with the file. At the far left, the status bar indicates the current view, in this case, Datasheet view.

Introduction to Database Concepts

Before you begin using Access to create the database for Cindi, you need to understand a few key terms and concepts associated with databases.

Organizing Data

Data is a valuable resource to any business. At Chatham Community Health Services, for example, important data includes patients' names and addresses, visit dates, and billing information. Organizing, storing, maintaining, retrieving, and sorting this type of data are critical activities that enable a business to find and use information effectively. Before storing data on a computer, however, you must organize the data.

Your first step in organizing data is to identify the individual fields. A **field** is a single characteristic or attribute of a person, place, object, event, or idea. For example, some of the many fields that Chatham Community Health Services tracks are patient ID, first name, last name, address, phone number, visit date, reason for visit, and invoice amount.

Next, you group related fields together into tables. A **table** is a collection of fields that describes a person, place, object, event, or idea. Figure 1-1 shows an example of a Patient table that contains the following four fields: PatientID, FirstName, LastName, and Phone. Each field is a column in the table, with the field name displayed as the column heading.

Figure 1-1	Data organization for a table of patients

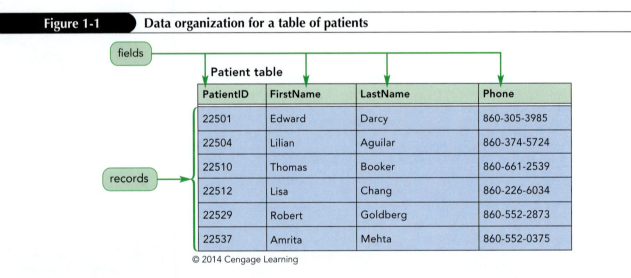

© 2014 Cengage Learning

The specific content of a field is called the **field value**. In Figure 1-1, the first set of field values for PatientID, FirstName, LastName, and Phone are, respectively: 22501; Edward; Darcy; and 860-305-3985. This set of field values is called a **record**. In the Patient table, the data for each patient is stored as a separate record. Figure 1-1 shows six records; each row of field values in the table is a record.

Databases and Relationships

A collection of related tables is called a **database**, or a **relational database**. In this tutorial, you will create the database for Chatham Community Health Services, and within that database, you'll create a table named Visit to store data about patient visits. Later on, you'll create two more tables, named Patient and Billing, to store related information about patients and their invoices.

As Cindi and her staff use the database that you will create, they will need to access information about patients and their visits. To obtain this information, you must have a way to connect records in the Patient table to records in the Visit table. You connect the records in the separate tables through a **common field** that appears in both tables.

In the sample database shown in Figure 1-2, each record in the Patient table has a field named PatientID, which is also a field in the Visit table. For example, Robert Goldberg is the fifth patient in the Patient table and has a PatientID field value of 22529. This same PatientID field value, 22529, appears in two records in the Visit table. Therefore, Robert Goldberg is the patient who made these two visits.

| Figure 1-2 | Database relationship between tables for patients and visits |

Patient table

PatientID	FirstName	LastName	Phone
22501	Edward	Darcy	860-305-3985
22504	Lilian	Aguilar	860-374-5724
22510	Thomas	Booker	860-661-2539
22512	Lisa	Chang	860-226-6034
22529	Robert	Goldberg	860-552-2873
22537	Amrita	Mehta	860-552-0375

primary keys

common field

foreign key

two visits for Robert Goldberg

Visit table

VisitID	PatientID	VisitDate	Reason
1539	22504	11/18/2015	Annual wellness visit
1549	22501	11/30/2015	Influenza
1564	22512	1/5/2016	Annual wellness visit
1610	22529	2/9/2016	Sinusitis
1613	22510	2/11/2016	Hypertension
1688	22529	4/12/2016	Annual wellness visit
1690	22537	4/13/2016	Varicella

© 2014 Cengage Learning

Each PatientID value in the Patient table must be unique so that you can distinguish one patient from another. These unique PatientID values also identify each patient's specific visits in the Visit table. The PatientID field is referred to as the primary key of the Patient table. A **primary key** is a field, or a collection of fields, whose values uniquely identify each record in a table. No two records can contain the same value for the primary key field. In the Visit table, the VisitID field is the primary key because Chatham Community Health Services assigns each visit a unique identification number.

When you include the primary key from one table as a field in a second table to form a relationship between the two tables, it is called a **foreign key** in the second table, as shown in Figure 1-2. For example, PatientID is the primary key in the Patient table and a foreign key in the Visit table. The PatientID field must have the same characteristics in both tables. Although the primary key PatientID contains unique values in the Patient table, the same field as a foreign key in the Visit table does not necessarily contain unique values. The PatientID value 22529, for example, appears two times in the Visit table because Robert Goldberg made two visits to the clinic. Each foreign key value, however, must match one of the field values for the primary key in the other table. In the example shown in Figure 1-2, each PatientID value in the Visit table must match a PatientID value in the Patient table. The two tables are related, enabling users to connect the facts about patients with the facts about their visits to the clinic.

Storing Data in Separate Tables

When you create a database, you must create separate tables that contain only fields that are directly related to each other. For example, in the Chatham database, the patient and visit data should not be stored in the same table because doing so would make the data difficult to update and prone to errors. Consider the patient Robert Goldberg and his visits to the clinic, and assume that he has many more than just two visits. If all the patient and visit data were stored in the same table, so that each record (row) contained all the information about each visit and the patient, the patient data would appear multiple times in the table. This causes problems when the data changes. For example, if Robert Goldberg's phone number changed, you would have to update the multiple occurrences of the phone number throughout the table. Not only would this be time-consuming, it would increase the likelihood of errors or inconsistent data.

Relational Database Management Systems

To manage its databases, a company uses a database management system. A **database management system (DBMS)** is a software program that lets you create databases and then manipulate the data they contain. Most of today's database management systems, including Access, are called relational database management systems. In a **relational database management system**, data is organized as a collection of tables. As stated earlier, a relationship between two tables in a relational DBMS is formed through a common field.

A relational DBMS controls the storage of databases and facilitates the creation, manipulation, and reporting of data, as illustrated in Figure 1-3.

Figure 1-3   **Relational database management system**

© 2014 Cengage Learning

Specifically, a relational DBMS provides the following functions:

- It allows you to create database structures containing fields, tables, and table relationships.
- It lets you easily add new records, change field values in existing records, and delete records.
- It contains a built-in query language, which lets you obtain immediate answers to the questions (or queries) you ask about your data.
- It contains a built-in report generator, which lets you produce professional-looking, formatted reports from your data.
- It protects databases through security, control, and recovery facilities.

An organization such as Chatham Community Health Services benefits from a relational DBMS because it allows users working in different groups to share the same data. More than one user can enter data into a database, and more than one user can retrieve and analyze data that other users have entered. For example, the database for Chatham Community Health Services will contain only one copy of the Visit table, and all employees will use it to access visit information.

Finally, unlike other software programs, such as spreadsheet programs, a DBMS can handle massive amounts of data and can be used to create relationships among multiple tables. Each Access database, for example, can be up to two gigabytes in size, can contain up to 32,768 objects (tables, reports, and so on), and can have up to 255 people using the database at the same time. For instructional purposes, the databases you will create and work with throughout this text contain a relatively small number of records compared to databases you would encounter outside the classroom, which would likely contain tables with very large numbers of records.

Starting Access and Creating a Database

Now that you've learned some database terms and concepts, you're ready to start Access and create the Chatham database for Cindi.

To start Access:

▶ **1.** Display the Windows Start screen, if necessary.

   Using Windows 7? To complete Step 1, click the Start button on the taskbar.

▶ **2.** Click the **Access 2013** tile. Access starts and displays the Recent screen in Backstage view. See Figure 1-4.

Figure 1-4   **Recent screen in Backstage view**

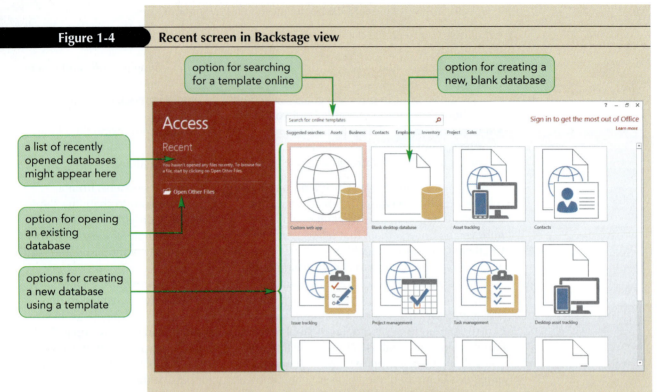

option for searching
for a template online

option for creating a
new, blank database

a list of recently
opened databases
might appear here

option for opening
an existing
database

options for creating
a new database
using a template

Trouble? If you don't see the Access 2013 tile on your Start screen, type Access to display the Apps screen with the Access 2013 tile highlighted, and then click the tile.

Using Windows 7? To complete Step 2, point to All Programs on the Start menu, click Microsoft Office 2013, and then click Access 2013.

When you start Access, the first screen that appears is Backstage view, which is the starting place for your work in Access. **Backstage view** contains commands that allow you to manage Access files and options. The Recent screen in Backstage view provides options for you to create a new database or open an existing database. To create a new database that does not contain any data or objects, you use the Blank desktop database option. If the database you need to create contains objects that match those found in common databases, such as databases that store data about contacts or tasks, you can use one of the templates provided with Access. A **template** is a predesigned database that includes professionally designed tables, reports, and other database objects that can make it quick and easy for you to create a database. You can also search for a template online using the Search box.

In this case, the templates provided do not match Cindi's needs for the clinic's database, so you need to create a new, blank database from scratch.

To create the new Chatham database:

1. Make sure you have the Access starting Data Files on your computer.

Trouble? If you don't have the starting Data Files, you need to get them before you can proceed. Your instructor will either give you the Data Files or ask you to obtain them from a specified location (such as a network drive). If you have any questions about the Data Files, see your instructor or technical support person for assistance.

2. Click the **Blank desktop database** option (see Figure1-4). The Blank desktop database screen opens.

Be sure to type **Chatham** or you'll create a database named Database1.

3. In the File Name box, type **Chatham** to replace the selected database name provided by Access, Database1. Next you need to specify the location for the file.

4. Click the **Browse** button 🗀 to the right of the File Name box. The File New Database dialog box opens.

5. Navigate to the drive and folder where you are storing your files, as specified by your instructor.

6. Make sure the "Save as type" box displays "Microsoft Access 2007 – 2013 Databases."

Trouble? If your computer is set up to show filename extensions, you will see the Access filename extension ".accdb" in the File name box.

TIP

If you don't type the filename extension, Access adds it automatically.

7. Click the **OK** button. You return to the Blank desktop database screen, and the File Name box now shows the name Chatham.accdb. The filename extension ".accdb" identifies the file as an Access 2007 - 2013 database.

8. Click the **Create** button. Access creates the new database, saves it to the specified location, and then opens an empty table named Table1.

Trouble? If you see only ribbon tab names and no buttons, click the HOME tab to expand the ribbon, and then in the bottom-right corner of the ribbon, click the Pin the ribbon button 📌.

Refer back to the Session 1.1 Visual Overview and spend some time becoming familiar with the components of the Access window.

INSIGHT

Understanding the Database File Type

Access 2013 uses the .accdb file extension, which is the same file extension used for databases created with Microsoft Access 2007 and 2010. To ensure compatibility between these earlier versions and the Access 2013 software, new databases created using Access 2013 have the same file extension and file format as Access 2007 and Access 2010 databases. This is why the File New Database dialog box provides the Microsoft Access 2007 - 2013 Databases option in the "Save as type" box. In addition, the notation "(Access 2007 - 2013 file format)" appears in the title bar next to the name of an open database in Access 2013, confirming that database files with the .accdb extension can be used in Access 2007, Access 2010, and Access 2013.

Working in Touch Mode

TIP

On a touch device, you tap instead of click.

If you are working on a touch device, such as a tablet, you can switch to Touch Mode in Access to make it easier for you to tap buttons on the ribbon and perform other touch actions. Your screens will not match those shown in the book exactly, but this will not cause any problems.

Note: The following steps assume that you are using a mouse. If you are instead using a touch device, please read these steps but don't complete them, so that you remain working in Touch Mode.

To switch to Touch Mode:

1. On the Quick Access Toolbar, click the **Customize Quick Access Toolbar** button. A menu opens listing buttons you can add to the Quick Access Toolbar as well as other options for customizing the toolbar.

   Trouble? If the Touch/Mouse Mode command on the menu has a checkmark next to it, press the Esc key to close the menu, and then skip to Step 3.

2. Click **Touch/Mouse Mode**. The Quick Access Toolbar now contains the Touch/Mouse Mode button, which you can use to switch between Mouse Mode, the default display, and Touch Mode.

3. On the Quick Access Toolbar, click the **Touch/Mouse Mode** button. A menu opens with two commands: Mouse, which shows the ribbon in the standard display and is optimized for use with the mouse; and Touch, which provides more space between the buttons and commands on the ribbon and is optimized for use with touch devices. The icon next to Mouse is shaded red to indicate that it is selected.

   Trouble? If the icon next to Touch is shaded red, press the Esc key to close the menu and skip to Step 5.

4. Click **Touch**. The display switches to Touch Mode with more space between the commands and buttons on the ribbon. See Figure 1-5.

Figure 1-5	Ribbon displayed in Touch Mode

Touch/Mouse Mode button on Quick Access Toolbar

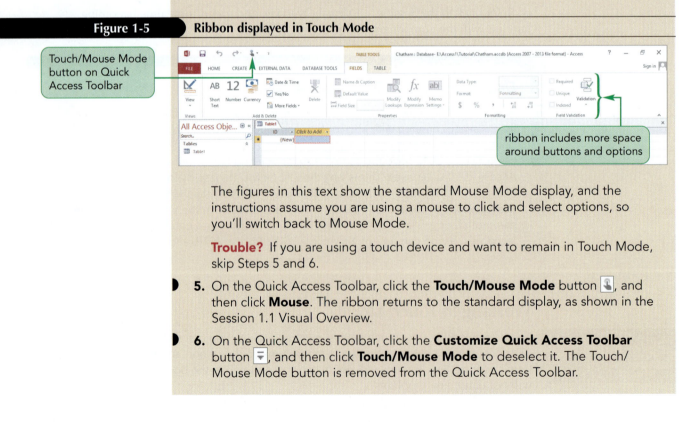

ribbon includes more space around buttons and options

The figures in this text show the standard Mouse Mode display, and the instructions assume you are using a mouse to click and select options, so you'll switch back to Mouse Mode.

Trouble? If you are using a touch device and want to remain in Touch Mode, skip Steps 5 and 6.

5. On the Quick Access Toolbar, click the **Touch/Mouse Mode** button, and then click **Mouse**. The ribbon returns to the standard display, as shown in the Session 1.1 Visual Overview.

6. On the Quick Access Toolbar, click the **Customize Quick Access Toolbar** button, and then click **Touch/Mouse Mode** to deselect it. The Touch/Mouse Mode button is removed from the Quick Access Toolbar.

Creating a Table in Datasheet View

Tables contain all the data in a database and are the fundamental objects for your work in Access. There are different ways to create a table in Access, including entering the fields and records for the table directly in Datasheet view.

REFERENCE

Creating a Table in Datasheet View

- On the ribbon, click the CREATE tab.
- In the Tables group, click the Table button.
- Rename the default ID primary key field and change its data type, if necessary; or accept the default ID field with the AutoNumber data type.
- In the Add & Delete group on the FIELDS tab, click the button for the type of field you want to add to the table (for example, click the Short Text button), and then type the field name; or, in the table datasheet, click the Click to Add column heading, click the type of field you want to add from the list that opens, and then press the Tab or Enter key to move to the next column in the datasheet. Repeat this step to add all the necessary fields to the table.
- In the first row below the field names, enter the value for each field in the first record, pressing the Tab or Enter key to move from one field to the next.
- After entering the value for the last field in the first record, press the Tab or Enter key to move to the next row, and then enter the values for the next record. Continue this process until you have entered all the records for the table.
- On the Quick Access Toolbar, click the Save button, enter a name for the table, and then click the OK button.

For Chatham Community Health Services, Cindi needs to track information about each patient visit at the clinic. She asks you to create the Visit table according to the plan shown in Figure 1-6.

Figure 1-6   **Plan for the Visit table**

Field	Purpose
VisitID	Unique number assigned to each visit; will serve as the table's primary key
PatientID	Unique number assigned to each patient; common field that will be a foreign key to connect to the Patient table
VisitDate	Date on which the patient visited the clinic
Reason	Reason/diagnosis for the patient visit
WalkIn	Whether the patient visit was a walk-in or a scheduled appointment

© 2014 Cengage Learning

As shown in Cindi's plan, she wants to store data about visits in five fields, including fields to contain the date of each visit, the reason for the visit, and if the visit was a walk-in or scheduled appointment. These are the most important aspects of a visit and, therefore, must be tracked. Also, notice that the VisitID field will be the primary key for the table; each visit at Chatham Community Health Services has a unique number assigned to it, so this field is the logical choice for the primary key. Finally, the PatientID field is needed in the Visit table as a foreign key to connect the information about visits to patients. The data about patients and their bills will be stored in separate tables, which you will create later.

Notice the name of each field in Figure 1-6. You need to name each field, table, and other object in an Access database.

Decision Making: Naming Fields in Access Tables

One of the most important tasks in creating a table is deciding what names to specify for the table's fields. Keep the following guidelines in mind when you assign field names:

- A field name can consist of up to 64 characters, including letters, numbers, spaces, and special characters, except for the period (.), exclamation mark (!), grave accent ('), and square brackets ([ ]).
- A field name cannot begin with a space.
- Capitalize the first letter of each word in a field name that combines multiple words, for example VisitDate.
- Use concise field names that are easy to remember and reference, and that won't take up a lot of space in the table datasheet.
- Use standard abbreviations, such as Num for Number, Amt for Amount, and Qty for Quantity, and use them consistently throughout the database. For example, if you use Num for Number in one field name, do not use the number sign (#) for Number in another.
- Give fields descriptive names so that you can easily identify them when you view or edit records.
- Although Access supports the use of spaces in field names (and in other object names), experienced database developers avoid using spaces because they can cause errors when the objects are involved in programming tasks.

By spending time obtaining and analyzing information about the fields in a table, and understanding the rules for naming Access fields, you can create a well-designed table that will be easy for others to use.

Renaming the Default Primary Key Field

As noted earlier, Access provides the ID field as the default primary key for a new table you create in Datasheet view. Recall that a primary key is a field, or a collection of fields, whose values uniquely identify each record in a table. However, according to Cindi's plan, the VisitID field should be the primary key for the Visit table. You'll begin by renaming the default ID field to create the VisitID field.

To rename the ID field to the VisitID field:

1. Right-click the **ID** column heading to open the shortcut menu, and then click **Rename Field**. The column heading ID is selected, so that whatever text you type next will replace it.

2. Type **VisitID** and then click the row below the heading. The column heading changes to VisitID, and the insertion point moves to the row below the heading. See Figure 1-7.

   Trouble? If you make a mistake while typing the field name, use the Backspace key to delete characters to the left of the insertion point or the Delete key to delete characters to the right of the insertion point. Then type the correct text. To correct a field name by replacing it entirely, press the Esc key, and then type the correct text.

Figure 1-7	ID field renamed to VisitID

The **insertion point** is a flashing cursor that shows where text you type will be inserted. In this case, it is hidden within the selected field value (New).

Notice that the TABLE TOOLS tab is active on the ribbon. This is an example of a **contextual tab**, which is a tab that appears and provides options for working with a specific object that is selected—in this case, the table you are creating. As you work with other objects in the database, other contextual tabs will appear with commands and options related to each selected object.

You have renamed the default primary key field, ID, to VisitID. However, the VisitID field still retains the characteristics of the ID field, including its data type. Your next task is to change the data type of this field.

Changing the Data Type of the Default Primary Key Field

Notice the Formatting group on the FIELDS tab. One of the options available in this group is the Data Type option (see Figure 1-7). Each field in an Access table must be assigned a data type. The **data type** determines what field values you can enter for the field. In this case, the AutoNumber data type is displayed. Access assigns the AutoNumber data type to the default ID primary key field because the **AutoNumber** data type automatically inserts a unique number in this field for every record, beginning with the number 1 for the first record, the number 2 for the second record, and so on. Therefore, a field using the AutoNumber data type can serve as the primary key for any table you create.

Visit numbers at Chatham Community Health Services are specific, four-digit numbers, so the AutoNumber data type is not appropriate for the VisitID field, which is the primary key field in the table you are creating. A better choice is the **Short Text** data type, which allows field values containing letters, digits, and other characters, and which is appropriate for identifying numbers, such as visit numbers, that are never used in calculations. So, Cindi asks you to change the data type for the VisitID field from AutoNumber to Short Text.

To change the data type for the VisitID field:

▶ **1.** Make sure that the VisitID column is selected. A column is selected when you click a field value, in which case the background color of the column heading changes to orange (the default color) and the insertion point appears in the field value. You can also click the column heading to select a column, in which case the background color of both the column heading and the field value changes (the default colors are gray and blue, respectively).

▶ **2.** In the Formatting group on the FIELDS tab, click the **Data Type arrow**, and then click **Short Text**. The VisitID field is now a Short Text field. See Figure 1-8.

| Figure 1-8 | Short Text data type assigned to the VisitID field |

Note the Unique check box in the Field Validation group. This check box is selected because the VisitID field assumed the characteristics of the default primary key field, ID, including the fact that each value in the field must be unique. Because this check box is selected, no two records in the Visit table will be allowed to have the same value in the VisitID field.

With the VisitID field created and established as the primary key, you can now enter the rest of the fields in the Visit table.

Adding New Fields

When you create a table in Datasheet view, you can use the options in the Add & Delete group on the FIELDS tab to add fields to your table. You can also use the Click to Add column in the table datasheet to add new fields. (See Figure 1-8.) You'll use both methods to add the four remaining fields to the Visit table. The next field you need to add is the PatientID field. Similar to the VisitID field, the PatientID field will contain numbers that will not be used in calculations, so it should be a Short Text field.

To add the rest of the fields to the Visit table:

1. In the Add & Delete group on the FIELDS tab, click the **Short Text** button. Access adds a new field named "Field1" to the right of the VisitID field. See Figure 1-9.

Figure 1-9	New Short Text field added to the table

The text "Field1" is selected, so you can simply type the new field name to replace it.

2. Type **PatientID**. The second field is added to the table. Next, you'll add the VisitDate field. Because this field will contain date values, you'll add a field with the **Date/Time** data type, which allows field values in a variety of date and time formats.

3. In the Add & Delete group, click the **Date & Time** button. Access adds a third field to the table, this time with the Date/Time data type.

4. Type **VisitDate** to replace the highlighted name "Field1." The fourth field in the Visit table is the Reason field, which will contain brief descriptions of the reason for the visit to the clinic. You'll add another Short Text field—this time using the Click to Add column.

5. Click the **Click to Add** column heading. Access displays a list of available data types from which you can choose the data type for the new field you're adding.

6. Click **Short Text** in the list. Access adds a fourth field to the table.

7. Type **Reason** to replace the highlighted name "Field1," and then press the **Enter** key. The Click to Add column becomes active and displays the list of field data types.

The fifth and final field in the Visit table is the WalkIn field, which will indicate whether or not the visit was a walk-in (that is, the patient did not have a scheduled appointment). The **Yes/No** data type is suitable for this field because it is used to define fields that store values representing one of two options—true/false, yes/no, or on/off.

TIP

You can also type the first letter of a data type to select it and close the Click to Add list.

8. Click **Yes/No** in the list, and then type **WalkIn** to replace the highlighted name "Field1."

   Trouble? If you pressed the Tab or Enter key after typing the WalkIn field name, press the Esc key to close the Click to Add list.

9. Click in the row below the VisitID column heading. All five fields are now entered for the Visit table. See Figure 1-10.

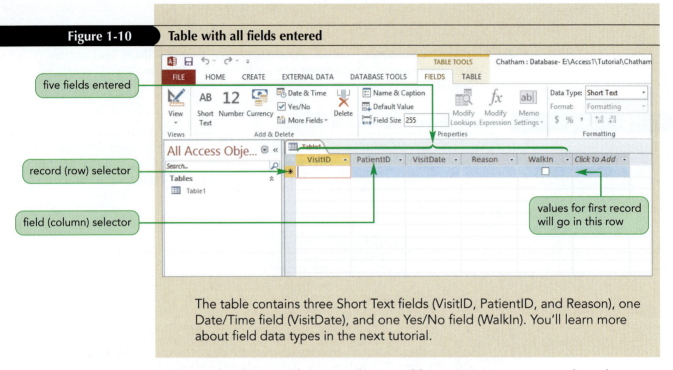

| Figure 1-10 | Table with all fields entered |

five fields entered

record (row) selector

field (column) selector

values for first record will go in this row

The table contains three Short Text fields (VisitID, PatientID, and Reason), one Date/Time field (VisitDate), and one Yes/No field (WalkIn). You'll learn more about field data types in the next tutorial.

As noted earlier, Datasheet view shows a table's contents in rows (records) and columns (fields). Each column is headed by a field name inside a field selector, and each row has a record selector to its left (see Figure 1-10). Clicking a **field selector** or a **record selector** selects that entire column or row (respectively), which you then can manipulate. A field selector is also called a **column selector**, and a record selector is also called a **row selector**.

Entering Records

With the fields in place for the table, you can now enter the field values for each record. Cindi requests that you enter eight records in the Visit table, as shown in Figure 1-11.

| Figure 1-11 | Visit table records |

VisitID	PatientID	VisitDate	Reason	WalkIn
1550	22549	12/1/2015	Influenza	Yes
1527	22522	11/9/2015	Allergies - environmental	Yes
1555	22520	12/7/2015	Annual wellness visit	No
1542	22537	11/24/2015	Influenza	Yes
1530	22510	11/10/2015	Seborrheic dermatitis	No
1564	22512	1/5/2016	Annual wellness visit	No
1575	22513	1/13/2016	Broken leg	Yes
1538	22500	11/17/2015	Migraine	Yes

© 2014 Cengage Learning

To enter records in a table datasheet, you type the field values below the column headings for the fields. The first record you enter will go in the first row (see Figure 1-10).

Be sure to type the numbers "0" and "1" and not the letters "O" and "l" in the field value.

To enter the first record for the Visit table:

1. In the first row for the VisitID field, type **1550** (the VisitID field value for the first record), and then press the **Tab** key. Access adds the field value and moves the insertion point to the right, into the PatientID column. See Figure 1-12.

Figure 1-12   **First field value entered**

Trouble? If you make a mistake when typing a value, use the Backspace key to delete characters to the left of the insertion point or the Delete key to delete characters to the right of the insertion point. Then type the correct value. To correct a value by replacing it entirely, press the Esc key, and then type the correct value.

Notice the pencil symbol that appears in the row selector for the new record. The **pencil symbol** indicates that the record is being edited. Also notice the star symbol that appears in the row selector for the second row. The **star symbol** identifies the second row as the next row available for a new record.

2. Type **22549** (the PatientID field value for the first record), and then press the **Tab** key. Access enters the field value and moves the insertion point to the VisitDate column.

3. Type **12/1/15** (the VisitDate field value for the first record), and then press the **Tab** key. Access displays the year as "2015" even though you entered only the final two digits of the year. This is because the VisitDate field has the Date/Time data type, which automatically formats dates with four-digit years.

   Trouble? Depending on your Windows date setting, your VisitDate field values might be displayed in a different format. This difference will not cause any problems.

4. Type **Influenza** (the Reason field value for the first record), and then press the **Tab** key to move to the WalkIn column.

   Recall that the WalkIn field is a Yes/No field. Notice the check box displayed in the WalkIn column. By default, the value for any Yes/No field is "No"; therefore, the check box is initially empty. For Yes/No fields with check boxes, you press the Tab key to leave the check box unchecked, or you press the spacebar to insert a checkmark in the check box. The record you are entering in the table is for a walk-in visit, so you need to insert a checkmark in the check box to indicate "Yes."

TIP

You can also click a check box in a Yes/No field to insert or remove a checkmark.

5. Press the **spacebar** to insert a checkmark, and then press the **Tab** key. The first record is entered into the table, and the insertion point is positioned in the VisitID field for the second record. The pencil symbol is removed from the first row because the record in that row is no longer being edited. The table is now ready for you to enter the second record. See Figure 1-13.

Figure 1-13	Datasheet with first record entered

next row available for a new record

value displayed with a four-digit year

field values for the first record entered

Now you can enter the remaining seven records in the Visit table.

To enter the remaining records in the Visit table:

TIP

You can also press the Enter key instead of the Tab key to move from one field to another, and to the next row.

1. Referring to Figure 1-11, enter the values for records 2 through 8, pressing the **Tab** key to move from field to field and to the next row for a new record. Keep in mind that you do not have to type all four digits of the year in the VisitDate field values; you can enter only the final two digits and Access will display all four. Also, for any WalkIn field values of "No," be sure to press the Tab key to leave the check box empty.

   Trouble? If you enter a value in the wrong field by mistake, such as entering a Reason field value in the VisitDate field, a menu might open with options for addressing the problem. If this happens, click the "Enter new value" option in the menu. You'll return to the field with the incorrect value highlighted, which you can then replace by typing the correct value.

   Notice that not all of the Reason field values are fully displayed. To see more of the table datasheet and the full field values, you'll close the Navigation Pane and resize the Reason column.

2. At the top of the Navigation Pane, click the **Shutter Bar Open/Close Button** ≪. The Navigation Pane closes, and only the complete table datasheet is displayed.

3. Place the pointer on the vertical line to the right of the Reason field name until the pointer changes to a ✛ shape, and then double-click the vertical line. All the Reason field values are now fully displayed. See Figure 1-14.

| Figure 1-14 | Datasheet with eight records entered |

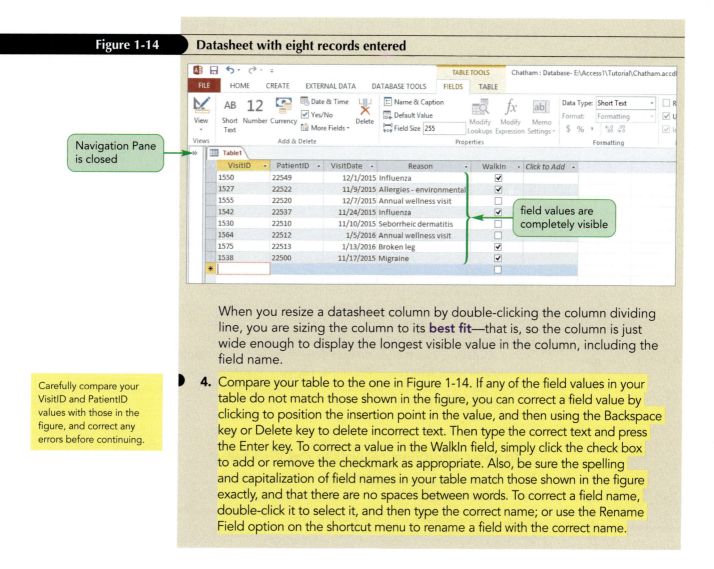

Navigation Pane is closed

field values are completely visible

When you resize a datasheet column by double-clicking the column dividing line, you are sizing the column to its **best fit**—that is, so the column is just wide enough to display the longest visible value in the column, including the field name.

Carefully compare your VisitID and PatientID values with those in the figure, and correct any errors before continuing.

4. Compare your table to the one in Figure 1-14. If any of the field values in your table do not match those shown in the figure, you can correct a field value by clicking to position the insertion point in the value, and then using the Backspace key or Delete key to delete incorrect text. Then type the correct text and press the Enter key. To correct a value in the WalkIn field, simply click the check box to add or remove the checkmark as appropriate. Also, be sure the spelling and capitalization of field names in your table match those shown in the figure exactly, and that there are no spaces between words. To correct a field name, double-click it to select it, and then type the correct name; or use the Rename Field option on the shortcut menu to rename a field with the correct name.

Saving a Table

The records you enter are immediately stored in the database as soon as you enter them; however, the table's design—the field names and characteristics of the fields themselves, plus any layout changes to the datasheet—are not saved until you save the table. When you save a new table for the first time, you should give it a name that best identifies the information it contains. Like a field name, a table name can contain up to 64 characters, including spaces.

REFERENCE

Saving a Table

- Make sure the table you want to save is open.
- On the Quick Access Toolbar, click the Save button. The Save As dialog box opens.
- In the Table Name box, type the name for the table.
- Click the OK button.

According to Cindi's plan, you need to save the table with the name "Visit."

To save and name the Visit table:

TIP

You can also use the Save command in Backstage view to save and name a new table.

1. On the Quick Access Toolbar, click the **Save** button 🖫. The Save As dialog box opens.

2. With the default name Table1 selected in the Table Name box, type **Visit**, and then click the **OK** button. The tab for the table now displays the name "Visit," and the Visit table design is saved in the Chatham database.

Notice that after you saved and named the Visit table, Access sorted and displayed the records in order by the values in the VisitID field because it is the primary key. If you compare your screen to Figure 1-11, which shows the records in the order you entered them, you'll see that the current screen shows the records in order by the VisitID field values.

Cindi asks you to add two more records to the Visit table. When you add a record to an existing table, you must enter the new record in the next row available for a new record; you cannot insert a row between existing records for the new record. In a table with just a few records, such as the Visit table, the next available row is visible on the screen. However, in a table with hundreds of records, you would need to scroll the datasheet to see the next row available. The easiest way to add a new record to a table is to use the New button, which scrolls the datasheet to the next row available so you can enter the new record.

To enter additional records in the Visit table:

1. If necessary, click the first record's VisitID field value (**1527**) to make it the current record.

2. On the ribbon, click the **HOME** tab.

3. In the Records group, click the **New** button. The insertion point is positioned in the next row available for a new record, which in this case is row 9. See Figure 1-15.

Figure 1-15 | **Entering a new record**

4. With the insertion point in the VisitID field for the new record, type **1548** and then press the **Tab** key.

5. Complete the entry of this record by entering each value shown below, pressing the **Tab** key to move from field to field:

    PatientID = **22519**

    VisitDate = **11/30/2015**

    Reason = **Hypertension**

    WalkIn = **No (unchecked)**

6. Enter the values for the next new record, as follows, and then press the **Tab** key after entering the WalkIn field value:

    VisitID = **1560**

    PatientID = **22514**

    VisitDate = **12/15/2015**

    Reason = **Influenza**

    WalkIn = **Yes (checked)**

    Your datasheet should now look like the one shown in Figure 1-16.

Figure 1-16	Datasheet with additional records entered

The new records you added appear at the end of the table, and are not sorted in order by the primary key field values. For example, VisitID 1548 should be the fifth record in the table, placed between VisitID 1542 and VisitID 1550. When you add records to a table datasheet, they appear at the end of the table. The records are not displayed in primary key order until you either close and reopen the table or switch between views.

7. Click the **Close** button ☒ on the object tab (see Figure 1-16 for the location of this button). The Visit table closes, and the main portion of the Access window is now blank because no database object is currently open. The Chatham database file is still open, as indicated by the filename in the Access window title bar.

Opening a Table

The tables in a database are listed in the Navigation Pane. You open a table, or any Access object, by double-clicking the object name in the Navigation Pane. Next, you'll open the Visit table so you can see the order of all the records you've entered.

To open the Visit table:

1. On the Navigation Pane, click the **Shutter Bar Open/Close Button** ⟫ to open the pane. Note that the Visit table is listed.

2. Double-click **Visit** to open the table in Datasheet view. See Figure 1-17.

Figure 1-17 | **Table with 10 records entered and displayed in primary key order**

Visit table object in the Chatham database

two records added now appear in primary key order

records listed in order by the values in the primary key field

Current Record box indicates the table contains 10 records

The two records you added, with VisitID field values of 1548 and 1560, now appear in the correct primary key order. The table now contains a total of 10 records, as indicated by the Current Record box at the bottom of the datasheet. The **Current Record box** displays the number of the current record as well as the total number of records in the table.

Each record contains a unique VisitID value because this field is the primary key. Other fields, however, can contain the same value in multiple records; for example, note the three values of "Influenza" in the Reason field.

Closing a Table and Exiting Access

When you are finished working in an Access table, it's a good idea to close the table so that you do not make unintended changes to the table data. You can close a table by clicking its Close button on the object tab, as you did earlier. Or, if you want to close the Access program as well, you can click the program's Close button. When you do, any open tables are closed, the active database is closed, and you exit the Access program.

TIP

To close a database without exiting Access, click the FILE tab to display Backstage view, and then click Close.

To close the Visit table and exit Access:

1. Click the **Close** button ☒ on the program window title bar. Access closes the Visit table and the Chatham database, and then the Access program closes.

INSIGHT

Saving a Database

Unlike the Save buttons in other Office programs, the Save button on the Quick Access Toolbar in Access does not save the active document (database). Instead, you use the Save button to save the design of an Access object, such as a table (as you saw earlier), or to save datasheet format changes, such as resizing columns. Access does not have a button or option you can use to save the active database.

Access saves changes to the active database automatically when you change or add a record or close the database. If your database is stored on a removable medium, such as a USB drive, you should never remove the drive while the database file is open. If you do, Access will encounter problems when it tries to save the database, which might damage the database. Make sure you close the database first before removing the drive.

Now that you've become familiar with database concepts and Access, and created the Chatham database and the Visit table, Cindi wants you to add more records to the table and work with the data stored in it to create database objects including a query, form, and report. You'll complete these tasks in the next session.

REVIEW

Session 1.1 Quick Check

1. A(n) _____ is a single characteristic of a person, place, object, event, or idea.
2. You connect the records in two separate tables through a(n) _____ that appears in both tables.
3. The _____, whose values uniquely identify each record in a table, is called a(n) _____ when it is placed in a second table to form a relationship between the two tables.
4. The _____ is the area of the Access window that lists all the objects in a database, and it is the main control center for opening and working with database objects.
5. What is the name of the field that Access creates, by default, as the primary key field for a new table in Datasheet view?
6. Which group on the FIELDS tab contains the options you use to add new fields to a table?
7. What does a pencil symbol at the beginning of a record represent? What does a star symbol represent?
8. Explain how the saving process in Access is different from saving in other Office programs.

Session 1.2 Visual Overview:

The **CREATE tab** provides options for creating various database objects, including tables, forms, and reports. The options appear on the tab grouped by object type.

The Forms group contains options for creating a **form**, which is a database object you use to enter, edit, and view records in a database.

The **Query Wizard button** opens a dialog box with different types of wizards that guide you through the steps to create a query. One of these, the **Simple Query Wizard**, allows you to select records and fields quickly to display in the query results.

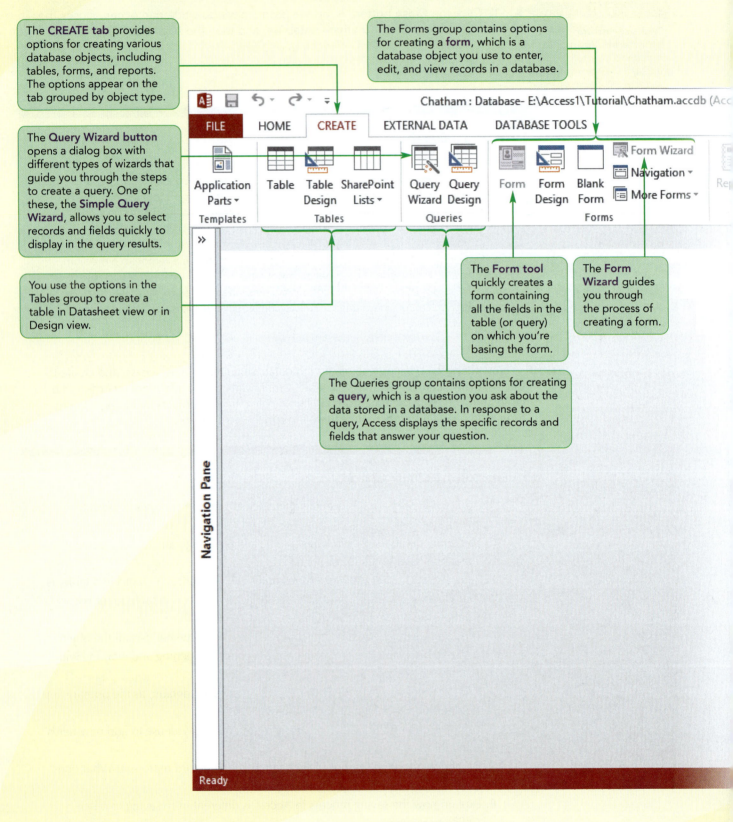

You use the options in the Tables group to create a table in Datasheet view or in Design view.

The **Form tool** quickly creates a form containing all the fields in the table (or query) on which you're basing the form.

The **Form Wizard** guides you through the process of creating a form.

The Queries group contains options for creating a **query**, which is a question you ask about the data stored in a database. In response to a query, Access displays the specific records and fields that answer your question.

Navigation Pane

Ready

The CREATE Tab Options

The Reports group contains options for creating a **report**, which is a formatted printout (or screen display) of the contents of one or more tables (or queries) in a database.

The Microsoft Access Help button opens the **Access Help** window, where you can find information about Access commands and features as well as instructions for using them.

The **Report tool** places all the fields from a selected table (or query) on a report, making it the quickest way to create a report.

The **Report Wizard** guides you through the process of creating a report.

You can enter words or phrases in the search box and the Access Help system will search online to find related topics.

The Popular searches section provides links to commonly searched Access Help topics.

Because the Access online Help system is a dynamic environment and subject to change, your Help screen might look slightly different from this one.

Copying Records from Another Access Database

When you created the Visit table, you entered records directly into the table datasheet. There are many other ways to enter records in a table, including copying and pasting records from a table into the same database or into a different database. To use this method, however, the two tables must have the same structure—that is, the tables must contain the same fields, with the same design, in the same order.

Cindi has already created a table named Appointment that contains additional records with visit data. The Appointment table is contained in a database named Cindi located in the Access1 ▶ Tutorial folder included with your Data Files. The Appointment table has the same table structure as the Visit table you created.

REFERENCE

Opening a Database

- Start Access and display the Recent screen in Backstage view.
- Click the name of the database you want to open in the list of recently opened databases.

or

- Start Access and display the Recent screen in Backstage view.
- In the navigation bar, click Open Other Files to display the Open screen.
- Click Computer, click the Browse button, and then navigate to the drive and folder containing the database file you want to open.
- Click the name of the database file you want to open, and then click the Open button.

Your next task is to copy the records from the Appointment table and paste them into your Visit table. To do so, you need to open the Cindi database.

To copy the records from the Appointment table:

1. Display the Windows Start screen, if necessary.

   Using Windows 7? To complete Step 1, click the Start button on the taskbar.

2. Click the **Access 2013** tile. Access starts and displays the Recent screen in Backstage view.

   Using Windows 7? To complete Step 2, click All Programs on the Start menu, click Microsoft Office 2013, and then click Access 2013.

3. Click **Open Other Files** to display the Open screen in Backstage view.

4. On the Open screen, click **Computer**. The right side of the screen now shows folder information for your computer.

   Trouble? If you are storing your files on SkyDrive, click SkyDrive, and then log in if necessary.

5. Click the **Browse** button, and then navigate to the drive that contains your Data Files.

6. Navigate to the **Access1 ▶ Tutorial** folder, click the database file named **Cindi**, and then click the **Open** button. The Cindi database opens in the Access program window. Note that the database contains only one object, the Appointment table.

Trouble? If a security warning appears below the ribbon indicating that some active content has been disabled, click the Enable Content button next to the warning. Access provides this warning because some databases might contain content that could harm your computer. Because the Cindi database does not contain objects that could be harmful, you can open it safely. If you are accessing the file over a network, you might also see a dialog box asking if you want to make the file a trusted document; click Yes.

7. In the Navigation Pane, double-click **Appointment** to open the Appointment table in Datasheet view. The table contains 76 records and the same five fields, with the same characteristics, as the fields in the Visit table. See Figure 1-18.

| Figure 1-18 | Appointment table in the Cindi database |

Cindi wants you to copy all the records in the Appointment table. You can select all the records by clicking the **datasheet selector**, which is the box to the left of the first field name in the table datasheet (see Figure 1-18).

8. Click the **datasheet selector** to the left of the VisitID field, as shown in Figure 1-18. Access selects all the records in the table.

9. In the Clipboard group on the HOME tab, click the **Copy** button. All the records are copied to the Clipboard.

10. Click the **Close 'Appointment'** button ⊠ on the object tab. A dialog box opens asking if you want to save the data you copied to the Clipboard. This dialog box opens only when you copy a large amount of data to the Clipboard.

11. Click the **Yes** button. The dialog box closes, and then the Appointment table closes.

With the records copied to the Clipboard, you can now paste them into the Visit table. First you need to close the Cindi database while still keeping the Access program open, and then open the Chatham database.

To close the Cindi database and then paste the records into the Visit table:

▶ **1.** Click the **FILE** tab to display Backstage view, and then click **Close** in the navigation bar to close the Cindi database. You return to the HOME tab in the Access program window.

▶ **2.** Click the **FILE** tab to return to Backstage view, and then click **Open** in the navigation bar. The Recent section of the Open screen shows a list of the recently opened database files. This list should include the Chatham database.

▶ **3.** In the Recent section of the screen, click **Chatham** to open the Chatham database file.

   Trouble? If the Chatham database file is not listed in the Recent section on your computer, click Computer, and then click Browse. In the Open dialog box, navigate to the drive and folder where you are storing your files, and then open the Chatham database file.

   Trouble? If the security warning appears below the ribbon, click the Enable Content button, and then, if necessary, click Yes to make the file a trusted document.

▶ **4.** In the Navigation Pane, double-click **Visit** to open the Visit table in Datasheet view.

▶ **5.** On the Navigation Pane, click the **Shutter Bar Open/Close Button** « to close the pane.

▶ **6.** Position the pointer on the star symbol in the row selector for row 11 (the next row available for a new record) until the pointer changes to a ➡ shape, and then click to select the row.

▶ **7.** In the Clipboard group on the HOME tab, click the **Paste** button. The pasted records are added to the table, and a dialog box opens asking you to confirm that you want to paste all the records (76 total).

   Trouble? If the Paste button isn't active, click the ➡ pointer on the row selector for row 11, making sure the entire row is selected, and then repeat Step 7.

▶ **8.** Click the **Yes** button. The dialog box closes, and the pasted records are highlighted. See Figure 1-19. Notice that the table now contains a total of 86 records—10 records that you entered and 76 records that you copied and pasted.

| Figure 1-19 | Visit table after copying and pasting records |

Not all the Reason field values are completely visible, so you need to resize this column to its best fit.

9. Place the pointer on the vertical line to the right of the Reason field name until the pointer changes to a ✛ shape, and then double-click the vertical line. The Reason field values are now fully displayed.

Navigating a Datasheet

The Visit table now contains 86 records, but only some of the records are visible on the screen. To view fields or records not currently visible on the screen, you can use the horizontal and vertical scroll bars shown in Figure 1-19 to navigate the data. The **navigation buttons**, shown in Figure 1-19 and also described in Figure 1-20, provide another way to move vertically through the records. The Current Record box appears between the two sets of navigation buttons and displays the number of the current record as well as the total number of records in the table. Figure 1-20 shows which record becomes the current record when you click each navigation button. Note the New (blank) record button, which works in the same way as the New button on the HOME tab you used earlier to enter a new record in the table.

| Figure 1-20 | Navigation buttons |

Navigation Button	Record Selected	Navigation Button	Record Selected
◄◄	First record	►►	Last record
◄	Previous record	►*	New (blank) record
►	Next record		

© 2014 Cengage Learning

Cindi suggests that you use the various navigation techniques to move through the Visit table and become familiar with its contents.

To navigate the Visit datasheet:

1. Click the first record's VisitID field value (**1527**). The Current Record box shows that record 1 is the current record.

2. Click the **Next record** navigation button ▶. The second record is now highlighted, which identifies it as the current record. Also, notice that the second record's value for the VisitID field is selected, and the Current Record box displays "2 of 86" to indicate that the second record is the current record.

3. Click the **Last record** navigation button ▶|. The last record in the table, record 86, is now the current record.

4. Drag the scroll box in the vertical scroll bar (see Figure 1-19) up to the top of the bar. Notice that record 86 is still the current record, as indicated in the Current Record box. Dragging the scroll box changes the display of the table datasheet, but does not change the current record.

5. Drag the scroll box in the vertical scroll bar back down until you can see the end of the table and the current record (record 86).

6. Click the **Previous record** navigation button ◀. Record 85 is now the current record.

7. Click the **First record** navigation button |◀. The first record is now the current record and is visible on the screen.

   As you moved through the datasheet, you might have noticed that not all the Reason field values are fully displayed. When you resize a column to its best fit, the column expands to fully display only the field values that are visible on the screen at that time. To make sure all field values are displayed for the entire table, you need to scroll through the datasheet and repeat the resizing process.

8. Drag the scroll box down to display more of the table, until you see other Reason field values that are not fully displayed. Then use the ✛ pointer to resize the field.

9. Repeat Step 8, as necessary, until you reach the bottom of the table and have resized all the Reason field values, and then drag the scroll box back up to display the beginning of the table.

The Visit table now contains all the data about patient visits for Chatham Community Health Services. To better understand how to work with this data, Cindi asks you to create simple objects for the other main types of database objects—queries, forms, and reports.

Creating a Simple Query

As noted earlier, a query is a question you ask about the data stored in a database. When you create a query, you tell Access which fields you need and what criteria it should use to select the records that will answer your question. Then Access displays only the information you want, so you don't have to navigate through the entire database for the information. In the Visit table, for example, Cindi might create a query to display only those records for visits that occurred in a specific month. Even though a query can display table information in a different way, the information still exists in the table as it was originally entered.

Cindi wants to see a list of all the visit dates and reasons for visits in the Visit table. She doesn't want the list to include all the fields in the table, such as PatientID and WalkIn. To produce this list for Cindi, you'll use the Simple Query Wizard to create a query based on the Visit table.

To start the Simple Query Wizard:

▶ **1.** On the ribbon, click the **CREATE** tab.

▶ **2.** In the Queries group on the CREATE tab, click the **Query Wizard** button. The New Query dialog box opens.

▶ **3.** Make sure **Simple Query Wizard** is selected, and then click the **OK** button. The first Simple Query Wizard dialog box opens. See Figure 1-21.

Figure 1-21 **First Simple Query Wizard dialog box**

Because the Visit table is the only object in the Chatham database, it is listed in the Tables/Queries box by default. If the database contained more objects, you could click the Tables/Queries arrow and choose another table or a query as the basis for the new query you are creating. The Available Fields box lists all the fields in the Visit table.

You need to select fields from the Available Fields box to include them in the query. To select fields one at a time, click a field and then click the > button. The selected (highlighted) field moves from the Available Fields box on the left to the Selected Fields box on the right. To select all the fields, click the >> button. If you change your mind or make a mistake, you can remove a field by clicking it in the Selected Fields box and then clicking the < button. To remove all fields from the Selected Fields box, click the << button.

Each Simple Query Wizard dialog box contains buttons on the bottom that allow you to move to the previous dialog box (Back button), move to the next dialog box (Next button), or cancel the creation process (Cancel button). You can also finish creating the object (Finish button) and accept the wizard's defaults for the remaining options.

Cindi wants her list to include data from only the following fields: VisitID, VisitDate, and Reason. You need to select these fields to include them in the query.

To create the query using the Simple Query Wizard:

TIP

You can also double-click a field to move it from the Available Fields box to the Selected Fields box.

1. Click **VisitID** in the Available Fields box to select the field (if necessary), and then click the ⎣ > ⎤ button. The VisitID field moves to the Selected Fields box.

2. Repeat Step 1 for the fields **VisitDate** and **Reason**, and then click the **Next** button. The second, and final, Simple Query Wizard dialog box opens and asks you to choose a name (title) for your query. Access suggests the name "Visit Query" because the query you are creating is based on the Visit table. You'll change the suggested name to "VisitList."

3. Click at the end of the suggested name, use the **Backspace** key to delete the word "Query" and the space, and then type **List**. Now you can view the query results.

4. Click the **Finish** button to complete the query. Access displays the query results in Datasheet view, on a new tab named "VisitList." A query datasheet is similar to a table datasheet, showing fields in columns and records in rows—but only for those fields and records you want to see, as determined by the query specifications you select.

5. Place the pointer on the vertical line to the right of the Reason field name until the pointer changes to a ✛ shape, and then double-click the vertical line to resize the Reason field. See Figure 1-22.

Figure 1-22	Query results

only the three selected fields are displayed in the query datasheet

all 86 records are included in the results

VisitID	VisitDate	Reason
1527	11/9/2015	Allergies - environmental
1528	11/9/2015	Diabetes mellitis Type 2 - initial diagnosis
1530	11/10/2015	Seborrheic dermatitis
1535	11/12/2015	Transverse fracture of left ulna
1536	11/17/2015	Gastroenteritis
1538	11/17/2015	Migraine
1539	11/18/2015	Annual wellness visit
1541	11/24/2015	Gastroenteritis - follow up
1542	11/24/2015	Influenza
1544	11/25/2015	Influenza
1548	11/30/2015	Hypertension
1549	11/30/2015	Influenza
1550	12/1/2015	Influenza
1552	12/3/2015	Annual wellness visit
1555	12/7/2015	Annual wellness visit
1557	12/10/2015	Annual wellness visit
1560	12/15/2015	Influenza
1562	12/22/2015	COPD management visit
1563	1/4/2016	Follow-up - cast removal
1564	1/5/2016	Annual wellness visit
1567	1/8/2016	Hypertension monitoring
1569	1/11/2016	COPD management visit
1570	1/11/2016	Nasopharyngitis
1572	1/13/2016	Acute sinusitis
1573	1/13/2016	Cardiac monitoring

Record: 14 ◄ 1 of 86 ► ►I ►☆ ⌄ No Filter Search

Datasheet View

The VisitList query datasheet displays the three selected fields for each record in the Visit table. The fields are shown in the order you selected them in the Simple Query Wizard, from left to right. The records are listed in order by the primary key field, VisitID. Even though the query datasheet displays only the three fields you chose for the query, the Visit table still includes all the fields for all records.

Notice that the navigation buttons are located at the bottom of the window. You navigate a query datasheet in the same way that you navigate a table datasheet.

▶ **6.** Click the **Last record** navigation button ⏮. The last record in the query datasheet is now the current record.

▶ **7.** Click the **Previous record** navigation button ◀. Record 85 in the query datasheet is now the current record.

▶ **8.** Click the **First record** navigation button ⏮. The first record is now the current record.

▶ **9.** Click the **Close 'VisitList'** button ⊠ on the object tab. A dialog box opens asking if you want to save the changes to the layout of the query. This dialog box opens because you resized the Reason column.

▶ **10.** Click the **Yes** button to save the query layout changes and close the query.

The query results are not stored in the database; however, the query design is stored as part of the database with the name you specified. You can re-create the query results at any time by opening the query again. When you open the query at a later date, the results displayed will reflect up-to-date information to include any new records entered in the Visit table.

Next, Cindi asks you to create a form for the Visit table so that Chatham Community Health Services employees can use the form to enter and work with data in the table easily.

Creating a Simple Form

As noted earlier, you use a form to enter, edit, and view records in a database. Although you can perform these same functions with tables and queries, forms can present data in many customized and useful ways.

Cindi wants a form for the Visit table that shows all the fields for one record at a time, with fields listed one below another in a column. This type of form will make it easier for her staff to focus on all the data for a particular visit. You'll use the Form tool to create this form quickly and easily.

To create the form using the Form tool:

▶ **1.** Make sure the Visit table is still open in Datasheet view. The table or other database object you're using as the basis for the form must either be open or selected in the Navigation Pane when you use the Form tool.

Trouble? If the Visit table is not open, click the Shutter Bar Open/Close Button ⟩⟩ to open the Navigation Pane. Then double-click Visit to open the Visit table in Datasheet view. Click the Shutter Bar Open/Close Button ⟨⟨ to close the pane.

▶ **2.** Make sure the CREATE tab is displayed.

▶ **3.** In the Forms group, click the **Form** button. The Form tool creates a simple form showing every field in the Visit table and places it on a tab named "Visit." Access assigns this name because the form is based on the Visit table. See Figure 1-23.

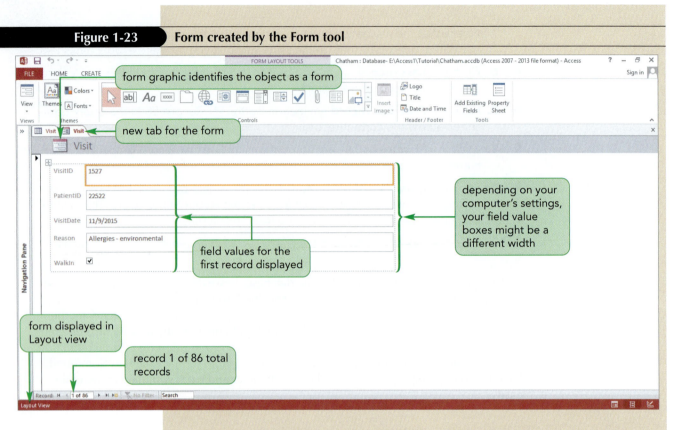

Figure 1-23 **Form created by the Form tool**

Trouble? Depending on the size of your monitor and your screen resolution settings, the fields in your form might appear in multiple columns instead of a single column. This difference will not present any problems.

The form displays one record at a time in the Visit table, providing another view of the data that is stored in the table and allowing you to focus on the values for one record. Access displays the field values for the first record in the table and selects the first field value (VisitID) by placing a border around the value. Each field name appears on a separate line and on the same line as its field value, which appears in a box to the right. Depending on your computer's settings, the field value boxes in your form might be wider or narrower than those shown in the figure. As indicated in the status bar, the form is displayed in Layout view. In **Layout view**, you can make design changes to the form while it is displaying data, so that you can see the effects of the changes you make immediately.

To view, enter, and maintain data using a form, you must know how to move from field to field and from record to record. Notice that the form contains navigation buttons, similar to those available in Datasheet view, which you can use to display different records in the form. You'll use these now to navigate the form; then you'll save and close the form.

To navigate, save, and close the form:

1. Click the **Next record** navigation button ▶. The form now displays the values for the second record in the Visit table.

2. Click the **Last record** navigation button ▶| to move to the last record in the table. The form displays the information for VisitID 1700.

3. Click the **Previous record** navigation button ◀ to move to record 85.

▶ 4. Click the **First record** navigation button ⏮ to return to the first record in the Visit table.

   Next, you'll save the form with the name "VisitData" in the Chatham database. Then the form will be available for later use.

▶ 5. On the Quick Access Toolbar, click the **Save** button 💾. The Save As dialog box opens.

▶ 6. In the Form Name box, click at the end of the highlighted word "Visit," type **Data**, and then press the **Enter** key. Access saves the form as VisitData in the Chatham database and closes the dialog box. The tab containing the form now displays the name VisitData.

▶ 7. Click the **Close 'VisitData'** button ✖ on the object tab to close the form.

INSIGHT

Saving Database Objects

In general, it is best to save a database object—query, form, or report—only if you anticipate using the object frequently or if it is time consuming to create, because all objects use storage space and increase the size of the database file. For example, you most likely would not save a form you created with the Form tool because you can re-create it easily with one mouse click. (However, for the purposes of this text, you usually need to save the objects you create.)

After attending a staff meeting, Cindi returns with another request. She would like to see the information in the Visit table presented in a more readable and professional format. You'll help Cindi by creating a report.

Creating a Simple Report

As noted earlier, a report is a formatted printout (or screen display) of the contents of one or more tables or queries. You'll use the Report tool to quickly produce a report based on the Visit table for Cindi. The Report tool creates a report based on the selected table or query.

To create the report using the Report tool:

▶ 1. With the Visit table open in Datasheet view, click the **CREATE** tab on the ribbon.

▶ 2. In the Reports group, click the **Report** button. The Report tool creates a simple report showing every field in the Visit table and places it on a tab named "Visit." Again, Access assigns this name because the object you created (the report) is based on the Visit table. See Figure 1-24.

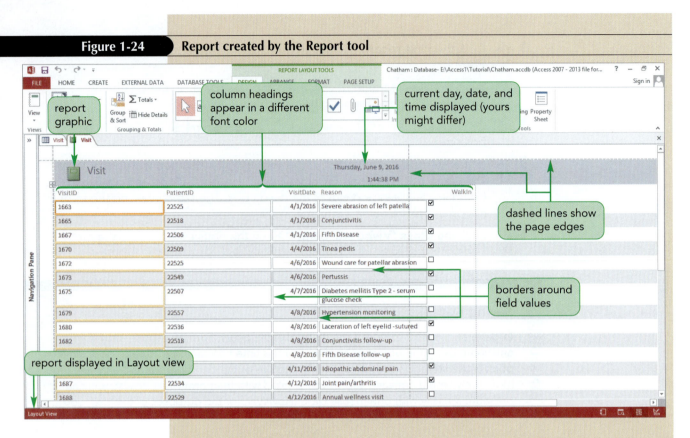

Figure 1-24   **Report created by the Report tool**

Trouble? The records in your report might appear in a different order from the records shown in Figure 1-24. This difference will not cause any problems.

The report shows each field in a column, with the field values for each record in a row, similar to a table or query datasheet. However, the report offers a more visually appealing format for the data, with the column headings in a different color, borders around each field value, a graphic of a report at the top left, and the current day, date, and time at the top right. Also notice the dashed horizontal and vertical lines on the top and right, respectively; these lines mark the edges of the page and show where text will print on the page.

The report needs some design changes to better display the data. The columns are much wider than necessary for the VisitID and PatientID fields, and the Reason and WalkIn field values and borders are not completely displayed within the page area defined by the dashed lines, which means they would not appear on the same page as the rest of the fields in the printed report. You can resize the columns easily in Layout view.

To resize the VisitID and PatientID columns:

1. Position the pointer on the right border of any field value in the VisitID column until the pointer changes to a ↔ shape.

2. Click and drag the mouse to the left; dark outlines surround the field name and each field value to show the column width as you change it. Drag to the left until the column is slightly wider than the VisitID field name.

3. Release the mouse button. The VisitID column is now narrower, and the other four columns have shifted to the left. The Reason and WalkIn fields, values, and borders are now completely within the page area. See Figure 1-25.

Figure 1-25   **Report after resizing the VisitID column**

field values and borders are now within the area marked by the dashed lines

column is now narrower

4. Click the first field value for PatientID to establish the field as the current field.

5. Position the pointer on the right border of the first value in the PatientID column until the pointer changes to ↔ , click and drag to the left until the column is slightly wider than its field name, and then release the mouse button.

6. Drag the scroll box on the vertical scroll bar all the way down to the bottom of the report to check its entire layout.

   The Report tool displays the number "86" at the bottom left of the report, showing the total number of records in the report and the table on which it is based—the Visit table. The Report tool also displays the page number at the bottom right, but the text "Page 1 of 1" appears cut off through the vertical dashed line. This will cause a problem when you print the report, so you need to move this text to the left.

7. Click anywhere on the words **Page 1 of 1**. An orange outline appears around the text, indicating it is selected. See Figure 1-26.

Figure 1-26   **Report page number selected**

text to the right of this dashed line would print on its own page

text is selected and can be moved to the left

shows total number of records in the report

With the text selected, you can use the keyboard arrow keys to move it.

8. Press the ← key repeatedly until the selected box containing the page number is to the left of the vertical dashed line (roughly 35 times). The page number text is now completely within the page area and will print on the same page as the rest of the report.

9. Drag the scroll box back up to redisplay the top of the report.

The report is displayed in Layout view, which doesn't show how many pages there are in the report. To see this, you need to switch to Print Preview.

To view the report in Print Preview:

1. In the Views group on the DESIGN tab, click the **View button arrow**, and then click **Print Preview**. The first page of the report is displayed in Print Preview. See Figure 1-27.

Figure 1-27 **First page of the report in Print Preview**

Print Preview shows exactly how the report will look when printed. Notice that Print Preview provides page navigation buttons at the bottom of the window, similar to the navigation buttons you've used to move through records in a table, query, and form.

2. Click the **Next Page** navigation button ▶. The second page of the report is displayed in Print Preview.

3. Click the **Last Page** navigation button ▶| to move to the last page of the report.

4. Drag the scroll box in the vertical scroll bar (see Figure 1-27) down until the bottom of the report page is displayed. The notation "Page 3 of 3" appears at the bottom of the page, indicating that you are on page 3 out of a total of 3 pages in the report.

   Trouble? Depending on the printer you are using, your report might have more or fewer pages, and some of the pages might be blank. If so, don't worry. Different printers format reports in different ways, sometimes affecting the total number of pages and the number of records printed per page.

> **5.** Click the **First Page** navigation button |◄| to return to the first page of the report, and then drag the scroll box in the vertical scroll bar back up so that the top of the report is displayed.
>
> Next you'll save the report as VisitDetails, and then print it.
>
> **6.** On the Quick Access Toolbar, click the **Save** button 🖫. The Save As dialog box opens.
>
> **7.** In the Report Name box, click at the end of the highlighted word "Visit," type **Details,** and then press the **Enter** key. Access saves the report as VisitDetails in the Chatham database and closes the dialog box. The tab containing the report now displays the name "VisitDetails."

Printing a Report

After creating a report, you might need to print it to distribute it to others who need to view the report's contents. You can print a report without changing any print settings, or display the Print dialog box and select options for printing.

Printing a Report

- Open the report in any view, or select the report in the Navigation Pane.
- Click the FILE tab to display Backstage view, click Print, and then click Quick Print to print the report with the default print settings.

or

- Open the report in any view, or select the report in the Navigation Pane.
- Click the FILE tab, click Print, and then click Print (or, if the report is displayed in Print Preview, click the Print button in the Print group on the PRINT PREVIEW tab). The Print dialog box opens, in which you can select the options you want for printing the report.

Cindi asks you to print the entire report with the default settings, so you'll use the Quick Print option in Backstage view.

Note: To complete the following steps, your computer must be connected to a printer. Check with your instructor first to see if you should print the report.

To print the report and then close it:

> **1.** On the ribbon, click the **FILE** tab to display Backstage view.
>
> **2.** In the navigation bar, click **Print**, and then click **Quick Print**. The report prints with the default print settings, and you return to the report in Print Preview.
>
> **Trouble?** If your report did not print, make sure that your computer is connected to a printer, and that the printer is turned on and ready to print. Then repeat Steps 1 and 2.
>
> **3.** Click the **Close 'VisitDetails'** button |X| on the object tab to close the report.
>
> **4.** Click the **Close 'Visit'** button |X| on the object tab to close the Visit table.
>
> **Trouble?** If you are asked to save changes to the layout of the table, click Yes.

You can also use the Print dialog box to print other database objects, such as table and query datasheets. Most often, these objects are used for viewing and entering data, and reports are used for printing the data in a database.

Viewing Objects in the Navigation Pane

The Chatham database now contains four objects—the Visit table, the VisitList query, the VisitData form, and the VisitDetails report. When you work with the database file—such as closing it, opening it, or distributing it to others—the file includes all the objects you created and saved in the database. You can view and work with these objects in the Navigation Pane.

To view the objects in the Chatham database:

1. On the Navigation Pane, click the **Shutter Bar Open/Close Button** >> to open the pane. See Figure 1-28.

Figure 1-28 Chatham database objects displayed in the Navigation Pane

The Navigation Pane currently displays the default category, **All Access Objects**, which lists all the database objects in the pane. Each object type (Tables, Queries, Forms, and Reports) appears in its own group. Each database object (the Visit table, the VisitList query, the VisitData form, and the VisitDetails report) has a unique icon to its left to indicate the type of object. This makes it easy for you to identify the objects and choose which one you want to open and work with.

The arrow on the All Access Objects bar displays a menu with options for various ways to group and display objects in the Navigation Pane. The Search box enables you to enter text for Access to find; for example, you could search for all objects that contain the word "Visit" in their names. Note that Access searches for objects only in the categories and groups currently displayed in the Navigation Pane.

As you continue to build the Chatham database and add more objects to it in later tutorials, you'll use the options in the Navigation Pane to manage those objects.

Using Microsoft Access Help

The Access program provides a Help system you can use to search for information about specific Access features. You start Help by clicking the Microsoft Access Help button in the top right of the Access window, or by pressing the F1 key. You'll use Help now to learn more about the Navigation Pane.

To search for information about the Navigation Pane in Help:

1. Click the **Microsoft Access Help** button ? on the title bar. The Access Help window opens, as shown earlier in the Session 1.2 Visual Overview.

2. Click in the search box, type **Navigation Pane**, and then press the **Enter** key. The Access Help window displays a list of topics related to the Navigation Pane.

3. Click the topic **Manage database objects in the Navigation Pane**. The Access Help window displays the article you selected. See Figure 1-29.

Figure 1-29   Article displayed in the Access Help window

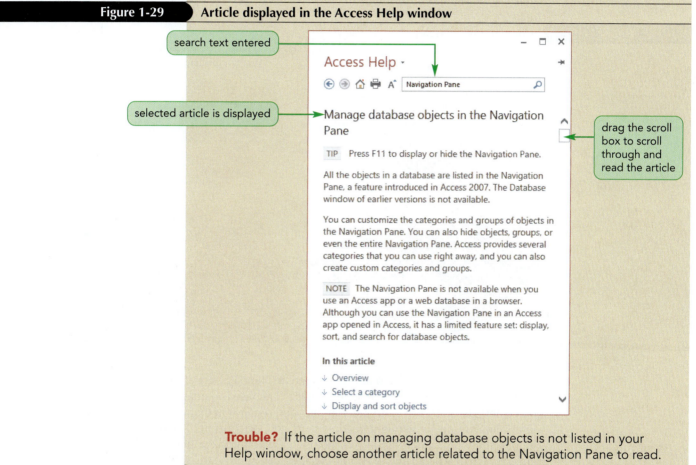

Trouble? If the article on managing database objects is not listed in your Help window, choose another article related to the Navigation Pane to read.

4. Scroll through the article to read detailed information about working with the Navigation Pane.

5. When finished, click the **Close** button ✖ on the Access Help window to close it.

The Access Help system is an important reference tool for you to use if you need additional information about databases in general, details about specific Access features, or support with problems you might encounter.

Managing a Database

One of the main tasks involved in working with database software is managing your databases and the data they contain. Some of the activities involved in database management include compacting and repairing a database and backing up and restoring a database. By managing your databases, you can ensure that they operate in the most efficient way, that the data they contain is secure, and that you can work with the data effectively.

Compacting and Repairing a Database

Whenever you open an Access database and work in it, the size of the database increases. Further, when you delete records or when you delete or replace database objects—such as queries, forms, and reports—the storage space that had been occupied by the deleted or replaced records or objects does not automatically become available for other records or objects. To make the space available, and also to increase the speed of data retrieval, you must compact the database. **Compacting** a database rearranges the data and objects in a database to decrease its file size, thereby making more storage space available and enhancing the performance of the database. Figure 1-30 illustrates the compacting process.

Figure 1-30 **Compacting a database**

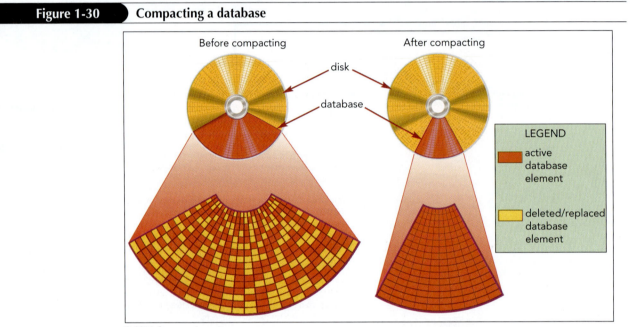

© 2014 Cengage Learning

When you compact a database, Access repairs the database at the same time, if necessary. In some cases, Access detects that a database is damaged when you try to open it and gives you the option to compact and repair it at that time. For example, the data in your database might become damaged, or corrupted, if you exit the Access program suddenly by turning off your computer. If you think your database might be damaged because it is behaving unpredictably, you can use the Compact & Repair Database option to fix it.

REFERENCE

Compacting and Repairing a Database

- Make sure the database file you want to compact and repair is open.
- Click the FILE tab to display the Info screen in Backstage view.
- Click the Compact & Repair Database button.

Access also allows you to set an option to compact and repair a database file automatically every time you close it. The Compact on Close option is available in the Current Database section of the Access Options dialog box, which you open from

Backstage view by clicking the Options command in the navigation bar. By default, the Compact on Close option is turned off.

Next, you'll compact the Chatham database manually using the Compact & Repair Database option. This will make the database smaller and allow you to work with it more efficiently. After compacting the database, you'll close it.

To compact and repair the Chatham database:

▶ **1.** On the ribbon, click the **FILE** tab to display the Info screen in Backstage view.

▶ **2.** Click the **Compact & Repair Database** button. Access closes Backstage view and returns to the HOME tab. Although nothing visible happens on the screen, Access compacts the Chatham database, making it smaller, and repairs it at the same time.

▶ **3.** Click the **FILE** tab to return to the Info screen, and then click **Close** in the navigation bar. Access closes the Chatham database.

Backing Up and Restoring a Database

Backing up a database is the process of making a copy of the database file to protect your database against loss or damage. The Back Up Database command enables you to back up your database file from within the Access program, while you are working on your database. To use this option, click the FILE tab to display the Info screen in Backstage view, click Save As in the navigation bar, click Back Up Database in the Advanced section of the Save Database As pane, and then click the Save As button. In the Save As dialog box that opens, Access provides a default filename for the backup copy that consists of the same filename as the database you are backing up (for example, "Chatham"), and an underscore character, plus the current date. This filenaming system makes it easy for you to keep track of your database backups and when they were created. To restore a backup database file, you simply copy the backup from the location where it is stored to your hard drive, or whatever device you use to work in Access, and start working with the restored database file. (You will not actually back up the Chatham database in this tutorial unless directed by your instructor to do so.)

INSIGHT

Planning and Performing Database Backups

Experienced database users make it a habit to back up a database before they work with it for the first time, keeping the original data intact. They also make frequent backups while continuing to work with a database; these backups are generally on flash drives, recordable CDs or DVDs, external or network hard drives, or cloud-based storage (such as SkyDrive). Also, it is recommended to store the backup copy in a different location from the original. For example, if the original database is stored on a flash drive, you should not store the backup copy on the same flash drive. If you lose the drive or the drive is damaged, you would lose both the original database and its backup copy.

If the original database file and the backup copy have the same name, restoring the backup copy might replace the original. If you want to save the original file, rename it before you restore the backup copy. To ensure that the restored database has the most current data, you should update the restored database with any changes made to the original between the time you created the backup copy and the time the original database became damaged or lost.

By properly planning for and performing backups, you can avoid losing data and prevent the time-consuming effort required to rebuild a lost or damaged database.

In the following tutorials, you'll help Cindi complete and maintain the Chatham database, and you'll use it to meet the specific information needs of the clinic's employees.

PROSKILLS

Decision Making: When to Use Access vs. Excel

Using a spreadsheet application like Microsoft Excel to manage lists or tables of information works well when the data is simple, such as a list of contacts or tasks. As soon as the data becomes complex enough to separate into tables that need to be related, you start to see the limitations of using a spreadsheet application. The strength of a database application such as Access is in its ability to easily relate one table of information to another. Consider a table of contacts that includes home addresses, with a separate row for each person living at the same address. When an address changes, it's too easy to make a mistake and not update the home address for each person who lives there. To ensure you have the most accurate data at all times, it's important to have only one instance of each piece of data. By creating separate tables that are related, and keeping only one instance of each piece of data, you'll ensure the integrity of the data. Trying to accomplish this in Excel is a complex process, whereas Access is specifically designed for this functionality.

Another limitation of using Excel instead of Access to manage data has to do with the volume of data. Although a spreadsheet can hold thousands of records, a database can hold millions. A spreadsheet containing thousands of pieces of information is cumbersome to use. Think of large-scale commercial applications such as enrollment at a college or tracking customers for a large company. It's hard to imagine managing such information in an Excel spreadsheet. Instead, you'd use a database. Finally, with an Access database, multiple users can access the information it contains at the same time. Although an Excel spreadsheet can be shared, there can be problems when users try to open and edit the same spreadsheet at the same time.

When you're trying to decide whether to use Excel or Access, ask yourself the following questions.

1. Do you need to store data in separate tables that are related to each other?
2. Do you have a very large amount of data to store?
3. Will more than one person need to access the data at the same time?

If you answer "yes" to any of these questions, an Access database is most likely the appropriate application to use.

REVIEW

Session 1.2 Quick Check

1. To copy the records from a table in one database to another table in a different database, the two tables must have the same _____.
2. A(n) _____ is a question you ask about the data stored in a database.
3. The quickest way to create a form is to use the _____.
4. Which view enables you to see the total number of pages in a report and navigate through the report pages?
5. In the Navigation Pane, each database object has a unique _____ to its left that identifies the object's type.
6. _____ a database rearranges the data and objects in a database to decrease its file size and enhance the speed and performance of the database.
7. _____ a database is the process of making a copy of the database file to protect the database against loss or damage.

ASSESS

SAM Projects

Put your skills into practice with SAM Projects! SAM Projects for this tutorial can be found online. If you have a SAM account, go to www.cengage.com/sam2013 to download the most recent Project Instructions and Start Files.

PRACTICE

Review Assignments

Data File needed for the Review Assignments: Company.accdb

For Chatham Community Health Services, Cindi asks you to create a new database to contain information about the vendors that the clinic works with to obtain medical supplies and equipment for the clinic, and the vendors who service and maintain the equipment. Complete the following steps:

1. Create a new, blank database named **Vendor** and save it in the folder where you are storing your files, as specified by your instructor.
2. In Datasheet view for the Table1 table, rename the default ID primary key field to **SupplierID**. Change the data type of the SupplierID field to Short Text.
3. Add the following 10 fields to the new table in the order shown; all of them are Short Text fields *except* InitialContact, which is a Date/Time field: **Company**, **Category**, **Address**, **City**, **State**, **Zip**, **Phone**, **ContactFirst**, **ContactLast**, and **InitialContact**. Resize the columns as necessary so that the complete field names are displayed. Save the table as **Supplier**.
4. Enter the records shown in Figure 1-31 in the Supplier table. For the first record, be sure to enter your first name in the ContactFirst field and your last name in the ContactLast field.

   Note: When entering field values that are shown on multiple lines in the figure, do not try to enter the values on multiple lines. The values are shown on multiple lines in the figure for page spacing purposes only.

Figure 1-31	Supplier table records

SupplierID	Company	Category	Address	City	State	Zip	Phone	ContactFirst	ContactLast	InitialContact
ARE318	Aresco Surgical, Inc.	Supplies	48 Vienna St	Bridgeport	CT	06601	203-774-3048	*Student First*	*Student Last*	9/2/2015
GRE364	Greinke Labs, Inc.	Supplies	451 Summit Dr	Tiverton	RI	02878	401-208-9843	Evan	Brighton	1/12/2016
DUR368	Durasurg Equipment, Inc.	Equipment	74 Jessie St	Roanoke	VA	24036	540-340-3829	Kristin	Taylor	12/1/2015
STE472	Sterile Labs of CT, Inc.	Service	938 Gormley Ave	North Branford	CT	06517	203-537-5940	Carmine	San Marcos	11/3/2015
GSE420	GSE Medical, Inc.	Equipment	583 Renovo Dr	Claremont	NH	03743	603-202-4951	John	Vereen	9/10/2015

© 2014 Cengage Learning

5. Cindi created a database named Company that contains a Business table with supplier data. The Supplier table you created has the same design as the Business table. Copy all the records from the **Business** table in the **Company** database (located in the Access1 ▶ Review folder provided with your Data Files) and then paste them at the end of the Supplier table in the Vendor database.

6. Resize all datasheet columns to their best fit, and then save the Supplier table.

7. Close the Supplier table, and then use the Navigation Pane to reopen it. Note that the records are displayed in primary key order by the values in the SupplierID field.

8. Use the Simple Query Wizard to create a query that includes the Company, Category, ContactFirst, ContactLast, and Phone fields (in that order) from the Supplier table. Name the query **SupplierList**, and then close the query.

9. Use the Form tool to create a form for the Supplier table. Save the form as **SupplierInfo**, and then close it.

10. Use the Report tool to create a report based on the Supplier table. In Layout view, resize all fields except the Company field, so that each field is slightly wider than the longest entry (either the field name itself or an entry in the field). Display the report in Print Preview and verify that all the fields fit across two pages in the report. Save the report as **SupplierDetails**, and then close it.

11. Close the Supplier table, and then compact and repair the Vendor database.

12. Close the Vendor database.

APPLY

Case Problem 1

Data File needed for this Case Problem: Program.accdb

GoGopher! Amol Mehta, a recent college graduate living in Boulder, Colorado, spent months earning money by running errands and completing basic chores for family members and acquaintances, while looking for full-time employment. As his list of customers needing such services continued to grow, Amol decided to start his own business called GoGopher! The business, which Amol operates completely online from his home, offers customers a variety of services—from grocery shopping and household chores to yard work and pet care—on a subscription basis. Clients become members of GoGopher! by choosing the plan that best suits their needs. Each plan provides a certain number of tasks per month to members, for a specified period of time. Amol wants to use Access to maintain information about the members who have joined GoGopher! and the types of plans offered. He needs your help in creating this database. Complete the following:

1. Create a new, blank database named **Gopher** and save it in the folder where you are storing your files, as specified by your instructor.

2. In Datasheet view for the Table1 table, rename the default primary key ID field to **PlanID**. Change the data type of the PlanID field to Short Text.

3. Add the following three fields to the new table in the order shown: **PlanDescription** (a Short Text field), **PlanCost** (a Currency field), and **FeeWaived** (a Yes/No field). Save the table as **Plan**.

4. Enter the records shown in Figure 1-32 in the Plan table. Note: When entering the PlanCost field values, you do not have to type the dollar signs, commas, or decimal places; Access will enter them automatically.

Figure 1-32 Plan table records

PlanID	PlanDescription	PlanCost	FeeWaived
301	20 tasks per month for 12 months	$6,000.00	Yes
311	10 tasks per month for 3 months	$750.00	No
304	10 tasks per month for 12 months	$3,000.00	Yes
303	15 tasks per month for 12 months	$4,500.00	Yes
312	8 tasks per month for 3 months	$600.00	No

when entering currency values, you do not have to type the dollar signs, commas, or decimal places

© 2014 Cengage Learning

5. Amol created a database named Program that contains a Service table with plan data. The Plan table you created has the same design as the Service table. Copy all the records from the **Service** table in the **Program** database (located in the Access1 ▸ Case1 folder provided with your Data Files) and then paste them at the end of the Plan table in the Gopher database.

6. Resize all datasheet columns to their best fit, and then save the Plan table.

7. Close the Plan table, and then use the Navigation Pane to reopen it. Note that the records are displayed in primary key order by the values in the PlanID field.

8. Use the Simple Query Wizard to create a query that includes the PlanID, PlanDescription, and PlanCost fields from the Plan table. In the second Simple Query Wizard dialog box, select the Detail option. (This option appears because the query includes a Currency field.) Save the query as **PlanData**, and then close the query.

9. Use the Form tool to create a form for the Plan table. Save the form as **PlanInfo**, and then close it.

10. Use the Report tool to create a report based on the Plan table. In Layout view, resize the PlanID field so it is slightly wider than the longest entry, which is the field name in this case. Also, resize the box containing the total amount that appears below the PlanCost column by clicking the box and then dragging its bottom border down so that the amount is fully displayed. (The Report Tool calculated this total automatically.) Display the report in Print Preview; then verify that all the fields are within the page area and all field values are fully displayed. Save the report as **PlanList**, print the report (only if asked by your instructor to do so), and then close it.

11. Close the Plan table, and then compact and repair the Gopher database.

12. Close the Gopher database.

Case Problem 2

Data File needed for this Case Problem: Consulting.accdb

APPLY

O'Brien Educational Services   After teaching English in a public high school for 15 years, Karen O'Brien decided to channel her experience in education in a new direction and founded O'Brien Educational Services, a small educational consulting company located in South Bend, Indiana. The company offers tutoring services to high school students to help prepare them for standardized tests, such as the SAT and the ACT. The company provides group, private, and semi-private tutoring sessions to best meet the needs of its students. As her business continues to expand, Karen wants to use Access to maintain information about the tutors who work for her, the students who sign up for tutoring, and the contracts they sign. She needs your help in creating this database. Complete the following steps:

1. Create a new, blank database named **OBrien** and save it in the folder where you are storing your files, as specified by your instructor.

2. In Datasheet view for the Table1 table, rename the default primary key ID field to **TutorID**. Change the data type of the TutorID field to Short Text.

3. Add the following five fields to the new table in the order shown; all of them are Short Text fields *except* HireDate, which is a Date/Time field: **FirstName**, **LastName**, **Degree**, **School**, and **HireDate**. Resize the columns, if necessary, so that the complete field names are displayed. Save the table as **Tutor**.

4. Enter the records shown in Figure 1-33 in the Tutor table. For the first record, be sure to enter your first name in the FirstName field and your last name in the LastName field.

| Figure 1-33 | Tutor table records |

TutorID	FirstName	LastName	Degree	School	HireDate
31-1200	*Student First*	*Student Last*	BA	Pierre University	8/2/2015
68-8234	Caitlin	Shea	MS	Towns University	1/5/2016
55-1234	Samuel	Glick	BA	Manoog College	7/23/2016
69-2254	Sachi	Hatanaka	MA	Wyman College	3/23/2015
71-1698	Richard	Keating	Ph.D	Hobert University	5/3/2015

© 2014 Cengage Learning

5. Karen created a database named Consulting that contains an Instructor table with tutor data. The Tutor table you created has the same design as the Instructor table. Copy all the records from the **Instructor** table in the **Consulting** database (located in the Access1 ▶ Case2 folder provided with your Data Files) and then paste them at the end of the Tutor table in the OBrien database.

6. Resize all datasheet columns to their best fit, and then save the Tutor table.

7. Close the Tutor table, and then use the Navigation Pane to reopen it. Note that the records are displayed in primary key order by the values in the TutorID field.

8. Use the Simple Query Wizard to create a query that includes the FirstName, LastName, and HireDate fields from the Tutor table. Save the query as **StartDate**, and then close the query.

9. Use the Form tool to create a form for the Tutor table. Save the form as **TutorInfo**, and then close it.

10. Use the Report tool to create a report based on the Tutor table. In Layout view, resize the TutorID, FirstName, LastName, and Degree fields so they are slightly wider than the longest entry (either the field name itself or an entry in the field). All six fields should fit within the page area after you resize the specified fields. At the bottom of the report, move the text "Page 1 of 1" to the left so it is within the page area. Display the report in Print Preview; then verify that the fields and page number fit within the page area, and that all field values are fully displayed. Save the report as **TutorList**, print the report (only if asked by your instructor to do so), and then close it.

11. Close the Tutor table, and then compact and repair the OBrien database.

12. Close the OBrien database.

CHALLENGE

Case Problem 3

Data File needed for this Case Problem: Animal.accdb

Rosemary Animal Shelter   Ryan Lang is the director of the Rosemary Animal Shelter in Cobb County, Georgia. The main goals of the shelter, which has several locations in the county, are to rescue dogs and cats and to find people who will adopt them. The shelter was established by Rosemary Hanson, who dedicated her life to rescuing pets and finding good homes for them. Residents of Cobb County generously donate money, food, and equipment in support of the shelter. Some of these patrons also adopt animals from the shelter. Ryan has asked you to create an Access database to manage information about the animals, patrons, and donations. Complete the following steps:

1. Create a new, blank database named **Shelter** and save it in the folder where you are storing your files, as specified by your instructor.

2. In Datasheet view for the Table1 table, rename the default primary key ID field to **PatronID**. Change the data type of the PatronID field to Short Text.

3. Add the following four Short Text fields to the new table in the order shown: **Title**, **FirstName**, **LastName**, and **Phone**. Save the table as **Patron**.

4. Enter the records shown in Figure 1-34 in the Patron table. For the first record, be sure to enter your title in the Title field, your first name in the FirstName field, and your last name in the LastName field.

Figure 1-34   Patron table records

PatronID	Title	FirstName	LastName	Phone
30405	*Student Title*	*Student First*	*Student Last*	770-427-9300
33287	Dr.	Ali	Haddad	770-528-8973
32189	Mrs.	Gini	Smith	770-499-2775
36028	Mr.	Michael	Carlucci	678-283-6334
30753	Ms.	Cynthia	Crosby	678-444-2676

© 2014 Cengage Learning

5. Ryan created a database named Animal that contains a Donor table with data about patrons. The Patron table you created has the same design as the Donor table. Copy all the records from the **Donor** table in the **Animal** database (located in the Access1 ▶ Case3 folder provided with your Data Files) and then paste them at the end of the Patron table in the Shelter database.

6. Resize all datasheet columns to their best fit, and then save the Patron table.

7. Close the Patron table, and then use the Navigation Pane to reopen it. Note that the records are displayed in primary key order by the values in the PatronID field.

✦ **Explore** 8. Use the Simple Query Wizard to create a query that includes all the fields in the Patron table *except* the Title field. (*Hint*: Use the `>>` and `<` buttons to select the necessary fields.) Save the query using the name **PatronPhoneList**.

✦ **Explore** 9. The query results are displayed in order by the PatronID field values. You can specify a different order by sorting the query. Display the HOME tab. Then, click the insertion point anywhere in the LastName column to make it the current field. In the Sort & Filter group on the HOME tab, click the Ascending button. The records are now listed in order by the values in the LastName field. Save and close the query.

✦ **Explore** 10. Use the Form tool to create a form for the Patron table. In the new form, navigate to record 15 (the record with PatronID 33765), and then print the form *for the current record only*. (*Hint*: You must use the Print dialog box in order to print only the current record. Go to Backstage view, click Print in the navigation bar, and then click Print to open the Print dialog box. Click the Selected Record(s) option button and then click the OK button to print the current record.) Save the form as **PatronInfo**, and then close it.

11. Use the Report tool to create a report based on the Patron table. In Layout view, resize each field so it is slightly wider than the longest entry (either the field name itself or an entry in the field). All five fields should fit within the page area after resizing. At the bottom of the report, move the text "Page 1 of 1" to the left so it is within the page area. Display the report in Print Preview, then verify that the fields and page number fit within the page area and that all field values are fully displayed. Save the report as **PatronList**. Print the report (only if asked by your instructor to do so), and then close it.

12. Close the Patron table, and then compact and repair the Shelter database.

13. Close the Shelter database.

CHALLENGE

Case Problem 4

Data File needed for this Case Problem: Tour.accdb

Stanley EcoTours   Janice and Bill Stanley live in Pocatello, Idaho, and are the proud owners and operators of Stanley EcoTours. Their passion is to encourage people to visit natural areas around the world in a responsible manner that does not harm the environment. Their advertising has drawn clients from Idaho, Wyoming, Montana, and Canada. As the interest in ecotourism grows, Janice and Bill's business is also expanding to include more tours in Africa and South America. Because of the growth in business that they anticipate, Janice and Bill realize their current recordkeeping system is inadequate. They would like you to build an Access database to manage information about guests, tours, and reservations. Complete the following:

1. Create a new, blank database named **Stanley** and save it in the folder where you are storing your files, as specified by your instructor.

2. In Datasheet view for the Table1 table, rename the default primary key ID field to **GuestID**. Change the data type of the GuestID field to Short Text.

3. Add the following eight Short Text fields to the new table in the order shown: **GuestFirst**, **GuestLast**, **Address**, **City**, **State/Prov**, **PostalCode**, **Country**, and **Phone**. Save the table as **Guest**.

4. Enter the records shown in Figure 1-35 in the Guest table. For the first record, be sure to enter your first name in the GuestFirst field and your last name in the GuestLast field.

Figure 1-35   **Guest table records**

GuestID	GuestFirst	GuestLast	Address	City	State/Prov	PostalCode	Country	Phone
401	*Student First*	*Student Last*	10 Winter Ave	Boise	ID	83702	USA	208-344-0975
417	Isabelle	Rouy	227 Front Ln	Calgary	AB	T1Y 2N7	Canada	403-226-0065
403	Brian	Anderson	5003 Grant Blvd	Great Falls	MT	59401	USA	406-761-4515
425	Kelly	Skolnik	15 Tobin Dr	Red Deer	AB	T4N 3D5	Canada	403-755-1597
420	Alberto	Lopez	991 Crestview Dr	Butte	MT	59701	USA	406-782-1183

© 2014 Cengage Learning

5. Bill created a database named Tour that contains a Customer table with data about guests. The Guest table you created has the same design as the Customer table. Copy all the records from the **Customer** table in the **Tour** database (located in the Access1 ▸ Case4 folder provided with your Data Files) and then paste them at the end of the Guest table in the Stanley database.

6. Resize all datasheet columns to their best fit, and then save the Guest table.

7. Close the Guest table, and then use the Navigation Pane to reopen it. Note that the records are displayed in primary key order.

8. Use the Simple Query Wizard to create a query that includes the following fields from the Guest table, in the order shown: GuestID, GuestLast, GuestFirst, State/Prov, and Phone. Name the query **GuestData**.

⊕ Explore 9. The query results are displayed in order by the GuestID field values. You can specify a different order by sorting the query. Display the HOME tab. Then, click the insertion point anywhere in the State/Prov column to make it the current field. In the Sort & Filter group on the HOME tab, click the Ascending button. The records are now listed in order by the values in the State/Prov field. Save and close the query.

⊕ Explore 10. Use the Form tool to create a form for the Guest table. In the new form, navigate to record 10 (the record with GuestID 412), and then print the form *for the current record only*. (*Hint*: You must use the Print dialog box in order to print only the current record. Go to Backstage view, click Print in the navigation bar, and then click Print to open the Print dialog box. Click the Selected Record(s) option button and then click the OK button to print the current record.) Save the form as **GuestInfo**, and then close it.

11. Use the Report tool to create a report based on the Guest table. In Layout view, resize each field so it is slightly wider than the longest entry (either the field name itself or an entry in the field). At the bottom of the report, move the text "Page 1 of 1" to the left so it is within the page area on the report's first page. Display the report in Print Preview and notice that the columns of the report are still spread across two pages, even after resizing the fields. Save the report as **GuestList**.

⊕ Explore 12. In the Close Preview group, click the Close Print Preview button to return to the report in Layout view. To make more room on the first page, you'll delete the Address, PostalCode, and Country columns from the report. Click anywhere in the Address column to make it active. Click the ARRANGE tab (one of the REPORT LAYOUT TOOLS contextual tabs), and then click the Select Column button in the Rows & Columns group. Click the HOME tab, and then click the Delete button in the Records group to delete the selected column from the report. Repeat this process to delete the PostalCode and Country columns. The remaining six fields should now all fit on the report's first page.

13. Display the report in Print Preview again, then verify that the fields and page number fit within the page area and that all field values are fully displayed.

14. Save the report, print it (only if asked by your instructor to do so), and then close it.

15. Close the Guest table, and then compact and repair the Stanley database.

16. Close the Stanley database.

Building a Database and Defining Table Relationships

Creating the Billing and Patient Tables

ACCESS

OBJECTIVES

Session 2.1
- Learn the guidelines for designing databases and setting field properties
- Create a table in Design view
- Define fields, set field properties, and specify a table's primary key
- Modify the structure of a table
- Change the order of fields in Design view
- Add new fields in Design view
- Change the Format property for a field in Datasheet view
- Modify field properties in Design view

Session 2.2
- Import data from an Excel worksheet
- Create a table by importing an existing table structure
- Add fields to a table with the Data Type gallery
- Delete and rename fields
- Change the data type for a field in Design view
- Set the Default Value property for a field
- Add data to a table by importing a text file
- Define a relationship between two tables

Case | *Chatham Community Health Services*

The Chatham database currently contains one table, the Visit table. Cindi Rodriguez also wants to track information about the clinic's patients and the invoices sent to them for services provided by Chatham Community Health Services. This information includes such items as each patient's name and address, and the amount and billing date for each invoice.

In this tutorial, you'll create two new tables in the Chatham database—named Billing and Patient—to contain the additional data Cindi wants to track. You will use two different methods for creating the tables, and learn how to modify the fields. After adding records to the tables, you will define the necessary relationships between the tables in the Chatham database to relate the tables, enabling Cindi and her staff to work with the data more efficiently.

STARTING DATA FILES

Tutorial	**Review**	**Case1**
Chatham.accdb *(cont.)*	Supplies.xlsx	Customers.txt
Invoices.xlsx	Vendor.accdb *(cont.)*	Gopher.accdb *(cont.)*
Kelly.accdb		
Patient.txt		

Case2	**Case3**	**Case4**
Agreements.xlsx	Animals.txt	Bookings.txt
Client.accdb	Donations.xlsx	Stanley.accdb *(cont.)*
OBrien.accdb *(cont.)*	Shelter.accdb *(cont.)*	Travel.accdb
Students.txt		

Session 2.1 Visual Overview:

Design view allows you to define or modify a table structure or the properties of the fields in a table.

The default name for a new table you create in Design view is Table1. This name appears on the tab for the new table.

The top portion of the Table window in Design view is called the **Table Design grid**. Here, you enter values for the Field Name, Data Type, and Description field properties.

After you assign a data type to a field, the General tab displays additional field properties for that data type. Initially, most field properties are assigned default values.

When defining the fields in a table, you can move from the Table Design grid to the Field Properties pane by pressing the **F6 key**.

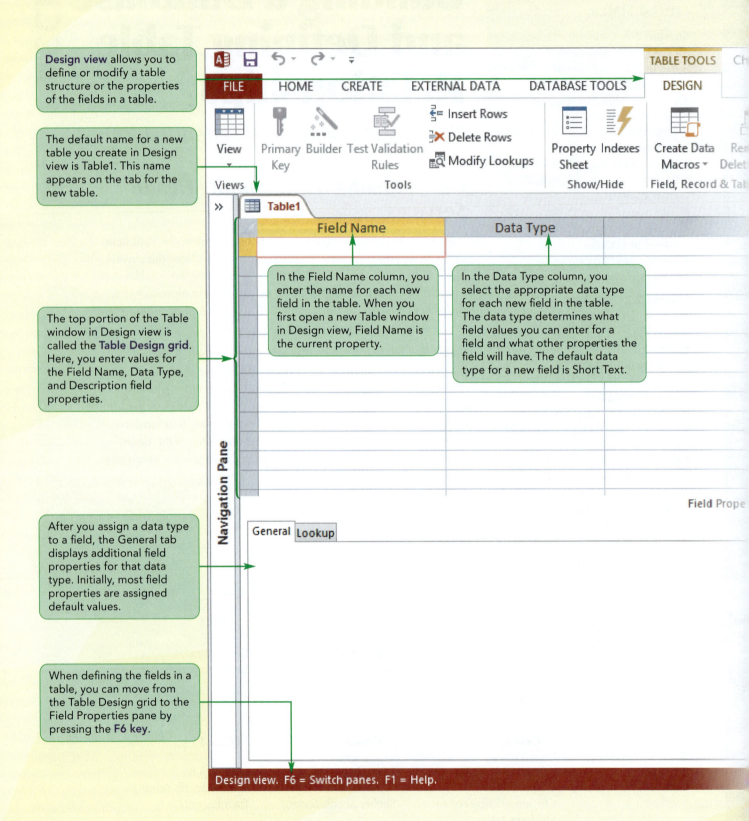

In the Field Name column, you enter the name for each new field in the table. When you first open a new Table window in Design view, Field Name is the current property.

In the Data Type column, you select the appropriate data type for each new field in the table. The data type determines what field values you can enter for a field and what other properties the field will have. The default data type for a new field is Short Text.

Design view. F6 = Switch panes. F1 = Help.

Table Window in Design View

Chatham : Database- E:\Access1\Tutorial\Chatham.accdb (Access...   ?   —   ⊡   ✕

Sign in

E TOOLS

ESIGN

ate Data   Rename/   Relationships   Object
acros ▾   Delete Macro   Dependencies

Record & Table Events   Relationships

Description (Optional)

You can use the **Description property** to enter an optional description for a field to explain its purpose or usage. A field's Description property can be up to 255 characters long, and its value appears on the status bar when you view the table datasheet.

The bottom portion of the Table window in Design view is called the **Field Properties pane**. Here, you select values for all other field properties, most of which are optional.

Field Properties

The purpose or characteristics of the current property (Field Name, in this case) appear in this section of the Field Properties pane.

A field name can be up to 64 characters long, including spaces. Press F1 for help on field names.

You can display more complete Help information about the current property by pressing the **F1 key**.

Guidelines for Designing Databases

A database management system can be a useful tool, but only if you first carefully design the database so that it meets the needs of its users. In database design, you determine the fields, tables, and relationships needed to satisfy the data and processing requirements. When you design a database, you should follow these guidelines:

- **Identify all the fields needed to produce the required information.** For example, Cindi needs information about patients, visits, and invoices. Figure 2-1 shows the fields that satisfy these information requirements.

Figure 2-1	Cindi's data requirements

VisitID	InvoiceDate
PatientID	Reason
InvoiceAmt	Phone
FirstName	WalkIn
LastName	Email
Address	VisitDate
City	InvoiceNum
State	InvoicePaid
Zip	BirthDate

© 2014 Cengage Learning

- **Organize each piece of data into its smallest useful part.** For example, Cindi could store each patient's complete name in one field called PatientName instead of using two fields called FirstName and LastName, as shown in Figure 2-1. However, doing so would make it more difficult to work with the data. If Cindi wanted to view the records in alphabetical order by last name, she wouldn't be able to do so with field values such as "Ben Li" and "Amanda Fox" stored in a PatientName field. She could do so with field values such as "Li" and "Fox" stored separately in a LastName field.
- **Group related fields into tables.** For example, Cindi grouped the fields related to visits into the Visit table, which you created in Tutorial 1. The fields related to invoices are grouped into the Billing table, and the fields related to patients are grouped into the Patient table. Figure 2-2 shows the fields grouped into all three tables for the Chatham database.

Figure 2-2	Cindi's fields grouped into tables

Visit table	Billing table	Patient table
VisitID	InvoiceNum	PatientID
PatientID	VisitID	LastName
VisitDate	InvoiceDate	FirstName
Reason	InvoiceAmt	BirthDate
WalkIn	InvoicePaid	Phone
		Address
		City
		State
		Zip
		Email

© 2014 Cengage Learning

- **Determine each table's primary key.** Recall that a primary key uniquely identifies each record in a table. For some tables, one of the fields, such as a credit card number, naturally serves the function of a primary key. For other tables, two or more fields might be needed to function as the primary key. In these cases, the primary key is called a **composite key**. For example, a school grade table would use a combination of student number, term, and course code to serve as the primary key. For a third category of tables, no single field or combination of fields can uniquely identify a record in a table. In these cases, you need to add a field whose sole purpose is to serve as the table's primary key. For Cindi's tables, VisitID is the primary key for the Visit table, InvoiceNum is the primary key for the Billing table, and PatientID is the primary key for the Patient table.

- **Include a common field in related tables.** You use the common field to connect one table logically with another table. For example, Cindi's Visit and Patient tables include the PatientID field as a common field. Recall that when you include the primary key from one table as a field in a second table to form a relationship, the field in the second table is called a foreign key; therefore, the PatientID field is a foreign key in the Visit table. With this common field, Cindi can find all visits to the clinic made by a particular patient; she can use the PatientID value for a patient and search the Visit table for all records with that PatientID value. Likewise, she can determine which patient made a particular visit by searching the Patient table to find the one record with the same PatientID value as the corresponding value in the Visit table. Similarly, the VisitID field is a common field, serving as the primary key in the Visit table and a foreign key in the Billing table.

- **Avoid data redundancy.** When you store the same data in more than one place, **data redundancy** occurs. With the exception of common fields to connect tables, you should avoid data redundancy because it wastes storage space and can cause inconsistencies. An inconsistency would exist, for example, if you type a field value one way in one table and a different way in the same table or in a second table. Figure 2-3, which contains portions of potential data stored in the Patient and Visit tables, shows an example of incorrect database design that has data redundancy in the Visit table. In Figure 2-3, the LastName field in the Visit table is redundant, and one value for this field was entered incorrectly, in three different ways.

Figure 2-3	Incorrect database design with data redundancy

Patient table

PatientID	Last Name	FirstName	Address
22542	Diaz	Anna	93 Gates Ln
22544	Sutherland	Max	48 Vine St
22546	Ingram	Julia	834 Kiefer Rd
22560	Lewis	Patrice	15 Prince Rd
22561	Shaw	Daniel	33 Agnes Ct

data redundancy

Visit table

VisitID	PatientID	Last Name	VisitDate	WalkIn
1535	22546	Ingraham	11/12/2015	Yes
1570	22561	Shaw	1/11/2016	Yes
1571	22546	Ingrams	1/15/2016	No
1591	22544	Sutherland	1/26/2016	Yes
1601	22542	Diaz	2/2/2016	No
1620	22546	Engram	3/7/2016	No
1638	22560	Lewis	3/11/2016	Yes

inconsistent data

© 2014 Cengage Learning

• **Determine the properties of each field.** You need to identify the **properties**, or characteristics, of each field so that the DBMS knows how to store, display, and process the field values. These properties include the field's name, data type, maximum number of characters or digits, description, valid values, and other field characteristics. You will learn more about field properties later in this tutorial.

The Billing and Patient tables you need to create will contain the fields shown in Figure 2-2. Before creating these new tables in the Chatham database, you first need to learn some guidelines for setting field properties.

Guidelines for Setting Field Properties

As just noted, the last step of database design is to determine which values to assign to the properties, such as the name and data type, of each field. When you select or enter a value for a property, you **set** the property. Access has rules for naming fields and objects, assigning data types, and setting other field properties.

Naming Fields and Objects

You must name each field, table, and other object in an Access database. Access stores these items in the database, using the names you supply. It's best to choose a field or object name that describes the purpose or contents of the field or object so that later you can easily remember what the name represents. For example, the three tables in the Chatham database are named Visit, Billing, and Patient because these names suggest their contents. Note that a table or query name must be unique within a database. A field name must be unique within a table, but it can be used again in another table.

Assigning Field Data Types

Each field must have a data type, which is either assigned automatically by Access or specifically by the table designer. The data type determines what field values you can enter for the field and what other properties the field will have. For example, the Billing table will include an InvoiceDate field, which will store date values, so you will assign the Date/Time data type to this field. Then Access will allow you to enter and manipulate only dates or times as values in the InvoiceDate field.

Figure 2-4 lists the most commonly used data types in Access, describes the field values allowed for each data type, explains when you should use each data type, and indicates the field size of each data type. You can find more complete information about all available data types in Access Help.

Figure 2-4	Common data types

Data Type	Description	Field Size
Short Text	Allows field values containing letters, digits, spaces, and special characters. Use for names, addresses, descriptions, and fields containing digits that are *not used in calculations*.	0 to 255 characters; default is 255
Long Text	Allows field values containing letters, digits, spaces, and special characters. Use for long comments and explanations.	1 to 65,535 characters; exact size is determined by entry
Number	Allows positive and negative numbers as field values. A number can contain digits, a decimal point, commas, a plus sign, and a minus sign. Use for fields that will be used in calculations, except those involving money.	1 to 15 digits
Date/Time	Allows field values containing valid dates and times from January 1, 100 to December 31, 9999. Dates can be entered in month/day/year format, several other date formats, or a variety of time formats, such as 10:35 PM. You can perform calculations on dates and times, and you can sort them. For example, you can determine the number of days between two dates.	8 bytes
Currency	Allows field values similar to those for the Number data type, but is used for storing monetary values. Unlike calculations with Number data type decimal values, calculations performed with the Currency data type are not subject to round-off error.	Accurate to 15 digits on the left side of the decimal point and to 4 digits on the right side
AutoNumber	Consists of integer values created automatically by Access each time you create a new record. You can specify sequential numbering or random numbering, which guarantees a unique field value, so that such a field can serve as a table's primary key.	9 digits
Yes/No	Limits field values to yes and no, on and off, or true and false. Use for fields that indicate the presence or absence of a condition, such as whether an order has been filled or whether an invoice has been paid.	1 character
Hyperlink	Consists of text used as a hyperlink address, which can have up to four parts: the text that appears in a field or control; the path to a file or page; a location within the file or page; and text displayed as a ScreenTip.	Up to 65,535 characters total for the four parts of the hyperlink

© 2014 Cengage Learning

Setting Field Sizes

The **Field Size property** defines a field value's maximum storage size for Short Text, Number, and AutoNumber fields only. The other data types have no Field Size property because their storage size is either a fixed, predetermined amount or is determined automatically by the field value itself, as shown in Figure 2-4. A Short Text field has a default field size of 255 characters; you can also set its field size by entering a number from 0 to 255. For example, the FirstName and LastName fields in the Patient table will be Short Text fields with sizes of 20 characters and 25 characters, respectively. These field sizes will accommodate the values that will be entered in each of these fields.

PROSKILLS

Decision Making: Specifying the Field Size Property for Number Fields

When you use the Number data type to define a field, you need to decide what the Field Size setting should be for the field. You should set the Field Size property based on the largest value that you expect to store in that field. Access processes smaller data sizes faster, using less memory, so you can optimize your database's performance and its storage space by selecting the correct field size for each field. Field Size property settings for Number fields are as follows:

- **Byte**: Stores whole numbers (numbers with no fractions) from 0 to 255 in one byte
- **Integer**: Stores whole numbers from –32,768 to 32,767 in two bytes
- **Long Integer** (default): Stores whole numbers from –2,147,483,648 to 2,147,483,647 in four bytes
- **Single**: Stores positive and negative numbers to precisely seven decimal places in four bytes
- **Double**: Stores positive and negative numbers to precisely 15 decimal places in eight bytes
- **Replication ID**: Establishes a unique identifier for replication of tables, records, and other objects in databases created using Access 2003 and earlier versions in 16 bytes
- **Decimal**: Stores positive and negative numbers to precisely 28 decimal places in 12 bytes

Choosing an appropriate field size is important to optimize efficiency. For example, it would be wasteful to use the Long Integer field size for a Number field that will store only whole numbers ranging from 0 to 255 because the Long Integer field size uses four bytes of storage space. A better choice would be the Byte field size, which uses one byte of storage space to store the same values. By first gathering and analyzing information about the number values that will be stored in a Number field, you can make the best decision for the field's Field Size property and ensure the most efficient user experience for the database.

Setting the Caption Property for Fields

The **Caption property** for a field specifies how the field name is displayed in database objects, including table and query datasheets, forms, and reports. If you don't set the Caption property, Access displays the field name as the column heading or label for a field. For example, field names such as InvoiceAmt and InvoiceDate in the Billing table can be difficult to read. Setting the Caption property for these fields to "Invoice Amt" and "Invoice Date" would make it easier for users to read the field names and work with the database.

INSIGHT

Setting the Caption Property vs. Naming Fields

Although Access allows you to include spaces in field names, this practice is not recommended because the spaces cause problems when you try to perform more complex tasks with the data in your database. Setting the Caption property allows you to follow best practices for naming fields, such as not including spaces in field names, while still providing users with more readable field names in datasheets, forms, and reports.

In Tutorial 1, you created the Chatham database file and, within that file, you created the Visit table working in Datasheet view. According to her plan for the Chatham database, Cindi also wants to track information about the invoices the clinic sends to its patients. Next, you'll create the Billing table for Cindi—this time, working in Design view.

Creating a Table in Design View

Creating a table in Design view involves entering the field names and defining the properties for the fields, specifying a primary key for the table, and then saving the table structure. Cindi documented the design for the new Billing table by listing each field's name and data type; each field's size and description (if applicable); and any other properties to be set for each field. See Figure 2-5.

Figure 2-5 | **Design for the Billing table**

Field Name	Data Type	Field Size	Description	Other
InvoiceNum	Short Text	5	Primary key	Caption = Invoice Num
VisitID	Short Text	4	Foreign key	Caption = Visit ID
InvoiceAmt	Currency			Format = Currency
				Decimal Places = 2
				Caption = Invoice Amt
InvoiceDate	Date/Time			Format = mm/dd/yyyy
				Caption = Invoice Date
InvoicePaid	Yes/No			Caption = Invoice Paid

© 2014 Cengage Learning

You'll use Cindi's design as a guide for creating the Billing table in the Chatham database.

To begin creating the Billing table:

1. Start Access and open the **Chatham** database you created in Tutorial 1.

   Trouble? If the security warning is displayed below the ribbon, click the Enable Content button.

2. If the Navigation Pane is open, click the **Shutter Bar Open/Close Button** « to close it.

3. On the ribbon, click the **CREATE** tab.

4. In the Tables group, click the **Table Design** button. A new table named Table1 opens in Design view. Refer to the Session 2.1 Visual Overview for a complete description of the Table window in Design view.

Defining Fields

When you first create a table in Design view, the insertion point is located in the first row's Field Name box, ready for you to begin defining the first field in the table. You enter values for the Field Name, Data Type, and Description field properties, and then select values for all other field properties in the Field Properties pane. These other properties will appear when you move to the first row's Data Type box.

REFERENCE

Defining a Field in Design View

- In the Field Name box, type the name for the field, and then press the Tab key.
- Accept the default Short Text data type, or click the arrow and select a different data type for the field. Press the Tab key.
- Enter an optional description for the field, if necessary.
- Use the Field Properties pane to type or select other field properties, as appropriate.

The first field you need to define is the InvoiceNum field. This field will be the primary key for the Billing table. Each invoice at Chatham Community Health Services is assigned a specific five-digit number. Although the InvoiceNum field will contain these number values, the numbers will never be used in calculations; therefore, you'll assign the Short Text data type to this field. Any time a field contains number values that will not be used in calculations—such as phone numbers, zip codes, and so on—you should use the Short Text data type instead of the Number data type.

To define the InvoiceNum field:

TIP

You can also press the Enter key to move from one property to the next in the Table Design grid.

1. Type **InvoiceNum** in the first row's Field Name box, and then press the **Tab** key to advance to the Data Type box. The default data type, Short Text, appears highlighted in the Data Type box, which now also contains an arrow, and the field properties for a Short Text field appear in the Field Properties pane. See Figure 2-6.

Figure 2-6 Table window after entering the first field name

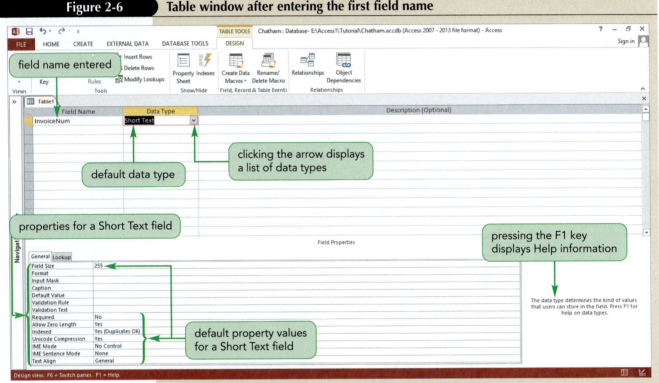

Notice that the right side of the Field Properties pane now provides an explanation for the current property, Data Type.

Trouble? If you make a typing error, you can correct it by clicking to position the insertion point, and then using either the Backspace key to delete characters to the left of the insertion point or the Delete key to delete characters to the right of the insertion point. Then type the correct text.

Because the InvoiceNum field values will not be used in calculations, you will accept the default Short Text data type for the field.

2. Press the **Tab** key to accept Short Text as the data type and to advance to the Description (Optional) box.

Next you'll enter the Description property value as "Primary key." The value you enter for the Description property will appear on the status bar when you view the table datasheet. Note that specifying "Primary key" for the Description property does *not* establish the current field as the primary key; you use a button on the ribbon to specify the primary key in Design view, which you will do later in this session.

3. Type **Primary key** in the Description (Optional) box.

   Notice the Field Size property for the field. The default setting of 255 for Short Text fields is displayed. You need to change this number to 5 because all invoice numbers at Chatham Community Health Services contain only five digits.

4. Double-click the number **255** in the Field Size property box to select it, and then type **5**.

   Finally, you need to set the Caption property for the field so that its name appears with a space, as "Invoice Num."

5. Click the **Caption** property box, and then type **Invoice Num**. The definition of the first field is complete. See Figure 2-7.

| Figure 2-7 | InvoiceNum field defined |

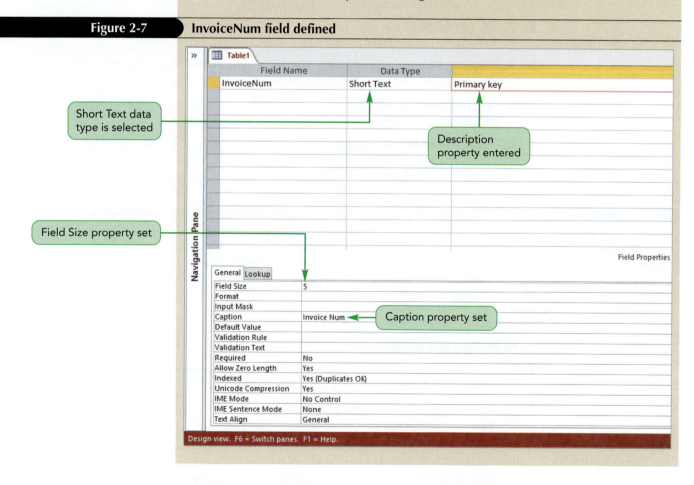

Short Text data type is selected

Description property entered

Field Size property set

Caption property set

Cindi's Billing table design (Figure 2-5) shows VisitID as the second field. Because Cindi and other staff members need to relate information about invoices to the visit data in the Visit table, the Billing table must include the VisitID field, which is the Visit table's primary key. Recall that when you include the primary key from one table as a field in a second table to connect the two tables, the field is a foreign key in the second table. The field must be defined in the same way in both tables—that is, the field properties, including field size and data type, must match exactly.

Next, you will define VisitID as a Short Text field with a field size of 4. Later in this session, you'll change the Field Size property for the VisitID field in the Visit table to 4 so that the field definition is the same in both tables.

To define the VisitID field:

▶ 1. In the Table Design grid, click the second row's Field Name box, type **VisitID** in the box, and then press the **Tab** key to advance to the Data Type box.

▶ 2. Press the **Tab** key to accept Short Text as the field's data type. Because the VisitID field is a foreign key to the Visit table, you'll enter "Foreign key" in the Description (Optional) box to help users of the database understand the purpose of this field.

▶ 3. Type **Foreign key** in the Description (Optional) box. Next, you'll change the Field Size property to 4.

▶ 4. Press the **F6** key to move to the Field Properties pane. The current entry for the Field Size property, 255, is highlighted.

▶ 5. Type **4** to set the Field Size property. Finally, you need to set the Caption property for this field.

▶ 6. Press the **Tab** key until the insertion point is in the Caption box, and then type **Visit ID** (be sure to include a space between the two words). You have completed the definition of the second field.

TIP

The quickest way to move back to the Table Design grid is to use the mouse.

The third field in the Billing table is the InvoiceAmt field, which will display the dollar amount of each invoice the clinic sends to its patients. Cindi wants the values to appear with two decimal places because invoice amounts include cents. She also wants the values to include dollar signs, so that the values will be formatted as currency when they are printed in bills sent to patients. The Currency data type is the appropriate choice for this field.

To define the InvoiceAmt field:

▶ 1. Click the third row's Field Name box, type **InvoiceAmt** in the box, and then press the **Tab** key to advance to the Data Type box.

▶ 2. Click the **Data Type** arrow, click **Currency** in the list, and then press the **Tab** key to advance to the Description (Optional) box.

According to Cindi's design (Figure 2-5), you do not need to enter a description for this field. If you've assigned a descriptive field name and the field does not fulfill a special function (such as primary key), you usually do not enter a value for the optional Description property. InvoiceAmt is a field that does not require a value for its Description property.

Cindi wants the InvoiceAmt field values to be displayed with two decimal places. The **Decimal Places property** specifies the number of decimal places that are displayed to the right of the decimal point.

TIP

You can display the arrow and the list simultaneously by clicking the right side of a box.

3. In the Field Properties pane, click the **Decimal Places** box to position the insertion point there. An arrow appears on the right side of the Decimal Places box. When you position the insertion point or select text in many boxes, Access displays an arrow, which you can click to display a list with options.

4. Click the **Decimal Places** arrow, and then click **2** in the list to specify two decimal places for the InvoiceAmt field values.

5. Press the **Tab** key until the insertion point is in the Caption box, and then type **Invoice Amt**. The definition of the third field is now complete. See Figure 2-8.

Figure 2-8   **Table window after defining the first three fields**

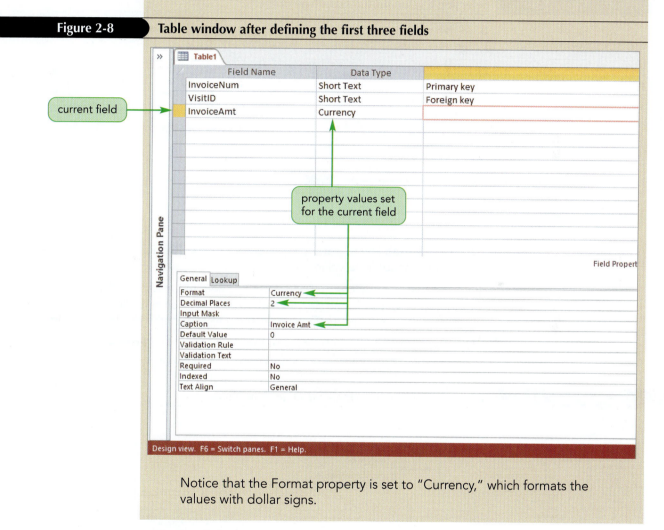

Notice that the Format property is set to "Currency," which formats the values with dollar signs.

The fourth field in the Billing table is the InvoiceDate field. This field will contain the dates on which invoices are generated for the clinic's patients. You'll define the InvoiceDate field using the Date/Time data type. Also, according to Cindi's design (Figure 2-5), the date values should be displayed in the format mm/dd/yyyy, which is a two-digit month, a two-digit day, and a four-digit year.

To define the InvoiceDate field:

▸ **1.** Click the fourth row's Field Name box, type **InvoiceDate**, and then press the **Tab** key to advance to the Data Type box.

You can select a value from the Data Type list as you did for the InvoiceAmt field. Alternately, you can type the property value in the box or type just the first character of the property value.

▸ **2.** Type **d**. The value in the fourth row's Data Type box changes to "date/Time," with the letters "ate/Time" highlighted. See Figure 2-9.

Figure 2-9 Selecting a value for the Data Type property

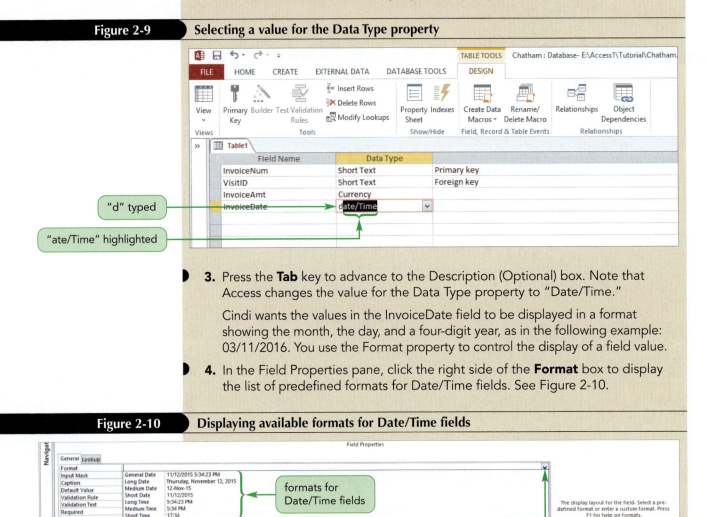

▸ **3.** Press the **Tab** key to advance to the Description (Optional) box. Note that Access changes the value for the Data Type property to "Date/Time."

Cindi wants the values in the InvoiceDate field to be displayed in a format showing the month, the day, and a four-digit year, as in the following example: 03/11/2016. You use the Format property to control the display of a field value.

▸ **4.** In the Field Properties pane, click the right side of the **Format** box to display the list of predefined formats for Date/Time fields. See Figure 2-10.

Figure 2-10 Displaying available formats for Date/Time fields

Trouble? If you see an arrow instead of a list of predefined formats, click the arrow to display the list.

As noted in the right side of the Field Properties pane, you can either choose a predefined format or enter a custom format. Even though the Short Date format seems to match the format Cindi wants, it displays only one digit for months that contain only one digit. For example, it would display the month of March with only the digit "3"—as in 3/11/2016—instead of displaying the month with two digits, as in 03/11/2016.

Because none of the predefined formats matches the exact layout Cindi wants for the InvoiceDate values, you need to create a custom date format. Figure 2-11 shows some of the symbols available for custom date and time formats.

| Figure 2-11 | Symbols for some custom date formats |

Symbol	Description
/	date separator
d	day of the month in one or two numeric digits, as needed (1 to 31)
dd	day of the month in two numeric digits (01 to 31)
ddd	first three letters of the weekday (Sun to Sat)
dddd	full name of the weekday (Sunday to Saturday)
w	day of the week (1 to 7)
ww	week of the year (1 to 53)
m	month of the year in one or two numeric digits, as needed (1 to 12)
mm	month of the year in two numeric digits (01 to 12)
mmm	first three letters of the month (Jan to Dec)
mmmm	full name of the month (January to December)
yy	last two digits of the year (01 to 99)
yyyy	full year (0100 to 9999)

© 2014 Cengage Learning

Cindi wants the dates to be displayed with a two-digit month (mm), a two-digit day (dd), and a four-digit year (yyyy). You'll enter this custom format now.

5. Click the **Format** arrow to close the list of predefined formats, and then type **mm/dd/yyyy** in the Format box.

6. Press the **Tab** key until the insertion point is in the Caption box, and then type **Invoice Date**. See Figure 2-12.

Figure 2-12 **Specifying the custom date format**

The fifth, and final, field to be defined in the Billing table is InvoicePaid. This field will be a Yes/No field to indicate the payment status of each invoice record stored in the Billing table. Recall that the Yes/No data type is used to define fields that store true/false, yes/no, and on/off field values. When you create a Yes/No field in a table, the default Format property is set to Yes/No.

To define the InvoicePaid field:

1. Click the fifth row's Field Name box, type **InvoicePaid**, and then press the **Tab** key to advance to the Data Type box.

2. Type **y**. Access completes the data type as "yes/No."

3. Press the **Tab** key to select the Yes/No data type and move to the Description (Optional) box. In the Field Properties pane, note that the default format of "Yes/No" is selected, so you do not have to change this property.

4. In the Field Properties pane, click the Caption box, and then type **Invoice Paid**.

You've finished defining the fields for the Billing table. Next, you need to specify the primary key for the table.

Specifying the Primary Key

As you learned earlier, the primary key for a table uniquely identifies each record in the table.

Specifying a Primary Key in Design View

- Display the table in Design view.
- Click in the row for the field you've chosen to be the primary key to make it the active field. If the primary key will consist of two or more fields, click the row selector for the first field, press and hold down the Ctrl key, and then click the row selector for each additional primary key field.
- In the Tools group on the DESIGN tab, click the Primary Key button.

According to Cindi's design, you need to specify InvoiceNum as the primary key for the Billing table. You can do so while the table is in Design view.

To specify InvoiceNum as the primary key:

1. Click in the row for the InvoiceNum field to make it the current field.

2. In the Tools group on the DESIGN tab, click the **Primary Key** button. The Primary Key button in the Tools group is now highlighted, and a key symbol appears in the row selector for the first row, indicating that the InvoiceNum field is the table's primary key. See Figure 2-13.

TIP

This button is a toggle; you can click it to remove the key symbol.

Figure 2-13   InvoiceNum field selected as the primary key

Primary Key button

key symbol indicates the table's primary key

Field Name	Data Type	
InvoiceNum	Short Text	Primary key
VisitID	Short Text	Foreign key
InvoiceAmt	Currency	
InvoiceDate	Date/Time	
InvoicePaid	Yes/No	

INSIGHT

Understanding the Importance of the Primary Key

Although Access does not require a table to have a primary key, including a primary key offers several advantages:

- A primary key uniquely identifies each record in a table.
- Access does not allow duplicate values in the primary key field. For example, if a record already exists in the Visit table with a VisitID value of 1550, Access prevents you from adding another record with this same value in the VisitID field. Preventing duplicate values ensures the uniqueness of the primary key field.
- When a primary key has been specified, Access forces you to enter a value for the primary key field in every record in the table. This is known as **entity integrity**. If you do not enter a value for a field, you have actually given the field a **null value**. You cannot give a null value to the primary key field because entity integrity prevents Access from accepting and processing that record.
- You can enter records in any order, but Access displays them by default in order of the primary key's field values. If you enter records in no specific order, you are ensured that you will later be able to work with them in a more meaningful, primary key sequence.
- Access responds faster to your requests for specific records based on the primary key.

Saving the Table Structure

The last step in creating a table is to name the table and save the table's structure. When you save a table structure, the table is stored in the database file (in this case, the Chatham database file). Once the table is saved, you can enter data into it. According to Cindi's plan, you need to save the table you've defined as "Billing."

To name and save the Billing table:

1. On the Quick Access Toolbar, click the **Save** button 🖫. The Save As dialog box opens.

2. Type **Billing** in the Table Name box, and then press the **Enter** key. Access saves the Billing table in the Chatham database. Notice that the tab for the table now displays the name "Billing" instead of "Table1."

Modifying the Structure of an Access Table

Even a well-designed table might need to be modified. Some changes that you can make to a table's structure in Design view include changing the order of fields and adding new fields.

After meeting with her assistant, Kelly Schwarz, and reviewing the structure of the Billing table, Cindi has changes she wants you to make to the table. First, she wants the InvoiceAmt field to be moved so that it appears right before the InvoicePaid field. Then, she wants you to add a new Short Text field named InvoiceItem to the table to include information about what the invoice is for, such as office visits, lab work, and so on. Cindi would like the InvoiceItem field to be inserted between the InvoiceDate and InvoiceAmt fields.

Moving a Field in Design View

To move a field, you use the mouse to drag it to a new location in the Table Design grid. Although you can move a field in Datasheet view by dragging its column heading to a new location, doing so rearranges only the *display* of the table's fields; the table structure is not changed. To move a field permanently, you must move the field in Design view.

Next, you'll move the InvoiceAmt field so that it is before the InvoicePaid field in the Billing table.

To move the InvoiceAmt field:

1. Position the pointer on the row selector for the InvoiceAmt field until the pointer changes to a ➡ shape.

2. Click the **row selector** to select the entire InvoiceAmt row.

3. Place the pointer on the row selector for the InvoiceAmt field until the pointer changes to ⍼, and then click and drag to the row selector for the InvoicePaid field. Notice that as you drag, the pointer changes to ⍼. See Figure 2-14.

Figure 2-14   Moving the InvoiceAmt field in the table structure

4. Release the mouse button. The InvoiceAmt field now appears between the InvoiceDate and InvoicePaid fields in the table structure.

    Trouble? If the InvoiceAmt field did not move, repeat Steps 1 through 4, making sure you hold down the mouse button during the drag operation.

Adding a Field in Design View

To add a new field between existing fields, you must insert a row. You begin by selecting the row below where you want the new field to be inserted.

REFERENCE

Adding a Field Between Two Existing Fields

- In the Table window in Design view, select the row below where you want the new field to be inserted.
- In the Tools group on the DESIGN tab, click the Insert Rows button.
- Define the new field by entering the field name, data type, optional description, and any property specifications.

Next, you need to add the InvoiceItem field to the Billing table structure between the InvoiceAmt and InvoicePaid fields.

To add the InvoiceItem field to the Billing table:

1. Click the **InvoicePaid** Field Name box. You need to establish this field as the current field so that the row for the new record will be inserted above this field.

2. In the Tools group on the DESIGN tab, click the **Insert Rows** button. Access adds a new, blank row between the InvoiceAmt and InvoicePaid fields. The insertion point is positioned in the Field Name box for the new row, ready for you to type the name for the new field. See Figure 2-15.

Figure 2-15	Table structure after inserting a row

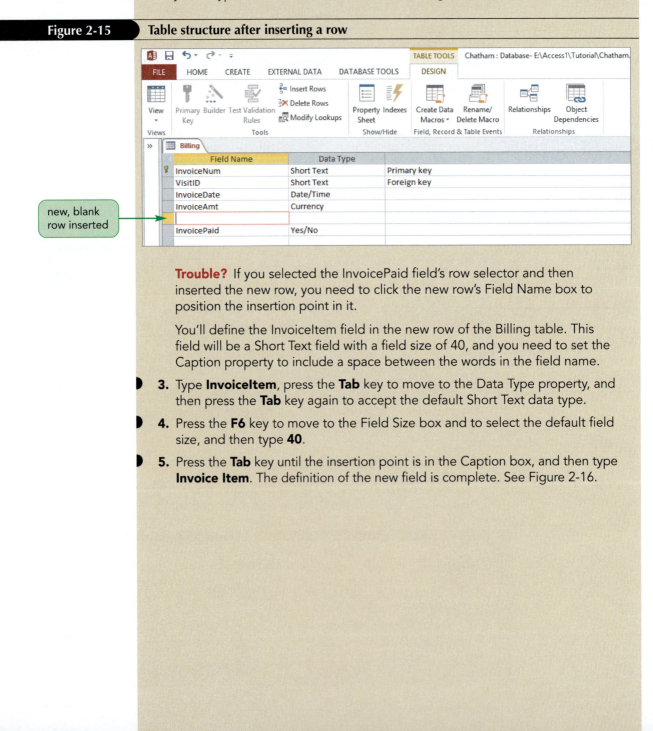

Trouble? If you selected the InvoicePaid field's row selector and then inserted the new row, you need to click the new row's Field Name box to position the insertion point in it.

You'll define the InvoiceItem field in the new row of the Billing table. This field will be a Short Text field with a field size of 40, and you need to set the Caption property to include a space between the words in the field name.

3. Type **InvoiceItem**, press the **Tab** key to move to the Data Type property, and then press the **Tab** key again to accept the default Short Text data type.

4. Press the **F6** key to move to the Field Size box and to select the default field size, and then type **40**.

5. Press the **Tab** key until the insertion point is in the Caption box, and then type **Invoice Item**. The definition of the new field is complete. See Figure 2-16.

Figure 2-16	InvoiceItem field added to the Billing table

new field →

	Field Name	Data Type	
🔑	InvoiceNum	Short Text	Primary key
	VisitID	Short Text	Foreign key
	InvoiceDate	Date/Time	
	InvoiceAmt	Currency	
	InvoiceItem	Short Text	
	InvoicePaid	Yes/No	

Field Size property set to 40

Field Properties

General Lookup

Field Size	40
Format	
Input Mask	
Caption	Invoice Item
Default Value	
Validation Rule	
Validation Text	
Required	No
Allow Zero Length	Yes
Indexed	No
Unicode Compression	Yes
IME Mode	No Control
IME Sentence Mode	None
Text Align	General

Caption property set

Design view. F6 = Switch panes. F1 = Help.

6. On the Quick Access Toolbar, click the **Save** button 💾 to save the changes to the Billing table structure.

7. Click the **Close 'Billing'** button ✖ on the object tab to close the Billing table.

Modifying Field Properties

With the Billing table design complete, you can now go back and modify the properties of the fields in the Visit table you created in Tutorial 1, as necessary. You can make some changes to properties in Datasheet view; for others, you'll work in Design view.

Changing the Format Property in Datasheet View

The Formatting group on the FIELDS tab in Datasheet view allows you to modify some formatting for certain field types. When you format a field, you change the way data is displayed, but not the actual values stored in the table.

Next, you'll check the properties of the VisitDate field in the Visit table to see if any changes are needed to improve the display of the date values.

To modify the VisitDate field's Format property:

1. On the Navigation Pane, click the **Shutter Bar Open/Close Button** ≫ to open the pane. Notice that the Billing table is listed above the Visit table in the Tables section. By default, objects are listed in the pane in alphabetical order.

2. Double-click **Visit** to open the Visit table in Datasheet view.

3. On the Navigation Pane, click the **Shutter Bar Open/Close Button** ≪ to close the pane. See Figure 2-17.

Figure 2-17 **Visit table datasheet**

Short Text field values are left-aligned

Date/Time field values are right-aligned

check boxes for Yes/No field are centered

Notice that the values in the three Short Text fields—VisitID, PatientID, and Reason—appear left-aligned within their boxes, and the values in the Date/Time field (VisitDate) appear right-aligned. In Access, values for Short Text fields are left-aligned, and values for Number, Date/Time, and Currency fields are right-aligned. The WalkIn field is a Yes/No field, so its values appear in check boxes that are centered within the column.

4. On the ribbon, click the **FIELDS** tab.

5. Click the first field value in the VisitDate column. The Data Type option shows that this field is a Date/Time field.

   By default, Access assigns the General Date format to Date/Time fields. Note the Format option in the Formatting group; this is the same as the Format property in the Field Properties pane in Design view. Even though the Format box is empty, the VisitDate field has the General Date format applied to it. The General Date format includes settings for date or time values, or a combination of date and time values. However, Cindi wants *only date values* to be displayed in the VisitDate field, so she asks you to specify the Short Date format for the field.

6. In the Formatting group, click the **Format arrow**, and then click **Short Date**. See Figure 2-18.

| Figure 2-18 | VisitDate field after modifying the format |

date picker

field values appear unchanged, but the format is applied

Short Date format specified

TIP

When working with date values, you can type dates directly or click the date picker shown in Figure 2-18 to select a date from an interactive calendar.

Although no change is apparent in the worksheet—the VisitDate field values already appear with the Short Date setting (for example, 11/9/2015), as part of the default General Date format—the field now has the Short Date format applied to it. This ensures that only date field values, and not time or date/time values, are allowed in the field.

Changing Properties in Design View

Recall that each of the Short Text fields in the Visit table—VisitID, PatientID, and Reason—still has the default field size of 255, which is too large for the data contained in these fields. Also, the VisitID and PatientID fields need descriptions to identify them as the primary and foreign keys, respectively, in the table. Finally, each of these fields needs a caption either to include a space between the words in the field name or to make the name more descriptive. You can make all of these property changes more easily in Design view.

To modify the Field Size, Description, and Caption field properties:

TIP

You can also click the Design View button in the far right of the status bar to switch to Design view.

1. In the Views group on the FIELDS tab, click the **View** button. The table is displayed in Design view with the VisitID field selected. You need to enter a Description property value for this field, the primary key in the table, and change its Field Size property to 4 because each visit number at Chatham Community Health Services consists of four digits.

2. Press the **Tab** key until the insertion point is in the Description (Optional) box, and then type **Primary key**.

3. Press the **F6** key to move to and select the default setting of 255 for the Field Size property, and then type **4**. Next you need to set the Caption property for this field.

4. Press the **Tab** key until the insertion point is in the Caption box, and then type **Visit ID**.

   Next you need to enter a Description property value for the PatientID field, a foreign key in the table, and set its Field Size property to 5 because each PatientID number at Chatham Community Health Services consists of five digits. You also need to set this field's Caption property.

5. Click the **Description (Optional)** box for the PatientID field, and then type **Foreign key**.

6. Press the **F6** key, type **5**, press the **Tab** key until the insertion point is in the Caption box, and then type **Patient ID**.

   Next you'll set the Caption property for the VisitDate field.

7. Click the **VisitDate** Field Name box, click the **Caption** box, and then type **Date of Visit**.

   For the Reason field, you will set the Field Size property to 60. This size can accommodate the longer values in the Reason field. You'll also set this field's Caption property to provide a more descriptive name.

8. Click the **Reason** Field Name box, press the **F6** key, type **60**, press the **Tab** key until the insertion point is in the Caption box, and then type **Reason/Diagnosis**.

   Finally, you'll set the Caption property for the WalkIn field.

9. Click the **WalkIn** Field Name box, click the **Caption** box, and then type **Walk-in?** See Figure 2-19.

Figure 2-19   **Visit table after modifying field properties**

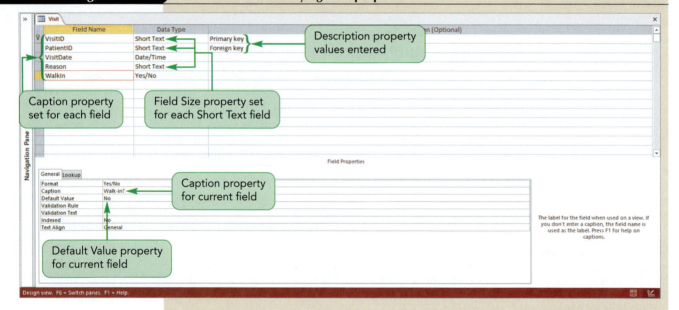

Notice that the WalkIn field's Default Value property is automatically set to "No," which means the check box for this field will be empty for each new record. This is the default for this property for any Yes/No field. You can set the Default Value property for other types of fields to make data entry easier. You'll learn more about setting this property in the next session.

The changes to the Visit table's properties are now complete, so you can save the table and view the results of your changes in Datasheet view.

To save and view the modified Visit table:

1. On the Quick Access Toolbar, click the **Save** button 💾 to save the modified table. A dialog box opens informing you that some data may be lost because you decreased the field sizes. Because all of the values in the VisitID, PatientID, and Reason fields contain the same number of or fewer characters than the new Field Size properties you set for each field, you can ignore this message.

2. Click the **Yes** button.

3. In the Views group on the DESIGN tab, click the **View** button to display the Visit table in Datasheet view. Notice that each column (field) heading now displays the text you specified in the Caption property for that field. See Figure 2-20.

Figure 2-20	Modified Visit table in Datasheet view

column headings display Caption property values

4. Click the **Close 'Visit'** button ☒ on the object tab to close the Visit table.

5. If you are not continuing to Session 2.2, click the **FILE** tab, and then click **Close** in the navigation bar to close the Chatham database.

You have created the Billing table and made modifications to its design. In the next session, you'll add records to the Billing table and create the Patient table in the Chatham database.

Session 2.1 Quick Check

REVIEW

1. What guidelines should you follow when designing a database?
2. What is the purpose of the Data Type property for a field?
3. The _____ property specifies how a field's name is displayed in database objects, including table and query datasheets, forms, and reports.
4. For which three types of fields can you assign a field size?
5. The default Field Size property setting for a Short Text field is _____.
6. In Design view, which key do you press to move from the Table Design grid to the Field Properties pane?
7. List three reasons why you should specify a primary key for an Access table.

Session 2.2 Visual Overview:

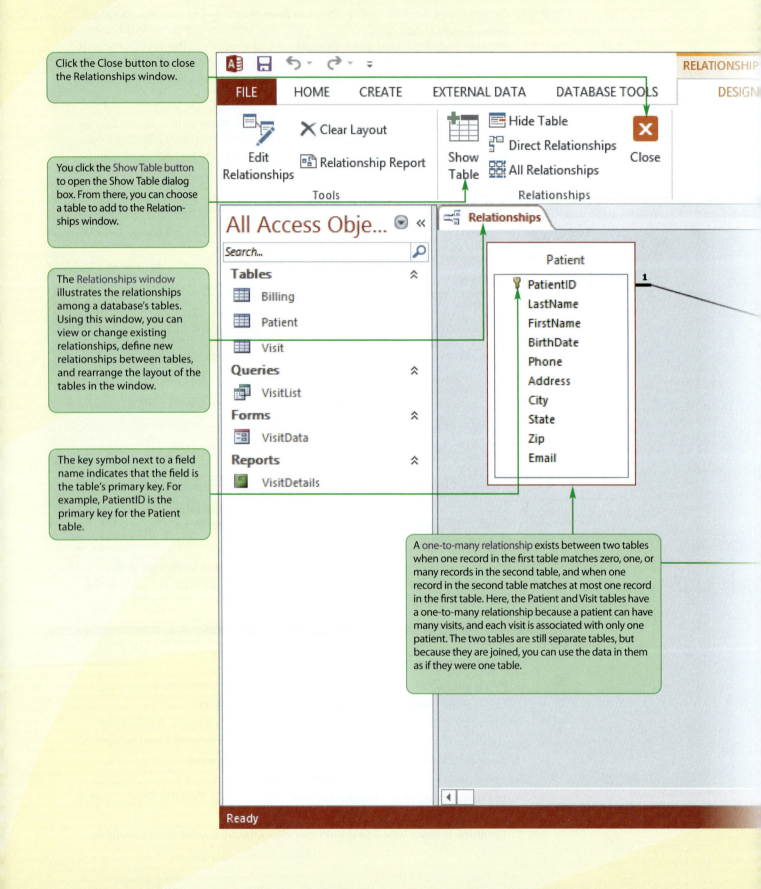

Click the Close button to close the Relationships window.

You click the Show Table button to open the Show Table dialog box. From there, you can choose a table to add to the Relationships window.

The Relationships window illustrates the relationships among a database's tables. Using this window, you can view or change existing relationships, define new relationships between tables, and rearrange the layout of the tables in the window.

The key symbol next to a field name indicates that the field is the table's primary key. For example, PatientID is the primary key for the Patient table.

A one-to-many relationship exists between two tables when one record in the first table matches zero, one, or many records in the second table, and when one record in the second table matches at most one record in the first table. Here, the Patient and Visit tables have a one-to-many relationship because a patient can have many visits, and each visit is associated with only one patient. The two tables are still separate tables, but because they are joined, you can use the data in them as if they were one table.

Understanding Table Relationships

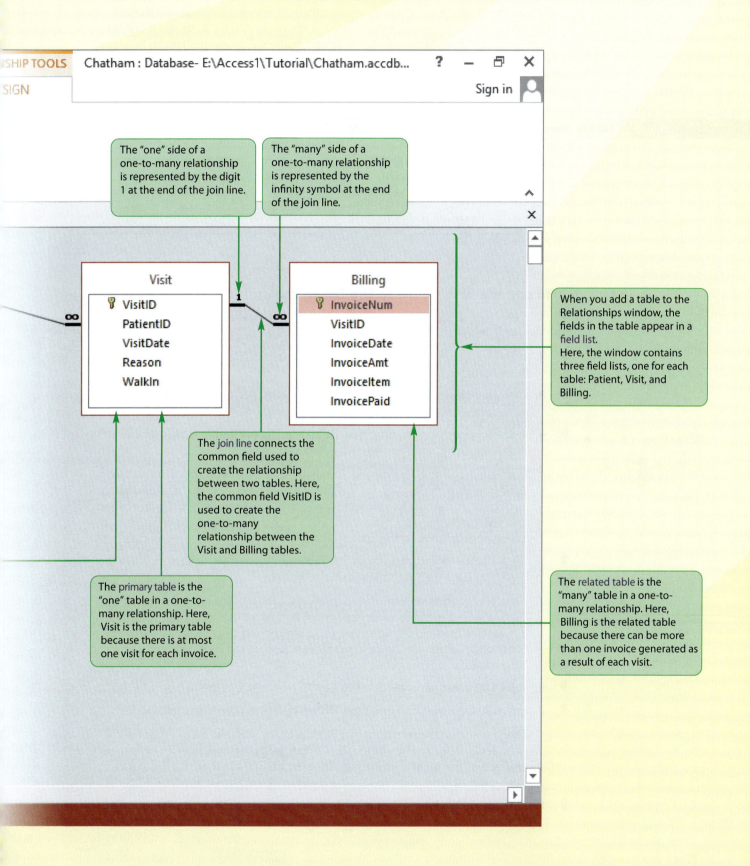

The "one" side of a one-to-many relationship is represented by the digit 1 at the end of the join line.

The "many" side of a one-to-many relationship is represented by the infinity symbol at the end of the join line.

When you add a table to the Relationships window, the fields in the table appear in a field list.
Here, the window contains three field lists, one for each table: Patient, Visit, and Billing.

The join line connects the common field used to create the relationship between two tables. Here, the common field VisitID is used to create the one-to-many relationship between the Visit and Billing tables.

The primary table is the "one" table in a one-to-many relationship. Here, Visit is the primary table because there is at most one visit for each invoice.

The related table is the "many" table in a one-to-many relationship. Here, Billing is the related table because there can be more than one invoice generated as a result of each visit.

Adding Records to a New Table

Before you can begin to define the table relationships illustrated in the Session 2.2 Visual Overview, you need to finish creating the tables in the Chatham database.

The Billing table design is complete. Now, Cindi would like you to add records to the table so it will contain the invoice data for Chatham Community Health Services. As you learned earlier, you add records to a table in Datasheet view by typing the field values in the rows below the column headings for the fields. You'll begin by entering the records shown in Figure 2-21.

Figure 2-21	Records to be added to the Billing table

Invoice Num	Visit ID	Invoice Date	Invoice Amt	Invoice Item	Invoice Paid
35801	1527	11/10/2015	$100.00	Office visit	Yes
35818	1536	11/18/2015	$100.00	Office visit	Yes
35885	1570	01/12/2016	$85.00	Pharmacy	No
35851	1550	12/02/2015	$85.00	Pharmacy	No

© 2014 Cengage Learning

To add the first record to the Billing table:

1. If you took a break after the previous session, make sure the Chatham database is open and the Navigation Pane is open.

2. In the Tables section of the Navigation Pane, double-click **Billing** to open the Billing table in Datasheet view.

3. Close the Navigation Pane, and then use the ✛ pointer to resize columns, as necessary, so that the field names are completely visible.

> Be sure to type the numbers "0" and "1" and *not* the letters "O" and "I" in the field values.

4. In the Invoice Num column, type **35801**, press the **Tab** key, type **1527** in the Visit ID column, and then press the **Tab** key.

   Next you need to enter the invoice date. Recall that you specified a custom date format, mm/dd/yyyy, for the InvoiceDate field. You do not need to type each digit; for example, you can type just "3" instead of "03" for the month, and you can type "16" instead of "2016" for the year. Access will display the full value according to the custom date format.

5. Type **11/10/15** and then press the **Tab** key. Notice that Access displays the date "11/10/2015" in the Invoice Date column.

   Next you need to enter the invoice amount for the first record. This is a Currency field with the Currency format and two decimal places specified. Because of the field's properties, you do not need to type the dollar sign, comma, or zeroes for the decimal places; Access will display these items automatically for you.

6. Type **100** and then press the **Tab** key. Access displays the value as "$100.00."

7. In the Invoice Item column, type **Office visit** and then press the **Tab** key.

   The last field in the table, InvoicePaid, is a Yes/No field. Recall that the default value for any Yes/No field is "No"; therefore, the check box is initially empty. For the record you are entering in the Billing table, the invoice has been paid, so you need to insert a checkmark in the check box.

8. Press the **spacebar** to insert a checkmark, and then press the **Tab** key. The values for the first record are entered. See Figure 2-22.

Figure 2-22   **First record entered in the Billing table**

field value displayed in the Currency format with two decimal places

field value displayed according to the custom date format

checkmark indicates a "Yes" value for the field

Now you can add the remaining three records. As you do, you'll learn a keyboard shortcut for inserting the value from the same field in the previous record. A **keyboard shortcut** is a key or combination of keys you press to complete an action more efficiently.

To add the next three records to the Billing table:

1. Refer to Figure 2-21 and enter the values in the second record's Invoice Num, Visit ID, and Invoice Date columns.

   Notice that the value in the second record's Invoice Amt column is $100.00. This value is the exact same value as in the first record. You can quickly insert the value from the same column in the previous record using the **Ctrl + '** (apostrophe) keyboard shortcut. To use this shortcut, you press and hold down the Ctrl key, press the ' key once, and then release both keys. (The plus sign in the keyboard shortcut indicates you're pressing two keys at once; you do not press the + key.)

2. With the insertion point in the Invoice Amt column, press the **Ctrl + '** keys. Access inserts the value "$100.00" in the Invoice Amt column for the second record.

3. Press the **Tab** key to move to the Invoice Item column. Again, the value you need to enter in this column—Office visit—is the same as the value for this column in the previous record. So, you can use the keyboard shortcut again.

4. With the insertion point in the Invoice Item column, press the **Ctrl + '** keys. Access inserts the value "Office visit" in the Invoice Item column for the second record.

5. Press the **Tab** key to move to the Invoice Paid column, press the **spacebar** to insert a checkmark in the check box, and then press the **Tab** key. The second record is entered in the Billing table.

6. Refer to Figure 2-21 to enter the values for the third and fourth records, using the Ctrl + ' keys to enter the values in the fourth record's Invoice Amt and Invoice Item columns. Also, for both records, the invoices have not been paid. Therefore, be sure to press the Tab key to leave the Invoice Paid column values unchecked (signifying "No"). Your table should look like the one in Figure 2-23.

| Figure 2-23 | Billing table with four records added |

To finish entering records in the Billing table, you'll use a method that allows you to import the data.

Importing Data from an Excel Worksheet

Often, the data you want to add to an Access table exists in another file, such as a Word document or an Excel workbook. You can bring the data from other files into Access in different ways. For example, you can copy and paste the data from an open file, or you can **import** the data, which is a process that allows you to copy the data from a source without having to open the source file.

Cindi had been using Excel to track invoice data for Chatham Community Health Services and already created a worksheet, named "Invoices," containing this data. You'll import this Excel worksheet into your Billing table to complete the entry of data in the table. To use the import method, the columns in the Excel worksheet must match the names and data types of the fields in the Access table.

INSIGHT

Caption Property Values and the Import Process

When you import data from an Excel worksheet into an Access table, any Caption property values set for the fields in the table are not considered in the import process. For example, your Access table could have fields such as InvoiceDate and InvoiceAmt with Caption property values of Invoice Date and Invoice Amt, respectively. If the Excel worksheet you are importing has the column headings Invoice Date and Invoice Amt, you might think that the data matches and you can proceed with the import. However, if the underlying field names in the Access table do not match the Excel worksheet column headings exactly, the import process will fail. It's a good idea to double-check to make sure that the actual Access field names—and not just the column headings displayed in a table datasheet (as specified by the Caption property)—match the Excel worksheet column headings. If there are differences, you can change the column headings in the Excel worksheet to match the Access table field names before you import the data, ensuring that the process will work correctly.

The Invoices worksheet contains the following columns: InvoiceNum, VisitID, InvoiceDate, InvoiceAmt, InvoiceItem, and InvoicePaid. These column headings match the field names in the Billing table exactly, so you can import the data. Before you import data into a table, you need to close the table.

To import the Invoices worksheet into the Billing table:

1. Click the **Close 'Billing'** button ✕ on the object tab to close the Billing table. A dialog box opens asking if you want to save the changes to the table layout. This dialog box opens because you resized the table columns.

2. Click the **Yes** button in the dialog box.

3. On the ribbon, click the **EXTERNAL DATA** tab.

4. In the Import & Link group on the EXTERNAL DATA tab, click the **Excel** button. The Get External Data - Excel Spreadsheet dialog box opens. See Figure 2-24.

Figure 2-24   Get External Data - Excel Spreadsheet dialog box

click to find the Excel workbook containing the data you want to import

you might see a different path here

option for adding records to an existing table

Trouble? If the Export - Excel Spreadsheet dialog box opens instead of the dialog box shown in Figure 2-24, you probably clicked the Excel button in the Export group. If so, click the Cancel button in the dialog box, and then repeat Step 4, being sure to click the Excel button in the Import & Link group.

The dialog box provides options for importing the entire worksheet as a new table in the current database, adding the data from the worksheet to an existing table, or linking the data in the worksheet to the table. You need to add, or append, the worksheet data to the Billing table.

5. Click the **Browse** button. The File Open dialog box opens. The Excel workbook file is named "Invoices" and is located in the Access1 ▸ Tutorial folder provided with your Data Files.

6. Navigate to the **Access1 ▸ Tutorial** folder, where your starting Data Files are stored, and then double-click the **Invoices** Excel file. You return to the dialog box.

7. Click the **Append a copy of the records to the table** option button. The box to the right of this option becomes active and displays the Billing table name, because it is the first table listed in the Navigation Pane.

Trouble? If another table name appears in this box, click the arrow on the box, and then click Billing.

> **8.** Click the **OK** button. The first Import Spreadsheet Wizard dialog box opens. See Figure 2-25.

Figure 2-25 **First Import Spreadsheet Wizard dialog box**

selected check box confirms that the first row contains column headings

data from the worksheet to be imported

The dialog box confirms that the first row of the worksheet you are importing contains column headings. The bottom section of the dialog box displays some of the data contained in the worksheet.

TIP

Carefully check the data to make sure it should be imported into the selected table.

> **9.** Click the **Next** button. The second, and final, Import Spreadsheet Wizard dialog box opens. Notice that the Import to Table box shows that the data from the spreadsheet will be imported into the Billing table.

> **10.** Click the **Finish** button. A dialog box opens asking if you want to save the import steps. If you needed to repeat this same import procedure many times, it would be a good idea to save the steps for the procedure. However, you don't need to save these steps because you'll be importing the data only one time. Once the data is in the Billing table, Cindi will no longer use Excel to track invoice data.

> **11.** Click the **Close** button in the dialog box to close it without saving the steps.

The data from the Invoices worksheet has been added to the Billing table. Next, you'll open the table to view the new records.

To open the Billing table and view the imported data:

> **1.** Open the Navigation Pane, and then double-click **Billing** in the Tables section to open the table in Datasheet view.

> **2.** Resize the Invoice Item column to its best fit, scrolling the worksheet and resizing, as necessary.

3. Press the **Ctrl + Home** keys to scroll to the top of the datasheet. Notice that the table now contains a total of 204 records—four records you entered plus 200 records imported from the Invoices worksheet. The records are displayed in primary key order by the values in the Invoice Num column. See Figure 2-26.

| Figure 2-26 | Billing table after importing data from Excel |

4. Save and close the Billing table, and then close the Navigation Pane.

Two of the tables—Visit and Billing—are now complete. According to Cindi's plan for the Chatham database, you need to create a third table, named "Patient," to track data about the clinic's patients. You'll use a different method to create this table.

Creating a Table by Importing an Existing Table Structure

If another Access database contains a table—or even just the design, or structure, of a table—that you want to include in your database, you can import the table and any records it contains or import only the table structure into your database.

Cindi documented the design for the new Patient table by listing each field's name and data type, as well as any applicable field size, description, and caption property values, as shown in Figure 2-27. Note that each field in the Patient table, except BirthDate, will be a Short Text field, and the PatientID field will be the table's primary key.

Figure 2-27	Design for the Patient table

Field Name	Data Type	Field Size	Description	Caption
PatientID	Short Text	5	Primary key	Patient ID
LastName	Short Text	25		Last Name
FirstName	Short Text	20		First Name
BirthDate	Date/Time			Date of Birth
Phone	Short Text	14		
Address	Short Text	35		
City	Short Text	25		
State	Short Text	2		
Zip	Short Text	10		
Email	Short Text	50		

© 2014 Cengage Learning

Cindi's assistant Kelly already created an Access database containing a Patient table design. She never entered any records into the table because she wasn't sure if the table design was complete or correct. After reviewing the table design, both Kelly and Cindi agree that it contains some of the fields they want to track, but that some changes are needed. So, you can import the table structure in Kelly's database to create the Patient table in the Chatham database, and then modify the imported table to produce the final table structure according to Cindi's design.

To create the Patient table by importing the structure of another table:

1. Make sure the EXTERNAL DATA tab is the active tab on the ribbon.

2. In the Import & Link group, click the **Access** button. The Get External Data - Access Database dialog box opens. This dialog box is similar to the one you used earlier when importing the Excel spreadsheet.

3. Click the **Browse** button. The File Open dialog box opens. The Access database file from which you need to import the table structure is named "Kelly" and is located in the Access1 ▸ Tutorial folder provided with your Data Files.

4. Navigate to the **Access1 ▸ Tutorial** folder, where your starting Data Files are stored, and then double-click the **Kelly** database file. You return to the dialog box.

5. Make sure the **Import tables, queries, forms, reports, macros, and modules into the current database** option button is selected, and then click the **OK** button. The Import Objects dialog box opens. The dialog box contains tabs for importing all the different types of Access database objects—tables, queries, forms, and so on. The Tables tab is the current tab.

6. Click the **Options** button in the dialog box to see all the options for importing tables. See Figure 2-28.

Figure 2-28   Import Objects dialog box

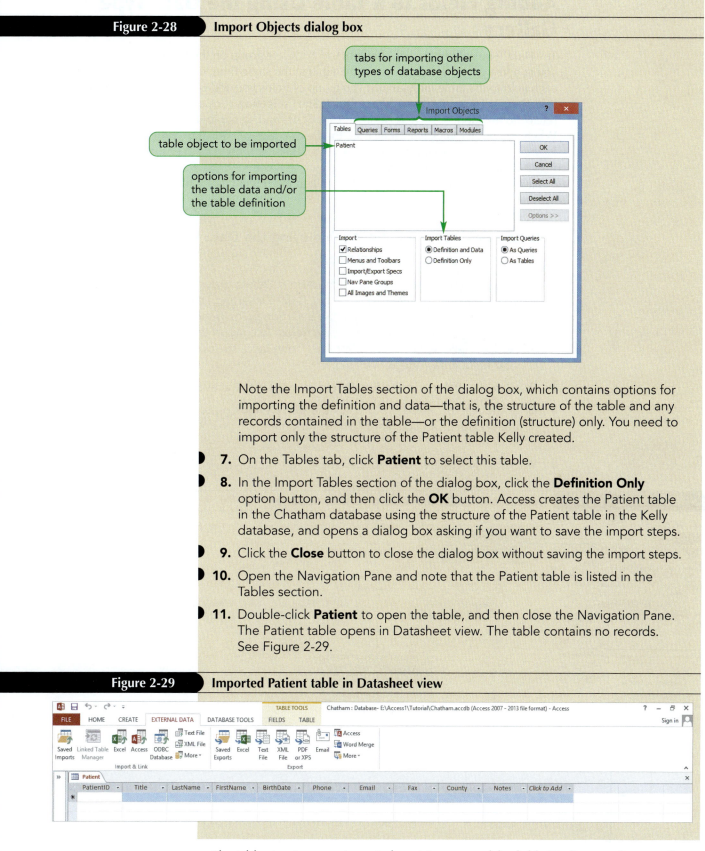

Note the Import Tables section of the dialog box, which contains options for importing the definition and data—that is, the structure of the table and any records contained in the table—or the definition (structure) only. You need to import only the structure of the Patient table Kelly created.

7. On the Tables tab, click **Patient** to select this table.

8. In the Import Tables section of the dialog box, click the **Definition Only** option button, and then click the **OK** button. Access creates the Patient table in the Chatham database using the structure of the Patient table in the Kelly database, and opens a dialog box asking if you want to save the import steps.

9. Click the **Close** button to close the dialog box without saving the import steps.

10. Open the Navigation Pane and note that the Patient table is listed in the Tables section.

11. Double-click **Patient** to open the table, and then close the Navigation Pane. The Patient table opens in Datasheet view. The table contains no records. See Figure 2-29.

Figure 2-29   Imported Patient table in Datasheet view

The table structure you imported contains some of the fields Cindi wants, but not all (see Figure 2-27); it also contains some fields Cindi does not want in the Patient table. You can add the missing fields using the Data Type gallery.

Adding Fields to a Table Using the Data Type Gallery

The **Data Type gallery**, available in the Add & Delete group on the FIELDS tab, allows you to add a group of related fields to a table at the same time, rather than adding each field to the table individually. The group of fields you add is called a **Quick Start selection**. For example, the **Address Quick Start selection** adds a collection of fields related to an address, such as Address, City, State, and so on, to the table at one time. When you use a Quick Start selection, the fields added already have properties set. However, you need to review and possibly modify the properties to ensure the fields match your design needs for the database.

Next, you'll use the Data Type gallery to add the missing fields to the Patient table.

To add fields to the Patient table using the Data Type gallery:

1. On the ribbon, click the **FIELDS** tab.

   Note the More Fields button in the Add & Delete group; this button allows you to display the Data Type gallery. Before inserting fields from the Data Type gallery, you need to place the insertion point in the field to the right of where you want to insert the new fields. According to Cindi's design, the Address field should come after the Phone field, so you need to make the next field, Email, the active field.

   > Make sure the correct field is active before adding new fields.

2. Click the first row in the **Email** field to make it the active field.

3. In the Add & Delete group, click the **More Fields** button. The Data Type gallery opens and displays options for different types of fields you can add to your table.

4. Scroll the gallery down so the Quick Start section is visible. See Figure 2-30.

Figure 2-30   Patient table with the Data Type gallery displayed

The Quick Start section provides options that will add multiple, related fields to the table at one time. The new fields will be inserted to the left of the current field.

▶ **5.** In the Quick Start section, click **Address**. Access adds five fields to the table: Address, City, State Province, ZIP Postal, and Country Region. See Figure 2-31.

Figure 2-31   **Patient table after adding fields from the Data Type gallery**

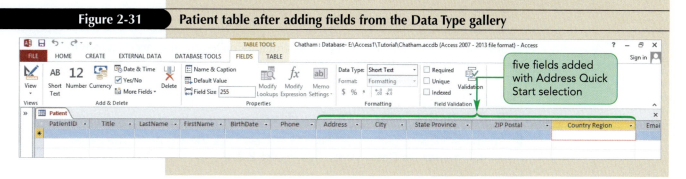

Modifying the Imported Table

Refer back to Cindi's design for the Patient table (Figure 2-27). To finalize the table design, you need to modify the imported table by deleting fields, renaming fields, and changing field data types. You'll begin by deleting fields.

Deleting Fields from a Table Structure

After you've created a table, you might need to delete one or more fields. When you delete a field, you also delete all the values for that field from the table. So, before you delete a field, you should make sure that you want to do so and that you choose the correct field to delete. You can delete fields in either Datasheet view or Design view.

REFERENCE

Deleting a Field from a Table Structure

- In Datasheet view, click anywhere in the column for the field you want to delete.
- In the Add & Delete group on the FIELDS tab, click the Delete button.

or

- In Design view, click the Field Name box for the field you want to delete.
- In the Tools group on the DESIGN tab, click the Delete Rows button.

The Address Quick Start selection added a field named "Country Region" to the Patient table. Cindi doesn't need a field to store country data because all Chatham Community Health Services patients are located in the United States. You'll begin to modify the Patient table structure by deleting the Country Region field.

To delete the Country Region field from the table in Datasheet view:

▶ **1.** Click the first row in the **Country Region** field (if necessary).

▶ **2.** In the Add & Delete group on the FIELDS tab, click the **Delete** button. The Country Region field is removed and the first field, PatientID, is now the active field.

You can also delete fields from a table structure in Design view. You'll switch to Design view to delete the other unnecessary fields.

To delete the fields in Design view:

▶ **1.** In the Views group on the FIELDS tab, click the **View** button. The Patient table opens in Design view. See Figure 2-32.

Figure 2-32	Patient table in Design view

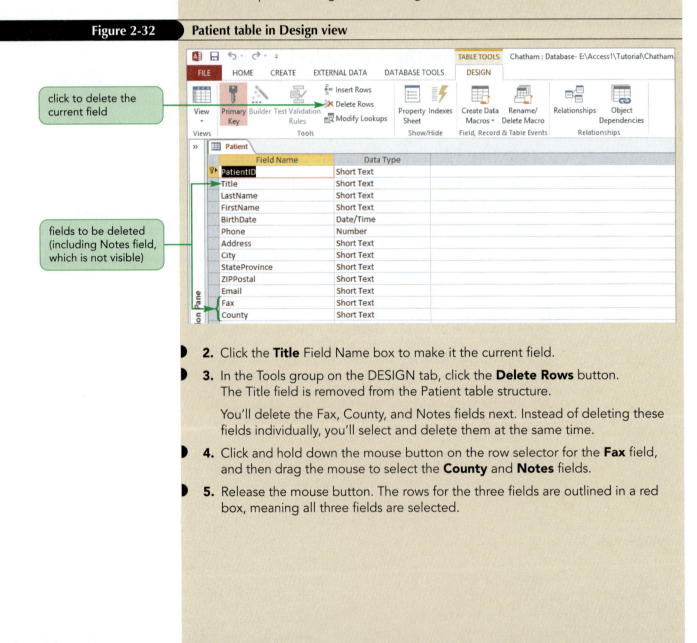

▶ **2.** Click the **Title** Field Name box to make it the current field.

▶ **3.** In the Tools group on the DESIGN tab, click the **Delete Rows** button. The Title field is removed from the Patient table structure.

You'll delete the Fax, County, and Notes fields next. Instead of deleting these fields individually, you'll select and delete them at the same time.

▶ **4.** Click and hold down the mouse button on the row selector for the **Fax** field, and then drag the mouse to select the **County** and **Notes** fields.

▶ **5.** Release the mouse button. The rows for the three fields are outlined in a red box, meaning all three fields are selected.

6. In the Tools group, click the **Delete Rows** button. See Figure 2-33.

Figure 2-33   **Patient table after deleting fields**

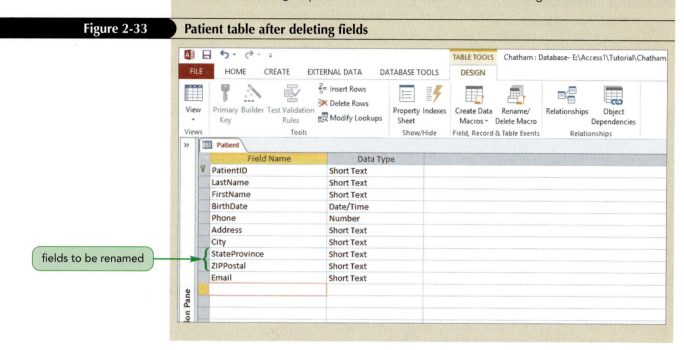

fields to be renamed

Renaming Fields in Design View

To match Cindi's design for the Patient table, you need to rename the StateProvince and ZIPPostal fields. In Tutorial 1, you renamed the default primary key field (ID) in Datasheet view. You can also rename fields in Design view by simply editing the names in the Table Design grid.

To rename the fields in Design view:

1. Click to position the insertion point to the right of the word **StateProvince** in the eighth row's Field Name box, and then press the **Backspace** key eight times to delete the word "Province." The name of the eighth field is now State.

You can also select an entire field name and then type new text to replace it.

2. In the ninth row's Field Name box, drag to select the text **ZIPPostal**, and then type **Zip**. The text you type replaces the original text. See Figure 2-34.

| Figure 2-34 | Patient table after renaming fields |

Changing the Data Type for a Field in Design View

According to Cindi's plan, all of the fields in the Patient table, except BirthDate, should be Short Text fields. The table structure you imported specifies the Number data type for the Phone field; you need to change this to Short Text. In Tutorial 1, you used an option in Datasheet view to change a field's data type. You can also change the data type for a field in Design view.

To change the data type of the Phone field in Design view:

▶ **1.** Click the right side of the **Data Type** box for the Phone field to display the list of data types.

▶ **2.** Click **Short Text** in the list. The Phone field is now a Short Text field. Note that, by default, the Field Size property is set to 255. According to Cindi's plan, the Phone field should have a Field Size property of 14. You'll make this change next.

▶ **3.** Press the **F6** key to move to and select the default Field Size property, and then type **14**.

Each of the remaining fields you added using the Address Quick Start selection—Address, City, State, and Zip—also has the default field size of 255. You need to change the Field Size property for these fields to match Cindi's design. You'll also delete any Caption property values for these fields because the field names match how Cindi wants them displayed, so captions are unnecessary.

To change the Field Size and Caption properties for the fields:

▶ **1.** Click the **Address** Field Name box to make it the current field.

▶ **2.** Press the **F6** key to move to and select the default Field Size property, and then type **35**.

Note that the Caption property setting for this field is the same as the field name. This field doesn't need a caption, so you can delete this value.

▶ **3.** Press the **Tab** key until the the word Address is selected in the Caption box, and then press the **Delete** key. The Caption property value is removed.

▶ **4.** Repeat Steps 1 through 3 to change the Field Size property for the City field to **25** and to delete its Caption property value.

▶ **5.** Change the Field Size property for the State field to **2**, and then delete its Caption property value.

▶ **6.** Change the Field Size property for the Zip field to **10**, and then delete its Caption property value.

▶ **7.** On the Quick Access Toolbar, click the **Save** button 🖫 to save your changes to the Patient table.

Finally, Cindi would like you to set the Description property for the Patient ID field and the Caption property for the PatientID, LastName, FirstName, and BirthDate fields. You'll make these changes now.

To enter the Description and Caption property values:

▶ **1.** Click the **Description (Optional)** box for the PatientID field, and then type **Primary key**.

▶ **2.** In the Field Properties pane, click the **Caption** box.

After you leave the Description (Optional) box, the Property Update Options button 📝 appears below this box for the PatientID field. When you change a field's property in Design view, you can use this button to update the corresponding property on forms and reports that include the modified field. For example, if the Chatham database included a form that contained the PatientID field, you could choose to **propagate**, or update, the modified Description property in the form by clicking the Property Update Options button, and then choosing the option to make the update everywhere the field is used. The text on the Property Update Options button varies depending on the task; in this case, if you click the button, the option is "Update Status Bar Text everywhere PatientID is used."

Because the Chatham database does not include any forms or reports that are based on the Patient table, you do not need to update the properties, so you can ignore the button for now. In most cases, however, it is a good idea to perform the update.

▶ **3.** In the Caption box for the PatientID field, type **Patient ID**.

▶ **4.** Click the **LastName** Field Name box to make it the current field.

▶ **5.** Click the **Caption** box, and then type **Last Name**.

▶ **6.** Click the **FirstName** Field Name box to make it the current field, click the **Caption** box, and then type **First Name**.

> **7.** Click the **BirthDate** Field Name box to make it the current field, click the **Caption** box, and then type **Date of Birth**. See Figure 2-35.

| Figure 2-35 | Patient table after entering description and captions |

> **8.** On the Quick Access Toolbar, click the **Save** button 🖫 to save your changes to the Patient table.

> **9.** In the Views group on the DESIGN tab, click the **View** button to display the table in Datasheet view.

> **10.** Resize each column to its best fit, and then click in the first row for the **Patient ID** column. See Figure 2-36.

| Figure 2-36 | Modified Patient table in Datasheet view |

After viewing the Patient table datasheet, both Cindi and Kelly agree that data entry would be made easier if the State field value of "CT" was automatically filled in for each new record added to the table, because all of the clinic's patients live in Connecticut. You can accomplish this by setting the Default Value property for the field.

Setting the Default Value Property for a Field

The **Default Value property** for a field specifies what value will appear, by default, for the field in each new record you add to a table. Recall the InvoicePaid field in the Billing table; this is a Yes/No field, which automatically includes a Default Value property setting of "No." That's why the check box for the InvoicePaid field is initially empty for a new record in the Billing table.

Because all the patients at Chatham Community Health Services live in Connecticut, you'll specify a default value of "CT" for the State field in the Patient table. With this setting, each new record in the Patient table will have the correct State field value entered automatically.

To set the Default Value property for the State field:

> **1.** In the Views group on the HOME tab, click the **View** button to display the Patient table in Design view.

> **2.** Click the **State** Field Name box to make it the current field.

> **3.** In the Field Properties pane, click the **Default Value** box, type **CT** and then press the Tab key. See Figure 2-37.

| Figure 2-37 | Specifying the Default Value property for the State field |

State field is current

Default Value property entered and enclosed within quotation marks

Note that a text entry in the Default Value property must be enclosed within quotation marks. If you do not type the quotation marks, Access adds them for you. However, for some entries, you would receive an error message indicating invalid syntax if you omitted the quotation marks. In such cases, you have to enter the quotation marks yourself.

4. On the Quick Access Toolbar, click the **Save** button 🖫 to save your changes to the Patient table.

TIP

You can change the value in a record from the default value to another value, if necessary.

5. In the Views group on the DESIGN tab, click the **View** button to display the table in Datasheet view. Note that the State field for the first row now displays the default value "CT" as specified by the Default Value property. Each new record entered in the table will automatically have this State field value entered.

With the Patient table design set, you can now enter records in it. You'll begin by entering two records, and then you'll use a different method to add the remaining records.

Note: *Be sure to enter your last name and first name where indicated.*

To add two records to the Patient table:

1. Enter the following values in the columns in the first record; note that you can press Tab to move past the default State field value:

   Patient ID = **22500**

   Last Name = *[student's last name]*

   First Name = *[student's first name]*

   Date of Birth = **2/28/1994**

   Phone = **860-938-2822**

   Address = **501 Perkins Dr**

   City = **Hartford**

   State = **CT**

   Zip = **06120**

   Email = **student1@example.edu**

2. Enter the following values in the columns in the second record:

   Patient ID = **22533**

   Last Name = **Rowe**

   First Name = **Christina**

   Date of Birth = **12/5/1941**

   Phone = **860-552-5920**

   Address = **27 Tracey Ct**

   City = **Windsor**

   State = **CT**

   Zip = **06095**

   Email = **c.rowe@example.com**

3. Resize columns to their best fit, as necessary, and then save and close the Patient table.

Before Cindi decided to store data using Access, Kelly managed the clinic's patient data in a different system. She exported that data into a text file and now asks you to import it into the new Patient table. You can import the data contained in this text file to add the remaining records to the Patient table.

Adding Data to a Table by Importing a Text File

There are many ways to import data into an Access database. So far, you've learned how to add data to an Access table by importing an Excel spreadsheet, and you've created a new table by importing the structure of an existing table. You can also import data contained in text files.

To complete the entry of records in the Patient table, you'll import the data contained in Kelly's text file. The file is named "Patient" and is located in the Access1 ▶ Tutorial folder provided with your Data Files.

To import the data contained in the Patient text file:

▶ **1.** On the ribbon, click the **EXTERNAL DATA** tab.

▶ **2.** In the Import & Link group, click the **Text File** button. The Get External Data - Text File dialog box opens. This dialog box is similar to the one you used earlier when importing the Excel spreadsheet and the Access table structure.

▶ **3.** Click the **Browse** button. The File Open dialog box opens.

▶ **4.** Navigate to the Access1 ▶ Tutorial folder, where your starting Data Files are stored, and then double-click the **Patient** file. You return to the dialog box.

▶ **5.** Click the **Append a copy of the records to the table** option button. The box to the right of this option becomes active. Next, you need to select the table to which you want to add the data.

▶ **6.** Click the arrow on the box, and then click **Patient**.

▶ **7.** Click the **OK** button. The first Import Text Wizard dialog box opens. The dialog box indicates that the data to be imported is in a delimited format. A **delimited text file** is one in which fields of data are separated by a character such as a comma or a tab. In this case, the dialog box shows that data is separated by the comma character in the text file.

▶ **8.** Make sure the **Delimited** option button is selected in the dialog box, and then click the **Next** button. The second Import Text Wizard dialog box opens. See Figure 2-38.

Figure 2-38   **Second Import Text Wizard dialog box**

fields in the text file are separated by commas

preview of the data being imported

This dialog box asks you to confirm the delimiter character that separates the fields in the text file you're importing. Access detects that the comma character is used in the Patient text file and selects this option. The bottom area of the dialog box provides a preview of the data you're importing.

TIP

Carefully check the data to make sure it should be imported into the selected table.

▶ **9.** Make sure the **Comma** option button is selected, and then click the **Next** button. The third, and final, Import Text Wizard dialog box opens. Notice that the Import to Table box shows that the data will be imported into the Patient table.

> **10.** Click the **Finish** button. A dialog box opens asking if you want to save the import steps. You'll only import the patient data once, so you can close the dialog box without saving the import steps.

> **11.** Click the **Close** button in the dialog box to close it without saving the import steps.

Cindi asks you to open the Patient table in Datasheet view so she can see the results of importing the text file.

To view the Patient table datasheet:

> **1.** Open the Navigation Pane, and then double-click **Patient** to open the Patient table in Datasheet view. The Patient table contains a total of 51 records.

> **2.** Close the Navigation Pane.

> **3.** Resize columns to their best fit, scrolling the table datasheet as necessary, so that all field values are displayed. When finished, scroll back to display the first fields in the table, and then click the first row's Patient ID field. See Figure 2-39.

Figure 2-39	Patient table after importing data from the text file

> **4.** Save and close the Patient table, and then open the Navigation Pane.

The Chatham database now contains three tables—Patient, Visit, and Billing—and the tables contain all the necessary records. Your final task is to complete the database design by defining the necessary relationships between its tables.

Defining Table Relationships

One of the most powerful features of a relational database management system is its ability to define relationships between tables. You use a common field to relate one table to another. The process of relating tables is often called performing a **join**. When you join tables that have a common field, you can extract data from them as if they were one larger table. For example, you can join the Patient and Visit tables by using the PatientID field in both tables as the common field. Then you can use a query, form, or report to extract selected data from each table, even though the data is contained in two separate tables, as shown in Figure 2-40. The PatientVisits query shown in Figure 2-40 includes the PatientID, LastName, and FirstName fields from the Patient table, and the VisitDate and Reason fields from the Visit table. The joining of records is based on the common field of PatientID. The Patient and Visit tables have a type of relationship called a one-to-many relationship.

Figure 2-40	One-to-many relationship and sample query

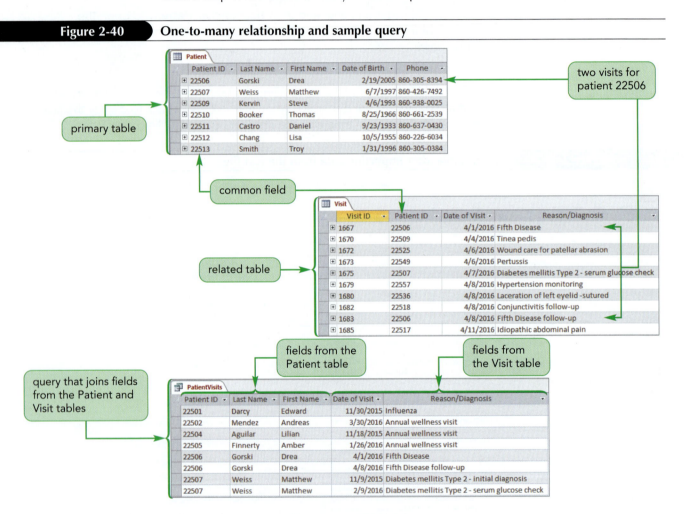

One-to-Many Relationships

As shown earlier in the Session 2.2 Visual Overview, a one-to-many relationship exists between two tables when one record in the first table matches zero, one, or many records in the second table, and when one record in the second table matches at most one record in the first table. For example, as shown in Figure 2-40, patient 22506 has two visits in the Visit table. Other patients have one or more visits. Every visit has a single matching patient.

Access refers to the two tables that form a relationship as the primary table and the related table. The primary table is the "one" table in a one-to-many relationship; in Figure 2-40, the Patient table is the primary table because there is only one patient for each visit. The related table is the "many" table; in Figure 2-40, the Visit table is the related table because a patient can have zero, one, or many visits.

Because related data is stored in two tables, inconsistencies between the tables can occur. Referring to Figure 2-40, consider the following three scenarios:

- Cindi adds a record to the Visit table for a new patient, Jack Perry, using PatientID 22570. She did not first add the new patient's information to the Patient table, so this visit does not have a matching record in the Patient table. The data is inconsistent, and the visit record is considered to be an **orphaned record**.
- In another situation, Cindi changes the PatientID in the Patient table for Drea Gorski from 22506 to 22601. Because there is no longer a patient with the PatientID 22506 in the Patient table, this change creates two orphaned records in the Visit table, and the database is inconsistent.
- In a third scenario, Cindi deletes the record for Drea Gorski, patient 22506, from the Patient table because this patient moved and no longer receives medical services from Chatham Community Health Services. The database is again inconsistent; two records for patient 22506 in the Visit table have no matching record in the Patient table.

You can avoid these types of problems and avoid having inconsistent data in your database by specifying referential integrity between tables when you define their relationships.

Referential Integrity

Referential integrity is a set of rules that Access enforces to maintain consistency between related tables when you update data in a database. Specifically, the referential integrity rules are as follows:

- When you add a record to a related table, a matching record must already exist in the primary table, thereby preventing the possibility of orphaned records.
- If you attempt to change the value of the primary key in the primary table, Access prevents this change if matching records exist in a related table. However, if you choose the **Cascade Update Related Fields option**, Access permits the change in value to the primary key and changes the appropriate foreign key values in the related table, thereby eliminating the possibility of inconsistent data.
- When you attempt to delete a record in the primary table, Access prevents the deletion if matching records exist in a related table. However, if you choose the **Cascade Delete Related Records option**, Access deletes the record in the primary table and also deletes all records in related tables that have matching foreign key values.

INSIGHT

Understanding the Cascade Delete Related Records Option

Although there are advantages to using the Cascade Delete Related Records option for enforcing referential integrity, its use does present risks as well. You should rarely select the Cascade Delete Related Records option because doing so might cause you to inadvertently delete records you did not intend to delete. It is best to use other methods for deleting records that give you more control over the deletion process.

Defining a Relationship Between Two Tables

When two tables have a common field, you can define a relationship between them in the Relationships window (see the Session 2.2 Visual Overview). Next, you need to define a one-to-many relationship between the Patient and Visit tables, with Patient as the primary table and Visit as the related table, and with PatientID as the common field (the primary key in the Patient table and a foreign key in the Visit table). You'll also define a one-to-many relationship between the Visit and Billing tables, with Visit as the primary table and Billing as the related table, and with VisitID as the common field (the primary key in the Visit table and a foreign key in the Billing table).

To define the one-to-many relationship between the Patient and Visit tables:

1. On the ribbon, click the **DATABASE TOOLS** tab.

2. In the Relationships group, click the **Relationships** button. The Show Table dialog box opens. See Figure 2-41.

Figure 2-41 **Show Table dialog box**

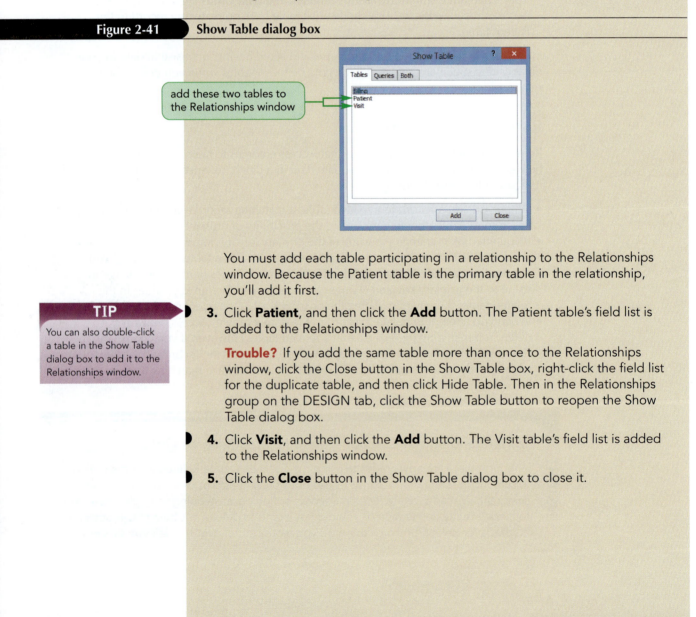

add these two tables to the Relationships window

You must add each table participating in a relationship to the Relationships window. Because the Patient table is the primary table in the relationship, you'll add it first.

3. Click **Patient**, and then click the **Add** button. The Patient table's field list is added to the Relationships window.

Trouble? If you add the same table more than once to the Relationships window, click the Close button in the Show Table box, right-click the field list for the duplicate table, and then click Hide Table. Then in the Relationships group on the DESIGN tab, click the Show Table button to reopen the Show Table dialog box.

4. Click **Visit**, and then click the **Add** button. The Visit table's field list is added to the Relationships window.

5. Click the **Close** button in the Show Table dialog box to close it.

So that you can view all the fields and complete field names, you'll resize the Patient table field list.

6. Use the ↕ pointer to drag the bottom of the Patient table field list to lengthen it until the vertical scroll bar disappears and all the fields are visible.

To form the relationship between the two tables, you drag the common field of PatientID from the primary table to the related table. Then Access opens the Edit Relationships dialog box, in which you select the relationship options for the two tables.

7. Click **PatientID** in the Patient field list, and then drag it to **PatientID** in the Visit field list. When you release the mouse button, the Edit Relationships dialog box opens. See Figure 2-42.

Figure 2-42	Edit Relationships dialog box

The primary table, related table, common field, and relationship type (One-To-Many) appear in the dialog box. Note that Access correctly identifies the "One" side of the relationship and places the primary table Patient in the Table/Query section of the dialog box; similarly, Access correctly identifies the "Many" side of the relationship and places the related table Visit in the Related Table/Query section of the dialog box.

8. Click the **Enforce Referential Integrity** check box.

After you click the Enforce Referential Integrity check box, the two cascade options become available. If you select the Cascade Update Related Fields option, Access will update the appropriate foreign key values in the related table when you change a primary key value in the primary table. You will *not* select the Cascade Delete Related Records option because doing so could cause you to delete records that you do not want to delete; this option is rarely selected.

9. Click the **Cascade Update Related Fields** check box.

10. Click the **Create** button to define the one-to-many relationship between the two tables and to close the dialog box. The completed relationship appears in the Relationships window, with the join line connecting the common field of PatientID in each table. See Figure 2-43.

Figure 2-43   Defined relationship in the Relationships window

Trouble? If a dialog box opens indicating a problem that prevents you from creating the relationship, you most likely made a typing error when entering the two records in the Patient table. If so, click the OK button in the dialog box and then click the Cancel button in the Edit Relationships dialog box. Refer back to the earlier steps instructing you to enter the two records in the Patient table and carefully compare your entries with those shown in the text, especially the PatientID field values. Make any necessary corrections to the data in the Patient table, and then repeat Steps 7 through 10. If you still receive an error message, ask your instructor for assistance.

Now you need to define the one-to-many relationship between the Visit and Billing tables. In this relationship, Visit is the primary ("one") table because there is at most one visit for each invoice. Billing is the related ("many") table because there are zero, one, or many invoices that are generated for each patient visit. For example, some visits require lab work or pharmacy charges, which are invoiced separately.

To define the relationship between the Visit and Billing tables:

1. In the Relationships group on the DESIGN tab, click the **Show Table** button. The Show Table dialog box opens.

2. Make sure the **Billing** table is selected on the Tables tab, click the **Add** button, and then click the **Close** button to close the Show Table dialog box. The Billing table's field list appears in the Relationships window to the right of the Visit table's field list.

TIP

You can also use the mouse to drag a table from the Navigation Pane to add it to the Relationships window.

3. Use the I pointer to drag the bottom of the Billing table field list to lengthen it until the vertical scroll bar disappears.

   Because the Visit table is the primary table in this relationship, you need to drag the VisitID field from the Visit field list to the Billing field list.

4. Click and drag the **VisitID** field in the Visit field list to the **VisitID** field in the Billing field list. When you release the mouse button, the Edit Relationships dialog box opens.

5. Click the **Enforce Referential Integrity** check box, and then click the **Cascade Update Related Fields** check box.

6. Click the **Create** button to define the one-to-many relationship between the two tables and to close the dialog box. The completed relationship appears in the Relationships window. See Figure 2-44.

Figure 2-44   **Both relationships defined**

Trouble? If a dialog box opens indicating a problem that prevents you from creating the relationship, you most likely made a typing error when entering the two records in the Visit table. If so, click the OK button in the dialog box and then click the Cancel button in the Edit Relationships dialog box. Refer back to the steps in Tutorial 1 instructing you to enter the records in the Visit table and carefully compare your entries with those shown in the text, especially the VisitID field values. Make any necessary corrections to the data in the Visit table, and then repeat Steps 4 through 6. If you still receive an error message, ask your instructor for assistance.

With both relationships defined, you have connected the data among the three tables in the Chatham database.

7. On the Quick Access Toolbar, click the **Save** button 💾 to save the layout in the Relationships window.

8. In the Relationships group on the DESIGN tab, click the **Close** button to close the Relationships window.

9. Click the **FILE** tab on the ribbon to display Backstage view.

10. Click the **Compact & Repair Database** button. Access compacts and repairs the Chatham database.

11. Click the **FILE** tab, and then click **Close** to close the Chatham database.

PROSKILLS

Problem Solving: Creating a Larger Database

When you create a small database that contains only a few tables, and the data and the reports you want to generate from it are fairly simple, you could follow the process outlined in this text: create the tables, populate them, and then define the necessary relationships between tables. This method, however, would not be suitable for creating a larger database. A larger database would most likely have many more tables and different types of relationships that can be quite complex. When creating a large database, a standard process to follow would include these steps:

1. Talk to people who will be using the data, and gather as much documentation as possible to try to understand how the data will be used. Gather sample reports, and ask the users to describe the data they require.
2. Gather some representative sample data, if possible.
3. Plan the tables, fields, data types, other properties, and the relationships between the tables.
4. Create the tables and define the relationships between them.
5. Populate the tables with sample data.
6. Design some queries, forms, and reports that will be needed, and then test them.
7. Modify the database structure, if necessary, based on the results of your tests.
8. Enter the actual data into the database tables.

Testing is critical at every stage of creating a database. Once the database is finalized and implemented, it's not actually finished. The design of a database evolves as new functionality is required and as the data that is gathered changes.

REVIEW

Session 2.2 Quick Check

1. What is the keyboard shortcut for inserting the value from the same field in the previous record into the current record?
2. _____ data is a process that allows you to copy the data from a source without having to open the source file.
3. The _____ gallery allows you to add a group of related fields to a table at the same time, rather than adding each field to the table individually.
4. What is the effect of deleting a field from a table structure?
5. A(n) _____ text file is one in which fields of data are separated by a character such as a comma or a tab.
6. The _____ is the "one" table in a one-to-many relationship, and the _____ is the "many" table in the relationship.
7. _____ is a set of rules that Access enforces to maintain consistency between related tables when you update data in a database.

SAM Projects

Put your skills into practice with SAM Projects! SAM Projects for this tutorial can be found online. If you have a SAM account, go to www.cengage.com/sam2013 to download the most recent Project Instructions and Start Files.

Review Assignments

Data Files needed for the Review Assignments: Vendor.accdb *(cont. from Tutorial 1)* **and Supplies.xlsx**

In addition to tracking information about the vendors Chatham Community Health Services works with, Cindi also wants to track information about their products and services. First, Cindi asks you to modify the necessary properties in the existing Supplier table in the Vendor database; then she wants you to create a new table in the Vendor database to contain product data. Complete the following:

1. Open the **Vendor** database you created in Tutorial 1.
2. Open the **Supplier** table in Design view, and set the field properties as shown in Figure 2-45.

Figure 2-45   Field properties for the Supplier table

Field Name	Data Type	Description	Field Size	Other
SupplierID	Short Text	Primary key	6	Caption = Supplier ID
Company	Short Text		50	
Category	Short Text		15	
Address	Short Text		35	
City	Short Text		25	
State	Short Text		2	
Zip	Short Text		10	
Phone	Short Text		14	Caption = Contact Phone
ContactFirst	Short Text		20	Caption = Contact First Name
ContactLast	Short Text		25	Caption = Contact Last Name
InitialContact	Date/Time			Format = Short Date
				Caption = Initial Contact

© 2014 Cengage Learning

3. Save the Supplier table. Click the Yes button when a message appears indicating some data might be lost. Switch to Datasheet view and resize columns, as necessary, to their best fit. Then save and close the Supplier table.
4. Create a new table in Design view, using the table design shown in Figure 2-46.

Figure 2-46   **Design for the Product table**

Field Name	Data Type	Description	Field Size	Other
ProductID	Short Text	Primary key	5	Caption = Product ID
SupplierID	Short Text	Foreign key	6	Caption = Supplier ID
ProductName	Short Text		75	Caption = Product Name
Price	Currency			Format = Standard
				Decimal Places = 2
TempControl	Yes/No			Caption = Temp Controlled?
Sterile	Yes/No			Caption = Sterile?
Units	Number		Integer	Decimal Places = 0
				Caption = Units/Case
				Default Value = [no entry]

© 2014 Cengage Learning

5. Specify ProductID as the primary key, and then save the table as **Product**.

6. Modify the table structure by adding a new field named **Weight** (data type: **Number**; field size: **Single**; Decimal Places: **2**; Caption: **Weight in Lbs**; Default Value: [no entry]) between the Price and TempControl fields. Then move the **Units** field so that it is positioned between the Price and Weight fields.

7. Enter the records shown in Figure 2-47 in the Product table. Resize all datasheet columns to their best fit. When finished, save and close the Product table.

Figure 2-47   **Records for the Product table**

Product ID	Supplier ID	Product Name	Price	Units/Case	Weight in Lbs	Temp Controlled?	Sterile?
SS582	DUR368	Stethoscopes	65.00	1	1	No	No
AL487	COU392	Alcohol wipes	15.00	1000	12	Yes	Yes

© 2014 Cengage Learning

8. Use the Import Spreadsheet Wizard to add data to the Product table. The data you need to import is contained in the Supplies workbook, which is an Excel file located in the Access1 ▶ Review folder provided with your Data Files.

   a. Specify the Supplies workbook as the source of the data.

   b. Select the option for appending the data.

   c. Select Product as the table.

   d. In the Import Spreadsheet Wizard dialog boxes, make sure Access confirms that the first row contains column headings, and import to the Product table. Do not save the import steps.

9. Open the **Product** table in Datasheet view and resize columns to their best fit, as necessary. Then save and close the Product table.

10. Define a one-to-many relationship between the primary Supplier table and the related Product table. Resize the table field lists so that all field names are visible. Select the referential integrity option and the cascade updates option for the relationship.

11. Save the changes to the Relationships window and close it, compact and repair the Vendor database, and then close the database.

Case Problem 1

Data Files needed for this Case Problem: Gopher.accdb (*cont. from Tutorial 1*) **and Customers.txt**

GoGopher! Amol Mehta wants to use the Gopher database to track information about members who join his online business, which provides a variety of services on a subscription basis, and the plans in which members are enrolled. He asks you to help maintain this database. Complete the following:

1. Open the **Gopher** database you created in Tutorial 1.
2. Open the **Plan** table in Design view, and change the following field properties:
   a. PlanID: Enter **Primary key** for the description, change the field size to **3**, and enter **Plan ID** for the caption.
   b. PlanDescription: Change the field size to **40** and enter **Plan Description** for the caption.
   c. PlanCost: Change the format to **Standard**, specify **0** decimal places, and enter **Plan Cost** for the caption.
   d. FeeWaived: Enter **Fee Waived** for the caption.
3. Save and close the Plan table. Click the Yes button when a message appears indicating some data might be lost.
4. Create a new table in Design view, using the table design shown in Figure 2-48.

Figure 2-48   Design for the Member table

Field Name	Data Type	Description	Field Size	Other
MemberID	Short Text	Primary key	4	Caption = Member ID
PlanID	Short Text	Foreign key	3	Caption = Plan ID
FirstName	Short Text		20	Caption = First Name
LastName	Short Text		25	Caption = Last Name
Phone	Short Text		14	
Expiration	Date/Time	Date when membership expires		Format = Short Date
				Caption = Expiration Date

© 2014 Cengage Learning

5. Specify MemberID as the primary key, and then save the table as **Member**.
6. Use the Address Quick Start selection in the Data Type gallery to add five fields between the LastName and Phone fields.
7. Switch to Design view, and then make the following changes to the Member table design:
   a. Address field: Change the name of this field to **Street**, change the field size to **40**, and delete the entry for the caption.
   b. City field: Change the field size to **25** and delete the entry for the caption.
   c. StateProvince field: Change the name of this field to **State**, change the field size to **2**, delete the entry for the caption, and enter **CO** for the default value.
   d. ZIPPostal field: Change the name of this field to **Zip**, change the field size to **10**, and delete the entry for the caption.
   e. Delete the **CountryRegion** field from the Member table structure.
   f. Add a new field named **DateJoined** (data type: **Date/Time**; format: **Short Date**; Caption: **Date Joined**) between the Phone and Expiration fields.
8. Enter the records shown in Figure 2-49 in the Member table. Be sure to enter your first and last names in the appropriate fields for the first new record. Resize all datasheet columns to their best fit. When finished, save and close the Member table.

Figure 2-49   Records for the Member table

Member ID	Plan ID	First Name	Last Name	Street	City	State	Zip	Phone	Date Joined	Expiration Date
1200	311	*Student First*	*Student Last*	45 Lakeview Dr	Boulder	CO	80301	303-559-1238	11/1/2015	2/1/2016
1210	312	Todd	Grant	6 Rosebriar Rd	Erie	CO	80516	303-674-2140	1/20/2016	4/20/2016

© 2014 Cengage Learning

9. Use the Import Text File Wizard to add data to the Member table. The data you need to import is contained in the Customers text file, which is located in the Access1 ▸ Case1 folder provided with your Data Files.

   a. Specify the Customers text file as the source of the data.

   b. Select the option for appending the data.

   c. Select Member as the table.

   d. In the Import Text File Wizard dialog boxes, choose the options to import delimited data, to use a comma delimiter, and to import the data into the Member table. Do not save the import steps.

10. Open the **Member** table in Datasheet view and resize columns to their best fit, as necessary. Then save and close the Member table.

11. Define a one-to-many relationship between the primary Plan table and the related Member table. Resize the Member table field list so that all field names are visible. Select the referential integrity option and the cascade updates option for this relationship.

12. Save the changes to the Relationships window and close it, compact and repair the Gopher database, and then close the database.

Case Problem 2

APPLY

Data Files needed for this Case Problem: OBrien.accdb *(cont. from Tutorial 1)*, Client.accdb, Students.txt, and Agreements.xlsx

O'Brien Educational Services   Karen O'Brien plans to use the OBrien database to maintain information about the students, tutors, and contracts for her educational services company. Karen asks you to help her build the database by updating one table and creating two new tables in the database. Complete the following:

1. Open the **OBrien** database you created in Tutorial 1.

2. Open the **Tutor** table in Design view, and set the field properties as shown in Figure 2-50.

Figure 2-50   Field properties for the Tutor table

Field Name	Data Type	Description	Field Size	Other
TutorID	Short Text	Primary key	7	Caption = Tutor ID
FirstName	Short Text		20	Caption = First Name
LastName	Short Text		25	Caption = Last Name
Degree	Short Text		7	
School	Short Text		50	
HireDate	Date/Time			Format = Short Date
				Caption = Hire Date

© 2014 Cengage Learning

3. Add a new field as the last field in the Tutor table with the field name **Groups**, the **Yes/No** data type, and the caption **Groups Only**.

4. Save the Tutor table. Click the Yes button when a message appears indicating some data might be lost.

5. In the table datasheet, specify that the following tutors conduct group tutoring sessions only: Student First/Student Last (i.e., your name), Amy Hawkins, Lori Burns, Samuel Glick, and Caitlin Shea. Close the Tutor table.

6. Karen created a table named Student in the Client database that is located in the Access1 ▶ Case2 folder provided with your Data Files. Import the structure of the Student table in the Client database into a new table named Student in the OBrien database. Do not save the import steps.

7. Open the **Student** table in Datasheet view, and then add the following two fields to the end of the table: **BirthDate** (Date/Time field) and **Gender** (Short Text field).

8. Use the Phone Quick Start selection in the Data Type gallery to add four fields related to phone numbers between the Zip and BirthDate fields. (*Hint:* Be sure to make the BirthDate field the active field before adding the new fields.)

9. Display the Student table in Design view, delete the BusinessPhone and FaxNumber fields, and then save and close the Student table.

10. Reopen the Student table and modify its design so that it matches the design in Figure 2-51, *including the revised field names and data types.*

    Note: You must type the quotation marks around the Default Property value for the State field.

Figure 2-51   Field properties for the Student table

Field Name	Data Type	Description	Field Size	Other
StudentID	Short Text	Primary key	7	Caption = Student ID
LastName	Short Text		25	Caption = Last Name
FirstName	Short Text		20	Caption = First Name
Address	Short Text		35	
City	Short Text		25	
State	Short Text		2	Default Value = "IN"
Zip	Short Text		10	
HomePhone	Short Text		14	
CellPhone	Short Text		14	Caption = Cell Phone
BirthDate	Date/Time			Format = Short Date
				Caption = Date of Birth
Gender	Short Text	F(emale), M(ale)	1	

© 2014 Cengage Learning

you must type the quotation marks for this Default Value property

11. Move the LastName field so it follows the FirstName field.

12. Save your changes to the table design, and then add the records shown in Figure 2-52 to the Student table.

Figure 2-52   Records for the Student table

Student ID	First Name	Last Name	Address	City	State	Zip	Home Phone	Cell Phone	Date of Birth	Gender
TUR8005	Lynne	Turner	6 Crowell Ct	South Bend	IN	46614	574-245-2125	574-245-8842	7/24/2002	F
CHA8034	Henry	Chang	1401 Lauren Dr	Oscela	IN	46561	574-607-3045	574-674-2410	10/5/1999	M

© 2014 Cengage Learning

13. Resize the fields to their best fit, and then save and close the Student table.

14. Use the Import Text File Wizard to add data to the Student table. The data you need to import is contained in the Students text file, which is located in the Access1 ▶ Case2 folder provided with your Data Files.

    a. Specify the Students text file as the source of the data.

    b. Select the option for appending the data.

c. Select Student as the table.

d. In the Import Text File Wizard dialog boxes, choose the options to import delimited data, to use a comma delimiter, and to import the data into the Student table. Do not save the import steps.

15. Open the **Student** table in Datasheet view, resize columns in the datasheet to their best fit (as necessary), and then save and close the table.

16. Create a new table in Design view, using the table design shown in Figure 2-53.

Figure 2-53	Design for the Contract table

Field Name	Data Type	Description	Field Size	Other
ContractID	Short Text	Primary key	4	Caption = Contract ID
StudentID	Short Text	Foreign key	7	Caption = Student ID
TutorID	Short Text	Foreign key	7	Caption = Tutor ID
SessionType	Short Text		15	Caption = Session Type
Length	Number		Integer	Decimal Places = 0 Caption = Length (Hrs) Default Value = [no entry]
NumSessions	Number		Integer	Decimal Places = 0 Caption = Number of Sessions Default Value = [no entry]
Cost	Currency			Format = Currency Decimal Places = 0 Default Value = [no entry]
Assessment	Yes/No	Pre-assessment exam complete		Caption = Assessment Complete

© 2014 Cengage Learning

17. Specify ContractID as the primary key, and then save the table using the name **Contract**.

18. Add a new field to the Contract table, between the TutorID and SessionType fields, with the field name **ContractDate**, the **Date/Time** data type, the description **Date contract is signed**, the **Short Date** format, and the caption **Contract Date**. Save and close the Contract table.

19. Use the Import Spreadsheet Wizard to add data to the Contract table. The data you need to import is contained in the Agreements workbook, which is an Excel file located in the Access1 ▶ Case2 folder provided with your Data Files.

a. Specify the Agreements workbook as the source of the data.

b. Select the option for appending the data to the table.

c. Select Contract as the table.

d. In the Import Spreadsheet Wizard dialog boxes, choose the Agreements worksheet, make sure Access confirms that the first row contains column headings, and import to the Contract table. Do not save the import steps.

20. Open the **Contract** table and add the records shown in Figure 2-54. (*Hint*: Use the New (blank) record button in the navigation buttons to add a new record.)

Figure 2-54	Records for the Contract table

Contract ID	Student ID	Tutor ID	Contract Date	Session Type	Length (Hrs)	Number of Sessions	Cost	Assessment Complete
5168	LUF8037	68-8234	8/30/2016	Group	3	12	$1,440	Yes
5172	GOS8029	71-1698	9/7/2016	Private	2	6	$720	Yes

© 2014 Cengage Learning

21. Resize columns in the datasheet to their best fit (as necessary), and then save and close the Contract table.

22. Define the one-to-many relationships between the database tables as follows: between the primary Student table and the related Contract table, and between the primary Tutor table and the related Contract table. Resize the table field lists so that all field names are visible. Select the referential integrity option and the cascade updates option for each relationship.

23. Save the changes to the Relationships window and close it, compact and repair the OBrien database, and then close the database.

Case Problem 3

CHALLENGE

Data Files needed for this Case Problem: Shelter.accdb *(cont. from Tutorial 1)*, **Donations.xlsx, and Animals.txt**

Rosemary Animal Shelter   Ryan Lang wants to use the Shelter database to maintain information about the patrons, animals, and donations for his not-for-profit agency. Ryan asks you to help him maintain the database by updating one table and creating two new ones. Complete the following:

1. Open the **Shelter** database you created in Tutorial 1.

2. Open the **Patron** table in Design view, and then change the following field properties:
   a. PatronID: Enter **Primary key** for the description, change the field size to **5**, and enter **Patron ID** for the caption.
   b. Title: Change the field size to **4**.
   c. FirstName: Change the field size to **20** and enter **First Name** for the caption.
   d. LastName: Change the field size to **25** and enter **Last Name** for the caption.
   e. Phone: Change the field size to **14.**

3. Save and close the Patron table. Click the Yes button when a message appears indicating some data might be lost.

✦ **Explore** 4. Use the Import Spreadsheet Wizard to create a table in the Shelter database. As the source of the data, specify the Donations workbook, which is located in the Access1 ▶ Case3 folder provided with your Data Files. Select the option to import the source data into a new table in the database.

✦ **Explore** 5. Complete the Import Spreadsheet Wizard dialog boxes as follows:
   a. Select Donation as the worksheet you want to import.
   b. Specify that the first row contains column headings.
   c. Accept the field options suggested by the wizard, and do not skip any fields.
   d. Choose DonationID as your own primary key.
   e. Import the data to a table named **Donation**, and do not save the import steps.

6. Open the Donation table in Datasheet view, and then delete the Requires Pickup field.

7. Open the Donation table in Design view, and then modify the table so it matches the design shown in Figure 2-55, including changes to data types, field name, and field position. For the Short Text fields, delete any formats specified in the Format property boxes.

Figure 2-55   **Design for the Donation table**

Field Name	Data Type	Description	Field Size	Other
DonationID	Short Text	Primary key	4	Caption = Donation ID
PatronID	Short Text	Foreign key	5	Caption = Patron ID
DonationDate	Date/Time			Format = mm/dd/yyyy
				Caption = Donation Date
Description	Short Text		30	
DonationValue	Currency	Dollar amount or estimated value		Format = Currency
				Decimal Places = 2
				Caption = Donation Value
				Default Value = [no entry]

© 2014 Cengage Learning

8. Save your changes to the table design, click Yes for the message about lost data, and then switch to Datasheet view.

9. Resize the columns in the Donation datasheet to their best fit.

✚ **Explore** 10. Ryan decides that the values in the Donation Value column would look better without the two decimal places. Make this field the current field in the datasheet. Then, in the Formatting group on the FIELDS tab, use the Decrease Decimals button to remove the two decimal places and the period from these values. Switch back to Design view, and note that the Decimal Places property for the DonationValue field is now set to 0.

11. Save and close the Donation table.

12. Use Design view to create a table using the table design shown in Figure 2-56.

Figure 2-56   **Design for the Animal table**

Field Name	Data Type	Description	Field Size	Other
AnimalID	Short Text	Primary key	3	Caption = Animal ID
AnimalName	Short Text		15	Caption = Animal Name
Age	Short Text		2	Caption = Age at Arrival
Gender	Short Text		6	
AnimalType	Short Text		5	Caption = Animal Type
Description	Short Text		60	
ArrivalDate	Date/Time			Format = Short Date
				Caption = Arrival Date
AdoptionDate	Date/Time			Format = Short Date
				Caption = Adoption Date
Adopted	Yes/No			
PatronID	Short Text		5	Caption = Patron ID

© 2014 Cengage Learning

---

13. Specify AnimalID as the primary key, save the table as **Animal**, and then close the table.

14. Use the Import Text File Wizard to add data to the Animal table. The data you need to import is contained in the Animals text file, which is located in the Access1 ▸ Case3 folder provided with your Data Files.

    a. Specify the Animals text file as the source of the data.

    b. Select the option for appending the data.

    c. Select Animal as the table.

    d. In the Import Text File Wizard dialog boxes, choose the options to import delimited data, to use a comma delimiter, and to import the data into the Animal table. Do not save the import steps.

15. Open the Animal table in Datasheet view, and resize all columns to their best fit.

16. Display the Animal table in Design view. Move the PatronID field to make it the second field in the table, and enter the description **Foreign key** for the PatronID field. Then move the Adopted field so it is positioned between the ArrivalDate and AdoptionDate fields. Save the modified Animal table design.

17. Switch to Datasheet view, and then add the records shown in Figure 2-57 to the Animal table. (*Hint*: Use the New (blank) record button in the navigation buttons to add a new record.) Close the table when finished.

Figure 2-57   **Records for the Animal table**

Animal ID	Patron ID	Animal Name	Age at Arrival	Gender	Animal Type	Description	Arrival Date	Adopted	Adoption Date
B45		Gizmo	12	Male	Dog	Hound mix	3/6/2016	No	
R39	38398	Simba	3	Female	Cat	Siamese	4/12/2016	Yes	5/14/2016

© 2014 Cengage Learning

18. Define the one-to-many relationships between the database tables as follows: between the primary Patron table and the related Animal table, and between the primary Patron table and the related Donation table. (*Hint:* Place the Patron table as the middle table in the Relationships window to make it easier to join the tables.) Resize the Animal field list so that all field names are visible. Select the referential integrity option and the cascade updates option for each relationship.

19. Save the changes to the Relationships window and close it, compact and repair the Shelter database, and then close the database.

Case Problem 4

Data Files needed for this Case Problem: Stanley.accdb (*cont. from Tutorial 1*), Travel.accdb, and Bookings.txt

Stanley EcoTours   Janice and Bill Stanley use the Stanley database to track the data about the tours they offer to clients of their ecotourism business. They ask you to help them maintain this database. Complete the following:

1. Open the **Stanley** database you created in Tutorial 1.

2. Open the **Guest** table in Design view and change the following field properties:

   a. GuestID: Enter **Primary key** for the description, change the field size to **3**, and enter **Guest ID** for the caption.

   b. GuestFirst: Change the field size to **20** and enter **Guest First Name** for the caption.

   c. GuestLast: Change the field size to **25** and enter **Guest Last Name** for the caption.

   d. Address: Change the field size to **35**.

   e. City: Change the field size to **25**.

   f. State/Prov: Change the field size to **2**.

   g. PostalCode: Change the field size to **10** and enter **Postal Code** for the caption.

   h. Country: Change the field size to **15**.

   i. Phone: Change the field size to **14**.

3. Save the Guest table, click the Yes button when a message appears indicating some data might be lost, resize the Guest First Name and Guest Last Name columns in Datasheet view to their best fit, and then save and close the table.

✦ Explore 4. In addition to importing the structure of an existing Access table, you can also import both the structure *and* the data contained in a table to create a new table. Import the **Trip** table structure and data from the **Travel** database into a new table in the **Stanley** database as follows:

   a. Start the process for importing an Access table structure.

   b. As the source of the data, specify the Travel database, which is located in the Access1 ▸ Case4 folder provided with your Data Files.

   c. Select the option button to import tables, queries, forms, reports, macros, and modules into the current database.

   d. In the Import Objects dialog box, select the Trip table, click the Options button, and then make sure that the correct option is selected to import the table's data and structure (definition).

   e. Do not save your import steps.

✦ Explore 5. Using a shortcut menu in the Navigation Pane, rename the Trip table as **Tour** to give this name to the new table in the Stanley database.

6. Open the **Tour** table in Design view, delete the VIPDiscount field, and then move the PricePerPerson field so that it appears between the Country and SingleSupplement fields.

CHALLENGE

7. Change the following properties:

   a. TourID: Enter the description **Primary key**, change the field size to **4**, and enter **Tour ID** for the caption.

   b. TourName: Enter **Tour Name** for the caption.

   c. PricePerPerson: Enter **Price Per Person** for the caption.

   d. SingleSupplement: Enter the description **Additional charge for single accommodation**, and enter **Single Supplement** for the caption.

   e. TourType: Change the field size to **15**, and enter **Tour Type** for the caption.

   f. Nights: Enter **Num of Nights** for the caption.

8. Save the modified table, click the Yes button when a message appears indicating some data might be lost, and then display the table in Datasheet view. Resize all datasheet columns to their best fit, and then save and close the table.

9. In Design view, create a table using the table design shown in Figure 2-58.

Figure 2-58   **Design for the Reservation table**

Field Name	Data Type	Description	Field Size	Other
ReservationID	Short Text	Primary key	3	Caption = Reservation ID
GuestID	Short Text	Foreign key	3	Caption = Guest ID
TourID	Short Text	Foreign key	4	Caption = Tour ID
StartDate	Date/Time			Caption = Start Date
People	Number	Number of people in the party	Integer	Decimal Places = 0
				Default Value = [no entry]

© 2014 Cengage Learning

---

10. Specify ReservationID as the primary key, and then save the table as **Reservation**.

✦ **Explore** 11. Refer back to Figure 2-11 to review the custom date formats. Change the Format property of the StartDate field to a custom format that displays dates in a format similar to 05/25/16. Save and close the Reservation table.

12. Use the Import Text File Wizard to add data to the Reservation table. The data you need to import is contained in the Bookings text file, which is located in the Access1 ▶ Case4 folder provided with your Data Files.

   a. Specify the Bookings text file as the source of the data.

   b. Select the option for appending the data.

   c. Select Reservation as the table.

   d. In the Import Text File Wizard dialog boxes, choose the options to import delimited data, to use a comma delimiter, and to import the data into the Reservation table. Do not save the import steps.

13. Resize columns in the **Reservation** table datasheet to their best fit (as necessary), verify that the date values in the StartDate field are displayed correctly according to the custom format, and then save and close the table.

14. Define the one-to-many relationships between the database tables as follows: between the primary Guest table and the related Reservation table, and between the primary Tour table and the related Reservation table. (*Hint:* Place the Reservation table as the middle table in the Relationships window to make it easier to join the tables.) Resize the Guest and Tour field lists so that all field names are visible. Select the referential integrity option and the cascade updates option for each relationship.

15. Save the changes to the Relationships window and close it, compact and repair the Stanley database, and then close the database.

ACCESS

OBJECTIVES

Session 3.1
- Find, modify, and delete records in a table
- Hide and unhide fields in a datasheet
- Work in the Query window in Design view
- Create, run, and save queries
- Update data using a query datasheet
- Create a query based on multiple tables
- Sort data in a query
- Filter data in a query

Session 3.2
- Specify an exact match condition in a query
- Use a comparison operator in a query to match a range of values
- Use the And and Or logical operators in queries
- Change the font size and alternate row color in a datasheet
- Create and format a calculated field in a query
- Perform calculations in a query using aggregate functions and record group calculations
- Change the display of database objects in the Navigation Pane

Maintaining and Querying a Database

Updating and Retrieving Information About Patients, Visits, and Invoices

Case | *Chatham Community Health Services*

At a recent meeting, Cindi Rodriguez and her staff discussed the importance of maintaining accurate information about the clinic's patients, visits, and invoices, and regularly monitoring the business activities of Chatham Community Health Services. For example, Kelly Schwarz, Cindi's assistant, needs to make sure she has up-to-date contact information, such as phone numbers and email addresses, for all the clinic's patients. The office staff also must monitor billing activity to ensure that invoices are paid on time and in full. Ethan Ward, a staff member who handles marketing and community outreach efforts for the clinic, tracks patient activity to develop new strategies for promoting services provided by the clinic. In addition, Cindi is interested in analyzing other aspects of the business related to patient visits and finances. You can satisfy all these informational needs for Chatham Community Health Services by updating data in the Chatham database and by creating and using queries that retrieve information from the database.

STARTING DATA FILES

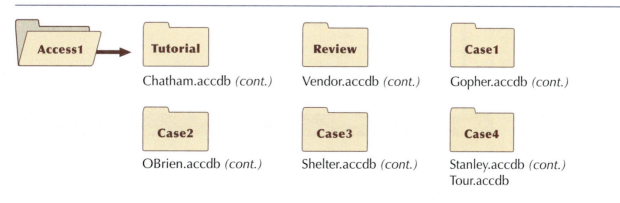

Access1 →	Tutorial	Review	Case1
	Chatham.accdb *(cont.)*	Vendor.accdb *(cont.)*	Gopher.accdb *(cont.)*
	Case2	Case3	Case4
	OBrien.accdb *(cont.)*	Shelter.accdb *(cont.)*	Stanley.accdb *(cont.)* Tour.accdb

Sorting on Multiple Fields in Design View

Sort fields can be unique or nonunique. A sort field is **unique** if the value in the sort field for each record is different. The PatientID field in the Patient table is an example of a unique sort field because each patient record has a different value in this primary key field. A sort field is **nonunique** if more than one record can have the same value for the sort field. For example, the City field in the Patient table is a nonunique sort field because more than one record can have the same City value.

When the sort field is nonunique, records with the same sort field value are grouped together, but they are not sorted in a specific order within the group. To arrange these grouped records in a specific order, you can specify a **secondary sort field**, which is a second field that determines the order of records that are already sorted by the **primary sort field** (the first sort field specified).

Access lets you select up to 10 different sort fields. When you use the buttons on the ribbon to sort by more than one field, the sort fields must be in adjacent columns in the datasheet. (Note that you cannot use an AutoFilter to sort on more than one field. This method works for a single field only.) You can specify only one type of sort—either ascending or descending—for the selected columns in the datasheet. You highlight the adjacent columns, and Access sorts first by the first column and then by each remaining highlighted column in order from left to right.

Kelly wants the records sorted first by the City field values, as they currently are, and then by the VisitDate values. The two fields are in the correct left-to-right order in the query datasheet, but they are not adjacent, so you cannot use the Ascending and Descending buttons on the ribbon to sort them. You could move the City field to the left of the VisitDate field in the query datasheet, but both columns would have to be sorted with the same sort order. This is not what Kelly wants—she wants the City field values sorted in ascending order so that they are in the correct alphabetical order, for ease of reference; and she wants the VisitDate field values to be sorted in descending order, so that she can focus on the most recent patient visits first. To sort the City and VisitDate fields with different sort orders, you must specify the sort fields in Design view.

In the Query window in Design view, Access first uses the sort field that is leftmost in the design grid. Therefore, you must arrange the fields you want to sort from left to right in the design grid, with the primary sort field being the leftmost. In Design view, multiple sort fields do not have to be adjacent to each other, as they do in Datasheet view; however, they must be in the correct left-to-right order.

REFERENCE

Sorting a Query Datasheet

- In the query datasheet, click the arrow on the column heading for the field you want to sort.
- In the menu that opens, click Sort A to Z for an ascending sort, or click Sort Z to A for a descending sort.

or

- In the query datasheet, select the column or adjacent columns on which you want to sort.
- In the Sort & Filter group on the HOME tab, click the Ascending button or the Descending button.

or

- In Design view, position the fields serving as sort fields from left to right.
- Click the right side of the Sort box for each field you want to sort, and then click Ascending or Descending for the sort order.

To achieve the results Kelly wants, you need to modify the query in Design view to specify the sort order for the two fields.

To select the two sort fields in Design view:

TIP

In Design view, the sort fields do not have to be adjacent, and fields that are not sorted can appear between the sort fields.

1. In the Views group on the HOME tab, click the **View** button to open the query in Design view. The fields are currently in the correct left-to-right order in the design grid, so you only need to specify the sort order for the two fields.

   First, you need to specify an ascending sort order for the City field. Even though the records are already sorted by the values in this field, you need to modify the query so that this sort order, and the sort order you will specify for the VisitDate field, are part of the query's design. Any time the query is run, the records will be sorted according to these specifications.

2. Click the right side of the **City Sort** box to display the arrow and the sort options, and then click **Ascending**. You've selected an ascending sort order for the City field, which will be the primary sort field. The City field is a Short Text field, and an ascending sort order will display the field values in alphabetical order.

3. Click the right side of the **VisitDate Sort** box, click **Descending**, and then click in one of the empty text boxes below the VisitDate field to deselect the setting. You've selected a descending sort order for the VisitDate field, which will be the secondary sort field because it appears to the right of the primary sort field (City) in the design grid. The VisitDate field is a Date/Time field, and a descending sort order will display the field values with the most recent dates first. See Figure 3-12.

Figure 3-12   **Selecting two sort fields in Design view**

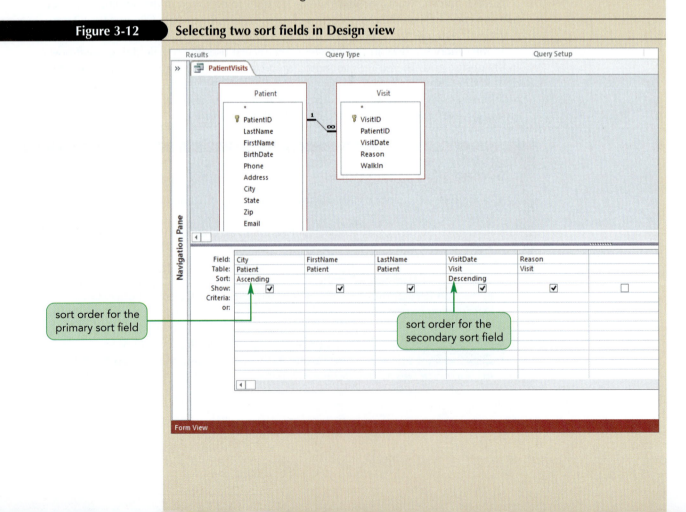

You have finished your query changes, so now you can run the query and then save the modified query with the same name.

▸ **4.** In the Results group on the DESIGN tab, click the **Run** button. Access runs the query and displays the query datasheet. The records appear in ascending order based on the values in the City field. Within groups of records with the same City field value, the records appear in descending order by the values of the VisitDate field. See Figure 3-13.

Figure 3-13	Datasheet sorted on two fields

primary sort field

secondary sort field

records grouped by City are shown in descending order by VisitDate

When you save the query, all of your design changes—including the selection of the sort fields—are saved with the query. The next time Kelly runs the query, the records will appear sorted by the primary and secondary sort fields.

▸ **5.** On the Quick Access Toolbar, click the **Save** button 🖫 to save the revised PatientVisits query.

Kelly knows that Chatham Community Health Services has seen an increase in the number of patients from Windsor. She would like to focus briefly on the information for patients in that city only. Also, she is interested in knowing how many patients from Windsor have had annual wellness exams. She is concerned that, although more patients are coming to the clinic from this city, not enough of them are scheduling wellness visits. Selecting only the records with a City field value of "Windsor" and a Reason field value beginning with "Annual" is a temporary change that Kelly wants in the datasheet, so you do not need to switch to Design view and change the query. Instead, you can apply a filter.

Filtering Data

A **filter** is a set of restrictions you place on the records in an open datasheet or form to *temporarily* isolate a subset of the records. A filter lets you view different subsets of displayed records so that you can focus on only the data you need. Unless you save a query or form with a filter applied, an applied filter is not available the next time you run the query or open the form.

The simplest technique for filtering records is Filter By Selection. **Filter By Selection** lets you select all or part of a field value in a datasheet or form, and then display only those records that contain the selected value in the field. You can also use the AutoFilter feature to filter records. When you click the arrow on a column heading, the menu that opens provides options for filtering the datasheet based on a field value or the selected part of a field value. Another technique for filtering records is to use **Filter By Form**, which changes your datasheet to display blank fields. Then you can select a value using the arrow that appears when you click any blank field to apply a filter that selects only those records containing that value.

REFERENCE

Using Filter By Selection

- In the datasheet or form, select the part of the field value that will be the basis for the filter; or, if the filter will be based on the entire field value, click anywhere within the field value.
- Make sure the HOME tab is displayed.
- In the Sort & Filter group, click the Selection button.
- Click the type of filter you want to apply.

For Kelly's request, you need to select a City field value of Windsor, and then use Filter By Selection to display only those records with this value. Then you will filter the records further by selecting only those records with a Reason value that begins with "Annual" (for Annual wellness visit).

To display the records using Filter By Selection:

▶ **1.** In the query datasheet, locate the first occurrence of a City field containing the value **Windsor**, and then click anywhere within that field value.

▶ **2.** In the Sort & Filter group on the HOME tab, click the **Selection** button. A menu opens with options for the type of filter to apply. See Figure 3-14.

Figure 3-14 **Using Filter By Selection**

options for the type of filter to apply →

current field is the basis for the filter →

The menu provides options for displaying only those records with a City field value that equals the selected value (in this case, Windsor); does not equal the value; contains the value somewhere within the field; or does not contain the value somewhere within the field. You want to display all the records whose City field value equals Windsor.

3. In the Selection menu, click **Equals "Windsor"**. Access displays the filtered results. Only the 24 records that have a City field value of Windsor appear in the datasheet. See Figure 3-15.

Figure 3-15 **Datasheet after applying the filter**

click to display more options for filtering the field →

indicate that a filter has been applied to the datasheet →

datasheet displays only records with a City value of Windsor →

The button labeled "Filtered" to the right of the navigation buttons and the notation "FILTERED" on the status bar both indicate that a filter has been applied to the datasheet. Also, notice that the Toggle Filter button in the Sort & Filter group on the HOME tab is active; you can click this button or the Filtered button next to the navigation buttons to toggle between the filtered and unfiltered displays of the query datasheet. The City column heading also has a filter icon on it; you can click this icon to display additional options for filtering the field.

Next, Kelly wants to view only those records with a Reason field value beginning with the word "Annual" so she can view the records for annual wellness visits. You need to apply an additional filter to the datasheet.

▶ 4. In any Reason field value beginning with the word "Annual," select only the word **Annual**.

▶ 5. In the Sort & Filter group, click the **Selection** button. The same four filter types are available for this selection as when you filtered the City field.

▶ 6. On the Selection menu, click **Begins With "Annual"**. The second filter is applied to the query datasheet, which now shows only the four records for customers located in Windsor who have had annual wellness visits at the clinic.

Now you can redisplay all the query records by clicking the Toggle Filter button, which you use to switch between the filtered and unfiltered displays.

TIP

The ScreenTip for this button is Remove Filter.

▶ 7. In the Sort & Filter group, click the **Toggle Filter** button. Access removes the filter and redisplays all 85 records in the query datasheet.

▶ 8. Close the PatientVisits query. Access asks if you want to save your changes to the design of the query—in this case, the filtered display, which is still available through the Toggle Filter button. Kelly does not want the query saved with the filter because she doesn't need to view the filtered information on a regular basis.

▶ 9. Click the **No** button to close the query without saving the changes.

▶ 10. If you are not continuing to Session 3.2, click the **FILE** tab, and then click **Close** in the navigation bar to close the Chatham database.

REVIEW

Session 3.1 Quick Check

1. In Datasheet view, what is the difference between navigation mode and editing mode?
2. What command can you use in Datasheet view to remove the display of one or more fields from the datasheet?
3. What is a select query?
4. Describe the field list and the design grid in the Query window in Design view.
5. How are a table datasheet and a query datasheet similar? How are they different?
6. For a Date/Time field, how do the records appear when sorted in ascending order?
7. When you define multiple sort fields in Design view, describe how the sort fields must be positioned in the design grid.
8. A(n) _____ is a set of restrictions you place on the records in an open datasheet or form to isolate a subset of records temporarily.

Session 3.2 Visual Overview:

When creating queries in Design view, you can enter criteria so that Access will display only selected records in the query results.

Field:	PatientID	LastName	FirstName	BirthDate	City
Table:	Patient	Patient	Patient	Patient	Patient
Sort:					
Show:	☑	☑	☑	☑	☑
Criteria:					"Bloomfield"
or:					

To define a condition for a field, you place the condition in the field's Criteria box in the design grid.

To tell Access which records you want to select, you must specify a condition as part of the query. A **condition** is a criterion, or rule, that determines which records are selected.

Field:	InvoiceNum	InvoiceDate	InvoiceAmt	
Table:	Billing	Billing	Billing	
Sort:				
Show:	☑	☑	☑	☐
Criteria:			>250	
or:				

A condition usually consists of an operator, often a comparison operator, and a value. A **comparison operator** asks Access to compare the value in a field to the condition value and to select all the records for which the condition is true.

Field:	VisitID	PatientID	VisitDate	Reason
Table:	Visit	Visit	Visit	Visit
Sort:				
Show:	☑	☑	☑	☑
Criteria:			Between #12/1/2015# And #12/31/2015#	
or:				

Most comparison operators (such as Between...And...) ask Access to select records that match a range of values for the condition—in this case, all records with dates that fall within the range shown.

Selection Criteria in Queries

The results of a query containing selection criteria include only the records that meet the specified criteria.

BloomfieldPatients

Patient ID	Last Name	First Name	Date of Birth	City
22501	Darcy	Edward	7/15/1986	Bloomfield
22506	Gorski	Drea	2/19/2005	Bloomfield
22513	Smith	Troy	1/31/1996	Bloomfield
22521	Engber	Cathy	4/7/2000	Bloomfield
22522	Li	Siyang	7/25/1986	Bloomfield
22549	Fielder	Pam	12/6/1978	Bloomfield
22557	Kirk	Isobel	11/18/1965	Bloomfield

The results of this query show only patients from Bloomfield because the condition "Bloomfield" in the City field's Criteria box specifies that Access should select records only with City field values of Bloomfield. This type of condition is called an **exact match** because the value in the specified field must match the condition exactly in order for the record to be included in the query results.

LargeInvoiceAmts

Invoice Num	Invoice Date	Invoice Amt
35815	11/16/2015	$300.00
35900	01/20/2016	$300.00
36002	03/15/2016	$450.00
36074	04/12/2016	$450.00
		$0.00

The results of this query show only those invoices with amounts greater than $250 because the condition >250, which uses the greater than comparison operator, specifies that Access should select records only with InvoiceAmt field values over $250.

DecemberVisits

Visit ID	Patient ID	Date of Visit	Reason/Diagnosis
1550	22549	12/1/2015	Influenza
1552	22511	12/3/2015	Annual wellness visit
1555	22520	12/7/2015	Annual wellness visit
1557	22526	12/10/2015	Annual wellness visit
1560	22514	12/15/2015	Influenza
1562	22516	12/22/2015	COPD management visit

The results of this query show only those patient visits that took place in December 2015 because the condition in the VisitDate's Criteria box specifies that Access should select records only with a visit date between 12/1/2015 and 12/31/2015.

Defining Record Selection Criteria for Queries

Cindi wants to display patient and visit information for all patients who live in Bloomfield. She is considering having the clinic hold a health fair in Bloomfield, with a special emphasis on hypertension, so she is interested in knowing more about the patients from this city. For this request, you could create a query to select the correct fields and all records in the Patient and Visit tables, select a City field value of Bloomfield in the query datasheet, and then click the Selection button and choose the appropriate filter option to display the information for only those patients in Bloomfield. However, a faster way of displaying the data Cindi needs is to create a query that displays the selected fields and only those records in the Patient and Visit tables that satisfy a condition.

Just as you can display selected fields from a database in a query datasheet, you can display selected records. To tell Access which records you want to select, you must specify a condition as part of the query, as illustrated in the Session 3.2 Visual Overview. A condition usually includes one of the comparison operators shown in Figure 3-16.

| Figure 3-16 | Access comparison operators |

Operator	Meaning	Example
=	equal to (optional; default operator)	="Hall"
<>	not equal to	<>"Hall"
<	less than	<#1/1/99#
<=	less than or equal to	<=100
>	greater than	>"C400"
>=	greater than or equal to	>=18.75
Between … And …	between two values (inclusive)	Between 50 And 325
In ()	in a list of values	In ("Hall", "Seeger")
Like	matches a pattern that includes wildcards	Like "706*"

© 2014 Cengage Learning

Specifying an Exact Match

For Cindi's request, you need to create a query that will display only those records in the Patient table with the value Bloomfield in the City field. This type of condition is an exact match because the value in the specified field must match the condition exactly in order for the record to be included in the query results. You'll create the query in Design view.

To create the query in Design view:

1. If you took a break after the previous session, make sure that the Chatham database is open and the Navigation Pane is closed.

2. On the ribbon, click the **CREATE** tab.

3. In the Queries group, click the **Query Design** button. The Show Table dialog box opens. You need to add the Patient and Visit tables to the Query window.

4. Click **Patient** in the Tables list, click the **Add** button, click **Visit**, click the **Add** button, and then click the **Close** button.

5. Use the ⬍ pointer to resize both field lists so that all the fields are displayed and the vertical scroll bars disappear.

6. Add the following fields from the Patient table to the design grid in the order shown: **LastName**, **FirstName**, **Phone**, **Address**, **City**, and **Email**.

   Cindi also wants information from the Visit table included in the query results.

7. Add the following fields from the Visit table to the design grid in the order shown: **VisitID**, **VisitDate**, and **Reason**. See Figure 3-17.

| Figure 3-17 | Design grid after adding fields from both tables |

The field lists for the Patient and Visit tables appear in the top portion of the window, and the join line indicating a one-to-many relationship connects the two tables. The fields you selected appear in the design grid.

To display the information Cindi wants, you need to enter the condition for the City field in its Criteria box (see Figure 3-17). Cindi wants to display only those records with a City field value of Bloomfield.

To enter the exact match condition, and then save and run the query:

1. Click the **City Criteria** box, type **Bloomfield**, and then press the **Enter** key. The condition changes to "Bloomfield".

   Access automatically enclosed the condition you typed in quotation marks. You must enclose text values in quotation marks when using them as selection criteria. If you omit the quotation marks, however, Access will include them automatically in most cases. Some words—including "in" and "select"—are special keywords in Access that are reserved for functions and commands. If you want to enter one of these keywords as the condition, you must type the quotation marks around the text or Access will display an error message and will not allow the condition to be entered.

2. On the Quick Access Toolbar, click the **Save** button 🖫 to open the Save As dialog box.

3. In the Query Name box, type **BloomfieldPatients** and then press the **Enter** key. Access saves the query with the specified name and displays the name on the object tab.

4. In the Results group on the DESIGN tab, click the **Run** button. Access runs the query and displays the selected field values for only those records with a City field value of Bloomfield. A total of 14 records is selected and displayed in the datasheet. See Figure 3-18.

Figure 3-18 **Datasheet displaying selected fields and records**

only records with a City
field value of Bloomfield
are selected

14 records
are selected

Cindi realizes that it's not necessary to include the City field values in the query results. The name of the query, BloomfieldPatients, indicates that the query design includes all patients who live in Bloomfield, so the City field values are unnecessary and repetitive. Also, she decides that she would prefer the query datasheet to show the fields from the Visit table first, followed by the Patient table fields. You need to modify the query to produce the results Cindi wants.

Modifying a Query

After you create a query and view the results, you might need to make changes to the query if the results are not what you expected or require. First, Cindi asks you to modify the BloomfieldPatients query so that it does not display the City field values in the query results.

To remove the display of the City field values:

1. In the Views group on the HOME tab, click the **View** button. The BloomfieldPatients query opens in Design view.

   You need to keep the City field as part of the query design because it contains the defined condition for the query. You only need to remove the display of the field's values from the query results.

2. Click the **City Show** check box to remove the checkmark. The query will still find only those records with the value Bloomfield in the City field, but the query results will not display these field values.

Next, you need to change the order of the fields in the query so that the visit information is listed first.

To move the Visit table fields to precede the Patient table fields:

1. Position the pointer on the VisitID field selector until the pointer changes to a ↓ shape, and then click to select the field. See Figure 3-19.

Figure 3-19   Selected VisitID field

Show check box is cleared

VisitID field selector

entire column is selected

2. Position the pointer on the VisitID field selector, and then click and hold down the mouse button; notice that the pointer changes to 🖑 and a black vertical line appears to the left of the selected field. This line represents the selected field when you drag the mouse to move it.

3. Drag to the left until the vertical line representing the selected field is positioned to the left of the LastName field. See Figure 3-20.

Figure 3-20   Dragging the field in the design grid

line representing selected field

drag pointer to here

selected field being moved

TIP

Instead of moving a field by dragging, you can also delete the field and then add it back to the design grid in the location you want.

4. Release the mouse button. The VisitID field moves to the left of the LastName field.

You can also select and move multiple fields at once. You need to select and move the VisitDate and Reason fields so that they follow the VisitID field in the query design. To select multiple fields, you click and drag the mouse over the field selectors for the fields you want.

5. Click and hold the pointer ↓ on the VisitDate field selector, drag the pointer to the right to select the Reason field, and then release the mouse button. Both fields are now selected. See Figure 3-21.

Figure 3-21 **Multiple fields selected to be moved**

6. Position the pointer anywhere near the top of the two selected fields, and then click and drag to the left until the vertical line representing the selected fields is positioned to the left of the LastName field.

7. Release the mouse button. The three fields from the Visit table are now the first three fields in the query design.

You have finished making the modifications to the query Cindi requested, so you can now run the query.

8. In the Results group on the DESIGN tab, click the **Run** button. Access displays the results of the modified query. See Figure 3-22.

Figure 3-22 **Results of the modified query**

fields from the Visit table are now listed first in the query datasheet

City field values are no longer displayed

Note that the City field values are no longer displayed in the query results.

9. Save and close the BloomfieldPatients query.

After viewing the query results, Cindi decides that she would like to see the same fields, but only for those records with a VisitDate field value before 1/1/2016. She is interested to know which patients of Chatham Community Health Services in all cities have not been to the clinic recently, so that her staff can follow up with these patients by sending them reminder notes or emails. To create the query that will produce the results Cindi wants, you need to use a comparison operator to match a range of values—in this case, any VisitDate value less than 1/1/2016.

Using a Comparison Operator to Match a Range of Values

After you create and save a query, you can double-click the query name in the Navigation Pane to run the query again. You can then click the View button to change its design. You can also use an existing query as the basis for creating another query. Because the design of the query you need to create next is similar to the BloomfieldPatients query, you will copy, paste, and rename this query to create the new query. Using this approach keeps the BloomfieldPatients query intact.

To create the new query by copying the BloomfieldPatients query:

1. Open the Navigation Pane. Note that the BloomfieldPatients query is listed in the Queries section.

   You need to use the shortcut menu to copy the BloomfieldPatients query and paste it in the Navigation Pane; then you'll give the copied query a different name.

2. In the Queries section of the Navigation Pane, right-click **BloomfieldPatients** to select it and display the shortcut menu.

3. Click **Copy** on the shortcut menu.

4. Right-click the empty area near the bottom of the Navigation Pane, and then click **Paste** on the shortcut menu. The Paste As dialog box opens with the text "Copy Of BloomfieldPatients" in the Query Name box. Because Cindi wants the new query to show data for patients who have not visited the clinic recently, you'll name the new query "EarlierVisits."

5. In the Query Name box, type **EarlierVisits** and then press the **Enter** key. The new query appears in the Queries section of the Navigation Pane.

6. Double-click the **EarlierVisits** query to open, or run, the query. The design of this query is currently the same as the original BloomfieldPatients query.

7. Close the Navigation Pane.

Next, you need to open the query in Design view and modify its design to produce the results Cindi wants—to display only those records with VisitDate field values that are earlier than, or less than, 1/1/2016.

To modify the design of the new query:

1. In the Views group on the HOME tab, click the **View** button to display the query in Design view.

2. Click the **VisitDate Criteria** box, type **<1/1/2016** and then press the **Tab** key. See Figure 3-23.

Figure 3-23	Criteria entered for the VisitDate field

new condition entered

original condition needs to be deleted

Note that Access automatically encloses the date criteria with number signs. The condition specifies that a record will be selected only if its VisitDate field value is less than (earlier than) 1/1/2016. Before you run the query, you need to delete the condition for the City field. Recall that the City field is part of the query, but its values are not displayed in the query results. When you modified the query to remove the City field values from the query results, Access moved the field to the end of the design grid. You need to delete the City field's condition, specify that the City field values should be included in the query results, and then move the field back to its original position following the Address field.

3. Press the **Tab** key six times until the condition for the City field is highlighted, and then press the **Delete** key. The condition for the City field is removed.

4. Click the **Show** check box for the City field to insert a checkmark so that the field values will be displayed in the query results.

5. Use the pointer to select the City field, drag the selected field to the left of the Email field, and then click in an empty box to deselect the City field. See Figure 3-24.

Figure 3-24   **Design grid after moving the City field**

6. In the Results group on the DESIGN tab, click the **Run** button. Access runs the query and displays the selected fields for only those records with a VisitDate field value less than 1/1/2016. The query displays a total of 18 records. See Figure 3-25.

| Figure 3-25 | Running the modified query |

only records with a VisitDate field value less than 1/1/2016 are selected

18 records are selected

7. Save and close the EarlierVisits query.

Cindi continues to analyze patient visits to Chatham Community Health Services. She is especially concerned about being proactive and reaching out to older patients well in advance of flu season. With this in mind, she would like to see a list of all patients who are age 60 or older and who have visited the clinic suffering from influenza. She wants to track these patients in particular so that her staff can contact them early for flu shots. To produce this list, you need to create a query containing two conditions—one for the patient's date of birth and another for the reason/diagnosis for each patient visit.

Defining Multiple Selection Criteria for Queries

Multiple conditions require you to use **logical operators** to combine two or more conditions. When you want a record selected only if two or more conditions are met, you need to use the **And logical operator**. In this case, Cindi wants to see only those records with a BirthDate field value less than or equal to 12/31/1956 *and* a Reason field value of "Influenza." If you place conditions in separate fields in the *same* Criteria row of the design grid, all conditions in that row must be met in order for a record to be included in the query results. However, if you place conditions in *different* Criteria rows, a record will be selected if at least one of the conditions is met. If none of the conditions are met, Access does not select the record. When you place conditions in different Criteria rows, you are using the **Or logical operator**. Figure 3-26 illustrates the difference between the And and Or logical operators.

Figure 3-26 **Logical operators And and Or for multiple selection criteria**

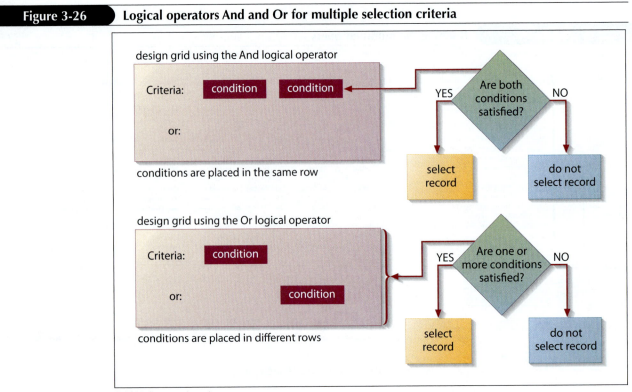

© 2014 Cengage Learning

The And Logical Operator

To create the query for Cindi, you need to use the And logical operator to show only the records for patients who were born on or before 12/31/1956 *and* who have visited the clinic because of influenza. You'll create a new query based on both the Patient and Visit tables to produce the necessary results. In the query design, both conditions you specify will appear in the same Criteria row; therefore, the query will select records only if both conditions are met.

To create a new query using the And logical operator:

1. On the ribbon, click the **CREATE** tab.

2. In the Queries group, click the **Query Design** button.

3. Add the **Patient** and **Visit** tables to the Query window, and then close the Show Table dialog box. Resize both field lists to display all the field names.

4. Add the following fields from the Patient field list to the design grid in the order shown: **FirstName**, **LastName**, **BirthDate**, **Phone**, and **City**.

5. Add the **VisitDate** and **Reason** fields from the Visit table to the design grid.

   Now you need to enter the two conditions for the query.

6. Click the **BirthDate Criteria** box, and then type **<=12/31/1956**.

7. Press the **Tab** key four times to move to the **Reason Criteria** box, type **Influenza**, and then press the **Tab** key. See Figure 3-27.

Figure 3-27   **Query to find older patients who have had influenza**

And logical operator with conditions entered in the same row

> **8.** Run the query. Access displays only those records that meet both conditions: a BirthDate field value less than or equal to 12/31/1956 *and* a Reason field value of Influenza. Two records are selected for two different patients. See Figure 3-28.

Figure 3-28   **Results of query using the And logical operator**

> **9.** On the Quick Access Toolbar, click the **Save** button 💾, and then save the query as **OlderAndFluPatients**.

> **10.** Close the query.

Cindi meets with staff member Ethan to discuss the issue of influenza and keeping patients informed about receiving flu shots at the clinic. After viewing the results of the OlderAndFluPatients query, Ethan suggests that the clinic should reach out to all elderly patients regarding flu shots, because this segment of the population is particularly susceptible to the flu. In addition, he thinks they should contact any patient who has visited the clinic suffering from influenza to keep these patients informed about flu shots well in advance of flu season. To help with their planning, Cindi and Ethan have asked you to produce a list of all patients who were born on or before 12/31/1956 or who visited the clinic because of influenza. To create this query, you need to use the Or logical operator.

The Or Logical Operator

To create the query that Cindi and Ethan requested, your query must select a record when either one of two conditions is satisfied or when both conditions are satisfied. That is, a record is selected if the BirthDate field value is less than or equal to 12/31/1956 *or* if the Reason field value is Influenza *or* if both conditions are met. You will enter the condition for the BirthDate field in the Criteria row and the condition for the Reason field in the "or" criteria row, thereby using the Or logical operator.

To display the information Cindi and Ethan want to view, you'll create a new query based on the existing OlderAndFluPatients query, since it already contains the necessary fields. Then you'll specify the conditions using the Or logical operator.

To create a new query using the Or logical operator:

1. Open the Navigation Pane. You'll use the shortcut menu to copy and paste the OlderAndFluPatients query to create the new query.

2. In the Queries section of the Navigation Pane, right-click **OlderAndFluPatients** to select it and display the shortcut menu.

3. Click **Copy** on the shortcut menu.

4. Right-click the empty area near the bottom of the Navigation Pane, and then click **Paste** on the shortcut menu. The Paste As dialog box opens with the text "Copy Of OlderAndFluPatients" in the Query Name box. Because Cindi wants the new query to show data for all older patients or patients who have visited the clinic due to influenza, you'll name the new query "OlderOrFluPatients."

5. In the Query Name box, type **OlderOrFluPatients** and then press the **Enter** key. The new query appears in the Queries section of the Navigation Pane.

6. In the Navigation Pane, right-click the **OlderOrFluPatients** query to select it and display the shortcut menu, and then click **Design View** on the shortcut menu to open the query in Design view.

7. Close the Navigation Pane.

   The query already contains all the fields Cindi and Ethan want to view, as well as the first condition—a BirthDate field value less than or equal to 12/31/1956. Because you want records selected if either the condition for the BirthDate field or the condition for the Reason field is satisfied, you must delete the existing condition for the Reason field in the Criteria row and then enter this same condition in the "or" row of the design grid for the Reason field.

8. In the design grid, click at the end of the **Reason Criteria** box and then press the **Backspace** key until the condition "Influenza" is deleted.

9. Press the ↓ key to move to the "or" row for the Reason field, type **Influenza**, and then press the **Tab** key. See Figure 3-29.

Figure 3-29   **Query window with the Or logical operator**

Field:	FirstName	LastName	BirthDate	Phone	City	VisitDate	Reason
Table:	Patient	Patient	Patient	Patient	Patient	Visit	Visit
Sort:							
Show:	✔	✔	✔	✔	✔	✔	✔
Criteria:			<=#12/31/1956#				
or:							"Influenza"

Or logical operator with conditions entered in different rows

Ready

Cindi wants the list displayed in descending order by BirthDate to better analyze the data.

10. Click the right side of the **BirthDate Sort** box, and then click **Descending**.

11. Run the query. Access displays only those records that meet either condition: a BirthDate field value less than or equal to 12/31/1956 *or* a Reason field value of Influenza. Access also selects records that meet both conditions. The query displays a total of 38 records. The records in the query datasheet appear in descending order based on the values in the BirthDate field. See Figure 3-30.

Figure 3-30	Results of query using the Or logical operator

datasheet selector

records with a Reason field value of Influenza

records that meet both criteria

records with BirthDate field values less than or equal to 12/31/1956

38 records are selected

Understanding the Results of Using And vs. Or

INSIGHT

When you use the And logical operator to define multiple selection criteria in a query, you *narrow* the results produced by the query because a record must meet more than one condition to be included in the results. For example, the OlderAndFluPatients query you created resulted in only 2 records. When you use the Or logical operator, you *broaden* the results produced by the query because a record must meet only one of the conditions to be included in the results. For example, the OlderOrFluPatients query you created resulted in 38 records. This is an important distinction to keep in mind when you include multiple selection criteria in queries, so that the queries you create will produce the results you want.

Cindi would like to spend some time reviewing the results of the OlderOrFluPatients query. To make this task easier, she asks you to change how the datasheet is displayed.

Changing a Datasheet's Appearance

You can make many formatting changes to a datasheet to improve its appearance or readability. Many of these modifications are familiar types of changes you can also make in Word documents or Excel spreadsheets, such as modifying the font type, size, color, and the alignment of text. You can also apply different colors to the rows and columns in a datasheet to enhance its appearance.

Modifying the Font Size

Depending on the size of the monitor you are using or the screen resolution, you might need to increase or decrease the size of the font in a datasheet to view more or fewer columns of data. Cindi asks you to change the font size in the query datasheet from the default 11 points to 14 points so that she can read the text more easily.

To change the font size in the datasheet:

1. In the Text Formatting group on the HOME tab, click the **Font Size** arrow, and then click **14**. The font size for the entire datasheet increases to 14 points.

   Next, you need to resize the columns to their best fit, so that all field values are displayed. Instead of resizing each column individually, you'll use the datasheet selector to select all the columns and resize them at the same time.

2. Click the **datasheet selector**, which is the box to the left of the First Name column heading (see Figure 3-30). All the columns in the datasheet are highlighted, indicating they are selected.

3. Position the pointer ↔ on the vertical line on the right of any column in the datasheet, and then double-click the vertical line. All the columns visible on the screen are resized to their best fit. Scroll down and repeat the resizing, as necessary, to make sure that all field values are fully displayed.

   Trouble? If all the columns are not visible on your screen, you need to scroll the datasheet to the right to make sure all field values for all columns are fully displayed. If you need to resize any columns, click a field value first to deselect the columns before resizing an individual column.

4. Click any value in the First Name column to make it the current field and to deselect the columns in the datasheet.

Changing the Alternate Row Color in a Datasheet

Access uses themes to format the objects in a database. A **theme** is a predefined set of formats including colors, fonts, and other effects that enhance an object's appearance and usability. When you create a database, Access applies the Office theme to objects as you create them. By default, the Office theme formats every other row in a datasheet with a gray background color to distinguish one row from another, making it easier to view and read the contents of a datasheet. The gray alternate row color provides a subtle difference compared to the rows that have the default white color. You can change the alternate row color in a datasheet to something more noticeable using the Alternate Row Color button in the Text Formatting group on the HOME tab. Cindi suggests that you change the alternate row color in the datasheet to see the effect of using this feature.

To change the alternate row color in the datasheet:

1. In the Text Formatting group on the HOME tab, click the **Alternate Row Color** button arrow ⊞ ▾ to display the gallery of color choices. See Figure 3-31.

Figure 3-31   **Gallery of color choices for alternate row color**

TIP

The name of the color appears in a ScreenTip when you point to a color in the gallery.

The Theme Colors section provides colors from the default Office theme, so that your datasheet's color scheme matches the one in use for the database. The Standard Colors section provides many standard color choices. You might also see a Recent Colors section, with colors that you have recently used in a datasheet. At the bottom of the gallery, you could also choose the No Color option, which sets each row's background color to white; or the More Colors option, which creates a custom color. You'll use one of the theme colors.

2. In the Theme Colors section, click the color box for **Orange, Accent 2, Lighter 60%** (third row, sixth color box). The alternate row color is applied to the query datasheet. See Figure 3-32.

Figure 3-32   **Datasheet formatted with alternate row color**

Every other row in the datasheet uses the selected theme color. Cindi likes how the datasheet looks with this color scheme, so she asks you to save the query.

▶ **3.** Save and close the OlderOrFluPatients query. The query is saved with both the increased font size and the orange alternate row color.

Next, Cindi turns her attention to some financial aspects of operating the clinic. She wants to use the Chatham database to perform calculations. She is considering imposing a 2% late fee on unpaid invoices and wants to know exactly what the late fee charges would be, should she decide to institute such a policy in the future. To produce the information for Cindi, you need to create a calculated field.

Creating a Calculated Field

In addition to using queries to retrieve, sort, and filter data in a database, you can use a query to perform calculations. To perform a calculation, you define an **expression** containing a combination of database fields, constants, and operators. For numeric expressions, the data types of the database fields must be Number, Currency, or Date/Time; the constants are numbers such as .02 (for the 2% late fee); and the operators can be arithmetic operators (+ − * /) or other specialized operators. In complex expressions, you can enclose calculations in parentheses to indicate which one should be performed first; any calculation within parentheses is completed before calculations outside the parentheses. In expressions without parentheses, Access performs basic calculations using the following order of precedence: multiplication and division before addition and subtraction. When operators have equal precedence, Access calculates them in order from left to right.

To perform a calculation in a query, you add a calculated field to the query. A **calculated field** is a field that displays the results of an expression. A calculated field that you create with an expression appears in a query datasheet or in a form or report; however, it does not exist in a database. When you run a query that contains a calculated field, Access evaluates the expression defined by the calculated field and displays the resulting value in the query datasheet, form, or report.

To enter an expression for a calculated field, you can type it directly in a Field box in the design grid. Alternately, you can open the Zoom box or Expression Builder and use either one to enter the expression. The **Zoom box** is a dialog box that you can use to enter text, expressions, or other values. To use the Zoom box, however, you must know all the parts of the expression you want to create. **Expression Builder** is an Access tool that makes it easy for you to create an expression; it contains a box for entering the expression, an option for displaying and choosing common operators, and one or more lists of expression elements, such as table and field names. Unlike a Field box, which is too narrow to show an entire expression at one time, the Zoom box and Expression Builder are large enough to display longer expressions. In most cases, Expression Builder provides the easiest way to enter expressions because you don't have to know all the parts of the expression; you can choose the necessary elements from the Expression Builder dialog box, which also helps to prevent typing errors.

Using Expression Builder

- Create and save the query in which you want to include a calculated field.
- Open the query in Design view.
- In the design grid, click the Field box in which you want to create an expression.
- In the Query Setup group on the DESIGN tab, click the Builder button.
- Use the expression elements and common operators to build the expression, or type the expression directly in the expression box.
- Click the OK button.

To produce the information Cindi wants, you need to create a new query based on the Billing and Visit tables and, in the query, create a calculated field that will multiply each InvoiceAmt field value by .02 to calculate the proposed 2% late fee.

To create the new query and the calculated field:

1. On the ribbon, click the **CREATE** tab.

2. In the Queries group, click the **Query Design** button. The Show Table dialog box opens.

   Cindi wants to see data from both the Visit and Billing tables, so you need to add these two tables to the Query window.

3. Add the **Visit** and **Billing** tables to the Query window, and then close the Show Table dialog box. The field lists appear in the Query window, and the one-to-many relationship between the Visit (primary) and Billing (related) tables is displayed.

4. Resize the two field lists so that all field names are visible.

5. Add the following fields to the design grid in the order given: **VisitID**, **PatientID**, and **VisitDate** from the Visit table; and **InvoiceItem**, **InvoicePaid**, and **InvoiceAmt** from the Billing table.

   Cindi is interested in viewing data only for unpaid invoices because a late fee would apply only to them, so you need to enter the necessary condition for the InvoicePaid field. Recall that InvoicePaid is a Yes/No field. The condition you need to enter is the word "No" in the Criteria box for this field, so that Access will retrieve the records for unpaid invoices only.

6. In the **InvoicePaid Criteria** box, type **No**. As soon as you type the letter "N," a menu appears with options for entering various functions for the criteria. You don't need to enter a function, so you can close this menu.

7. Press the **Esc** key to close the menu.

> You must close the menu or you'll enter a function, which will cause an error.

8. Press the **Tab** key. The query name you'll use will indicate that the data is for unpaid invoices, so you don't need to include the InvoicePaid values in the query results.

9. Click the **InvoicePaid Show** check box to remove the checkmark.

10. Save the query with the name **UnpaidInvoiceLateFee**.

Now you can use Expression Builder to create the calculated field for the InvoiceAmt field.

To create the calculated field:

1. Click the blank Field box to the right of the InvoiceAmt field. This field will contain the expression.

2. In the Query Setup group on the DESIGN tab, click the **Builder** button. The Expression Builder dialog box opens.

The insertion point is positioned in the large box at the top of the dialog box, ready for you to enter the expression. The Expression Categories section of the dialog box lists the fields from the query so you can include them in the expression. The Expression Elements section contains options for including other elements in the expression, including functions, constants, and operators. If the expression you're entering is a simple one, you can type it in the box; if it's more complex, you can use the options in the Expression Elements section to help you build the expression.

The expression for the calculated field will multiply the InvoiceAmt field values by the numeric constant .02 (which represents a 2% late fee).

3. In the Expression Categories section of the dialog box, double-click **InvoiceAmt**. The field name is added to the expression box, within brackets and with a space following it. In an expression, all field names must be enclosed in brackets.

Next you need to enter the multiplication operator, which is the asterisk (*), followed by the constant.

4. Type * (an asterisk) and then type **.02**. You have finished entering the expression. See Figure 3-33.

Figure 3-33   **Completed expression for the calculated field**

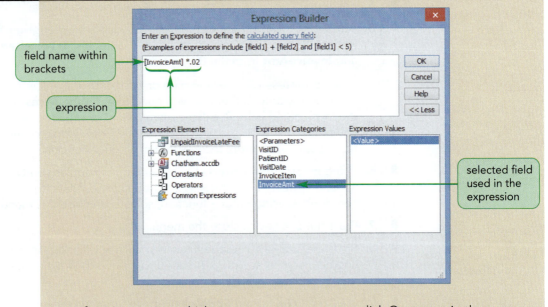

If you're not sure which operator to use, you can click Operators in the Expression Elements section to display a list of available operators in the center section of the dialog box.

5. Click the **OK** button. Access closes the Expression Builder dialog box and adds the expression to the design grid in the Field box for the calculated field.

When you create a calculated field, Access uses the default column name "Expr1" for the field. You need to specify a more meaningful column name so it will appear in the query results. You'll enter the name "LateFee," which better describes the field's contents.

6. Click to the left of the text "Expr1:" at the beginning of the expression, and then press the **Delete** key five times to delete the text **Expr1**. *Do not delete the colon*; it is needed to separate the calculated field name from the expression.

7. Type **LateFee**. Next, you'll set this field's Caption property so that the field name will appear as "Late Fee" in the query datasheet.

8. In the Show/Hide group on the DESIGN tab, click the **Property Sheet** button. The Property Sheet for the current field, LateFee, opens on the right side of the window. See Figure 3-34.

Figure 3-34	Property Sheet for the calculated field

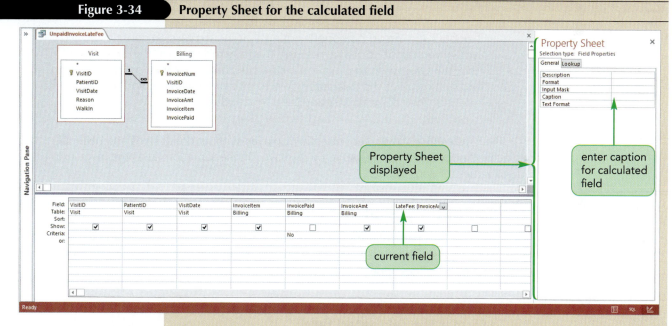

9. Click in the Caption box of the Property Sheet, type **Late Fee** and then close the Property Sheet.

10. Run the query. Access displays the query datasheet, which contains the specified fields and the calculated field with the caption "Late Fee." See Figure 3-35.

Figure 3-35 Datasheet displaying the calculated field

specified caption for the calculated field

calculated field values

Trouble? If a dialog box opens noting that the expression contains invalid syntax, you might not have included the required colon in the expression. Click the OK button to close the dialog box, resize the column in the design grid that contains the calculated field to its best fit, change your expression to LateFee: [InvoiceAmt]*0.02 and then repeat Step 10.

The LateFee field values are currently displayed without dollar signs and decimal places. Cindi wants these values to be displayed in the same format as the InvoiceAmt field values for consistency.

Formatting a Calculated Field

You can specify a particular format for a calculated field, just as you can for any field, by modifying its properties. Next, you'll change the format of the LateFee calculated field so that all values appear in the Currency format.

To format the calculated field:

1. Switch to Design view.

2. In the design grid, click in the **LateFee** calculated field to make it the current field, if necessary.

3. In the Show/Hide group on the DESIGN tab, click the **Property Sheet** button to open the Property Sheet for the calculated field.

   You need to change the Format property to Currency, which displays values with a dollar sign and two decimal places.

4. In the Property Sheet, click the right side of the **Format** box to display the list of formats, and then click **Currency**.

5. Close the Property Sheet for the calculated field, and then run the query. The amounts in the LateFee calculated field are now displayed with dollar signs and two decimal places.

6. Save and close the UnpaidInvoiceLateFee query.

PROSKILLS

Problem Solving: Creating a Calculated Field vs. Using the Calculated Field Data Type

You can also create a calculated field using the Calculated Field data type, which lets you store the result of an expression as a field in a table. However, database experts caution users against storing calculations in a table for several reasons. First, storing calculated data in a table consumes valuable space and increases the size of the database. The preferred approach is to use a calculated field in a query; with this approach, the result of the calculation is not stored in the database—it is produced only when you run the query—and it is always current. Second, the Calculated Field data type provides limited options for creating a calculation, whereas a calculated field in a query provides more functions and options for creating expressions. Third, including a field in a table using the Calculated Field data type limits your options if you need to upgrade the database at some point to a more robust DBMS, such as Oracle or SQL Server, that doesn't support this data type; you would need to redesign your database to eliminate this data type. Finally, most database experts agree that including a field in a table whose value is dependent on other fields in the table violates database design principles. To avoid such problems, it's best to create a query that includes a calculated field to perform the calculation you want, instead of creating a field in a table that uses the Calculated Field data type.

To better analyze costs at Chatham Community Health Services, Cindi wants to view more detailed information about patient invoices. Specifically, she would like to know the minimum, average, and maximum invoice amounts. She asks you to determine these statistics from data in the Billing table.

Using Aggregate Functions

You can calculate statistical information, such as totals and averages, on the records displayed in a table datasheet or selected by a query. To do this, you use the Access aggregate functions. **Aggregate functions** perform arithmetic operations on selected records in a database. Figure 3-36 lists the most frequently used aggregate functions.

| Figure 3-36 | Frequently used aggregate functions |

Aggregate Function	Determines	Data Types Supported
Average	Average of the field values for the selected records	AutoNumber, Currency, Date/Time, Number
Count	Number of records selected	AutoNumber, Currency, Date/Time, Long Text, Number, OLE Object, Short Text, Yes/No
Maximum	Highest field value for the selected records	AutoNumber, Currency, Date/Time, Number, Short Text
Minimum	Lowest field value for the selected records	AutoNumber, Currency, Date/Time, Number, Short Text
Sum	Total of the field values for the selected records	AutoNumber, Currency, Date/Time, Number

© 2014 Cengage Learning

Working with Aggregate Functions Using the Total Row

If you want to quickly perform a calculation using an aggregate function in a table or query datasheet, you can use the Totals button in the Records group on the HOME tab. When you click this button, a row labeled "Total" appears at the bottom of the datasheet. You can then choose one of the aggregate functions for a field in the datasheet, and the results of the calculation will be displayed in the Total row for that field.

Cindi wants to know the total amount of all invoices for the clinic. You can quickly display this amount using the Sum function in the Total row in the Billing table datasheet.

To display the total amount of all invoices in the Billing table:

1. Open the Navigation Pane, open the **Billing** table in Datasheet view, and then close the Navigation Pane.

2. Make sure the HOME tab is displayed.

3. In the Records group, click the **Totals** button. Access adds a row with the label "Total" to the bottom of the datasheet.

4. Scroll to the bottom of the datasheet to view the last records in the datasheet and the Total row. You want to display the sum of all the values in the Invoice Amt column.

5. In the Total row, click the **Invoice Amt** column. An arrow appears on the left side of the field.

6. Click the **arrow** to display the menu of aggregate functions. The functions displayed depend on the data type of the current field; in this case, the menu provides functions for a Currency field. See Figure 3-37.

Figure 3-37	**Using aggregate functions in the Total row**

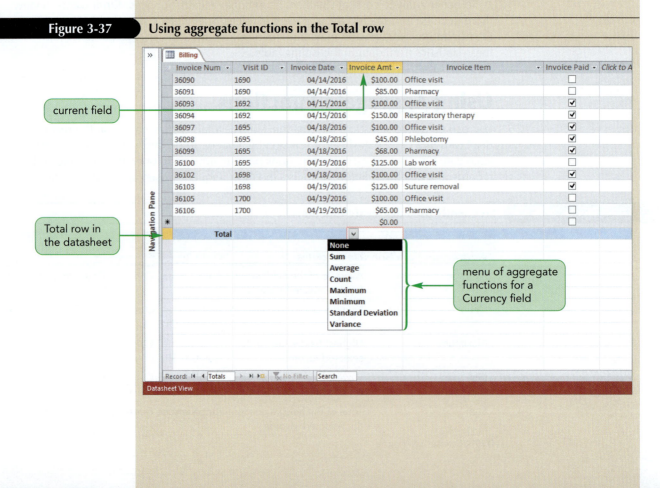

Datasheet View

7. Click **Sum** in the menu. Access adds all the values in the Invoice Amt column and displays the total $20,603.00 in the Total row for the column.

   Cindi doesn't want to change the Billing table to always display this total. You can remove the Total row by clicking the Totals button again; this button works as a toggle to switch between the display of the Total row with the results of any calculations in the row, and the display of the datasheet without this row.

8. In the Records group, click the **Totals** button. Access removes the Total row from the datasheet.

9. Close the Billing table without saving the changes.

Cindi wants to know the minimum, average, and maximum invoice amounts for Chatham Community Health Services. To produce this information for Cindi, you need to use aggregate functions in a query.

Creating Queries with Aggregate Functions

Aggregate functions operate on the records that meet a query's selection criteria. You specify an aggregate function for a specific field, and the appropriate operation applies to that field's values for the selected records.

To display the minimum, average, and maximum of all the invoice amounts in the Billing table, you will use the Minimum, Average, and Maximum aggregate functions for the InvoiceAmt field.

To calculate the minimum of all invoice amounts:

1. Create a new query in Design view, add the **Billing** table to the Query window, and then close the Show Table dialog box. Resize the Billing field list to display all fields.

   To perform the three calculations on the InvoiceAmt field, you need to add the field to the design grid three times.

2. In the Billing field list, double-click **InvoiceAmt** three times to add three copies of the field to the design grid.

   You need to select an aggregate function for each InvoiceAmt field. When you click the Totals button in the Show/Hide group on the DESIGN tab, a row labeled "Total" is added to the design grid. The Total row provides a list of the aggregate functions that you can select.

3. In the Show/Hide group on the DESIGN tab, click the **Totals** button. A new row labeled "Total" appears between the Table and Sort rows in the design grid. The default entry for each field in the Total row is the Group By operator, which you will learn about later in this tutorial. See Figure 3-38.

| Figure 3-38 | Total row inserted in the design grid |

In the Total row, you specify the aggregate function you want to use for a field.

4. Click the right side of the first column's **Total** box, and then click **Min**. This field will calculate the minimum amount of all the InvoiceAmt field values.

When you run the query, Access automatically will assign a datasheet column name of "MinOfInvoiceAmt" for this field. You can change the datasheet column name to a more descriptive or readable name by entering the name you want in the Field box. However, you must also keep the InvoiceAmt field name in the Field box because it identifies the field to use in the calculation. The Field box will contain the datasheet column name you specify followed by the field name (InvoiceAmt) with a colon separating the two names.

5. In the first column's Field box, click to the left of InvoiceAmt, and then type **MinimumInvoiceAmt:** (including the colon).

6. Using the ✛ pointer, double-click the column dividing line between the first two columns so that you can see the complete field name, MinimumInvoiceAmt:InvoiceAmt.

Next, you need to set the Caption property for this field so that the field name appears with spaces between words in the query datatsheet.

7. In the Show/Hide group on the DESIGN tab, click the **Property Sheet** button to open the Property Sheet for the current field.

8. In the Caption box, type **Minimum Invoice Amt** and then close the Property Sheet.

Be sure to type the colon following the name or the query will not work correctly.

You'll follow the same process to complete the query by calculating the average and maximum invoice amounts.

To calculate the average and maximum of all invoice amounts:

1. Click the right side of the second column's **Total** box, and then click **Avg**. This field will calculate the average of all the InvoiceAmt field values.

2. In the second column's Field box, click to the left of InvoiceAmt, and then type **AverageInvoiceAmt:**.

3. Resize the second column to fully display the field name, AverageInvoiceAmt:InvoiceAmt.

4. Open the Property Sheet for the current field, and then set its Caption property to **Average Invoice Amt**. Leave the Property Sheet open.

5. Click the right side of the third column's **Total** box, and then click **Max**. This field will calculate the maximum amount of all the InvoiceAmt field values.

6. In the third column's Field box, click to the left of InvoiceAmt, and then type **MaximumInvoiceAmt:**.

7. Resize the third column to fully display the field name, MaximumInvoiceAmt:InvoiceAmt.

8. In the Property Sheet for the current field, set the Caption property to **Maximum Invoice Amt** and then close the Property Sheet. See Figure 3-39.

| Figure 3-39 | Query with aggregate functions entered |

functions entered and columns resized

Trouble? Carefully compare your field names to those shown in the figure to make sure they match exactly; otherwise the query will not work correctly.

9. Run the query. Access displays one record containing the three aggregate function results. The single row of summary statistics represents calculations based on all the records selected for the query—in this case, all 203 records in the Billing table.

10. Resize all columns to their best fit so that the column names are fully displayed, and then click the field value in the first column to deselect the value and view the results. See Figure 3-40.

| Figure 3-40 | Result of the query using aggregate functions |

11. Save the query as **InvoiceAmtStatistics**.

Cindi would like to view the same invoice amount statistics (minimum, average, and maximum) as they relate to both scheduled appointments and walk-in visits to the clinic.

Using Record Group Calculations

In addition to calculating statistical information on all or selected records in selected tables, you can calculate statistics for groups of records. For example, you can determine the number of patients in each city or the average invoice amount by city.

To create a query for Cindi's latest request, you can modify the current query by adding the WalkIn field and assigning the Group By operator to it. The **Group By operator** divides the selected records into groups based on the values in the specified field. Those records with the same value for the field are grouped together, and the datasheet displays one record for each group. Aggregate functions, which appear in the other columns of the design grid, provide statistical information for each group.

You need to modify the current query to add the Group By operator to the WalkIn field from the Visit table. The Group By operator will display the statistical information grouped by the values of the WalkIn field for all the records in the query datasheet. To create the new query, you will save the InvoiceAmtStatistics query with a new name, keeping the original query intact, and then modify the new query.

To create a new query with the Group By operator:

1. Display the InvoiceAmtStatistics query in Design view. Because the query is open, you can use Backstage view to save it with a new name, keeping the original query intact.

2. Click the **FILE** tab to display Backstage view, and then click **Save As** in the navigation bar. The Save As screen opens.

3. In the File Types section on the left, click **Save Object As**. The right side of the screen changes to display options for saving the current database object as a new object.

4. Click the **Save As** button. The Save As dialog box opens, indicating that you are saving a copy of the InvoiceAmtStatistics query.

5. Type **InvoiceAmtStatisticsByWalkIn** to replace the highlighted name, and then press the **Enter** key. The new query is saved with the name you specified and displayed in Design view.

   You need to add the WalkIn field to the query. This field is in the Visit table. To include another table in an existing query, you open the Show Table dialog box.

TIP

You could also open the Navigation Pane and drag the Visit table from the pane to the Query window.

6. In the Query Setup group on the DESIGN tab, click the **Show Table** button to open the Show Table dialog box.

7. Add the **Visit** table to the Query window, close the Show Table dialog box, and then resize the Visit field list.

8. Drag the **WalkIn** field from the Visit field list to the first column in the design grid. When you release the mouse button, the WalkIn field appears in the design grid's first column, and the existing fields shift to the right. Group By, the default option in the Total row, appears for the WalkIn field.

9. Run the query. Access displays 2 records—one for each WalkIn group, Yes and No. Each record contains the WalkIn field value for the group and the three aggregate function values. The summary statistics represent calculations based on the 203 records in the Billing table. See Figure 3-41.

Figure 3-41   **Aggregate functions grouped by WalkIn**

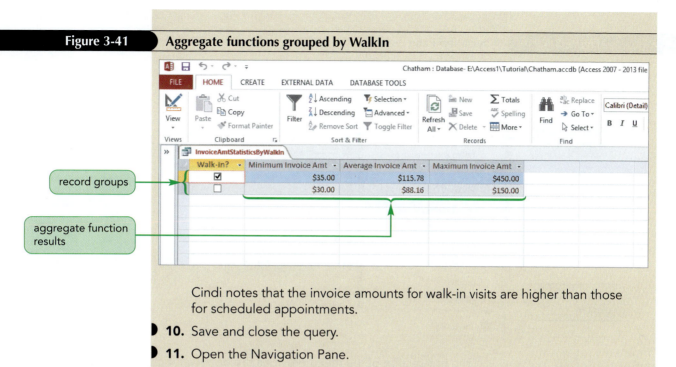

Cindi notes that the invoice amounts for walk-in visits are higher than those for scheduled appointments.

▶ **10.** Save and close the query.

▶ **11.** Open the Navigation Pane.

You have created and saved many queries in the Chatham database. The Navigation Pane provides options for opening and managing the queries you've created, as well as the other objects in the database, such as tables, forms, and reports.

Working with the Navigation Pane

As noted earlier, the Navigation Pane is the main area for working with the objects in a database. As you continue to create objects in your database, you might want to display and work with them in different ways. The Navigation Pane provides options for grouping database objects in various ways to suit your needs. For example, you might want to view only the queries created for a certain table or all the query objects in the database.

The Navigation Pane divides database objects into categories, and each category contains groups. The groups contain one or more objects. The default category is **Object Type**, which arranges objects by type—tables, queries, forms, and reports. The default group is **All Access Objects**, which displays all objects in the database. You can also choose to display only one type of object, such as tables.

The default group name, All Access Objects, appears at the top of the Navigation Pane. Currently, each object type—Tables, Queries, Forms, and Reports—is displayed as a heading, and the objects related to each type are listed below the heading. To group objects differently, you can select another category by using the Navigation Pane menu. You'll try this next.

TIP

You can hide the display of a group's objects by clicking the button to the right of the group name; click the button again to expand the group and display its objects.

To group objects differently in the Navigation Pane:

▶ **1.** At the top of the Navigation Pane, click the **All Access Objects** button ⊙. A menu is displayed for choosing different categories and groups. See Figure 3-42.

Figure 3-42   Navigation Pane menu

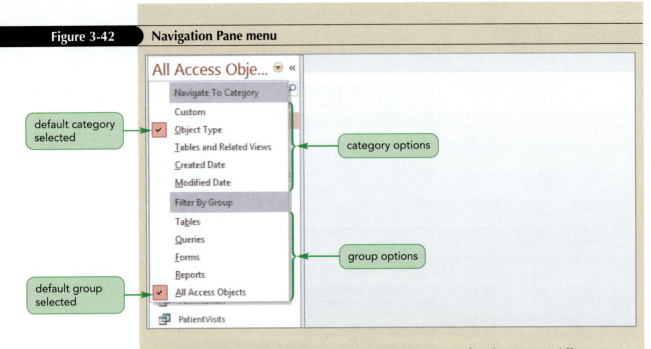

The top section of the menu provides the options for choosing a different category. The Object Type category has a checkmark next to it, signifying that it is the currently selected category. The lower section of the menu provides options for choosing a different group; these options might change depending on the selected category.

2. In the top section of the menu, click **Tables and Related Views**. The Navigation Pane is now grouped into categories of tables, and each table in the database—Visit, Billing, and Patient—is its own group. All database objects related to a table are listed below the table's name. See Figure 3-43.

| Figure 3-43 | Database objects grouped by table in the Navigation Pane |

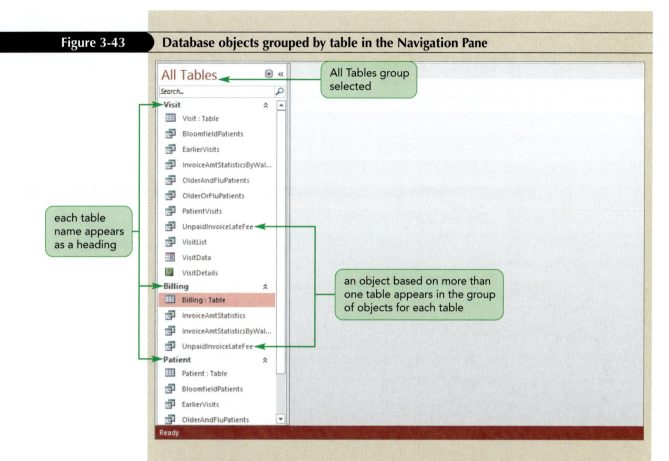

Some objects appear more than once. When an object is based on more than one table, that object appears in the group for each table. For example, the UnpaidInvoiceLateFee query is based on both the Visit and Billing tables, so it is listed in the group for both tables.

You can also choose to display the objects for only one table to better focus on that table.

3. At the top of the Navigation Pane, click the **All Tables** button ⊙ to display the Navigation Pane menu, and then click **Patient**. The Navigation Pane now shows only the objects related to the Patient table—the table itself plus the six queries you created that include fields from the Patient table.

4. At the top of the Navigation Pane, click the **Patient** button ⊙, and then click **Object Type** to return to the default display of the Navigation Pane.

5. Compact and repair the Chatham database, and then close the database.

Trouble? If a dialog box opens and warns that this action will cause Microsoft Access to empty the Clipboard, click the Yes button to continue.

The default All Access Objects category is a predefined category. You can also create custom categories to group objects in the way that best suits how you want to manage your database objects. As you continue to build a database and the list of objects grows, creating a custom category can help you to work more efficiently with the objects in the database.

The queries you've created and saved will help Cindi, Kelly, Ethan, and other staff members to monitor and analyze the business activity of Chatham Community Health Services and its patients. Now any staff member can run the queries at any time, modify them as needed, or use them as the basis for designing new queries to meet additional information requirements.

REVIEW

Session 3.2 Quick Check

1. A(n) _____ is a criterion, or rule, that determines which records are selected for a query datasheet.
2. In the design grid, where do you place the conditions for two different fields when you use the And logical operator, and where do you place them when you use the Or logical operator?
3. To perform a calculation in a query, you define a(n) _____ containing a combination of database fields, constants, and operators.
4. Which Access tool do you use to create an expression for a calculated field in a query?
5. What is an aggregate function?
6. The _____ operator divides selected records into groups based on the values in a field.
7. What is the default category for the display of objects in the Navigation Pane?

SAM Projects

Put your skills into practice with SAM Projects! SAM Projects for this tutorial can be found online. If you have a SAM account, go to www.cengage.com/sam2013 to download the most recent Project Instructions and Start Files.

ASSESS

PRACTICE

Review Assignments

Data File needed for the Review Assignments: Vendor.accdb *(cont. from Tutorial 2)*

Cindi asks you to update some information in the Vendor database and also to retrieve specific information from the database. Complete the following:

1. Open the **Vendor** database you created and worked with in Tutorials 1 and 2, and then click the Enable Content button next to the security warning, if necessary.

2. Open the **Supplier** table in Datasheet view, and then change the following field values for the record with the Supplier ID GRE364: Address to **1550 W Main St**, Contact Phone to **401-625-2745**, Contact First Name to **Andrew**, and Contact Last Name to **Kline**. Close the table.

3. Create a query based on the Supplier table. Include the following fields in the query, in the order shown: Company, Category, ContactFirst, ContactLast, Phone, and InitialContact. Sort the query in ascending order based on the Category field values. Save the query as **ContactList**, and then run the query.

4. Use the ContactList query datasheet to update the Supplier table by changing the Phone field value for Aresco Surgical, Inc. to **203-335-0054**.

5. Change the size of the font in the ContactList query datasheet to 12 points. Resize columns, as necessary, so that all field values and column headings are visible.

6. Change the alternate row color in the ContactList query datasheet to the Theme Color named Green, Accent 6, Lighter 60%, and then save and close the query.

7. Create a query based on the Supplier and Product tables. Select the Company, Category, and State fields from the Supplier table, and the ProductName, Price, Units, and Weight fields from the Product table. Sort the query results in descending order based on price. Select only those records with a State field value of CT, but do not display the State field values in the query results. Save the query as **CTSuppliers**, run the query, and then close it.

8. Create a query that lists all products that cost more than $200 and are sterile. Display the following fields from the Product table in the query results: ProductID, ProductName, Price, Units, and TempControl. (*Hint:* The Sterile field is a Yes/No field that should not appear in the query results.) Save the query as **HighPriceAndSterile**, run the query, and then close it.

9. Create a query that lists information about suppliers who sell equipment or products that require temperature control. Include the Company, Category, ContactFirst, and ContactLast fields from the Supplier table; and the ProductName, Price, TempControl, and Sterile fields from the Product table. Save the query as **EquipmentOrTempControl**, run the query, and then close it.

10. Create a query that lists only those products that cost $1000 or more, along with a 5% discount amount based on the price of the product. Include the Company field from the Supplier table and the following fields from the Product table in the query: ProductID, ProductName, and Price. Save the query as **HighPriceWithDiscount**. Display the discount in a calculated field named **DiscountAmt** that determines a 5% discount based on the Price field values. Set the Caption property **Discount Amt** for the calculated field. Display the query results in descending order by Price. Save and run the query.

11. Modify the format of the DiscountAmt field in the HighPriceWithDiscount query so that it uses the Standard format and two decimal places. Run the query, resize all columns in the datasheet to their best fit, and then save and close the query.

12. Create a query that calculates the lowest, highest, and average prices for all products using the field names **LowestPrice**, **HighestPrice**, and **AveragePrice**, respectively. Set the Caption property for each field to include a space between the two words in the field name. Run the query, resize all columns in the datasheet to their best fit, save the query as **PriceStatistics**, and then close it.

13. In the Navigation Pane, copy the PriceStatistics query, and then rename the copied query as **PriceStatisticsBySupplier**.

14. Modify the PriceStatisticsBySupplier query so that the records are grouped by the Company field in the Supplier table. The Company field should appear first in the query datasheet. Save and run the query, and then close it.

15. Compact and repair the Vendor database, and then close it.

Case Problem 1

Data File needed for this Case Problem: Gopher.accdb *(cont. from Tutorial 2)*

APPLY

GoGopher! Amol Mehta needs to modify a few records in the Gopher database and analyze the data for members enrolled in his company's various plans. To help Amol, you'll update the Gopher database and create queries to answer his questions. Complete the following:

1. Open the **Gopher** database you created and worked with in Tutorials 1 and 2, and then click the Enable Content button next to the security warning, if necessary.

2. In the **Member** table, find the record for MemberID 1251, and then change the Street value to **75 Hemlock Ln** and the Phone to **303-553-1847**.

3. In the **Member** table, find the record for MemberID 1228, and then delete the record. Close the Member table.

4. Create a query that lists members who did not have to pay a fee when they joined. In the query results, display the FirstName, LastName, and DateJoined fields from the Member table, and the PlanCost field from the Plan table. Sort the records in descending order by the date joined. Select records only for members whose fees were waived. (*Hint:* The FeeWaived field is a Yes/No field that should not appear in the query results.) Save the query as **NoFees**, and then run the query.

5. Use the NoFees query datasheet to update the Member table by changing the Last Name value for Kara Murray to **Seaburg**.

6. Use the NoFees query datasheet to display the total Plan Cost for the selected members. Save and close the query.

7. Create a query that lists the MemberID, FirstName, LastName, DateJoined, PlanDescription, and PlanCost fields for members who joined GoGopher! between April 1, 2016 and April 30, 2016. Save the query as **AprilMembers**, run the query, and then close it.

8. Create a query that lists all members who live in Louisville and whose memberships expire on or after 1/1/2017. Display the following fields from the Member table in the query results: MemberID, FirstName, LastName, Phone, and Expiration. (*Hint:* The City field values should not appear in the query results.) Sort the query results in ascending order by last name. Save the query as **LouisvilleAndExpiration**, run the query, and then close it.

9. Copy and paste the LouisvilleAndExpiration query to create a new query named **LouisvilleOrExpiration**. Modify the new query so that it lists all members who live in Louisville or whose memberships expire on or after 1/1/2017. Display the City field values in the query results following the Phone field values, and sort the query results in ascending order by city (this should be the only sort in the query). Save and run the query.

10. Change the size of the font in the LouisvilleOrExpiration query datasheet to 14 points. Resize columns, as necessary, so that all field values and column headings are visible.

11. Change the alternate row color in the LouisvilleOrExpiration query datasheet to the Theme Color named Blue, Accent 1, Lighter 80%, and then save and close the query.

12. Create a query that calculates the lowest, highest, and average cost for all plans using the field names **LowestCost**, **HighestCost**, and **AverageCost**, respectively. Set the Caption property for each field to include a space between the two words in the field name. Run the query, resize all columns in the datasheet to their best fit, save the query as **CostStatistics**, and then close it.

13. Copy and paste the CostStatistics query to create a new query named **CostStatisticsByCity**.

14. Modify the CostStatisticsByCity query to display the same statistics grouped by City, with City appearing as the first field. (*Hint:* Add the Member table to the query.) Run the query, and then save and close it.

15. Compact and repair the Gopher database, and then close it.

Case Problem 2

Data File needed for this Case Problem: OBrien.accdb *(cont. from Tutorial 2)*

O'Brien Educational Services   After reviewing the OBrien database, Karen O'Brien wants to modify some records and then view specific information about the students, tutors, and contracts for her educational services company. She asks you to update and query the OBrien database to perform these tasks. Complete the following:

1. Open the **OBrien** database you created and worked with in Tutorials 1 and 2, and then click the Enable Content button next to the security warning, if necessary.

2. In the **Tutor** table, change the following information for the record with TutorID 79-0678: Degree is **BA** and Hire Date is **9/15/2015**. Close the table.

3. In the **Student** table, find the record with the StudentID MCS8051, and then delete the related record in the subdatasheet for this student. Delete the record for StudentID MCS8051, and then close the Student table.

4. Create a query based on the Student table that includes the LastName, FirstName, and CellPhone fields, in that order. Save the query as **StudentCellList**, and then run the query.

5. In the results of the StudentCellList query, change the cell phone number for Haley Gosnold to **574-252-1973**. Close the query.

6. Create a query based on the Tutor and Contract tables. Display the LastName field from the Tutor table, and the StudentID, ContractDate, SessionType, Length, and Cost fields, in that order, from the Contract table. Sort first in ascending order by the tutor's last name, and then in ascending order by the StudentID. Save the query as **SessionsByTutor**, run the query, and the close it.

7. Copy and paste the SessionsByTutor query to create a new query named **GroupSessions**. Modify the new query so that it displays the same information for records with a Group session type only. Do not display the SessionType field values in the query results. Save and run the query, and then close it.

8. Create and save a query that produces the results shown in Figure 3-44. Close the query when you are finished.

Figure 3-44   **SouthBendPrivate query results**

show only records for students from South Bend who are taking private sessions

sort by Last Name

format with a font size of 12 and the Gold, Accent 4, Lighter 60% alternate row Theme Color

9. Create and save a query that produces the results shown in Figure 3-45. Close the query when you are finished.

Figure 3-45   **OscelaOrSemi query results**

sort in descending order by Contract Date

show only records for students from Oscela or students taking semi-private sessions

Student ID	First Name	Last Name	Contract Date	Cost
DRO8048	Emma	Drouin	9/15/2016	$720
NAS8012	Andre	Nastasia	9/12/2016	$800
GUS8002	Michael	Gustafson	9/10/2016	$900
RIV8011	Marco	Rivera	8/10/2016	$1,080
DEN8042	David	DeNardo	8/1/2016	$800
CAR8059	Carol	Carlson	7/15/2016	$1,200
YEN8035	Lila	Yen	6/22/2016	$1,440
MAS8056	Kimberly	Mase	5/8/2016	$960
STI8038	Lily	Stiefel	3/15/2016	$720
BIE8000	Joshua	Biega	3/14/2016	$1,800
HIN8040	Erica	Hinkle	3/1/2016	$960
NAS8012	Andre	Nastasia	2/1/2016	$960
GUS8002	Michael	Gustafson	1/28/2016	$720
MUE8041	Bart	Mueller	1/15/2016	$1,440
YEN8035	Lila	Yen	1/7/2016	$1,280
HEC8018	Eric	Hecht	12/17/2015	$900
WOO8071	Jon	Woodburn	12/15/2015	$1,800
NUN8084	Rodrigo	Nunez	9/30/2015	$800
Total				$19,280

Total row shows the sum of the Cost values

10. Create and save a query to display statistics for the Cost field, as shown in Figure 3-46. Close the query when you are finished.

Figure 3-46   **CostStatistics query results**

set captions to include spaces between words

Minimum Cost	Average Cost	Maximum Cost
720.00	1,086.67	1,920.00

format values as Standard with two decimal places

11. Copy and paste the CostStatistics query to create a new query named **CostStatisticsByCity**.

12. Modify the CostStatisticsByCity query to display the same statistics grouped by City, with City appearing as the first field. (*Hint:* Add the Student table to the query.) Run the query, and then save and close it.

13. Compact and repair the OBrien database, and then close it.

Case Problem 3

CHALLENGE

Data File needed for this Case Problem: Shelter.accdb *(cont. from Tutorial 2)*

Rosemary Animal Shelter   Ryan Lang needs to modify some records in the Shelter database, and then he wants to find specific information about the animals, patrons, and donations for his not-for-profit agency. Ryan asks you to help him update the database and create queries to find the information he needs. Complete the following:

1. Open the **Shelter** database you created and worked with in Tutorials 1 and 2, and then click the Enable Content button next to the security warning, if necessary.

⊕ **Explore** 2. In the **Patron** table, delete the record with PatronID 36064. (*Hint:* Delete the related record in the Donation subdatasheet first, which you need to display using the Insert Subdatasheet dialog box.) Close the Patron table without saving changes to the table layout.

3. Create a query based on the Animal table that includes the AnimalID, AnimalName, AnimalType, Gender, and ArrivalDate fields, in that order. Save the query as **AnimalsByType**, and then run it.

4. Modify the AnimalsByType query design so that it sorts records in ascending order first by AnimalType and then by Gender. Save and run the query.

5. In the AnimalsByType query datasheet, find the record for the animal with Animal ID D23, and then change the arrival date for this animal to **5/19/2016**. Close the query.

6. Create a query that displays the PatronID, FirstName, and LastName fields from the Patron table, and the Description and DonationValue fields from the Donation table for all donations over $150. Sort the query in ascending order by donation value. Save the query as **LargeDonations**, run the query, and then close it.

7. Copy and paste the LargeDonations query to create a new query named **LargeCashDonations**.

⊕ **Explore** 8. Modify the LargeCashDonations query to display only those records with donations valuing more than $150 in cash. Do not include the Description field values in the query results. Use the query datasheet to calculate the average cash donation. Save and close the query.

9. Create a query that displays the PatronID, FirstName, and LastName fields from the Patron table, and the AnimalName, AnimalType, Age, Gender, and Adopted fields from the Animal table. Specify that the results show records for only those animals that have been adopted. Do not display the Adopted field values in the query results. Save the query as **CatAdoptions**, and then run the query.

10. Filter the results of the CatAdoptions query datasheet to display records for cats only.

⊕ **Explore** 11. Format the datasheet of the CatAdoptions query so that it does not display gridlines, uses an alternate row Standard Color of Purple 2, and displays a font size of 12. (*Hint*: Use the Gridlines button in the Text Formatting group on the HOME tab to select the appropriate gridlines option.) Resize the columns to display the complete field names and values, if necessary. Save and close the query.

⊕ **Explore** 12. Create a query that displays the PatronID, FirstName, and LastName fields from the Patron table, and the Description, DonationDate, and DonationValue fields from the Donation table. Specify that the query include records for noncash donations only or for donations made in the month of June 2016. Sort the records first in ascending order by the patron's last name, and then in descending order by the donation value. Save the query as **NonCashOrJuneDonations**, run the query, and then close it.

13. Copy and paste the NonCashOrJuneDonations query to create a new query named **DonationsAfterStorageCharge**.

⊕ **Explore** 14. Modify the DonationsAfterStorageCharge query so that it displays records for noncash donations made on all dates. Create a calculated field named **NetDonation** that displays the results of subtracting $3.50 from the DonationValue field values to account for the cost of storing each noncash donated item. Set the Caption property **Net Donation** for the calculated field. Display the results in ascending order by donation value. Run the query, and then modify it to format both the DonationValue field and the calculated field as Currency with two decimal places. Run the query again and resize the columns in the datasheet to their best fit, as necessary. Save and close the query.

⊕ **Explore** 15. Create a query based on the **Donation** table that displays the sum, average, and count of the DonationValue field for all donations. Then complete the following:

   a. Specify field names of **TotalDonations**, **AverageDonation**, and **NumberofDonations**. Then specify captions to include spaces between words.

   b. Save the query as **DonationStatistics**, and then run it. Resize the query datasheet columns to their best fit.

   c. Modify the field properties so that the values in the Total Donations and Average Donation columns display two decimal places and the Standard format. Run the query again, and then save and close the query.

   d. Copy and paste the DonationStatistics query to create a new query named **DonationStatisticsByDescription**.

   e. Modify the DonationStatisticsByDescription query to display the sum, average, and count of the DonationValue field for all donations grouped by Description, with Description appearing as the first field. Sort the records in descending order by Total Donations. Save, run, and then close the query.

16. Compact and repair the Shelter database, and then close it.

TROUBLESHOOT

Case Problem 4

Data File needed for this Case Problem: Stanley.accdb *(cont. from Tutorial 2)* and Tour.accdb

Stanley EcoTours   Janice and Bill Stanley need your help to maintain and analyze data about the clients, reservations, and tours for their ecotourism business. Additionally, you'll troubleshoot some problems in another database containing tour information. Complete the following:

1. Open the **Stanley** database you created and worked with in Tutorials 1 and 2, and then click the Enable Content button next to the security warning, if necessary.

2. In the **Guest** table, change the phone number for Paul Barry to **406-497-1068**, and then close the table.

3. Create a query based on the Tour table that includes the TourName, Location, Country, PricePerPerson, and TourType fields, in that order. Sort in ascending order based on the PricePerPerson field values. Save the query as **ToursByPrice**, and then run the query.

4. Use the ToursByPrice query datasheet to display the total Price Per Person for the tours. Save and close the query.

5. Create a query that displays the GuestLast, City, and State/Prov fields from the Guest table, and the ReservationID, StartDate, and People fields from the Reservation table. Save the query as **GuestTourDates**, and then run the query. Change the alternate row color in the query datasheet to the Theme Color Green, Accent 6, Lighter 40%. In Datasheet view, use an AutoFilter to sort the query results from oldest to newest Start Date. Save and close the query.

6. Create a query that displays the GuestFirst, GuestLast, City, ReservationID, TourID, and StartDate fields for all guests from Montana (MT). Do not include the State/Prov field in the query results. Sort the query in ascending order by the guest's last name. Save the query as **MontanaGuests** and then run it. Close the query.

7. Create a query that displays data from all three tables in the database, as follows: the GuestLast, City, State/Prov, and Country fields from the Guest table; the StartDate field from the Reservation table; and the TourName, Location, and TourType fields from the Tour table. Specify that the query select only those records for guests from Canada or guests who are taking Jeep tours. Sort the query in ascending order by Location. Save the query as **CanadaOrJeep**, and then run the query. Resize datasheet columns to their best fit, as necessary, and then save and close the query.

8. Copy and paste the CanadaOrJeep query to create a new query named **IdahoAndJuly**.

9. Modify the IdahoAndJuly query to select all guests from Idaho who are taking a tour starting sometime in the month of July 2016. Do not include the State/Prov field values or the Country field values in the query results. Run the query. Resize datasheet columns to their best fit, as necessary, and then save and close the query.

10. Create a query that displays the ReservationID, StartDate, and People fields from the Reservation table, and the TourName, Location, Country, PricePerPerson, and SingleSupplement fields from the Tour table for all reservations with a People field value of 1. Save the query as **SingleReservations**. Add a field to the query named **TotalCost** that displays the results of adding the SingleSupplement field values to the PricePerPerson field values. Set the Caption property **Total Cost** for the calculated field. Display the results in descending order by TotalCost. Do not include the People field values in the query results. Run the query. Modify the query by formatting the TotalCost field to show 0 decimal places. Run the query, resize datasheet columns to their best fit, as necessary, and then save and close the query.

11. Create a query based on the Tour table that determines the minimum, average, and maximum price per person for all tours. Then complete the following:

   a. Specify field names of **LowestPrice**, **AveragePrice**, and **HighestPrice**.

   b. Set the Caption property for each field to include a space between the two words in the field name.

   c. Save the query as **PriceStatistics**, and then run the query.

   d. In Design view, specify the Standard format and two decimal places for each column.

   e. Run the query, resize all the datasheet columns to their best fit, save your changes, and then close the query.

   f. Create a copy of the PriceStatistics query named **PriceStatisticsByTourType**.

   g. Modify the PriceStatisticsByTourType query to display the price statistics grouped by TourType, with TourType appearing as the first field. Save your changes and then run and close the query.

12. Compact and repair the Stanley database, and then close it.

☼ **Troubleshoot** 13. Open the **Tour** database located in the Access1 ▸ Case4 folder provided with your Data Files, and then click the Enable Content button next to the security warning, if necessary. Run the BookingByDateAndState query in the Tour database. The query is not producing the desired results. Fix the query so that the data from the Booking table is listed first, the data is sorted only by StartDate in ascending order, and the results do not display country values. Save and close the corrected query.

Troubleshoot 14. Run the WYGuestsFewerPeople query, which displays no records in the results. This query is supposed to show data for guests from Wyoming with fewer than four people in their booking. Find and correct the error in the query design, run the query, and then close it.

Troubleshoot 15. Run the CanadaOrSeptStart query. This query should display the records for all guests who are from Canada or whose booking start date is on or after 9/1/2016. Find and correct the errors in the query design, run the query, and then close it. Compact and repair the Tour database, and then close it.

Teamwork

Working with a Team to Create a Database

Teamwork is the collaborative effort of individuals working together to achieve a goal. Most organizations rely on teams to complete work tasks, regardless of whether those teams are formal and ongoing or informally organized to achieve a specific goal. Some teams might even be virtual, such as teams that use telecommunications technologies and social networks to complete tasks from different corporate or geographical locations.

When an organization decides to use a database to manage information, the database is rarely planned, created, and maintained by a single individual. In most cases, a team of individuals is assigned to work on different stages of database development. For example, a team might research the needs of the organization, the best database management system to use to meet those needs, and the skills required of the team members to create, update, and maintain the database. Then another team might take over the task of actually creating the database and its objects, inputting the data, and installing the database on the organization's network. Finally, yet another team might conduct training sessions to teach users how to use the database to extract the data they require to perform their jobs.

Regardless of the type of database being created, the roles that individual team members play when working on a team are similar to what you might expect in any situation that requires a collaborative effort.

The Roles of Team Members

If a team is to be successful, individual members must see the value in their respective contributions and what the team as a whole gets out of each member's contribution. This means two important requirements must be met: task performance and social satisfaction. Task performance usually is handled by one or more members who are task specialists. Task specialists spend a lot of time and effort ensuring that the team achieves its goals. They initiate ideas, give opinions, gather information, sort details, and provide motivation to keep the team on track.

Social satisfaction is handled by individuals who strengthen the team's social bonds through encouragement, empathy, conflict resolution, compromise, and tension reduction. Have you ever been on a team where the tension was high, and someone stepped in to tell a joke or tried to soften the blow of criticism? That person held the role of managing social satisfaction.

Both the task specialist and social satisfaction specialist are important roles on teams. These are not the only roles, however. Other roles include team leaders, work coordinators, idea people, and critics. The roles of individual team members are not always mutually exclusive. For example, the task specialist might also be the team leader, and the idea person might also fill the social satisfaction role. As you begin working with your team in this exercise, watch how these roles are filled and how they change as your team completes its work. Perhaps you'll want to discuss upfront which role each member is comfortable filling to see how complementary your collective skill sets turn out to be. What if your team lacks a role? Then you'll need to figure out, as a team, how to move forward so you can complete your work successfully. The following are tips that everyone should respect as work on a team begins:

- Remember that everyone brings something of value to the team.
- Respect and support each other as you work toward the common goal.
- When criticism or questions arise, try to see things from the other person's perspective.
- If someone needs assistance, find ways to encourage or support that person so the team is not affected.
- Deal with negative or unproductive attitudes immediately so they don't damage team energy and attitude.
- Get outside help if the team becomes stuck and can't move forward.
- Provide periodic positive encouragement or rewards for contributions.

The Importance of Technology in Teamwork

Many teams now depend on technology to accomplish work tasks. For example, corporate intranets and networks, email and voice mail, texting and instant messaging, teleconferencing and software collaboration tools, social networks, and cell phones can support teamwork. Each time you work in a group, decide at the outset how the team will use different technologies to communicate and document work activities. Determine how the team will organize and combine deliverable documents or presentation materials. Use whatever technology tools make the most sense for your team, your task, and your skills.

PROSKILLS

Create a Database

Many organizations use Access to manage business data, but Access can also be a valuable tool to track personal data. For example, you might create an Access database to store information about items in a personal collection, such as CDs, DVDs, or books; items related to a hobby, such as coin or stamp collecting, travel, or family history; or items related to sports teams, theater clubs, or other organizations to which you might belong. In this exercise, you'll work with your team members to create a database that will contain information of your choice, using the Access skills and features presented in Tutorials 1 through 3. As a group, you'll choose something the team is interested in tracking, such as members and activities of a college service organization or recruiters and job opportunities at your school.

Using Templates

Access includes templates for creating databases. A **database template** is a database containing predefined tables, queries, forms, and reports. Using a database template can save you time and effort when creating a database. For example, if the database objects available in one of the database templates are suitable for the data you want to store, you can use the template to quickly create a database with the objects already created for you. You can then modify them, as necessary, to suit your needs. Before you begin to create a database with your team members, review the following steps for using a database template.

To create a database using a database template:

1. Make sure the New screen is displayed in Backstage view.
2. Click one of the available Desktop templates, or use the box at the top of the screen to search for templates online. (Note that templates without the word "Desktop" in their names require Sharepoint, so do not choose one of those.)
3. Specify the name for your database and a location in which to save the database file.
4. Click the Create button.
5. Use the resulting database objects to enter, modify, or delete data or database objects.

Work in a Team to Create a Database

Working with your team members, you can decide to use a database template for this exercise if the template fits the data you want to track. Note, however, that you still need to create the additional database objects indicated in the following steps—tables, queries, forms, and reports—to complete the exercise successfully.

Note: Please be sure *not* to include any personal information of a sensitive nature in the database you create to be submitted to your instructor for this exercise. Later on, you can update the data in your database with such information for your own personal use.

1. Meet with your team to determine what data you want to track in your new Access database. Determine how many tables you need and what data will go into each table. Be sure that the data you choose to track lends itself to at least three groupings of related data, that at least twenty items are available to track within each group, and that you'll be able to track multiple types of data. Sketch the layout of the columns (fields) and rows (records) for each table.

Also discuss the field properties for each field, so that team members can document the characteristics needed for each field as they collect data. Consider using a standard form to help each person as he or she collects the necessary data.

Next, assign data gathering and documentation tasks to each team member and set a deadline for finishing this initial task. Consider using Excel workbooks for this task, as you can use them to import the data later when working in Access. When all the data for the fields is collected, meet again as a team to examine the data collected and determine the structure of the database you will create. Finally, assign each team member specific tasks for creating the database objects discussed in the following steps.

2. Create a new Access database to contain the data your team wants to track.

3. Create two or three tables in the database that can be joined through one-to-many relationships.

4. Using the preliminary design work done by team members, define the properties for each field in each table. Make sure to include a mix of data types for the fields (for example, do not include only Short Text fields in each table).

5. As a team, discuss and specify a primary key for each table.

6. Define the necessary one-to-many relationships between the tables in the database with referential integrity enforced.

7. Enter 20 to 30 records in each table. If appropriate, your team can import the data for a table from another source, such as an Excel workbook or a text file.

8. Create 5 to 10 queries based on single tables and multiple tables. Be sure that some of the queries include some or all of the following: exact match conditions, comparison operators, and logical operators.

9. For some of the queries, use various sorting and filtering techniques to display the query results in various ways. Save these queries with the sort and/or filter applied.

10. If possible, and depending on the data your team is tracking, create at least one calculated field in one of the queries.

11. If possible, and depending on the data your team is tracking, use aggregate functions to produce summary statistics based on the data in at least one of the tables.

12. Create a simple form for each table in the database.

13. Create a simple report based on each table in the database.

14. Submit your team's completed database to your instructor as requested. Include printouts of any database objects, such as reports, if required. Also, provide written documentation that describes the role of each team member and his or her contributions to the team. This documentation should include descriptions of any challenges the team faced while completing this exercise and how the team members worked together to overcome those challenges.

OBJECTIVES

Session 1.1
- Plan and create a new presentation
- Create a title slide and slides with lists
- Edit and format text
- Move and copy text
- Convert a list to a SmartArt diagram
- Duplicate, rearrange, and delete slides
- Close a presentation

Session 1.2
- Open an existing presentation
- Change the theme and theme variant
- Insert and crop photos
- Modify photo compression options
- Resize and move objects
- Create speaker notes
- Check the spelling
- Run a slide show
- Print slides, handouts, speaker notes, and the outline

Creating a Presentation

Presenting Information About Community Supported Agriculture

POWERPOINT

Case | *Valley Falls CSA*

Isaac DeSoto graduated from Claflin University in Orangeburg, South Carolina, with a degree in Agriculture Production Technology. He began his career working for the South Carolina Department of Agriculture. Recently, he bought a large farm near Spartanburg, South Carolina, and started a community-supported agriculture program, or CSA. In a CSA, people buy shares each season and, in return, receive weekly portions of produce from the farm. Isaac also created a partnership with other local farmers and founded Valley Falls CSA. Isaac wants to use a PowerPoint presentation to attract new co-op members.

Microsoft PowerPoint 2013 (or simply **PowerPoint**) is a computer program you use to create a collection of slides that can contain text, charts, pictures, sounds, movies, multimedia, and so on. In this tutorial, you'll use PowerPoint to create a presentation that Isaac can use to explain what Valley Falls CSA is and what it has to offer to potential members and the community. After Isaac reviews it, you'll add graphics and speaker notes to the presentation. Finally, you'll check the spelling, run the slide show to evaluate it, and print the file.

STARTING DATA FILES

Tutorial

People.jpg
Produce1.jpg
Produce2.jpg
Revised Membership.pptx

Review

Farmland.jpg
Field Volunteer.jpg
Office Volunteer.jpg
Revised Volunteer Info.pptx

Case1

Orientation.pptx
4 .jpg files

Case2

Olympiad.pptx
Tangrams.jpg
Winner.jpg

Case3

Floating Houses.jpg
Karl.jpg
Peru.pptx
11 Region .jpg files

Case4

Loading1.mp4
Loading2.mp4
6 .jpg files

Session 1.1 Visual Overview:

The **Quick Access Toolbar** contains buttons for frequently used commands. You can click the Customize Quick Access Toolbar button (the small arrow on the right) to add and remove commands.

The ribbon is organized into tabs. Each **tab** contains buttons related to particular activities or tasks.

The **ribbon** contains buttons that you click to execute commands you need to work with PowerPoint.

PowerPoint files consist of **slides**, which are similar to pages in a document.

Each tab is organized into **groups** of related commands.

The **Slides tab** shows a column of numbered slide thumbnails so you can see a visual representation of several slides at once.

A **placeholder** is a region of a slide reserved for inserting text or graphics.

The **status bar** provides information about the file and contains commands for viewing the presentation in different ways and for zooming in on the view.

The PowerPoint Window

The title bar contains the filename of the current presentation. A temporary filename "Presentation" followed by a number appears until you save the file.

You click the Ribbon Display Options button to select commands to display and hide the ribbon.

You use the window buttons to minimize, maximize, and close the PowerPoint window.

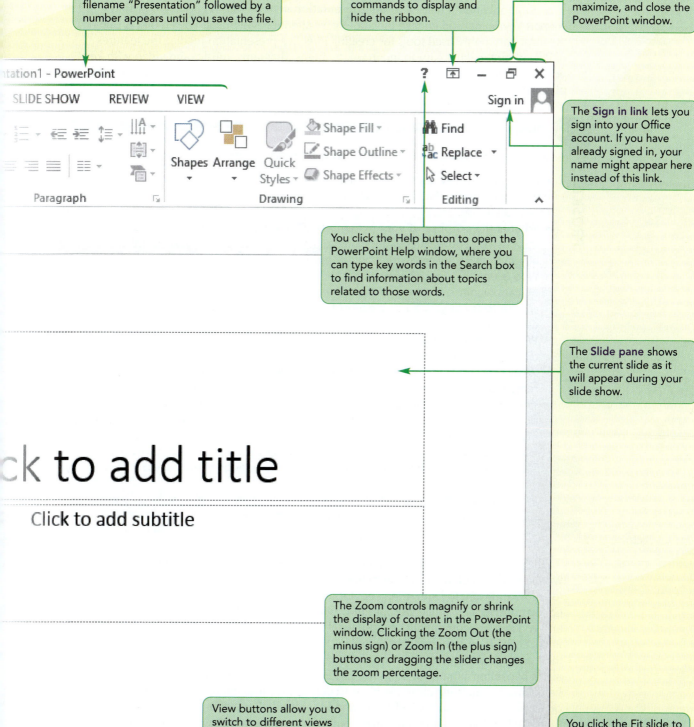

The **Sign in link** lets you sign into your Office account. If you have already signed in, your name might appear here instead of this link.

You click the Help button to open the PowerPoint Help window, where you can type key words in the Search box to find information about topics related to those words.

The **Slide pane** shows the current slide as it will appear during your slide show.

The Zoom controls magnify or shrink the display of content in the PowerPoint window. Clicking the Zoom Out (the minus sign) or Zoom In (the plus sign) buttons or dragging the slider changes the zoom percentage.

View buttons allow you to switch to different views of the presentation.

You click the Fit slide to current window button to resize the slide in the Slide pane to fit in the window.

Planning a Presentation

A **presentation** is a talk (lecture) or prepared file in which the person speaking or the person who prepared the file—the presenter—wants to communicate with an audience to explain new concepts or ideas, sell a product or service, entertain, train the audience in a new skill or technique, or any of a wide variety of other topics.

Most people find it helpful to use **presentation media**—visual and audio aids to support key points and engage the audience's attention. Microsoft PowerPoint is one of the most commonly used tools for creating effective presentation media. The features of PowerPoint make it easy to incorporate photos, diagrams, music, and video with key points of a presentation. Before you create a presentation, you should spend some time planning its content.

PROSKILLS

Verbal Communication: Planning a Presentation

Answering a few key questions will help you create a presentation using appropriate presentation media that successfully delivers its message or motivates the audience to take an action.

- **What is the purpose of your presentation?** In other words, what action or response do you want your audience to have? For example, do you want them to buy something, follow instructions, or make a decision?
- **Who is your audience?** Think about the needs and interests of your audience as well as any decisions they'll make as a result of what you have to say. What you choose to say to your audience must be relevant to their needs, interests, and decisions or it will be forgotten.
- **What are the main points of your presentation?** Identify the information that is directly relevant to your audience.
- **What presentation media will help your audience absorb the information and remember it later?** Do you need lists, photos, charts, or tables?
- **What is the format for your presentation?** Will you deliver the presentation orally or will you create a presentation file that your audience members will view on their own, without you present?
- **How much time do you have for the presentation?** Keep that in mind as you prepare the presentation content so that you have enough time to present all of your key points.
- **Will your audience benefit from handouts?** **Handouts** are printed documents you give to your audience before, during, or after your presentation.

The purpose of Isaac's presentation is to sell shares in the new CSA. His audience will be members of the local community who are interested in the benefits of belonging to a CSA and want to learn more about it. His key points are that being a member of a CSA is good for consumers because they will be eating fresher, more nutritious food, and good for the community because local farms are supported and there is less of an impact on the environment. He also plans to explain pricing and how members get their produce so that audience members have enough information to make a decision about becoming a member. Isaac will use PowerPoint to display lists and graphics to help make his message clear. He plans to deliver his presentation orally to small groups of people in a classroom-sized room, and his presentation will be 15 to 20 minutes long. For handouts, he plans to have membership applications available to distribute to anyone who is interested, but he will not distribute anything before his presentation because he wants the audience's full attention to be on him and the details are not complex enough that the audience will need a sheet to refer to as he is speaking.

Once you know what you want to say or communicate, you can prepare the presentation media to help communicate your ideas.

Starting PowerPoint and Creating a New Presentation

Microsoft PowerPoint 2013 is a tool you can use to create and display visual and audio aids on slides to help clarify the points you want to make in your presentation or to create a presentation that people view on their own without you being present.

When PowerPoint starts, the Recent screen in Backstage view is displayed. **Backstage view** contains commands that allow you to manage your presentation files and PowerPoint options. When you first start PowerPoint, the only actions available to you in Backstage view are to open an existing PowerPoint file or create a new file. You'll start PowerPoint now.

To start PowerPoint:

1. Display the Windows Start screen, if necessary.

   Using Windows 7? To complete Step 1, click the Start button on the taskbar.

2. Click the **PowerPoint 2013** tile. PowerPoint starts and displays the Recent screen in Backstage view. See Figure 1-1. In the orange bar on the left is a list of recently opened presentations, and on the right are options for creating new presentations.

Figure 1-1	**Recent screen in Backstage view**

if you recently worked on a presentation file, it might be listed here

click to open a new, blank presentation

the choices on your screen might differ

Trouble? If you don't see the PowerPoint 2013 tile, type PowerPoint to display the Apps screen with the PowerPoint 2013 tile highlighted, and then click the tile.

Using Windows 7? To complete Step 2, point to All Programs on the Start menu, click Microsoft Office 2013, and then click PowerPoint 2013.

3. Click **Blank Presentation**. Backstage view closes and a new presentation window appears. The temporary filename "Presentation1" appears in the title bar. There is only one slide in the new presentation—Slide 1.

Trouble? If you do not see the area on the ribbon that contains buttons and you see only the ribbon tab names, click the HOME tab to expand the ribbon and display the commands, and then in the bottom-right corner of the ribbon, click the Pin the ribbon button ⊞ that appears.

Trouble? If the window is not maximized, click the Maximize button ⬜ in the upper-right corner.

When you create a new presentation, it is displayed in Normal view. **Normal view** displays slides one at a time in the Slide pane, allowing you to see how the text and graphics look on each slide, and displays **thumbnails**—miniature images—of all the slides in the presentation in the Slides tab on the left. The HOME tab on the ribbon is orange to indicate that it is selected when you first open or create a presentation. The Session 1.1 Visual Overview identifies elements of the PowerPoint window.

Working in Touch Mode

In Office 2013, you can work with a mouse or, if you have a touch screen, you can work in Touch Mode. In **Touch Mode** the ribbon increases in height so that there is more space around each button on the ribbon, making it easier to use your finger to tap the specific button you need. Also, in the main part of the PowerPoint window, the instructions telling you to "Click" are replaced with instructions to "Tap." Note that the figures in this text show the screen with Mouse Mode on. You'll switch to Touch Mode and then back to Mouse Mode now.

Note: The following steps assume that you are using a mouse. If you are instead using a touch device, please read these steps but don't complete them, so that you remain working in Touch Mode.

To switch between Touch Mode and Mouse Mode:

▶ **1.** On the Quick Access Toolbar, click the **Customize Quick Access Toolbar** button ⯯. A menu opens. The Touch/Mouse Mode command near the bottom of the menu does not have a checkmark next to it.

   Trouble? If the Touch/Mouse Mode command has a checkmark next to it, press the Esc key to close the menu, and then skip Step 2.

▶ **2.** On the menu, click **Touch/Mouse Mode**. The menu closes and the Touch/Mouse Mode button appears on the Quick Access Toolbar.

▶ **3.** On the Quick Access Toolbar, click the **Touch/Mouse Mode** button ⬚. A menu opens listing Mouse and Touch, and the icon next to Mouse is shaded orange to indicate it is selected.

   Trouble? If the icon next to Touch is shaded orange, press the Esc key to close the menu and skip Step 4.

▶ **4.** On the menu, click **Touch**. The menu closes and the ribbon increases in height so that there is more space around each button on the ribbon. Notice that the instructions in the main part of the PowerPoint window changed by replacing the instruction to "Click" with the instruction to "Tap." See Figure 1-2. Now you'll change back to Mouse Mode.

| Figure 1-2 | PowerPoint window with Touch mode active |

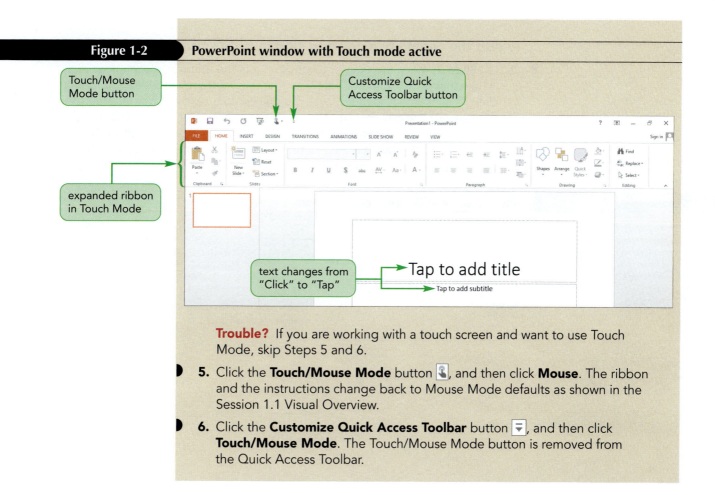

Trouble? If you are working with a touch screen and want to use Touch Mode, skip Steps 5 and 6.

5. Click the **Touch/Mouse Mode** button 👆, and then click **Mouse**. The ribbon and the instructions change back to Mouse Mode defaults as shown in the Session 1.1 Visual Overview.

6. Click the **Customize Quick Access Toolbar** button ⏷, and then click **Touch/Mouse Mode**. The Touch/Mouse Mode button is removed from the Quick Access Toolbar.

Creating a Title Slide

The **title slide** is the first slide in a presentation. It generally contains the title of the presentation plus any other identifying information you want to include, such as a company's slogan, the presenter's name, or a company name. The **font**—a set of characters with the same design—used in the title and subtitle may be the same or may be different fonts that complement each other.

The title slide contains two objects called text placeholders. A placeholder is a region of a slide reserved for inserting text or graphics. A **text placeholder** is a placeholder designed to contain text. Text placeholders usually display text that describes the purpose of the placeholder and instructs you to click so that you can start typing in the placeholder. The larger text placeholder on the title slide is designed to hold the presentation title, and the smaller text placeholder is designed to contain a subtitle. Once you enter text into a text placeholder, it is no longer a placeholder and becomes an object called a **text box**.

When you click in the placeholder, the **insertion point**, which indicates where text will appear when you start typing, appears as a blinking line in the center of the placeholder. In addition, a contextual tab, the DRAWING TOOLS FORMAT tab, appears on the ribbon. A **contextual tab** appears only in context—that is, when a particular type of object is selected or active—and contains commands for modifying that object.

You'll add a title and subtitle for Isaac's presentation now. Isaac wants the title slide to contain the company name and slogan.

To add the company name and slogan to the title slide:

1. On **Slide 1**, move the pointer to position it in the title text placeholder (where it says "Click to add title") so that the pointer changes to I, and then click. The insertion point replaces the placeholder text; the border around the text placeholder changes to a dotted line, and the DRAWING TOOLS FORMAT contextual tab appears as the rightmost tab on the ribbon. Note that in the Font group on the HOME tab, the Font box identifies the title font as Calibri Light. See Figure 1-3.

Figure 1-3	Title text placeholder after clicking in it

Trouble? The insertion point might appear as a thin, blue rectangle with the Mini toolbar above and to the right of it. Ignore this and continue with Step 2.

2. Type **Valley Farms CSA**. The placeholder is now a text box.

3. Click a blank area of the slide. The border of the text box disappears, and the DRAWING TOOLS FORMAT tab no longer appears on the ribbon.

4. Click in the **subtitle text placeholder** (where it says "Click to add subtitle"), and then type **Freshest, most delicious food!**. Notice in the Font group that the subtitle font is Calibri, a font which works well with the Calibri Light font used in the title text.

5. Click a blank area of the slide.

Saving and Editing a Presentation

Once you have created a presentation, you should name and save the presentation file. You can save the file on a hard drive or a network drive, on an external drive such as a USB drive, or to your account on SkyDrive, Microsoft's free online storage area.

To save the presentation for the first time:

▶ **1.** On the Quick Access Toolbar, point to the **Save** button 🖫. The button becomes shaded and its ScreenTip appears. A **ScreenTip** identifies the names of buttons; sometimes they also display a key combination you can press instead of clicking the button and information about how to use the button. In this case, the ScreenTip displays the word "Save" and the key combination for the Save command, Ctrl+S.

▶ **2.** Click the **Save** button 🖫. The Save As screen in Backstage view appears. See Figure 1-4. Because a presentation is open, more commands are available in Backstage view than when you started PowerPoint. The **navigation bar** on the left contains commands for working with the file and program options.

Figure 1-4	Save As screen in Backstage view

if you need to return to the presentation window, click this button

Save As selected

navigation bar

you might have additional folders in this list; if the folder you want to save in is listed, click it to open the Save As dialog box to that folder

click to open the Save As dialog box

▶ **3.** Click **Computer**, if necessary, and then click the **Browse** button. The Save As dialog box opens, similar to the one shown in Figure 1-5.

Figure 1-5	Save As dialog box

the current folder on your screen might differ

suggested filename

your user name will appear here

Trouble? If you are saving your files to your SkyDrive account, click SkyDrive on the Save As screen, log in to your account if necessary, and then click the Browse button.

4. Navigate to the drive and folder where you are storing your Data Files, and then click in the **File name** box. The suggested filename, Valley Falls CSA, is selected.

5. Type **Membership Info**. The text you type replaces the selected text in the File name box.

6. Click the **Save** button. The file is saved, the dialog box and Backstage view close, and the presentation window appears again with the new filename in the title bar.

Once you have created a presentation, you can make changes to it. For example, if you need to change text in a text box, you can easily edit it. The Backspace key deletes characters to the left of the insertion point, and the Delete key deletes characters to the right of the insertion point.

If you mistype or misspell a word, you might not need to correct it because the **AutoCorrect** feature automatically corrects many commonly mistyped and misspelled words after you press the spacebar or the Enter key. For instance, if you type "cna" and then press the spacebar, PowerPoint corrects the word to "can." If you want AutoCorrect to stop making a particular change, you can display the AutoCorrect Options menu, and then click Stop making the change. (The exact wording will differ depending on the change made.)

After you make changes to a presentation, you will need to save the file again so that the changes are stored. Because you have already saved the presentation with a permanent filename, using the Save command does not open the Save As dialog box; it simply saves the changes you made to the file.

To edit the text on Slide 1 and save your changes:

1. On Slide 1, click the **title**, and then use the ← and → keys as needed to position the insertion point to the right of the word "Farms."

2. Press the **Backspace** key three times. The three characters to the left of the insertion point, "rms," are deleted.

3. Type **lls** to change the second word to "Falls."

4. Click to the left of the word "Freshest" in the subtitle text box to position the insertion point in front of that word, type **Teh**, and then press the **spacebar**. PowerPoint corrects the word you typed to "The."

5. Move the pointer on top of the word **The**. A small, very faint rectangle appears below the first letter of the word. This indicates that an AutoCorrection has been made.

6. Move the pointer on top of the AutoCorrection indicator box so that it changes to the AutoCorrect Options button 📝 ▾, and then click the **AutoCorrect Options button** 📝 ▾. A menu opens, as shown in Figure 1-6. You can change the word back to what you originally typed, instruct PowerPoint to stop making this type of correction in this file, or open the AutoCorrect dialog box.

Trouble? If you can't see the AutoCorrection indicator box, point to the letter T, and then slowly move the pointer down until it is on top of the box and changes it to the AutoCorrect Options button.

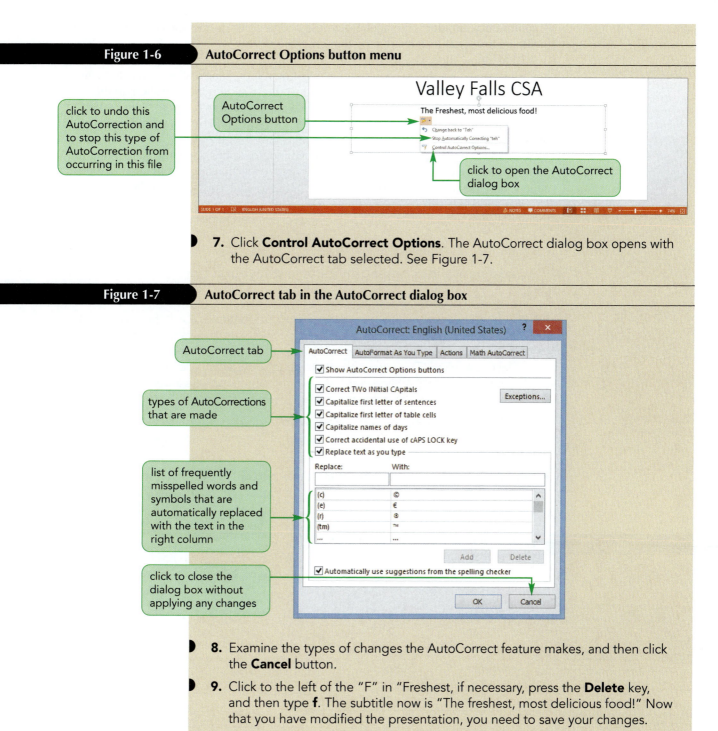

Figure 1-6   **AutoCorrect Options button menu**

click to undo this AutoCorrection and to stop this type of AutoCorrection from occurring in this file

AutoCorrect Options button

click to open the AutoCorrect dialog box

Valley Falls CSA

The Freshest, most delicious food!

Change back to "Teh"
Stop Automatically Correcting "teh"
Control AutoCorrect Options...

7. Click **Control AutoCorrect Options**. The AutoCorrect dialog box opens with the AutoCorrect tab selected. See Figure 1-7.

Figure 1-7   **AutoCorrect tab in the AutoCorrect dialog box**

AutoCorrect tab

types of AutoCorrections that are made

list of frequently misspelled words and symbols that are automatically replaced with the text in the right column

click to close the dialog box without applying any changes

AutoCorrect: English (United States)

AutoCorrect | AutoFormat As You Type | Actions | Math AutoCorrect

☑ Show AutoCorrect Options buttons

☑ Correct TWo INitial CApitals   Exceptions...
☑ Capitalize first letter of sentences
☑ Capitalize first letter of table cells
☑ Capitalize names of days
☑ Correct accidental use of cAPS LOCK key
☑ Replace text as you type

Replace: With:

(c)   ©
(e)   €
(r)   ®
(tm)   ™
...   …

Add   Delete

☑ Automatically use suggestions from the spelling checker

OK   Cancel

8. Examine the types of changes the AutoCorrect feature makes, and then click the **Cancel** button.

9. Click to the left of the "F" in "Freshest, if necessary, press the **Delete** key, and then type **f**. The subtitle now is "The freshest, most delicious food!" Now that you have modified the presentation, you need to save your changes.

10. On the Quick Access Toolbar, click the **Save** button 🖫. The changes you made are saved to the file you named Membership Info.

Adding New Slides

Now that you've created the title slide, you need to add more slides. Every slide has a **layout**, which is the arrangement of placeholders on the slide. The title slide uses the Title Slide layout. A commonly used layout is the Title and Content layout, which contains a title text placeholder for the slide title and a content placeholder.

A **content placeholder** is a placeholder designed to hold several types of slide content including text, a table, a chart, a picture, or a video.

To add a new slide, you use the New Slide button in the Slides group on the HOME tab. When you click the top part of the New Slide button, a new slide is inserted with the same layout as the current slide, unless the current slide is the title slide; in that case the new slide has the Title and Content layout. If you want to create a new slide with a different layout, click the bottom part of the New Slide button to open a gallery of layouts, and then click the layout you want to use.

You can change the layout of a slide at any time. To do this, click the Layout button in the Slides group to display the same gallery of layouts that appears in the Add Slide gallery, and then click the slide layout you want to apply to the selected slide.

As you add slides, you can switch from one slide to another by clicking the slide thumbnails in the Slides tab. You need to add several new slides to the file.

To add new slides and apply different layouts:

1. Make sure the HOME tab is displayed on the ribbon.

2. In the Slides group, click the **New Slide** button (that is, click the top part of the button). A new slide appears in the Slide pane and its thumbnail appears in the Slides tab below Slide 1. The new slide has the Title and Content layout applied. This layout contains a title text placeholder and a content placeholder. In the Slides tab, an orange border appears around the new Slide 2, indicating that it is the current slide.

3. In the Slides group, click the **New Slide** button again. A new Slide 3 is added. Because Slide 2 had the Title and Content layout applied, Slide 3 also has that layout applied.

4. In the Slides group, click the **New Slide button arrow** (that is, click the bottom part of the New Slide button). A gallery of the available layouts appears. See Figure 1-8.

Figure 1-8   **Gallery of layouts on the New Slide button menu**

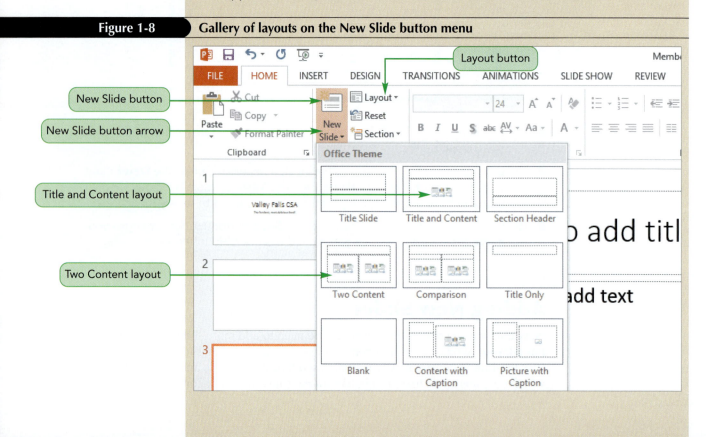

5. In the gallery, click the **Two Content** layout. The gallery closes and a new Slide 4 is inserted with the Two Content layout applied. This layout includes three objects: a title text placeholder and two content placeholders.

6. In the Slides group, click the **New Slide** button. A new Slide 5 is added to the presentation. Because Slide 4 had the Two Content layout applied, that layout is also applied to the new slide. You need to change the layout of Slide 5.

7. In the Slides group, click the **Layout** button. The same gallery of layouts that appeared when you clicked the New Slide button arrow appears. The Two Content layout is selected, as indicated by the orange shading behind it, showing you that this is the layout applied to the current slide, Slide 5.

8. Click the **Title and Content** layout. The layout of Slide 5 is changed to Title and Content.

9. In the Slides group, click the **New Slide** button three more times to add three more slides with the Title and Content layout. There are now eight slides in the presentation. In the Slides tab, Slides 1 through 3 have scrolled up out of view, and vertical scroll bars are now visible in both the Slides tab and in the Slide pane.

10. In the Slides tab, drag the **scroll box** to the top of the vertical scroll bar, and then click the **Slide 2** thumbnail. Slide 2 becomes the current slide—it appears in the Slide pane and is selected in the Slides tab. See Figure 1-9.

Figure 1-9   **Slide 2 with the Title and Content layout**

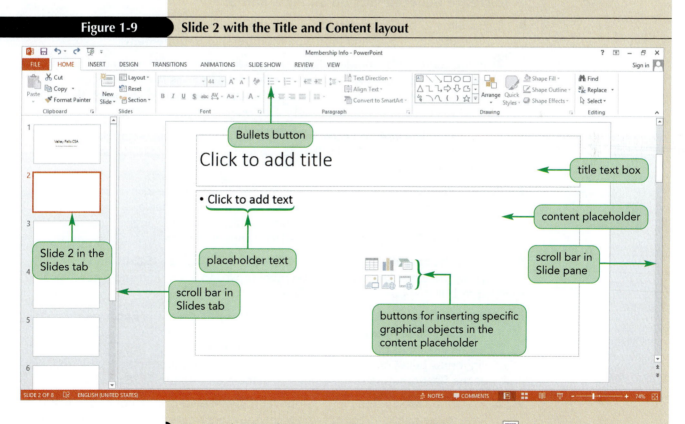

11. On the Quick Access Toolbar, click the **Save** button. The changes you made are saved in the file.

If you accidentally close a presentation without saving changes and need to recover it, you can do so by clicking the FILE tab, clicking Open in the navigation bar, and then clicking the Recover Unsaved Presentations button.

Creating Lists

One way to help explain the topic or concept you are describing in your presentation is to use lists. For oral presentations, the intent of lists is to enhance the oral presentation, not replace it. In self-running presentations, items in lists might need to be longer and more descriptive. However, keep in mind that PowerPoint is a presentation graphics program intended to help you present information in a visual, graphical manner, not create a written document in an alternate form.

Items in a list can appear at different levels. A **first-level item** is a main item in a list; a **second-level item**—sometimes called a **subitem**—is an item beneath and indented from a first-level item. Usually, the font size—the size of the text—in subitems is smaller than the size used for text in the level above. Text is measured in **points**, which is a unit of measurement. Text in a book is typically printed in 10- or 12-point type; text on a slide needs to be much larger so the audience can easily read it.

Creating a Bulleted List

A **bulleted list** is a list of items with some type of bullet symbol in front of each item or paragraph. When you create a subitem in the list, a different or smaller symbol is often used. You need to create a bulleted list that describes the requirements of a membership in Valley Farms CSA.

To create bulleted lists on Slides 2 and 3:

1. On **Slide 2**, click in the **title text placeholder** (with the placeholder text "Click to add title"), and then type **Membership Requirements**.

2. In the content placeholder, click any area where the pointer is shaped as I; in other words, anywhere except on one of the buttons in the center of the placeholder. The placeholder text "Click to add text" disappears, the insertion point appears, and a light gray bullet symbol appears.

   Trouble? The insertion point might appear as a thin, blue rectangle with a rectangle called the Mini toolbar above and to the right of it. Ignore this and continue with Step 3.

3. Type **Purchase**. As soon as you type the first character, the icons in the center of the content placeholder disappear, the bullet symbol darkens, and the content placeholder changes to a text box. On the HOME tab, in the Paragraph group, the Bullets button is shaded orange to indicate that it is selected.

4. Press the **spacebar**, type **full-share ($425) or half-share ($250)**, and then press the **Enter** key. The insertion point moves to a new line and a new, light gray bullet appears on the new line.

5. Type **Volunteer minimum two hours per month**, press the **Enter** key, type **Pick up share once per week**, and then press the **Enter** key. The bulleted list now consists of three first-level items, and the insertion point is next to a light gray bullet on the fourth line in the text box. Notice on the HOME tab, in the Font group, that the point size in the Font Size box is 28 points.

6. Press the **Tab** key. The bullet symbol and the insertion point indent one-half inch to the right, the bullet symbol changes to a smaller size, and the number in the Font Size box changes to 24. See Figure 1-10.

Figure 1-10   **Subitem created on Slide 2**

font size of subitems is 24 points

bullet for subitem

insertion point

7. Type **Fridays, 3 p.m. - 5 p.m.** and then press the **Enter** key. When you pressed the spacebar key after typing 5, AutoCorrect changed the dash to an en-dash, a typographical character slightly longer than a hyphen.

8. Type **Saturdays, 7 a.m. - noon**, and then press the **Enter** key. A third subitem is created. You will change it to a first-level item using a key combination. In this book, when you need to press two keys together, the keys will be listed separated by a plus sign. You don't need to press the keys at exactly the same time—press and hold the first key, press and release the second key, and then release the first key.

9. Press the **Shift+Tab** keys. The bullet symbol and the insertion point shift back to the left margin of the text box, the bullet symbol changes back to the larger size, and 28 again appears in the Font Size box because this line is now a first-level bulleted item.

TIP

Avoid putting information on the bottom quarter of the slide because people in the back of a large room will not be able to see it.

10. Type **Or have it delivered (additional fee)**, press the **Enter** key, and then type **October community celebration**.

11. In the Slides tab, click the **Slide 3** thumbnail to display Slide 3 in the Slide pane, click in the **title text placeholder**, and then type **Members Receive**.

12. In the content placeholder, click the **placeholder text**, type **Share of pre-selected produce**, press the **Enter** key, and then type **Self-selected items**.

If you add more text than will fit in the text box with the default font sizes and line spacing, **AutoFit** adjusts these features to make the text fit. When AutoFit is activated, the AutoFit Options button appears below the text box. You can click this button and then select from among several options, including turning off AutoFit for this text box and splitting the text between two slides. Although AutoFit can be helpful, be aware that it also allows you to crowd text on a slide, making the slide less effective.

PROSKILLS

Written Communication: How Much Text Should I Include?

Text can help audiences retain the information you are presenting by allowing them to read the main points while hearing you discuss them. But be wary of adding so much text to your slides that your audience can ignore you and just read the slides. Try to follow the 7x7 rule—no more than seven items per slide, with no more than seven words per item. A variation of this rule is 6x6, and some presenters even prefer 4x4. If you create a self-running presentation (a presentation file others will view on their own) you will usually need to add more text than you would if you were presenting the material in person.

Creating a Numbered List

A **numbered list** is similar to a bulleted list except that numbers appear in front of each item instead of bullet symbols. Generally you should use a numbered list when the order of the items is important—for example, if you are presenting a list of step-by-step instructions that need to be followed in sequence in order to complete a task successfully. You need to create a numbered list on Slide 5 to explain how members can order items in addition to their regular CSA share.

To create a numbered list on Slide 5:

1. In the Slides tab, click the **Slide 5** thumbnail to display Slide 5 in the Slide pane, and then type **Placing Your Order for Additional Items** as the title text.

2. In the content placeholder, click the **placeholder text**.

3. On the HOME tab, in the Paragraph group, click the **Numbering** button. The Numbering button is selected, the Bullets button is deselected, and in the content placeholder, the bullet symbol is replaced with the number 1 followed by a period.

   Trouble? If a menu containing a gallery of numbering styles appears, you clicked the Numbering button arrow on the right side of the button. Click the Numbering button arrow again to close the menu, and then click the left part of the Numbering button.

4. Type **Place online by Wednesday**, and then press the **Enter** key. As soon as you start typing, the number 1 darkens to black. After you press the Enter key, the insertion point moves to the next line, next to the light gray number 2.

5. Type **Verify payment information**, and then press the **Enter** key. The number 3 appears on the next line.

6. In the Paragraph group, click the **Increase List Level** button. The third line is indented to be a subitem under the second item, and the number 3 that had appeared changes to a number 1 in a smaller size than the first-level items. Clicking the Increase List Level button is an alternative to pressing the Tab key to create a subitem.

7. Type **Credit card**, press the **Enter** key, type **Debit from checking account**, press the **Enter** key.

8. In the Paragraph group, click the **Decrease List Level** button. The fifth line is now a first-level item and the number 3 appears next to it. Clicking the Decrease List Level button is an alternative to pressing the Shift+Tab keys to promote a subitem.

9. Type **Submit**. The list now consists of three first-level numbered items and two subitems under number 2.

10. In the second item, click before the word "Verify," and then press the **Enter** key. A blank line is inserted above the second item.

11. Press the ↑ key. A light-gray number 2 appears in the blank line. The item on the third line in the list is still numbered 2.

12. Type **Specify pickup or delivery**. As soon as you start typing, the new number 2 darkens in the second line and the third item in the list is numbered 3. Compare your screen to Figure 1-11.

| Figure 1-11 | Numbered list on Slide 5 |

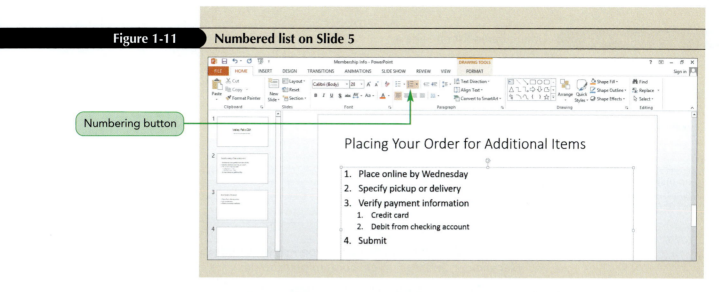

Numbering button

Creating an Unnumbered List

An **unnumbered list** is a list that does not have bullets or numbers preceding each item. Unnumbered lists are useful in slides when you want to present information on multiple lines without actually itemizing the information. For example, contact information for the presenter, including his or her email address, street address, city, and so on would be clearer if it were in an unnumbered list.

As you have seen, items in a list have a little extra space between each item to visually separate bulleted items. Sometimes, you don't want the extra space between lines. If you press the Shift+Enter keys instead of just the Enter key, a new line is created, but it is still considered to be part of the item above it. Therefore, there is no extra space between the lines. Note that this also means that if you do this in a bulleted or numbered list, the new line will not have a bullet or number next to it because it is not a new item.

You need to create a slide that defines CSA. Also, Isaac asks you to create a slide containing contact information.

To create unnumbered lists on Slides 4 and 7:

1. In the Slides tab, click the **Slide 4** thumbnail to display Slide 4 in the Slide pane. Slide 4 has the Two Content layout applied.

2. Type **What Is a CSA?** as the title text, and then in the left content placeholder, click the **placeholder text**.

3. On the HOME tab, in the Paragraph group, click the **Bullets** button. The button is no longer selected, and the bullet symbol disappears from the content placeholder.

4. Type **Community**, press the **Enter** key, type **Supported**, press the **Enter** key, and then type **Agriculture**. Compare your screen to Figure 1-12.

Figure 1-12   Unnumbered list on Slide 4

neither the Bullets or Numbering button is selected

no bullet symbol or number appears

5. Display **Slide 7** in the Slide pane, type **For More Information** in the title text placeholder, and then in the content placeholder, click the **placeholder text**.

6. In the Paragraph group, click the **Bullets** button ▤ to remove the bullets, type **Valley Falls CSA**, and then press the **Enter** key. A new line is created, but there is extra space above the insertion point. This is not how addresses usually appear.

7. Press the **Backspace** key to delete the new line and move the insertion point back to the end of the first line, and then press the **Shift+Enter** keys. The insertion point moves to the next line and, this time, there is no extra space above it.

8. Type **300 County Fair Road**, press the **Shift+Enter** keys, and then type **Spartanburg, SC 29301**. You need to insert the phone number on the next line, the general email address for the group on the line after that, and the website address on the last line. The extra space above these lines will set this information apart from the address and make it easier to read.

9. Press the **Enter** key to create a new line with extra space above it, type **(864) 555-FOOD**, press the **Enter** key, type **csainfo@valleyfallscsa.example.org**, and then press the **Enter** key. The insertion point moves to a new line with extra space above it, and the email address you typed changes color to blue and is underlined.

   When you type text that PowerPoint recognizes as an email or website address and then press the spacebar or Enter key, it automatically formats it as a link that can be clicked during a slide show, and changes its color and adds the underline to indicate this. You can only click links during a slide show.

10. Type **www.valleyfallscsa.example.org**, and then press the **spacebar**. The text is formatted as a link. Isaac plans to click the link during his presentation to show the audience the website, so he wants it to stay formatted as a link. However, there is no need to have the email address formatted as a link because no one will click it during the presentation.

11. Right-click **csainfo@valleyfallscsa.example.org**. A shortcut menu opens.

12. On the shortcut menu, click **Remove Hyperlink**. The email address is no longer formatted as a hyperlink. Compare your screen to Figure 1-13.

| Figure 1-13 | List on Slide 7 |

no space between lines

normal space between items

link formatting removed from email address

text formatted as a link

For More Information

Valley Falls CSA
300 County Fair Road
Spartanburg, SC 29301

(864) 555-FOOD

csainfo@valleyfallscsa.example.org
www.valleyfallscsa.example.org

▶ **13.** On the Quick Access Toolbar, click the **Save** button 🖫 to save the changes.

Formatting Text

Slides in a presentation should have a cohesive look and feel. For example, the slide titles and the text in content placeholders should be in complementary fonts. However, there are times when you need to change the format of text. For instance, you might want to make specific words bold to make them stand out more.

To apply a format to text, either the text or the text box must be selected. If you want to apply the same formatting to all the text in a text box, you can click the border of the text box. When you do this, the dotted line border changes to a solid line to indicate that the contents of the entire text box are selected.

The commands in the Font group on the HOME tab are used to apply formatting to text. Some of these commands are also available on the Mini toolbar, which appears when you select text with the mouse. The **Mini toolbar** contains commonly used buttons for formatting text. If the Mini toolbar appears, you can use the buttons on it instead of those in the Font group.

Some of the commands in the Font group use the Microsoft Office **Live Preview** feature, which previews the change on the slide so you can instantly see what the text will look like if you apply that format.

Isaac wants the contact information on Slide 7 to be larger. He also wants the first letter of each item in the unnumbered list on Slide 4 ("What Is a CSA?") formatted so they are more prominent.

TIP

To remove all formatting from selected text, click the Clear All Formatting button in the Font group.

To format the text on Slides 4 and 7:

▶ **1.** On **Slide 7** ("For More Information"), position the pointer on the text box border so that it changes to 🔭, and then click the border of the text box containing the contact information. The border changes to a solid line to indicate that the entire text box is selected.

▶ **2.** On the HOME tab, in the Font group, click the **Increase Font Size** button 🅰 twice. All the text in the text box increases in size with each click.

▶ **3.** Display **Slide 4** ("What Is a CSA?") in the Slide pane.

4. In the unnumbered list, click to the left of "Community," press and hold the **Shift** key, press the → key, and then release the **Shift** key. The letter "C" is selected. See Figure 1-14.

Figure 1-14   Text selected to be formatted

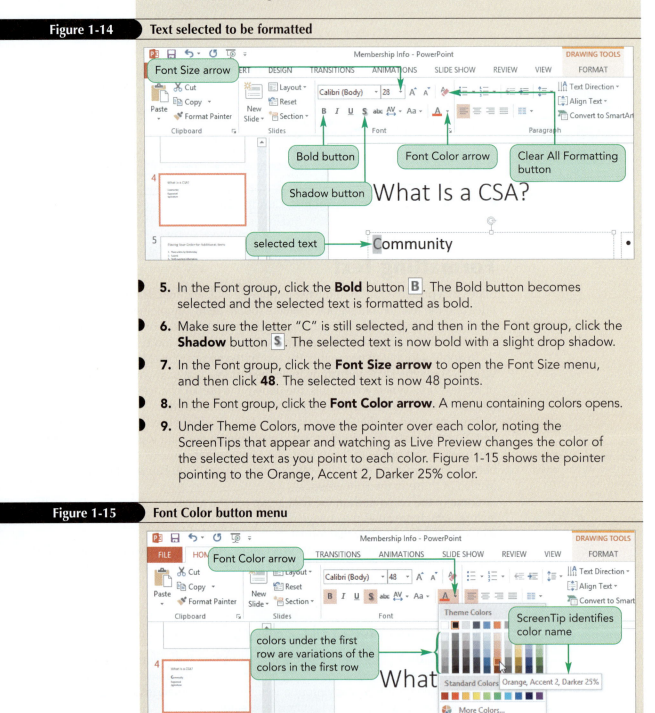

5. In the Font group, click the **Bold** button B. The Bold button becomes selected and the selected text is formatted as bold.

6. Make sure the letter "C" is still selected, and then in the Font group, click the **Shadow** button S. The selected text is now bold with a slight drop shadow.

7. In the Font group, click the **Font Size arrow** to open the Font Size menu, and then click **48**. The selected text is now 48 points.

8. In the Font group, click the **Font Color arrow**. A menu containing colors opens.

9. Under Theme Colors, move the pointer over each color, noting the ScreenTips that appear and watching as Live Preview changes the color of the selected text as you point to each color. Figure 1-15 shows the pointer pointing to the Orange, Accent 2, Darker 25% color.

Figure 1-15   Font Color button menu

10. Using the ScreenTips, locate the **Orange, Accent 2, Darker 25%** color and then click it. The selected text changes to the orange color you clicked.

Now you need to format the first letters in the other words in the list to match the letter "C." You can repeat the steps you did when you formatted the letter "C," or you use the Format Painter to copy all the formatting of the letter "C" to the other letters you need to format.

Also, Isaac wants the text in the unnumbered list to be as large as possible. Because the first letters of each word are larger than the rest of the letters, the easiest way to do this is to select all of the text, and then use the Increase Font Size button. All of the letters will increase in size by four points with each click.

To use the Format Painter to copy and apply formatting on Slide 4:

▶ **1.** Make sure the letter "C" is still selected.

▶ **2.** On the HOME tab, in the Clipboard group, click the **Format Painter** button, and then move the pointer back to the Slide pane. The button is selected, and the pointer changes to 🖌.

▶ **3.** Position the pointer before the letter "S" in "Supported," press and hold the mouse button, drag over the letter **S**, and then release the mouse button. The formatting you applied to the letter "C" is copied to the letter "S" and the Mini toolbar appears. See Figure 1-16. The Mini toolbar appears whenever you drag over text to select it.

Figure 1-16	The Mini toolbar

TIP

If you need to copy formatting to more than one location, double-click the Format Painter button to keep it selected until you deselect it.

▶ **4.** On the Mini toolbar, click the **Format Painter** button 🖌, and then drag across the letter **A** in Agriculture.

▶ **5.** Click the border of the text box to select the entire text box, and then in the Font group, click the **Increase Font Size** button A̲ five times. In the Font group, the Font Size button indicates that the text is 48+ points. This means that in the selected text box, the text that is the smallest is 48 points and there is some text that is a larger point size.

▶ **6.** On the Quick Access Toolbar, click the **Save** button 💾 to save the changes.

INSIGHT

Undoing and Redoing Actions

If you make a mistake or change your mind about an action as you are working, you can reverse the action by clicking the Undo button on the Quick Access Toolbar. You can undo up to the most recent 20 actions by continuing to click the Undo button, or by clicking the Undo button arrow and then selecting as many actions in the list as you want. You can also Redo an action that you undid by clicking the Redo button on the Quick Access Toolbar.

When there are no actions that can be redone, the Redo button changes to the Repeat button. You can use the Repeat button to repeat an action, such as formatting text as bold. If the Repeat button is light gray, this means it is unavailable because there is no action to repeat (or to redo).

Moving and Copying Text

You can move or copy text and objects in a presentation using the Clipboard. The **Clipboard** is a temporary storage area available to all Windows programs on which text or objects are stored when you cut or copy them. To **cut** text or objects—that is, remove the selected text or objects from one location so that you can place it somewhere else—you select the text or object, and then use the Cut button in the Clipboard group on the HOME tab to remove the selected text or object and place it on the Clipboard. To **copy** selected text or objects, you use the Copy button in the Clipboard group on the HOME tab, which leaves the original text or object on the slide and places a copy of it on the Clipboard. You can then **paste** the text or object stored on the Clipboard anywhere in the presentation, or, in fact, in any file in any Windows program.

You can paste an item on the Clipboard as many times and in as many locations as you like. However, the Clipboard can hold only the most recently cut or copied item. As soon as you cut or copy another item, it replaces the previously cut or copied item on the Clipboard.

Note that cutting text or an object is different from using the Delete or Backspace key to delete it. Deleted text and objects are not placed on the Clipboard; this means they cannot be pasted.

Isaac wants a few changes made to Slides 5 and 3. You'll use the Clipboard as you make these edits.

To copy and paste text using the Clipboard:

1. Display **Slide 5** ("Placing Your Order for Additional Items") in the Slide pane, and then double-click the word **Order** in the title text. The word "Order" is selected.

2. On the HOME tab, in the Clipboard group, click the **Copy** button. The selected word is copied to the Clipboard.

3. In the last item in the numbered list, click after the word "Submit," and then press the **spacebar**.

4. In the Clipboard group, click the **Paste** button. The text is pasted and picks up the formatting of its destination; that is, the pasted text is the 28-point Calibri font, the same font and size as the rest of the first-level items in the list, instead of 44-point Calibri Light as in the title. The Paste Options button [(Ctrl) ▾ appears below the pasted text.

5. Click the **Paste Options** button [(Ctrl) ▾. A menu opens with four buttons on it. See Figure 1-17.

Figure 1-17 | Buttons on the Paste Options button menu when text is on the Clipboard

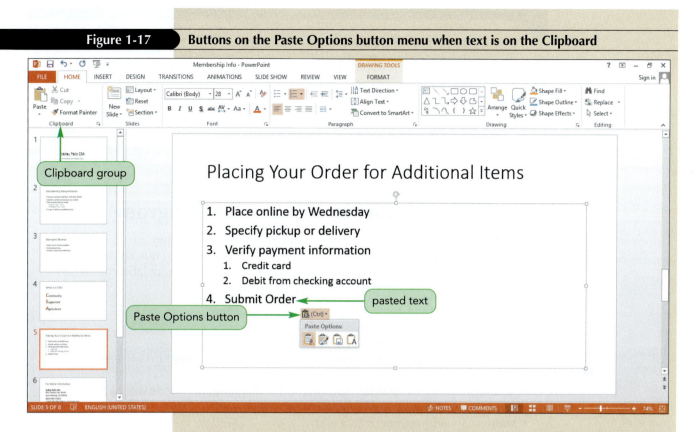

6. Point to each button on the menu, reading the ScreenTips and watching to see how the pasted text changes in appearance. The first button is the Use Destination Theme button, and this is the default choice when you paste text.

7. Click a blank area of the slide to close the menu without making a selection, click to the left of "Order" in the last item in the numbered list, press the **Delete** key, and then type **o**. The word "order" in in the numbered list is now all lowercase.

8. Display **Slide 2** ("Membership Requirements") in the Slide pane. The last bulleted item ("October community celebration") belongs on Slide 3.

9. In the last bulleted item, position the pointer on top of the bullet symbol so that the pointer changes to ✛, and then click. The entire bulleted item is selected.

10. In the Clipboard group, click the **Cut** button. The last bulleted item is removed from the slide and placed on the Clipboard.

11. Display **Slide 3** ("Members Receive") in the Slide pane, click after the second bulleted item, and then press the **Enter** key to create a third line.

12. In the Clipboard group, click the **Paste** button. The bulleted item you cut is pasted as the third bulleted item on Slide 3 using the default Paste option of Use Destination Theme. The insertion point appears next to a fourth bulleted item.

13. Press the **Backspace** key twice. The extra line is deleted.

Using the Office Clipboard

The **Office Clipboard** is a special Clipboard available only to Microsoft Office applications. Once you activate the Office Clipboard, you can store up to 24 items on it and then select the item or items you want to paste. To activate the Office Clipboard, click the HOME tab. In the Clipboard group, click the Dialog Box Launcher (the small square in the lower-right corner of the Clipboard group) to open the Clipboard task pane to the left of the Slide pane.

Converting a List to a SmartArt Diagram

A **diagram** visually depicts information or ideas and shows how they are connected. **SmartArt** is a feature that allows you to create diagrams easily and quickly. In addition to shapes, SmartArt diagrams usually include text to help describe or label the shapes. You can create the following types of diagrams using SmartArt:

- **List**—Shows a list of items in a graphical representation
- **Process**—Shows a sequence of steps in a process
- **Cycle**—Shows a process that is a continuous cycle
- **Hierarchy** (including organization charts)—Shows the relationship between individuals or units
- **Relationship** (including Venn diagrams, radial diagrams, and target diagrams)— Shows the relationship between two or more elements
- **Matrix**—Shows information in a grid
- **Pyramid**—Shows foundation-based relationships
- **Picture**—Provides a location for a picture or pictures that you insert

There is also an Office.com category of SmartArt, which, if you are connected to the Internet, displays additional SmartArt diagrams available in various categories on Office.com, a Microsoft website that contains tools for use with Office programs.

A quick way to create a SmartArt diagram is to convert an existing list. When you select an existing list and then click the Convert to SmartArt Graphic button in the Paragraph group on the HOME tab, a gallery of SmartArt layouts appears. For SmartArt, a **layout** is the arrangement of the shapes in the diagram. Each first-level item in the list is converted to a shape in the SmartArt diagram. If the list contains subitems, you might need to experiment with different layouts to find one that best suits the information in your list.

Converting a Bulleted List into a SmartArt Diagram

- Click anywhere in the bulleted list.
- In the Paragraph group on the HOME tab, click the Convert to SmartArt Graphic button, and then click More SmartArt Graphics.
- In the Choose a SmartArt Graphic dialog box, select the desired SmartArt type in the list on the left.
- In the center pane, click the SmartArt diagram you want to use.
- Click the OK button.

Isaac wants the numbered list on Slide 5 converted into a SmartArt diagram.

To convert the list on Slide 5 into a SmartArt diagram:

1. Display **Slide 5** ("Placing Your Order for Additional Items") in the Slide pane, and then click anywhere on the numbered list to make the text box border appear.

2. On the HOME tab, in the Paragraph group, click the **Convert to SmartArt Graphic** button. A gallery of SmartArt layouts appears.

3. Point to the first layout. The ScreenTip identifies this layout as the Vertical Bullet List layout, and Live Preview shows you what the numbered list will look like with that layout applied. See Figure 1-18. Notice that the subitems are not included in a shape in this diagram.

Figure 1-18	Live Preview of the Vertical Bullet List SmartArt Layout

4. Point to several other layouts in the gallery, observing the Live Preview of each one. In some of the layouts, the subitems are included in a shape.

5. At the bottom of the gallery, click **More SmartArt Graphics**. The Choose a SmartArt Graphic dialog box opens. See Figure 1-19. You can click a type in the left pane to filter the middle pane to show only that type of layout.

Figure 1-19 | Choose a SmartArt Graphic dialog box

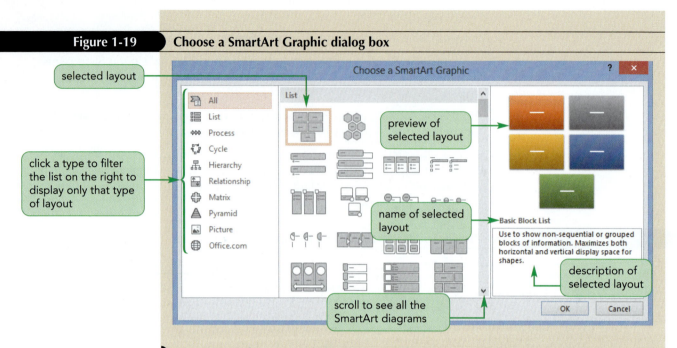

6. In the left pane, click **Process**, and then in the middle pane, click the **Continuous Block Process** layout, using the ScreenTips to identify it (it's the first layout in the third row). The right pane changes to show a description of that layout.

7. Click the **OK** button. The dialog box closes, and each of the first level items in the list appears in the square shapes in the diagram. The items also appear as a bulleted list in the Text pane, which is open to the left of the diagram. The SMARTART TOOLS contextual tabs appear on the ribbon. See Figure 1-20.

In this layout, the subitems below "Verify payment information" are included in the third square; they are not placed in their own shapes in the diagram. Isaac decides the information in the subitems does not need to be on the slide because people will see those options on the website when they log in.

Trouble? If you do not see the Text pane, click the Text pane button ◄ on the left border of the selected SmartArt diagram.

Figure 1-20   **SmartArt diagram with the Continuous Block Process layout**

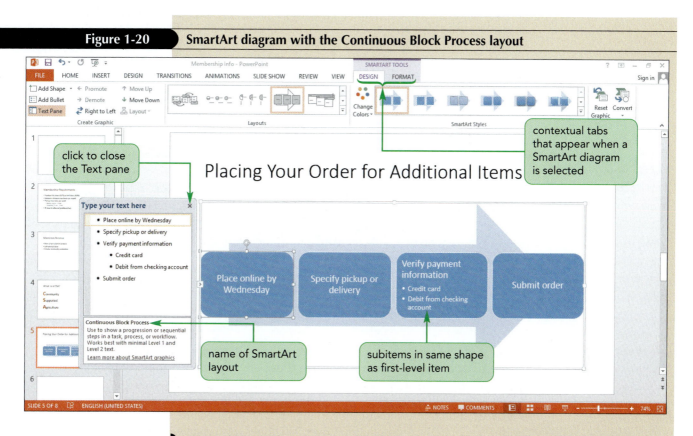

8. In the "Verify payment information shape," select **Debit from checking account**, and then press the **Delete** key. The text is deleted from the shape and from the Text pane.

9. In the Text pane, click after the word "card," press the **Backspace** key as many times as necessary to delete all of the bullet text, and then press the **Backspace** key once more. The bullet changes to a first-level bullet and a new square shape is inserted in the diagram.

10. Press the **Backspace** key one more time. The empty bullet and the blank line are deleted in the Text pane, and the newly added shape is removed from the diagram. The "Verify payment information" square now contains only the first-level item. Notice that AutoFit increased the size of the text in all the boxes so that the text still fills the boxes and is as large as possible.

11. Click a blank area of the slide to deselect the diagram, and then on the Quick Access Toolbar, click the **Save** button to save your changes.

Manipulating Slides

You can manipulate the slides in a presentation to suit your needs. For instance, if you need to create a slide that is similar to another slide, you can duplicate the existing slide and then modify the copy. If you decide that slides need to be rearranged, you can reorder them. And if you no longer want to include a slide in your presentation, you can delete it.

To duplicate, rearrange, or delete slides, you select the slides in the Slides tab in Normal view or switch to Slide Sorter view. In **Slide Sorter view** all the slides in the presentation are displayed as thumbnails in the window; the Slides tab does not appear. You already know that to select a single slide you click its thumbnail. You can also select more than one slide at a time. To select sequential slides, click the first slide, press and hold the Shift key, and then click the last slide you want to select. To select nonsequential slides, click the first slide, press and hold the Ctrl key, and then click any other slides you want to select.

Isaac wants to show the slide that explains what the letters "CSA" stand for at the end of the presentation. You will duplicate that slide instead of recreating it.

To duplicate Slide 4:

1. In the Slides tab, click the **Slide 4** ("What Is a CSA?") thumbnail to display Slide 4 in the Slide pane.

2. On the HOME tab, in the Slides group, click the **New Slide button arrow**, and then click **Duplicate Selected Slides**. Slide 4 is duplicated and the copy is inserted as a new Slide 5 in the Slides tab. Slide 5 is now the current slide. If more than one slide were selected, they would all be duplicated. The duplicate slide doesn't need the title; Isaac just wants to reinforce the term.

3. Click in the title "What Is a CSA?", click the text box border to select the text box, and then press the **Delete** key. The title and the title text box are deleted and the title text placeholder reappears.

You could delete the title text placeholder, but it is not necessary. When you display the presentation to an audience as a slide show, any unused placeholders will not appear.

Next you need to rearrange the slides. You need to move the duplicate of the "What Is a CSA?" slide so it is the last slide in the presentation because Isaac wants to leave it displayed after the presentation is over. He hopes this visual will reinforce for the audience that CSAs are good for the entire community. Isaac also wants the "Members Receive" slide moved so it appears before the "Membership Requirements" slide, and he wants the original "What Is a CSA?" slide to be the second slide in the presentation.

To move slides in the presentation:

1. In the Slides tab, scroll up, if necessary, so that you can see Slides 2 and 3, and then drag the **Slide 3** ("Members Receive") thumbnail above the Slide 2 ("Membership Requirements") thumbnail. As you drag, the Slide 3 thumbnail follows the pointer and Slide 2 moves down. The "Members Receive" slide is now Slide 2 and "Membership Requirements" is now Slide 3. You'll move the other two slides in Slide Sorter view.

2. On the status bar, click the **Slide Sorter** button ⊞. The view switches to Slide Sorter view. Slide 2 has an orange border, indicating that it is selected.

3. On the status bar, click the **Zoom Out** button ▬ as many times as necessary until you can see all nine slides in the presentation. See Figure 1-21.

TIP

You can also use the buttons in the Presentation Views group on the VIEW tab to switch views.

Figure 1-21	Slide Sorter view

4. Drag the **Slide 4** ("What Is a CSA?") thumbnail between Slides 1 and 2. As you drag, the other slides move out of the way. The slide is repositioned and the slides are renumbered so that the "What Is a CSA?" slide is now Slide 2.

5. Drag the **Slide 5** (the CSA slide without a title) thumbnail so it becomes the last slide in the presentation (Slide 9).

Now you need to delete the two blank slides. To delete a slide, you need to right-click its thumbnail to display a shortcut menu.

To delete slides:

1. Click **Slide 6** (a blank slide), press and hold the **Shift** key, and then click **Slide 8** (the other blank slide), and then release the **Shift** key. The two slides you clicked are selected, as well as the slide between them. You want to delete only the two blank slides.

2. Click a blank area of the window to deselect the slides, click **Slide 6**, press and hold the **Ctrl** key, click **Slide 8**, and then release the **Ctrl** key. Only the two slides you clicked are selected.

3. Right-click either selected slide. A shortcut menu appears. See Figure 1-22.

Figure 1-22 **Shortcut menu for selected slides**

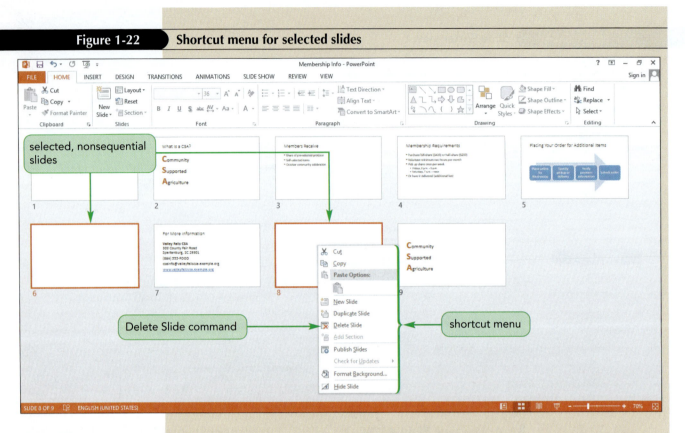

4. On the shortcut menu, click **Delete Slide**. The shortcut menu closes and the two selected slides are deleted. The presentation now contains seven slides.

5. On the status bar, click the **Normal** button. The presentation appears in Normal view.

6. On the Quick Access Toolbar, click the **Save** button to save the changes to the presentation.

Closing a Presentation

When you are finished working with a presentation, you can close it and leave PowerPoint open. To do this, you click the FILE tab to open Backstage view, and then click the Close command. If you click the Close button in the upper-right corner of the PowerPoint window and only one presentation is open, you will not only close the presentation, you will exit PowerPoint as well.

You're finished working with the Membership Info file for now, so you will close it. First you will add your name to the title slide.

To close the Membership Info presentation:

1. Display **Slide 1** (the title slide) in the Slide pane, click the **subtitle**, position the insertion point after "food!," press the **Enter** key, and then type your full name.

2. On the ribbon, click the **FILE** tab. Backstage view appears with the Info screen displayed. See Figure 1-23. The Info screen contains information about the current presentation, including the name, drive, and folder of the current presentation.

Figure 1-23	Info screen in Backstage view

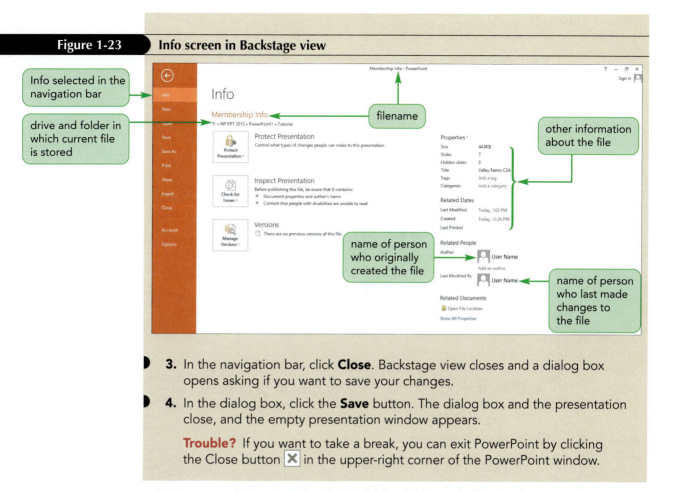

3. In the navigation bar, click **Close**. Backstage view closes and a dialog box opens asking if you want to save your changes.

4. In the dialog box, click the **Save** button. The dialog box and the presentation close, and the empty presentation window appears.

Trouble? If you want to take a break, you can exit PowerPoint by clicking the Close button ☒ in the upper-right corner of the PowerPoint window.

You've created a presentation that includes slides to which you added bulleted, numbered, and unnumbered lists. You also edited and formatted text, converted a list to a SmartArt diagram, and duplicated, rearranged, and deleted slides. You are ready to give the presentation draft to Isaac to review.

REVIEW

Session 1.1 Quick Check

1. Define "presentation."

2. How do you display Backstage view?

3. What is the main area of the PowerPoint window called?

4. What is a layout?

5. In addition to a title text placeholder, what other placeholder do most layouts contain?

6. What is the term for an object that contains text?

7. What is the difference between the Clipboard and the Office Clipboard?

8. How do you convert a list to a SmartArt diagram?

Session 1.2 Visual Overview:

In **Slide Show view**, each slide fills the screen, one after another.

Benefits of CSAs

▶ CSAs provide fresh, locally grown produce
  ▶ Tastes better
  ▶ More nutritious
  ▶ Better for the environment
▶ Your membership supports local farms

The pointer is not visible in Slide Show view until you move it or right-click it. When you move the pointer, this faint row of buttons appears in the lower left corner of the screen. All of these buttons are also available in Presenter view.

Click the More slide show options button to display additional commands.

Click the Zoom into the slide button to zoom into a portion of the slide during the slide show.

Click the Return to the previous slide and Advance to the next slide buttons to move from slide to slide in Slide Show view.

Click the See all slides button to display all the slides, similar to Slide Sorter view.

Slide Show and Presenter Views

Click this button to display the Windows taskbar so that you can switch to another program.

Click this button to swap the monitors showing Slide Show view and Presenter views.

In **Presenter view**, the left pane shows the current slide. On the second monitor or on the projection screen, this slide fills the screen in Slide Show view and is what the audience sees.

The timer shows how long the presentation has been running.

The next slide appears in the right pane in Presenter view.

Use these buttons to pause and restart the timer.

This is the Zoom into the slide button in Presenter view.

Click the More slide show options button to display additional commands.

Click the Black or unblack slide show button to display a black slide during the slide show and then return to the current slide.

Click the See all slides button to display all the slides, similar to Slide Sorter view.

These are the Return to the previous slide and Advance to the next slide buttons in Presenter view.

This part of the Presenter view window displays the speaker notes for the current slide.

Opening a Presentation and Saving It with a New Name

If you have closed a presentation, you can always reopen it to modify it. To do this, you can double-click the file in a Windows Explorer window, or you can open Backstage view in PowerPoint and use the Open command.

Isaac reviewed the presentation you created in Session 1.1. He added a slide listing the benefits of CSAs and made a few additional changes. You will continue modifying this presentation.

To open the revised presentation:

▶ 1. Click the **FILE** tab on the ribbon to display Backstage view. Because there is no open presentation, the Open screen is displayed. Recent Presentations is selected, and you might see a list of the 25 most recently opened presentations on the right.

Trouble? If PowerPoint is not running, start PowerPoint, and then in the navigation bar on the Recent screen, click the Open Other Presentations link.

Trouble? If another presentation is open, click Open in the navigation bar in Backstage view.

▶ 2. Click **Computer**. The list of recently opened files is replaced with a list of recently accessed folders on your computer and a Browse button.

Trouble? If you are storing your files on your SkyDrive, click SkyDrive, and then log in if necessary.

▶ 3. Click the **Browse** button. The Open dialog box appears. It is similar to the Save As dialog box.

▶ 4. Navigate to the drive that contains your Data Files, navigate to the **PowerPoint1 ▶ Tutorial** folder, click **Revised Membership** to select it, and then click the **Open** button. The Open dialog box closes and the Revised Membership presentation opens in the PowerPoint window, with Slide 1 displayed in the Slide pane.

Trouble? If you don't have the starting Data Files, you need to get them before you can proceed. Your instructor will either give you the Data Files or ask you to obtain them from a specified location (such as a network drive). If you have any questions about the Data Files, see your instructor or technical support person for assistance.

If you want to edit a presentation without changing the original, you need to create a copy of it. To do this, you use the Save As command to open the Save As dialog box, which is the same dialog box you saw when you saved your presentation for the first time. When you save a presentation with a new name, a copy of the original presentation is created, the original presentation is closed, and the newly named copy remains open in the PowerPoint window.

To save the Revised Membership presentation with a new name:

▶ 1. Click the **FILE** tab, and then in the navigation bar, click **Save As**. The Save As screen in Backstage view appears.

▶ 2. Click **Computer**, if necessary. On the right under Computer is a list of recently accessed folders with the folder containing the current file at the top.

> **3.** If the folder in which you are saving your Data Files is listed on the right, click it; if the folder in which you are saving your files is not listed, click the **Browse** button. The Save As dialog box opens.

> **4.** If necessary, navigate to the drive and folder where you are storing your Data Files.

> **5.** In the File name box, change the filename to **CSA New Member**, and then click the **Save** button. The Save As dialog box closes, a copy of the file is saved with the new name CSA New Member, and the CSA New Member presentation appears in the PowerPoint window.

Changing the Theme and the Theme Variant

A **theme** is a coordinated set of colors, fonts, backgrounds, and effects. All presentations have a theme. If you don't choose one, the default Office theme is applied; that is the theme currently applied to the CSA New Member presentation.

You saw the Office theme set of colors when you changed the color of the text on the "What Is a CSA?" slide. You have also seen the Office theme fonts in use on the slides. In the Office theme, the font of the slide titles is Calibri Light and the font of the text in content text boxes is Calibri. In themes, the font used for slide titles is the Headings font, and the font used for the content text boxes is the Body font.

In PowerPoint, each theme has several variants with different coordinating colors and sometimes slightly different backgrounds. A theme and its variants are called a **theme family**. PowerPoint comes with several installed themes, and many more themes are available online at Office.com. In addition, you can use a custom theme stored on your computer or network.

You can select a different installed theme when you create a new presentation by clicking one of the themes on the New or Recent screen in Backstage view instead of clicking Blank Presentation, and then clicking one of the variants. If you want to change the theme of an open presentation, you can choose an installed theme on the DESIGN tab or you can apply a custom theme stored on your computer or network. When you change the theme, the colors, fonts, and slide backgrounds change to those used in the new theme.

Isaac wants the theme of the CSA New Member presentation changed to one that has more color in the background. First you'll display Slide 2 in the Slide pane so you can see the effect a different theme has on the text formatted with a theme color.

To examine the current theme and then change the theme and theme variant:

> **1.** Display **Slide 2** ("What Is a CSA?") in the Slide pane, and then, in the unnumbered list select the orange letter **C**.

> **2.** On the HOME tab, in the Font group, click the **Font Color arrow**. Look at the colors under Theme Colors and note the second to last color is selected in the column containing shades of orange. Notice also the row of Standard Colors below the theme colors.

> **3.** In the Font group, click the **Font arrow**. A menu of fonts installed on the computer opens. At the top under Theme Fonts, Calibri (Body) is selected because the letter C that you selected is in a content text box. See Figure 1-24.

Figure 1-24 Theme fonts on the Font box menu

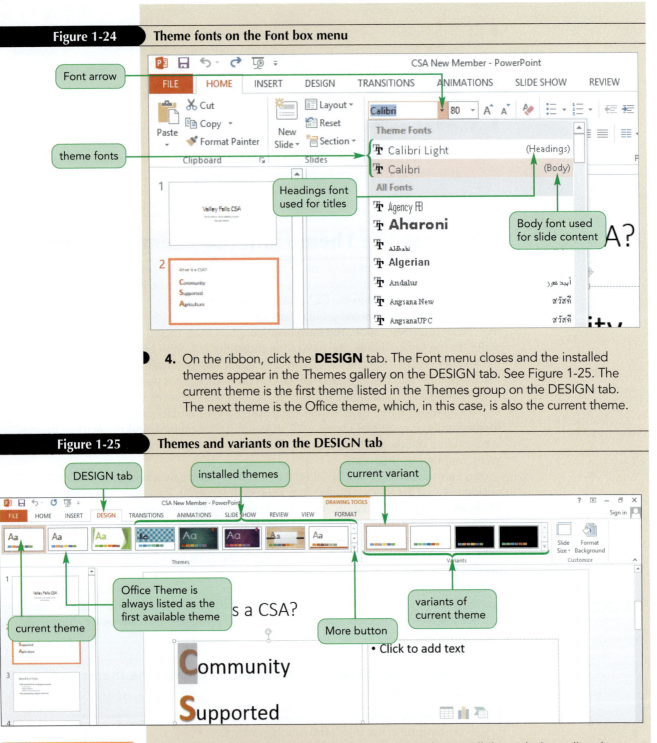

4. On the ribbon, click the **DESIGN** tab. The Font menu closes and the installed themes appear in the Themes gallery on the DESIGN tab. See Figure 1-25. The current theme is the first theme listed in the Themes group on the DESIGN tab. The next theme is the Office theme, which, in this case, is also the current theme.

Figure 1-25 Themes and variants on the DESIGN tab

To see all of the installed themes, you need to scroll through the gallery by clicking the up and down scroll buttons on the right end of the gallery or clicking the More button to expand the gallery to see all of the themes at once. The **More button** appears on all galleries that contain additional items or commands that don't fit in the group on the ribbon.

5. In the Themes group, click the **More** button ⬇. The gallery of themes opens. See Figure 1-26. When the gallery is open, the theme applied to the current presentation appears in the first row. In the next row, the first theme is the Office theme, and then the rest of the installed themes appear. Some of these themes appear on the Recent and New screens in Backstage view.

Figure 1-26   **Theme gallery expanded**

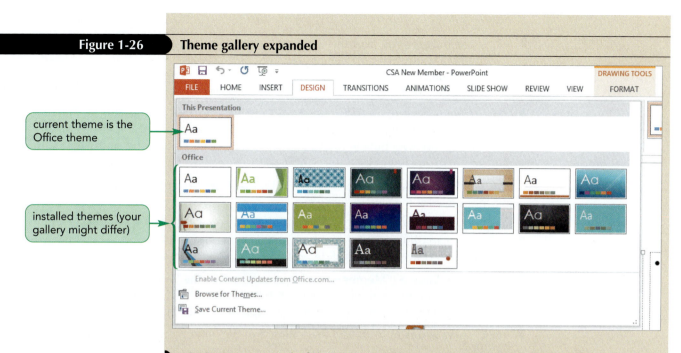

current theme is the Office theme

installed themes (your gallery might differ)

6. Point to several of the themes in the gallery to display their ScreenTips and to see a Live Preview of the theme applied to the current slide, and then click the **Facet** theme. The gallery closes and the Facet theme is applied to all the slides with the default variant (the first variant in the Variants group).

   The title text on each slide changes from black to green, the letters that you had colored orange on Slide 2 are dark green, the bullet symbols change from black circles to green triangles, and in the Slides tab, you can see on the Slide 6 thumbnail that the SmartArt shapes are now green as well.

7. In the Variants group, point to the other three variants to see a Live Preview of each of them. Isaac likes the default green variant best, so you will not change it.

8. Click the **HOME** tab, and then in the Font group, click the **Font Color arrow**. The selected color—the color of the selected letter "C"—is now a shade of green in the Theme Colors of the Facet theme. Notice also that the row of Standard Colors is the same as it was when the Office theme was applied.

9. In the Font group, click the **Font arrow**. You can see that the Theme Fonts are now Trebuchet MS for both Headings (slide titles) and the Body (content text boxes).

10. Press the **Esc** key. The Font menu closes.

After you apply a new theme, you should examine your slides to make sure that they look the way you expect them to. The font sizes used in the Facet theme are considerably smaller than those used in the Office theme. You know that Isaac wants the slides to be legible and clearly visible from a distance, so you will increase the font sizes on some of the slides. The title slide and Slide 2 are fine, but you need to examine the rest of the slides.

To examine the slides with the new theme and adjust font sizes:

1. Display **Slide 3** ("Benefits of CSAs") in the Slide pane, and then in the bulleted list, click the first bulleted item. (This is the new slide that Isaac added.) In the Font group, the font size is 18 points, quite a bit smaller than the font size of first-level bulleted items in the Office theme, which is 28 points. You can see that the font size of the subitems is also fairly small.

2. In the bulleted list, click the text box border to select the entire text box. In the Font group, 16+ appears in the Font Size box. The smallest font size used in the selected text box—the font size of the subitems—is 16, and the plus sign indicates that there is text in the selected text box larger than 16 points.

3. In the Font group, click the **Increase Font Size** button A˙ three times. The font size of the first-level bullets changes to 28 points, and the font size of the second-level bullets changes to 24 points. This is the same as the font sizes used in lists in the Office theme.

   Trouble? If the DRAWING TOOLS FORMAT tab becomes selected on the ribbon, click the HOME tab.

4. Display **Slide 4** ("What Do CSA Members Receive?") in the Slide pane, and then increase the size of the text in the bulleted list to 28 points. There are misspelled words on this slide and on Slide 5; ignore them for now.

5. Display **Slide 5** ("Membership Requirements") in the Slide pane, and then increase the font size of the text in the bulleted list so that the font size of the first-level items is 28 points and of the subitems is 24 points.

6. Display **Slides 6, 7, 8,** and then **Slide 1** in the Slide pane. These remaining slides look fine.

7. On the Quick Access Toolbar, click the **Save** button 🖫. The changes to the presentation are saved.

INSIGHT

Understanding the Difference Between Themes and Templates

As explained earlier, a theme is a coordinated set of colors, fonts, backgrounds, and effects. A **template**, like any presentation, has a theme applied, but it also contains text, graphics, and placeholders to help direct you in creating content for a presentation. You can create and save your own custom templates or find everything from calendars to marketing templates among the thousands of templates available on Office.com. To find a template on Office.com, display the Recent or New screen in Backstage view, type key words in the Search box or click one of the category links below the Search box to display templates related to the search terms or category. If you create a new presentation based on a template, you can make any changes you want to the slides.

If a template is stored on your computer, you can apply the theme used in the template to an existing presentation. However, if you want to apply the theme used in a template on Office.com to an existing presentation, you need to download and save the template to your computer first, and then you can apply it to an existing presentation.

Working with Photos

Most people are exposed to multimedia daily and expect to have information conveyed visually as well as verbally. In many cases, graphics are more effective than words for communicating an important point. For example, if a sales force has reached its sales goals for the year, including a photo in your presentation of a person reaching the top of a mountain can convey a sense of exhilaration to your audience.

Inserting Photos Stored on Your Computer or Network

Content placeholders contain buttons that you can use to insert things other than a list, including photos stored on your hard drive, a network drive, a USB drive, an SD card from a digital camera, or any other medium to which you have access. You can also use the Picture button in the Images group on the INSERT tab to add photos to slides.

Isaac has photos showing produce from his farm that he wants inserted on two of the slides in the presentation. He also wants a photo of people volunteering on the farm to appear on the last slide in the presentation.

To insert photos stored on your computer or network on slides:

1. Display **Slide 2** ("What Is a CSA?") in the Slide pane, and then in the content placeholder on the right, click the **Pictures** button 🖾. The Insert Picture dialog box appears. This dialog box is similar to the Open dialog box.

2. Navigate to the **PowerPoint1 ▸ Tutorial** folder included with your Data Files, click **Produce1**, and then click the **Insert** button. The dialog box closes, and a picture of produce in bins appears in the placeholder and is selected. The contextual PICTURE TOOLS FORMAT tab appears on the ribbon to the right of the VIEW tab and is the active tab. See Figure 1-27.

Figure 1-27	Picture inserted on Slide 2

Photo courtesy of S. Scott Zimmerman

3. Display **Slide 3** ("Benefits of CSAs") in the Slide pane. This slide uses the Title and Content layout and does not have a second content placeholder. You can change the layout to include a second content placeholder or you can use a command on the ribbon to insert a photo.

4. Click the **INSERT** tab, and then in the Images group, click the **Pictures** button. The Insert Picture dialog box opens.

5. In the PowerPoint1 ▸ Tutorial folder, click **Produce2**, and then click the **Insert** button. The dialog box closes and the picture is added to the center of the slide, covering much of the bulleted list. You will fix this later.

6. Display **Slide 8** (the copy of the "What Is a CSA?" slide), and then click the **INSERT** tab on the ribbon.

7. In the Images group, click the **Pictures** button, click **People** in the PowerPoint1 ▸ Tutorial folder, and then click the **Insert** button. The picture replaces the content placeholder on the slide.

Cropping Photos

Sometimes you want to display only part of a photo. For example, if you insert a photo of a party scene that includes a bouquet of colorful balloons, you might want to show only the balloons. To do this, you can **crop** the photo—cut out the parts you don't want to include. In PowerPoint, you can crop it manually to any size you want, crop it to a preset ratio, or crop it to a shape.

On Slide 2, Isaac wants you to crop the photo to a diamond shape to make it more interesting, and to crop the photo on Slide 3 to make the dimensions of the final photo smaller without making the images in the photo smaller.

To crop the photos on Slides 2 and 3:

1. Display **Slide 3** ("Benefits of CSAs") in the Slide pane, click the photo to select it, and then click the **PICTURE TOOLS FORMAT** tab, if necessary.

2. In the Size group, click the **Crop** button. The Crop button is selected, and crop handles appear around the edges of the photo just inside the sizing handles. See Figure 1-28.

Figure 1-28 **Photo with crop handles**

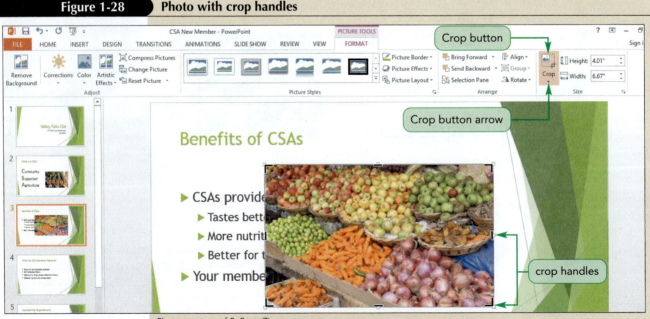

Photo courtesy of S. Scott Zimmerman

3. Position the pointer directly on top of the **left-middle crop handle** so that it changes to ⊣, press and hold the mouse button, and then drag the crop handle to the right approximately two inches.

4. Drag the crop handles on the bottom and right of the photo to match the cropped photo shown in Figure 1-29.

Figure 1-29   **Cropped photo**

Photo courtesy of S. Scott Zimmerman

5. Click the **Crop** button again. The Crop feature is turned off, but the photo is still selected and the FORMAT tab is still the active tab. The photo is still on top of the bulleted list, but you'll fix this later.

6. Display **Slide 2** ("What Is a CSA?") in the Slide pane, click the photo to select it, and then click the **FORMAT** tab, if necessary.

7. In the Size group, click the **Crop button arrow**. The Crop button menu opens. See Figure 1-30.

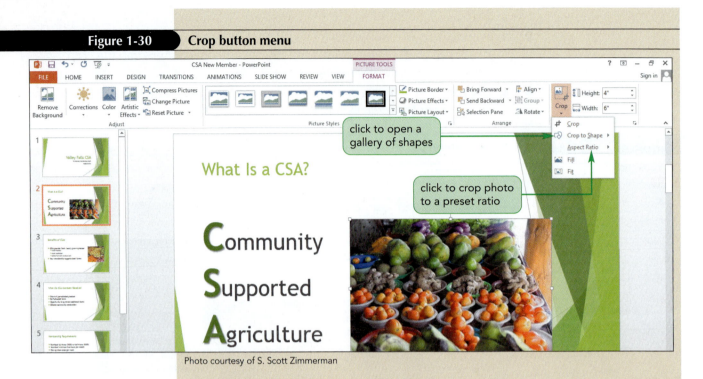

Figure 1-30   Crop button menu

Photo courtesy of S. Scott Zimmerman

▶ **8.** Point to **Crop to Shape** to open a gallery of shapes, and then under Basic Shapes, click the **Diamond** shape. The photo is cropped to a diamond shape. Notice that the rectangular selection border of the original photo is still showing.

▶ **9.** In the Size group, click the **Crop** button. You can now see the cropped portions of the original, rectangle photo that are shaded gray.

▶ **10.** Click a blank area of the slide. The picture is no longer selected and the HOME tab is the active tab on the ribbon.

Modifying Photo Compression Options

When you save a presentation that contains photos, PowerPoint automatically compresses the photos to a resolution of 220 pixels per inch (ppi). (For comparison, photos printed in magazines are typically 300 ppi.) Compressing photos reduces the size of the presentation file, but it also reduces the quality of the photos. See Figure 1-31 for a description of the compression options available. If an option in the dialog box is gray, the photo is a lower resolution than that setting. Note that many monitors and projectors are capable of displaying resolutions only a little higher (98 ppi) than the resolution designated for email (96 ppi).

Figure 1-31 | **Photo compression settings**

Compression Setting	Description
220 ppi	Photos are compressed to 220 pixels per inch; use when you need to maintain the quality of the photograph when the slides are printed. This is the default setting for PowerPoint presentations. (Note that although this setting compresses the photos minimally, they are still compressed, and if photograph quality is the most important concern, do not compress photos at all.)
150 ppi	Photos are compressed to 150 pixels per inch; use when the presentation will be viewed on a monitor or screen projector.
96 ppi	Photos are compressed to 96 pixels per inch; use for presentations that need to be emailed or uploaded to a Web page or when it is important to keep the overall file size small.
Document resolution	Photos are compressed to the resolution specified on the Advanced tab in the PowerPoint Options dialog box. The default setting is 220 ppi.
No compression	Photos are not compressed at all; used when it is critical that photos remain at their original resolution.

© 2014 Cengage Learning

You can change the compression setting for each photo that you insert or you can change the settings for all the photos in the presentation. If you cropped photos, you also can discard the cropped areas of the photo to make the presentation file size smaller. (Note that when you crop to a shape, the cropped portions are not discarded.) If you insert additional photos or crop a photo after you apply the new compression settings to all the slides, you will need to apply the new settings to the new photos.

REVIEW

Modifying Photo Compression Settings and Removing Cropped Areas

- After all photos have been added to the presentation file, click any photo in the presentation to select it.
- Click the PICTURE TOOLS FORMAT tab. In the Adjust group, click the Compress Pictures button.
- Click the option button next to the resolution you want to use.
- To apply the new compression settings to all the photos in the presentation, click the Apply only to this picture check box to deselect it.
- To keep cropped areas of photos, click the Delete cropped area of pictures check box to deselect it.
- Click the OK button.

You will adjust the compression settings to make the file size of the presentation as small as possible so that Isaac can easily send it or post it for others without worrying about file size limitations on the receiving server.

To modify photo compression settings and remove cropped areas from photos:

1. On **Slide 2** ("What Is a CSA?"), click the photo, and then click the **PICTURE TOOLS FORMAT** tab, if necessary.

2. In the Adjust group, click the **Compress Pictures** button. The Compress Pictures dialog box opens. See Figure 1-32. Under Target output, the Use document resolution option button is selected.

Figure 1-32   **Compress Pictures dialog box**

3. Click the **E-mail (96 ppi)** option button. This setting compresses the photos to the smallest possible size. At the top of the dialog box under Compression options, the Delete cropped area of pictures check box is already selected. This option is not applied to cropped photos until you open this dialog box and then click the OK button to apply it. Because you want the presentation file size to be as small as possible, you do want cropped portions of photos to be deleted, so you'll leave this selected. The Apply only to this picture check box is also selected; however, you want the settings applied to all the photos in the file.

4. Click the **Apply only to this picture** check box to deselect it.

5. Click the **OK** button.

Be sure you are satisfied with the way you cropped the photo on Slide 3 before you delete the cropped areas.

The dialog box closes and the compression settings are applied to all the photos in the presentation. You can confirm that the cropped areas of photos were removed by examining the photo on Slide 3. (The photo on Slide 2 was cropped to a shape, so the cropped areas on it were not removed.)

6. Display **Slide 3** ("Benefits of CSAs") in the Slide pane, click the photo to select it, click the **FORMAT** tab, if necessary, and then in the Size group, click the **Crop** button. The Crop handles appear around the photo, but the portions of the photo that you cropped out no longer appear.

7. Click the **Crop** button again to deselect it, and then save the changes to the presentation.

<hr />

INSIGHT

Keeping Photos Uncompressed

Suppose you are a photographer and want to create a presentation to show your photos. In that case, you would want to display them at their original, uncompressed resolution. To do this, you need to change a setting in the PowerPoint Options dialog box before you add photos to slides. Click the FILE tab to open Backstage view, click Options in the navigation bar to open the PowerPoint Options dialog box, click Advanced in the navigation bar, and then locate the Image Size and Quality section. To keep images at their original resolution, click the Do not compress images in file check box to select it. Note that you can also change the default compression setting for photos in this dialog box; you can increase the compression or choose to automatically discard cropped portions of photos. Note that these changes affect only the current presentation.

Resizing and Moving Objects

You can resize and move any object to best fit the space available on a slide. One way to resize an object is to drag a sizing handle. **Sizing handles** are the small squares that appear in the corners and in the middle of the sides of the border of a selected object. When you use this method, you can adjust the size of the object so it best fits the space visually. If you need to size an object to exact dimensions, you can modify the measurements in the Size group on the FORMAT tab that appears when you select the object.

You can also drag an object to reposition it anywhere on the slide. If more than one object is on a slide, **smart guides**, dashed red lines, appear as you drag to indicate the center and the top and bottom borders of the objects. Smart guides can help you position objects so they are aligned and spaced evenly.

In addition to using the smart guides, it can be helpful to display rulers and gridlines in the window. The rulers appear along the top and left sides of the Slide pane. Gridlines are one-inch squares made up of dots one-sixth of an inch apart. As you drag an object, it snaps to the grid, even if it is not visible.

Resizing and Moving Pictures

Pictures and other objects that cause the PICTURE TOOLS FORMAT tab to appear when selected have their aspect ratios locked by default. The **aspect ratio** is the ratio of the object's height to its width. When the aspect ratio is locked, if you resize the photo by dragging a corner sizing handle or if you change one dimension in the Size group on the PICTURE TOOLS FORMAT tab, the other dimension will change by the same percentage. However, if you drag one of the sizing handles in the middle of an object's border, you will override the locked aspect ratio setting and resize the object only in the direction you drag. Generally you do not want to do this with photos because the images will become distorted.

You need to resize and move the cropped photo on Slide 3 so it is not obscuring the text. You also want to resize and move the photos you inserted on Slides 2 and 8 so the slides are more attractive. You'll display the rulers and gridlines to help you as you do this.

To move and resize the photos:

1. Click the **VIEW** tab, and then in the Show group, click the **Ruler** and the **Gridlines** check boxes. Rulers appear along the top and left sides of the Slide pane, and the gridlines appear in the Slide pane.

2. On **Slide 3** ("Benefits of CSAs"), select the photo, if necessary, and then position the pointer on the photo anywhere except on a sizing handle so that the pointer changes to ⤧.

3. Press and hold the mouse button, drag the photo down and to the right so that the right edge of the photo is approximately one inch from the right side of the slide and a smart guide appears indicating that the top of the photo and the top of the bulleted list text box are aligned, as shown in Figure 1-33.

TIP

If you don't want objects you are moving to snap to the grid, press and hold the Alt key while you are dragging.

Figure 1-33 Repositioning photo on Slide 3 using smart guides and gridlines

Photo courtesy of S. Scott Zimmerman

4. **Release the mouse button.** The photo is repositioned to the right of the bulleted list.

5. Display **Slide 2** ("What Is a CSA?") in the Slide pane, click the photo to select it, and then click the **PICTURE TOOLS FORMAT** tab if necessary. Instead of the border and sizing handles being on the diamond border, a rectangular border appears representing the original, uncropped photo's borders. (Remember that cropped portions of photos that are cropped to a shape are not removed.)

6. In the Size group, click in the **Height** box to select the current measurement, type **4**, and then press the **Enter** key. The measurement in the Width box in the Size group changes proportionately, and the new measurements are applied to the photo.

7. Drag the photo up and to the left until a horizontal smart guide appears indicating the alignment of the middle of the text box and the middle of the photo, and a vertical smart guide appears on the left side of the photo indicating the alignment of the left edge of the photo and the right edge of the bulleted list text box, as shown in Figure 1-34.

Figure 1-34   Moving resized photo on Slide 2

Photo courtesy of S. Scott Zimmerman

8. Display **Slide 8** (the last slide in the presentation) in the Slide pane, click the photo to select it, position the pointer on the top-middle sizing handle to that it changes to ↕, press and hold the mouse button, and then drag the sizing handle approximately two inches up. The photo is two inches taller, but the image is distorted.

9. On the Quick Access Toolbar, click the **Undo** button ↺. You need to resize the photo by dragging a corner sizing handle to maintain the aspect ratio.

10. Click the **FORMAT** tab, and note the measurements in the Size group. The photo is 3.05 inches high and 4.58 inches wide.

11. Position the pointer on the bottom-right corner sizing handle so that it changes to ⬉, press and hold the mouse button, and then drag the sizing handle down. Even though you are dragging in only one direction, because you are dragging a corner sizing handle, both the width and height are changing proportionately.

12. When the photo is approximately four inches high and six inches wide, release the mouse button. Note that the measurements in the Height and Width boxes changed to reflect the picture's new size.

13. Drag the photo up until the top of the photo aligns with the 2-inch mark on the ruler on the left and the right edge of the photo is aligned with the 6-inch mark on the ruler at the top of the Slide pane. You are done using the ruler and gridlines so you can turn these features off.

14. Click the **VIEW** tab, and then click the **Ruler** and **Gridlines** check boxes to deselect them.

Resizing and Moving Text Boxes

The themes and layouts installed with PowerPoint are designed by professionals, so much of the time it's a good idea to use the layouts as provided to be assured of a cohesive look among the slides. However, occasionally there will be a compelling reason to adjust the layout of objects on a slide, by either resizing or repositioning them.

Text boxes and other objects that cause the DRAWING TOOLS FORMAT tab to appear when selected do not have their aspect ratios locked by default. This means that when you resize an object by dragging a corner sizing handle or changing one dimension in the Size group, the other dimension is not affected.

Like any other object on a slide, you can reposition text boxes. To do this, you must position the pointer on the text box border, anywhere except on a sizing handle, to drag it to its new location.

To improve the appearance of Slide 8, you will resize the text box containing the unnumbered list so it vertically fills the slide.

To resize the text box on Slide 8 and increase the font size:

1. On Slide 8, click the unnumbered list to display the text box border.

2. Position the pointer on the top-middle sizing handle so that it changes to ↕, and then drag the sizing handle up until the top edge of the text box is aligned with the top edge of the title text placeholder.

3. Drag the right-middle sizing handle to the right until the right edge of the text box is touching the left edge of the photo.

4. Click the **HOME** tab, and then in the Font group, click the **Increase Font Size** button A˙ three times. Even though the title text placeholder will not appear during a slide show, you will delete it so that it is easier to see how the final slide will look.

5. Click the title text placeholder border, and then press the **Delete** key. See Figure 1-35 and adjust the position of the photo if necessary.

| Figure 1-35 | Slide 8 with resized text box |

Photo courtesy of moodboard/Getty Images

▌ **6.** Save the changes to the presentation.

Adding Speaker Notes

Speaker notes, or simply **notes**, are information you add about slide content to help you remember to bring up specific points during the presentation. Speaker notes should not contain all the information you plan to say during your presentation, but they can be a useful tool for reminding you about facts and details related to the content on specific slides. You add notes in the **Notes pane**, which you can display below the Slide pane in Normal view, or you can switch to **Notes Page view**, in which an image of the slide appears in the top half of the presentation window and the notes for that slide appear in the bottom half.

To add notes to Slides 3 and 7:

▌ **1.** Display **Slide 7** ("For More Information") in the Slide pane, and then, on the status bar, click the **NOTES** button. The Notes pane appears below the Slide pane with "Click to add notes" as placeholder text. See Figure 1-36.

Figure 1-36 **Notes pane below the Slide pane**

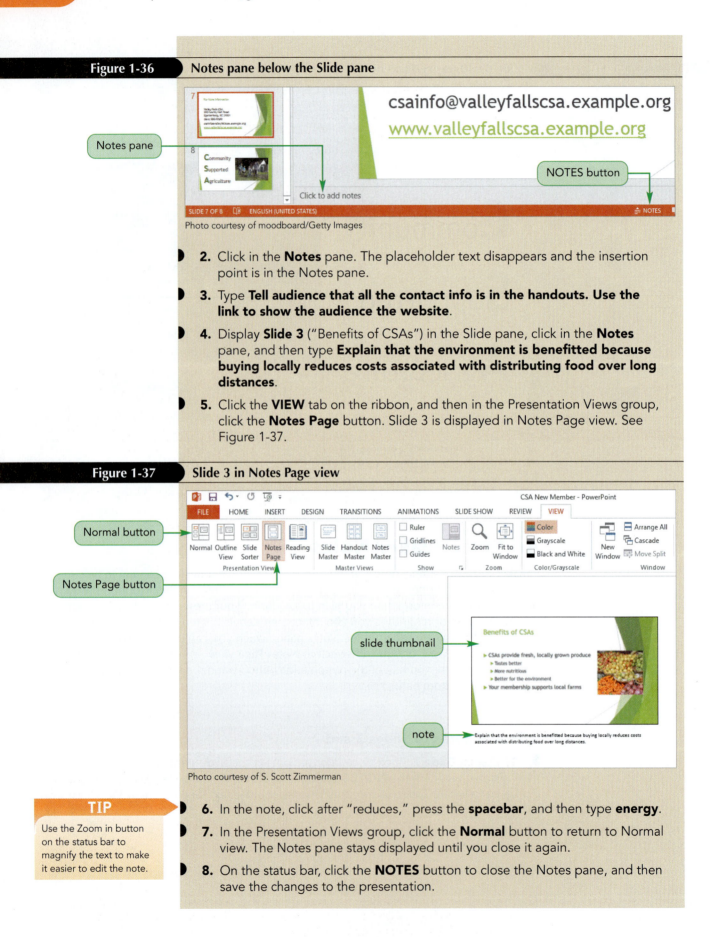

Notes pane

NOTES button

Click to add notes

SLIDE 7 OF 8   ENGLISH (UNITED STATES)   ≜ NOTES

Photo courtesy of moodboard/Getty Images

2. Click in the **Notes** pane. The placeholder text disappears and the insertion point is in the Notes pane.

3. Type **Tell audience that all the contact info is in the handouts. Use the link to show the audience the website**.

4. Display **Slide 3** ("Benefits of CSAs") in the Slide pane, click in the **Notes** pane, and then type **Explain that the environment is benefitted because buying locally reduces costs associated with distributing food over long distances**.

5. Click the **VIEW** tab on the ribbon, and then in the Presentation Views group, click the **Notes Page** button. Slide 3 is displayed in Notes Page view. See Figure 1-37.

Figure 1-37 **Slide 3 in Notes Page view**

Normal button

Notes Page button

slide thumbnail

Benefits of CSAs

▸ CSAs provide fresh, locally grown produce
  ▸ Tastes better
  ▸ More nutritious
  ▸ Better for the environment
▸ Your membership supports local farms

note

Explain that the environment is benefitted because buying locally reduces costs associated with distributing food over long distances.

Photo courtesy of S. Scott Zimmerman

6. In the note, click after "reduces," press the **spacebar**, and then type **energy**.

7. In the Presentation Views group, click the **Normal** button to return to Normal view. The Notes pane stays displayed until you close it again.

8. On the status bar, click the **NOTES** button to close the Notes pane, and then save the changes to the presentation.

TIP

Use the Zoom in button on the status bar to magnify the text to make it easier to edit the note.

Checking Spelling

You should always check the spelling and grammar in your presentation before you finalize it. To make this task easier, you can use PowerPoint's spelling checker. You can quickly tell if there are words on slides that are not in the built-in dictionary by looking at the Spelling button at the left end of the status bar. If there are no words flagged as possibly misspelled, the button is [icon]; if there are flagged words, the button changes to [icon]. To indicate that a word might be misspelled, a wavy red line appears under it.

To correct misspelled words, you can right-click a flagged word to see a list of suggested spellings on the shortcut menu, or you can check the spelling of all the words in the presentation. To check the spelling of all the words in the presentation, you click the Spelling button in the Proofing group on the REVIEW tab. This opens the Spelling task pane to the right of the Slide pane and starts the spell check from the current slide. A **task pane** is a pane that opens to the right or left of the Slide pane and contains commands and options related to the task you are doing. When a possible misspelled word is found, suggestions are displayed for the correct spelling. Synonyms for the selected correct spelling are also listed.

To check the spelling of words in the presentation:

▶ 1. Display **Slide 4** ("What Do CSA Members Receive?") in the Slide pane, and then right-click the misspelled word **Oportunity**. A shortcut menu opens listing spelling options. See Figure 1-38.

| Figure 1-38 | Shortcut menu for a misspelled word |

Photos courtesy of S. Scott Zimmerman and moodboard/Getty Images

▶ 2. On the shortcut menu, click **Opportunity**. The menu closes and the spelling is corrected.

TIP

You can also click the Spelling button on the status bar to start the spell check.

▶ 3. Click the **REVIEW** tab, and then in the Proofing group, click the **Spelling** button. The Spelling task pane opens to the right of the Slide pane, and the next slide that contains a possible misspelled word, Slide 5 ("Membership Requirements"), appears in the Slide pane with the flagged word, "minmum," highlighted. See Figure 1-39. In the Spelling task pane, the first suggested correct spelling is selected. The selected correct spelling also appears at the bottom of the task pane with synonyms for the word listed below it and a speaker icon next to it.

Figure 1-39 Spelling task pane displaying a misspelled word

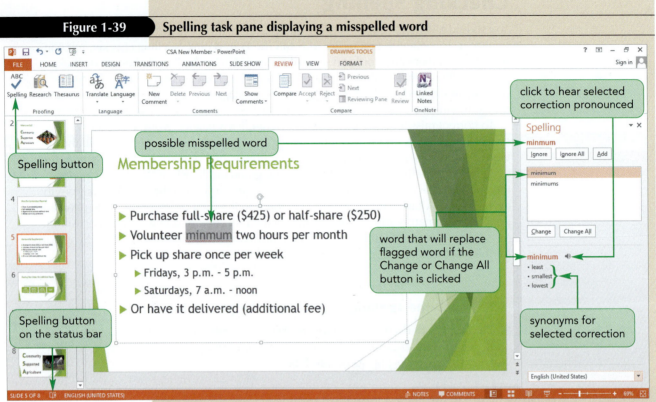

Photos courtesy of S. Scott Zimmerman and moodboard/Getty Images

▸ **4.** In the Spelling task pane, click the **speaker** icon 🔊. A male voice says the word "minimum."

▸ **5.** In the list of suggested corrections, click **minimums**. The word at the bottom of the task pane changes to "minimums," and the synonyms change also.

▸ **6.** In the list of suggested corrections, click **minimum**, and then click the **Change** button. The word is corrected and the next slide containing a possible misspelled word, Slide 1, appears in the Slide pane with the flagged word, "DeSoto," highlighted and listed in the Spelling task pane. This is Isaac's last name so you want the spell checker to ignore this.

Trouble? If the spell checker finds any other misspelled words, correct them.

▸ **7.** In the task pane, click the **Ignore All** button. Because that was the last flagged word in the presentation, the Spelling task pane closes and a dialog box opens telling you that the spell check is complete.

▸ **8.** Click the **OK** button. The dialog box closes. The last flagged word, DeSoto, is still selected on Slide 1.

▸ **9.** Click a blank area of the slide to deselect the text, and then save the changes to your presentation.

Running a Slide Show

After you have created and proofed your presentation, you should view it as a slide show to see how it will appear to your audience. There are several ways to do this—Slide Show view, Presenter view, and Reading view.

Using Slide Show View and Presenter View

You can use Slide Show view if your computer has only one monitor and you don't have access to a screen projector. If your computer is connected to a second monitor or a screen projector, Slide Show view is the way an audience will see your slides. Refer to the Session 1.2 Visual Overview for more information about Slide Show view.

Isaac asks you to review the slide show in Slide Show view to make sure the slides look good.

TIP

To start the slide show from the current slide, click the Slide Show button on the status bar.

To use Slide Show view:

1. On the Quick Access Toolbar, click the **Start From Beginning** button. Slide 1 appears on the screen in Slide Show view. Now you need to advance the slide show.

2. Press the **spacebar**. Slide 2 ("What Is a CSA?") appears on the screen.

3. Click the mouse button. The next slide, Slide 3 ("Benefits of CSAs"), appears on the screen.

4. Press the **Backspace** key. The previous slide, Slide 2, appears again.

5. Type **7**, and then press the **Enter** key. Slide 7 ("For More Information") appears on the screen.

6. Move the mouse to display the pointer, and then position the pointer on the website address **www.valleyfoodscsa.example.org**. The pointer changes to 🖑 to indicate that this is a link, and the ScreenTip that appears shows the full website address including "http://". If this were a real website, you could click the link to open your Web browser and display the website to your audience. Because you moved the pointer, a very faint row of buttons appears in the lower-left corner. See Figure 1-40.

Figure 1-40   Link and buttons in Slide Show view

pointer on a link in Slide Show view

row of buttons that appears when you move the pointer

(864) 555-FOOD

csainfo@valleyfallscsa.example.org

www.valleyfallscsa.example.org

http://www.valleyfallscsa.example.org/

ScreenTip identifying the link

7. Move the pointer again, if necessary, to display the row of buttons that appears in the lower left corner of the screen, and then click the **Return to the previous slide** button four times to return to Slide 3 ("Benefits of CSAs").

Trouble? If you can't see the buttons on the toolbar, move the pointer to the lower left corner so it is on top of the first button to darken that button, and then move the pointer to the right to see the rest of the buttons.

8. Display the faint row of buttons again, and then click the **Zoom into the slide** button. The pointer changes to ⊕ and three-quarters of the slide is darkened. See Figure 1-41.

Figure 1-41 **Zoom feature activated in Slide Show view**

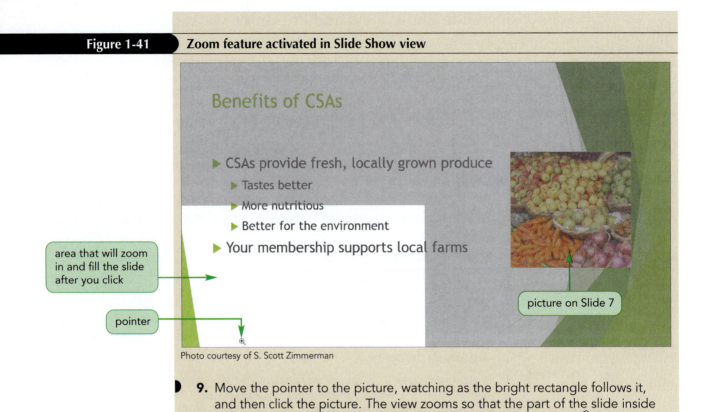

Photo courtesy of S. Scott Zimmerman

9. Move the pointer to the picture, watching as the bright rectangle follows it, and then click the picture. The view zooms so that the part of the slide inside the bright rectangle fills the screen, and the pointer changes to 🖑.

10. Press and hold the mouse button to change the pointer to 🖐, and then drag down and to the right to pull another part of the zoomed in slide into view.

11. Press the **Esc** key to zoom back out to see the whole slide.

Presenter view provides additional tools for running a slide show. In addition to seeing the current slide, you can also see the next slide, speaker notes, and a timer showing you how long the slide show has been running. Refer to the Session 1.2 Visual Overview for more information about Presenter view. Because of the additional tools available in Presenter view, you should consider using it if your computer is connected to a second monitor or projector. If, for some reason, you don't want to use Presenter view in that circumstance, you can switch to Slide Show view.

If your computer is connected to a projector or second monitor, and you start a slide show in Slide Show view, Presenter view starts on the computer and Slide Show view appears on the second monitor or projection screen. If you want to practice using Presenter view when your computer is not connected to a second monitor or projector, you can switch to Presenter view from Slide Show view.

Isaac wants you to switch to Presenter view and familiarize yourself with the tools available there.

To use Presenter view to review the slide show:

1. Move the pointer to display the row of buttons in the lower left corner of the screen, click the **More slide show options** button ⊙ to open a menu of commands, and then click **Show Presenter View**. The screen changes to show the presentation in Presenter view.

2. Below the current slide, click the **See all slides** button ▦. The screen changes to show thumbnails of all the slides in the presentation, similar to Slide Sorter view.

3. Click the **Slide 4** thumbnail. Presenter view reappears, displaying Slide 4 ("What Do CSA Members Receive?") as the current slide.

4. Click anywhere on the current slide, Slide 4. The slide show advances to display Slide 5.

5. At the bottom of the screen, click the **Advance to the next slide** button ⏵. Slide 6 ("Placing Your Order for Additional Items") appears.

6. Press the **spacebar** twice. The slide show advances again to display Slides 7 and then 8.

7. Press the **spacebar** again. A black slide appears. As noted on the slide, the black screen indicates the end of the slide show.

8. Press the **spacebar** once more. Presentation view closes and you return to Normal view.

PROSKILLS

Decision Making: Displaying a Blank Slide During a Presentation

Sometimes during a presentation, the audience has questions about the material and you want to pause the slide show to respond to their questions. Or you might want to refocus the audience's attention on you instead of on the visuals on the screen. In these cases, you can display a blank slide (either black or white). When you do this, the audience, with nothing else to look at, will shift all of their attention to you. Some presenters plan to use blank slides and insert them at specific points during their slide shows. Planning to use a blank slide can help you keep your presentation focused and remind you that the purpose of the PowerPoint slides is to provide visual aids to enhance your presentation; the slides themselves are not the presentation.

If you did not create blank slides in your presentation file, but during your presentation you feel you need to display a blank slide, you can easily do this in Slide Show or Presenter view by pressing the B key to display a blank black slide or the W key to display a blank white slide. You can also click the Menu button in the row of buttons or right-click the screen to open a menu, point to Screen on the menu, and then click Black or White. To remove the black or white slide and redisplay the slide that had been on the screen before you displayed the blank slide, press any key on the keyboard or click anywhere on the screen. In Presenter view, you can also use the Black or unblack slide show button 🔳 to toggle a black slide on or off.

An alternative to redisplaying the slide that had been displayed prior to the blank slide is to click the Advance to the next slide button ⏵. This can be more effective than redisplaying the slide that was onscreen before the blank slide because, after you have grabbed the audience's attention and prepared them to move on, you won't lose their focus by displaying a slide they have already seen.

Using Reading View

Reading view displays the slides so that they almost fill the screen, similar to Slide Show view; however, in Reading view, a status bar appears identifying the number of the current slide and providing buttons to advance the slide show. You can also resize the window in Reading view to allow you to work in another window on the desktop.

To use Reading view to review the presentation:

1. Display **Slide 2** ("What Is a CSA?"), in the Slide pane, and then on the status bar, click the **Reading View** button 📖. The presentation changes to Reading view with Slide 2 displayed. See Figure 1-42.

Figure 1-42   **Slide 2 in Reading view**

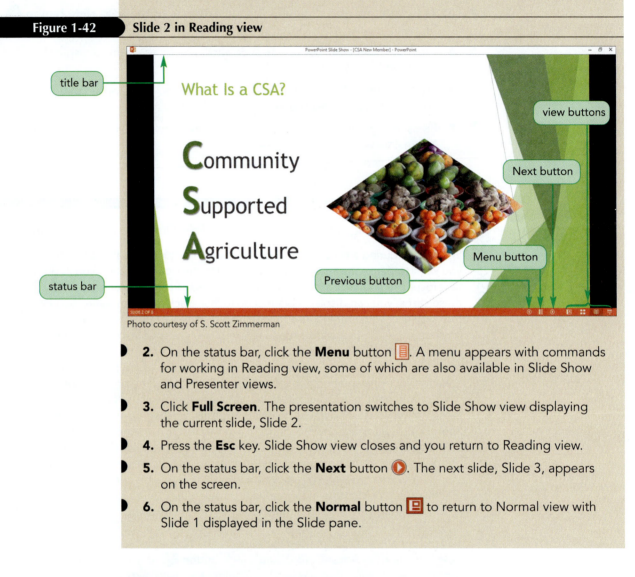

Photo courtesy of S. Scott Zimmerman

2. On the status bar, click the **Menu** button 📑. A menu appears with commands for working in Reading view, some of which are also available in Slide Show and Presenter views.

3. Click **Full Screen**. The presentation switches to Slide Show view displaying the current slide, Slide 2.

4. Press the **Esc** key. Slide Show view closes and you return to Reading view.

5. On the status bar, click the **Next** button ⊙. The next slide, Slide 3, appears on the screen.

6. On the status bar, click the **Normal** button 🖬 to return to Normal view with Slide 1 displayed in the Slide pane.

Printing a Presentation

Before you deliver your presentation, you might want to print it. PowerPoint provides several printing options. For example, you can print the slides in color, grayscale (white and shades of gray), or pure black and white, and you can print one, some, or all of the slides in several formats.

You use the Print screen in Backstage view to set print options such as specifying a printer and color options.

First, you will replace Isaac's name on Slide 1 with your name.

To choose a printer and color options:

1. Display **Slide 1** in the Slide pane, and then replace Isaac's name in the subtitle with your name.

2. Click the **FILE** tab to display Backstage view, and then click **Print** in the navigation bar. Backstage view changes to display the Print screen. The Print screen contains options for printing your presentation, and a preview of the first slide as it will print with the current options. See Figure 1-43.

| Figure 1-43 | Print screen in Backstage view |

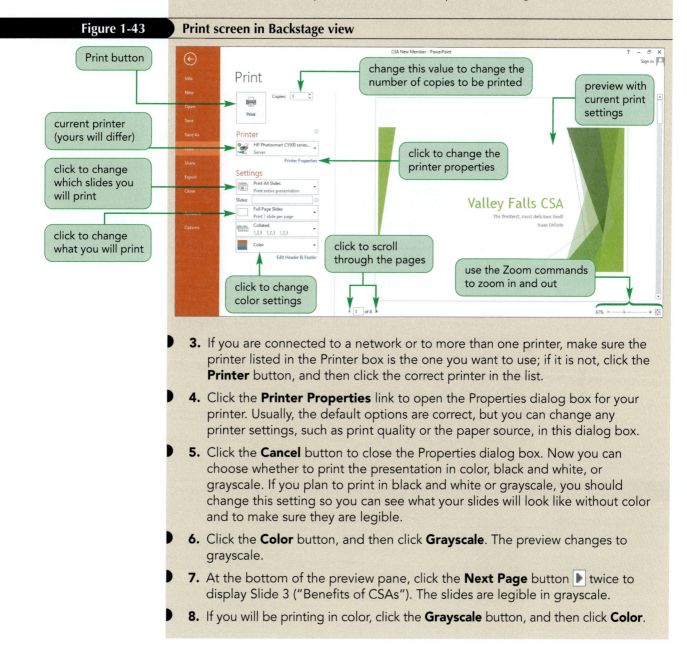

3. If you are connected to a network or to more than one printer, make sure the printer listed in the Printer box is the one you want to use; if it is not, click the **Printer** button, and then click the correct printer in the list.

4. Click the **Printer Properties** link to open the Properties dialog box for your printer. Usually, the default options are correct, but you can change any printer settings, such as print quality or the paper source, in this dialog box.

5. Click the **Cancel** button to close the Properties dialog box. Now you can choose whether to print the presentation in color, black and white, or grayscale. If you plan to print in black and white or grayscale, you should change this setting so you can see what your slides will look like without color and to make sure they are legible.

6. Click the **Color** button, and then click **Grayscale**. The preview changes to grayscale.

7. At the bottom of the preview pane, click the **Next Page** button ▶ twice to display Slide 3 ("Benefits of CSAs"). The slides are legible in grayscale.

8. If you will be printing in color, click the **Grayscale** button, and then click **Color**.

In the Settings section on the Print screen, you can click the Full Page Slides button to choose from among several choices for printing the presentation, as described below:

- **Full Page Slides**—Prints each slide full size on a separate piece of paper.
- **Notes Pages**—Prints each slide as a notes page.
- **Outline**—Prints the text of the presentation as an outline.
- **Handouts**—Prints the presentation with one or more slides on each piece of paper. When printing four, six, or nine slides, you can choose whether to order the slides from left to right in rows (horizontally) or from top to bottom in columns (vertically).

Isaac wants you to print the title slide as a full page slide so that he can use it as a cover page for his handouts.

To print the title slide as a full page slide:

1. At the bottom of the preview pane, click the **Previous Page** button ◀ three times to display Slide 1 (the title slide) as the preview.

2. If the second button in the Settings section is not labeled "Full Page Slides," click it, and then click **Full Page Slides**. Note that below the preview of Slide 1, it indicates that you are viewing Slide 1 of eight slides to print.

3. In the Settings section, click the **Print All Slides** button. Note on the menu that opens that you can print all the slides, selected slides, the current slide, or a custom range. You want to print just the title slide as a full page slide.

4. Click **Print Current Slide**. Slide 1 appears in the preview pane, and at the bottom, it now indicates that you will print only one slide.

5. Click the **Print** button. Backstage view closes and Slide 1 prints.

Next, Isaac wants you to print the slides as a handout, with all eight slides on a single sheet of paper.

To print the slides as a handout:

1. Click the **FILE** tab, and then click **Print** in the navigation bar.

2. In the Settings section, click the **Full Page Slides** button. A menu opens listing the various ways you can print the slides. See Figure 1-44.

Figure 1-44   **Print screen in Backstage view with print options menu open**

click to print slides as notes pages

click to print full page-sized slides

options for printing handouts

options you can toggle on or off

click to print the text of the presentation as an outline

click to print 3 slides per page with lines next to each slide for notes

Valley Falls CSA
The freshest, most delicious food!

3. In the Handouts section, click **9 Slides Horizontal**. The preview changes to show Slide 1 in the upper-left corner. You need to specify that all eight slides will print.

4. Click the **Print Current Slide** button, and then click **Print All Slides**. All eight slides appear in the preview pane, arranged in order horizontally, that is, in three rows from left to right. Notice that the current date appears in the top-right corner and a page number appears in the bottom-right corner.

5. At the top of the Print section, click the **Print** button. Backstage view closes and the handout prints.

Recall that you created speaker notes on Slides 3 and 7. Isaac would like you to print these slides as notes pages.

To print the nonsequential slides containing speaker notes:

1. Open the Print screen in Backstage view again, and then click the **9 Slides Horizontal** button. The menu opens. "9 Slides Horizontal" appeared on the button because that was the last printing option you chose.

2. In the Print Layout section of the menu, click **Notes Pages**. The menu closes and the preview displays Slide 1 as a Notes Page.

3. In the Settings section, click in the **Slides** box, type **3,7** and then click a blank area of the Print screen.

4. Scroll through the preview to confirm that Slides 3 and 7 will print, and then click the **Print** button. Backstage view closes and Slides 3 and 7 print as notes pages.

Finally, Isaac would like you to print the outline of the presentation. Recall that Slide 8 is designed to be a visual Isaac can leave displayed at the end of the presentation, so you don't need to include it in the outline.

To print Slides 1 through 7 as an outline on a single page:

1. Open the Print tab in Backstage view, click the **Notes Pages** button, and then in the Print Layout section, click **Outline**. The text on Slides 3 and 7 appears as an outline in the preview pane.

2. Click in the **Slides** box, type **1-7**, and then click a blank area of the Print screen. See Figure 1-45.

Figure 1-45   Print screen in Backstage view with Slides 1-7 previewed as an outline

text of Slides 1-7 as an outline

3. At the top of the Print section, click the **Print** button. Backstage view closes and the text of Slides 1-7 prints on one sheet of paper.

Exiting PowerPoint

When you are finished working with your presentation, you can exit PowerPoint. If there is only one presentation open, you click the Close button ☒ in the upper-right corner of the program window to exit the program. If more than one presentation is open, clicking this button will only close the current presentation; to exit PowerPoint, you would need to click the Close button in each of the open presentation's windows.

To exit PowerPoint:

1. In the upper-right corner of the program window, click the **Close** button ☒. A dialog box opens asking if you want to save your changes. This is because you did not save the file after you replaced Isaac's name with your own.

2. In the dialog box, click the **Save** button. The dialog box closes, the changes are saved, and PowerPoint exits.

In this session, you opened an existing presentation and saved it with a new name, changed the theme, added and cropped photos and adjusted the photo compression, and resized and moved objects. You have also added speaker notes and checked the spelling. Finally, you printed the presentation in several forms and exited PowerPoint. Your work will help Isaac give an effective presentation to potential customers of Valley Farms CSA.

REVIEW

Session 1.2 Quick Check

1. Explain what a theme is and what changes with each variant.

2. Describe what happens when you crop photos.

3. Describe sizing handles.

4. Describe smart guides.

5. Why is it important to maintain the aspect ratio of photos?

6. What is the difference between Slide Show view and Presenter view?

7. List the four formats for printing a presentation.

ASSESS

SAM Projects

Put your skills into practice with SAM Projects! SAM Projects for this tutorial can be found online. If you have a SAM account, go to www.cengage.com/sam2013 to download the most recent Project Instructions and Start Files.

PRACTICE

Review Assignments

Data Files needed for the Review Assignments: Farmland.jpg, Field Volunteer.jpg, Office Volunteer.jpg, Revised Volunteer Info.pptx

Chris Kopache is the Volunteer Coordinator for Valley Falls CSA. He needs to create a presentation for CSA members to explain the various ways they can volunteer. He will give the presentation to small groups. He doesn't want to overwhelm people, but he wants them to have enough information about each type of job so that they can choose one that best suits their abilities. He asks you to begin creating the presentation.

1. Start PowerPoint and create a new, blank presentation. On the title slide, type **Information for Volunteers** as the title, and then type your name as the subtitle. Save the presentation as **Volunteer Info** to the drive and folder where you are storing your files.

2. Edit the title by adding **Valley Falls CSA** before the word "Volunteers."

3. Add a new Slide 2 with the Title and Content layout, type **Jobs for Volunteers** as the slide title, and then in the content placeholder type the following:
   - **Field work**
   - **Work in store**
   - **Deliver shares**
   - **Office work**
     - **Must be familiar with Excel and Word**
     - **Only 3 positions available**

4. Create a new Slide 3 with the Title and Content layout. Add **Expectations** as the slide title, and then type the following as a numbered list on the slide:
   1. **Submit job preferences with membership application**
   2. **Volunteer minimum two hours per month**
   3. **Submit shift changes one week in advance**
   4. **Contact Chris Kopache**

5. Create a new Slide 4 using the Two Content layout. Add **Questions?** as the slide title.

6. Use the Cut and Paste commands to move the last bulleted item on Slide 3 ("Contact Chris Kopache") to the left content placeholder on Slide 4.

7. On Slide 4, remove the bullet symbol from the text you pasted, and then add the following as the next two items in the unnumbered list:
   Email: c_kopache@example.org
   Cell: 803-555-8723

8. Click after "Kopache" in the first item in the list, and then create a new line below it without creating a new item in the list and so that there is no extra space above the new line. On the new line, type **Volunteer Coordinator**.

9. Remove the hyperlink formatting from the email address.

10. Create a new Slide 5 using the Title and Content layout. Delete the title text placeholder. In the content placeholder, type **Thank You!** as a single item in an unnumbered list. Increase the size of the text "Thank You!" to 96 points, and then change the color of this text to Blue, Accent 1.

11. On Slide 3 ("Expectations"), change the numbered list to a SmartArt graphic. Use the Vertical Curved List layout, which is a List type of diagram.

12. Save your changes, and then close the presentation.

13. Open the file **Revised Volunteer Info**, located in the PowerPoint1 ▶ Review folder included with your Data Files, add your name as the subtitle on the title slide, and then save it as **New CSA Volunteers** to the drive and location where you are storing your files.

14. Change the theme to Wisp and keep the default variant. On Slide 2, change the size of the text in the bulleted list so that the size of the text of the first-level items is 28 points.

15. On Slide 1 (the title slide), insert the photo **Farmland**, located in the PowerPoint1 ▶ Review folder included with your Data Files. Resize the photo, maintaining the aspect ratio, so that it is the same width as the slide, and then reposition the photo so that the top of the photo aligns with the top of the slide. Crop the photo from the bottom, up to the base of the trees on the right, leaving approximately one-quarter inch between the bottom of the photo and the slide title.

16. Change the layout of Slide 4 ("Volunteer in the Fields") to Title and Content, and then duplicate Slide 4. In the title of Slide 5 (the duplicate slide), replace "Fields" with **Office**.

17. On Slide 4, insert the photo **Field Volunteer**, located in the PowerPoint1 ▶ Review folder. Resize the photo so it is 4.9 inches high, maintaining the aspect ratio, and reposition it so it is approximately centered in the space below the slide title.

18. On Slide 5, insert the photo **Office Volunteer**. Crop the top portion of the photo so that there is approximately one-half inch of wall above the top of the paintings in the photo. Resize the cropped photo so it is 5.1 inches high, maintaining the aspect ratio, and then reposition the photo as you did for the photo on Slide 4.

19. Move Slide 5 ("Volunteer in the Office") so it becomes Slide 7.

20. On Slide 9 ("Questions?"), crop the photo to the Oval shape. Increase the size of the text in the unnumbered list to 24 points, and then resize the text box to make it wide enough so that the line containing the email address fits on one line.

21. Compress all the photos in the slides to 96 ppi and delete cropped areas of pictures.

22. Display Slide 3 ("Description of Volunteer Jobs") in the Slide pane and review the information on this slide. Chris wants to include this information as notes on Slides 4 through 7 instead of displaying it as a bulleted list. He has already added the notes to Slides 5 and 6. Display Slide 4 ("Volunteer in the Fields") in the Slide pane, display the Notes pane, and then add **Field workers pull weeds and participate in harvesting produce.** in the Notes pane. Then display Slide 7 ("Volunteer in the Office") in the Slide pane, and add **Office workers use Excel to maintain volunteer schedules and use Word to publish the newsletter.** as a note on this slide.

23. Delete Slide 3 ("Description of Volunteer Jobs") and the last slide (the blank slide).

24. Correct the two spelling errors on Slide 2 and the error on Slide 7, and ignore all instances of Chris's last name. If you made any additional spelling errors, correct them as well. Save the changes to the presentation.

25. Review the slide show in Slide Show, Presenter, and Reading views.

26. View the slides in grayscale, and then print the following: the title slide as a full page-sized slide in color or in grayscale depending on your printer; Slides 1–9 as a handout on a single piece of paper with the slides in order horizontally; Slides 3 and 6 as notes pages, and Slides 1–8 as an outline. Close the presentation when you are finished.

Case Problem 1

Data Files needed for this Case Problem: Apartment.jpg, Center.jpg, Couple.jpg, Orientation.pptx, Room.jpg

Wind Lake Assisted Living Center Sylvia Prater is director of human resources at Wind Lake Assisted Living Center in Muskego, Wisconsin. She is in charge of hiring employees and training them. She decided to create a presentation that she will give to new employees as part of their orientation. She asks you to help her create PowerPoint slides that she will use while she gives her presentation. Complete the following steps:

1. Open the presentation named **Orientation**, located in the PowerPoint1 ▸ Case1 folder included with your Data Files, and then save it as **Employee Orientation** to the drive and folder where you are storing your files.

2. Insert a new slide using the Title Slide layout. Move this new slide so it is Slide 1. Type **Employee Orientation** as the presentation title on the title slide. In the subtitle text placeholder, type your name.

3. Create a new Slide 2 with the Title and Content layout. Type **What Is Assisted Living?** as the slide title, and **Residence for people who need some assistance with daily living activities**. as the only item in the content placeholder. Change this to an unnumbered list.

4. Apply the View theme, and then apply its third variant. (If the View theme is not listed in the Themes gallery, choose any other theme and variant that uses a white or mostly white background, places the slide titles at the top of the slides, uses bullet symbols for first-level bulleted items, and positions the content in the bulleted lists starting at the top of the content text box, not the middle.)

5. On Slide 2 ("What Is Assisted Living?"), increase the size of the text of the in the text box below the slide titles to 28 points. On Slide 3 ("What Do We Provide?") increase the size of the text in the bulleted list so it is 24 points. On Slide 4 ("Our Employees") and Slide 7 ("Our Residents"), increase the size of the text in the bulleted list so that the first-level items are 28 points.

6. On Slide 2, insert the photo **Center**, located in the PowerPoint1 ▸ Case1 folder. Crop the top part of the photo off so that there is about one inch of sky above the building. Position the photo so the bottom of the photo aligns with the bottom of the slide and the left edge of the photo aligns with the right edge of the gray bar on the left. Resize the photo, maintaining the aspect ratio, so that it stretches from the gray bar on the left to the orange bar on the right. (If you used a different theme, center the photo horizontally in the space at the bottom of the slide.)

7. On Slide 3 ("What Do We Provide?"), add the speaker note **Personal care, such as bathing, grooming, and dressing, is provided by certified personal care attendants**.

8. On Slide 6 ("Living Quarters"), change the layout to the Comparison layout, which includes two content placeholders and a small text placeholder above each content placeholder. In the large content placeholder on the left, insert the photo **Room**, and in the large content placeholder on the right, insert the photo **Apartment**. Resize the Room photo so it is approximately the same height as the Apartment photo, maintaining the aspect ratio, and then reposition it, if needed, so that it is center-aligned with the caption placeholder above it and top-aligned with the Room photo on the left.

9. On Slide 5 ("Our Facility"), cut the first bulleted item, and then paste it in on Slide 6 in the small text placeholder on the left. If a blank line is added below the pasted text, delete it. On Slide 5, cut the remaining bulleted item, and then paste it on Slide 6 in the small text placeholder on the right, deleting the blank line if necessary.

10. On Slide 7 ("Our Residents"), add **Age** as the third bulleted item in the list, and then add **Minimum 60 years** and **Average 78 years** as subitems under the "Age" first-level item. Change the layout to Two Content.

11. On Slide 7, in the content placeholder, insert the photo **Couple**, located in the PowerPoint1 ► Case1 folder. Crop off the part of the photo to the right of the man, resize the photo so it is 5 inches high, maintaining the aspect ratio, and then reposition it as needed so that the top of the photo and the top of the content text box are aligned.

12. Compress all the photos in the presentation to 96 ppi and delete cropped portions of photos.

13. On Slide 8 ("New Employee To Do List"), change the list to a numbered list, and then add the following as a new item 2:

    2. Attend certification seminars
      1. First aid
      2. CPR

14. On Slide 8, convert the numbered list to a SmartArt diagram using the Vertical Block List layout, which is a List type of diagram. In the Text pane, click before "Confidentiality agreement," and then press the Tab key to make it a subitem under "Fill out paperwork." Change "W-4 and other personnel forms" to a second subitem under "Fill out paperwork."

15. Delete Slide 5 ("Our Facility"). Move Slide 4 ("Our Employees") so it becomes Slide 6.

16. Check the spelling in the presentation, and then read the text in the presentation carefully. On Slide 3 ("What Do We Provide?"), change the incorrect word "sight" to **site**.

17. Save the changes to the presentation, view the slide show in Presenter view, and then print the title slide as a full page slide, print Slides 2–7 as a handout using the 6 Slides Horizontal arrangement, and print Slide 3 as a notes page.

Case Problem 2

Data Files needed for this Case Problem: Olympiad.pptx, Tangrams.jpg, Winner.jpg

TROUBLESHOOT

Chandler, AZ School District Manuel Resendez is the Director of Science Curriculum Development for the Chandler, Arizona school district. One of his responsibilities is to organize an annual district-wide Math and Science Olympiad, during which school children in grades 4 through 6 can demonstrate their skills in math and science. To make sure that the teachers, coaches, parents, and volunteers at the Olympiad understand the purpose of the event and the activities the students will be doing, he plans to visit each school and give a presentation to those involved. He created a PowerPoint presentation with text describing the event, and he asks you to finish it by inserting photos from the previous year's event. Complete the following steps:

1. Open the file named **Olympiad**, located in the PowerPoint1 ► Case2 folder included with your Data Files, and then save it as **Math-Science Olympiad** to the drive and folder where you are storing your files. Add your name as the subtitle on Slide 1.

2. Apply the Frame theme. Change the variant to the third variant.

⚙ **Troubleshoot** 3. Evaluate the problem that the theme change caused on the title slide and fix it.

4. On Slide 3, in the first item in the bulleted list, move "9:00 a.m. to 8:00 p.m." to a new line below the first line starting with "When" without creating a new bulleted item. Do the same with "180 S. Arizona Ave." in the second item.

5. Move Slide 4 ("Rules") so it becomes Slide 10.

6. On Slide 10 ("Rules"), change the bulleted list to a numbered list. Add as a new item 4 **Only event administrators allowed on the contest floor**. Change the size of the text in the numbered list to 28 points.

7. Change the layout of Slide 9 ("Tangrams") to Two Content, and then insert the photo **Tangrams**, located in the PowerPoint1 ▸ Case2 folder, in the content placeholder. Increase the size of the picture, maintaining the aspect ratio, and reposition it so it better fills the space on the right.

8. Change the layout of Slide 11 ("Awards") to Two Content, and then insert the photo **Winner**, located in the PowerPoint1 ▸ Case2 folder, in the content placeholder.

⚙ **Troubleshoot** 9. One of the slides contains information that should be explained orally rather than presented as a list. Review the presentation to identify this slide and change that information to a speaker note on that slide. Make any other adjustments necessary to make this an effective slide.

⚙ **Troubleshoot** 10. Review the presentation to identify the slide that contains information that is repeated in the presentation and delete that slide.

⚙ **Troubleshoot** 11. Consider how changing the theme in Step 2 affected the readability of the lists on the slides. Make the appropriate changes to the slides.

12. Compress all the photos in the presentation to 96 ppi, check the spelling in the presentation, and then save the changes. (*Hint:* If the E-mail (96 ppi) option in the Compress Pictures dialog box is gray and not available, close the dialog box, select a different picture, and try again.)

13. View the slide show in Presenter view, zooming in on the pictures of the different events.

14. Print the title slide as a full page slide in grayscale. Print Slides 1–3 and Slides 5–10 as an outline by typing **1-3, 5-10** in the Slides box.

CREATE

Case Problem 3

Data Files needed for this Case Problem: Floating Houses.jpg, Karl.jpg, Peru.pptx, Region1.jpg – Region8 Right.jpg

Karl Benson Photography Karl Benson is a photographer who specializes in scenic photos. He also teaches a course for beginner photographers. Karl recently returned from a trip to Peru. On his trip, he was very interested to learn that Peru has eight distinct regions with different geography and climates. Karl asks you to create a presentation that contains some of the photos he took on his trip. He will not be giving an oral presentation using this file. Instead, he wants his students to view the slides on their own, so he prepared a file with text describing the photos and the regions in Peru. Slides 2 through 10 of the final presentation are shown in Figure 1-46. Refer to Figure 1-46 as you complete the following steps:

Figure 1-46 **Slides 2-11 of Peruvian Regions presentation**

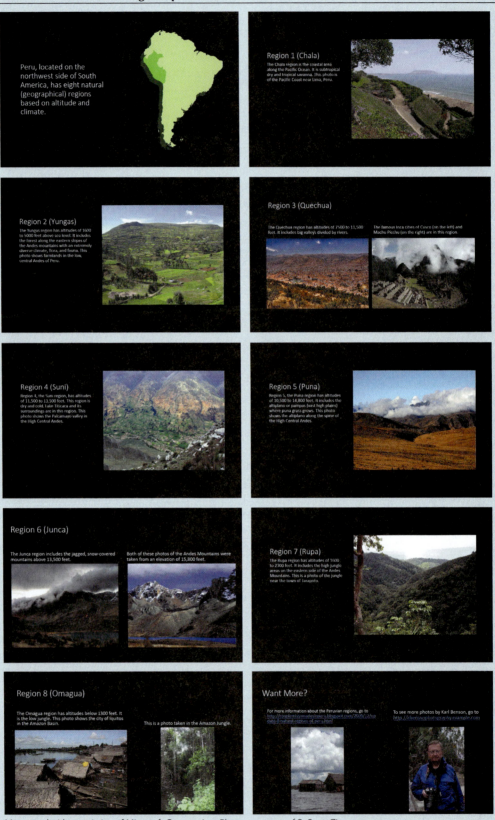

Maps used with permission of Microsoft Corporation; Photos courtesy of S. Scott Zimmerman

1. Open the file named **Peru**, located in the PowerPoint1 ▶ Case3 folder included with your Data Files, and then save it as **Peruvian Regions** to the drive and folder where you are storing your files.

2. Add a new slide with the Title Slide layout, and move it so it is Slide 1. Type **The Eight Regions of Peru** as the title and your name as the subtitle.

3. Change the variant of the Office theme to the third variant.

4. On Slide 2, drag the map of Peru on top of the map of South America as in Figure 1-46. (Use the left edges of the maps as a guide.) Resize the title text box to 4" x 5", change the font size of the text in the title text box to 32 points, and then position it on the left side of the slide, approximately centered vertically.

5. Change the layout of Slides 3 through 7 to Picture with Caption. On all five slides, change the font size of the captions in the text boxes below the titles from 16 points to 18 points.

6. Use the Region numbers on the slides to reorder Slides 3 through 10 in order by Region, starting with Region 1 on Slide 3 and ending with Region 8 on Slide 10.

7. On Slides 3 through 10, insert the photos provided in the PowerPoint1 ▶ Case3 folder that correspond to the region numbers described on each slide. Refer to Figure 1-46 as needed.

8. On Slide 11 ("Want More?"), insert the **Floating Houses** photo, located in the PowerPoint1 ▶ Case3 folder, in the content placeholder on the left and the **Karl** photo, located in the PowerPoint1 ▶ Case3 folder, in the content placeholder on the right.

9. Karl needs to post this presentation to a website that has file size limitations, so he needs the presentation file size to be as small as possible, even though he realizes that compressing the photos will reduce their quality. Compress all the photos in the presentation to 96 ppi.

10. Save the changes to the presentation, and then view the presentation in Reading view.

Case Problem 4

Data Files needed for this Case Problem: Cargo.jpg, Corpus Christi.jpg, Freight.jpg, Loading1.mp4, Loading2.mp4, Submit.jpg, URL.jpg, Woman.jpg

CHALLENGE

Corpus Christi Freight Transport, Inc. Quentin Hershey is a customer relations representative for Corpus Christi Freight Transport, Inc., a large shipping company headquartered in Corpus Christi, Texas, and with offices in Argentina and Sydney. He wants you to help him create a PowerPoint presentation to explain features of the company and the services it offers. Quentin wants to give the presentation to organizations that require shipping services to U.S. waterways and to foreign ports. Complete the following steps:

✦ **Explore** 1. Create a new presentation using the Striped black border presentation template from Office.com. (*Hint*: Use **striped black border** as the search term. If you get no results, type **white** as the search term, and then choose a template with a simple theme.)

2. Replace the title text on the title slide with **Corpus Christi Freight Transport, Inc**. and replace the subtitle text with your name. Save the presentation as **Freight Transport** to the drive and folder where you are storing your files.

3. Delete all the slides except the title slide.

4. Add a new Slide 2 with the Two Content layout. Type **Who We Are** as the title, and then type the following as a bulleted list in the left content placeholder:

   • **International shipping company**
   • **Licensed by Federal Maritime Commission**
   • **Bonded as international freight transporter**
   • **Registered as cosmetic freight forwarder**

5. On Slide 2, in the right content placeholder, insert the photo **Freight**, located in the PowerPoint1 ▶ Case4 folder included with your Data Files. Resize it, maintaining the aspect ratio, so it is 4.8 inches high, and then reposition it as needed so that the middle of the photo and the middle of the bulleted list text box are aligned.

6. Add a new Slide 3 with the Title and Content layout. Type **Online Scheduling** as the title, and then type the following as a bulleted list in the content placeholder:

   • **Register at www.freight.example.com**
   • **Enter type and amount**
   • **Submit information**
   • **Receive confirmation within 24 hours**

7. On Slide 3, remove the link formatting from the website address in the first bulleted item.

8. On Slide 3, convert the bulleted list to a SmartArt diagram with the Vertical Picture List layout, which is a List type of diagram.

⊕ **Explore** 9. Change the colors of the diagram to Colored Fill – Accent 3 by using the Change Colors button in the SmartArt Styles group on the SMARTART TOOLS DESIGN tab.

⊕ **Explore** 10. Insert the following pictures, located in the PowerPoint1 ▸ Case4 folder, in the picture placeholders in the SmartArt diagram, in order from top to bottom: **URL, Cargo, Submit,** and **Woman**.

11. Add a new Slide 4 with the Two Content layout. Type **U.S. Office** as the title. In the content placeholder on the left, type the following as an unnumbered list without extra space between the lines:

   Corpus Christi Freight
   2405 Shoreline Road
   Corpus Christi, TX 78401

12. On Slide 4, add the phone number **(361) 555-1254** and the website address **www.freight.example.com** as new items in the unnumbered list. Press the spacebar after typing the website address to format it as a link.

13. On Slide 4, add the photo **Corpus Christi**, located in the PowerPoint1 ▸ Case4 folder, to the content placeholder on the right. Resize it so it is 3.9 inches high, maintaining the aspect ratio, and then position it so the top edge aligns with the top edge of the text box on the left and there is approximately one inch of space between the right side of the photo and the right edge of the slide.

14. Compress all the photos in the presentation to 96 ppi, and then save the changes.

15. Add a new Slide 5 with the Comparison layout. Type **How Are Containers Loaded?** as the title, type **First a container is selected** in the small text placeholder on the left, and then type **Then it is transported to the ship and loaded** in the small text placeholder on the right. Move this slide so it becomes Slide 4.

⊕ **Explore** 16. On Slide 4 ("How Are Containers Loaded?"), insert the video **Loading1**, located in the PowerPoint1 ▸ Case4 folder, in the left content placeholder, and insert the video **Loading2**, located in the same folder, in the right content placeholder. (The video objects might be filled with black when they are inserted.)

⊕ **Explore** 17. Open the Info tab in Backstage view. Use the Compress Media command to compress the videos to the lowest quality possible. Use the Back button at the top of the navigation bar in Backstage view to return to Normal view.

18. Run the slide show in Slide Show view. When Slide 4 ("How Are Containers Loaded?") appears, point to each video to make a Play button appear, and then click the Play button to play each video. Note that there is no sound in the videos. (*Hint*: Point to the video as it plays to display the play bar again.)

Aa Verbal Communication

Rehearsing Your Presentation

The best presentations are planned well in advance of their delivery. Once the content has been created, enhanced, and perfected, it is time to prepare you, the presenter. Presenters who try to stand up and "wing it" in front of a crowd usually reveal this amateur approach the moment they start speaking—by looking down at their notes, rambling off topic, or turning their back on the audience frequently to read from the slides displayed on-screen.

To avoid being seen as an amateur, you need to rehearse your presentation. Even the most knowledgeable speakers rehearse to ensure they know how the topic flows, what the main points are, how much time to spend on each slide, and where to place emphasis. Experienced presenters understand that while practice may not make them perfect, it will certainly make them better.

Where you practice isn't that important. You can talk to a mirror, your family, or a group of friends. If you have a video camera, you can record yourself and then review the video. Watching video evidence of your performance often reveals the weaknesses you don't want your audience to see and that your friends or family may be unwilling or unable to identify. Whatever you choose to do, the bottom line is this: If you practice, you will improve.

As you rehearse, you should remember to focus on the following steps:

- Practice speaking fluently.
- Work on your tone of voice.
- Decide how to involve your audience.
- Become aware of your body language.
- Check your appearance.

Speaking Fluently

Be sure to speak in an easy, smooth manner, and avoid using nonwords and fillers. Nonwords consist of ums, ahs, hms, and other such breaks in speech. Fillers are phrases that don't add any value yet add length to sentences. Both can dilute a speaker's message because they are not essential to the meaning of what's being spoken. At best, they can make you sound unprofessional. At worst, they can distract your audience and make your message incomprehensible.

Considering Your Tone of Voice

When delivering your presentation, you usually want to speak passionately, with authority, and with a smile. If you aren't excited about your presentation, how will your audience feel? By projecting your voice with energy, passion, and confidence, your audience will automatically pay more attention to you. Smile and look directly at your audience members and make eye contact. If your message is getting across, they will instinctively affirm what you're saying by returning your gaze, nodding their heads, or smiling. There's something compelling about a confident speaker whose presence commands attention. However, be careful not to overdo it. Speaking too loudly or using an overly confident or arrogant tone will turn off an audience and make them stop listening altogether.

Involving Your Audience

If you involve your audience in your presentation, they will pay closer attention to what you have to say. When an audience member asks a question, be sure to affirm them before answering. For example, you could respond with "That's a great question. What do the rest of you think?" or "Thanks for asking. Here's what my research revealed." An easy way to get the audience to participate is to start with a question and invite responses, or to stop partway through to discuss a particularly important point.

Being Aware of Your Body Language

Although the content of your presentation plays a role in your message delivery, it's your voice and body language during the presentation that make or break it. Maintain eye contact to send the message that you want to connect and that you can be trusted. Stand up straight to signal confidence. Conversely, avoid slouching, which can convey laziness, lack of energy, or disinterest, and fidgeting or touching your hair, which can signal nervousness. Resist the temptation to glance at your watch; you don't want to send a signal that you'd rather be someplace else. Finally, be aware of your hand movements. The best position for your hands is to place them comfortably by your side, in a relaxed position. As you talk, it's fine to use hand gestures to help make a point, but be careful not to overdo it.

Evaluating Your Appearance

Just as a professional appearance makes a good impression during a job interview, an audience's first impression of a speaker is also based on appearance. Before a single word is spoken, the audience sizes up the way the presenter looks. You want to make sure you look professional and competent. Make sure your appearance is neat, clean, and well-coordinated, and dress in appropriate clothing.

As you spend time practicing your presentation, you will naturally develop appropriate body language, tone of voice, and a fluent delivery, ensuring a clear connection with your audience and a professional delivery of your presentation's message.

PROSKILLS

Create and Deliver a Training Presentation

If you hold a job for any length of time, as part of your employment, you might have to train new employees in their work tasks. For example, if you work in a library, you might have to explain how to process returned books, or if you work in a chemistry stockroom at a college, you might have to describe how to make up solutions for the school's chemistry laboratories. A PowerPoint presentation can be an effective way to start the training process. With a presentation, you can give an overview of the job without needing to repeat yourself to explain detailed aspects. Then you can customize the rest of the training to fit the needs of the specific employee.

In this exercise, you'll create a presentation containing information of your choice, using the PowerPoint skills and features presented in Tutorial 1, and then you will practice techniques for delivering the presentation.

Note: Please be sure not to include any personal information of a sensitive nature in the documents you create to be submitted to your instructor for this exercise. Later on, you can update the documents with such information for your own personal use.

1. Create a new PowerPoint presentation and apply an appropriate theme. Make sure you choose a theme that is relevant to the job you are describing and to your audience. Consider using a template from Office.com.
2. On Slide 1, make the presentation title the same as the title of your job or the job for which you are giving the training. Add your name as a subtitle.
3. Create a new slide for each major category of tasks. For example, task categories for a library job might be "Punching In," "Checking in with Your Supervisor," "Gathering Books from Drop-Off Stations," "Scanning Returned Books into the Computer," "Checking Books for Damage or Marks," "Processing Abused Books," "Processing Late Books," "Sorting Books," "Shelving Books," and "Punching Out."
4. On each slide, create a bulleted list to explain the particular task category or to provide the steps required to perform the task, or consider if a graphic, such as a SmartArt diagram, would better illustrate your point.
5. Where applicable, include photographs. For example, you might include a photograph of the punch clock (time clock) used by hourly workers in the library, or a photograph of a book with serious damage relative to one with normal wear. Resize and reposition the photographs as needed.

6. Examine your slides. Are you using too many words? Can any of your bulleted lists be replaced with a graphic?

7. Reevaluate the theme you chose. Do you think it is still appropriate? Does it fit the content of your presentation? If not, apply a different theme.

8. Add speaker notes to help you remember important points that you want to make.

9. Check the spelling of your presentation, and then proofread it to check for errors that would not be caught by the spell check. Save the final presentation.

10. Rehearse the presentation. Try using Presenter view to keep your speaker notes visible. Consider adding a blank slide in your presentation at a point where you want the audience to focus on you exclusively.

11. Consider your appearance, and decide on the appropriate clothing to wear.

12. Practice the delivery of your presentation in front of a mirror and friends or family, and if you can, create a video of yourself. Notice and fine tune your body language, tone of voice, and fluency to fully engage your audience.

OBJECTIVES

Session 1
- Explore the Outlook window
- Navigate between Outlook components
- Set up Outlook for email
- Create and send email messages
- Create and edit contact information

Session 2
- Read and respond to email messages
- Attach files to email messages
- File, sort, save, and archive messages
- Delete items from Outlook folders

Communicating with Outlook 2013

Sending and Receiving Email Messages

Case | *Geoff's Mobile Bike Repairs*

Geoff Landry has a special knack for repairing bicycles. After noticing that friends, and friends of friends, were constantly calling asking him to come over and fix their bicycles, he decided to turn his skill into a business. Geoff outfitted his bike with a special trailer that fits all of his tools and materials he might need for bicycle maintenance and repairs. He now cycles to client's homes around Portland, Oregon. As he travels to and from clients, the sign on his bike trailer works as advertising as does word-of-mouth references from his satisfied clients.

To coordinate all the activities involved in running Geoff's Mobile Bike Repairs, Geoff relies on **Microsoft Outlook 2013**, or **Outlook**, an information management and communication program.

You will use Outlook to help Geoff with a variety of tasks. In this tutorial, you'll explore the Outlook window and its components. You'll use email to send messages to Geoff's suppliers. You'll set up contact information for clients and suppliers. You'll receive, read, and respond to email messages. Finally, you'll organize messages by filing, sorting, and archiving them.

STARTING DATA FILES

Invoice.xlsx   Workshops.docx   Doris Brandt.vcf   (none)

Session 1 Visual Overview:

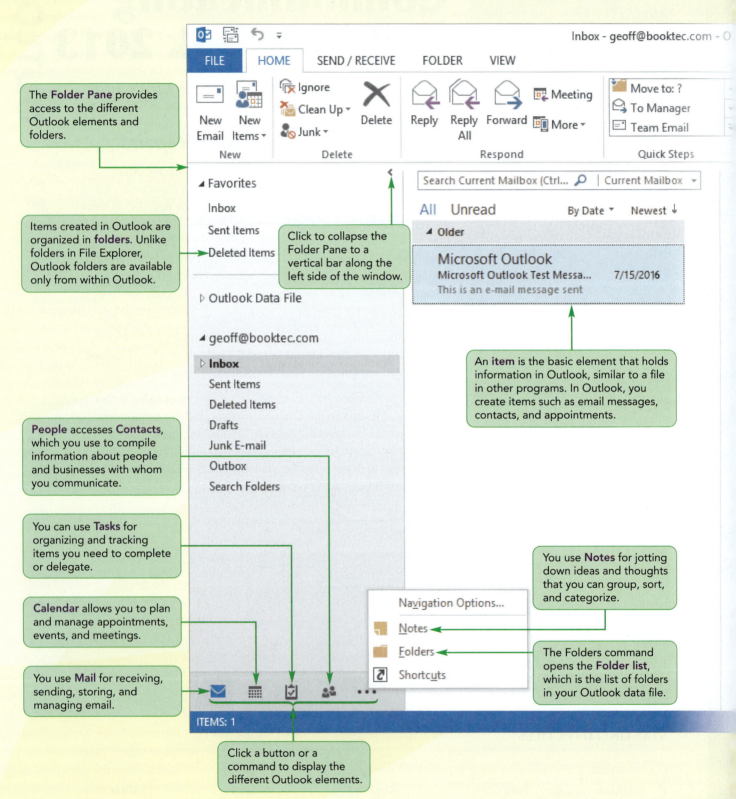

The **Folder Pane** provides access to the different Outlook elements and folders.

Items created in Outlook are organized in **folders**. Unlike folders in File Explorer, Outlook folders are available only from within Outlook.

Click to collapse the Folder Pane to a vertical bar along the left side of the window.

An **item** is the basic element that holds information in Outlook, similar to a file in other programs. In Outlook, you create items such as email messages, contacts, and appointments.

People accesses **Contacts**, which you use to compile information about people and businesses with whom you communicate.

You can use **Tasks** for organizing and tracking items you need to complete or delegate.

You use **Notes** for jotting down ideas and thoughts that you can group, sort, and categorize.

Calendar allows you to plan and manage appointments, events, and meetings.

The Folders command opens the **Folder list**, which is the list of folders in your Outlook data file.

You use **Mail** for receiving, sending, storing, and managing email.

Click a button or a command to display the different Outlook elements.

Outlook Window

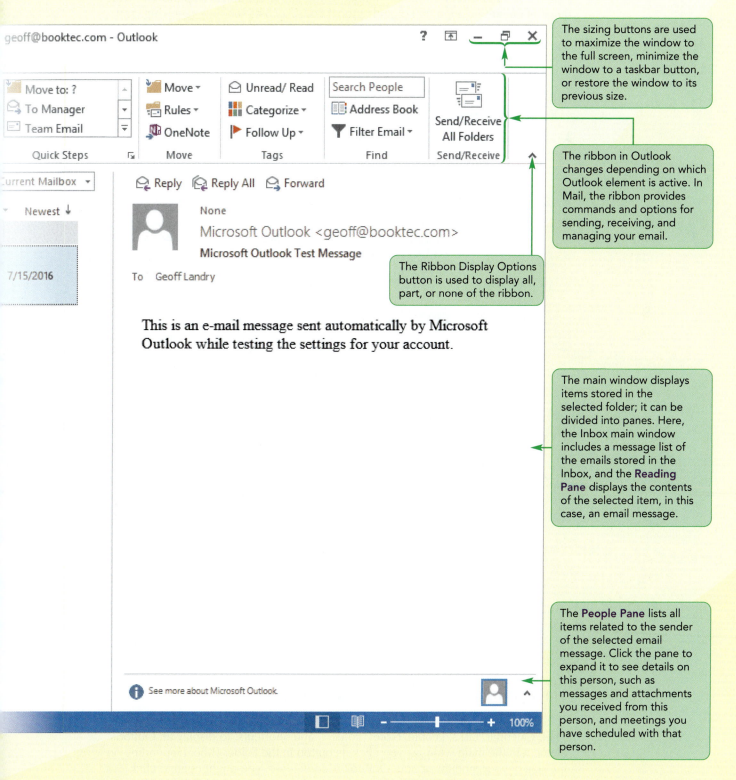

The sizing buttons are used to maximize the window to the full screen, minimize the window to a taskbar button, or restore the window to its previous size.

The ribbon in Outlook changes depending on which Outlook element is active. In Mail, the ribbon provides commands and options for sending, receiving, and managing your email.

The Ribbon Display Options button is used to display all, part, or none of the ribbon.

The main window displays items stored in the selected folder; it can be divided into panes. Here, the Inbox main window includes a message list of the emails stored in the Inbox, and the **Reading Pane** displays the contents of the selected item, in this case, an email message.

The **People Pane** lists all items related to the sender of the selected email message. Click the pane to expand it to see details on this person, such as messages and attachments you received from this person, and meetings you have scheduled with that person.

Exploring Outlook

Outlook is a powerful information manager. You can use Outlook to perform a wide range of communication and organizational tasks, such as sending, receiving, and organizing email; organizing contact information; scheduling appointments, events, and meetings; creating a to-do list and delegating tasks; and writing notes.

You start Outlook the same way as any other program—using the Start screen.

To start Outlook:

▶ **1.** Display the Windows Start screen, if necessary.

Using Windows 7? To complete Step 1, click the Start button on the taskbar.

▶ **2.** Click the **Outlook 2013** tile. The Outlook program window opens.

Using Windows 7? To complete Step 2, point to All Programs on the Start menu, click the Microsoft Office folder, and then click Outlook 2013.

Trouble? If you don't see the Outlook 2013 tile on your screen, type Outlook to display the Apps screen with the Outlook 2013 tile highlighted, and then click the tile.

Trouble? If the Welcome to Microsoft Outlook 2013 dialog box opens to guide you through the process of adding your email to Outlook, you don't have an email account set up. Click the Next button to go to the Microsoft Outlook Account Setup dialog box, click the No option button, and then click the Next button to go to the Cancel Email Account Setup dialog box, click the Use Outlook without an email account check box, and then click the Finish button. You'll set up an email account shortly.

▶ **3.** If your Outlook window is not maximized, click the **Maximize** button ☐ on the title bar.

▶ **4.** If the Folder Pane is minimized along the left side of the Outlook window, click the **Expand the Folder Pane** button ▶ in the minimized Folder Pane. The Session 1 Visual Overview shows the maximized Outlook window with the Folders Pane expanded.

Trouble? Depending on how Outlook is configured on your computer, you might see different folders in the Folder Pane, but you should see the default folders–Inbox, Drafts, Sent Items, Deleted Items, and Outbox.

Trouble? If you see something other than emails in the Outlook window, a different element is active. You'll learn to switch between Outlook elements next.

Navigating Between Outlook Elements

The Folder Pane contains buttons for the most commonly used Outlook elements—Mail, Calendar, Tasks, People, Notes, Folders, and Shortcuts. To display an Outlook element in the main window, you click its button in the Folder Pane. Depending on the size of your monitor or how Outlook is configured, you might need to click ⋯ at the bottom of the Folder Pane to access the Notes, Folders, and Shortcuts buttons.

TIP

You can point to the Calendar, Tasks, or People button to get a sneak peek of its contents.

To navigate between the Outlook elements:

1. In the Folder Pane, click the **Calendar** button to display the Calendar element in the main window. If the Calendar button was already selected, your view does not change.

2. On the HOME tab, in the Arrange group, click the **Work Week** button, if necessary. The planner appears in the main window and the Date Navigator with calendars for the current month and next month appears at the top of the Folder Pane. See Figure 1.

Figure 1	**Calendar**

3. In the Folder Pane, click the **People** button to display the Contacts element in the main window.

4. On the HOME tab, in the Current View group, click the **People** button, if necessary. The list of contacts appears in the center pane; if you don't have any contacts entered, you see only the buttons that you use to display the contacts that start with the selected number or letter. If you have contacts in your list, information about the selected contact appears in the Reading Pane. See Figure 2.

Figure 2	**Contacts**

5. In the Folder Pane, click the **Tasks** button to display the Tasks element in the main window. The to-do list appears in the center pane. If you have tasks on your to-do list, information about the selected task appears in the Reading Pane. See Figure 3.

| Figure 3 | Tasks |

6. In the Folder Pane, click the **Mail** button, and then click the **Inbox** folder, if necessary. If you already have messages in your Inbox, a list of email messages appears in the middle pane, and the content of the selected message appears in the Reading Pane. Refer back to the Session 1 Visual Overview to see the Inbox selected in the Folder Pane.

A second way to navigate the Outlook elements is with the Folder list. You can click any item in the Folder list to display its contents in the main window. In the Folder Pane, click ..., and then click Folders. The Folder list appears in the Folder Pane, and you can click any icon to display that Outlook element or folder contents in the main window.

Setting Up Outlook for Email

The main window shows the contents of the Inbox folder, where you receive, create, and send email. **Email**, the electronic transfer of messages between computers, is a simple and inexpensive way to communicate with people near or far. The messages you send are delivered immediately and stored until recipients can read those messages at their convenience. Geoff uses email to correspond with his clients and suppliers because it is fast, convenient, and inexpensive. It is also portable, as he can access his email from his cell phone, laptop, and tablet.

Before you can send and receive email messages with Outlook, you must have access to an email server or Internet service provider (ISP), an email address, and a password. An **email address** is a username and a domain name separated by @. A **username** (or account name) is a unique name that identifies you to your mail server. A user name can include uppercase and lowercase letters, numbers, and periods; although symbols are allowed, you should avoid them because some ISPs may not accept them. The **domain name** is the name of your ISP's server on the Internet. For example, in the email address "geoff@example.com," "geoff" is the username and "example.com" is the domain name. Although many people might use the same ISP, each username is unique, so that the ISP can distinguish one user from another. A **password** is a private code that you enter to access your account. (In this tutorial, you will use your own email address to send all messages.)

You'll set up an Outlook email account. If you already have an Outlook email account, skip Steps 1 through 4 in the following set of steps, and begin with Step 5.

To set up an Outlook email account:

1. On the ribbon, click the **FILE** tab to open Backstage view, and then click **Info** in the navigation bar, if necessary.

2. On the Account Information screen, click the **Add Account** button. The Add Account dialog box opens. See Figure 4.

| Figure 4 | Add Account dialog box |

select this option to set up your account based on your email address and password

enter your information here

Be sure to enter the information carefully; a mistyped address or password will prevent Outlook from configuring your server settings.

3. Make sure the **E-mail Account** option button is selected, enter your name, email address, and password in the appropriate boxes, and then click the **Next** button. Outlook connects to your email account to determine the rest of the server settings needed to configure your email account.

   Trouble? If you are unsure what information to enter in the Add Account dialog box or if Outlook was unable to configure your server settings, ask your instructor or technical support person for help.

4. Click the **Finish** button to confirm that Outlook has successfully set up your email account.

5. In the Folder Pane, to the left of **Outlook Data File**, click the **Collapse** button ◢ to hide the default folders, and then click the **Expand** button ▷ to the left of your email address to display the folders for your email address, if necessary.

6. In the Folder Pane, below your email address, click **Inbox**. You might see a Microsoft Outlook Test Message that was sent when you set up your email account.

Choosing a Message Format

Outlook can send and receive messages in three formats: HTML, Rich Text, and plain text. Although you specify one of these formats as the default for your messages, you can always switch formats for an individual message. HTML provides the most formatting features and options (text formatting, numbering, bullets, alignment, horizontal lines, backgrounds, HTML styles, and web pages). Rich Text provides some formatting options (text formatting, bullets, and alignment), which can be read only by Outlook and Microsoft Exchange Client versions 4 and 5. Outlook converts Rich Text messages to HTML for any other recipients, which retains the formatting. With both HTML and Rich Text, some recipients will not be able to see the formatting if their email software is not set up to handle formatted messages. All email applications support plain text messages, which include no formatting, and the recipient specifies which font is used for the message. When you reply to a message, Outlook uses the same format in which the message was created, unless you specify otherwise. For example, if you reply to a message sent to you in plain text, Outlook sends your response in plain text.

Geoff wants you to set the message format to HTML so you can apply formatting options to the messages.

To choose HTML as the default message format:

▶ **1.** On the ribbon, click the **FILE** tab to open Backstage view, and then click **Options** in the navigation bar. The Outlook Options dialog box opens.

▶ **2.** In the left pane, click **Mail**. The Mail options appear in the right pane.

▶ **3.** If necessary, click the **Compose messages in this format** arrow, and then click **HTML**. Outlook will use the HTML format each time you create a message, unless you select a different format for that message. See Figure 5.

Figure 5	Mail options in the Outlook Options dialog box

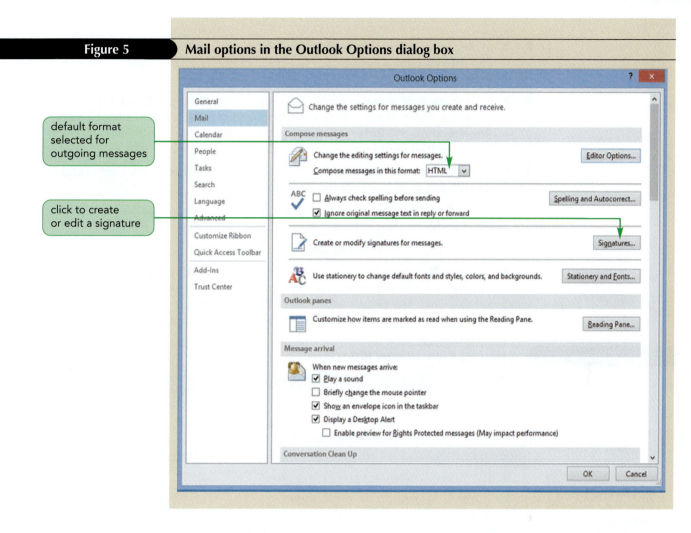

default format selected for outgoing messages

click to create or edit a signature

Adding a Signature

A **signature** is text that is automatically added to every email message you send. A signature can contain any text you want. For example, you might create a signature with your name, job title, company name, and phone number. Geoff might create a signature containing a paragraph that describes the services he offers. You can create more than one signature for an email account, and you can create different signatures for each email account you have. Although you can attach a signature to a message in any format, the HTML and Rich Text formats enable you to apply font and paragraph formatting.

You can customize your messages with a signature. Note that the figures in this book show the name Geoff Reynolds, whose email address is geoff@booktec.com. Because you selected the HTML message format, you can add formatting to the signature. You'll create a formatted signature.

To create a formatted signature:

1. In the Outlook Options dialog box, click the **Signatures** button. The Signatures and Stationery dialog box opens with the E-mail Signature tab displayed.

2. Click the **New** button. The New Signature dialog box opens.

3. In the Type a name for this signature box, type **Geoff's Mobile Bike Repairs**, and then click the **OK** button. The signature name is selected in the Select signature to edit box.

4. Click in the **Edit signature** box, type your name, press the **Enter** key to move the insertion point to the next line, and then type **Geoff's Mobile Bike Repairs**, press the **Enter** key to move the insertion point to the next line, and then type **Pedaling bike repairs to you**.

5. Select **Geoff's Mobile Bike Repairs**, click the **Font** arrow, click **Calibri Light (Headings)**, and then click the **Bold** button **B**.

6. Select **Pedaling bike repairs to you** and then click the **Italic** button **I**. The selected text is reformatted.

7. If necessary, click the **E-mail account** arrow, and then click your email address.

8. Click the **New messages** arrow, and then click **Geoff's Mobile Bike Repairs** (the name of the signature you just set up). Leave the Replies/forwards box set to (none). The Geoff's Mobile Bike Repairs signature will be added to new messages you create, but not to messages you respond to. See Figure 6.

Figure 6	Signatures and Stationary dialog box

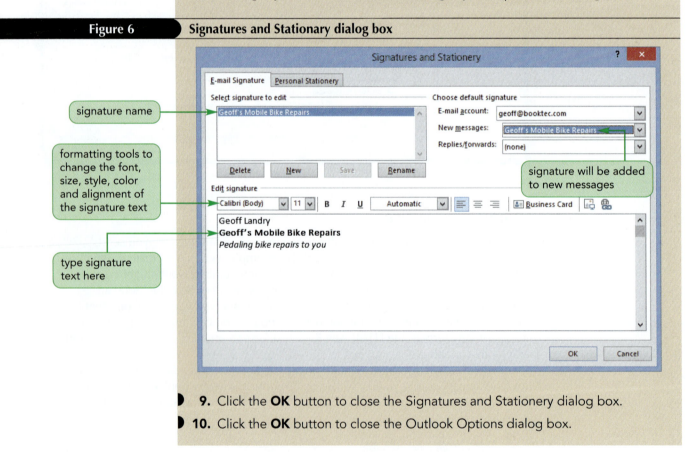

9. Click the **OK** button to close the Signatures and Stationery dialog box.

10. Click the **OK** button to close the Outlook Options dialog box.

Using Stationery and Themes

Stationery and themes are a way to quickly distinguish your HTML messages with a preset design. **Stationery** is an HTML file that includes complementary background colors, images, or patterns. A **theme** includes complementary backgrounds as well as other design elements such as fonts, bullets, colors, and effects. Stationery and themes increase the size of the outgoing message. Stationery uses HTML message format, so recipients whose email programs don't read HTML email will see the message but not the stationery.

To add stationery or a theme to a message, click the New Items button in the New group on the HOME tab, point to E-mail Message Using, click More Stationery to open the Theme or Stationery dialog box, and then select the one you want to use. Previously selected stationeries and themes appear above the More Stationery command. To add the same stationery or theme to all your outgoing messages, you can click Mail in the left pane of the Outlook Options dialog box, click the Stationery and Fonts button in the right pane, and then click the Theme button on the Personal Stationery tab of the Signatures and Stationery dialog box. Select the theme in the Theme or Stationery dialog box, and then click the OK button in each dialog box. You also can create your own stationery.

Creating and Sending Email Messages

An email message includes Date, To, From, Cc, and Subject lines followed by the message. Outlook fills in the Date line with the date on which you send the message and the From line with your name or email address; these lines are not visible in the window in which you create your email message. You complete the other lines. The To line lists the email addresses of all recipients. The Cc line lists the email addresses of anyone who will receive a courtesy copy of the message. An optional Bcc line lists the email addresses of anyone who will receive a blind courtesy copy of the message; Bcc recipients are not visible to each other or to the To and Cc recipients. The Subject line provides a quick overview of the message topic, similar to a headline. The main part of the email is the message body.

REFERENCE

Creating and Sending an Email Message

- On the HOME tab, in the New group, click the New Email button.
- In the To box, type a recipient email address; for each additional recipient type a semicolon and then the email address.
- In the Cc box and the Bcc box, type recipient email addresses, as needed.
- In the Subject box, type a topic.
- In the message body, type the message text and then format it as needed.
- Click the Send button.

You'll create an email message to Simon Wilson, the owner of Bicycle Parts PDX. You usually send messages to other people; in this tutorial, you will send messages to yourself so you can practice sending and receiving messages.

To create an email message:

1. On the HOME tab, in the New group, click the **New Email** button. An untitled Message window opens with the insertion point in the To box. Your signature appears in the message body; you'll type your message above the signature.

2. In the To box, type your email address.

   To send an email message to multiple recipients, type a comma or semicolon between addresses.

3. Click in the **Subject** box, type **This Week's Order** and then press the **Tab** key. The insertion point moves to the message body just above the signature. As soon as you move the insertion point out of the Subject box, the title bar shows the subject of the message.

4. Type **Hi Simon**, as the salutation, press the **Enter** key twice, **Please add one 21.1mm Freestyle Stem to my order.** (including the period), press the **Enter** key twice, and then type **Thank you.** (including the period).

You don't need to type your name because you included it as part of the signature. Before sending this message, you will add some text formatting. You have access to the standard text formatting features available in all the Office programs. For example, you can apply bold, underline, and italics; change the font, font size, and font color; align and indent text; create a bulleted or numbered list; and even apply paragraph styles. People whose email programs cannot read formatted email will still be able to read your messages in plain text.

To format text in the message body:

1. Select **21.1mm Freestyle Stem** in the message body. You'll make this text bold and blue.

2. On the MESSAGE tab, in the Basic Text group, click the **Bold** button B. The text changes to boldface.

3. In the Basic Text group, click the **Font Color** arrow A, and then click the **Blue, Accent 5** color (the ninth color in the first row of the Theme Colors section in the Font Color gallery). The text changes to blue.

4. Press the ↓ key to deselect the text and move the insertion point to the next line.

TIP

You can also apply formatting from the Mini Toolbar that appears when you select text.

Geoff's message conveys the new item to be added to the order, and the formatting helps the details of this new item to stand out from the rest of the message.

Setting the Importance and Sensitivity Levels

You can add icons that appear in the message pane of the Inbox to provide clues to the recipient about the importance and sensitivity of the message. You can specify an importance level of High or Low or leave the message set at the default Normal importance level. High importance tells the recipient that the message needs prompt attention, whereas a Low importance tells the recipient that the message can wait for a response. Use the importance level appropriately. If you send all messages with a High importance, recipients will learn to disregard the status.

You'll change the message importance level to High.

To change the message importance level to High:

1. On the MESSAGE tab, in the Tags group, click the **High Importance** button. The button remains selected to indicate the importance level you selected for the message. See Figure 7.

Figure 7	Completed email message

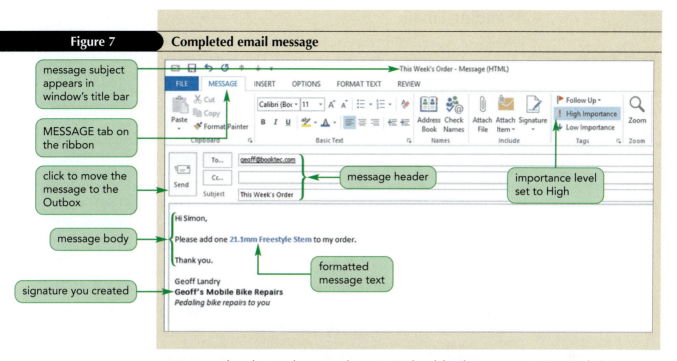

You can also change the normal sensitivity level for the message to Personal, Private, or Confidential. This is another way to help recipients determine the content of a message before reading it. To set the sensitivity level, click the Dialog Box Launcher in the Tags group on the MESSAGE tab to open the Properties dialog box, click the Sensitivity button in the Settings section, select the sensitivity level for the message, and then click the Close button. You'll leave the sensitivity set to Normal for this message.

INSIGHT

Creating Effective Messages

Keep the following guidelines in mind to create effective, professional messages:

- **Focus on one topic per email.** A distinct conversation thread makes it simpler to find messages related to a topic.

- **Include a short, descriptive subject line.** A clear subject quickly tells recipients the main point of a message (and reminds you when they reply). Also, some people decide whether to read a message based on its subject line.

- **Write a concise, complete message.** An effective message conveys information quickly and fully, so the entire contents appear in the Reading Pane. People receive many messages each day, and tend to save poorly written or rambling messages to deal with later.

- **Format to enhance rather than decorate.** Recipients may see a message that looks very different from the one you sent with variations in colors or fonts. Add emphasis with bold, italic, and other basic formatting as needed. Use white or a light colored background with black or a dark colored text. Choose common fonts and sizes, such as 10 or 12 point Arial and Times New Roman.

- **Use an attachment for complex content.** If you want to send a more elaborately formatted message, an attached Word document or PDF file might be a better option.

Sending Email

When your computer is connected to your email server, the messages you write are sent immediately when you click the Send button in the Message window. After you send the message to your email server, a copy of the message is stored in the Sent Items folder, which provides a record of all the messages you sent. The time your email takes to arrive at its destination varies, depending on the size of the message, the speed of your Internet connection, and the number of other users on the Internet.

If you are working **offline** (not connected to your email server), the messages you write move to the Outbox folder when you click the Send button in the Message window. The outgoing messages remain in the Outbox folder until you choose to send them. You can set a schedule for Outlook to automatically send and receive messages at regular intervals that you specify (such as every 15 minutes or every few hours). You must then click the Send/Receive All Folders button in the Send/Receive group on the HOME tab to check for and deliver new messages.

To send the completed message:

1. Click the **Send** button in the message header area. The message is sent to your email server, and you return to the Inbox. You could receive the email message you sent at any point; if a notification box appears or a sound plays informing you of incoming mail, ignore it for now. You'll work with the received message in Session 2.

2. Click **Sent Items** in the Folder Pane. The message in the Sent Items folder appears in the main window. See Figure 8.

Figure 8   Sent Items folder with the sent message

Trouble? If the message wasn't sent, you are probably working offline. On the SEND/RECEIVE tab, in the Preferences group, click the Work Online button. In the Send & Receive group, click the Send/Receive All Folders button to send all the messages in the Outbox to your email server. The Outlook Send/Receive Progress dialog box remains open until all the messages in the Outbox are sent. You can tell when the messages are sent because the Outbox will be empty.

Trouble? If Outlook requests a password, you need to enter your password before you can send and receive messages. Type your password, and then click the OK button.

The message is sent to Simon, Geoff's main contact at Bike Parts PDX, with the addition to his order.

PROSKILLS

Written Communication: Following Netiquette Guidelines

Email, like other types of communication, is governed by its own customs of behavior, called **netiquette** (short for Internet etiquette), which helps prevent miscommunication. As you write and send email messages, keep in mind the following guidelines:

- **Think before you send.** Your words can have a lasting impact. Be sure they convey the thoughts you intend and want attributed to you. Your name and email address are attached to every message you send, and your message can be forwarded easily to others.
- **Be concise.** The recipient should be able to read and understand your message quickly.
- **Use standard capitalization.** Excessive use of uppercase is considered shouting, and exclusive use of lowercase is incorrect; both are difficult to read.
- **Check spelling and grammar.** Create and maintain a professional image by using standard spelling and grammar. What you say is just as important as how you say it.
- **Avoid sarcasm.** Without vocal intonations and body language, a recipient may read your words with emotions or feelings you didn't intend. You can use punctuation marks and other characters to create **emoticons**—also called **smileys**—such as :-), to convey the intent of your words. (Tilt your head to the left to look at the emoticon sideways to see the "face"—in this case, a smile.) To learn additional emoticons, search the web for emoticon or smiley dictionaries.
- **Don't send confidential information.** Email is not private; once you send a message, you lose control over where it may go and who might read it. Also, employers and schools usually can legally access their employees' and students' email messages, even after a message is deleted from an Inbox.

The adage "Act in haste; repent in leisure" is particularly apt for writing email. For more email netiquette guidelines, search the web for email etiquette or netiquette websites.

Organizing Contact Information

The Contacts element is an address book where you store information about the people and businesses with whom you communicate. Each person or organization is called a **contact**. You can store business-related information about each contact, including job title, phone and fax numbers, postal and web addresses, and email addresses, as well as more personal information, such as birthdays, anniversaries, and spouse and children's names.

Each piece of information you enter about a contact is called a **field**. For example, a complete contact name, such as Mr. Paul L. Ruiz, Sr., consists of a Title field, First field, Middle field, Last field, and Suffix field. The field's name, or label, identifies what information is stored in that field. You can use fields to sort, group, or look up contacts by any part of the name.

Creating Contacts

You can create contacts for anyone you communicate with. To create a contact or access information for existing contacts, you click the People button in the Folder Pane. Geoff asks you to create new contacts for several suppliers.

TIP

To create a new contact when working in another Outlook element, click the New Items button in the New group on the HOME tab, and then click Contact.

To create a contact:

1. In the Folder Pane, click the **People** button 👥. The Folder Pane changes to display the My Contacts list, and the ribbon changes to provide the commands and options for working with contacts.

2. On the HOME tab, in the New group, click the **New Contact** button. A Contact window opens in which you can enter the contact information.

The Contact window provides options for entering and working with general information about a contact. Contact information is divided into General and Details, available by clicking the corresponding buttons in the Show group on the CONTACT tab. General information includes the most pertinent information about a contact, including the contact's name, job title and company, phone numbers, and addresses. Details are less frequently needed items, such as the names of the contact's department, manager, assistant, and spouse/partner, as well as the contact's birthday, anniversary, and nickname.

REFERENCE

Creating a Contact

- In the Folder Pane, click the People button.
- On the HOME tab, in the New group, click the New Contact button to open the Contact window.
- Enter the contact's information, such as name, job title, company, email and webpage addresses, phone numbers, and mailing addresses.
- On the CONTACT tab, in the Show group, click the Details button, and then enter other business or personal data as needed.
- In the Actions group, click the Save & New button to create another contact or click the Save & Close button if you have no other contacts to create.
- If the Duplicate Contact Detected dialog box opens, select whether to add the contact anyway or merge with existing contact, and then click the OK button.

Geoff wants you to create a contact for Paul who is in charge of orders at Bicycle Parts PDX. You'll start by entering his name and company.

To enter the first contact's name and company:

1. Type **Mr. Paul L. Ruiz, Sr.** in the Full Name box, and then press the **Enter** key. The insertion point moves to the Company box, and the contact name appears in the File as box as "Ruiz, Paul L." By default, Outlook organizes contacts by their last names.

   The contact's name also appears at the top of the business card on the right and in the title bar of the Contact window. The business card is a graphic that displays all of the contact information as you enter it in a standard business card format.

2. Click the **Full Name** button. The Check Full Name dialog box opens. Although you entered the contact name in one box, Outlook stores each part of the name as a separate field. See Figure 9.

Figure 9	Check Full Name dialog box

full name split into fields

Check Full Name

Name details

Title   Mr.

First   Paul

Middle   L.

Last   Ruiz

Suffix   Sr.

☑ Show this again when name is incomplete or unclear

OK   Cancel

▶ **3.** Click the **Cancel** button to close the dialog box without making any changes.

▶ **4.** Click in the **Company** box, and then type **Bicycle Parts PDX**.

▶ **5.** Press the **Tab** key to move to the Job title box, and then type **Manager**.

Next, you'll enter Paul Ruiz's contact information. You can enter up to three email addresses for each contact in the Internet section of the Contact window. In most cases, each email address would be unique. For this tutorial, you'll use your email address for all of the contacts.

In the Phone numbers section, you can display only four phone fields at a time, but you can use any of the four available phone number boxes to continue to enter and store up to 19 phone numbers per contact. No matter how you enter the numbers— with or without spaces, hyphens, or parentheses—Outlook formats them consistently in the format (503) 555-3928. Next to each phone number box is an arrow button you can click to change the name of the phone field to help you identify the phone number. For example, you could choose Home Fax as the third type of phone number instead of Business Fax if the contact had only a home fax number.

In the Addresses section of the window, you can enter a business, home, and other address for each contact. As soon as you start typing the first address, a checkmark appears in the "This is the mailing address" check box. Outlook sets the first address you enter for a contact as the mailing address. However, you can specify any one of the addresses you enter as the mailing address.

To enter the contact's email address, phone numbers, and mailing address:

TIP

The Auto-Complete List displays suggested names and email addresses as you begin to type. To select a suggested name or address, click it.

▶ **1.** Click in the **E-mail** box, type your email address, and then press the **Tab** key to move the insertion point to the Display as box. The email address you typed is underlined in the E-mail box and appears in both the Display as box and on the business card in the Contact window.

The Display as box shows how the email address will appear in the To box of email messages as well as how it will be displayed within Outlook. Geoff prefers the email address to be displayed with the contact's full name preceding the actual email address and with the address enclosed in parentheses. You'll edit the address in the Display as box to include the contact's name.

▶ **2.** If necessary, click in the **Display as** box before your email address, type **Paul Ruiz (** to identify the email address, click after your email address, and then type **)** to enter the closing parenthesis.

3. In the Phone numbers section, click in the **Business** box, type **503 555 9753**, and then press the **Tab** key. Outlook formats the phone number with parentheses around the area code and a hyphen between the main parts of the number, even though you didn't type these punctuation symbols, and underlines it. Note also that the phone number appears on the business card with the label "Work" because you entered the phone number in the Business box.

4. Click the **Home button arrow** to display the phone number field labels, click **Assistant** to change the field label, type **503-555-9752** for the phone number of Paul's assistant, and then press the **Tab** key. The phone number is formatted to match the business phone number, and appears on the business card with the label "Assistant."

Geoff wants you to store the name of Paul's assistant and his department, so you need to switch to the Details page.

5. On the CONTACT tab, in the Show group, click the **Details** button. The Details page appears in the Contact window.

6. In the Department box, type **Orders** as the name of Paul's department.

7. Click in the **Assistant's name** box, and then type **Alyssa Walsh** as the name of Paul's assistant.

8. In the Show group, click the **General** button to return to the General information, and then type **503-555-6441** as the Business Fax.

9. In the Addresses section, click in the **Business** box, type **180 Grand Ave.**, press the **Enter** key to move the insertion point to the next line within the box, and then type **Portland, OR 97202**. You could verify that Outlook recorded the address in the correct fields by clicking the Business button, but you don't need to do so for a simple address.

10. Press the **Tab** key. The address appears on the business card. See Figure 10.

Figure 10	Completed Contact window for Paul L. Ruiz, Sr.

contact name appears in the title bar

General information is displayed

how the contact will be displayed in the Contact list

how the email address will be displayed in Outlook

indicates the Business address is the mailing address

You have completed the contact information for Paul. Geoff asks you to create additional contacts. You can close Paul's Contact window and open a new Contact window in the same step.

To create additional contacts:

1. On the CONTACT tab, in the Actions group, click the **Save & New** button to save Paul's contact information and open a new Contact window.

2. Enter the following information: full name **Pam Murphy**, company **Tires, Tubes, and Wheels**, job title **Manager**, your email address, display as **Pam Murphy (*your email address*)**, business phone **503-555-1224**, business fax **503-555-4331**, and business address **21 SE Fairfield St., Beaverton, OR 97005**.

Trouble? If your email address or the "Display as" entry is shown with the text "Paul Ruiz" at the beginning, edit the entry to delete this text. This text might appear because of the "Display as" entry you completed for the contact Paul Ruiz earlier. Because you are using your email address for multiple contacts, this could happen each time you add a new contact. Continue to edit the email and "Display as" entries so they match those provided in the steps. When doing so, you might not be able to press the Tab key after typing in the Email box; you might need to click in the "Display as" box to be able to enter your email address correctly.

3. In the Actions group, click the **Save & New** button. Outlook detects that another contact already has the same email address as Paul Ruiz and opens the Duplicate Contact Detected dialog box. You can add the contact as a new contact or update the information of the selected contact.

4. Click the **Add new contact** option button, and then click the **Add** button. The new Contact window appears.

5. Enter the following new contact information: full name **Tom Quinlan**, company **The Bike Tool Shop**, your email address, display as **Tom Quinlan** (*your email address*), business phone **971-555-9797**, and business address **4207 NE Alberta St., Portland, OR 97212**.

6. In the Actions group, click the **Save & New** button, click the **Add new contact** option button in the Duplicate Contact Detected dialog box, and then click the **Add** button to add Tom Quinlan as a new contact.

    For your work in this tutorial, you need to create a contact for Geoff as well.

7. Enter the following new contact information: full name **Geoff Landry**, company **Geoff's Mobile Bike Repairs**, your email address, and display as **Geoff Landry** (*your email address*).

8. In the Actions group, click the **Save & Close** button, and then add Geoff Landry as a new contact. Geoff's contact information is saved, and you return to the Contacts folder. The four contacts you added appear in the Contacts main window, sorted alphabetically by last name. See Figure 11.

Figure 11   **Contacts in People view**

Trouble? If your contacts are in a different view, this is not a problem. You'll change the view next.

Switching Contact Views

Views specify how information in an Outlook element is organized and which details are visible. Each Outlook element has a set of standard views from which you can choose. There are a variety of ways to look at the information in Contacts for example. All of the information about a contact is called a **contact card**. People view displays the names in a list. Business Card view displays the names and addresses in a standard business card format. Card view displays names and addresses in blocks. Phone view displays details about your contacts, such as name, company, and telephone numbers, in columns. List view displays additional information in column format, but grouped by company name.

Currently the contacts are shown in People view. Geoff wants to see how the contact information appears in different views. You'll change the Contacts view.

To change the view of Contacts:

1. On the HOME tab, in the Current View group, click the **Business Card** button. Business Card view displays a business card for each contact. Unless you customize it, the business card includes the contact's name; company; job title; department; phone numbers for work, home, mobile, and assistant; email address; and mailing address.

2. Click the **Card** button. Card view displays more contact information than is shown in Business Card view, such as the business fax number.

3. In the Contacts window, point to the vertical bar to the right of the contact cards until the pointer changes to ◀▮▶, and then drag the vertical bar to the right until the cards are wide enough to display all of the address text. See Figure 12.

| Figure 12 | Contacts in Card view |

In the People, Business Card, Card, and List views, Outlook organizes your contacts in alphabetical order by last name, as specified in the File as box in the Contact window. When you have many contacts, you can find a specific contact quickly by typing the contact's name in the Search Contacts box, which appears below the ribbon, and then click the Search button. This **Instant Search** feature finds all items in the selected folder that match the keywords you enter. You can also click the letter button in the middle pane that corresponds to the first letter of a contact's last name, and then scroll as needed to display that contact.

Editing Contacts

Many aspects of a contact's information might change over time, or you might discover that you entered information incorrectly. Rather than deleting the contact and starting over, you can update the existing contact. You can double-click the contact to open its Contact window, and then edit the information as needed.

The zip code for The Bike Tool Shop was entered incorrectly; it is 97211. Geoff asks you to correct the zip code. You'll make this change in Card view.

To edit Tom Quinlan's contact card:

1. Click the **q** button along the left side of the Contacts main window to select the first contact card that starts with Q—in this case, Tom Quinlan's contact card.

   Trouble? If your contacts list has additional contacts, the first contact beginning with "q" will be selected. Scroll until you can see Tom Quinlan's contact card.

2. Double-click Tom Quinlan's contact card. The Tom Quinlan Contact window opens.

3. In the Address box, select the final **2** in the zip code, and then type **1**. The zip code is corrected.

4. Save and close Tom Quinlan's contact card.

Sending Contact Information by Email

If you need to send some of your contacts to others, you can forward the contact information. When you forward contact information as a business card, it includes only the data displayed in Business Card view. The file that is created is known as a vCard (short for virtual business card), and is in Internet Format, which is compatible with popular communication and information management programs. If you forward the Outlook contact, it contains all the information in the contact card. The recipient can then drag the contact into his or her Contacts folder to create a new contact card with all the forwarded information. Keep in mind that the recipient must use Outlook to open and read the contact information.

To forward a contact, select the contact, click the Forward Contact button in the Share group on the HOME tab, and then click As a Business Card or As an Outlook Contact. A new Message window opens with the contact included as an attachment to the message in the format you specified.

Creating and Modifying a Contact Group

Sometimes you need to repeatedly send one email message—such as a weekly progress report or company updates—to the same group of people. Rather than selecting the names one by one from the Contacts list, you can create a contact group. A **contact group**, also called a distribution list, is a group of people to whom you frequently send the same messages, such as all suppliers. A contact group saves you time and ensures that you don't inadvertently omit someone. You can create multiple contact groups to meet your needs, and individuals can be included in more than one contact group. You send a message to a contact group just as you would to an individual contact.

Creating a Contact Group

- In the Contacts window, on the HOME tab, in the New group, click the New Contact Group button to open the Contact Group window.
- Click in the Name box, and then type a name for the contact group.
- On the CONTACT GROUP tab, in the Members group, click the Add Members button, and then click From Outlook Contacts.
- In the Select Members: Contacts dialog box, click the Address Book arrow, and then click Contacts, if necessary.
- Double-click each contact in the list to add to the contact group, and then click the OK button.
- On the CONTACT GROUP tab, in the Actions group, click the Save & Close button.

Geoff asks you to create a contact group with the three suppliers so he can send messages to all of them using the contact group instead of individual email addresses.

To create the suppliers contact group:

1. On the HOME tab, in the New group, click the **New Contact Group** button. The Contact Group window opens.

2. In the Name box, type **Suppliers** as the name for the contact group.

3. On the CONTACT GROUP tab, in the Members group, click the **Add Members** button, and then click **From Outlook Contacts.** The Select Members: Contacts dialog box opens. A separate entry is listed for each email address and fax number for each contact.

4. Double-click the **Tom Quinlan** entry (the email address entry) to enter this contact in the Members box. Instead of double-clicking an entry, you can also click it and then click the Members button to move the entry to the list in the Members box.

5. Click the email address entry for **Pam Murphy**, and then click the **Members** button; then double-click the email address entry for **Paul L. Ruiz Sr.** Both email addresses are added as members of the Suppliers contact group, which now includes the three email addresses separated by semicolons. See Figure 13.

Figure 13   Select Members: Contacts dialog box

Pam Murphy's email address entry

Paul Ruiz's email address entry

contacts available to add to the contact group

contacts selected as members of the contact group (your email address will appear here)

6. Click the **OK** button. The three suppliers appear as members of the Suppliers contact group in the Contact Group window. Note that the names appear in alphabetical order by first name. See Figure 14.

Figure 14   Suppliers – Contact Group window

click to delete a selected contact from the group

click to add existing contacts to the group

descriptive name for the contact group

current members of the contact group

TIP

To send a message to all members of the group, type the contact group name in the To or Cc box of the message.

7. In the Actions group, click the **Save & Close** button. The contact group is filed as "Suppliers" in Contacts. The group icon in the upper-right corner of the contact card indicates that this is a contact group rather than an individual contact.

Modifying a Contact Group

At times, you'll need to update a contact group. You might need to add a new contact to the group or delete a contact from the group. First, double-click the contact group in the Contacts window to open its Contact Group window. Then, click the Add Members button in the Members group on the CONTACT GROUP tab to add contacts to the group or click the Remove Member button to delete a selected contact from the group. Removing a member from a contact group only deletes the contact from the group; the individual's contact card remains intact in your Contacts. If you need to update the information for an existing contact, you do so in the individual's contact card. If you no longer need a contact group, select the contact group in the Contacts window, and then click the Delete button in the Delete group on the HOME tab.

So far, you have sent an email message and created contacts for Geoff. In the next session, you send and receive emails with and without attachments, organize your messages, and then store the messages.

Session 1 Quick Check

REVIEW

1. Describe the purposes of the Inbox and the Outbox.
2. Define email.
3. What are two benefits of using email?
4. What is a signature?
5. List five types of contact information that you can store in Outlook.
6. Explain the purpose of a contact group.

Session 2 Visual Overview:

You print selected messages from the Print tab in Backstage view.

Reply All responds to the sender and all recipients (including any Bcc recipients).

Forward sends a copy of the message to one or more recipients you specify.

Reply responds to the sender.

Rather than searching through multiple folders, you can have Instant Search find messages (or other Outlook items).

Sorting is a way to arrange items in a specific order—either ascending or descending.

You can create subfolders to better organize messages and other Outlook items.

The message header includes the sender's name, the subject line, the date the message was received, the first few words of the message, as well as icons that provide information about the message (such as its importance level).

Search Folders are folders that display any email messages that match specific search criteria. You can choose a preset Search folder or create your own.

You can use one of the six preset color categories or add others to organize or rank your messages.

A flag is an icon that appears in the message header to indicate the item has been added as a task; text appears in the Reading Pane with a reminder of the start date and deadline.

Email Messages and Attachments

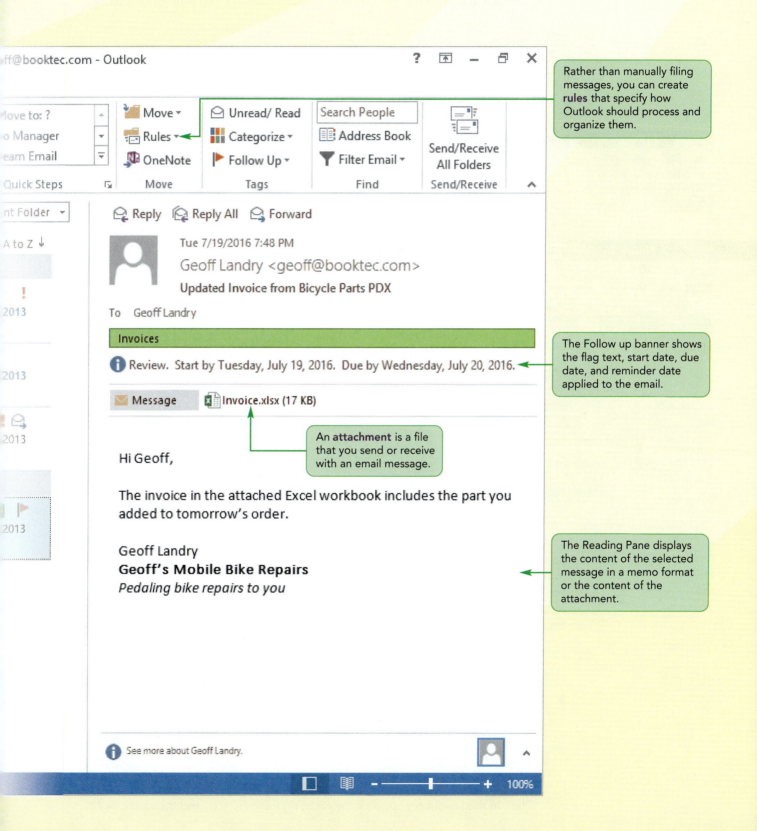

Rather than manually filing messages, you can create **rules** that specify how Outlook should process and organize them.

The Follow up banner shows the flag text, start date, due date, and reminder date applied to the email.

An **attachment** is a file that you send or receive with an email message.

The Reading Pane displays the content of the selected message in a memo format or the content of the attachment.

Receiving Email

When you check for new email messages, Outlook connects to your email server, if necessary, sends any messages in the Outbox, and receives any incoming messages that have arrived since you last checked. New messages are delivered into the Inbox. You'll switch to the Inbox folder and download the message you sent yourself earlier.

To receive the This Week's Order email you sent earlier:

1. If you took a break after the previous session, make sure Outlook is running.

2. In the Folder Pane, click the **Mail** button ✉, and then click the **Inbox** folder for your email address, if necessary.

> **TIP**
>
> You can also click the Send/Receive All Folders button on the Quick Access Toolbar.

3. On the HOME tab, in the Send/Receive group, click the **Send/Receive All Folders** button. If you are not already connected to the Internet, connect now.

4. Watch for new messages to appear in the Inbox. The number of unread messages in the Inbox appears next to the Inbox folder in the Folder Pane. See Figure 15. Your Inbox might contain a different number of messages.

Figure 15   Received message in the Inbox

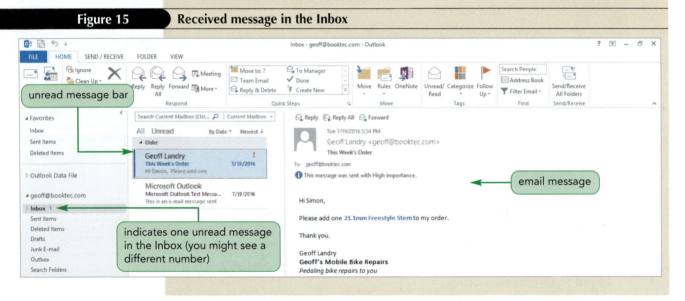

After a message arrives, you can read it. The Inbox window is divided into two panes. The left pane lists all the email messages that you have received, along with information about the message in the message header. The date and time the message was received, the sender, the subject, the importance level, and all the recipients (except Bcc recipients) appear at the top of the message in the Reading Pane. You can resize the panes by dragging the border between the panes.

To read the This Week's Order message:

1. Click the **This Week's Order** message in the left pane to display its contents in the Reading Pane, if necessary. When you select a different message, the Unread message bar along the left side of the message header will disappear and the subject changes from blue to black and will no longer be in boldface.

   Trouble? If the Reading Pane does not appear on your screen or if it appears on the bottom of the screen, you need to set it. On the ribbon, click the VIEW tab. In the Layout group, click the Reading Pane button, and then click Right.

> **2.** Read the message in the Reading Pane. Because Outlook can view HTML messages, the formatting added to the message is visible. If you don't see the HTML formatting, your email server might not preserve the HTML formatting in email messages; continue with the tutorial.

After you read a message, you have several options—you can leave the message in the Inbox and deal with it later, reply to the message, forward the message to others, print it, file it, or delete it.

Replying To and Forwarding Messages

Many messages you receive require some sort of response—for example, confirmation you received the information, the answer to a question, or sending the message to another person. The quickest way to respond to messages is to use the Reply, Reply to All, and Forward features. Reply responds to the sender, and Reply to All responds to the sender and all recipients (including any Bcc recipients); Outlook inserts the email addresses into the appropriate boxes. Forward sends a copy of the message to one or more recipients you specify; you enter the email addresses in the To or Cc box. With both Reply and Forward, the original message is included for reference, separated from your new message by a line and the original message header information. By default, new text you type is added at the top of the message body, above the original message. This makes it simpler for recipients to read your message because they don't have to scroll through the original message to find the new text.

You'll reply to the This Week's Order message, as if you were Simon, the recipient, responding to Geoff.

To reply to the This Week's Order message:

> **TIP**
>
> You can also click the Reply, Reply All, or Forward button above the message in the Reading Pane to respond to the message.

> **1.** On the HOME tab, in the Respond group, click the **Reply** button. A Message window opens with the recipient's name and email address in the To box (in this case, your name and address) and RE: (short for Regarding) inserted at the beginning of the Subject line. The body of the original message appears in the message body pane below a divider line, and the insertion point is above the message, ready for you to type your reply.

> **2.** Type **Hi Geoff,** as the salutation, press the **Enter** key twice, type **We'll add this part to your order for pick up tomorrow.** as the reply message, press the **Enter** key twice, and then type your name (remember that your signature is not added for replies). Your reply message appears in blue because you selected HTML format. Notice that [Draft] appears in the message header in the message list.
>
> **Trouble?** Depending on how your computer is configured, you might not see the HTML formatting.

> **3.** Click the **Send** button to send the message. In the message list, the icon appears in the upper-right corner of the message header to indicate you replied to this message.

Next, you'll forward the message for Simon to Paul Ruiz at Bicycle Parts PDX. Because Paul's contact information is in your Contacts, you can address the message to him quickly.

To forward the This Week's Order message:

▶ **1.** On the HOME tab, in the Respond group, click the **Forward** button. This time, the insertion point is in the empty To box and FW: (for Forward) is inserted at the beginning of the Subject line.

▶ **2.** In the To box, type **Paul Ruiz**.

▶ **3.** Click at the top of the message body, above the forwarded message, and then type **Hi Paul,** as the salutation, press the **Enter** key twice, type **Please add the item listed below to Geoff's order. He'll pick up the complete order tomorrow morning.** as the message, press the **Enter** key twice, and then type your name.

▶ **4.** Click the **Send** button to send the message. The Check Names dialog box opens because Paul Ruiz has multiple contact information—an email address and a fax number.

▶ **5.** Click the first **Paul Ruiz**, the entry with his email address (if necessary), and then click the **OK** button. In the message list, the icon 🔄 now appears in the upper-right corner of the message header to indicate that this message has been forwarded.

▶ **6.** In the Send/Receive group, click the **Send/Receive All Folders** button to send the messages to your email server. The messages you just sent might appear in your Inbox.

Printing Messages

Although email eliminates the need for paper messages, sometimes you might require printed documentation of a correspondence or to read when you're away from your computer. You can use the Print screen in Backstage view to preview and print a selected message. From the Print screen, you specify a printer and select settings such as the print style. Memo Style prints the contents of the selected item—in this case, the email message. Table Style prints the view of the selected folder—in this case, the Inbox folder. Other Outlook elements have different print style options. The Print Options button opens the Print dialog box, where you can select the page range, number of copies, and other options for printing.

Geoff asks you to print the This Week's Order message for future reference.

To print the This Week's Order message:

▶ **1.** On the ribbon, click the **FILE** tab to open Backstage view, and then click **Print** in the navigation bar.

▶ **2.** In the Printer section, make sure that the printer you want to use is listed.

▶ **3.** In the Settings section, click **Memo Style** to select it, if necessary.

▶ **4.** Click the **Print** button. The message prints, and the Inbox folder is redisplayed.

Working with Attachments

You'll often want to send information that is stored in a variety of files on your computer. Some of this information could be typed into an email message, but the original file might be long with complex formatting that is inappropriate for email. Also, some kinds of files (such as photos and spreadsheets) cannot be inserted into email messages. Instead, you can send files as attachments.

Attachments can be any type of file, including documents (such as a Word document, Excel workbook, or PowerPoint presentation), images, sounds, and programs. Recipients can then save and open the file; the recipient must have the original program or a program that can read that file type. You'll send an attachment containing the updated invoice from Bicycle Parts PDX to Geoff.

TIP

Many ISPs don't accept messages with attachments over a certain size. You might not be notified that the recipient didn't receive your message.

To attach the updated invoice file to an email message:

1. On the HOME tab, in the New group, click the **New Email** button to open a Message window.

2. Click the **To** button. The Select Names: Contacts dialog box opens. You will select which contacts should receive the message.

3. Click **Geoff Landry** in the list of contacts (if necessary), and then click the **To** button at the bottom of the dialog box. Geoff's name is added to the To list.

4. Click the **OK** button. The To box in the Message window now contains Geoff's email address.

5. In the Subject box, type **Updated Invoice from Bicycle Parts PDX**.

6. In the message body, type **Hi Geoff,** as the salutation, press the **Enter** key twice, and then type **The invoice in the attached Excel workbook includes the part you added to tomorrow's order.** as the message.

7. On the MESSAGE tab, in the Include group, click the **Attach File** button. The Insert File dialog box opens, which functions like the Open dialog box.

8. Navigate to the **Outlook ▸ Tutorial** folder included with your Data Files.

   Trouble? If you don't have the starting Data Files, you need to get them before you can proceed. Your instructor will either give you the Data Files or ask you to obtain them from a specified location (such as a network drive). If you have any questions about the Data Files, see your instructor or technical support person for assistance.

9. Double-click **Invoice** in the file list. The file is attached to your email message. See Figure 16.

Figure 16   **Email message with an attached file**

Figure 16   Email message with an attached file

Excel workbook attached to the message

10. Click the **Send** button to send the message.

A message with an attachment might take a bit longer to send and receive because its file size is larger than an email message without an attachment. Messages with attached files display a paper clip icon in the message header. If the appropriate program is installed on your computer, you can open the attached file from the message itself. You can also save the attachment to your computer and then open, edit, and move it like any other file on your computer. You can reply to or forward any message with an attachment, but the attachment is included only in the forwarded message because it's unlikely that you'll want to return the same file to the sender.

After you receive the message with the Invoice workbook attachment, you'll save the attachment and then view it from within the message.

To save and view the Updated Invoice from Bicycle Parts PDX message attachment:

1. If the Updated Invoice from Bicycle Parts PDX message (with the attachment) is not already in your Inbox folder, on the Quick Access Toolbar, click the **Send/Receive All Folders** button ⊞.

TIP

You can double-click a message header in the Inbox to open the message in its own window.

2. Click the **Updated Invoice from Bicycle Parts PDX** message in the Inbox. The attachment icon 📎 appears in the upper-right corner of the message header. The message is displayed in the Reading Pane, and the attached file's icon and name appear below the message header.

3. In the Reading Pane, click **Invoice.xlsx** below the message header. The attached file replaces the message text in the Reading Pane, so you can view its contents, and the ATTACHMENT TOOLS ATTACHMENTS contextual tab appears on the ribbon. See Figure 17.

Figure 17   **Invoice.xlsx attachment displayed in the Reading Pane**

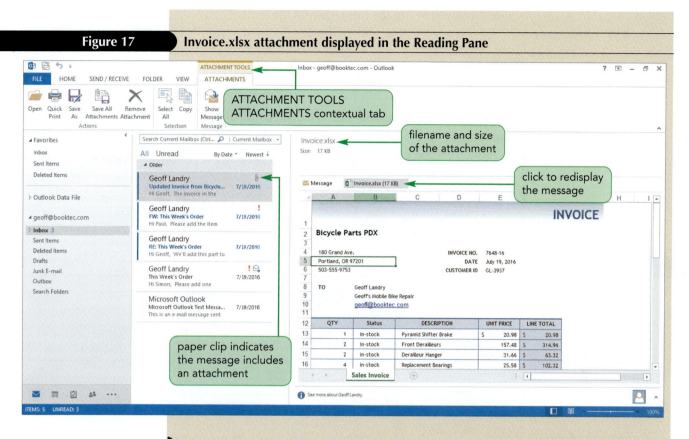

4. On the ATTACHMENTS tab, in the Actions group, click the **Save As** button. The Save Attachment dialog box opens, where you can select the location to save the attachment.

5. Navigate to the location specified by your instructor, change the filename to **Updated Invoice** and then click the **Save** button. The attached file is saved. You can work with this file just as you would any other file on disk.

6. In the Reading Pane, review the worksheet, and then click the **Message** button. The email message reappears in the Reading Pane, and the HOME tab is redisplayed on the ribbon.

Flagging and Color Coding Messages

Some messages you receive require a specific response or action. Although the subject should be informative and the message can provide explicit instructions, often a more obvious reminder would better draw attention to messages that require action. A flag in the message header indicates that the item has been added as a task; text appears in the Reading Pane with a reminder of the start date and deadline. To add a flag, point to the upper-right area of the message header and click the flag icon that appears, click Add Reminder to open the Custom dialog box, then choose preset flag text or enter your own text, and select a specific due date or enter descriptive words such as "tomorrow," which Outlook converts to the correct date. Outlook will then display a reminder about the flag at the appropriate time. After you have performed the requested action, you can mark the flag completed by right-clicking the flag icon in the message header, and then clicking Mark Complete on the shortcut menu. You can also choose from six preset color categories or add others to better organize or rank your messages.

Geoff asks you to flag the message with the updated invoice and add it to the green color category. Geoff wants to use the green color category for all messages related to invoices. The flag will cause Outlook to display a reminder of the item that needs your attention on the date specified.

To flag and color code the Updated Invoice from Bicycle Parts PDX message:

▶ **1.** Make sure the **Updated Invoice from Bicycle Parts PDX** message is selected in the Inbox.

▶ **2.** On the HOME tab, in the Tags group, click the **Follow Up** button to open a menu of preset flag options, and then click **Add Reminder**. The Custom dialog box opens. See Figure 18 (your dates will differ).

Figure 18   Custom dialog box

- start date set to today (your date will differ)
- select or type reminder day and time
- select or type flag text
- select or type due date

▶ **3.** Click the **Flag to** arrow to display the preset flag options, and then scroll down and click **Review** to set the flag message.

▶ **4.** Click the **Due date** arrow to open a calendar showing this month with today's date highlighted, and then click the date for the next workday. A reminder is set for the next workday.

▶ **5.** Click the **OK** button. The Custom dialog box closes. A banner appears at the top of the Reading Pane showing the selections you made.

▶ **6.** On the HOME tab, in the Tags group, click the **Categorize** button, and then click **Green Category** in the menu. The Rename Category dialog box opens. You can choose to enter a descriptive category name or keep the default name.

Trouble? If the Rename Category dialog box doesn't open, you need to use the Color Categories dialog box. In the Tags group, click the Categorize button, and then click All Categories. Continue with Step 7.

Geoff asks you to specify the name "Invoices" for the green category to clarify the purpose of the category. When you rename a category, your version of Outlook will retain the name; in this case, the green category will retain the name "Invoices" unless it is renamed in the future.

▶ **7.** In the Name box, type **Invoices**, and then click the **Yes** button. The message has a green category icon in the message header. Also, a green bar labeled "Invoices" appears at the top of the message in the Reading Pane; this indicates that the message is in the Invoices category. See Figure 19.

Figure 19   Updated Invoice from Bicycle Parts PDX message with a flag and green color category

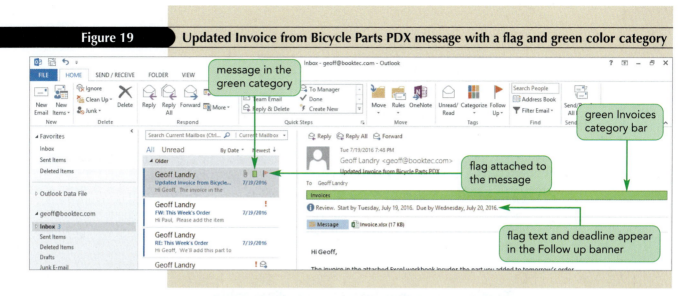

Figure 19   Updated Invoice from Bicycle Parts PDX message with a flag and green color category

Organizing and Managing Messages

So far, all the messages you received are stored in the Inbox folder. As you can see, messages can collect quickly in your Inbox. Even if you respond to each message as it arrives, all the original messages still remain in your Inbox folder. Some messages you'll want to file and store; other messages you'll want to delete.

Creating a Folder

The Folder List acts like an electronic file cabinet. You should create a logical folder structure in which to store your messages. For example, Geoff might create subfolders named "Customers" and "Suppliers" within the Inbox folder. You can create folders at the same level as the default folders, such as Inbox, Outbox, and Sent Messages, or you can create subfolders within these folders. For now, you'll create one subfolder named "Suppliers" in the Inbox folder.

Note: If you are using a web-based email account and store messages on your mail server, you will not be able to create folders in Outlook. Please read the following sections related to creating folders, but do not attempt to complete the steps.

To create the Suppliers subfolder in the Inbox:

1. On the ribbon, click the **FOLDER** tab. The ribbon displays options for working with the selected folder—in this case, the Inbox.

2. In the New group, click the **New Folder** button. The Create New Folder dialog box opens.

3. In the Name box, type **Suppliers**. Because you opened the dialog box from the Inbox, the Folder contains box lists Mail and Post Items. You can also create subfolders to store other items, such as contacts, notes, and tasks.

4. In the Select where to place the folder box, click **Inbox** if it is not already selected.

5. Click the **OK** button. The new folder appears indented below the Inbox folder in the Folder Pane.

Trouble? If you don't see the Suppliers folder, the Inbox is probably collapsed. Click the Expand button next to the Inbox.

Trouble? If a dialog box opens to notify you that you cannot create the folder, you are probably using a web-based email account. Click the OK button, and then read but do not complete the steps in the next two sections.

Moving Messages into Folders

One method for keeping messages organized and the Inbox uncluttered is to move a message out of the Inbox as soon as you have dealt with it. This leaves the Inbox filled only with messages you still need to deal with. You'll file messages related to suppliers in the new subfolder.

To move messages into the Suppliers folder:

1. In the message list, make sure the **Updated Invoice from Bicycle Parts PDX** message is still selected. It is the first message that you will move.

2. On the ribbon, click the **HOME** tab. In the Move group, click the **Move** button, and then click **Suppliers** (note that the Suppliers folder name includes your email address). The selected message moves to the Suppliers subfolder.

   You could continue to move each message individually, but it is faster to move all of them at once. You press the Ctrl key to select nonadjacent messages and the Shift key to select a block of adjacent messages.

3. Click the **This Week's Order** message header, the first message you want to file.

4. Press and hold the **Ctrl** key, click the **RE: This Week's Order** message header, click the **FW: This Week's Order** message header, and then release the **Ctrl** key. The three messages are selected.

5. In the Move group, click the **Move** button, and then click **Suppliers**. The three selected messages move from the Inbox into the Suppliers subfolder. You might see a number next to the Suppliers subfolder, depending on whether any messages in the folder remain unread.

TIP

You can also drag selected messages from one folder to another.

The Inbox folder is now empty of messages related to Geoff's Mobile Bike Repair. However, the Updated Invoice from Bicycle Parts PDX message does not belong in the Suppliers folder. You'll create a new folder named "Invoices" to store that message.

To create a subfolder named "Invoices":

1. In the Folder Pane, right-click the **Inbox** folder, and then click **New Folder** on the shortcut menu. A box for the subfolder name appears in the Folder Pane below the Inbox folder. Because you created this subfolder for the Inbox, it is already set for storing mail and post items.

2. In the box, type **Invoices** as the folder name, and then press the **Enter** key. The Invoices subfolder appears indented below the Inbox folder. Note that subfolders you create are listed in alphabetical order below the main folder.

Creating Rules

Rather than manually filing messages, you can create rules that specify how Outlook should process and organize them. For example, you can use rules to move messages to a folder based on their subjects, flag messages about a particular topic, or forward messages to a person or a distribution list.

Each **rule** includes three parts: the conditions that determine if a message is to be acted on, the actions that should be applied to qualifying messages, and any exceptions that remove a message from the qualifying group. A rule might state that all messages you receive from Paul Ruiz (condition) are moved to the Suppliers folder (action) except for ones marked as High importance (exception). Outlook can apply rules to incoming, outgoing, or stored messages.

You can create a simple rule from common conditions and actions in the Create Rule dialog box. Or you can use the Rules Wizard, which is a feature that steps you through the rule-writing process, to write more complex rules that also include exceptions.

Geoff asks you to create a rule to move all messages related to invoices to the Invoices subfolder. A message must be selected in order for the Create Rule button to be available. You can select any message to create a rule. Note that the information from the selected message automatically appears as conditions in the Create Rule dialog box.

To create a rule to move all invoice messages to the Invoices subfolder:

1. In the Folder Pane, click the **Suppliers** subfolder, and then click the **Updated Invoice from Bicycle Parts PDX** message in the message list to select it, if necessary.

2. On the HOME tab, in the Move group, click the **Rules** button, and then click **Create Rule**. The Create Rule dialog box opens. You need to create a rule that will move any message that includes "Invoice" in the subject into the Invoices subfolder.

3. Click the **Subject contains** check box to insert a checkmark. The Subject contains box already contains the subject from the selected message.

4. Delete **Updated** and **from Bicycle Parts PDX** from the Subject contains box. You've specified the first part of the rule, the condition—the Subject of the message must contain the text "Invoice."

5. Click the **Move the item to folder** check box. The Rules and Alerts dialog box opens.

6. In the Choose a folder box, expand the Inbox folder for your email account, click the **Invoices** folder, and then click the **OK** button. You've specified the second part of the rule, the action—move the message to the Invoices folder. There are no exceptions needed for this rule, so the settings are complete. See Figure 20.

Figure 20   Completed Create Rule dialog box

set conditions for the rule

rule will search for this text in the Subject field of messages

set actions for the rule

click to open the Rules Wizard

rule will move all messages that meet conditions to this folder

7. Click the **OK** button. The Success dialog box opens, indicating that the rule "Invoice" has been created.

Trouble? If a dialog box opens and displays the message, "This rule is a client-only rule, and will process only if Outlook is running," you are set up to run Outlook with Exchange Server. This message appears because Outlook has determined that the rule requires access to your computer to run. Click the OK button. Outlook saves the rule and adds "(client only)" after the name of the rule in the Rules and Alerts dialog box to remind you that your computer must be logged onto Exchange for the rule to be run. If you have any questions about Exchange Server, ask your instructor or technical support person for assistance.

So you can see how to run a rule at any time, you'll deselect the option for running the rule immediately and then use another option to run it.

8. Click the **Run this rule now on messages already in the current folder** check box to remove the checkmark, if necessary, and then click the **OK** button.

You'll use the Rules and Alerts dialog box to run the Invoice rule on the messages in the Suppliers subfolder. The dialog box gives you options for running the rule on specified folders as well as any subfolders.

To run the Invoice rule:

1. On the HOME tab, in the Move group, click the **Rules** button, and then click **Manage Rules & Alerts**. The Rules and Alerts dialog box opens with the E-mail Rules tab displayed.

2. On the E-mail Rules tab, click the **Run Rules Now** button. The Run Rules Now dialog box opens.

3. Click the **Invoice** check box to insert a checkmark, and then read the rule description.

4. Click the **Run Now** button. The rule runs on the messages in the Suppliers folder and the Updated Invoice from Bicycle Parts PDX message is moved to the Invoices folder.

5. Click the **Close** button in the Run Rules Now dialog box, and then click the **OK** button in the Rules and Alerts dialog box.

6. In the Folder Pane, click the **Invoices** folder to see that the Updated Invoice from Bicycle Parts PDX message is now in the Invoices folder, having been moved there from the Suppliers subfolder.

Rearranging Messages

As your folder structure becomes more complex and you have more stored messages, it might become difficult to locate a specific message you filed. Searching, sorting, and changing views provide different ways to locate and organize your messages.

Searching for Messages

Rather than searching through multiple folders, you can use Instant Search to find the desired message (or any other Outlook item). You select the folder you want to search, and then enter text in the Search box. As you type, items with that search text appear in the main window with the search text highlighted. Attachments are also searched, but the search text is not highlighted in them. To narrow your search, you can select additional criteria in the Refine group on the SEARCH TOOLS SEARCH tab, which appears when you click in the Search box.

You'll use Instant Search to look for messages containing the word "complete" in the Suppliers folder.

To search for messages with the word "complete":

1. In the Folder Pane, click the **Suppliers** subfolder to display its contents in the main window.

2. Click in the **Instant Search** box in the main window. The SEARCH TOOLS SEARCH tab appears on the ribbon with tools for searching Outlook items.

3. Type **complete** in the Search box. As you type, any text in the message headers and the Reading Pane that matches the search text is highlighted. Only one message contains the search text. See Figure 21.

| Figure 21 | Instant Search results |

4. In the Search box, click the **Close Search** button [X]. The highlighting is removed and all the messages in the folder are redisplayed.

Using Search Folders

Another way to find specific messages is with Search Folders. Outlook has preset Search Folders. For example, the Categorized Mail Search Folder displays messages grouped by their color categories, the Large Mail Search Folder displays any messages larger than 100 KB, and the Unread Mail Search Folder displays all messages that have an unread icon. Messages that meet a Search Folder's criteria are displayed in that Search Folder but remain stored in their current folders. This lets you open one folder to view messages with similar characteristics, but store them logically in other folders based upon their contents. A message can appear in more than one Search Folder. For example, a message in the blue category that is 200 KB and marked as unread will appear in at least three Search Folders: Categorized Mail, Large Mail, and Unread Mail. You can use the preset Search Folders, customize them to better fit your needs, or create your own Search Folders.

If you delete a Search Folder, the messages that were displayed in that folder are not deleted because they are actually stored in other Outlook folders. However, if you delete an individual message from within a Search Folder, the message is also deleted from the folder in which it is actually stored.

You'll use Search Folders to look for categorized messages and unread messages.

To use the Categorized Mail and Unread Mail Search Folders:

TIP

You can also right-click Search Folders in the Folder Pane, and then click New Search Folder to open the New Search Folder dialog box.

1. On the ribbon, click the **FOLDER** tab. In the New group, click **New Search Folder**. The New Search Folder dialog box opens.

2. Scroll down the Select a Search Folder box until you see the **Organizing Mail** section, and then click **Categorized mail**.

3. Click the **OK** button. The Categorized Mail Search Folder appears in the Folder Pane below the Search Folders.

4. In the Folder Pane, click the **Categorized Mail** Search Folder if it is not already selected. One message header appears under the green group heading "Invoices." See Figure 22. If you had more than one message categorized and used different colors, the messages would appear grouped according to their color categories.

Figure 22   Categorized Mail Search Folder

5. In the New group, click the **New Search Folder** button, click **Unread mail** in the Reading Mail section of the Select a Search Folder box, and then click the **OK** button. The Unread Mail Search Folder is added to the Folder Pane. Any messages you haven't yet read are listed in the main window when the Unread Mail Search Folder is selected.

Switching Views and Arrangements

Another way to manage messages is to change the view or arrangement. You are already familiar with views, which specify how items for an Outlook element are organized and which details are visible. Each Outlook element has a set of standard views from which you can choose. An **arrangement** is a predefined organization of how items in a view are displayed. Views and arrangements enable you to see the same items in different ways.

To switch the arrangement of the Suppliers folder:

1. In the Folder Pane, click **Suppliers** to display the contents of this folder in the main window. All the messages appear in the folder arranged according to the date they were received.

2. On the ribbon, click the **VIEW** tab. In the Arrangement group, click the **More** button to open the Arrangement gallery, and then click **Subject**. All the messages appear in the main window grouped according to the text in their Subject boxes.

3. Above the message list, click the **By Subject** arrow to display the list of default arrangements, and then click **Importance**. The messages are now grouped according to their importance levels, in this case High or Normal. The messages with High importance appear first in the list, followed by messages with Normal importance.

Sorting Messages

Sorting arranges items in either ascending or descending order. **Ascending order** arranges messages alphabetically from A to Z, chronologically from earliest to latest, or numerically from lowest to highest. **Descending order** arranges messages in reverse alphabetical, chronological, or numerical order. By default, all messages are sorted in descending order by their Received date and time. You can, however, change the field by which messages are sorted; for example, you might sort email messages alphabetically by sender. You can also sort messages by multiple fields. For example, you might sort email messages alphabetically by sender and then by subject.

To sort the messages in the Suppliers folder by importance:

1. On the VIEW tab, in the Arrangement group, click the **Reverse Sort** button. The Importance sort order changes to ascending, as indicated by the text "Low" and the down arrow icon in the column heading. See Figure 23. Note that your screen might show a different message selected in the main window and its contents in the Reading Pane.

| Figure 23 | Messages in the Suppliers folder sorted in ascending order by importance |

Trouble? If the column heading changes to "High" and the arrow icon points up, the sort order was already ascending. Repeat Step 1.

TIP
To select additional sort columns, press the Shift key as you click the corresponding column links.

2. In the Suppliers main window, click the **Low** column heading. The Importance sort order returns to descending (High on top), as indicated by the text and the down arrow icon in the column heading.

3. In the Suppliers main window, click the **By Importance** link, and then click **Date**. The messages are redisplayed in the original order.

Storing Messages

After a time, you might not need immediate access to the messages you have compiled in the Outlook folders. You can store messages by saving them in other file formats or by archiving them.

Saving Messages

You can use the Save As command to save messages and other Outlook items in other file formats so that you can store them separately from Outlook in a specific location on your hard drive or removable storage device (such as a USB flash drive) just as you save other files, and then delete them from Outlook. You can open such messages with other programs. For example, you can save an email message as a Text Only (.txt) file that most word processing programs can read. You can also save HTML messages as HTML (.htm) files to preserve their original formatting.

INSIGHT

Understanding Save As File Formats in Outlook

Sometimes you will want to access and manipulate items created in Outlook using other programs, or you might want to share items created in Outlook with others who might not have Outlook installed on their device. To be able to do this effectively, you need to understand the types of file formats available and some of the limitations associated with each.

- **Outlook Template**, **Outlook Message Format**, **Outlook Message Format – Unicode** are Outlook formats that can be read only by Outlook. These formats limit your options in sharing the saved files you save.
- **Text Only** saves the message as plain text but loses any formatting and images. Most word processing programs can read this format. Select this format when you want to save the content of a message without its formatting or images.
- **HTML** saves the message with all its formatting but stores images in a subfolder. Most web browsers can read this format. Select this format when you want to save a message's content as well as its formatting and images.
- **MHT files** is a Microsoft format that saves the message with all its formatting and images into a single file that Internet Explorer and most desktop search programs can read. Select this format if you want to consolidate the file and know that you and others with whom you want to share the file have a program that can read this format.

You'll save the This Week's Order message as a text file.

To save the This Week's Order message as a text file:

1. Click the **This Week's Order** message in the Inbox folder to select it.

2. On the ribbon, click the **FILE** tab, and then click **Save As** in the navigation bar. The Save As dialog box opens, with the message's subject in the File name box.

3. Navigate to the location specified by your instructor.

4. Click the **Save as type** button to display the available file formats from which you can choose, and then click **Text Only** to select that file format.

5. Click the **Save** button. The message is saved as a text file.

TIP

To save a message as a Word document, select and copy the message, paste it into an open document, and then save the document from Word.

Archiving Mail Messages

Eventually, even the messages in your subfolders can become too numerous to manage easily. More often than not, you don't need immediate access to older messages. Rather than reviewing filed messages and moving older ones to a storage file, you can archive them. When you **archive** a folder, you transfer messages or other items stored in a folder (such as an attachment in the email folder) to an Outlook data file when the items have reached the age you specify. An **Outlook data file**—which has the file extension .pst and can be accessed only from Outlook—stores folders, messages, files, and other items. Outlook calculates the age of an email message from the date the message was sent or received, whichever is later.

When you create an archive, your existing folder structure from Outlook is recreated in the archive file and all the messages are moved from Outlook into the archive file. If you want to archive only a subfolder, the entire folder structure is still recreated in the archive file; however, only the messages from the selected subfolder are moved into the archive file. For example, if you archive the Suppliers folder, the archive file will include both the Inbox folder and the Suppliers subfolder, but only the messages in the Suppliers subfolder will be moved. Any messages in the Inbox folder remain in the Outlook Inbox. All folders remain in place within Outlook after archiving—even empty ones.

You can manually archive a folder at any time, such as when you finish a project or event. You specify which folders to archive, the age of items to archive, and the name and location of the archive file.

To manually archive the Suppliers and Invoices folders:

1. On the ribbon, click the **FILE** tab, and then click **Info** in the navigation bar, if necessary.

2. Click the **Cleanup Tools** button, and then click **Archive**. The Archive dialog box opens.

3. If necessary, click the **Archive this folder and all subfolders** option button.

4. Expand your email's **Inbox** to display the subfolders, and then click the **Suppliers** folder.

5. Select the text in the Archive items older than box, type **tomorrow** to replace the selected text, and then press the **Tab** key. The text is replaced with the next day's date, which means Outlook will move any files dated with today's date or earlier to the archive file.

6. Click the **Browse** button. The Open Outlook Data Files dialog box opens.

7. Navigate to location specified by your instructor, type **Suppliers Archive** in the File name box, and then click the **OK** button. The Archive dialog box reappears. See Figure 24.

Figure 24	Archive dialog box

folder selected to archive →

date set to tomorrow (your date will differ)

path to the folder in which to save the archive (yours will differ)

▶ **8.** Click the **OK** button. A dialog box opens warning that all the items in the folder could be archived because you entered a date in the future.

▶ **9.** Click the **Yes** button to confirm that you want to archive all the items in the folder. All the messages in the Suppliers folder are moved into the archive file you specified. The empty Suppliers folder remains in the folder structure.

▶ **10.** Repeat Steps 2 through 9 to create an archive for the Invoices folder named **Invoices Archive**.

▶ **11.** In Backstage view, click the **Back** button ⬅ to return to the main Outlook window.

The two archive folders you created appear in the Folder Pane. You can display the subfolders and select items in them from the Folder Pane. If you don't need immediate access to an archive, you can close it. You can access items in a closed archive from the Open screen in Backstage view. To work with the files from the Folder Pane, use the Open Outlook Data File command to open the file, and then drag the items you need from the archive to a current folder. To restore all of the items in the archive file, use the Import command.

To view and close the Suppliers and Invoices archive folders:

▶ **1.** On the ribbon, click the **HOME** tab. Two folders named Archives are listed in the Folder Pane, one for each folder you archived.

▶ **2.** In the Folder Pane, expand the first **Archives** folder, expand its **Inbox** folder, and then click the **Suppliers** folder to see the contents of the archive folder.

▶ **3.** Repeat Step 2 to view the contents of the Invoices archive folder.

▶ **4.** In the Folder Pane, right-click each **Archives** folder, and then click **Close "Archives"** to close each folder.

Deleting Items and Exiting Outlook

After you finish working with Outlook, you should exit the program. Unlike with other programs, you don't need to save or close any files. Before you exit, however, you'll delete the rule and each of the items you created in this tutorial. Deleted items are moved into the Deleted Items folder. This folder acts like the Recycle Bin in Windows. Items you delete stay in this folder until you empty it.

To delete the rule, items you created, and your signature:

1. On the HOME tab, in the Move group, click the **Rules** button, and then click **Manage Rules & Alerts**. The Rules and Alerts dialog box opens with the E-mail Rules tab active.

2. In the Rule box, click **Invoice** to select the rule, and then click the **Delete** button on the toolbar above the Rule box.

3. Click the **Yes** button to confirm the deletion, and then click the **OK** button to close the Rules and Alerts dialog box.

4. In the Folder Pane, click the **Invoices** folder.

5. On the ribbon, click the **FOLDER** tab. In the Actions group, click the **Delete Folder** button. A dialog box opens to confirm that you want to move the folder and all of its messages to the Deleted Items folder.

6. Click the **Yes** button.

7. Repeat Steps 4 through 6 to delete the **Suppliers** folder, the **Categorized Mail** folder, and the **Unread Mail** folder.

8. In the Folder Pane, click the **Sent Items** folder, click the first message you sent in this tutorial, press and hold the **Ctrl** key as you click each additional message you sent in this tutorial, and then release the **Ctrl** key. All the messages you sent in the tutorial are selected.

9. On the ribbon, click the **HOME** tab. In the Delete group, click the **Delete** button. The selected messages move to the Deleted Items folder.

10. In the Folder Pane, click the **People** button 👥, press and hold the **Ctrl** key as you click each of the four contacts and the Suppliers contact group you created in this tutorial, release the **Ctrl** key, and then click the **Delete** button in the Delete group. The contacts you created for this tutorial are deleted.

11. On the ribbon, click the **FILE** tab to open Backstage view, and then click **Info** in the navigation bar, if necessary.

12. On the Account Information screen, click the **Cleanup Tools** button, click **Empty Deleted Items Folder**, and then click the **Yes** button to confirm that you want to permanently delete all the items and subfolders in the Deleted Items folder.

13. Click **Options** in the navigation bar to open the Outlook Options dialog box, and then click **Mail** in the left pane.

14. Click the **Signatures** button in the right pane, click **Geoff's Mobile Bike Repairs** in the Select signature to edit box, and then click the **Delete** button.

15. Click the **Yes** button to confirm that you want to delete this signature.

16. Click the **OK** button in the Signatures and Stationery dialog box, and then click the **OK** button in the Outlook Options dialog box.

You have deleted all of the items you created in this tutorial—email messages, contacts, Search Folders, a rule, a signature, and emptied the Deleted Items folder.

PROSKILLS

Teamwork: Communicating Effectively with a Group

Email is a common way for team members to communicate. As teams work on a project, many messages about a variety of topics related to that project will be exchanged. When you are part of a team (or communicating with a group for a one-time purpose), keep in mind the following guidelines as you send and receive messages:

- **Check the recipient list.** Are all team members included? Has anyone else been added to the exchange? If so, should that person be part of the ongoing communication? For example, a customer should be removed from the internal discussion about how to deal with the customer's complaint, and be sent only the resolution.
- **Reread the message chain.** Is the entire conversation appropriate for all recipients? For example, an upcoming surprise retirement party should not be mentioned in an email chain that includes the retiree. Also, is the message chain getting very long? If so, it might be appropriate to delete the earliest part of the chain.
- **Use one subject per message chain.** Is the discussion veering to a new topic? Start a new email with an appropriate subject line to reflect the new topic. This makes it simpler to track the different conversations.
- **Check attachment content.** Is the attachment appropriate for all recipients? For example, you want to make sure that confidential or proprietary information, such as budgets and items under development, are not forwarded to customers or competitors.
- **Understand Reply vs. Reply All vs. Forward.** Who do you want to include in the message chain? Use Reply when you want to respond only to the sender. Use Reply All when you want to respond to everyone who received the message chain. Use Forward when you want to send the message chain to someone not already on the list. Keep in mind that you can add or remove recipients each time you send a response.

Thanks to your help, Geoff is set up to use Outlook to communicate more effectively with his suppliers and manage the email messages that he sends and receives.

REVIEW

Session 2 Quick Check

1. Explain the difference between Reply and Reply to All.
2. What two things can you do with a file attached to an email message from within Outlook?
3. How do you move an email message from the Inbox to a subfolder?
4. What is a Search Folder?
5. What is the purpose of a rule?
6. What does it mean to archive a folder?

Review Assignments

Data File needed for the Review Assignments: Workshops.docx

Geoff Landry asks you to help him with customer communication for Geoff's Mobile Bike Repairs. Complete the following steps:

1. Create a signature that uses your name and the company name **Geoff's Mobile Bike Repairs**. Format the company name with bold and italics. Apply the signature to new messages and replies and forwards.

2. Create a new email message addressed to your email address with the subject **Appointment Reminder** and the message **Hello. I'll arrive tomorrow at 10 am for your bike tune-up.**

3. In the message body, format "10 am" with bold and a red font.

4. Send the email.

5. Create a contact card for **Geoff Landry** at **Geoff's Mobile Bike Repairs** using your email address, an appropriate display as entry, a fictional business phone number, and a fictional business mailing address.

6. Create contact cards for the following three customers at their home addresses and phone numbers, using your email address and an appropriate display as entry. (*Hint*: Click the arrow button in the address section, and then click Home.)
   - **Lilah Devlin, 5002 SE Belmont Street, Portland, OR 97215, 503-555-1232**
   - **Tristan Buckman, 9281 Stark Avenue, Portland, OR 97216, 971-555-0907**
   - **Eva Chiuso, 8201 SE Woodstock Boulevard, Portland, OR 97206, 971-555-6497**

7. Create a contact group named **Clients** that includes Lilah Devlin, Tristan Buckman, and Eva Chiuso.

8. Edit Tristan's contact card to change the address to **9281 Stark Street**.

9. Create an email message addressed to **Geoff Landry** with **Workshops** as the subject and **Are you teaching any workshops soon?** as the message body. Send the message.

10. Download your messages. If the Workshops message hasn't arrived, wait a few minutes and try again.

11. Reply to the Workshops message with the text **The attached flyer describes the upcoming workshops. Let me know if you are interested in signing up.**

12. Attach the **Workshops** document located in the Outlook ▸ Review folder included with your Data Files to the file, and then send the message.

13. Forward the **Workshops** message to Geoff Landry with the message **Interest is starting to build for your workshops.** Mark the message as High importance. Send the message.

14. Create a new folder named **Clients** that contains Mail and Post Items placed in the Inbox folder.

15. Create a rule to move messages you receive from yourself to the Clients folder. Run the rule now.

16. Download your messages, and verify that the Appointment reminder message and the three Workshops messages were filed in the Clients subfolder.

17. Add a blue color category to the Workshops message, using the default category name.

18. Find the three messages in the Customers folder that contain the word **workshop**.

19. Save each message that was found in HTML format using the subject as the filename (if your server does not support HTML, save the messages in Text Only format).

20. Review the attachment in the RE: Workshops message, and then save the attachment as **Spring Workshops** in the location specified by your instructor.

21. Print the RE: Workshops message and its attachment. (*Hint:* Click the Print Options button to open the Print dialog box, and check the Print attached files check box.)

22. Archive all the messages in the Clients folder using the filename **Clients Archive**. Close the archive folder.

23. Delete each Outlook item you created: the signature, the rule, the subfolder, the four messages in the Sent Items folder, and the four contacts, the contact group, and then empty the Deleted Items folder.

Case Problem 1

Data File needed for this Case Problem: Doris Brandt.vcf

Neighborhood Tool Library   Many homeowners find that they need a specific tool to complete a one-time home repair or do-it-yourself project. Rather than purchase new tools each time, homeowners in Patchogue, New York, can become members of the Neighborhood Tool Library and borrow the tools they need. The Neighborhood Tool Library accepts donations of new and used tools, and has an extensive collection of tools from hammers and drills to saws and ladders to cement mixers and wheelbarrows. Local residents join for free but pay late fees if they don't return the tools they have signed out by the end of one week. You'll use Outlook to send email to some of Neighborhood Tool Library's members. Complete the following steps:

1. Display the Contacts window, and then create the following new contacts, using the Save & New button to create each new contact:
   - Full name **Carrie Holmes**; company name **Ace Home Care**; job title **Nurse**; your email address; an appropriate display as entry; mobile phone **631-555-8712**; home mailing address **17 University Ave.**, **Patchogue, NY 11772**; spouse **Evan Lorenson**
   - Full name **Walt Camden**; home phone **631-555-6741**; home mailing address **841 Carpenter St.**, **Patchogue, NY 11772**
   - Full name **Michael Richards**; job title **Student**; your email address; an appropriate display as entry; mobile phone **631-555-2145**; home mailing address **8 Carpenter St.**, **Patchogue, NY 11772**; nickname **Mike**
   - Full name **Troy Delancey**; company name **Neighborhood Tool Library**; job title **President**; your email address; an appropriate display as entry; business phone **631-555-9797**; business fax **631-555-9701**; pager **631-555-2157**; business mailing address **2949 Broad St.**, **Patchogue, NY 11772**

2. View the contacts in Card view.

3. Edit Walt Camden's contact card to add **631-555-6110** as his mobile phone number.

4. Create a contact group called **Library Members** that includes all members with an email address; do not include Troy Delancey.

5. Send Troy Delancey's contact information as a business card. Select Troy's contact card. On the HOME tab, in the Share group, click the Forward Contact button, and then click As a Business Card. A Message window opens with the contact card included as an attachment. Send the message to the Library Members contact group, use **Troy Delancey** as the subject, and include the message **Attached is Troy's contact information. Please direct any questions or comments about the Library to him.** followed by your name on a separate line.

6. Send a new email message to Troy Delancey with the subject **Doris Brandt's contact** and no message; attach the vCard file **Doris Brandt** located in the Outlook ▶ Case1 folder included with your Data Files.

7. Download your messages, select the Doris Brandt's contact message, view the business card attachment in the Reading Pane, click the Copy button in the Selection group on the ATTACHMENT TOOLS ATTACHMENTS tab, switch to the Contacts folder, press the Ctrl+V keys to create a contact card based on the attachment, and then save and close the new contact card.

8. Create a new folder named **Library** that contains Mail and Post Items placed in the Inbox folder.

9. Search for all messages in the Inbox related to the subject **contact**.

10. Save the two messages you found as HTML files, and then file them in the Library folder.

11. Archive the Library subfolder as **Library Archive**, and then close the archive.

12. Delete the Library folder, the two messages in the Sent Items folder, and the five contacts and the contact group, and then empty the Deleted Items folder.

CHALLENGE

Case Problem 2

There are no Data Files needed for this Case Problem.

Always Soccer Aiden Robert owns Always Soccer, an indoor soccer field that hosts classes, leagues, and tournaments. Aiden has collected a list of customers who have expressed interest in joining a soccer league. He is planning an open scrimmage where these potential league members can meet and create a new team. Complete the following steps:

1. Create contact cards for five potential league members. Include their names, mailing addresses, phone numbers, and email addresses (using your email address for each contact) and appropriate display as entries. Create a contact card for Aiden Robert that includes his name, company name, your email address, and an appropriate display as entry.

2. Create a contact group named **Potential Members** that includes the contact cards of all the potential league members.

3. Edit at least two contacts to include one item of personal information, such as a birthday or spouse.

⊕ **Explore** 4. Create an email message using stationery for the open scrimmage invitation.

5. Address the invitation to the Potential Members contact group. Type an appropriate subject. Enter an appropriate message for the invitation; be sure to include the day, time, and place of the scrimmage. Format the message text appropriately. Send the message.

6. Switch to Contacts, and then change the view to Business Card.

⊕ **Explore** 7. Create a new folder named **Team** that contains Contact Items placed in Contacts, and then move the contact cards you created for this Case Problem into it. (*Hint:* Make sure you change the Folder contains box to Contact Items in the Create New Folder dialog box.)

⊕ **Explore** 8. Export your contact list. Click the FILE tab on the ribbon, click Open & Export in the navigation bar, and then click Import/Export. In the Import and Export Wizard, click Export to a file, and then click the Next button. Click Comma Separated Values as the file type, and then click the Next button. If necessary, expand the Contacts folder, select the Team subfolder, and then click the Next button. Use the Browse button to save the file as **Soccer List** to the location specified by your instructor. Click the Next button, and then click the Finish button. The contact list is exported.

9. Create a new folder named **Soccer** that contains Mail and Post Items placed in the Inbox folder, and then move the invitation email into the subfolder.

10. Save the invitation email as an HTML file in the location specified by your instructor. (You might receive only one message because you used the same email addresses for all your contacts.)

11. Archive the messages in the Soccer subfolder as **Soccer Archive** in the location specified by your instructor.

12. Delete the Soccer subfolder and the messages in the Sent Items folder, delete the Teams subfolder and the contacts, and then empty the Deleted Items folder.

Introduction to Cloud Computing

Sharing Files and Collaborating with Others Online

OBJECTIVES

- Learn about Office 365 and Office on Demand
- Determine if you have a Microsoft account
- Understand the SkyDrive app and the SkyDrive desktop application
- Learn how to upload files to and download files from SkyDrive
- Learn how to share files and folders on SkyDrive
- Learn how to access Office Web Apps to create and edit files

The **cloud** refers to powerful computers called servers connected to the Internet that allow you to store and share files and access data, applications, and resources rather than storing these resources on your own computer. People store files in the cloud so they can access them from any device that has Internet access. Files stored in the cloud are also accessible to others with whom you want to share. **SkyDrive** is free storage provided in the cloud by Microsoft. SkyDrive is like having a personal hard drive in the cloud. You store files on your SkyDrive in folders, similar to the folders on your computer. You can store many types of files on your SkyDrive, including Office documents, photos, and videos. You can also sync files between your SkyDrive and your computer. Software that is stored in the cloud is accessible through a browser from any computer or device that can access the Internet. Examples of software stored in the cloud are **Office Web Apps** (sometimes referred to as **SkyDrive apps** or **Office 365 apps**), which are versions of Microsoft Office applications with basic functionality. Other examples include Google Docs and Zoho.

In this appendix, you will learn about cloud computing. You will also learn how to determine if you have a Microsoft account. Then you will learn about uploading files to and managing files in your storage space in the cloud, and how to use the Office Web Apps and share files with others.

> **Note:** SkyDrive and Office Web Apps are dynamic webpages, and might change over time, including the way they are organized and how commands are performed. The information provided in this appendix, including the information about Office 365 subscriptions, was accurate at the time this book was published.

STARTING DATA FILES

There are no starting data files for this appendix.

Overview of Office 365 and Office on Demand

Office 365 is a subscription to Microsoft cloud services. There are different plans available for home and business users. **Office on Demand** is a benefit of some Office 365 subscription plans. With Office on Demand, you can access Office programs from any computer, even if that computer does not have Office installed. For details on the various subscription plans, go to www.microsoft.com. (Only some of the plans include Office 2013.) Pricing and installation options for each plan differ.

To subscribe to Office 365, you need a Microsoft account. A **Microsoft account** is a free account that you can create that associates your email address and a password with Microsoft cloud services, such as Outlook.com for email, Xbox Live for games, and SkyDrive for file storage.

Determining If You Have a Microsoft Account

In order to access any of Microsoft's cloud services, you must sign in to your Microsoft account. Even if you think you did not sign up for one, you might already have a Microsoft account. You have a Microsoft account if you have one of the following:

- a subscription to Office 365
- a Hotmail account
- a live.com email account
- a SkyDrive account
- an Xbox account
- a Windows phone
- a Windows 8 user account with a user name that is an email address and that requires a password

If you are not sure if your Windows 8 user account is a Microsoft account, you can check on the PC settings screen. To do this, display the Start screen, display the Charms bar, click the Settings charm, and then click Change PC settings to display the PC settings screen. On the left, click Users to display options for managing Windows 8 user accounts. If you are currently signed in to Windows 8 with a local account, your user name appears as shown in Figure A-1.

Figure A-1   **Users screen showing a local account signed in**

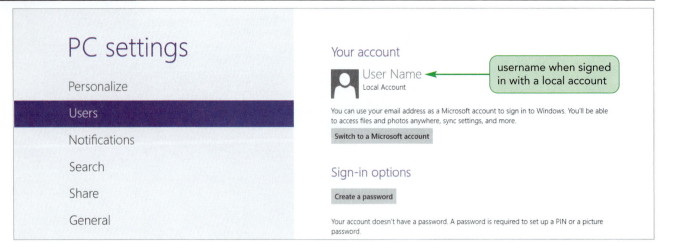

If you are currently signed in to Windows 8 with a Microsoft account, your user name will appear as an email address. See Figure A-2. If your Windows 8 user account is a Microsoft account, every time you use your computer, you are signed into your Microsoft account and you have access to SkyDrive and other Microsoft cloud services.

Figure A-2 | **Users screen showing a Microsoft account signed in**

If you do not have a Microsoft account, you will need to create one in order to access SkyDrive and other Microsoft cloud services. When you attempt to access a Microsoft cloud service—for example, when you try to save to SkyDrive from Backstage view in Microsoft Word, Excel, or PowerPoint, or when you try to use an app such as Mail, People, or Messaging—and you are not signed in to a Microsoft account, a screen will appear asking you to sign in or to create a new Microsoft account. Click the Sign up link, and then follow the instructions to create your account.

INSIGHT

How to Determine if You Are Signed In To Your Microsoft Account in an Office Application

If your Windows 8 account is a Microsoft account, when you start Office 2013 applications, you will be signed in to your Microsoft account. Your user name will appear in the upper-right corner, and you will be able to save to your SkyDrive from Backstage view in Word, Excel, and PowerPoint without signing in again. If your Windows 8 account is not a Microsoft account, you might see a Sign in link in the upper-right corner of the Office applications. You can click this to sign in to your Microsoft account. Or, if you try to save to SkyDrive, you will be prompted to sign in, and then your user name will replace the Sign in link in the upper-right corner.

Understanding the SkyDrive App and the SkyDrive Desktop Application

The **SkyDrive app** comes with Windows 8 and runs like any other app in Windows 8. The SkyDrive tile appears on the Start screen and you click it to run the app. If you are signed in to your Microsoft account, the folders on your SkyDrive appear. If you are not signed in to a Microsoft account, you will be prompted to sign in. Figure A-3 shows one user's SkyDrive in the SkyDrive app. Using the SkyDrive app, you can click a file to open it in the appropriate app or desktop application on your computer. For example, if you click a photo, the Photo app will start and the photo will appear in the Photo app; if you click a Word document, Word will start and the document will open in Word. You can also download files from your SkyDrive to your computer or upload files from your computer to your SkyDrive. You can also create new folders on your SkyDrive or delete folders from it.

| Figure A-3 | Folders and files on SkyDrive in SkyDrive app |

The **SkyDrive desktop application** is available for download from the Windows 8 App Store. (Note that the SkyDrive desktop application is named "Microsoft SkyDrive" in the Windows 8 store.) It runs on the desktop and looks like any other folder in File Explorer. See Figure A-4.

Figure A-4	File Explorer window after installing SkyDrive desktop application

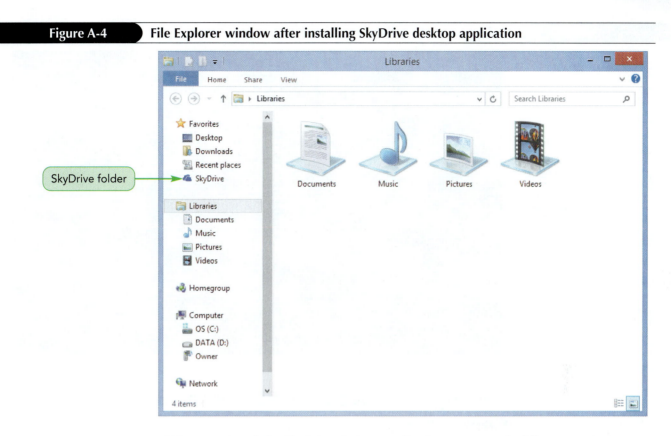

SkyDrive folder

When you install the SkyDrive desktop application, you are asked if you want to sync all the folders on your SkyDrive to your computer. If you do not, you can deselect the folders you do not want to sync. Once the SkyDrive application is installed, any files you place in the SkyDrive folder are automatically uploaded and saved to your SkyDrive. If you edit one of these files on your computer, the edited file is synced with the version on your SkyDrive. If you access the file on your SkyDrive, either through a browser or from another computer, and make changes to it, the changes are automatically synced to the copy on your computer the next time you start your computer.

When you search for SkyDrive from the Start screen, both the SkyDrive app and the SkyDrive desktop application are named "SkyDrive," but the icons are different. Refer to Figure A-5 to see the difference.

Figure A-5   **SkyDrive app and desktop application on the Apps screen**

SkyDrive app

SkyDrive desktop application

Moving Files Between SkyDrive and Your Computer

Once you are signed in to your Microsoft account, you can store files on your SkyDrive. You can do this from within Word, Excel, or PowerPoint, you can use the SkyDrive app or the SkyDrive desktop application, or you can use your browser to go to www.skydrive.com, log in, and then use the commands on the website. Each file that you upload can be a maximum size of 300 GB if you upload it using a browser or 2 GB if you upload it using the SkyDrive desktop application or SkyDrive app.

> **TIP**
> You cannot save to SkyDrive from Backstage view in Access.

To upload a file from within Word, Excel, or PowerPoint, display the file in the application window, click the FILE tab to display Backstage view, and then click Save As in the navigation bar. On the Save As screen, click SkyDrive. (Note that your Microsoft account user name will appear before SkyDrive; for example, "John Smith's Skydrive.") Then click the Browse button to open the Save As dialog box with the current location as your SkyDrive. Figure A-6 shows the Save As dialog box open on the Save As screen in Backstage view in Word. The folders on the user's SkyDrive are listed in the dialog box. Double-click a folder to make it the current folder, and then save the file to this folder on your SkyDrive in the same manner that you save files to a folder on your computer.

Figure A-6   **Save As dialog box open on the Save As screen in Word's Backstage view**

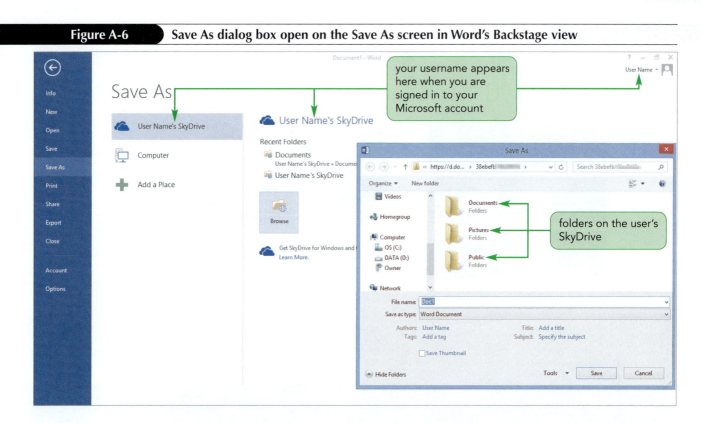

To upload files using the SkyDrive app, start the app from the Start screen. Each of the tiles on the screen represents a folder. Click the folder to which you want to upload the file to open that folder, or right-click anywhere on the screen to display the Apps bar at the bottom of the screen, as shown in Figure A-7 and then use the New Folder button to create a new folder. To upload a file, display the Apps bar, and then click the Upload button. This displays the Files screen, which lists all the files in the current folder (usually the Documents folder). You can select a file in this folder or switch to another folder. After you click a file to select it, click the Add to SkyDrive button at the bottom of the screen. To download files, right-click the file on SkyDrive to select it, and then click the Download button on the Apps bar.

Figure A-7   **Apps bar in SkyDrive app**

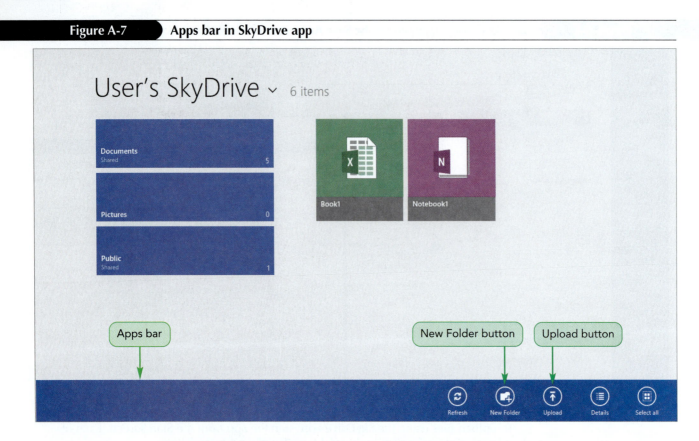

To upload a file using the SkyDrive desktop application, you either save a file to the SkyDrive folder from within an application, or copy or move a file from another folder to the SkyDrive folder. The file will be automatically synced to your SkyDrive. Likewise, to download a file, simply copy it from the SkyDrive folder to any other folder on your computer.

You can also move files between your SkyDrive and your computer by opening a browser window, going to www.skydrive.com, and signing in to your Microsoft account from that webpage. If your SkyDrive is not the current page, click SkyDrive at the top. Figure A-8 shows a typical SkyDrive page. As in the SkyDrive app, each of the tiles in your SkyDrive window represents a folder. To open a folder, click the folder tile. Then you can use the Upload button at the top of the screen to open the Choose File to Upload dialog box, which is very similar to the Save As dialog box. To download a file, point to it to display a check box in the upper-right corner, and then click the check box to display additional commands at the top of the browser including the Download command.

Figure A-8	SkyDrive in Internet Explorer browser

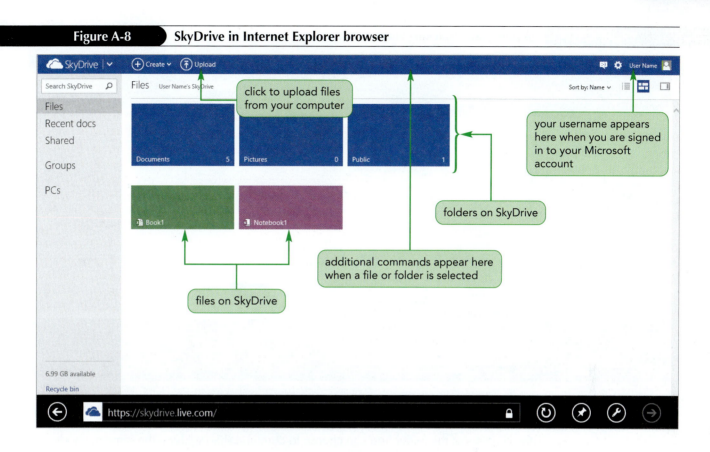

Sharing Files and Folders on Your SkyDrive

One of the great advantages of working with SkyDrive is that you can share your files with others. Suppose, for example, that you want a colleague to review and edit a presentation you created in PowerPoint. You can upload the PowerPoint file to SkyDrive, and then give your colleague access to the file.

You can choose to share individual files or folders on your SkyDrive. Keep in mind that if you share folders, you are granting permission to whomever you are sharing access to all of the files in that folder.

To share files and folders on your SkyDrive, you need to access your SkyDrive from a browser. To share a single file, point to it to display a check box in the upper-right corner of the file tile, and then click the check box to select the file. When you do this, additional commands appear at the top of the browser screen or window. Click the Sharing command to display a screen similar to the one shown in Figure A-9. You can then send an email to someone, which will include a direct link to the item you are sharing. You can also choose to post the link to one of the social media sites listed, or you can copy the link and paste it anywhere you choose. Finally, you can choose whether the people with whom you are sharing can edit the files or only read them.

TIP

You can also share a file from within the corresponding Office Web App. To do this, click the FILE tab, and then click Share in the navigation pane.

| Figure A-9 | SkyDrive after clicking Share command |

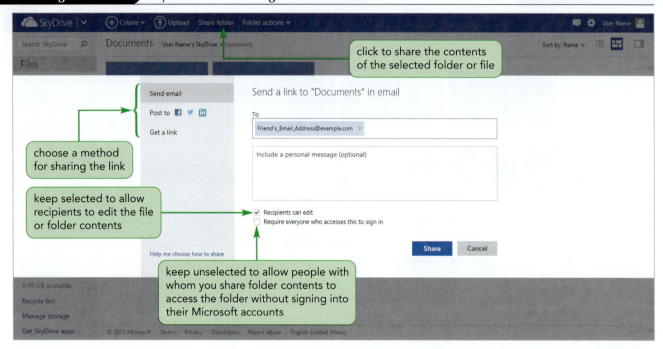

To share a folder, click the folder to open it, and then click the Sharing command at the top of the browser. A warning appears reminding you that you will be sharing all of the contents of the folder. You can choose to continue sharing using the same methods you use to share a file or cancel the sharing request. Note that files stored in the Public folder are viewable by anyone who has the link to them.

Because people with whom you share a file or folder click a direct link to access the file or folder, they do not need to sign in to their Microsoft accounts in order to view or download the files stored in it (unless you require it by selecting that option when you share the file or folder). However, if they want to use the Office Web Apps to edit those files, they do need to sign in to a Microsoft account.

INSIGHT

Viewing Photos and Videos on SkyDrive

You can use SkyDrive as a photo viewer and video player. When you click a photo or a video stored in a folder on SkyDrive, the screen changes to show the photo or the video much larger on the screen. At the bottom, thumbnails of the other photos and videos in the folder appear. You can click each thumbnail to display that photo or video on the screen, or move the pointer to display scroll arrows on the left or right edges of the screen, and then click these to scroll through the photos and videos in the folder.

Using Office Web Apps

When you sign in to your SkyDrive using a browser, you also have access to Office Web Apps. The programs included in Office Web Apps are limited versions of Microsoft Word, Excel, PowerPoint, and **OneNote** (an electronic notebook program). You can use the Office Web Apps from any computer that is connected to the Internet, even if Microsoft Office is not installed on that computer. Although the interface for each Office Web App is similar to the interface of the full-featured program on your computer, only a limited number of commands are available for editing documents using the Office Web App. Figure A-10 shows the Word Web App.

Figure A-10   **Word Web App**

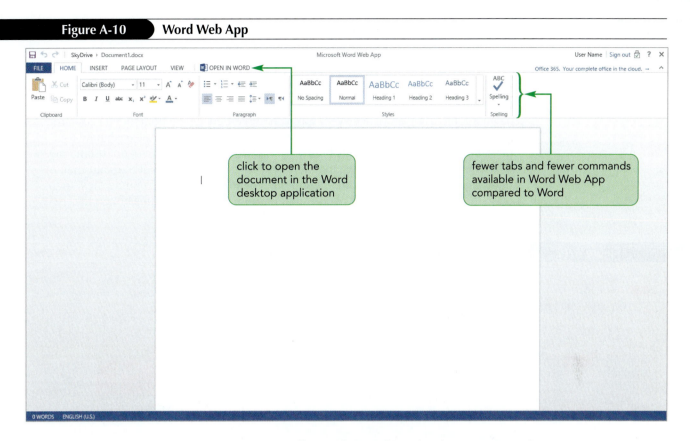

You cannot access Office Web Apps from the SkyDrive App. When you access SkyDrive from the browser, you can choose to open the file in the corresponding Web App, or the corresponding Office desktop application installed on your computer.

To create new files on SkyDrive using an Office Web App, sign in to your SkyDrive in a browser, and then click the Create button at the top of the browser. See Figure A-11. A menu opens allowing you to create a new folder, Word document, Excel workbook, PowerPoint presentation, OneNote notebook, or an Excel survey (an Excel template that allows you to create a survey and collect the responses in an Excel workbook). Select the Office Web App you want to use to open a new file in Edit mode in that Web App.

Figure A-11   **Create button menu listing Office Web Apps**

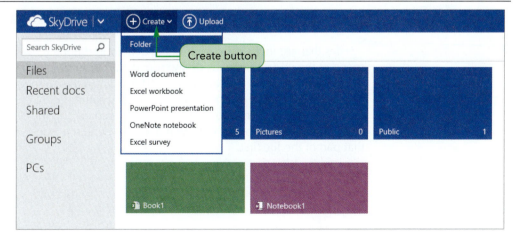

When you work in an Office Web app, you do not need to save your changes. All changes are saved automatically.

Coauthoring with the Office Web Apps

The ability to work on files at the same time as others is called **coauthoring**. When you coauthor a file using an Office Web App, you and others with whom the file is shared open the file in the appropriate Web App on your own computers. As each new user opens the file, a message appears briefly telling you the Microsoft account username of the person who is now editing the file with you. On the left end of the status bar, a button appears indicating that the file is being coauthored, and the number next to the button indicates the number of people coauthoring. You can click this button to see a list of their Microsoft account usernames. See Figure A-12.

| Figure A-12 | File open in PowerPoint Web App with two people editing it |

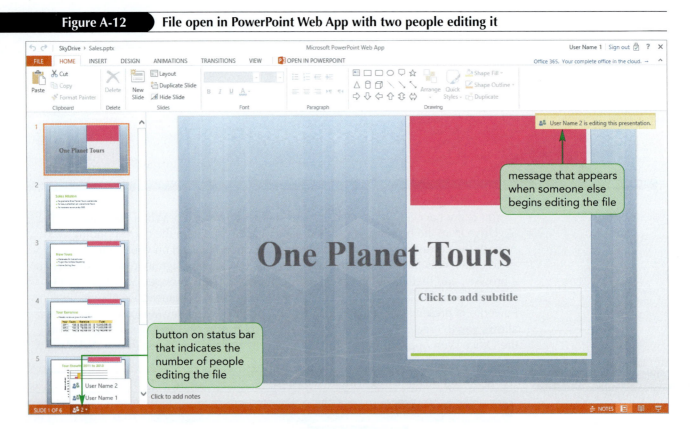

Files that are in the process of being coauthored update every few minutes. The speed of the update depends on the speed of your Internet connection and the size of the file. There can be a delay of up to 10 minutes if the connection is very slow or the files are very large. If two people try to edit the same part of the file at the same time, the edits of the person who started first are accepted and the other user sees a message telling them that his or her edits will not be accepted because another user was editing that part of the file first.

GLOSSARY/INDEX

P

page break
    automatic, EX 97
    inserting, EX 116–117
    manual, EX 96
    Page Break Preview, EX 114–115
    removing, EX 116, EX 117

Page Break Preview The Excel view that shows the location of page breaks in the printed sheet. EX 31, EX 97, EX 114–115

PAGE LAYOUT tab, EX 30, EX 96
    adjusting margin, WD 23–25
    Clear All Formatting button, WD 30
    Themes button, EX 108

Page Layout view The Excel view that shows how the sheet will appear when printed. EX 31

page number, inserting and modifying, WD 98–100

page number field An instruction that tells Word to insert a page number on each page of a document, no matter how many pages you eventually add to the document. WD 98

page orientation, WD 37–38
    worksheets, EX 53

Page Setup dialog box, EX 118, EX 120, EX 122, WD 24–25

pane, Windows Explorer, FM 8

paragraph Anything preceding a nonprinting paragraph mark; can be a group of words that is many lines long, a single word, or even a blank line, in which case you *see* a paragraph mark alone on a single line. WD 18
    indenting, WD 96–98
    selecting multiple paragraphs, WD 22
    spacing between paragraphs, WD 21

paragraph border An outline around one or more paragraphs in a document. WD 45–47

paragraph formatting Formatting that affects an entire paragraph, including paragraph and line spacing. WD 31, WD 85

paragraph mark (¶) Nonprinting character that indicates the end of a paragraph. WD 2, WD 17

paragraph spacing The space, measured in points, that appears directly above and below a paragraph. WD 18–20

paragraph-level formatting. *See* paragraph formatting

password A confidential series of characters that you must enter before you can work with Windows. WIN 7

password A private code that you enter to access your account. OUT 6

Paste Options button, EX 103–104

Paste Options menu, PPT 22–23

Paste Special, EX 104

pasting Placing a copy of the contents of the Clipboard into the document at the insertion point. PPT 22, WD 75
    formulas, EX 35–36

PDF document A file in the Portable Document Format that usually includes text and graphics. WIN 14

pencil symbol The symbol that appears in a row selector to indicate that the record is being edited. AC 17

People The button used to access Contacts. OUT 2

People Pane, OUT 3

Percent style The number format for percentages that adds the % symbol after the number and no decimal places. EX 68

percentage, formatting, EX 85–86

photo, PPT 38–44
    compression options, modifying, PPT 42–44
    cropping, PPT 40–42
    keeping uncompressed, PPT 44
    removing cropped areas, PPT 43
    stored on computer or network, inserting, PPT 39–40
    viewing on SkyDrive, APP A10

picture A photo or other type of image that you insert into a document. WD 49–52
    inline, WD 52
    resizing and moving, PPT 45–47

Picture button, PPT 39

picture diagram, PPT 24

picture style A collection of formatting options-such as a frame, a rounded shape, and a shadow-that changes a picture's overall appearance. WD 51

PICTURE TOOLS FORMAT tab
    Compress Pictures button, PPT 43–44
    Size group, PPT 45

Pictures button A button in the Illustrations group on the INSERT tab used to insert a photo or other picture in a document. WD 30

pinching, WIN 6

pinning To always display a button, icon, or tile in a certain location, such as the Start screen or taskbar. WIN 3

pixel Small dot of color that makes up a graphic displayed on a computer screen. EX 25

placeholder A region of a slide reserved for inserting text or graphics. PPT 2

planning
    presentations, PPT 4
    workbooks, EX 13–14

planning analysis sheet A series of questions that help you think about a workbook's purpose and how to achieve your desired results. EX 13

plus sign (+) (Access) In a datasheet, a symbol indicating that a record has related records in another table. AC 123–124

plus sign (+) (Excel), addition operator, EX 32

point A unit of measurement for measuring fonts and graphics; a point is equal to 1/72 of an inch. EX 29, PPT 14, WD 18

pointer A small object, such as an arrow, that moves on the screen when you move your mouse. PPT 32, WIN 5

pointing To move the mouse pointer over an object on the screen using a pointing device. WIN 5

pointing device A device, such as a mouse or trackball, that is connected to a computer and helps you interact with objects by controlling the pointer. WIN 4–5

Popular searches section, Access Help, AC 24

Portable Document Format file. *See* PDF

portrait orientation The orientation where the page is taller than it is wide. EX 53, WD 38

pound sign (#)
    error values, EX 150
    numbers exceeding cell size, EX 24, EX 84

PowerPoint. *See* Microsoft PowerPoint 2013

presentation A talk (lecture) or prepared file in which the person speaking or the person who prepared the file-the presenter-wants to communicate with an audience to explain new concepts or ideas, sell a product or service, entertain, train the audience in a new skill or technique, or any of a wide variety of other topics. PPT 4
    closing, PPT 30–31
    displaying blank slides, PPT 55
    editing, PPT 10–11
    moving slides in, PPT 28–29
    opening, PPT 34
    planning, PPT 4
    printing, PPT 56–60
    saving, PPT 9–10, PPT 11
    saving with new name, PPT 34–35
    slides. *See* slide

presentation media Visual and audio aids that can be used to support key points and engage the audience's attention. PPT 4

Presenter view A view in PowerPoint that allows you to view your slides with speaker notes on one monitor, while the audience sees only the slides in ordinary Slide Show view on another monitor or screen. PPT 33, PPT 54–55

TASK REFERENCE

TASK	PAGE #	RECOMMENDED METHOD
Absolute reference, create	EX 154	Type a $ before both the row and column references
Access, start	AC 7	Click the Access 2013 tile on the Windows Start screen
Action, reverse last in WordPad	WIN 21	Click ▦ on the Quick Access Toolbar
Action, undo or redo	EX 19	Click ↶ or ↷ on the Quick Access Toolbar
Aggregate functions, use in a datasheet	AC 162	Open the table or query in Datasheet view, in Records group on HOME tab click Totals button, click Total field row, click function
Aggregate functions, use in a query	AC 163	Display the query in Design view, click the Totals button in the Show/Hide group on the DESIGN tab
Application, close	WIN 27	Press Alt+F4
Application, start	WIN 13	*See Reference box: Starting an Application*
Apps screen, display	WIN 15	Right-click a blank area on the Start screen, click All apps
Archive folder, close	OUT 61	In the Folder Pane, right-click the Archives folder, click Close "Archives"
Arrangement, switch	OUT 55	Click the More button in the Arrangement group on the View tab, click an arrangement
Attachment, add to email	OUT 39	In the Message window, click the Attach File button in the Include group on the Message tab, double-click the file to insert
Attachment, save	OUT 41	In the Reading Pane, click the attachment file icon, click the Save As button in Actions group on Attachments tab, select a save location, enter a filename, click Save
Attachment, view in Reading Pane	OUT 42	In the Reading Pane, click the attachment file icon
AutoCorrect, change	PPT 10	Click 🖉 ▾, click command on menu
AutoSum feature, enter function with	EX 37	Click a cell, click Σ AutoSum ▾ in the Editing group on the HOME tab, click a function, verify the range, press Enter
Bibliography, insert	WD 109	Create citations in the document, click the desired location for the bibliography, click Bibliography button in Citations & Bibliography group on REFERENCES tab, click a bibliography style
Bold text, enter in WordPad	WIN 21	Click **B** in the Font group on the Home tab
Border, add to cells	EX 50	Select a range, click ▦ ▾ in the Font group on the HOME tab, click a border
Border, insert around paragraph	WD 45	Click in a paragraph, click ▦ ▾ in the Paragraph group on the HOME tab, click a border style
Bulleted or numbered item, demote	PPT 14, 16	Click bullet or number, click ⇥
Bulleted or numbered item, promote	PPT 15, 16	Click bullet or number, click ⇤
Bullets, add to paragraph	WD 71	Select paragraphs, click ⁝≡ in the Paragraph group on the HOME tab
Calculated field, add to a query	AC 157	*See Reference box: Using Expression Builder*
Cell, change fill color	EX 76	Click 🖌 ▾ in the Font group on the HOME tab, click a color
Cell, clear contents of	EX 58	Select a cell, press Delete

TASK	PAGE #	RECOMMENDED METHOD
Cell, delete	EX 46	Select a cell, range, column, or row; click Delete button in the Cells group on the HOME tab
Cell, edit	EX 19	Double-click a cell, enter changes
Cell, go to	EX 10	Click Find & Select button in the Editing group on the HOME tab, click Go To
Cell contents, align within a cell	EX 87	Click ▤, ▤, or ▤ in the Alignment group on the HOME tab
Cell contents, change indent of	EX 88	Click ▤ or ▤ in the Alignment group on the HOME tab
Cell contents, rotate	EX 91	Click ▨ ▾ in the Alignment group on the HOME tab, click angle
Cells, merge and center	EX 90	Select adjacent cells, click ▤ in the Alignment group on the HOME tab
Charms bar, display	WIN 11	Point to the upper-right or lower-right corner of screen
Citations, create and edit	WD 103	See Reference box: Creating Citations
Clipboard task pane, open	WD 76	In Clipboard group on HOME tab, click the Dialog Box Launcher
Column, change width	EX 25	Drag the right border of the column heading left or right
Column, resize width in a datasheet	AC 18	Double-click ✛ on the right border of the column heading
Column, select	EX 26	Click the column heading
Comments, display and insert	WD 67	See Reference box: Working with Comments
Compressed folder, extract all files and folders from	FM 27	Click the compressed folder, click the Compressed Folder Tools Extract tab, click the Extract all button
Compressed folder, open	FM 27	Double-click the compressed folder
Conditional format, apply	EX 108	See Reference box: Highlighting a Cell with a Conditional Format
Contact, create	OUT 20	See Reference box: Creating a Contact
Contact, edit	OUT 28	In the Contacts window, double-click a contact card, edit as needed, save and close the contact card
Contact group, create	OUT 30	See Reference box: Creating a Contact Group
Contacts view, change	OUT 27	On the HOME tab, in the Current View group, click a view
Data Type gallery, add fields to a table with	AC 86	Click the FIELDS tab, click More Fields in the Add & Delete group, click the field or Quick Start selection to add
Database, compact and repair	AC 42	See Reference box: Compacting and Repairing a Database
Database, create a blank	AC 7	Start Access, click Blank desktop database, type the database name, select the drive and folder, click OK, click Create
Database, open	AC 26	See Reference box: Opening a Database
Datasheet view for tables, switch to	AC 75	In the Views group on the DESIGN tab, click the View button
Date, enter into a cell	EX 23	Click a cell, type the date, press Enter or Tab
Date, insert the current	EX 167	Enter TODAY() or NOW() function in cell
Deleted Items folder, empty	OUT 62	Click the File tab, click Info, click the Cleanup Tools button, click Empty Deleted Items Folder, click Yes
Design view, switch to	AC 73	In the Views group on the FIELDS tab, click the View button
Desktop application, close inactive	WIN 26	Right-click the application's button on taskbar, click Close window
Desktop application, switch to another open	WIN 23	Click the application's button on taskbar

TASK	PAGE #	RECOMMENDED METHOD
Document, print	WD 25	Click FILE tab, click Print, click Print button
Documents library, open	FM 10	In File Explorer, click ▷ next to Libraries, click ▷ next to Documents
Email account, set up new	OUT 7	Click the File tab, click Info, click the Add Account button, follow the steps to set up an account
Email message, create	OUT 12	*See* Reference box: Creating and Sending an Email Message
Email message, forward	OUT 37	Select a message in the Inbox, click the Forward button in the Respond group on the HOME tab, enter recipient email address(es), type a message, click the Send button
Email message, print	OUT 38	Select a message in the Inbox, click the FILE tab, click Print, verify printer, select print style, click the Print button
Email message, reply or reply all	OUT 36	Select a message in the Inbox, click the Reply or Reply All button in the Respond group on the HOME tab, type a reply message, click the Send button
Email message, set importance	OUT 14	In the Message window, on the MESSAGE tab, in the Tags group, click the appropriate button
Email messages, receive	OUT 34	Click the Send/Receive All Folders button on the Quick Access toolbar
Envelope, create and save in current document	WD 28	Click the MAILINGS tab, click the Envelopes button in the Create group, enter return address, if necessary, enter delivery address, click Add to Document
Excel worksheet, import data from	AC 81	Click the EXTERNAL DATA tab, click Excel in the Import & Link group, complete the import dialog boxes
Excel, start	EX 4	Click the Excel 2013 title on the Start screen
Field, add to a table	AC 69	*See* Reference box: Adding a Field Between Two Existing Fields
Field, define in a table	AC 59	*See* Reference box: Defining a Field in Design View
Field, delete from a table	AC 87	*See* Reference box: Deleting a Field from a Table Structure
Field, move to a new location in a table	AC 69	Display the table in Design view, click the field's row selector, drag the field with the pointer
Field property change, update	AC 91	Click 🖋, select the option for updating the field property
File Explorer, open	FM 10	Click 🗀 on the taskbar
File Explorer, return to a previous location	FM 14	Click ⬅
File list, sort	FM 14	Click the column heading button
File, copy	FM 24	Right-click the file, click Copy, right-click destination, click Paste
File, delete	FM 25	Right-click the file, click Delete
File, move	FM 21	Drag the file to the folder
File, open from File Explorer	FM 15	Right-click the file, point to Open with, click an application
File, rename	FM 26	Right-click the file, click Rename, type the new filename, press Enter
File, save with new name in WordPad	FM 18	Click the File tab, click Save as, enter the filename, click Save
Files and folders, compress	FM 27	Select the files to compress, click the Share tab, click the Zip button in the Send group

TASK	PAGE #	RECOMMENDED METHOD
Files, select multiple	FM 24	Press and hold the Ctrl key and click the files
Files, view in Large Icons view	FM 13	Click the View tab, click in the Layout group
Fill handle, use	EX 162	*See Reference box: Copying Formulas and Formats with AutoFill*
Filter By Selection, activate	AC 136	*See Reference box: Using Filter By Selection*
Find and replace, text or format	EX 104	Click Find & Select in the Editing group on the HOME tab, click Replace
Flag, add reminder to message in Inbox	OUT 43	Select a message in the Inbox, click the Follow Up button in the Tags group on the HOME tab, click Add Reminder, select or type Flag to text, select a due date, click OK
Flash Fill, apply	EX 49	Type a few entries in a column to establish a pattern, Flash Fill adds the remaining entries
Folder, create	FM 19	Click the New folder button in the New group on the Home tab
Folder, create	OUT 45	Click the New Folder button in the New group on the Folder tab, type the folder name, select where to place the folder, click OK
Folder, delete	OUT 62	Click a folder in the Folder Pane, click the Delete Folder button in the Actions group on the Folder tab, click Yes
Folder List, display	OUT 6	In the Folder Pane, click , click Folders
Folder Pane, use	OUT 5	Click a button in the Folder Pane
Font, change color	EX 73	Click in the Font group on the HOME tab, click a color
Font, change size	EX 71	Click the Font Size arrow in the Font group on the HOME tab, click a point size
Font, change style	EX 71	Click , , or in the Font group on the HOME tab
Font, change typeface	EX 71	Click the Font arrow in the Font group on the HOME tab, click a font
Format Painter, use	PPT 21	Select formatted text or object, click HOME tab, in Clipboard group click Format Painter, select object to format
Formula, enter	EX 32	Click the cell, type = and then a formula, press Enter or Tab
Formulas, display in a worksheet	EX 56	Press Ctrl+`
Function, insert	EX 145	Click a function category in the Function Library group on the FORMULAS tab, click a function, enter arguments, click OK
Goal seek, perform	EX 180	*See Reference box: Performing What-if Analysis and Goal Seek*
Graphic object, resize	WD 50	Click graphic object, click the FORMAT tab, change the height and width settings in the Size group
Help, search for topic	WIN 29	On the Help home page, click in the Search box, type word or phrase, press Enter
Help, start	WIN 27	On the Start screen, type help, click Help and Support on the Apps screen
Help, use Browse help list	WIN 29	On the Help home page, click Browse help
Help, view Get started topics	WIN 28	On the Help home page, click Get started link
Hyperlink, remove	WD 12	Right-click hyperlink, click Remove Hyperlink
Item(s), delete	OUT 62	Select item(s), click the Delete button in the Delete group on the HOME tab, click Yes if needed
Layout, change	PPT 13	Click HOME tab, in Slides group click Layout button, click layout

TASK	PAGE #	RECOMMENDED METHOD
Line spacing, change	WD 18	Select text, click ⬚ in the Paragraph group on HOME tab, click a spacing option
Margins, change	WD 23	Click PAGE LAYOUT tab, click the Margins button in the Page Setup group on HOME tab, click a margins option
Margins, set	EX 121	Click the Margins button in the Page Setup group on the PAGE LAYOUT tab, select a margin size
Message format, choose	OUT 9	Click the File tab, click Options, click Mail, select HTML in the Compose messages in this format list, click OK
Message(s), move into folder	OUT 46	Select message(s) in the Inbox, click the Move button in Move group on the HOME tab, click a destination folder
Messages, save	OUT 58	Select a message in the Inbox, click the File tab, click Save As, select a folder, type a filename if needed, select a file format, click Save
Messages, search for	OUT 51	See Reference box: Searching for Messages
Messages, sort	OUT 55	Click a column heading above the message list in a mail folder
Microsoft Access Help, search	AC 41	Click ⬚ on the title bar, enter the search text in the search box, press Enter
Mixed reference, create	EX 154	Type $ before either the row or column reference
My Documents folder, open	FM 10	In File Explorer, click ⬚ next to Libraries, click ⬚ next to Documents, click My Documents
Number format, apply	EX 82	Click ⬚, ⬚, ⬚, or the Number Format arrow in the Number group on the HOME tab
Number, enter as text	EX 21	Type ' and then type the number
Numbered list, create	PPT 16	Select list, click HOME tab, in Paragraph group click ⬚
Numbering, add to paragraphs	WD 72	Select paragraphs, click ⬚ in the Paragraph group on HOME tab
Object, delete	PPT 48	Click object, press Delete
Object, move	PPT 45	Click object, drag to new position with ⬚
Object, open	AC 22	Double-click the object in the Navigation Pane
Object, save	AC 20	Click ⬚, type the object name, click OK
Page break, insert	WD 108	Click where you want to insert a page break, click INSERT tab, click the Page Break button in the Pages group
Page break, insert or remove	EX 116	See Reference box: Inserting and Removing Page Breaks
Page number, insert	WD 98	Click INSERT tab, click the Page Number button in the Header & Footer group, select options from menu
Page orientation, change	WD 38	Click PAGE LAYOUT tab, click the Orientation button in the Page Setup group, click an orientation
Paragraph spacing, add or remove default	WD 18	Click paragraph, click ⬚ in the Paragraph group on HOME tab, click options to add or remove space before or after paragraphs
Paragraph spacing, select specific setting	WD 48	Click paragraph, click PAGE LAYOUT tab, adjust settings in the Spacing Before and After boxes in Paragraph group
Photo compression options, change	PPT 43	See Reference box: Modifying Photo Compression Settings and Removing Cropped Areas

TASK	PAGE #	RECOMMENDED METHOD
Picture style, apply	WD 51	Click a picture, click FORMAT tab, click the More button in the Picture Styles group, click a style
Picture, crop	PPT 40	Click picture, click PICTURE TOOLS FORMAT tab, in Size group, click Crop, drag Crop handles, click Crop
Picture, insert	WD 49	Click INSERT tab, click Pictures button in the Illustrations group, select picture file, click Insert button
Picture, insert from your computer	PPT 39	In content placeholder click , navigate to picture file location, click picture file, click Insert
Picture, resize	PPT 46	Click object, drag a corner sizing handle
PowerPoint, exit	PPT 60	Click
Presentation, close	PPT 30	Click FILE tab, click Close
Presentation, open	PPT 34	Click FILE tab, click Open, click Computer, click Browse, navigate to location of file, click file, click Open
Presentation, print	PPT 57	Click FILE tab, click Print, select options, click Print
Presentation, save changes	PPT 11	On Quick Access Toolbar, click
Presentation, save for the first time	PPT 9	On Quick Access Toolbar, click , on Save As screen click Computer, type filename, navigate to location, click Save
Presentation, save with a new name	PPT 34	Click FILE tab, click Save As, on Save As screen click Computer, type filename, navigate to location, click Save
Primary key, specify	AC 67	*See* Reference box: Specifying a Primary Key in Design View
Print area, set	EX 115	Select range, click the Print Area button in the Page Setup group on PAGE LAYOUT tab, click Set Print Area
Print dialog box, open in WordPad	WIN 21	Click the File tab, click Print
Print titles, add	EX 117	Click the Print Titles button in the Page Setup group on the PAGE LAYOUT tab, click Rows to repeat at top, select a range, click OK
Property sheet, open	AC 159	Make the object current in Design view, click the Property Sheet button in the Show/Hide group on the DESIGN tab
Query, define	AC 125	Click the CREATE tab, click the Query Design button in the Queries group
Query, run	AC 127	Double-click the query in the Navigation Pane or, in the Results group on the DESIGN tab, click the Run button
Query results, sort	AC 133	*See* Reference box: Sorting a Query Datasheet
Quick Start selection, add	AC 86	Click the FIELDS tab, click More Fields in the Add & Delete group, click the Quick Start selection
Range, select adjacent	EX 11	Click a cell, drag the pointer from the selected cell to the cell in the lower-right corner of the range
Range, select nonadjacent	EX 12	Select a cell or an adjacent range, press the Ctrl key as you select additional cells or adjacent ranges
Record, add new	AC 20	In the Records group on the HOME tab, click the New button
Record, delete	AC 122	*See* Reference box: Deleting a Record
Record, move to first	AC 30	Click
Record, move to last	AC 30	Click
Record, move to next	AC 30	Click

TASK	PAGE #	RECOMMENDED METHOD
Record, move to previous	AC 30	Click ◀
Records, redisplay all after filter	AC 138	In Sort & Filter group on HOME tab, click the Toggle Filter button
Recycle Bin, open	WIN 22	Double-click the Recycle Bin icon on desktop
Relative reference, create	EX 150	Type the cell reference as it appears in the worksheet
Report, print	AC 39	*See Reference box: Printing a Report*
Ribbon, expand in File Explorer	FM 13	Click ⌄
Row, change height	EX 29	Drag the bottom border of the row heading up or down
Row, select	EX 26	Click the row heading
Rows, repeat in printout	EX 118	Click the Print Titles button in the Page Setup group on the PAGE LAYOUT tab, click Rows to repeat at top, select range, click OK
Rule, create	OUT 49	Click the Rules button in the Move group on the HOME tab, click Create Rule, set rule conditions, set rule actions, click OK
Rule, delete	OUT 62	Click the Rules button in the Move group on the HOME tab, click Manage Rules & Alerts, select a rule, click the Delete button, click Yes, click OK
Search Folder, add new	OUT 53	Click the New Search Folder button in the New group on the Folder tab, select a search folder, click OK
Series, create with AutoFill	EX 162	Enter the first few entries in a series, drag the fill handle over the adjacent range
Settings menu, open	WIN 11	Display the Charms bar, click Settings
Shading, apply to paragraph	WD 45	Click in paragraph, click ⬛⌄ in Paragraph group on HOME tab, click color
Shortcut menu, open	WIN 15	Right-click the object
Signature, create new	OUT 10	Click the FILE tab, click Options, click Mail, click the Signatures button, click the New button, type a name, click OK, type and format the signature text, click OK, click OK
Signature, delete	OUT 62	Click the File tab, click Options, click Mail, click the Signatures button, click your signature, click the Delete button, click Yes, click OK, click OK
Signature, select for email account	OUT 11	Click the FILE tab, click Options, click Mail, click Signatures button, select an email account, select a signature in for new messages and for replies/forwards, click OK, click OK
Slide show, run from current slide	PPT 53	On the status bar, click 🖳
Slide show, run from Slide 1	PPT 53	On the Quick Access Toolbar, click 🖳
Slide show, run in Presenter view	PPT 54	In Slide Show view, click ⬤, click Show Presenter View
Slide show, run in Reading view	PPT 56	On status bar, click 📖
Slide, add	PPT 12	Click HOME tab, in Slides group click New Slide button arrow, click layout
Slide, delete	PPT 29	Right-click slide thumbnail, click Delete Slide
Slide, duplicate	PPT 28	Click slide thumbnail, click HOME tab, in Slides group click New Slide button arrow, click Duplicate Selected Slides
Slide, move	PPT 28	Drag slide thumbnail to new location

TASK	PAGE #	RECOMMENDED METHOD
SmartArt diagram, convert from list	PPT 24	*See Reference box:* Converting a Bulleted List into a SmartArt Diagram
Sort, specify ascending in datasheet	AC 132	Click a column heading arrow, click Sort A to Z
Sort, specify descending in datasheet	AC 132	Click a column heading arrow, click Sort Z to A
Speaker notes, add	PPT 49	On status bar click NOTES, click in Notes pane, type note
Spelling and grammar, correct for entire document	WD 36	Click the REVIEW tab, click the Spelling & Grammar button in the Proofing group
Spelling, check entire presentation	PPT 51	Click REVIEW tab, in Proofing group click Spelling
Spelling, correct flagged word	PPT 51	Right-click flagged word, click correct spelling
Start PowerPoint	PPT 5	On Windows Start screen, click the PowerPoint 2013 tile
Start screen, scroll	WIN 9	Move the pointer, drag the scroll bar
Start screen, zoom	WIN 2	Move the pointer, click ▬ on the Start screen
Style, apply	WD 85	Select text, click a style in the Styles group on HOME tab or click ⬇ in the Styles group on HOME tab and click a style
Switch List, display	WIN 24	Point to the upper-left corner of the screen, move the pointer down along left edge of the screen
Table, create in Datasheet view	AC 11	*See Reference box:* Creating a Table in Datasheet View
Table, open in a database	AC 22	Double-click the table in the Navigation Pane
Table, save in a database	AC 19	*See Reference box:* Saving a Table
Text Effects, apply	WD 42	Select text, click [A ▾] in the Font group on HOME tab, click a text effect
Text file, import data from	AC 96	Click the EXTERNAL DATA tab, click Text File in the Import & Link group, complete the import dialog boxes
Text, change format of	PPT 19	Select text, click HOME tab, in Font group click appropriate button to apply formatting
Text, enter into a cell	EX 18	Click cell, type entry, press Enter or Tab
Text, enter multiple lines in a cell	EX 28	Type the first line of the entry, press Alt+Enter, type the next line
Text, move or copy	PPT 22	Select text, click HOME tab, in Clipboard group click Cut or Copy, click at new location, in Clipboard group click Paste
Text, wrap within a cell	EX 28	Select the cell, click [⧉] in the Alignment group on the HOME tab
Theme and theme variant, change	PPT 36	Click DESIGN tab, in Themes group click theme
Theme, change for workbook	EX 107	Click the Themes button in the Themes group on the PAGE LAYOUT tab, click a theme
Theme, select new	WD 89	Click DESIGN tab, click Themes button in the Document Formatting group, click a theme
Touch Mode, switch to	PPT 6	On Quick Access Toolbar, click [⬇], click Touch/Mouse mode if not selected, click [👆], click Touch
Touch mode, turn on	WD 5	Click [⬇] on the Quick Access toolbar, click Touch/Mouse Mode, click Touch
Unnumbered list, create	PPT 17	Select list or placeholder, click HOME tab, in Paragraph group click [▤] or [▤] to deselect it
View, change in File Explorer	FM 12	*See Reference box:* Changing the View in File Explorer
Window, close	WIN 26	Click [✕]

TASK	PAGE #	RECOMMENDED METHOD
Window, maximize	WIN 19	Click ▢
Window, minimize	WIN 19	Click ▬
Window, move	WIN 19	Drag the title bar
Window, resize	WIN 19	Drag the edge or the corner of the window
Window, restore	WIN 19	Click ▣
Windows 8 application, close	WIN 27	Press Alt+F4
Windows 8 application, snap	WIN 16	Point to the upper-left corner of the screen, right-click the thumbnail, click Snap left or click Snap right
Windows 8 application, start	WIN 13	Click the application's tile on the Start screen
Windows 8 application, switch to another open	WIN 24	Display the Switch List, click the application's thumbnail
Windows 8 application, unsnap	WIN 16	Drag the separator bar to left or right
Windows 8 desktop, display	WIN 2	Click the Desktop tile on the Start screen
Windows 8, start	WIN 8	Turn on the computer
Windows 8, turn off	WIN 30	Display the Charms bar, click Settings, click Power, click Shut down
Workbook, close	EX 13	Click the FILE tab, click Close
Workbook, create a new	EX 15	Click the FILE tab, click New
Workbook, open an existing	EX 4	Click the FILE tab, click Open, select the workbook file
Workbook, preview and print	EX 55	Click the FILE tab, click Print
Workbook, save	EX 17	Click 🖫 on the Quick Access Toolbar
Worksheet, change orientation	EX 53	Click the Orientation button in the Page Setup group on the PAGE LAYOUT tab, click Landscape or Portrait
Worksheet, change view	EX 52	Click ▦, ▣, or ⬚ on the status bar
Worksheet, copy	EX 16	Hold down Ctrl and drag a sheet tab to a new location
Worksheet, delete	EX 17	Right-click a sheet tab, click Delete
Worksheet, insert	EX 16	Click ⊕
Worksheet, move	EX 16	Drag the sheet tab to a new location
Worksheet, rename	EX 16	Double-click the sheet tab, type a new name, press Enter
Worksheet, scale for printing	EX 54	Set the width and height in the Scale to Fit group on the PAGE LAYOUT tab
Worksheets, move between	EX 8	Click a sheet tab or click a tab scrolling button and then click a sheet tab